CLASSIC
PHILOSOPHICAL
QUESTIONS

CLASSIC PHILOSOPHICAL QUESTIONS

TWELFTH EDITION

Edited by

JAMES A. GOULD
University of South Florida

ROBERT J. MULVANEY
University of South Carolina

Upper Saddle River, New Jersey 07458

Library of Congress Cataloging-in-Publication Data

Classic philosophical questions / edited by James A. Gould, Robert J.
Mulvaney.—12th ed.
   p. cm.
Includes bibliographical references.
ISBN 0-13-194961-6
1. Philosophy—Introductions.   2. Philosophy.   I. Gould, James A.,   II. Mulvaney, Robert J.
BD21.C594 2007
100—dc22

2005034623

Editorial Director: Charlyce Jones-Owen
Editor-in-Chief: Sarah Touborg
Senior Acquisitions Editor: Mical Moser
Editorial Assistant: Carla Worner
Director of Marketing: Brandy Dawson
Assistant Marketing Manager: Andrea Messineo
Marketing Assistant: Vicki DeVita
Managing Editor: Joanne Riker
Production Liaison: Joanne Hakim
Manufacturing Buyer: Christina Helder
Cover Art Director: Jayne Conte
Cover Design: Bruce Kenselaar
Manager, Cover Visual Research & Permissions: Karen Sanatar
Cover Photo: "The Death of Socrates" by Jacques-Louis David. © Francis G. Mayer/CORBIS
Full-Service Project Management: Penny Walker / TechBooks/ GTS
Printer/Binder: The Courier Companies

Pearson Education LTD., London
Pearson Education Singapore, Pte. Ltd
Pearson Education, Canada, Ltd
Pearson Education–Japan
Pearson Education Australia PTY, Limited

Pearson Education North Asia Ltd
Pearson Educación de Mexico, S.A. de C.V.
Pearson Education Malaysia, Pte. Ltd
Pearson Education, Upper Saddle River,
   New Jersey

10 9 8 7 6 5 4 3 2 1
ISBN 0-13-194961-6

To Leslie, Francesca, and Stephanie for art, beauty, courage, and joy.

James A. Gould

To my children, Norah, Evan, and Kieran.

Robert J. Mulvaney

Contents

PART 3   PHILOSOPHY OF RELIGION

PART 4   ETHICS

PART 8   APPLIED SOCIAL AND ETHICAL PROBLEMS

PART 9   AESTHETICS

PART 10 THE MEANING OF LIFE

Preface

The American philosopher and psychologist William James once wrote: "Philosophy was meant to be not a bill of fare, but a hearty meal." This twelfth edition of *Classic Philosophical Questions* is intended to offer that hearty meal, one consisting of many courses, all of them enjoyable and beneficial. It is true that this analogy breaks down at some important junctures. For instance, the "courses" offered in this meal need not be taken in any particular order. Dessert can come first! But the reader, teacher, or student must decide which course is dessert and which one is the main course. There is considerable latitude in this matter, and we have made every effort to maintain the independence of the various parts of our work. Although we begin with Socrates, we try not to assume that everyone has read him before taking up the issues of knowledge, metaphysics, ethics, and so on. We hope the instructor will be able to arrange the order of topics to suit individual needs and wishes. Philosophy has no preferred starting point. Like a circle, it can begin and end anywhere. All the readings are selected for beginners in philosophy, especially at the undergraduate level but including even advanced secondary school students. The issues include fundamental philosophical problems of interest to such students, and are drawn from classic and contemporary sources. None of the material is technical. Introductions and study questions precede the essays and alert students to which ideas are important to grasp. At the end of the essays, the unique "To Think About" questions and quotations provide material for spirited debates or for written assignments. Also at the end of each essay is a reading list that can be used for writing assignments and term papers. At the end of the book there is a glossary of philosophical terms.

We make every effort to present as many points of view on the issues covered as possible. Generally, we offer at least two essays on each question, one giving an affirmative response, the other a negative one. Where this is not explicitly done, we choose articles that present both sides of a given issue. At the least, we attempt to incorporate dissenting opinion into our introductions and into the "To Think About" sections at the end of the readings. In every case, we focus on argument and the rational justification of opinions presented. Philosophy necessarily involves the expression of reasoned opinion. This anthology is faithful to that essential element of the discipline.

The reception of earlier editions of this anthology has been enthusiastic. This reflects in part many suggestions from both students and teachers. We have included some of their ideas in this twelfth edition, with new or additional material from St. Thomas Aquinas, Virginia Held, Parmenides, Lao-Tzu, John Dewey, Rosemarie Tong, Alexis de Tocqueville, Karl Popper, and Peter Singer. We wish to thank the following reviewers for their help in strengthening this edition: Martin Weatherston, East Stroudsburg University; Michael Strawser, University of Central Florida; John Michael Atherton, Seton Hall University; Bruce Landesman, University of Utah; Michael W. Austin, Eastern Kentucky University; and Robert Kent Bunch, Bloomfield College. Ross Miller was of great editorial help in the earlier stages of preparing this anthology. Charlyce Jones-Owen, Vice-President and Editorial Director at Prentice-Hall, Sarah Touborg, Editor-in-Chief of Prentice Hall's Arts and Humanities division and their team, especially Wendy Yurash and Carla Worner, saw this edition of our anthology through most of its developmental stages. Mical Moser, our new editor, guided the work through its conclusion, with a number of excellent suggestions. Joanne Hakim, production liaison, and Penny Walker of TechBooks, project manager, are to be credited for their attention to the many details involved in the production of the text. Helen Greenberg did the scrupulous copyediting. The professionalism, courtesy and generosity of all these individuals were indispensable in bringing this project to completion. In addition, recognition is due the following for their assistance in the search for a suitable image for our cover: Anne Day, the distinguished photographer, Donna Urschel of the Library of Congress's public affairs office, Martin Donougho of the University of South Carolina and Ellen Todd of James Mason University. We could not use all their fine suggestions, but we thank them sincerely for their interest in the book. All deserve our gratitude for their encouragement and support.

James A. Gould
Robert J. Mulvaney

CLASSIC
PHILOSOPHICAL
QUESTIONS

What Is Philosophy?

1
Euthyphro: Defining Philosophical Terms

Plato (427?–347 B.C.), one of the great Greek philosophers, has exerted more influence on the development of Western philosophy than any other writer, with the possible exception of Aristotle, his student. Plato established the Academy in Athens, the first of the major schools of ancient Greece. His works, written in dialogue form and featuring his teacher Socrates (469–399 B.C.) as the principal figure, have continued to be widely read not only for their intellectual content, but also for their literary merit. Among his writings are Euthyphro, Apology, Crito, Phaedo, Republic, Protagoras, Gorgias, *and* Philebus.

In *Euthyphro,* Socrates, in the law courts on his way to his trial, encounters Euthyphro, a smug fool who is about to bring an indictment against his father for murder and impiety. This leads to a dialogue on the nature of piety. To us, to be impious means to be irreligious, whereas for the Athenians the term was an amalgamation of responsibility, trustworthiness, piety, and loyalty. Hence, this dialogue is not only a prelude to Socrates' trial, but also an excellent example of a philosophic search for the meaning of an important term.

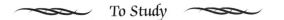 To Study

1. For what is Socrates being prosecuted?
2. For what is Euthyphro prosecuting his father? How did the idea of impiety arise?

From Plato, *Euthyphro, Apology, Crito.* trans. by F. J. Church. Copyright © 1956. Reprinted by permission of Prentice Hall, Inc., Upper Saddle River, New Jersey.

3. What is the first definition of piety offered? What is Socrates' objection to it?
4. What is the second definition of piety? What is Socrates' objection to it?
5. What definition of piety does Socrates himself offer? What is his own refutation of this?
6. What problem regarding piety finally remains?

CHARACTERS *Socrates and Euthyphro*
SCENE *The Hall of the King*

Euthyphro. What in the world are you doing here in the king's hall, Socrates? Why have you left your haunts in the Lyceum? You surely cannot have a suit before him, as I have.

Socrates. The Athenians, Euthyphro, call it an indictment, not a suit.

Euth. What? Do you mean that someone is prosecuting you? I cannot believe that you are prosecuting anyone yourself.

Socr. Certainly I am not.

Euth. Then is someone prosecuting you?

Socr. Yes.

Euth. Who is he?

Socr. I scarcely know him myself, Euthyphro; I think he must be some unknown young man. His name, however, is Meletus, and his district Pitthis.

Euth. I don't know him, Socrates. But tell me, what is he prosecuting you for?

Socr. What for? Not on trivial grounds, I think. It is no small thing for so young a man to have formed an opinion on such an important matter. For he, he says, knows how the young are corrupted, and who are their corrupters. He must be a wise man who, observing my ignorance, is going to accuse me to the state, as his mother, of corrupting his friends. I think that he is the only one who begins at the right point in his political reforms; for his first care is to make the young men as good as possible, just as a good farmer will take care of his young plants first, and, after he has done that, of the others. And so Meletus, I suppose, is first clearing us away who, as he says, corrupt the young men growing up; and then, when he has done that, of course he will turn his attention to the older men, and so become a very great public benefactor. . . .

Euth. I hope it may be so, Socrates, but I fear the opposite. It seems to me that in trying to injure you, he is really setting to work by striking a blow at the foundation of the state. But how, tell me, does he say that you corrupt the youth?

Socr. In a way which sounds absurd at first, my friend. He says that I am a maker of gods; and so he is prosecuting me, he says, for inventing new gods and for not believing in the old ones.

Euth. I understand, Socrates. It is because you say that you always have a divine guide. So he is prosecuting you for introducing religious reforms; and he is going into court to arouse prejudice against you, knowing that the multitude are easily prejudiced about such matters. . . . Well, Socrates, I dare say that nothing will come of it. Very likely you will be successful in your trial, and I think that I shall be in mine.

Socr.   And what is this suit of yours, Euthyphro? Are you suing, or being sued?

Euth.   I am suing.

Socr.   Whom?

Euth.   A man whom people think I must be mad to prosecute.

Socr.   What? Has he wings to fly away with?

Euth.   He is far enough from flying; he is a very old man.

Socr.   Who is he?

Euth.   He is my father.

Socr.   Your father, my good man?

Euth.   He is indeed.

Socr.   What are you prosecuting him for? What is the accusation?

Euth.   Murder, Socrates.

Socr.   Good heavens, Euthyphro! Surely the multitude are ignorant of what is right. I take it that it is not everyone who could rightly do what you are doing; only a man who was already well advanced in wisdom.

Euth.   That is quite true, Socrates.

Socr.   Was the man whom your father killed a relative of yours? But, of course, he was. You would never have prosecuted your father for the murder of a stranger?

Euth.   You amuse me, Socrates. What difference does it make whether the murdered man were a relative or a stranger? The only question that you have to ask is, did the murderer kill justly or not? . . . In the present case the murdered man was a poor laborer of mine, who worked for us on our farm in Naxos. While drunk he got angry with one of our slaves and killed him. My father therefore bound the man hand and foot and threw him into a ditch, while he sent to Athens to ask the priest what he should do. While the messenger was gone, he entirely neglected the man, thinking that he was a murderer, and that it would be no great matter, even if he were to die. And that was exactly what happened; hunger and cold and his bonds killed him before the messenger returned. And now my father and the rest of my family are indignant with me because I am prosecuting my father for the murder of this murderer. They assert that he did not kill the man at all; and they say that, even if he had killed him over and over again, the man himself was a murderer, and that I ought not to concern myself about such a person because it is impious for a son to prosecute his father for murder. So little, Socrates, do they know the divine law of piety and impiety.

Socr.   And do you mean to say, Euthyphro, that you think that you understand divine things and piety and impiety so accurately that, in such a case as you have stated, you can bring your father to justice without fear that you yourself may be doing something impious?

Euth.   If I did not understand all these matters accurately, Socrates, I should not be worth much. . . .

Socr.   Then, my dear Euthyphro, I cannot do better than become your pupil and challenge Meletus on this very point before the trial begins. I should say that I had always thought it very important to have knowledge about divine things; and that now, when he says that I offend by speaking carelessly about them, and by introducing reforms, I have become your pupil. And I should say, "Meletus, if you acknowledge Euthyphro to be wise in these matters and to hold the correct belief, then think the same of me and do not put me on trial; but if you do not, then bring a suit, not against me, but against my master, for corrupting his elders—namely, myself whom he corrupts by his teaching, and his own father whom he corrupts by admonishing and punishing him." And if I did not succeed in persuading him to release me from the suit or to indict you in my place, then I could repeat my challenge in court.

Euth.   Yes, by Zeus! Socrates, I think I should find out his weak points if he were to try to indict me. I should have a good deal to say about him in court long before I spoke about myself.

Socr.   Yes, my dear friend, and knowing this I am anxious to become your pupil. I see that Meletus here, and others too, seem not to notice you at all, but he sees through me without difficulty and at once prosecutes me for impiety. Now, therefore, please explain to me what you were so confident just now that you knew. Tell me what are righteousness and sacrilege with respect to murder and everything else. I suppose that piety is the same in all actions, and that impiety is always the opposite of piety, and retains its identity, and that, as impiety, it always has the same character, which will be found in whatever is impious.

Euth.   Certainly, Socrates, I suppose so.

Socr.   Tell me, then, what is piety and what is impiety?

Euth.   Well, then, I say that piety means prosecuting the unjust individual who has committed murder or sacrilege, or any other such crime, as I am doing now, whether he is your father or your mother or whoever he is; and I say that impiety means not prosecuting him. And observe, Socrates, I will give you a clear proof, which I have already given to others, that it is so, and that doing right means not letting off unpunished the sacrilegious man, whosoever he may be. Men hold Zeus to be the best and the most just of the gods; and they admit that Zeus bound his own father, Cronos, for wrongfully devouring his children; and that Cronos, in his turn, castrated his father for similar reasons. And yet these same men are incensed with me because I proceed against my father for doing wrong. So, you see, they say one thing in the case of the gods and quite another in mine.

Socr.   Is not that why I am being prosecuted, Euthyphro? I mean, because I find it hard to accept such stories people tell about the gods? I expect that I shall be found at fault because I doubt those stories. Now if you who understand all these matters so well agree in holding all those tales true, then I suppose that I must yield to your authority. What could I say when I admit myself that I know nothing about them? But tell me, in the name of friendship, do you really believe that these things have actually happened?

Euth.   Yes, and more amazing things too, Socrates, which the multitude do not know of.

Socr.   Then you really believe that there is war among the gods, and bitter hatreds, and battles, such as the poets tell of. . . .

Euth.   Yes, Socrates, and more besides. As I was saying, I will report to you many other stories about divine matters, if you like, which I am sure will astonish you when you hear them.

Socr.   I dare say. You shall report them to me at your leisure another time. At present please try to give a more definite answer to the question which I asked you just now. What I asked you, my friend, was, What is piety? and you have not explained it to me to my satisfaction. You only tell me that what you are doing now, namely, prosecuting your father for murder, is a pious act.

Euth.   Well, that is true, Socrates.

Socr.   Very likely. But many other actions are pious, are they not, Euthyphro?

Euth.   Certainly.

Socr.   Remember, then, I did not ask you to tell me one or two of all the many pious actions that there are; I want to know what is characteristic of piety which makes all pious actions pious. You said, I think, that there is one characteristic which makes all pious actions pious, and another characteristic which makes all impious actions impious. Do you not remember?

Euth.   I do.

Socr.   Well, then, explain to me what is this characteristic, that I may have it to turn to, and to use as a standard whereby to judge your actions and those of other men, and be able to say that whatever action resembles it is pious, and whatever does not, is not pious.

Euth.   Yes, I will tell you that if you wish. Socrates. . . . What is pleasing to the gods is pious, and what is not pleasing to them is impious.

Socr.   Fine, Euthyphro. Now you have given me the answer that I wanted. Whether what you say is true, I do not know yet. But, of course, you will go on to prove that it is true.

Euth.   Certainly.

Socr.   Come, then, let us examine our statement. The things and the men that are pleasing to the gods are pious, and the things and the men that are displeasing to the gods are impious. But piety and impiety are not the same; they are as opposite as possible—was not that what he said?

Euth.   Certainly. . . .

Socr.   Have we not also said, Euthyphro, that there are quarrels and disagreements and hatreds among the gods?

Euth.   We have.

Socr.   But what kind of disagreement, my friend, causes hatred and anger? Let us look at the matter thus. If you and I were to disagree as to whether one number were more than another, would that make us angry and enemies? Should we not settle such a dispute at once by counting?

Euth.   Of course.

Socr.   And if we were to disagree as to the relative size of two things, we should measure them and put an end to the disagreement at once, should we not? . . . And should we not settle a question about the relative weight of two things by weighing them?

Euth.   Of course.

Socr.   Then what is the question which would make us angry and enemies if we disagreed about it, and could not come to a settlement? Perhaps you have not an answer ready; but listen to mine. Is it not the question of the just and unjust, of the honorable and the dishonorable, of the good and the bad? Is it not questions about these matters which make you and me and everyone else quarrel, when we do quarrel, if we differ about them and can reach no satisfactory agreement?

Euth.   Yes. Socrates, it is disagreements about these matters.

Socr.   Well, Euthyphro, the gods will quarrel over these things if they quarrel at all, will they not?

Euth.   Necessarily.

Socr.   Then, my good Euthyphro, you say that some of the gods think one thing just, the others, another; and that what some of them hold to be honorable or good, others hold to be dishonorable or evil. For there would not have been quarrels among them if they had not disagreed on these points, would there?

Euth.   You are right.

Socr.   And each of them loves what he thinks honorable, and good, and just; and hates the opposite, does he not?

Euth.   Certainly.

Socr.   But you say that the same action is held by some of them to be just, and by others to be unjust; and that then they dispute about it, and so quarrel and fight among themselves. Is it not so?

Euth.   Yes.

Socr.   Then the same thing is hated by the gods and loved by them; and the same thing will be displeasing and pleasing to them.

Euth.   Apparently.

Socr.   Then, according to your account, the same thing will be pious and impious.

Euth.   So it seems.

Socr.   Then, my good friend, you have not answered my question. I did not ask you to tell me what action is both pious and impious; but it seems that whatever is pleasing to the gods is also displeasing to them. And so, Euthyphro, I should not be surprised if what you are doing now in punishing your father is an action well pleasing to Zeus, but hateful to Cronos and Uranus, and acceptable to Hephaestus, but hateful to Hera; and if any of the other gods disagree about it, pleasing to some of them and displeasing to others.

Euth.   But on this point, Socrates, I think that there is no difference of opinion among the gods: they all hold that if one man kills another unjustly, he must be punished.

Socr.   What, Euthyphro? Among mankind, have you never heard disputes whether a man ought to be punished for killing another man unjustly, or for doing some other unjust deed?

Euth.   Indeed, they never cease from these disputes, especially in courts of justice. They do all manner of unjust things; and then there is nothing which they will not do and say to avoid punishment.

Socr.   Do they admit that they have done something unjust, and at the same time deny that they ought to be punished, Euthyphro?

Euth.   No, indeed, that they do not.

Socr.   Then it is not the case that there is nothing which they will not do and say. I take it, they do not dare to say or argue that they must not be punished if they have done something unjust. What they say is that they have not done anything unjust, is it not so?

Euth.   That is true.

Socr.   Then they do not disagree over the question that the unjust individual must be punished. They disagree over the question, who is unjust, and what was done and when, do they not?

Euth.   That is true.

Socr.   Well, is not exactly the same thing true of the gods if they quarrel about justice and injustice, as you say they do? Do not some of them say that the others are doing something unjust, while the others deny it? No one, I suppose, my dear friend, whether god or man, dares to say that a person who has done something unjust must not be punished.

Euth.   No, Socrates, that is true, by and large.

Socr.   I take it, Euthyphro, that the disputants, whether men or gods, if the gods do disagree, disagree over each separate act. When they quarrel about any act, some of them say that it was just, and others that it was unjust. Is it not so?

Euth.   Yes.

Socr.   Come, then, my dear Euthyphro, please enlighten me on this point. What proof have you that all the gods think that a laborer who has been imprisoned for murder by the master of the man whom he has murdered, and who dies from his imprisonment before the master has had time to learn from the religious authorities what he should do, dies unjustly? How do you know that it is just for a son to indict his father and to prosecute him for the murder of such a man? Come, see if you can make it clear to me that the gods necessarily agree in thinking that this action of yours is just; and if you satisfy me, I will never cease singing your praises for wisdom.

Euth.   I could make that clear enough to you, Socrates; but I am afraid that it would be a long business.

Socr.   I see you think that I am duller than the judges. To them, of course, you will make it clear that your father has committed an unjust action, and that all the gods agree in hating such actions.

Euth.   I will indeed, Socrates, if they will only listen to me.

Socr.   They will listen if they think that you are a good speaker. But while you were talking, it occurred to me to ask myself this question: suppose that Euthyphro were to prove to me as clearly as possible that all the gods think such a death unjust, how has he brought me any nearer to understanding what piety and impiety are? This particular act, perhaps, may be displeasing to the gods, but then we have just seen that piety and impiety cannot be defined in that way; for we have seen that what is displeasing to the gods is also pleasing to them. So I will let you off on this point. Euthyphro; and all the gods shall agree in thinking your father's action wrong and in hating it, if you like. But shall we correct our definition and say that whatever all the gods hate is impious, and whatever they all love is pious; while whatever some of them love, and others hate, is either both or neither? Do you wish us now to define piety and impiety in this manner?

Euth. Why not, Socrates?

Socr. There is no reason why I should not, Euthyphro. It is for you to consider whether that definition will help you to teach me what you promised.

Euth. Well, I should say that piety is what all the gods love, and that impiety is what they all hate.

Socr. Are we to examine this definition, Euthyphro, and see if it is a good one? . . .

Euth. For my part I think that the definition is right this time.

Socr. We shall know that better in a little while, my good friend. Now consider this question. Do the gods love piety because it is pious, or is it pious because they love it?

Euth. I do not understand you, Socrates.

Socr. I will try to explain myself: we speak of a thing being carried and carrying, and being led and leading, and being seen and seeing; and you understand that all such expressions mean different things, and what the difference is.

Euth. Yes, I think I understand.

Socr. And we talk of a thing being loved, of a thing loving, and the two are different?

Euth. Of course.

Socr. Now tell me, is a thing which is being carried in a state of being carried because it is carried, or for some other reason?

Euth. No, because it is carried.

Socr. And a thing is in a state of being led because it is led, and of being seen because it is seen?

Euth. Certainly.

Socr. Then a thing is not seen because it is in a state of being seen: it is in a state of being seen because it is seen; and a thing is not led because it is in a state of being led: it is in a state of being led because it is led; and a thing is not carried because it is in a state of being carried: it is in a state of being carried because it is carried. Is my meaning clear now, Euthyphro? I mean this: if anything becomes or is affected, it does not become because it is in a state of becoming: it is in a state of becoming because it becomes; and it is not affected because it is in a state of being affected: it is in a state of being affected because it is affected. Do you not agree?

Euth. I do.

Socr. Is not that which is being loved in a state either of becoming or of being affected in some way by something?

Euth. Certainly.

Socr. Then the same is true here as in the former cases. A thing is not loved by those who love it because it is in a state of being loved; it is in a state of being loved because they love it.

Euth. Necessarily.

Socr.   Well, then, Euthyphro, what do we say about piety? Is it not loved by all the gods, according to your definition?

Euth.   Yes.

Socr.   Because it is pious, or for some other reason?

Euth.   No, because it is pious.

Socr.   Then it is loved by the gods because it is pious; it is not pious because it is loved by them?

Euth.   It seems so.

Socr.   But, then, what is pleasing to the gods is pleasing to them, and is in a state of being loved by them, because they love it?

Euth.   Of course.

Socr.   Then piety is not what is pleasing to the gods, and what is pleasing to the gods is not pious, as you say, Euthyphro. They are different things.

Euth.   And why, Socrates?

Socr.   Because we are agreed that the gods love piety because it is pious, and that it is not pious because they love it. Is not this so?

Euth.   Yes.

Socr.   And that what is pleasing to the gods because they love it, is pleasing to them by reason of this same love, and that they do not love it because it is pleasing to them.

Euth.   True.

Socr.   Then, my dear Euthyphro, piety and what is pleasing to the gods are different things. If the gods had loved piety because it is pious, they would also have loved what is pleasing to them because it is pleasing to them; but if what is pleasing to them had been pleasing to them because they loved it, then piety, too, would have been piety because they loved it. But now you see that they are opposite things, and wholly different from each other. For the one is of a sort to be loved because it is loved, while the other is loved because it is of a sort to be loved. My question, Euthyphro, was, What is piety? But it turns out that you have not explained to me the essential character of piety; you have been content to mention an effect which belongs to it— namely, that all gods love it. You have not yet told me what its essential character is. Do not, if you please, keep from me what piety is; begin again and tell me that. Never mind whether the gods love it, or whether it has other effects: we shall not differ on that point. Do your best to make clear to me what is piety and what is impiety.

Euth.   But, Socrates, I really don't know how to explain to you what is on my mind. Whatever statement we put forward always somehow moves round in a circle, and will not stay where we put it. . . .

Socr.   Then we must begin again and inquire what piety is. I do not mean to give in until I have found out. Do not regard me as unworthy; give your whole mind to the question, and this time tell me the truth. For if anyone knows it, it is you; and you are a Proteus whom I must not let go until you have told me. It cannot be that you would ever have undertaken to prosecute your aged father for the murder of a laboring man unless you had known exactly what piety and impiety are. You would have feared to risk the anger of the gods, in case you should be doing wrong, and you would have been afraid of what men would say. But now I am sure that you think that you know exactly what is pious and what is not; so tell me, my good Euthyphro, and do not conceal from me what you think.

Euth.   Another time, then, Socrates, I am in a hurry now, and it is time for me to be off.

~~~~~ To Think About ~~~~~

1. How does one determine the definition of a term such as *piety* or *murder*?

2. Do the ways a word is used in a particular society always represent its correct meaning? Can you think of an exception?

3. "There is only one thing a philosopher can be relied upon to do, and that is to contradict other philosophers."   **William James**

4. "We are discussing no small matter, but how we ought to live."   **Socrates**

5. "Why worry about death, when you don't concern yourself about your nothingness before your birth?"   **James Gould**

6. "Since ignorance is no guarantee of security, and in fact only makes our insecurity still worse, it is probably better despite our fear to know where the danger lies. To ask the right question is already half the solution of a problem. . . . Discerning persons have realized for some time that external . . . conditions, of whatever kind, are only . . . jumping-off grounds, for the real dangers that threaten our lives."   **C. G. Jung**

7. "We do not err because truth is difficult to see. It is visible at a glance. We err because this is more comfortable."   **Alexander Solzhenitsyn**

8. "The life-blood of philosophy is argument and counter-argument. Plato and Aristotle thought of this occurring in what they called *dialectic discussion.* Today, it might be argued that it is just the same, except that it operates on a much wider scale, both historically and geographically. Argument and counter-argument in books and journals is the modern version of dialectic."   **D. W. Hamlyn**

9. "Every word is a prejudice."   **James Gould**

10. "Wonder is a feeling of a philosopher and philosophy begins in wonder."
                               Plato

11. "Philosophy consoles us for the small achievements in life, and the decline of strength and beauty; it arms us against poverty, old age, sickness and death, against fools and evil sneerers."   **Jean de la Bruyère**

12. "To philosophize is to doubt."   **Michel Eyquem de Montaigne**

2

The Apology, Phaedo, and Crito: The Trial, Immortality, and Death of Socrates

*Apology,** *Phaedo,* and *Crito* are thought to be among Plato's earliest writings. They portray Socrates, Plato's teacher, as he appeared when tried before the Athenian people in 399 B.C. Socrates spent his life wandering the streets of Athens questioning the citizens he encountered about their ideas and ideals. Because he questioned the ideas of the elders, and because some of his acquaintances had warred against Athens, he was not liked by city powers, who brought him to trial, as noted in the *Euthyphro* selection.

Apology, Phaedo, and *Crito* raise a number of interesting questions about the different demands of private and public spheres. They are especially concerned with the role of the critic in a free society and with speaking the truth as opposed to saying what is merely persuasive and pleasing. Predominant in both writings are Socrates himself and the attitudes that he judged appropriate to a person who is free in the deepest sense.

 To Study

1. What are the charges against Socrates?
2. What has caused prejudice to arise against Socrates?
3. How does Socrates refute the charge that he corrupts the young?
4. What is Socrates' argument that he believes in God?

*In the fourth century B.C. the word *apology* meant "a debate" or "dispute." [ED.]

From Plato, *The Apology, Phaedo, and Crito.* Taken from *Dialogues of Plato,* 3rd ed., trans. by Benjamin Jowett (Oxford University Press, 1896).

5. What has Socrates spent his whole life doing?
6. Socrates says he is a "gadfly." Explain.
7. Why doesn't Socrates plead for his life or accept exile?
8. What argument does Socrates use to show that death is good?
9. State Socrates' arguments about why he should not escape.
10. What is Socrates' argument for immortality of the soul?

CHARACTERS   *Socrates and Meletus*
SCENE   *The Court of Justice*

Socr.   I cannot tell what impression my accusers have made upon you, Athenians. For my own part, I know that they nearly made me forget who I was, so believable were they; and yet they have scarcely uttered one single word of truth. But of all their many falsehoods, the one which astonished me most was when they said that I was a clever speaker, and that you must be careful not to let me mislead you. I thought that it was most impudent of them not to be ashamed to talk in that way; for as soon as I open my mouth they will be refuted, and I shall prove that I am not a clever speaker in any way at all—unless, indeed, by a clever speaker they mean a man who speaks the truth. If that is their meaning, I agree with them that I am a much greater orator than they. My accusers, then I repeat, have said little or nothing that is true; but from me you shall hear the whole truth. Certainly you will not hear an elaborate speech, Athenians, dressed up, like theirs, with words and phrases. I will say to you what I have to say, without preparation, and in the words which come first, for I believe that my cause is just; so let none of you expect anything else. Indeed, my friends, it would hardly be seemingly for me, at my age, to come before you like a young man with his specious phrases. But there is one thing, Athenians, which I do most earnestly beg and entreat of you. Do not be surprised and do not interrupt with shouts if in my defense I speak in the same way that I am accustomed to speak in the marketplace, at the tables of the moneychangers, where many of you have heard me, and elsewhere. The truth is this. I am more than seventy years old, and this is the first time that I have ever come before a law court; so your manner of speech here is quite strange to me. If I had been really a stranger, you would have forgiven me for speaking in the language and the fashion of my native country; and so now I ask you to grant me what I think I have a right to claim. Never mind the style of my speech—it may be better or it may be worse—give your whole attention to the question, Is what I say just, or is it not? That is what makes a good judge, as speaking the truth makes a good advocate.

I have to defend myself, Athenians, first against the old false accusations of my old accusers, and then against the later ones of my present accusers. For many men have been accusing me to you, and for very many years, who have not uttered a word of truth; and I fear them more than I fear Anytus and his associates, formidable as they are. But, my friends, those others are still more formidable; for they got hold of most of you when you were children, and they have been more persistent in accusing me untruthfully and have persuaded you that there is a certain Socrates, a wise man, who speculates about the heavens, and who investigates things that are beneath the earth, and who can make the weaker reason appear the stronger. These men, Athenians, who spread abroad this report are the accusers whom I fear; for their hearers think that persons who pursue such inquiries never believe in the gods. Then they are many, and their attacks have been going on for a long time, and they spoke to you when you were at the age most readily to believe them, for you were all young, and many of you were children, and there was no one to answer them when they attacked me. And the most unreasonable thing of all is that I do not even know their names: I cannot tell you who they are except when one happens to be a comic poet. But all the rest who have persuaded you, from motives of resentment and prejudice, and sometimes, it may be, from conviction, are hardest to cope with. For I cannot call any one of them forward in court to cross-examine him. I have, as it were, simply to spar with shadows in my defense, and to put questions which there is no one to answer. I ask you, therefore, to believe that, as I say, I have been attacked by two kinds of accusers—first, by Meletus and his associates, and, then, by those older ones of whom I have spoken. And, with your leave, I will defend myself first against my old accusers; for you heard their accusations first, and they were much more forceful than my present accusers are.

Well, I must make my defense, Athenians, and try in the short time allowed me to remove the prejudice which you have been so long a time acquiring. I hope that I may manage to do this, if it be good for you and for me, and that my defense may be successful; but I am quite aware of the nature of my task, and I know that it is a difficult one. Be the outcome, however, as is pleasing to God, I must obey the law and make my defense.

Let us begin from the beginning, then, and ask what is the accusation which has given rise to the prejudice against me, which was what Meletus relied on when he brought his indictment. What is the prejudice which my enemies have been spreading about me? I must assume that they are formally accusing me, and read their indictment. It would run somewhat in this fashion: Socrates is a wrongdoer, who meddles with inquiries into things beneath the earth and in the heavens, and who makes the weaker reason appear the stronger, and who teaches others these same things. That is what they say; and in the comedy of Aristophanes [*Clouds*] you yourselves saw a man called Socrates swinging round in a basket and saying that he walked on the air, and prattling a great deal of nonsense about matters of which I understand nothing, either more or less. I do not mean to disparage that kind of knowledge if there is anyone who is wise about these matters. I trust Meletus may never be able to prosecute me for that. But the truth is, Athenians, I have nothing to do with these matters, and almost all of you are yourselves my witnesses of this. I beg all of you who have heard me discussing, and they are many, to inform your neighbors and tell them if any of you have ever heard me discussing such matters, either more or less. That will show you that the other common stories about me are as false as this one.

But the fact is that not one of these is true. And if you have heard that I undertake to educate men, and make money by so doing, that is not true either, though I think that it would be a fine thing to be able to educate men. . . .

Perhaps some of you may reply: But, Socrates, what is the trouble with you? What has given rise to these prejudices against you? You must have been doing something out of the ordinary. All these stories and reports of you would never have arisen if you had not been doing something different from other men. So tell us what it is, that we may not give our verdict in the dark. I think that that is a fair question, and I will try to explain to you what it is that has raised these prejudices against me and given me this reputation. Listen, then: some of you, perhaps, will think that I am joking, but I assure you that I will tell you the whole truth. I have gained this reputation, Athenians, simply by reason of a certain wisdom. But by what kind of wisdom? It is by just that wisdom which is perhaps human wisdom. In that, it may be, I am really wise. . . .

You remember Chaerephon. From youth upwards he was my comrade; and also a partisan of your democracy, sharing your recent exile and returning with you. You remember, too, Chaerephon's character—how vehement he was in carrying through whatever he took in hand. Once he went to Delphi and ventured to put this question to the oracle—I entreat you again, my friends, not to interrupt me with your shouts— he asked if there was any man who was wiser than I. The priestess answered that there was no one. Chaerephon himself is dead, but his brother here will confirm what I say.

Now see why I tell you this. I am going to explain to you how the prejudice against me has arisen. When I heard of the oracle I began to reflect: What can the god mean by this riddle? I know very well that I am not wise, even the smallest degree. Then what can he mean by saying that I am the wisest of men? It cannot be that he is speaking falsely, for he is a god and cannot lie. For a long time I was at a loss to understand his meaning. Then, very reluctantly, I turned to seek for it in this manner: I went to a man who was reputed to be wise, thinking that there, if anywhere, I should prove the answer wrong, and meaning to point out to the oracle its mistake, and to say, You said that I was the wisest of men, but this man is wiser than I am. So I examined the man—I need not tell you his name, he was a politician—but this was the result, Athenians. When I conversed with him I came to see that, though a great many persons, and most of all he himself, thought that he was wise, yet he was not wise. Then I tried to prove to him that he was not wise, though he fancied that he was; and by so doing I made him indignant, and many of the bystanders. So when I went away, I thought to myself, I am wiser than this man: neither of us knows anything that is really worthwhile, but he thinks that he has knowledge when he has not, while I, having no knowledge, do not think that I have. I seem, at any rate, to be a little wiser than he is on this point: I do not think that I know what I do not know. Next I went to another man who was reputed to be still wiser than the last, with exactly the same result. And there again I made him, and many other men, indignant.

Then I went on to one man after another, seeing that I was arousing indignation every day, which caused me much pain and anxiety. Still I thought that I must set the god's command above everything. So I had to go to every man who seemed to possess any knowledge, and investigate the meaning of the oracle. Athenians, I must tell you the truth; by the god, this was the result of the investigation which I made at the god's bidding: I found that the men whose reputation for wisdom stood highest were nearly the most lacking in it, while others who were looked down on as common people were much more intelligent. Now I must describe to you the wanderings which I undertook, like Heraclean labors, to prove the oracle irrefutable. After the politicians, I went to the poets, tragic, dithyrambic, and others, thinking that there I should find myself manifestly more ignorant than they. So I took up the poems on which I thought that they had spent most pains, and asked them what they meant, hoping at the same time to learn something from them. I am ashamed to tell you the truth, my friends, but I must say it. Almost anyone of the bystanders could have talked about the works of these poets better than the poets themselves. So I soon found that it is not by wisdom that the poets create their works, but by a certain innate power and by inspiration, like soothsayers and prophets, who say many fine things, but who understand nothing of what they say. The poets seemed to me to be in a similar situation. And at the same time I perceived that, because of their poetry, they thought that they were the wisest of men in other matters, too, which they were not. So I went away again, thinking that I had the same advantage over the poets that I had over the politicians.

Finally, I went to the artisans, for I knew very well that I possessed no knowledge at all worth speaking of, and I was sure that I should find that they knew many fine things. And in that I was not mistaken. They knew what I did not know, and so far they were wiser than I. But, Athenians, it seemed to me that the skilled artisans made the same mistakes as the poets. Each of them believed himself to be extremely wise in matters of the greatest importance because he was skillful in his own art: and this presumption of theirs obscured their real wisdom. So I asked myself, on behalf of the oracle, whether I would choose to remain as I was, without either their wisdom or their ignorance, or to possess both, as they did. And I answered to myself and to the oracle that it was better for me to remain as I was.

From this examination, Athenians, has arisen much fierce and bitter indignation, and from this a great many prejudices about me, and people say that I am "a wise man." For the bystanders always think that I am wise myself in any matter wherein I refute another. But, my friends, I believe that the god is really wise, and that by this oracle he meant that human wisdom is worth little or nothing. I do not think that he meant that Socrates was wise. He only made use of my name, and took me as an example, as though he would say to men: He among you is the wisest who, like Socrates, knows that in truth his wisdom is worth nothing at all. Therefore I still go about testing and examining every man whom I think wise, whether he be a citizen or a stranger, as the god has commanded me; and whenever I find that he is not wise, I point out to him, on the god's behalf, that he is not wise. I am so busy in this pursuit that I have never had leisure to take any path worth mentioning in public matters or to look after my private affairs. I am in great poverty as the result of my service to the god.

Besides this, the young men who follow me about, who are the sons of wealthy persons and have the most leisure, take pleasure in hearing men cross-examined. They often imitate me among themselves; then they try their hands at cross-examining other people. And, I imagine, they find plenty of men who think that they know a great deal when in fact they know little or nothing. Then the persons who are cross-examined get angry with me instead of with themselves, and say that Socrates is an abomination and corrupts the young. When they are asked, Why, what does he do? what does he teach? they do not know what to say; but, not to seem at a loss, they repeat the stock charges against all philosophers, and allege that he investigates things in the air and under the earth, and that he teaches people to disbelieve in the gods, and to make the weaker reason appear the stronger. For, I suppose, they would not like to confess the truth, which is that they are shown up as ignorant pretenders to knowledge that they do not possess. So they have been filling your ears with their bitter prejudices for a long time, for they are ambitious, energetic, and numerous; and they speak vigorously and persuasively against me. Relying on this, Meletus, Anytus, and Lycon have attacked me. Meletus is indignant with me on the part of the poets, Anytus on the part of the artisans and politicians, and Lycon on the part of the orators. And so, as I said at the beginning, I shall be surprised if I am able, in the short time allowed me for my defense, to remove from your minds this prejudice which has grown so strong. What I have told you, Athenians, is the truth: I neither conceal nor do I suppress anything, small or great. Yet I know that it is just this plainness of speech which rouses indignation. But that is only a proof that my words are true, and that the prejudice against me, and the causes of it, are what I have said. And whether you look for them now or hereafter, you will find that they are so.

What I have said must suffice as my defense against the charges of my first accusers. I will try next to defend myself against Meletus, that "good patriot," as he calls himself, and my later accusers. Let us assume that they are a new set of accusers, and read their indictment, as we did in the case of the others. It runs thus. He says that Socrates is a wrongdoer who corrupts the youth, and who does not believe in the gods whom the state believes in, but in other new divinities. Such is the accusation. Let us examine each point in it separately. Meletus says that I do wrong by corrupting the youth. But I say, Athenians, that he is doing wrong, for he is playing a solemn joke by lightly bringing men to trial, and pretending to have zealous interest in matters to which he has never given a moment's thought. Now I will try to prove to you that it is so.

Come here, Meletus. Is it not a fact that you think it very important that the young should be as excellent as possible?

Mel.   It is.

Socr.   Come then, tell the judges who is it who improves them? You care so much, you must know. You are accusing me, and bringing me to trial, because, as you say, you have discovered that I am the corrupter of the youth. Come now, reveal to the gentlemen who improves them. You see, Meletus, you have nothing to say; you are silent. But don't you think that this is shameful? Is not your silence a conclusive proof of what I say—that you have never cared? Come, tell us, my good sir, who makes the young better citizens?

Mel.   The laws.

Socr.   That, my friend, is not my question. What man improves the young, who starts with the knowledge of the laws?

Mel.   The judges here, Socrates.

Socr.   What do you mean, Meletus? Can they educate the young and improve them?

Mel.   Certainly.

Socr.   All of them? or only some of them?

Mel.   All of them.

Socr.   By Hera, that is good news! Such a large supply of benefactors! And do the listeners here improve them, or not?

Mel.   They do.

Socr.   And do the senators?

Mel.   Yes.

Socr.   Well then, Meletus, do the members of the assembly corrupt the young or do they again all improve them?

Mel.   They, too, improve them.

Socr.   Then all the Athenians, apparently, make the young into good men except me, and I alone corrupt them. Is that your meaning?

Mel.   Most certainly; that is my meaning.

Socr.   You have discovered me to be most unfortunate. Now tell me: do you think that the same holds good in the case of horses? Does one man do them harm and everyone else improve them? On the contrary, is it not one man only, or a very few—namely, those who are skilled with horses—who can improve them, while the majority of men harm them if they use them and have anything to do with them? Is it not so, Meletus, both with horses and with every other animal? Of course it is, whether you and Anytus say yes or no. The young would certainly be very fortunate if only one man corrupted them, and everyone else did them good. The truth is, Meletus, you prove conclusively that you have never thought about the youth in your life. You exhibit your carelessness in not caring for the very matters about which you are prosecuting me.

Now be so good as to tell us, Meletus, is it better to live among good citizens or bad ones? Answer, my friend. I am not asking you at all a difficult question. Do not the bad harm their associates and the good do them good?

Mel.   Yes.

Socr.   Is there any man who would rather be injured than benefited by his companions? Answer, my good sir; you are obliged by the law to answer. Does any one like to be injured?

Mel.   Certainly not.

Socr.   Well then, are you prosecuting me for corrupting the young and making them worse, intentionally or unintentionally?

Mel.   For doing it intentionally.

Socr.   What, Meletus? Do you mean to say that you, who are so much younger than I, are yet so much wiser than I that you know that bad citizens always do evil, and that good citizens do good, to those with whom they come in contact, while I am so extraordinarily stupid as not to know that, if I make any of my companions evil, he will probably injure me in some way, and as to commit this great evil, as you allege, intentionally? You will not make me believe that, nor anyone else either, I should think. Either I do not corrupt the young at all or, if I do, I do so unintentionally: so that you are lying in either case. And if I corrupt them unintentionally, the law does not call upon you to prosecute me for an error which is unintentional, but to take me aside privately and reprove and instruct me. For, of course, I shall cease from doing wrong involuntarily, as soon as I know that I have been doing wrong. But you avoided associating with me and educating me; instead you bring me up before the court, where the law sends persons, not for instruction, but for punishment.

The truth is, Athenians, as I said, it is quite clear that Meletus has never cared at all about these matters. However, now tell us, Meletus, how do you say that I corrupt the young? Clearly, according to your indictment, by teaching them not to believe in the gods the state believes in, but other new divinities instead. You mean that I corrupt the young by that teaching, do you not?

Mel.   Yes, most certainly I mean that.

Socr.   Then in the name of these gods of whom we are speaking, explain yourself a little more clearly to me and to these gentlemen here. I cannot understand what you mean. Do you mean that I teach the young to believe in some gods, but not in the gods of the state? Do you accuse me of teaching them to believe in strange gods? If that is your meaning, I myself believe in some gods, and my crime is not that of absolute atheism. Or do you mean that I do not believe in the gods at all myself, and I teach other people not to believe in them either?

Mel.   I mean that you do not believe in the gods in any way whatever.

Socr.   You amaze me, Meletus! Why do you say that? Do you mean that I believe neither the sun nor the moon to be gods, like other men?

Mel.   I swear he does not, judges; he says that the sun is a stone, and the moon earth.

Socr.   My dear Meletus, do you think that you are prosecuting Anaxagoras? You must have a very poor opinion of these men, and think them illiterate, if you imagine that they do not know that the works of Anaxagoras of Clazomenae are full of these doctrines. And so young men learn these things from me, when they can often buy places in the theatre for a drachma at most, and laugh at Socrates were he to pretend that these doctrines, which are very peculiar doctrines, too, were his own. But please tell me, do you really think that I do not believe in the gods at all?

Mel.   Most certainly I do. You are a complete atheist.

Socr.   No one believes that, Meletus, not even you yourself. It seems to me, Athenians, that Meletus is very insolent and reckless, and that he is prosecuting me simply out of insolence, recklessness and youthful bravado. For he seems to be testing me, by asking me a riddle that has no answer. Will this wise Socrates, he says to himself, see that I am joking and contradicting myself? or shall I outwit him and everyone else who hears me? Meletus seems to me to contradict himself in his indictment: it is as if he were to say, Socrates is a wrongdoer who does not believe in the gods, but who believes in the gods. But that is mere joking.

Now, my friends, let us see why I think that this is his meaning. Do you answer me, Meletus; and do you, Athenians, remember the request which I made to you at the start, and do not interrupt me with shouts if I talk in my usual way.

Is there any man, Meletus, who believes in the existence of things pertaining to men and not in the existence of men? Make him answer the question, my friends, without these interruptions. Is there any man who believes in the existence of horsemanship and not in the existence of horses? or in flute-playing and not in flute-players? There is not, my friend. If you will not answer, I will tell both you and the judges. But you must answer my next question. Is there any man who believes in the existence of divine things and not in the existence of divinities?

Mel.   There is not.

Socr.   I am very glad that these gentlemen have managed to extract an answer from you. Well then, you say that I believe in divine beings, whether they be old or new ones, and that I teach others to believe in them; at any rate, according to your statement, I believe in divine beings. That you have sworn in your indictment. But if I believe in divine beings, I suppose it follows necessarily that I believe in divinities. Is it not so? It is. I assume that you grant that, as you do not answer. But do we not believe that divinities are either gods themselves or the children of the gods? Do you admit that?

Mel.   I do.

Socr.   Then you admit that I believe in divinities. Now, if these divinities are gods, then, as I say, you are joking and asking a riddle, and asserting that I do not believe in the gods, and at the same time that I do, since I believe in divinities. But if these divinities are the illegitimate children of the gods, either by the nymphs or by other mothers, as they are said to be, then, I ask, what men could believe in the existence of the children of the gods, and not in the existence of the gods? That would be as strange as believing in the existence of the offspring of horses and asses, and not in the existence of horses and asses. You must have indicted me in this manner, Meletus, either to test me or because you could not find any crime that you could accuse me of with truth. But you will never contrive to persuade any man with any sense at all that a belief in divine things and things of the gods does not necessarily involve a belief in divinities, and in the gods, and in heroes.

But in truth, Athenians, I do not think that I need say very much to prove that I have not committed the crime for which Meletus is prosecuting me. What I have said is enough to prove that. But I repeat it is certainly true, as I have already told you, that I have aroused much indignation. That is what will cause my condemnation if I am condemned; not Meletus nor Anytus either, but that prejudice and suspicion of the multitude which have been the destruction of many good men before me, and I think will be so again. There is no fear that I shall be the last victim.

Perhaps someone will say: Are you not ashamed, Socrates, of leading a life which is very likely now to cause your death? I should answer him with justice, and say: My friend, if you think that a man of any worth at all ought to reckon the chances of life and death when he acts, or that he ought to think of anything but whether he is acting rightly or wrongly, and as a good or a bad man would act, you are mistaken. According to you, the demigods who died at Troy would be foolish, and among them the son of Thetis, who thought nothing of danger when the alternative was disgrace. For when his mother—and she was a goddess—addressed him, when he was burning to slay Hector, in this fashion, "My son, if you avenge the death of your comrade Patroclus and slay Hector, you will die yourself, for 'fate awaits you straightway after Hector's death' "; when he heard this, he scorned danger and death; he feared much more to live a coward and not to avenge his friend. "Let me punish the evildoer and straightway die," he said, "that I may not remain here by the beaked ships jeered at, encumbering the earth." Do you suppose that he thought of danger or of death? For this, Athenians, I believe to be the truth. Wherever a man's station is, whether he has chosen it of his own will, or whether he has been placed at it by his commander, there it is his duty to remain and face the danger without thinking of death or of any other thing except dishonor.

When the generals whom you chose to command me, Athenians, assigned me my station at Potidaea and at Amphipolis and at Delium, I remained where they placed me and ran the risk of death, like other men. It would be very strange conduct on my part if I were to desert my station now from fear of death or of any other thing when God has commanded me—as I am persuaded that he has done—to spend my life in searching for wisdom, and in examining myself and others. That would indeed be a very strange thing: then certainly I might with justice be brought to trial for not believing in the gods, for I should be disobeying the oracle, and fearing death and thinking myself wise when I was not wise. For to fear death, my friends, is only to think ourselves wise without really being wise, for it is to think that we know what we do not know. For no one knows whether death may not be the greatest good that can happen to man. But men fear it as if they knew quite well that it was the greatest of evils. And what is this but that shameful ignorance of thinking that we know what we do not know? In this matter, too, my friends, perhaps I am different from the multitude; and if I were to claim to be at all wiser than others, it would be because, not knowing very much about the other world, I do not think I know. But I do know very well that it is evil and disgraceful to do wrong, and to disobey my superior, whoever he is, whether man or god. I will never do what I know to be evil, and shrink in fear from what I do not know to be good or evil. Even if you acquit me now, and do not listen to Anytus' argument that, if I am to be acquitted, I ought never to have been brought to trial at all, and that, as it is, you are bound to put me to death because, as he said, if I escape, all your sons will be utterly corrupted by practising what Socrates teaches. If you were therefore to say to me: Socrates, this time we will not listen to Anytus; we will let you go, but on this condition, that you give up this investigation of yours, and philosophy; if you are found following those pursuits again, you shall die. I say, if you offered to let me go on these terms, I should reply: Athenians, I hold you in the highest regard and affection, but I will be persuaded by the god rather than by you; and as long as I have breath and strength I will not give up philosophy and exhorting you and declaring the truth to every one of you whom I meet, saying, as I am accustomed, "My good friend, you are a citizen of Athens, a city which is very great and very famous for its wisdom and strength—are you not ashamed of caring so much for the making of money and for fame and prestige, when you neither think nor care about wisdom and truth and the improvement of your soul?" And if he disputes my words and says that he does care about these things, I shall not at once release him and go away: I shall question him and cross-examine him and test him. If I think that he does not possess virtue, though he says that he does, I shall reproach him for undervaluing the most valuable things, and overvaluing those that are less valuable. This I shall do to everyone whom I meet, young or old, citizen or stranger, but especially to citizens, for they are more nearly akin to me. For know that the god has commanded me to do so. And I think that no greater good has ever befallen you in Athens than my service to the god. For I spend my whole life in going about and persuading you all give your first and greatest care to the improvement of your souls, and not till you have done that to think of your bodies or your wealth; and telling you that virtue does not come from wealth, but that wealth, and every other good thing which men have, whether in public or in private, comes from virtue. If then I corrupt the youth by this teaching, these things must be harmful; but if any man says that I teach anything else, there is nothing in what he says. And therefore, Athenians, I say, whether you are persuaded by Anytus or not, whether you acquit me or not, be sure I shall not change my way of life; no, not if I have to die for it many times.

Do not interrupt me, Athenians, with your shouts. Remember the request which I made to you, and do not interrupt my words. I think that it will profit you to hear them. I am going to say something more to you, at which you may be inclined to protest, but do not do that. Be sure that if you put me to death, who am what I have told you that I am, you will do yourselves more harm than me. Meletus and Anytus can do me no harm: that is impossible, for I am sure it is not allowed that a good man be injured by a worse. They may indeed kill me, or drive me into exile, or deprive me of my civil rights; and perhaps Meletus and others think those things great evils. But I do not think so. I think it is a much greater evil to do what he is doing now, and to try to put a man to death unjustly. And now, Athenians, I am not arguing in my own defense at all, as you might expect me to do, but rather in yours in order [that] you may not make a mistake about the gift of the god to you by condemning me. For if you put me to death, you will not easily find another who, if I may use a ludicrous comparison, clings to the state as a sort of gadfly to a horse that is large and well-bred but rather sluggish from its size, and needing to be aroused. It seems to me that the god has attached me like that to the state, for I am constantly alighting upon you at every point to rouse, persuade, and reproach each of you all day long. You will not easily find anyone else, my friends, to fill my place; and if you are persuaded by me, you will spare my life. You are indignant, as drowsy persons are, when they are awakened, and, of course, if you are persuaded by Anytus, you could easily kill me with a single blow, and then sleep on undisturbed for the rest of your lives, unless the god in his care for you sends another to rouse you. And you may easily see that it is the god who has given me to your city; for it is not human the way in which I have neglected all my own interests and permitted my private affairs to be neglected now for so many years, while occupying myself unceasingly in your interests, going to each of you privately, like a father or an elder brother, trying to persuade him to care for virtue. There would have been a reason for it, if I had gained any advantage by this, or if I had been paid for my exhortations; but you see yourselves that my accusers, though they accuse me of everything else without shame, have not had the impudence to say that I ever either exacted or demanded payment. Of that they have no evidence. And I think that I have sufficient evidence of the truth of what I say—my poverty.

Perhaps it may seem strange to you that, though I go about giving this advice privately and meddling in others' affairs, yet I do not venture to come forward in the assembly and advise the state. You have often heard me speak of my reason for this, and in many places: it is that I have a certain divine sign, which is what Meletus has caricatured in his indictment. I have had it from childhood. It is a kind of voice which, whenever I hear it, always turns me back from something which I was going to do, but never urges me to act. It is this which forbids me to take part in politics. And I think it does well to forbid me. For, Athenians, it is quite certain that, if I had attempted to take part in politics, I should have perished at once and long ago without doing any good either to you or to myself. And do not be indignant with me for telling the truth. There is no man who will preserve his life for long, either in Athens or elsewhere, if he firmly opposes the multitude, and tries to prevent the commission of much injustice and illegality in the state. He who would really fight for justice must do so as a private citizen, not as an office-holder, if he is to preserve his life, even for a short time.

I will prove to you that this is so by very strong evidence, not by mere words, but by what you value highly, actions. Listen then to what has happened to me, that you may know that there is no man who could make me consent to do wrong from the fear of death, but that I would perish at once rather than give way. What I am going to tell you may be a commonplace in the law court; nevertheless it is true. The only office that I ever held in the state, Athenians, was that of Senator. When you wished to try the ten generals who did not rescue their men after the battle of Arginusae, as a group, which was illegal, as you all came to think afterwards, the tribe Antiochis, to which I belong, held the presidency. On that occasion I alone of all the presidents opposed your illegal action and gave my vote against you. The speakers were ready to suspend me and arrest me; and you were clamoring against me, and crying out to me to submit. But I thought that I ought to face the danger, with law and justice on my side, rather than join with you in your unjust proposal, from fear of imprisonment or death. That was when the state was democratic. When the oligarchy came in, the Thirty sent for me, with four others, to the council-chamber, and ordered us to bring Leon the Salaminian from Salmis, that they might put him to death. They were in the habit of frequently giving similar orders, to many others, wishing to implicate as many as possible in their crimes. But, then, I again proved, not by mere words, but by my actions, that, if I may speak bluntly, I do not care a straw for death; but that I do care very much indeed about not doing anything unjust or impious. That government with all its powers did not terrify me into doing anything unjust; but when we left the council-chamber, the other four went over to Salamis and brought Leon across to Athens; and I went home. And if the rule of the Thirty had not been destroyed soon afterwards, I should very likely have been put to death for what I did then. Many of you will be my witnesses in this matter.

Now do you think that I could have remained alive all these years if I had taken part in public affairs, and had always maintained the cause of justice like an honest man, and had held it a paramount duty, as it is, to do so? Certainly not, Athenians, nor could any other man. But throughout my whole life, both in private and in public, whenever I have had to take part in public affairs, you will find I have always been the same and have never yielded unjustly to anyone; no, not to those whom my enemies falsely assert to have been my pupils. But I was never anyone's teacher. I have never withheld myself from anyone, young or old, who was anxious to hear me discuss while I was making my investigation; neither do I discuss for payment, and refuse to discuss without payment. I am ready to ask questions of rich and poor alike, and if any man wishes to answer me, and then listen to what I have to say, he may. And I cannot justly be charged with causing these men to turn out good or bad, for I never either taught or professed to teach any of them any knowledge whatever.[1] And if any man asserts that he ever learned or heard anything from me in private which everyone else did not hear as well as he, be sure that he does not speak the truth.

---

[1] Socrates is saying that he only brings forth what is already latently known by a person. This is a central Socratic doctrine. [ED.]

Why is it, then, that people delight in spending so much time in my company? You have heard why, Athenians. I told you the whole truth when I said that they delight in hearing me examine persons who think that they are wise when they are not wise. It is certainly very amusing to listen to that. And, I say, the god has commanded me to examine men, in oracles and in dreams and in every way in which the divine will was ever declared to man. This is the truth, Athenians, and if it were not the truth, it would be easily refuted. For if it were really the case that I have already corrupted some of the young men, and am now corrupting others, surely some of them, finding as they grew older that I had given them bad advice in their youth, would have come forward today to accuse me and take their revenge. Or if they were unwilling to do so themselves, surely their relatives, their fathers or brothers, or others, would, if I had done them any harm, have remembered it and taken their revenge. Certainly I see many of them in Court. Here is Crito, of my own deme and of my own age, the father of Critobulus; here is Lysanias of Sphettus, the father of Aeschines; . . . And I can name many others to you, some of whom Meletus ought to have called as witnesses in the course of his own speech; but if he forgot to call them then, let him call them now—I will yield the floor to him—and tell us if he has any such evidence. No, on the contrary, my friends, you will find all these men ready to support me, the corrupter, the injurer, of their relatives, as Meletus and Anytus call me. Those of them who have been already corrupted might perhaps have some reason for supporting me, but what reason can their relatives have who are grown up, and who are uncorrupted, except the reason of truth and justice— that they know very well that Meletus is a liar, and that I am speaking the truth?

Well, my friends, this, and perhaps more like this, is pretty much what I have to say in my defense. There may be some one among you who will be indignant when he remembers how, even in a less important trial than this, he begged and entreated the judges, with many tears, to acquit him, and brought forward his children and many of his friends and relatives in Court in order to appeal to your feelings; and then finds that I shall do none of these things, though I am in what he would think the supreme danger. Perhaps he will harden himself against me when he notices this: it may make him angry, and he may cast his vote in anger. If it is so with any of you— I do not suppose that it is, but in case it should be so—I think that I should answer him reasonably if I said: My friend, I have relatives, too, for, in the words of Homer, "I am not born of an oak or a rock" but of flesh and blood; and so, Athenians, I have relatives, and I have three sons, one of them a lad, and the other two still children. Yet I will not bring any of them forward before you and implore you to acquit me. And why will I do none of these things? It is not from arrogance, Athenians, nor because I lack respect for you—whether or not I can face death bravely is another question— but for my own good name, and for your good name, and for the good name of the whole state. I do not think it right, at my age and with my reputation, to do anything of that kind. Rightly or wrongly, men have made up their minds that in some way Socrates is different from the mass of mankind. And it will be shameful if those of you who are thought to excel in wisdom, or in bravery, or in any other virtue, are going to act in this fashion. I have often seen men of reputation behaving in an extraordinary way at their trial, as if they thought it a terrible fate to be killed, and as though they expected to live forever if you did not put them to death. Such men seem to me to bring shame upon the state, for any stranger would suppose that the best and most eminent Athenians, who are selected by their fellow citizens to hold office, and for other honors, are no better than women. Those of you, Athenians, who have any reputation at all ought not to do these things, and you ought not to allow us to do them; you should show that you will be much more ready to condemn men who make the state ridiculous by these pitiful pieces of acting, than men who remain quiet.

But apart from the question of reputation, my friends, I do not think that it is right to entreat the judge to acquit us, or to escape condemnation in that way. It is our duty to convince him by reason. He does not sit to give away justice as a favor, but to pronounce judgment; and he has sworn, not to favor any man whom he would like to favor, but to judge according to law. And, therefore, we ought not to encourage you in the habit of breaking your oaths; and you ought not to allow yourselves to fall into this habit, for then neither you nor we would be acting piously. Therefore, Athenians, do not require me to do these things, for I believe them to be neither good nor just nor pious; and, more especially, do not ask me to do them today when Meletus is prosecuting me for impiety. For were I to be successful and persuade you by my entreaties to break your oaths, I should be clearly teaching you to believe that there are no gods, and I should be simply accusing myself by my defense of not believing in them. But, Athenians, that is very far from the truth. I do believe in the gods as no one of my accusers believes in them: and to you and to God I commit my cause to be decided as is best for you and for me.

(*He is found guilty by 281 votes to 220.*)

I am not indignant at the verdict which you have given, Athenians, for many reasons. I expected that you would find me guilty; and I am not so much surprised at that as at the numbers of the votes. I certainly never thought that the majority against me would have been so narrow. But now it seems that if only thirty votes had changed sides, I should have escaped. So I think that I have escaped Meletus, as it is; and not only have I escaped him, for it is perfectly clear that if Anytus and Lycon had not come forward to accuse me, too, he would not have obtained the fifth part of the votes, and would have had to pay a fine of a thousand drachmae.

So he proposes death as the penalty. Be it so. And what alternative penalty shall I propose to you, Athenians? What I deserve, of course, must I not? What then do I deserve to pay or to suffer for having determined not to spend my life in ease? I neglected the things which most men value, such as wealth, and family interests, and military commands, and popular oratory, and all the political appointments, and clubs, and factions, that there are in Athens; for I thought that I was really too honest a man to preserve my life if I engaged in these matters. So I did not go where I should have done no good either to you or to myself. I went, instead, to each one of you privately to do him, as I say, the greatest of services, and tried to persuade him not to think of his affairs until he had thought of himself and tried to make himself as good and wise as possible, nor to think of the affairs of Athens until he had thought of Athens herself; and to care for other things in the same manner. Then what do I deserve for such a life? Something good, Athenians, if I am really to propose what I deserve; and something good which it would be suitable to me to receive. Then what is a suitable reward to be given to a poor benefactor who requires leisure to exhort you? There is no reward, Athenians, so suitable for him as a public maintenance in the Prytaneum. It is a much more suitable reward for him than for any of you who has won a victory at the Olympic games with his horse or his chariots. Such a man only makes you seem happy, but I make you really happy; and he is not in want, and I am. So if I am to propose the penalty which I really deserve, I propose this—a public maintenance in the Prytaneum.

Perhaps you think me stubborn and arrogant in what I am saying now, as in what I said about the entreaties and tears. It is not so, Athenians; it is rather that I am convinced that I never wronged any man intentionally, though I cannot persuade you of that, for we have discussed together only a little time. If there were a law at Athens, as there is elsewhere, not to finish a trial of life and death in a single day, I think that I could have persuaded you; but now it is not easy in so short a time to clear myself of great prejudices. But when I am persuaded that I have never wronged any man, I shall certainly not wrong myself, or admit that I deserve to suffer any evil, or propose any evil for myself as a penalty. Why should I? Lest I should suffer the penalty which Meletus proposes when I say that I do not know whether it is a good or an evil? Shall I choose instead of it something which I know to be an evil, and propose that as a penalty? Shall I propose imprisonment? And why should I pass the rest of my days in prison, the slave of successive officials? Or shall I propose a fine, with imprisonment until it is paid? I have told you why I will not do that. I should have to remain in prison, for I have no money to pay a fine with. Shall I then propose exile? Perhaps you would agree to that. Life would indeed be very dear to me if I were unreasonable enough to expect that strangers would cheerfully tolerate my discussions and reasonings when you who are my fellow citizens cannot endure them, and have found them so irksome and odious to you that you are seeking now to be relieved of them. No, indeed, Athenians, that is not likely. A fine life I should lead for an old man if I were to withdraw from Athens and pass the rest of my days in wandering from city to city, and continually being expelled. For I know very well that the young men will listen to me wherever I go, as they do here; and if I drive them away, they will persuade their elders to expel me; and if I do not drive them away, their fathers and kinsmen will expel me for their sakes.

Perhaps someone will say, "Why cannot you withdraw from Athens, Socrates, and hold your peace?" It is the most difficult thing in the world to make you understand why I cannot do that. If I say that I cannot hold my peace because that would be to disobey the god, you will think that I am not in earnest and will not believe me. And if I tell you that no better thing can happen to a man than to discuss virtue every day and the other matters about which you have heard me arguing and examining myself and others, and that an unexamined life is not worth living, then you will believe me still less. But that is so, my friends, though it is not easy to persuade you. And, what is more, I am not accustomed to think that I deserve any punishment. If I had been rich, I would have proposed as large a fine as I could pay: that would have done me no harm. But I am not rich enough to pay a fine unless you are willing to fix it at a sum within my means. Perhaps I could pay you a mina, so I propose that. Plato here, Athenians, and Crito, and Critobulus, and Apollodorus bid me propose thirty minae, and they will be sureties for me. So I propose thirty minae. They will be sufficient sureties to you for the money.

(*He is condemned to death.*)

You have not gained very much time, Athenians, and, as the price of it, you will have an evil name for all who wish to revile the state, and they will say that you put Socrates, a wise man, to death. For they will certainly call me wise, whether I am wise or not, when they want to reproach you. If you would have waited for a little while, your wishes would have been fulfilled in the course of nature; for you see that I am an old man, far advanced in years, and near to death. I am saying this not to all of you, only to those who have voted for my death. And to them I have something else to say. Perhaps, my friends, you think that I have been convicted because I was wanting in the arguments by which I could have persuaded you to acquit me, if, that is, I had thought it right to do or to say anything to escape punishment. It is not so. I have been convicted because I was wanting, not in arguments, but in impudence and shamelessness—because I would not plead before you as you would have liked to hear me plead, or appeal to you with weeping and wailing, or say and do many other things which I maintain are unworthy of me, but which you have been accustomed to from other men. But when I was defending myself, I thought that I ought not to do anything unworthy of a free man because of the danger which I ran, and I have not changed my mind now. I would very much rather defend myself as I did, and die, than as you would have had me do, and live. Both in a lawsuit and in war, there are some things which neither I nor any other man may do in order to escape from death. In battle, a man often sees that he may at least escape from death by throwing down his arms and falling on his knees before the pursuer to beg for his life. And there are many other ways of avoiding death in every danger if a man is willing to say and to do anything. But, my friends, I think that it is a much harder thing to escape from wickedness than from death, for wickedness is swifter than death. And now I, who am old and slow, have been overtaken by the slower pursuer: and my accusers, who are clever and swift, have been overtaken by the swifter pursuer—wickedness. And now I shall go away, sentenced by you to death; and they will go away, sentenced by truth to wickedness and injustice. And I abide by this award as well as they. Perhaps it was right for these things to be so; and I think that they are fairly measured.

And now I wish to prophesy to you, Athenians, who have condemned me. For I am going to die, and that is the time when men have most prophetic power. And I prophesy to you who have sentenced me to death that a far more severe punishment than you have inflicted on me will surely overtake you as soon as I am dead. You have done this thing, thinking that you will be relieved from having to give an account of your lives. But I say that the result will be very different. There will be more men who will call you to account, whom I have held back, though you did not recognize it. And they will be harsher toward you than I have been, for they will be younger, and you will be more indignant with them. For if you think that you will restrain men from reproaching you for not living as you should, by putting them to death, you are very much mistaken. That way of escape is neither possible nor honorable. It is much more honorable and much easier not to suppress others, but to make yourselves as good as you can. This is my parting prophecy to you who have condemned me.

With you who have acquitted me I should like to discuss this thing that has happened, while the authorities are busy, and before I go to the place where I have to die. So, remain with me until I go: there is no reason why we should not talk with each other while it is possible. I wish to explain to you, as my friends, the meaning of what has happened to me. A wonderful thing has happened to me, judges—for you I am right in calling judges. The prophetic sign has been constantly with me all through my life till now, opposing me in quite small matters if I were not going to act rightly. And now you yourselves see what has happened to me—a thing which might be thought, and which is sometimes actually reckoned, the supreme evil. But the divine sign did not oppose me when I was leaving my house in the morning, nor when I was coming up here to the court, nor at any point in my speech when I was going to say anything; though at other times it has often stopped me in the very act of speaking. But now, in this matter, it has never once opposed me, either in my words or my actions. I will tell you what I believe to be the reason. This thing that has come upon me must be a good; and those of us who think that death is an evil must needs be mistaken. I have a clear proof that that is so; for my accustomed sign would certainly have opposed me if I had not been going to meet with something good.

And if we reflect in another way, we shall see that we may well hope that death is a good. For the state of death is one of two things: either the dead man wholly ceases to be and loses all consciousness or, as we are told, it is a change and a migration of the soul to another place. And if death is the absence of all consciousness, and like the sleep of one whose slumbers are unbroken by any dreams, it will be a wonderful gain. For if a man had to select that night in which he slept so soundly that he did not even dream, and had to compare with it all the other nights and days of his life, and then had to say how many days and nights in his life he had spent better and more pleasantly than this night, I think that a private person, nay, even the great King himself, would find them easy to count, compared with the others. If that is the nature of death, I for one count it a gain. For then it appears that all time is nothing more than a single night. But if death is a journey to another place, and what we are told is true—that there are all who have died—what good could be greater than this, my judges? Would a journey not be worth taking, at the end of which, in the other world, we should be released from the self-styled judges here and should find the true judges who are said to sit in judgment below, such as Minos and Rhadamanthus and Aeacus and Triptolemus, and the other demigods who were just in their own lives? Or what would you not give to discuss with Orpheus and Musaeus and Hesiod and Homer? I am willing to die many times if this be true. And for my own part I should find it wonderful to meet there Palamedes, and Ajax, the son of Telamon, and the other men of old who have died through an unjust judgment, and in comparing my experiences with theirs. That I think would be no small pleasure. And, above all, I could spend my time in examining those who are there, as I examine men here, and in finding out which of them is wise, and which of them thinks himself wise when he is not wise. What would we not give, my judges, to be able to examine the leader of the great expedition against Troy, or Odysseus, or Sisyphus, or countless other men and women whom we could name? It would be an infinite happiness to discuss with them and to live with them and to examine them. Assuredly there they do not put men to death for doing that. For besides the other ways in which they are happier than we are, they are immortal, at least if what we are told is true.

And you, too, judges, must face death hopefully, and believe this as a truth that no evil can happen to a good man, either in life or after death. His fortunes are not neglected by the gods; and what has happened to me today has not happened by chance. I am persuaded that it was better for me to die now, and to be released from trouble; and that was the reason why the sign never turned me back. And so I am not at all angry with my accusers or with those who have condemned me to die. Yet it was not with this in mind that they accused me and condemned me, but meaning to do me an injury. So far I may blame them.

Yet I have one request to make of them. When my sons grow up, punish them, my friends, and harass them in the same way that I have harassed you, if they seem to you to care for riches or for any other thing more than virtue; and if they think that they are something when they are really nothing, reproach them, as I have reproached you, for not caring for what they should, and for thinking that they are great men when really they are worthless. And if you will do this, I myself and my sons will have received justice from you.

But now the time has come, and we must go away—I to die, and you to live. Whether life or death is better is known to God, and to God only.

(*Socrates was given the opportunity to escape, but he refused, pointing out to Crito that to do so would violate his principles. This is from the* Crito.)

Socr. Then, my good friend, we must not think so much of what the many will say of us; we must think of what the one man who understands justice and injustice, and of what truth herself, will say of us. And so you are mistaken, to begin with, when you invite us to regard the opinion of the multitude concerning the just and the honorable and the good, and their opposites. But, it may be said, the multitude can put us to death?

Crito. Yes, that is evident. That may be said, Socrates.

Socr. True. But, my good friend, to me it appears that the conclusion which we have just reached is the same as our conclusion of former times. Now consider whether we still hold to the belief that we should set the highest value, not on living, but on living well?

Crito. Yes, we do.

Socr. And living well and honorably and justly mean the same thing: do we hold to that or not?

Crito. We do.

Socr. Then, starting from these premises, we have to consider whether it is just or not for me to try to escape from prison, without the consent of the Athenians. If we find that it is just, we will try; if not, we will give up the idea.

. . . shall we be acting justly if we give money and thanks to the men who are to aid me in escaping, and if we ourselves take our respective parts in my escape? Or shall we in truth be acting unjustly if we do all this?

Then, my next point, or rather my next question, is this: Ought a man to carry out his just agreements, or may he shuffle out of them?

Crito. He ought to carry them out.

Socr. Then consider. If I escape without the state's consent, shall I be injuring those whom I ought least to injure, or not? Shall I be abiding by my just agreements or not?

Crito. I cannot answer your question, Socrates. I do not understand it.

Socr.   Consider it in this way. Suppose the laws and the commonwealth were to come and appear to me as I was preparing to run away (if that is the right phrase to describe my escape) and were to ask, "Tell us, Socrates, what have you in your mind to do? What do you mean by trying to escape but to destroy us, the laws and the whole state, so far as you are able? Do you think that a state can exist and not be overthrown, in which the decisions of law are of no force, and are disregarded and undermined by private individuals?" . . . Shall I reply, "But the state has injured me by judging my case unjustly"? Shall we say that?

Crito.   Certainly we will, Socrates.

Socr.   And suppose the laws were to reply, "Was that our agreement? Or was it that you would abide by whatever judgments the state should pronounce?" . . . What answer shall we make, Crito? Shall we say that the laws speak the truth, or not?

Crito.   I think that they do.

Socr.   "Then consider, Socrates," perhaps they would say, "if we are right in saying that by attempting to escape you are attempting an injustice. We brought you into the world, we raised you, we educated you, we gave you and every other citizen a share of all the good things we could. Yet we proclaim that if any man of the Athenians is dissatisfied with us, he may take his goods and go away wherever he pleases; we give that privilege to every man who chooses to avail himself of it, so soon as he has reached manhood, and sees us, the laws, and the administration of our state. No one of us stands in his way or forbids him to take his goods and go wherever he likes, whether it be to an Athenian colony or to any foreign country, if he is dissatisfied with us and with the state. But we say that every man of you who remains here, seeing how we administer justice, and how we govern the state in other matters, has agreed, by the very fact of remaining here, to do whatsoever we tell him. And, we say, he who disobeys us acts unjustly on three counts: he disobeys us who are his parents, and he disobeys us who reared him, and he disobeys us after he has agreed to obey us, without persuading us that we are wrong.

". . . if you had wished, you might at your trial have offered to go into exile. At that time you could have done with the state's consent what you are trying now to do without it. But then you gloried in being willing to die. You said that you preferred death to exile. And now you do not honor those words: you do not respect us, the laws, for you are trying to destroy us; and you are acting just as a miserable slave would act, trying to run away, and breaking the contracts and agreement which you made to live as our citizen. First, therefore, answer this question. Are we right, or are we wrong, in saying that you have agreed not in mere words, but in your actions, to live under our government?" What are we to say, Crito? Must we not admit that it is true?

Crito.   We must, Socrates.

Socr.   Then they would say, "Are you not breaking your contracts and agreements with us? And you were not led to make them by force or by fraud. You did not have to make up your mind in a hurry. You had seventy years in which you might have gone away if you had been dissatisfied with us, or if the agreement had seemed to you unjust. But you preferred neither Sparta nor Crete, though you are fond of saying that they are well governed, nor any other state, either of the Greeks or the Barbarians. . . . Clearly you, far more than other Athenians, were satisfied with the state, and also with us who are its laws; for who would be satisfied with a state which has no laws? And now will you not abide by your agreement? If you take our advice, you will, Socrates; then you will not make yourself ridiculous by going away from Athens.

"Reflect now. What good will you do yourself or your friends by thus transgressing and breaking your agreement? It is tolerably certain that they, on their part, will at least run the risk of exile, and of losing their civil rights, or of forfeiting their property. You yourself might go to one of the neighboring states, to Thebes or to Megara, for instance—for both of them are well governed—but, Socrates, you will come as an enemy to these governments, and all who care for their city will look askance at you, and think that you are a subverter of law. You will confirm the judges in their opinion, and make it seem that their verdict was a just one. For a man who is a subverter of law may well be supposed to be a corrupter of the young and thoughtless. Then will you avoid well-governed states and civilized men? Will life be worth having, if you do? Will you associate with such men, and converse without shame— about what, Socrates? About the things which you talk of here? Will you tell them that excellence and justice and institutions and law are the most valuable things that men can have? And do you not think that that will be a disgraceful thing for Socrates?"

Crito.   I have nothing more to say, Socrates.

Socr.   Then let it be, Crito, and let us do as I say, since the god is our guide.

But I suppose that I may, and must, pray to the gods that my journey hence may be prosperous. That is my prayer; may it be granted.

(Thus Socrates preferred to die rather than go against his principles.)

(After being sentenced Socrates spent several days in prison talking to his friends before having the poison administered to him. Among the topics they discussed were man's possible knowledge of God and whether or not man has an immortal soul. Socrates believed man has an immortal soul because the soul can perceive and share in truth, goodness, and beauty, which are eternal. The following is from the Phaedo.)*

And were we not saying long ago that the soul when using the body as an instrument of perception, that is to say, when using the sense of sight or hearing or some other sense (for the meaning of perceiving through the body is perceiving through the senses)—were we not saying that the soul too is then dragged by the body into the region of the changeable, and wanders and is confused; the world spins round her, and she is like a drunkard, when she touches change?

Very true.

But when returning into herself she reflects, then she passes into the other world, the region of purity, and eternity, and immortality, and unchangeableness, which are her kindred, and with them she ever lives, when she is by herself and is not let or hindered; then she ceases from her erring ways, and being in communion with the unchanging is unchanging. And this state of the soul is called wisdom?

That is well and truly said, Socrates, he replied.

*From Plato, *Apology, Phaedo,* and *Crito.* Taken from *Dialogues of Plato,* 3d ed., trans. Benjamin Jowett (Oxford: Oxford University Press, 1896).

And to which class is the soul more nearly alike and akin, as far as may be in-ferred from this argument, as well as from the preceding one?

I think, Socrates, that, in the opinion of everyone who follows the argument, the soul will be infinitely more like the unchangeable—even the most stupid person will not deny that.

And the body is more like the changing?

Yes.

Yet once more consider the matter in another light: When the soul and the body are united, then nature orders the soul to rule and govern, and the body to obey and serve. Now which of these two functions is akin to the divine? and which to the mor-tal? Does not the divine appear to you to be that which naturally orders and rules, and the mortal to be that which is subject and servant?

True.

And which does the soul resemble?

The soul resembles the divine, and the body the mortal—there can be no doubt of that, Socrates.

Then reflect, Cebes: of all which has been said is not this the conclusion?—that the soul is in the very likeness of the divine, and immortal, and intellectual, and uni-form, and indissoluble, and unchangeable; and that the body is in the very likeness of the human, and mortal, and unintellectual, and multiform, and dissoluble, and change-able. Can this, my dear Cebes, be denied?

It cannot.

But if it be true, then is not the body liable to speedy dissolution? and is not the soul almost or altogether indissoluble?

Certainly.

Must we not, said Socrates, ask ourselves what that is which, as we imagine, is liable to be scattered, and about which we fear? and what again is that about which we have no fear? And then we may proceed further to inquire whether that which suf-fers dispersion is or is not of the nature of soul—our hopes and fears as to our own souls will turn upon the answers to these questions.

Very true, he said.

Now the compound or composite may be supposed to be naturally capable, as of being compounded, so also of being dissolved; but that which is uncompounded, and that only, must be, if anything is, indissoluble.

Yes; I should imagine so, said Cebes.

And the uncompounded may be assumed to be the same and unchanging, whereas the compound is always changing and never the same.

I agree, he said.

Then now let us return to the previous discussion. Is that idea or essence, which in the dialectical process we define as essence or true existence—whether essence of equality, beauty, or anything else—are these essences, I say, liable at times to some degree of change? or are they each of them always what they are, having the same simple self-existent and unchanging forms, not admitting of variation at all, or in any way, or at any time?

They must be always the same, Socrates, replied Cebes.

And what would you say of the many beautiful—whether men or horses or garments or any other things which are named by the same names and may be called equal or beautiful,—are they all unchanging and the same always, or quite the reverse? May they not rather be described as almost always changing and hardly ever the same, either with themselves or with one another?

The latter, replied Cebes; they are always in a state of change.

And these you can touch and see and perceive with the senses, but the unchanging things you can only perceive with the mind—they are invisible and are not seen?

That is very true, he said.

Well then, added Socrates, let us suppose that there are two sorts of existences—one seen, the other unseen.

Let us suppose them.

The seen is the changing, and the unseen is the unchanging?

That may be also supposed.

And, further, is not one part of us body, another part soul?

To be sure.

And to which class is the body more alike and akin?

Clearly to the seen—no one can doubt that.

And is the soul seen or not seen?

Not by man, Socrates.

And what we mean by "seen" and "not seen" is that which is or is not visible to the eye of man?

Yes, to the eye of man.

And is the soul seen or not seen?

Not seen.

Unseen then?

Yes.

Then the soul is more like to the unseen, and the body to the seen?

That follows necessarily, Socrates.

 To Think About

1. Define atheism. Was Socrates an atheist? Name some famous historical and contemporary atheists.

2. Do you believe Socrates was entirely guiltless of the charges? Did the Athenians have a case at all?

3. Think about the metaphor of the gadfly. Who are the gadflies in today's world? Name a liberal gadfly and a conservative one.

4. Socrates said that an "unexamined life is not worth living." What do you think this means? Can you think of people who haven't examined their lives? Has the average person examined his or her life?

5. Do Socrates' reasons for not fearing death satisfy you? Do you fear death? Who do you know that doesn't fear it?

6. "The chief task of philosophy is to prevent mankind from losing itself in the ideas and activities which the existing organizations of society instill in its members." Discuss.   ***Max Horkheimer***

7. "You see me as an atheist. God sees me as the loyal opposition."

    Woody Allen

8. "If I had my life to live over again, I would have made it a rule to read some poetry and listen to some music at least every week. . . . The loss of these tastes is a loss of happiness, and may possibly be injurious to the intellect, and more probably to the moral character, by enfeebling the emotional part of our nature."   ***Charles Darwin***

9. "Philosophy is man's quest for the unity of knowledge: it consists in a perpetual struggle to create the concepts in which the universe can be conceived as a universe and not a multiverse."   ***William Halverson***

10. "Philosophy means liberation from the two dimensions of routine, soaring above the well known, seeing it in new perspectives, arousing wonder and the wish to fly."   ***Walter Kaufmann***

11. "Plato . . . knew that our reason, if left to itself, tries to soar up to knowledge to which no object that experience may give can ever correspond; but which is nonetheless real, and by no means a cobweb of the brain."

    Immanuel Kant

12. What is the best argument establishing immortality?

13. "The true lover of knowledge is always striving after *being*. . . . He will not rest at those multitudinous phenomena whose existence is appearance only."

    Plato

 Readings

Socrates

BENSON, H. H., ed. *Essays on the Philosophy of Socrates.* New York: Oxford University Press, 1992.

GUTHRIE, W. K. C. *Socrates.* London: Cambridge University Press, 1972.

MONTGOMERY, J. D. *Socrates versus the State.* New York, 1954.

SANTAS, GEORGE. *Socrates.* Boston, 1978.

TAYLOR, A. E. *Socrates.* Garden City, NY: Doubleday, 1953.

VLASTOS, G., ed. *The Philosophy of Socrates.* Garden City, NY: Anchor Books, 1971.

Plato

CROMBIE, I. M. *An Examination of Plato's Doctrines.* 2 vols. London: Routledge & Kegan Paul, 1962–63.

GRUBE, G. M. A. *Plato's Thought.* 2d ed. London: Hackett, 1980.

IRWIN, T. *Plato's Ethics.* New York: Oxford University Press, 1995.

KRAUT, R., ed. *The Cambridge Companion to Plato.* Cambridge: Cambridge University Press, 1992.

ROSS, W. D. *Plato's Theory of Ideas.* Oxford: Clarendon Press, 1951.

SHOREY, P. *What Plato Said.* Chicago: University of Chicago Press, 1933.

TAYLOR, A. E. *Plato, the Man and His Work.* London: Methuen, 1926.

~~~~~~

What Is the Value of Philosophy?

3
The Value of Philosophy

Bertrand Russell (1872–1970), the grandson of Lord John Russell, a prime minister under Queen Victoria, was born in Wales. He studied mathematics and philosophy at Trinity College, Cambridge, from 1890 to 1894. He was a fellow at Trinity from 1895 to 1901 and a lecturer in philosophy there from 1910 to 1916. In 1916, Russell was dismissed from his position because of his pacifist activities. Then, in 1918, he was sentenced to six months in prison because of an allegedly libelous article in which he expressed his opposition to World War I and his desire for peace. Russell was a fellow of the Royal Society, an honorary fellow of the British Academy, and a recipient of the Order of Merit. He was awarded the Nobel Prize for literature in 1950. In the area of logic, Russell wrote Principles of Mathematics *(1903)*, Principia Mathematica *(with A. N. Whitehead; three volumes, 1910–13), and* Introduction to Mathematical Philosophy *(1919). His works in epistemology and metaphysics include* Our Knowledge of the External World *(1914),* The Analysis of Matter *(1927), and* Human Knowledge, Its Scope and Limits *(1948). Among his books on social issues are* Marriage and Morals *(1929) and* Education and the Social Order *(1932).*

"Practical" people often dismiss philosophy because they see it as vague and uncertain. Russell agrees that philosophy deals with issues with uncertain answers. Yet in this uncertainty, he sees philosophy's chief value—that in contemplating the great questions one is freed from narrow personal interests alone. Russell believes that unless the individual can escape from his "instinctive Self," the self concerned only with immediate personal needs, he or she will be assaulted and damaged by the events outside that private world. The "practical" person who scorns philosophy does have

From Bertrand Russell, *The Problems of Philosophy* (Oxford: Oxford University Press, 2001). Reprinted by permission of Oxford University Press, UK.

a philosophy—usually "rugged individualism"—a philosophy Russell argues is inadequate, in part because it fails to meet one's mental needs.

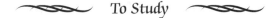 To Study

1. Describe the "practical" person.
2. Why must we free ourselves from the prejudices of the "practical" individual?
3. At what does philosophy aim?
4. With what types of questions does philosophy deal? Give an example.
5. According to Russell, where does the chief value of philosophy lie?
6. Describe the instinctive person.
7. How does the "Self" enlarge itself?
8. What is the relation of the philosophic mind to the world of action and justice? Can you suggest an example of an individual so concerned?

Having now come to the end of our brief and very incomplete review of the problems of philosophy, it will be well to consider, in conclusion, what is the value of philosophy and why it ought to be studied. It is the more necessary to consider this question, in view of the fact that many men, under the influence of science or of practical affairs, are inclined to doubt whether philosophy is anything better than innocent but useless trifling, hair-splitting distinctions, and controversies on matters concerning which knowledge is impossible.

This view of philosophy appears to result, partly from a wrong conception of the ends of life, partly from a wrong conception of the kind of goods which philosophy strives to achieve. Physical science, through the medium of inventions, is useful to innumerable people who are wholly ignorant of it; thus the study of physical science is to be recommended, not only, or primarily, because of the effect on mankind in general. This utility does not belong to philosophy. If the study of philosophy has any value at all for others than students of philosophy, it must be only indirectly, through its effects upon the lives of those who study it. It is in these effects, therefore, if anywhere, that the value of philosophy must be primarily sought.

But further, if we are not to fail in our endeavour to determine the value of philosophy, we must first free our minds from the prejudices of what are wrongly called "practical" men. The "practical" man, as this word is often used, is one who recognizes only material needs, who realizes that men must have food for the body, but is oblivious of the necessity of providing food for the mind. If all men were well off, if poverty and disease had been reduced to their lowest possible point, there would still remain much to be done to produce a valuable society; and even in the existing world the goods of the mind are at least as important as the goods of the body. It is exclusively among the goods of the mind that the value of philosophy is to be found; and only those who are not indifferent to these goods can be persuaded that the study of philosophy is not a waste of time.

Philosophy, like all other studies, aims primarily at knowledge. The knowledge it aims at is the kind of knowledge which gives unity and system to the body of the sciences, and the kind which results from a critical examination of the grounds of our convictions, prejudices, and beliefs. But it cannot be maintained that philosophy has had any very great measure of success in its attempts to provide definite answers to its questions. If you ask a mathematician, a mineralogist, a historian, or any other man of learning, what definite body of truths has been ascertained by his science, his answer will last as long as you are willing to listen. But if you put the same question to a philosopher, he will, if he is candid, have to confess that his study has not achieved positive results such as have been achieved by other sciences. It is true that this is partly accounted for by the fact that, as soon as definite knowledge concerning any subject becomes possible, this subject ceases to be called philosophy, and becomes a separate science. The whole study of the heavens, which now belongs to astronomy, was once included in philosophy; Newton's great work was called "the mathematical principles of natural philosophy." Similarly, the study of the human mind, which was, until very lately, a part of philosophy, has now been separated from philosophy and has become the science of psychology. Thus, to a great extent, the uncertainty of philosophy is more apparent than real: those questions which are already capable of definite answers are placed in the sciences, while those only to which, at present, no definite answer can be given, remain to form the residue which is called philosophy.

This is, however, only a part of the truth concerning the uncertainty of philosophy. There are many questions—and among them those that are of the profoundest interest to our spiritual life—which, so far as we can see, must remain insoluble to the human intellect unless its powers become of quite a different order from what they are now. Has the universe any unity of plan or purpose, or is it a fortuitous concourse of atoms? Is consciousness a permanent part of the universe, giving hope of indefinite growth in wisdom, or is it a transitory accident on a small planet on which life must ultimately become impossible? Are good and evil of importance to the universe or only to man? Such questions are asked by philosophy, and variously answered by various philosophers. But it would seem that, whether answers be otherwise discoverable or not, the answers suggested by philosophy are none of them demonstrably true. Yet, however slight may be the hope of discovering an answer, it is part of the business of philosophy to continue the consideration of such questions, to make us aware of their importance, to examine all the approaches to them, and to keep alive that speculative interest in the universe which is apt to be killed by confining ourselves to definitely ascertainable knowledge.

Many philosophers, it is true, have held that philosophy could establish the truth of certain answers to such fundamental questions. They have supposed that what is of most importance in religious beliefs could be proved by strict demonstration to be true. In order to judge of such attempts, it is necessary to take a survey of human knowledge, and to form an opinion as to its methods and its limitations. On such a subject it would be unwise to pronounce dogmatically; but if the investigations of our previous chapters have not led us astray, we shall be compelled to renounce the hope of finding philosophical proofs of religious beliefs. We cannot, therefore, include as part of the value of philosophy any definite set of answers to such questions. Hence, once more, the value of philosophy must not depend upon any supposed body of definitely ascertainable knowledge to be acquired by those who study it.

The value of philosophy is, in fact, to be sought largely in its very uncertainty. The man who has no tincture of philosophy goes through life imprisoned in the prejudices derived from common sense, from the habitual beliefs of his age or his nation, and from convictions which have grown up in his mind without the co-operation or consent of his deliberate reason. To such a man the world tends to become definite, finite, obvious; common objects rouse no questions, and unfamiliar possibilities are contemptuously rejected. As soon as we begin to philosophise, on the contrary, we find, as we saw in our opening chapters, that even the most everyday things lead to problems to which only very incomplete answers can be given. Philosophy, though unable to tell us with certainty what is the true answer to the doubts which it raises, is able to suggest many possibilities which enlarge our thoughts and free them from the tyranny of custom. Thus, while diminishing our feeling of certainty as to what things are, it greatly increases our knowledge as to what they may be; it removes the somewhat arrogant dogmatism of those who have never travelled into the region of liberating doubt, and it keeps alive our sense of wonder by showing familiar things in an unfamiliar aspect.

Apart from its utility in showing unsuspected possibilities, philosophy has a value—perhaps its chief value—through the greatness of the objects which it contemplates, and the freedom from narrow and personal aims resulting from this contemplation. The life of the instinctive man is shut up within the circle of his private interests: family and friends may be included, but the outer world is not regarded except as it may help or hinder what comes within the circle of instinctive wishes. In such a life there is something feverish and confined, in comparison with which the philosophic life is calm and free. The private world of instinctive interests is a small one, set in the midst of a great and powerful world which must, sooner or later, lay our private world in ruins. Unless we can so enlarge our interests as to include the whole outer world, we remain like a garrison in a beleaguered fortress, knowing that the enemy prevents escape and that ultimate surrender is inevitable. In such a life there is no peace, but a constant strife between the insistence of desire and the powerlessness of will. In one way or another, if our life is to be great and free, we must escape this prison and this strife.

One way of escape is by philosophic contemplation. Philosophic contemplation does not, in its widest survey, divide the universe into two hostile camps—friends and foes, helpful and hostile, good and bad—it views the whole impartially. Philosophic contemplation, when it is unalloyed, does not aim at proving that the rest of the universe is akin to man. All acquisition of knowledge is an enlargement of the Self, but this enlargement is best attained when it is not directly sought. It is obtained when the desire for knowledge is alone operative, by a study which does not wish in advance that its objects should have this or that character, but adapts the Self to the characters which it finds in its objects. This enlargement of Self is not obtained when, taking the Self as it is, we try to show that the world is so similar to this Self that knowledge of it is possible without any admission of what seems alien. The desire to prove this is a form of self-assertion, and like all self-assertion, it is an obstacle to the growth of Self which it desires, and of which the Self knows that it is capable. Self-assertion, in philosophic speculation as elsewhere, views the world as a means to its own ends; thus it makes the world of less account than Self, and the Self sets bounds to the greatness of its goods. In contemplation, on the contrary, we start from the not-Self, and through its greatness the boundaries of Self are enlarged, through the infinity of the universe the mind which contemplates it achieves some share in infinity.

For this reason greatness of soul is not fostered by those philosophies which assimilate the universe to Man. Knowledge is a form of union of Self and not-Self; like all union, it is impaired by dominion, and therefore by any attempt to force the universe into conformity with what we find in ourselves. There is a widespread philosophical tendency toward the view which tells us that man is the measure of all things, that truth is man-made, that space and time and the world of universals are properties of the mind, and that, if there be anything not created by the mind, it is unknowable and of no account for us. This view, if our previous discussions were correct, is untrue; but in addition to being untrue, it has the effect of robbing philosophic contemplation of all that gives it value, since it fetters contemplation to Self. What it calls knowledge is not a union with the not-Self, but a set of prejudices, habits, and desires, making an impenetrable veil between us and the world beyond. The man who finds pleasure in such a theory of knowledge is like the man who never leaves the domestic circle for fear his word might not be law.

The true philosophic contemplation, on the contrary, finds its satisfaction in every enlargement of the not-Self, in everything that magnifies the objects contemplated, and thereby the subject contemplating. Everything, in contemplation, that is personal or private, everything that depends upon habit, self-interest, or desire, distorts the object, and hence impairs the union which the intellect seeks. By thus making a barrier between subject and object, such personal and private things become a prison to the intellect. The free intellect will see as God might see, without a *here* and *now*, without hopes and fears, without the trammels of customary beliefs and traditional prejudices, calmly, dispassionately, in the sole and exclusive desire of knowledge—knowledge as impersonal, as purely contemplative, as it is possible for man to attain. Hence also the free intellect will value more the abstract and universal knowledge into which the accidents of private history do not enter, than the knowledge brought by the senses, and dependent, as such knowledge must be, upon an exclusive and personal point of view and a body whose sense-organs distort as much as they reveal.

The mind which has become accustomed to the freedom and impartiality of philosophic contemplation will preserve something of the same freedom and impartiality in the world of action and emotion. It will view its purposes and desires as parts of the whole, with the absence of insistence that results from seeing them as infinitesimal fragments in a world of which all the rest is unaffected by any one man's deeds. The impartiality which, in contemplation, is the unalloyed desire for truth, is the very same quality of mind which, in action, is justice, and in emotion is that universal love which can be given to all, and not only to those who are judged useful or admirable. Thus contemplation enlarges not only the objects of our thoughts, but also the objects of our actions and our affections: it makes us citizens of the universe, not only of one walled city at war with all the rest. In this citizenship of the universe consists man's true freedom, and his liberation from the thraldom of narrow hopes and fears.

Thus, to sum up our discussion of the value of philosophy: Philosophy is to be studied, not for the sake of any definite answers to its questions, since no definite answers can, as a rule, be known to be true, but rather for the sake of the questions themselves; because these questions enlarge our conception of what is possible, enrich our intellectual imagination, and diminish the dogmatic assurance which closes the mind against speculation; but above all because, through the greatness of the universe which philosophy contemplates, the mind also is rendered great, and becomes capable of that union with the universe which constitutes its highest good.

To Think About

1. "There is no private life that is not determined by a wider public life."
   George Eliot

2. "The idealist deals with facts as much as the realist. He merely sees them differently." **Margaret Halsey,** in *Pseudo Ethic*

3. "Utopianism is the growing edge of society." **A. J. Muste**

4. " 'Realistic people' who pursue 'practical aims' are rarely as realistic or practical, in the long run of life, as the dreamers who pursue their dreams." **Hans Selye**

5. "Philosophy is the eternal search for truth, a search which inevitably fails and yet is never defeated; which continually eludes us, but which always guides us." **William James**

6. "Jesus Christ was a realist." **James Gould**

7. "The philosopher is not a citizen of any community of ideas. That is what made him a philosopher." **Ludwig Wittgenstein**

8. "[T]he ideas of economists and political philosophers, both when they are right and when they are wrong, are more powerful than is commonly understood. Indeed the world is ruled by little else. Practical men, who believe themselves to be quite exempt from any intellectual influences, are usually the slaves of some defunct economist. Madmen in authority, who hear voices in the air, are distilling their frenzy from some academic scribbler of a few years back. I am sure that the power of vested interests is vastly exaggerated compared with the gradual encroachment of ideas."
   John Maynard Keynes's frequently quoted concluding paragraph from *The General Theory*

9. "We all have our philosophies, whether or not we are aware of this fact. . . . The impact of our philosophies upon our actions and our lives is often devastating. This makes it necessary to try to improve our philosophies by criticism. This is the only apology for the continued existence of philosophy which I am able to offer." **Karl R. Popper,** in *Objective Knowledge*

10. "Spiritual growth is a journey out of the microcosm into an ever greater microcosm. . . . To develop a broader vision we must be willing to forsake, to kill, our narrower vision. In the short run it is more comfortable not to do this—to stay where we are, to keep using the same microcosmic map, to avoid suffering the death of cherished notions. The road of spiritual growth, however, lies

in the opposite direction. We begin by distrusting what we already believe, by actively seeking the threatening and unfamiliar, by deliberately challenging the validity of what we have previously been taught and hold dear. The path to holiness lies through questioning *everything.*"

M. Scott Peck, in *The Road Less Traveled*

11. "The ideal of philosophical ability is to see the entire universe of possible assertions in all their inferential relationships to one another, and thus to be able to construct, or criticize, any argument." ***Richard Rorty***

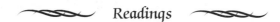

Readings

DEWEY, JOHN. *The Bertrand Russell Case.* New York: Viking Press, 1941.

GOULD, JAMES. "Philosophy as Institutional Critic." *Religious Humanism* 13 (Winter 1979): 19–25.

MONRO, D. "Russell's Moral Theories." *Philosophy* 35 (1960): 30–50.

RUSSELL, BERTRAND. *Autobiography.* 3 vols. New York: Simon & Schuster, 1967.

WOOD, A. *Bertrand Russell.* New York: St. Martin's Press, 1956.

4

Four Approaches
to Philosophy

Charles Sanders Peirce (1839–1914) is regarded by many as the most profound and original of American philosophers. His genius was not recognized in his own lifetime, and he never held a permanent university position. Peirce published a number of philosophical essays during his career, but never a book on philosophy.

Every individual has a philosophy, a system of beliefs about philosophic issues such as love, the "good life," death, the value of money, duty to country, and the role of government. One may form these beliefs by getting ideas from parents, peers, or church, or perhaps even from reading various philosophers. But the development of a philosophy rests ultimately on the individual. Whether one's philosophy is sophisticated or elementary, enduring or changeable, it cannot be a task delegated to others. A mature philosophy consists of reflection on experience in search of underlying meanings and principles that can guide one's life.

The particular approach used to confront a philosophical problem in large measure determines the particular answer found for each problem. There are several approaches to the various problems. In his essay "The Fixation of Belief," Peirce distinguishes four methods by which we habitually fix our beliefs. The first is the *method of tenacity,* which is fixing one's beliefs according to environment or personal relationships. The second Peirce calls the *method of authority,* which involves fixing one's beliefs according to a person, an institution, or a state. One believes that what this authority states is true. Third, Peirce notes the *a priori* method, or the *method of intuition.* Those who follow this method arrive at their beliefs independent of experience, that is, by intuition. Peirce rejects each of these three methods.

Peirce favors what he calls the *method of science.* This method involves the sound reasoning and painstaking observation that is used in any science to establish

From Charles Sanders Peirce, "The Fixation of Belief," *Popular Science Monthly* 15 (New York: Appleton-Century-Crofts, 1877): 1–15.

the nature of the real. Peirce argues that the scientific method is the only one of the four approaches that can distinguish the true from the false. It alone can settle disagreements in belief.

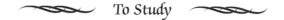

To Study

1. Why do few people study logic?
2. What determines whether we draw one inference rather than another?
3. What distinguishes doubt from belief?
4. What is the role of inquiry?
5. What is the method of tenacity? What are its weaknesses?
6. What is the method of authority? What are its weaknesses?
7. What is the *a priori* method? What are its weaknesses?
8. What is the method of science? What are its advantages?

Few persons care to study logic, because everybody conceives himself to be proficient enough in the art of reasoning already. But I observe that this satisfaction is limited to one's own ratiocination, and does not extend to that of other men.

We come to the full possession of our power of drawing inferences, the last of all our faculties, for it is not so much a natural gift as a long and difficult art. The history of its practice would make a grand subject for a book.

We are, doubtless, in the main logical animals, but we are not perfectly so. Most of us, for example, are naturally more sanguine and hopeful than logic would justify. We seem to be so constituted that, in the absence of any facts to go upon, we are happy and self-satisfied; so that the effect of experience is continually to counteract our hopes and aspirations. Yet a lifetime of the application of this corrective does not usually eradicate our sanguine disposition. Where hope is unchecked by any experience, it is likely that our optimism is extravagant. Logicality in regard to practical matters is the most useful quality an animal can possess, and might, therefore, result from the action of natural selection; but outside of these, it is probably of more advantage to the animal to have his mind filled with pleasing and encouraging visions, independently of their truth; and thus, upon unpractical subjects, natural selection might occasion a fallacious tendency of thought.

That which determines us, from given premises, to draw one inference rather than another, is some habit of mind, whether it be constitutional or acquired. The habit is good or otherwise, according as it produces true conclusions from true premises or not; and an inference is regarded as valid or not, without reference to the truth or falsity of its conclusion specially, but according as the habit which determines it is such as to produce true conclusions in general or not. The particular habit of mind which governs this or that inference may be formulated in a proposition whose truth depends on the validity of the inferences which the habit determines; and such a formula is called a *guiding principle* of inference. . . .

We generally know when we wish to ask a question and when we wish to pronounce a judgment, for there is a dissimilarity between the sensation of doubting and that of believing.

But this is not all which distinguishes doubt from belief. There is a practical difference. Our beliefs guide our desires and shape our actions. The Assassins, or followers of the Old Man of the Mountain, used to rush into death at his least command, because they believed that obedience to him would ensure everlasting felicity. Had they doubted this, they would not have acted as they did. So it is with every belief, according to its degree. The feeling of believing is a more or less sure indication of the being established in our nature some habit which will determine our actions. Doubt never has such an effect.

Nor must we overlook a third point of difference. Doubt is an uneasy and dissatisfied state from which we struggle to free ourselves and pass into the state of belief; while the latter is a calm and satisfactory state which we do not wish to avoid, or to change to a belief in anything else. On the contrary, we cling tenaciously, not merely to believing, but to believing just what we do believe.

Thus, both doubt and belief have positive effects upon us, though very different ones. Belief does not make us act at once, but puts us into such a condition that we shall behave in a certain way, when the occasion arises. Doubt has not the least effect of this sort, but stimulates us to action until it is destroyed. This reminds us of the irritation of a nerve and the reflex action produced thereby; while for the analogue of belief, in the nervous system, we must look to what are called nervous associations— for example, to that habit of the nerves in consequence of which the smell of a peach will make the mouth water.

The irritation of doubt causes a struggle to attain a state of belief. I shall term this struggle *inquiry,* though it must be admitted that this is sometimes not a very apt designation.

The irritation of doubt is the only immediate motive for the struggle to attain belief. It is certainly best for us that our beliefs should be such as may truly guide our actions so as to satisfy our desires; and this reflection will make us reject any belief which does not seem to have been so formed as to ensure this result. But it will only do so by creating doubt in the place of that belief. With the doubt, therefore, the struggle begins, and with the cessation of doubt it ends. Hence, the sole object of inquiry is the settlement of opinion. We may fancy that this is not enough for us, and that we seek, not merely an opinion, but a true opinion. But put this fancy to the test, and it proves groundless; for as soon as a firm belief is reached we are entirely satisfied, whether the belief be false or true. And it is clear that nothing out of the sphere of our knowledge can be our object, for nothing which does not affect the mind can be a motive for mental effort. The most that can be maintained is that we seek for a belief that we shall *think* to be true. But we think each one of our beliefs to be true, and, indeed, it is mere tautology to say so.

That the settlement of opinion is the sole end of inquiry is a very important proposition. It sweeps away, at once, various vague and erroneous conceptions of proof. A few of these may be noticed here.

1. Some philosophers have imagined that to start an inquiry it was only necessary to utter a question or set it down on paper, and have even recommended us to

begin our studies with questioning everything! But the mere putting of a proposition into the interrogative form does not stimulate the mind to any struggle after belief. There must be a real and living doubt, and without this all discussion is idle.

2. It is a very common idea that a demonstration must rest on some ultimate and absolutely indubitable propositions. These, according to one school, are first principles of a general nature; according to another, are first sensations. But, in point of fact, an inquiry, to have that completely satisfactory result called demonstration, has only to start with propositions perfectly free from all actual doubt. If the premises are not in fact doubted at all, they cannot be more satisfactory than they are.

3. Some people seem to love to argue a point after all the world is fully convinced of it. But no further advance can be made. When doubt ceases, mental action on the subject comes to an end; and, if it did go on, it would be without a purpose.

If the settlement of opinion is the sole object of inquiry, and if belief is of the nature of a habit, why should we not attain the desired end by taking any answer to a question, which we may fancy, and constantly reiterating it to ourselves, dwelling on all which may conduce to that belief, and learning to turn with contempt and hatred from anything which might disturb it? This simple and direct method is really pursued by many men. I remember once being entreated not to read a certain newspaper lest it might change my opinion upon free trade. "Lest I might be entrapped by its fallacies and misstatements," was the form of expression. "You are not," my friend said, "a special student of political economy. You might, therefore, easily be deceived by fallacious arguments upon the subject. You might, then, if you read this paper, be led to believe in protection. But you admit that free trade is the true doctrine; and you do not wish to believe what is not true." I have often known this system to be deliberately adopted. Still oftener, the instinctive dislike of an undecided state of mind, exaggerated into a vague dread of doubt, makes men cling spasmodically to the views they already take. The man feels that, if he only holds to his belief without wavering, it will be entirely satisfactory. Nor can it be denied that a steady and immovable faith yields great peace of mind. It may, indeed, give rise to inconveniences, as if a man should resolutely continue to believe that fire would not burn him, or that he would be eternally damned if he received his *ingesta* otherwise than through a stomach-pump. But then the man who adopts this method will not allow that its inconveniences are greater than its advantages. He will say, "I hold steadfastly to the truth and the truth is always wholesome." And in many cases it may very well be that the pleasure he derives from his calm faith overbalances any inconveniences resulting from its deceptive character. Thus, if it be true that death is annihilation, then the man who believes that he will certainly go straight to heaven when he dies, provided he has fulfilled certain simple observances in this life, has a cheap pleasure which will not be followed by the least disappointment. A similar consideration seems to have weight with many persons in religious topics, for we frequently hear it said, "Oh, I could not believe so-and-so, because I should be wretched if I did." When an ostrich buries its head in the sand as danger approaches, it very likely takes the happiest course. It hides from the danger, and then calmly says there is no danger; and, if it feels perfectly sure there is none, why should it raise its head to see? A man may go through life systematically keeping out of view all that might cause a change in his opinions, and if he only succeeds—basing his method, as he does, on two fundamental psychological laws—I do not see what can be said against his doing so. It would be an egotistical impertinence to object that his procedure is irrational, for that only amounts to saying that his method of settling belief is not ours. He does not propose to himself to be rational, and, indeed, will often talk with scorn of man's weak and illusive reason. So let him think as he pleases.

But this method of fixing belief, which may be called the method of tenacity, will be unable to hold its ground in practice. The social impulse is against it. The man who adopts it will find that other men think differently from him, and it will be apt to occur to him in some saner moment that their opinions are quite as good as his own, and this will shake his confidence in his belief. This conception, that another man's thought or sentiment may be equivalent to one's own, is a distinctly new step, and a highly important one. It arises from an impulse too strong in man to be suppressed without danger of destroying the human species. Unless we make ourselves hermits, we shall necessarily influence each other's opinions, so that the problem becomes how to fix belief, not in the individual merely, but in the community.

Let the will of the state act, then, instead of that of the individual. Let an institution be created which shall have for its object to keep correct doctrines before the attention of the people, to reiterate them perpetually, and to teach them to the young; having at the same time power to prevent contrary doctrines from being taught, advocated, or expressed. Let all possible causes of a change of mind be removed from men's apprehensions. Let them be kept ignorant, lest they should learn of some reason to think otherwise than they do. Let their passions be enlisted, so that they may regard private and unusual opinions with hatred and horror. Then, let all men who reject the established belief be terrified into silence. Let the people turn out and tar-and-feather such men, or let inquisitions be made into the manner of thinking of suspected persons, and, when they are found guilty of forbidden beliefs, let them be subjected to some signal punishment. When complete agreement could not otherwise be reached, a general massacre of all who have not thought in a certain way has proved a very effective means of settling opinion in a country. If the power to do this be wanting, let a list of opinions be drawn up, to which no man of the least independence of thought can assent, and let the faithful be required to accept all these propositions, in order to segregate them as radically as possible from the influence of the rest of the world.

This method has, from the earliest times, been one of the chief means of upholding correct theological and political doctrines, and of preserving their universal or catholic character. In Rome, especially, it has been practiced from the days of Numa Pompilius to those of Pius Nonus. This is the most perfect example in history; but wherever there is a priesthood—and no religion has been without one—this method has been more or less made use of. Wherever there is an aristocracy, or a guild, or any association of a class of men whose interests depend, or are supposed to depend, on certain propositions, there will be inevitably found some traces of this natural product of social feeling. Cruelties always accompany this system; and when it is consistently carried out, they become atrocities of the most horrible kind in the eyes of any rational man. Nor should this occasion surprise, for the officer of a society does not feel justified in surrendering the interests of that society for the sake of mercy, as he might his own private interests. It is natural, therefore, that sympathy and fellowship should thus produce a most ruthless power.

In judging this method of fixing belief, which may be called the method of authority, we must, in the first place, allow its immeasurable mental and moral superiority to the method of tenacity. Its success is proportionately greater; and, in fact, it has over and over again worked the most majestic results. The mere structures of stone which it has caused to be put together—in Siam, for example, in Egypt, and in Europe—have many of them a sublimity hardly more than rivalled by the greatest works of Nature. And, except the geological epochs, there are no periods of time so vast as those which are measured by some of these organized faiths. If we scrutinize the matter closely, we shall find that there has not been one of their creeds which has remained always the same; yet the change is so slow as to be imperceptible during one person's life, so that individual belief remains sensibly fixed. For the mass of mankind, then, there is perhaps no better method than this. If it is their highest impulse to be intellectual slaves, then slaves they ought to remain.

But no institution can undertake to regulate opinions upon every subject. Only the most important ones can be attended to, and on the rest men's minds must be left to the action of natural causes. This imperfection will be no source of weakness so long as men are in such a state of culture that one opinion does not influence another—that is, so long as they cannot put two and two together. But in the most priest-ridden states some individuals will be found who are raised above that condition. These men possess a wider sort of social feeling; they see that men in other countries and in other ages have held to very different doctrines from those which they themselves have been brought up to believe; and they cannot help seeing that it is the mere accident of their having been taught as they have, and of their having been surrounded with the manners and associations they have, that has caused them to believe as they do and not far differently. Nor can their candor resist the reflection that there is no reason to rate their own views at a higher value than those of other nations and other centuries; thus giving rise to doubts in their minds.

They will further perceive that such doubts as these must exist in their minds with reference to every belief which seems to be determined by the caprice either of themselves or of those who originated the popular opinions. The willful adherence to a belief, and the arbitrary forcing of it upon others, must, therefore, both be given up. A different new method of settling opinions must be adopted, that shall not only produce an impulse to believe, but shall also decide what proposition it is which is to be believed. Let the action of natural preferences be unimpeded, then, and under their influence let men, conversing together and regarding matters in different lights, gradually develop beliefs in harmony with natural causes. This method resembles that by which conceptions of art have been brought to maturity. The most perfect example of it is to be found in the history of metaphysical philosophy. Systems of this sort have not usually rested upon any observed facts, at least not in any great degree. They have been chiefly adopted because their fundamental propositions seemed "agreeable to reason." This is an apt expression; it does not mean that which agrees with experience, but that which we find ourselves inclined to believe. Plato, for example, finds it agreeable to reason that the distances of the celestial spheres from one another should be proportional to the different lengths of strings which produce harmonious chords. Many philosophers have been led to their main conclusions by considerations like this; but this is the lowest and least developed from which the method takes, for it is clear that another man might find Kepler's theory, that the celestial spheres are proportional to the inscribed and circumscribed spheres of the different regular solids, more agreeable to *his* reason. But the shock of opinions will soon lead men to rest on preferences of a far more universal nature. Take, for example, the doctrine that man only acts selfishly—that is, from the consideration that acting in one way will afford him more pleasure than acting in another. This rests on no fact in the world, but it has had a wide acceptance as being the only reasonable theory.

This method is far more intellectual and respectable from the point of view of reason than either of the others which we have noticed. But its failure has been the most manifest. It makes of inquiry something similar to the development of taste; but taste, unfortunately, is always more or less a matter of fashion, and accordingly metaphysicians have never come to any fixed agreement, but the pendulum has swung backward and forward between a more material and a more spiritual philosophy, from the earliest times to the latest. And so from this, which has been called the *a priori* method, we are driven, in Lord Bacon's phrase, to a true induction. We have examined this *a priori* method as something which promised to deliver our opinions from their accidental and capricious element. But development, while it is a process which eliminates the effect of some casual circumstances, only magnifies that of others. This method, therefore, does not differ in a very essential way from that of authority. The government may not have lifted its finger to influence my convictions; I may have been left outwardly quite free to choose, we will say, between monogamy and polygamy, and, appealing to my conscience only, I may have concluded that the latter practice is in itself licentious. But when I come to see that the chief obstacle to the spread of Christianity among a people of as high culture as the Hindus has been a conviction of the immorality of our way of treating women, I cannot help seeing that, though governments do not interfere, sentiments in their development will be very greatly determined by accidental causes. Now, there are some people, among whom I must suppose that my reader is to be found, who, when they see that any belief of theirs is determined by any circumstance extraneous to the facts, will from that moment not merely admit in words that that belief is doubtful, but will experience a real doubt of it, so that it ceases in some degree to be a belief.

To satisfy our doubts, therefore, it is necessary that a method should be found by which our beliefs may be caused by nothing human, but by some external permanency—by something upon which our thinking has no effect. Some mystics imagine that they have such a method in a private inspiration from on high. But that is only a form of the method of tenacity, in which the conception of truth as something public is not yet developed. Our external permanency would not be external, in our sense, if it was restricted in its influence to one individual. It must be something which affects, or might affect, every man. And, though these affections are necessarily as various as are individual conditions, yet the method must be such that the ultimate conclusion of every man shall be the same. Such is the method of science. Its fundamental hypothesis, restated in more familiar language, is this: There are Real things, whose characters are entirely independent of our opinions about them; those realities affect our senses according to regular laws, and, though our sensations are as different as are our relations to the objects, yet, by taking advantage of the laws of perception, we can ascertain by reasoning how things really are; and any man, if we have sufficient experience and he reason enough about it, will be led to the one True conclusion. The new conception here involved is that of Reality. It may be asked how I know that there are any realities. If this hypothesis is the sole support of my method of inquiry, my method of inquiry must not be used to support my hypothesis. The reply is this: 1. If investigation cannot be regarded as proving that there are Real things, it at least does not lead to a contrary conclusion; but the method and the conception on which it is based remain ever in harmony. No doubts of the method, therefore, necessarily arise from its practice, as is the case with all the others. 2. The feeling which gives rise to any method of fixing belief is a dissatisfaction at two repugnant propositions. But here already is a vague concession that there is some *one* thing to which a proposition should conform. Nobody, therefore, can really doubt that there are realities, for, if he did, doubt would not be a source of dissatisfaction. The hypothesis, therefore, is one which every mind admits. So that the social impulse does not cause men to doubt it. 3. Everybody uses the scientific method about a great many things, and only ceases to use it when he does not know how to apply it. 4. Experience of the method has not led us to doubt it, but, on the contrary, scientific investigation has had the most wonderful triumphs in the way of settling opinion. These afford the explanation of my not doubting the method or the hypothesis which it supposes; and not having any doubt, nor believing that anybody else whom I could influence has, it would be the merest babble for me to say more about it. If there be anybody with a living doubt upon the subject, let him consider it. . . .

This is the only one of the four methods which presents any distinction of a right and a wrong way. If I adopt the method of tenacity, and shut myself out from all influences, whatever I think necessary to doing this, is necessary according to that method. So with the method of authority: the state may try to put down heresy by means which, from a scientific point of view, seem very ill-calculated to accomplish its purposes; but the only test *on that method* is what the state thinks; so that it cannot pursue the method wrongly. So with the *a priori* method. The very essence of it is to think as one is inclined to think. All metaphysicians will be sure to do that, however they may be inclined to judge each other to be perversely wrong. Hegel's system of Nature represents tolerably the science of that day; and one may be sure that whatever scientific investigation has put out of doubt will presently receive *a priori* demonstration on the part of the metaphysicians. But with the scientific method the case is different. I may start with known and observed facts to proceed to the unknown; and yet the rules which I follow in doing so may not be such as investigation would approve. The test of whether I am truly following the method is not an immediate appeal to my feelings and purposes, but, on the contrary, itself involves the application of the method. Hence it is that bad reasoning as well as good reasoning is possible; and this fact is the foundation of the practical side of logic.

It is not to be supposed that the first three methods of settling opinion present no advantage whatever over the scientific method. On the contrary, each has some peculiar convenience of its own. The *a priori* method is distinguished for its comfortable conclusions. It is the nature of the process to adopt whatever belief we are inclined to, and there are certain flatteries to the vanity of man which we all believe by nature, until we are awakened from our pleasing dream by rough facts. The method of authority will always govern the mass of mankind; and those who wield the various forms of organized force in the state will never be convinced that dangerous reasoning ought not to be suppressed in some way. If liberty of speech is to be untrammelled from the grosser forms of constraint, then uniformity of opinion will be secured by a moral terrorism to which the respectability of society will give its thorough approval. Following the method of authority is the path of peace. Certain nonconformities are permitted; certain others (considered unsafe) are forbidden. These are different in different countries and in different ages; but, wherever you are, let it be known that you seriously hold a tabooed belief, and you may be perfectly sure of being treated with a cruelty less brutal but more refined than hunting you like a wolf. Thus, the greatest intellectual benefactors of mankind have never dared, and dare not now, to utter the whole of their thought; and thus a shade of *prima facie* doubt is cast upon every proposition which is considered essential to the security of society. Singularly enough, the persecution does not all come from without; but a man torments himself and is oftentimes more distressed at finding himself believing propositions which he has been brought up to regard with aversion. The peaceful and sympathetic man will, therefore, find it hard to resist the temptation to submit his opinions to authority. But most of all I admire the method of tenacity for its strength, simplicity, and directness. Men who pursue it are distinguished for their decision of character, which becomes very easy with such a mental rule. They do not waste time in trying to make up their minds what they want, but, fastening like lightning upon whatever alternative comes first, they hold it to the end, whatever happens, without an instant's irresolution. This is one of the splendid qualities which generally accompany brilliant, unlasting success. It is impossible not to envy the man who can dismiss reason, although we know how it must turn out at last.

Such are the advantages which the other methods of settling opinion have over scientific investigation. A man should consider well of them; and then he should consider that, after all, he wishes his opinions to coincide with the fact and that there is no reason why the result of those three methods should do so. To bring about this effect is the prerogative of the method of science. Upon such considerations he has to make his choice—a choice which is far more than the adoption of any intellectual opinion, which is one of the ruling decisions of his life, to which, when once made, he is bound to adhere. The force of habit will sometimes cause a man to hold on to old beliefs, after he is in a condition to see that they have no sound basis. But reflection upon the state of the case will overcome these habits, and he ought to allow reflection its full weight. People sometimes shrink from doing this, having an idea that beliefs are wholesome which they cannot help feeling rest on nothing. But let such persons suppose an analogous though different case from their own. Let them ask themselves what they would say to a reformed Mussulman who should hesitate to give up his old notions in regard to the relations of the sexes; or to a reformed Catholic who should still shrink from reading the Bible. Would they not say that these persons ought to consider the matter fully, and clearly understand the new doctrine, and then ought to embrace it, in its entirety? But, above all, let it be considered that what is more wholesome than any particular belief is integrity of belief, and that to avoid looking into the support of any belief from a fear that it may turn out rotten is quite as immoral as it is disadvantageous. The person who confesses that there is such a thing as truth, which is distinguished from falsehood simply by this, that if acted on it will carry us to the point we aim at and not astray, and then, though convinced of this, dares not know the truth and seeks to avoid it, is in a sorry state of mind indeed.

Yes, the other methods do have their merits: a clear logical conscience does cost something—just as any virtue, just as all that we cherish, costs us dear. But we should not desire it to be otherwise. The genius of a man's logical method should be loved and reverenced as his bride, whom he has chosen from all the world. He need not condemn the others; on the contrary, he may honor them deeply, and in doing so he only honors her the more. But she is the one that he has chosen, and he knows that he was right in making that choice. And having made it, he will work and fight for her, and will not complain that there are blows to take, hoping that there may be as many and as hard to give, and will strive to be the worthy knight and champion of her from the blaze of whose splendors he draws his inspiration and his courage.

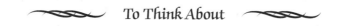

To Think About

1. "Custom is the source of our strongest and most believed proofs. It persuades the mind without its thinking about the matter. It is custom that makes so many men Christians, . . . Turks, etc."   ***Blaise Pascal,*** *in Pensées*

2. "The common sense world is the preeminent reality for us."   ***William James***

3. "We believe a philosophy when it satisfies certain desires."   ***William James***

4. "A belief is a statement that we are willing to act upon."   ***C. S. Peirce***

5. "Man can either remain within his 'accidental' reference frame and unquestioningly accept the meaning it has to offer, or he can boldly emerge from his psycho-epistemological cocoon and broaden his reality image. The need for man to break out of his capsule is crucial, for encapsulation may well be the essence of contemporary man's spiritual emptiness."   ***Joseph R. Royce***

6. "Faith can move mountains, or lead a man endlessly down a blind path."   ***James E. Gunn***

7. "It is only charlatans who are certain. . . . Doubt is not a very agreeable state, but certainty is a ridiculous one."   ***Voltaire***

8. "There is not *a* philosophical method, though there are indeed methods, like different therapies."   ***Ludwig Wittgenstein***

9. "I can live with doubt and uncertainty. I think it's much more interesting to live *not* knowing than to have answers which might be wrong."   ***Richard Feynman***

10. "Anyone who conducts an argument by appealing to authority is not using his intelligence; he is just using his memory."   ***Leonardo da Vinci***

11. "What are man's truths ultimately? Merely his *irrefutable* errors."
                                                                    Friedrich Nietzsche

12. "In broad terms, the destiny of man on earth has been made clear by evolution-
     ary biology. It is to be the agent of the world process of evolution, the sole agent
     capable of leading it to new heights, and enabling it to realize new possibilities."
                                                                    Sir Julian Huxley

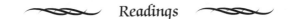

Readings

BRENT, J. *Charles Sanders Peirce: A Life.* Bloomington: Indiana University Press, 1998.

FISCH, M. *Peirce, Semeiotic and Pragmatism.* Bloomington: Indiana University Press, 1986.

GOULD, JAMES A. "Patriotism, Tenacity and Authority." *Darshana International Quarterly* (1961):

HAUSER, N., AND C. KLOESEL, eds. *The Essential Peirce.* Bloomington: Indiana University Press, 1992.

HOOKWAY, C. J. *Peirce.* London, Routledge & Kegan Paul, 1985.

KLOESEL, C., ET AL., eds. *Writings of Charles S. Peirce: A Chronological Edition.* Bloomington: Indiana University Press, 1993.

PEIRCE, C. S. *Reasoning and the Logic of Things,* ed. by Kenneth Laine Ketner. Cambridge, MA: Harvard University Press, 1992.

5

The Scientific Approach

Herbert Feigl (1902–88) was educated at the University of Vienna when the scientific philosophy of logical positivism was at its height. He taught at the University of Minnesota until he retired in 1971. He is well known for his many publications in the philosophy of science.

Peirce argued that the scientific approach was the best way to establish a personal philosophy. Feigl's essay shows this approach in more detail. Feigl discusses the relationship between science and the humanities as well as the basic characteristics of the scientific method. He identifies the aims of science as description, explanation, and prediction. Furthermore, he conceives science to be regulated by certain criteria: intersubjectiveness, testing ability, sufficient degree of confirmation, precision, coherence, and comprehensiveness. All of these give science its progressive character and sense of experimental certainty. He also contends that science can contribute to better value judgments.

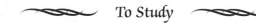 To Study

1. What is the difference between the formal and the factual sciences?
2. What are the three aims of science?
3. Explain *intersubjective testability.*
4. Explain *reliability* in science.
5. Explain both coherence and comprehensiveness as related to a scientific system.
6. Discuss at least one misconception of science with which you either strongly agree or disagree.
7. Discuss Feigl's view of the relation between science and values.

From Herbert Feigl, "Naturalism and Humanism," *American Quarterly* 1:3 (1949): 135–48. The American Studies Association. Reprinted with permission of The Johns Hopkins University Press.

The main purpose of this essay is to dispel certain confusions and misunderstandings which still prevent the much-needed constructive synthesis and mutual supplementation of the scientific and humanistic elements in general education. It is my contention that the philosophical foundations of both science and the humanities are widely misconceived; and that the frequently held claim of their basic incompatibilities arises out of philosophical prejudices which, owing to cultural lag, have unfortunately not as yet been completely relegated to oblivion. Science is still identified with an absurd mechanistic reductionism, but this is the caricature of science drawn by representatives of the humanities who are largely ignorant of the nature of modern science and also of the more recent scientific outlook in philosophy. The defenders of the humanities often enough increase the existing tension by holding an equally distorted view of the philosophical basis of the humanities. . . .

CRITERIA OF THE SCIENTIFIC METHOD

What, then, are the basic characteristics of the scientific method? The often alleged difficulties of an adequate definition of science seem to me mainly a matter of terminology. We must first distinguish between pure mathematics as an exclusively formal-conceptual discipline, and the factual (or empirical, that is, the natural and the social-cultural) sciences. The certainty, complete exactitude, and necessity of pure mathematics depends precisely on its detachment from empirical fact. Mathematics as applied in the factual sciences merely lends its forms and deductive structures to the contents furnished by experience. But no matter how predominant mathematics may be in the formulations and derivations of empirical facts, factual knowledge cannot attain either the absolute precision or necessity of pure mathematics. The knowledge claimed in the natural and the social sciences is a matter of successive approximations and of increasing degrees of confirmation. Warranted assertibility or probability is all that we can conceivably secure in the sciences that deal with the facts of experience. It is empirical science, thus conceived as an unending quest (its truth-claims to be held only "until further notice"), which is under consideration here. Science in this sense differs only in degree from the knowledge accumulated throughout the ages by sound and common sense.

The aims of science are description, explanation, and prediction. The first aim is basic and indispensable, the second and third (closely related to each other) arise as the most desirable fruits of scientific labors whenever inquiry rises beyond the mere fact-gathering stage. History, often and nowadays quite fashionably declared an art, is scientific to the extent that it ascertains its facts concerning past events by a meticulous scrutiny of present evidence. Causal interpretation of these facts (in history, but similarly also in psychology, sociology, cultural anthropology, and economics) is usually much more difficult than, but in principle not logically different from, causal interpretation (that is, explanation) in the natural sciences. The aims of the pure (empirical) sciences are then essentially the same throughout the whole field. What the scientists are seeking are descriptions, explanations, and predictions which are as adequate and accurate as possible in the given context of research.

The quest for scientific knowledge is therefore regulated by certain standards or criteria which may best be formulated in the form of ideals to be approximated, but perhaps never fully attained. The most important of these regulative ideals are:

1. *Intersubjective Testability.*   This is only a more adequate formulation of what is generally meant by the "objectivity" of science. What is here involved is not only the freedom from personal or cultural bias or partiality, but—even more fundamentally— the requirement that the knowledge claims of science be in principle capable of test (confirmation or disconfirmation, at the least indirectly and to some degree) on the part of any person properly equipped with intelligence and the technical devices of observation or experimentation. The term *intersubjective* stresses the social nature of the scientific enterprise. If there be any "truths" that are accessible only to privileged individuals, such as mystics or visionaries—that is, knowledge-claims which by their very nature cannot independently be checked by anyone else—then such "truths" are not of the kind that we seek in the sciences. The criterion of intersubjective testability thus delimits the scientific from the nonscientific activities of man.

Religious ecstasy, the elations of love, the inspiration of the artist, yes, even the flash of insight on the part of a scientific genius are not in themselves scientific activities. All these processes may eventually become subject matter for scientific study. But in themselves they do not validate knowledge-claims. They may, as in the case of the scientific intuition (or empathy in the psychological-cultural field) be instrumental in the generation of knowledge-claims. But it is these knowledge-claims which have to be, first, formulated in an intersubjectively intelligible (or communicable) manner, and, second, subjected to the appropriate kind of tests in order to ascertain their validity. Beliefs transcending all possible tests by observation, self-observation, experiment, measurement, or statistical analysis are recognized as theological or metaphysical and therefore devoid of the type of meaning that we all associate with the knowledge-claims of common sense or factual science. From the point of view of the scientific outlook in philosophy it may be suggested that the sort of significance with which the in-principle-unconfirmable assertions of transcendent theology and metaphysics impress so many people is largely emotive. The pictorial, emotional, and motivational appeals of language, no matter how indispensable or valuable in the contexts of practical life, art, education, persuasion, and propaganda, must, however, not be confused with the cognitive meanings (purely formal and/or factual-empirical) that are of the essence of science. Each type of significance has its function, and in most uses of language both are combined or even fused. The only point stressed here is that they must not be *confused,* that is, mistaken for one another, if we wish to be clear as to what we are about.

2. *Reliability, or a Sufficient Degree of Confirmation.*   This second criterion of scientific knowledge enables us to distinguish what is generally called "mere opinion" (or worse still, "superstition") from knowledge (well-substantiated belief). It may be considered as the delimitation of the scientific from the unscientific knowledge-claims. Clearly, in contrast to the first criterion, we face here a distinction of degree. There is no sharp line of demarcation between the well-confirmed laws, theories, or hypotheses of science, and the only poorly substantiated hunches and

ideas-on-trial which may ultimately either be included in the corpus of scientific knowledge or else rejected as unconfirmed. Truth-claims which we repudiate as "superstition," and, quite generally, as judgments based upon hasty generalization or weak analogy (if they fulfill the criterion of testability), differ from what we accept as "scientific truth" in the extremely low degree of probability to which they are supported by the available evidence. Astrology or alchemy, for example, are not factually meaningless, but they are considered false to fact in that all available evidence speaks overwhelmingly against them. Modern techniques of experimentation and of statistical analysis are the most powerful tools we have in the discernment between chance and law and hence the best means of enhancing the reliability of knowledge.

3. *Definiteness and Precision.*   This obvious standard of scientific method requires that the concepts used in the formulation of scientific knowledge-claims be as definitely delimited as possible. On the level of the qualitative-classificatory sciences this amounts to the attempt to reduce all border-zone vagueness to a minimum. On the level of quantitative science the exactitude of the concepts is enormously enhanced through the application of the techniques of measurement. The mensurational devices usually also increase the degree of objectivity. This is especially clear when they are contrasted with purely impressionistic ways of estimating magnitudes. Of course, there is no point in sharpening precision to a higher degree than the problem in hand requires. (You need no razor to cut butter.)

4. *Coherence or Systematic Structure.*   This is what T. H. Huxley had in mind when he defined science as "organized common-sense." Not a mere collection of miscellaneous items of information, but a well-connected account of the facts is what we seek in science. On the descriptive level this results, for example, in systems of classification or division, in diagrams, statistical charts, and the like. On the explanatory levels of science sets of laws, or theoretical assumptions, are utilized. Explanation in science consists in the hypothetico-deductive procedure. The laws, theories, or hypotheses form the premises from which we derive logically, or logico-mathematically, the observed or observable facts. These facts, often belonging to heterogeneous domains, thus become integrated into a coherent, unifying structure. (Theological and metaphysical systems have, frequently enough, ambitiously tried to imitate this feature of science; but even if they succeeded in proceeding *more geometrico,* the important difference from science remains: they either lack testability or else reliability in the senses specified in our previous points.)

5. *Comprehensiveness or Scope of Knowledge.*   This final point in our enumeration of criteria of science also characterizes scientific knowledge as different in degree (often enormously) from common-sense knowledge. Not only through bold and sweeping hypotheses, but especially through the ingenious devices by means of which they are tested, science acquires a reach far beyond the limits of our unaided senses. With telescopes, microscopes, spectroscopes, Geiger Counters, lie detectors, and the thousands of other contrivances of modern science we manage to amplify our senses and thus open up avenues of at least indirect access to the worlds of the very distant, the very large, the extremely small, or the disguised and concealed. The

resulting increase in the completeness of our knowledge is, of course, popularly the most impressive feature of science. It must be kept in mind, however, that the scope thus achieved is a product of hard labor, and not to be confused with the sham completeness metaphysicians procure for their world pictures by verbal magic. Instead of presenting a finished account of the world, the genuine scientist keeps his unifying hypotheses open to revision and is always ready to modify or abandon them if evidence should render them doubtful. This self-corrective aspect of science has rightly been stressed as its most important characteristic and must always be kept in mind when we refer to the comprehensiveness or the unification achieved by the scientific account of the universe. It is a sign of one's maturity to be able to live with an unfinished world view.

The foregoing outline of the criteria of science has been set down in a somewhat dogmatic tone. But this was done only for the sake of brevity.[1] The spirit behind it is that of a humble account of what, I think, an impartial and elaborate study of the history of thought from magic to science would reveal. In any case, these criteria seem unquestionably the guiding ideals of present-day empirical science. They may therefore be used in a definition of science as we understand this term today. It seems rather useless to speculate about just what this term, by a change of meaning, might come to connote in the future.

It should be remembered that the criteria listed characterize the *pure* factual (empirical) sciences. The aims of the *applied* sciences—the technologies, medicine, social and economic planning, and others—are practical control, production, guidance, therapy, reform, and so forth. Responsible activity in the application of science clearly presupposes information which is fairly well substantiated by the methods of the pure sciences. (These remarks intend to draw merely a logically important distinction. The obvious practical interpenetration and important mutual fertilization of the pure and the applied disciplines is of course not denied here.)

CRITIQUE OF MISCONCEPTIONS

Having indicated at least in broad outline the nature of scientific method we may now turn to the critique of some of the misconceptions to which it is all too commonly exposed. In what follows, a dozen typical charges against science are stated and answered consecutively.[2]

> Science arises exclusively out of practical and social needs and has its only value in serving them in turn. (Dialectical Materialism and Vocationalism)

---

[1] A thorough discussion of the logical, epistemological, methodological, and historical issues connected with the criteria would require a whole book, not just another essay.

[2] These charges are not straw men. In more than twenty years of reading, listening, teaching, and argument I have encountered them again and again in Europe and just as frequently in this country. If space permitted and time were less valuable, I could quote many well-known writers in connection with each charge.

While this is important it does not tell the whole story. Science has always also been the pursuit of knowledge, the satisfaction of a deep-rooted curiosity. It should be recognized as one of the cultural values along with art, literature, and music. Better teaching of the sciences and their history can redress the balance. Fuller utilization of results and suggestions from the history and the philosophy of science would give the student a deeper appreciation of the evolution of scientific knowledge and of the scientific point of view. Through proper instruction, the student could be led to rediscover some of the important results of science. The intellectual gratification that comes with a grasp of the order of nature, with the understanding of its processes by means of laws and theories, is one of the most powerful incentives in the pursuit of pure knowledge.

Science cannot furnish a secure basis for human affairs since it is unstable. It changes its views continually. (Traditionalism)

While there is constant evolution, and occasionally a revolution, in the scientific outlook, the charge is a superficial (usually journalistic) exaggeration. The typical progress of science reveals that later views often contain much of the earlier views (to the extent that these have stood the test of repeated examination). The more radical or revolutionary changes usually amount to a revision of the conceptual frame of a scientific discipline. The criticism often also presupposes other sources of certainty which will simply not bear critical scrutiny. The quest for absolute certainty is an immature, if not infantile, trait of thinking. The best knowledge we have can be established only by the method of trial and error. It is of the essence of science to make such knowledge as reliable as is humanly and technically possible.

Science rests on uncritical or uncriticized presuppositions. It validates its outlook by its own standards. It therefore begs the question as regards alternative approaches for settling problems of knowledge and action.

Science has been clarifying and revising its basic assumptions throughout its development. Particularly since the beginning of the modern age and still more intensively since the beginning of our century, an increasing awareness of, and critical attitude toward, the fundamental presuppositions has been most fruitfully applied in the repudiation of dogmatic prejudices and in the articulation of the conceptual frame of scientific method. It can be shown (through logical analysis) that the procedure of science is the only one we are *certain* will yield the results (reliable knowledge, that is, valid explanation and predictions) *if* such results can at all be achieved. Any alleged rival method—theology, metaphysics, mysticism, intuition, dialectics—if it made any contributions at all could not be examined and appraised on any basis other than the usual inductive criteria of science. Generally, it seems that these alleged alternatives do not even aim primarily at knowledge but, like the arts, at the enrichment of experience. They may therefore more properly be said to be *non*scientific, rather than *un*scientific.

Science distorts the facts of reality. In its Procrustean manner it introduces discontinuities where there is continuity (and vice versa). The abstractions and idealizations used in science can never do justice to the richness and complexities of experience.

Since the task of science is to discover reliable and precise knowledge of what happens under what conditions, it always tries to approximate the facts as closely as the problem on hand requires and permits. Both continuity and discontinuity can be formulated mathematically and be given an adequate formulation only with the help of modern mathematics.

Science can deal only with the measurable and therefore tends to "explain away" that which it cannot measure.

While measure is eminently desirable in order to enhance the precision and objectivity of knowledge, it is not indispensable in many branches of science or, at least, on their more qualitative levels of analysis. Science does not explain away the qualities of experience. It aims at, and often succeeds in, making these qualities more predictable.

Science never explains, it merely describes the phenomena of experience. The reality beyond the appearances is also beyond the reach of science.

This is partly a terminological issue and partly a result of the (traditional but most misleading and useless) metaphysical distinction between appearance and reality. In the sense in which the word *explaining* is used in common life, science *does* explain facts—it deduces them from laws or theoretical assumptions. Questions which are in principle incapable of being answered by the scientific method turn out, on closer analysis, not to be questions of knowledge. They are expressions of emotional tensions or of the wish for soothing (or exciting) experience.

Science and the scientific attitude are incompatible with religion and the religious attitude.

If by religion one refers to an explanation of the universe and a derivation of moral norms from theological premises, then indeed there is logical incompatibility with the results, methods, and general outlook of science. But if religion means an attitude of sincere devotion to human values, such as justice, peace, relief from suffering, there is not only no conflict between religion and science but rather a need for mutual supplementation.

Science is responsible for the evils and maladjustments of our civilization. It is creating ever more powerful weapons of destruction. The employment of scientific techniques in the machine age has contributed to the misery, physical and mental, of the multitudes. Moreover, the biological facts of evolution imply the negation of all morality: the law of the jungle.

These are particularly superficial charges. It is the social-political-economic structure of a society that is responsible for these various evils. Scientific knowledge itself is socially and morally neutral. But the manner in which it is applied, whether for the benefit or to the detriment of humanity, depends entirely on ourselves. Scientists are becoming increasingly aware that they, even more than the average citizen, have to work for enlightenment toward the proper use of knowledge. The facts and theories of evolution have been construed in many ways as regards their implications for ethics. Julian Huxley reads them very differently from the way his grandfather Thomas Henry did.[3] It should be easy to see that the forces active on the level of human civilization and intelligent communal life are not completely reducible to those involved in the ruthless struggle for survival.

> *The ethical neutrality of scientific truth and the ivory tower situation of the pure researcher is apt to generate an attitude of indifference toward the pressing problems of humanity.*

Only maladjusted individuals are unable to combine the detachment necessary for the pursuit of truth with an ardent interest in the improvement of the condition of humanity.

> *Scientific method, while eminently successful in the explanation, prediction, and control of physical phenomena, is distinctly less successful in regard to the facts of organic life and almost altogether hopeless in the mental and social realm. The methods of the physical sciences are essentially mechanistic (if not materialistic) and therefore reductionistic; they cannot do justice to the complex organismic, teleological, and emergent features of life and mind.*

"Scientism" as a slogan of criticism and reproach is very fashionable these days. It is true that some scientists and especially some of the popularizers of science have indulged in reductive fallacies of various sorts. But the true scientific spirit as exemplified in some of the foremost researchers is free from that impatience and simplemindedness that tries to finish the unfinished business of science by hasty speculation. Admittedly, there are tremendous problems yet to be solved. On the other hand what method is there but the method of science to solve them? Explanations of the mechanistic type (in *one* sense of the term) have been abandoned even in physics. But mechanistic explanation in the wider sense of a search for law (deterministic or statistical) is still the indispensable procedure of all sciences that have gone beyond the purely classificatory level. Organic wholeness, teleology, and emergence can be understood, if at all, only by causal analysis on the usual empirical basis. Purposiveness and freedom of choice, far from being incompatible with causality, presuppose causal order.

> *The methods of science can never replace the intuitive insight or empathic understanding of the practical psychologist, psychiatrist, cultural anthropologist, or historian. This claim is made particularly wherever the object of knowledge is the individual, the unique, and unrepeatable.*

---

[3] Compare Julian Huxley, *Touchstone for Ethics* (Harper, 1947); but see also C. D. Broad, "Review of Julian S. Huxley's Evolutionary Ethics" (*Mind* 53, 1944), reprinted in H. Feigl and W. Sellars, *Readings in Philosophical Analysis* (Appleton-Century-Crofts, 1949).

It is only through the scientific method that the validity and reliability of the intuitive approach can be gauged. There is, on this ground, some doubt as to its more exaggerated claims. However, there is nothing in the principles of scientific method that would deny the occasional, or even frequent, efficacy of intuitive judgments based, as they must be, on a rich (but often not articulated) background of experience in the given field. Aside from the mere artistic contemplation of the unique and individual, knowledge, in the proper sense of the word, always means the subsumption of the specific case under general concepts or laws. This holds in the social sciences just as much as in the natural sciences.

> *Science cannot determine values. Since scientific knowledge can (at best) find out only what is the case, it can, by its very nature, never tell what ought to be.*

This final challenge often comes from theology or metaphysics. It usually maintains that questions of aims, goals, and ideals cannot be settled by the methods of science but rather require recourse either to divine revelation, the voice of conscience, or some metaphysical *a priori* truths. The answer to this in a scientific age would seem to be that a mature mankind should be able to determine its own value standards on the basis of its needs, wants, and the facts of the social condition of man. But it is true that science cannot dictate value standards. It can, as in social psychology, ascertain the actual evaluations of groups and individuals, study their compatibilities and incompatibilities, and recommend (that is *applied* science!) ways and means of harmonizing conflicting evaluations. True enough, in many of the urgent issues that confront us, we do not possess enough scientific knowledge to warrant a course of action. This means that we have to act, as so often in life, on the highest probabilities available even if these probabilities be low in themselves. But such estimates of probabilities will still be made most reliable by the scientific method. Common life experience and wisdom, when freed from its adherence to prescientific thought patterns, is not fundamentally different from scientific knowledge. In both we find the procedure of self-correction, so essentially needed if knowledge is to be a guide for action. There is an important common element in mature thinking (as we find it in science) and mature social action (as we find it in democracy): progress arises out of the peaceful competition of ideas as they are put to intersubjective test. Cooperative planning of the basis of the best and fullest knowledge available is the only path left to an awakened humanity that has embarked on the adventure of science and civilization.

To Think About

1. Do you think that Newton, Darwin, Einstein, or Freud had Feigl's basic aims of science? Give examples. Do their theories attain Feigl's "regulative ideals"?

2. "Science is meaningless because it gives no answer to our question, the only question important to us: 'What shall we do and how shall we live?'"
   W. Runciman, in *Social Science and Political Theory,* quoting Leo Tolstoy

3. Can you cite a recent controversy regarding a scientific or technical matter in which a value judgment was fundamentally involved?

4. Do you believe a scientist should be allowed to do any unmonitored research? Should research such as germ warfare be regulated? Gene research?

5. Do novels reveal traits about human beings that the sciences (psychology, etc.) cannot?

6. "We can continue to give ourselves over to the great hope of Western reason. But that hope is now a more modest one as a result of the discovery of the plurality of both language and knowledge and the ambiguities of all histories, including the history of reason itself."   ***Arnold Toynbee***

7. Does creationism fit Feigl's conception of science?

8. "Knowledge is never finished."   ***Maurice Merleau-Ponty***

9. "We are drowning in information, but starved for knowledge."   ***John Naisbitt***

10. "Never accept a fact until it is verified by a theory!"   ***Sir Arthur Eddington***

11. "The knowledge of science fails in the face of all ultimate questions."
    Karl Jaspers

12. "The essential point in science is not complicated mathematical formula or a ritualized experimentation. Rather the heart of science is a kind of shrewd honesty that springs from really wanting to know what the hell is going on!" ***Saul-Paul Sirag***

13. "Reality is the real business of physics."   ***Albert Einstein***

14. "Science and industry, and their progress, might turn out to be the most enduring thing in the modern world. Perhaps any speculation about a coming collapse of science and industry is . . . nothing but a dream; perhaps science and industry, having caused infinite misery in the process, will unite the world—I mean condense it into a single unit, though one in which peace is the last thing that will find a home. Because science and industry do decide wars, or so it seems."   ***Ludwig Wittgenstein***

15. "Many a scientist has patiently designed experiments for the *purpose* of substantiating his belief that animal operations are motivated by no purposes. He has perhaps spent his spare time in writing articles to prove that human beings are as other animals, so that 'purpose' is a category irrelevant for the explanation of their bodily activities, his own activities included. Scientists animated by the purpose of proving that they are purposeless constitute an interesting subject for study."   ***Alfred North Whitehead***

16. "One of the gross deficiencies of science is that it has not yet defined what sets man apart from other animals."   ***René Dubos***

17. "It is true that the whole scientific inquiry starts from the familiar world and in the end it must return to the familiar world; but the part of the journey over which the physicist has charge is in foreign territory."   ***Sir Arthur Eddington***

18. "He claimed that science was a method, while I said it was a body of knowledge."
    Unknown

19.   "Science is neither a method nor a body of knowledge. It is a body of changing, learned opinion, aspiring to be true. There are certain facts about nature and history; our grasp of those facts is constantly changing."   ***George Santayana***

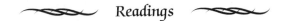

Readings

CAMPBELL, NORMAN. *What Is Science?* New York: Dover, 1930.

COPI, IRVING M., AND CARL COHEN. *Introduction to Logic.* 12th ed. Upper Saddle River, NJ: Prentice Hall, 2005.

HEMPEL, CARL G. *Philosophy of Natural Science.* Upper Saddle River, NJ: Prentice Hall, Foundations of Philosophy Series, 1966.

NAGEL, ERNEST. *The Structure of Science.* New York: Harcourt, 1961.

RESCHER, NICHOLAS. *Philosophical Reasoning: A Study in the Methodology of Philosophizing.* Oxford: Blackwell, 2001.

PART 3

Can We Prove That God Exists?

6
The Ontological Argument

St. Anselm (1033–1109) of Canterbury was born in Aosta, Italy. In 1093 he was made Archbishop of Canterbury. During his years in the abbey he wrote the two works for which he is best known, The Monologium *and* The Proslogium. *Anselm's name will forever be associated with the* ontological *argument for God's existence, which holds that the idea of God in one's mind is evidence of a genuinely existing being.*

Philosophy and religion have always had a close but uneasy relationship. For some, the two mean practically the same thing, since the concept of a way of life seems essential to both of them. Both religion and philosophy seem to share the aim of searching for the key to living well. On the other hand, many have argued that philosophy has no need of a special revelation, or even of the concept of a supreme being, whereas religion seems to require both. And some claim that philosophy is regulated by canons of logical procedure, whereas many religions are based sheerly on emotion and feeling. As you think through your own conception of religion, you will want to consider two ways in which philosophers have always thought they could add something to religion. The first of these is a consideration of arguments for God's existence, and the other is a treatment of the definition or nature of God, particularly as it concerns the great problem of human evil and suffering.

Most people believe that God exists, and many have attempted to give rational arguments or proofs for his existence. The German philosopher Immanuel Kant (1724–1804) said that there are only three possible bases on which to prove God's existence: no experience, many experiences, and one experience. He called the first of these the *ontological* argument, the second the *cosmological* argument, and the third the *teleological* argument. The ontological argument was first given

From St. Anselm, *Proslogium,* trans. Sidney Norton Deane (La Salle, IL: Open Court, 1903).

by St. Anselm, who claims that once we understand the nature of God as a "being than which nothing greater can be conceived," we realize that his essence implies his existence. One might put the argument in other words and argue that God is a perfect being, and it is an imperfection not to exist. Hence, since God is perfect, he must exist.

In the following selections Anselm's extended argument for God's existence is presented along with a counterargument by a certain monk named Gaunilo, who claimed that, if Anselm is correct, then we must conclude the existence of a perfect island, or indeed a perfect anything at all. If it is greater to exist than not to exist, then there must be a greatest member of any class of beings whatsoever. Anselm's response focuses on his position that God alone cannot be conceived not to exist. Anything else can be so conceived. Therefore the argument works only in the case of God.

To Study

1. What is St. Anselm's conception of God?
2. What argument does St. Anselm offer as proof that this God exists? State it in a formal manner.
3. According to St. Anselm, in what way may God be conceived not to exist?
4. State Gaunilo's criticism. What is Anselm's reply?

. . . Lord, I acknowledge and I thank thee that thou has created me in this, thine image, in order that I may be mindful of thee, may conceive of thee, and love thee; but that image has been so consumed and wasted away by vices, and obscured by the smoke of wrong-doing, that it cannot achieve that for which it was made, except thou renew it, and create it anew. I do not endeavor, O Lord, to penetrate thy sublimity, for in no wise do I compare my understanding with that; but I long to understand in some degree thy truth, which my heart believes and loves. For I do not seek to understand that I may believe, but I believe in order to understand. For this also I believe—that unless I believed, I should not understand. . . .

And so, Lord, do thou, who dost give understanding to faith, give me, so far as thou knowest it to be profitable, to understand that thou art as we believe; and that thou art that which we believe. And, indeed, we believe that thou art a being than which nothing greater can be conceived. Or is there no such nature, since the fool hath said in his heart, there is no God? . . . But, at any rate, this very fool, when he hears of this being of which I speak—a being than which nothing greater can be conceived—understands what he hears, and what he understands is in his understanding; although he does not understand it to exist.

For, it is one thing for an object to be in the understanding, and another to understand that the object exists. When a painter first conceives of what he will afterwards perform, he has it in his understanding, but he does not yet understand it to be, because he has not yet performed it. But after he has made the painting, he both has it in his understanding, and he understands that it exists, because he has made it.

Hence, even the fool is convinced that something exists in the understanding, at least, than which nothing greater can be conceived. For, when he hears of this, he understands it. And whatever is understood exists in the understanding. And assuredly that than which nothing greater can be conceived cannot exist in the understanding alone. For, suppose it exists in the understanding alone: then it can be conceived to exist in reality; which is greater.

Therefore, if that than which nothing greater can be conceived exists in the understanding alone, the very being than which nothing greater can be conceived is one than which a greater can be conceived. But obviously this is impossible. Hence, there is no doubt that there exists a being than which nothing greater can be conceived, and it exists both in the understanding and in reality.

And it assuredly exists so truly that it cannot be conceived not to exist. For, it is possible to conceive of a being which cannot be conceived not to exist; and this is greater than one which can be conceived not to exist. Hence, if that than which nothing greater can be conceived can be conceived not to exist, it is not that than which nothing greater can be conceived. But this is an irreconcilable contradiction. There is, then, so truly a being than which nothing greater can be conceived to exist, that it cannot even be conceived not to exist; and this being thou art, O Lord, our God.

So truly, therefore, dost thou exist, O Lord, my God, that thou canst not be conceived not to exist; and rightly. For, if a mind could conceive of a being better than thee, the creature would rise above the Creator; and this is most absurd. And, indeed, whatever else there is, except thee alone, can be conceived not to exist. To thee alone, therefore, it belongs to exist more truly than all other beings, and hence in a higher degree than all others. For, whatever else exists does not exist so truly, and hence in a less degree it belongs to it to exist. Why, then, has the fool said in his heart, there is no God . . . since it is so evident, to a rational mind, that thou dost exist in the highest degree of all? Why, except that he is dull and a fool?

But how has the fool said in his heart what he could not conceive; or how is it that he could not conceive what he said in his heart? Since it is the same to say in the heart, and to conceive.

But, if really, nay, since really, he both conceived, because he said in his heart, and did not say in his heart, because he could not conceive, there is more than one way in which a thing is said in the heart or conceived. For, in one sense, an object is conceived when the word signifying it is conceived; and in another, when the very entity which the object is, is understood.

In the former sense, then, God can be conceived not to exist; but in the latter, not at all. For no one who understands what fire and water are can conceive fire to be water, in accordance with the nature of the facts themselves, although this is possible according to the words. So, then, no one who understands what God is can conceive that God does not exist; although he says these words in his heart, either without any, or with some, foreign signification. For, God is that than which a greater cannot be conceived. And he who thoroughly understands this assuredly understands that this being so truly exists, that not even in concept can it be non-existent. Therefore, he who understands that God so exists cannot conceive that he does not exist.

I thank thee, gracious Lord, I thank thee; because what I formerly believed by thy bounty, I now so understand by thine illumination, that if I were unwilling to believe that thou dost exist, I should not be able not to understand this to be true.

GAUNILO'S CRITICISM

For example: it is said that somewhere in the ocean is an island, which, because of the difficulty, or rather the impossibility, of discovering what does not exist, is called the lost island. And they say that this island has an inestimable wealth of all manner of riches and delicacies in greater abundance than is told of the Islands of the Blest; and that having no owner or inhabitant, it is more excellent than all other countries, which are inhabited by mankind, in the abundance with which it is stored.

Now if some one should tell me that there is such an island, I should easily understand his words, in which there is no difficulty. But suppose that he went on to say, as if by a logical inference: "You can no longer doubt that this island which is more excellent than all lands exists somewhere, since you have no doubt that it is in your understanding. And since it is more excellent not to be in the understanding alone, but to exist both in the understanding and in reality, for this reason it must exist. For if it does not exist, any land which really exists will be more excellent than it; and so the island already understood by you to be more excellent will not be more excellent."

If a man should try to prove to me by such reasoning that this island truly exists, and that its existence should no longer be doubted, either I should believe that he was jesting, or I know not which I ought to regard as the greater fool: myself, supposing that I should allow this proof; or him, if he should suppose that he had established with any certainty the existence of this island. For he ought to show first that the hypothetical excellence of this island exists as a real and indubitable fact, and in no wise as any unreal object, or one whose existence is uncertain, in my understanding.

ST. ANSELM'S REJOINDER

A criticism of Gaunilo's example, in which he tries to show that in this way the real existence of a lost island might be inferred from the fact of its being conceived.

But, you say, it is as if one should suppose an island in the ocean, which surpasses all lands in its fertility, and which, because of the difficulty, or rather the impossibility, of discovering what does not exist, is called a lost island; and should say that there can be no doubt that this island truly exists in reality, for this reason, that one who hears it described easily understands what he hears.

Now I promise confidently that if any man shall devise anything existing either in reality or in concept alone (except that than which a greater cannot be conceived) to which he can adapt the sequence of my reasoning, I will discover that thing, and will give him lost island, not to be lost again.

But it now appears that this being than which a greater is inconceivable cannot be conceived not to be, because it exists on so assured a ground of truth; for otherwise it would not exist at all.

Hence, if any one says that he conceives this being not to exist, I say that at the time when he conceives of this either he conceives of a being than which a greater is inconceivable, or he does not conceive at all. If he does not conceive, he does not conceive of the non-existence of that of which he does not conceive. But if he does conceive, he certainly conceives of a being which cannot be conceived not to exist. For if it could be conceived not to exist, it could be conceived to have a beginning and an end. But this is impossible.

He, then, who conceives of this being conceives of a being which cannot be even conceived not to exist; but he who conceives of this being does not conceive that it does not exist; else he conceives what is inconceivable. The non-existence, then, of that than which a greater cannot be conceived is inconceivable.

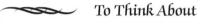 To Think About

1. "Is not the God of the Jewish and Christian scriptures a God profoundly involved in humanity's struggle to the point where God not merely affects but is affected by the struggle?"   ***Charles Hartshorne***

2. "A great temptation is to say that there is only one way to practice any religion. That may sound benign . . . because it simplifies things, but it really leads to ban the books, change the faculties in the seminaries and universities and, at the limit, mount a crusade."   ***James Gould***

3. An anti-God argument from ***James Rachels:***

    a.   If any being is God, he must be a fitting object of worship.

    b.   No being could possibly be a fitting object of worship, since worship requires the abandonment of one's role as an autonomous moral agent.

    c.   Therefore, there cannot be any being who is God.

4. "Father's criticism of Billy Sunday, the evangelist, was, 'He preaches against the sins of the poor, not of the rich.' "   ***Charles Hartshorne***

5. ***Norman Malcolm's*** ontological argument:

    > *God is an unlimited being.*
    > *The existence of an unlimited being is either impossible or necessary.*
    > *The concept of an unlimited being is not self-contradictory, so such a being is not impossible.*
    > *Therefore such a being is necessary.*

6. "If one is prepared to concede that something—God—can exist without an external cause, why go that far along the chain? Why can't the universe exist without an external cause? Does it require any greater suspension of

disbelief to suppose that the universe causes itself than to suppose that God causes himself?"   ***Paol Davis***

7.   "I think that it is a mistake to think that God is interested only or even chiefly in religion."   ***William Temple***

8.   "John Calvin's creed is not about sex; it is about God's infinite glory and ab-solute authority and our utter dependence upon his free grace rather than on our own phony virtue for salvation. True, regulating sexual behavior is almost the last remaining concern of contemporary American religion. But that has little to do with real Christianity—or Judaism or Islam or Buddhism either. When re-ligious conservatives again show serious interest in feeding the hungry, cloth-ing the naked, sheltering the homeless, tending the sick ... (Matthew 25:35–36), perhaps they will be given power to speak to us again with author-ity about sex. Until then, condemning physical expressions of love will only drive more people out of church."   ***A. Hugh Jones***

9.   "I wish however, to emphasize my conviction that my chief contentions about the ontological argument can be put, and to some extent evaluated, in-formally. For one thing, this argument is not by itself the chief, or even one of the chief, reasons for theistic belief. My two primary reasons for belief are the arguments: (1) without God we cannot understand how cosmic order as such is possible; and (2) without God as recipient and objective immortalizer of our achievements, 'all experience is a passing whiff of insignificance,' considering our mortality and other basic aspects of animal life."

Charles Hartshorne

10.   "If religion is a delusion due to wishes (Freud) or bad society (Marx) can't the same be said of atheism?"   ***Unknown***

11.   "Another fundamental error [is] . . . the unnatural distinction Christianity makes between man and the animal world to which he really belongs. It sets up man as all important, and looks upon animals as merely things. . . . Christianity contains in fact a great and essential imperfection in limiting its precepts to man, and in refusing rights to the entire animal world."   ***Arthur Schopenhauer***

 Readings

BARNES, JONATHAN. *The Ontological Argument.* London: Macmillan, 1972.

HARTSHORNE, CHARLES. *Anselm's Discovery: A Re-examination of the Ontological Proof for God's Existence.* La Salle, IL: Open Court, 1965.

HICK, JOHN, ed. *The Many-Faced Argument: Recent Studies on the Ontological Argument for the Existence of God.* New York: Macmillan, 1967.

OPPY, GRAHAM. *Ontological Arguments and Belief in God.* Cambridge: Cambridge University Press, 1995.

7

The Cosmological Argument

St. Thomas Aquinas (1225–74), born in Roccasicca (lower Italy), received his education at the Monte Cassino Abbey and in Naples, Cologne, and Paris; he taught theology in Paris, Rome, and other cities. He is generally regarded as the greatest of the Scholastic theologians. His two major works are Summa Theologica *and* Summa Contra Gentiles, *which respectively synthesized Aristotelian and Christian doctrines and attempted to answer the objections against Catholicism.*

St. Anselm's line of argument can be described as nonexperiential, or *a priori* in character. But many philosophers have claimed that arguments for existence must be "empirical," or based on experience. The proof of God's existence that argues on the basis of many experiences is called the *cosmological* or *first cause* argument. This argues that all things in the world must have had a cause, and since there cannot be an infinity of causes, there must be a first cause, which is God. St. Thomas Aquinas is most famous for arguing in this manner. In the following essays, he argues that five arguments (or "ways") can be used to demonstrate the existence of God. The first four of these arguments take the basic form of causal argumentation. Some things in the world are caused, but nothing can be caused unless caused by something else. There must then be either an infinite series of causes or a first uncaused cause. Since the infinite series is impossible, the only alternative is a first cause, itself uncaused, which we commonly call God.

We begin this section with St. Thomas's critique of the ontological argument, a more formal and precise statement of Gaunilo's objection made to St. Anselm (see page 68 above). It is clear that St. Thomas thinks that some arguments for God's existence are sound and others are unsound. A critical approach of this kind shows the difference between a philosophical approach to these issues and an apologetic one. St. Thomas is interested in the cogency of arguments, not in making converts or pros- elytizing.

Finally, you will notice that Aquinas structures his argument by introducing two "objections" to the existence of God and answering them at the end of his essay. Note that the first of these objections is the problem of evil, which we shall consider in Readings 11 and 12. And finally, the fifth "way" or argument, although drawn from experience, is properly a different kind of argument from the others. It is really a form of the "teleological" argument, which we shall consider next.

⌒⌒⌒ To Study ⌒⌒⌒

1. What does Aquinas mean by claiming that the existence of God is "self-evident in itself, though not to us?"
2. State the two objections Aquinas gives that are used to deny God's existence.
3. What are the five ways in which Aquinas claims that the existence of God can be proven? Construct three of the arguments in logical form.
4. What are Aquinas's replies to the objections stated at the beginning of the discussion?

WHETHER THE EXISTENCE OF GOD IS SELF-EVIDENT?

Objection 1.   It seems that the existence of God is self-evident. For those things are said to be self-evident to us the knowledge of which exists naturally in us, as we can see in regard to first principles. But as Damascene says, *the knowledge of God is naturally implanted in all.* Therefore the existence of God is self-evident.

Obj. 2.   Further, those things are said to be self-evident which are known as soon as the terms are known, which the Philosopher says is true of the first principles of demonstration. Thus, when the nature of a whole and of a part is known, it is at once recognized that every whole is greater than its part. But as soon as the signifi- cation of the name *God* is understood, it is at once seen that God exists. For by this name is signified that thing than which nothing greater can be conceived. But that which exists actually and mentally is greater than that which exists only mentally. Therefore, since as soon as the name *God* is understood it exists mentally, it also fol- lows that it exists actually. Therefore the proposition *God exists* is self-evident.

Obj. 3.   Further, the existence of truth is self-evident. For whoever denies the existence of truth grants that truth does not exist: and, if truth does not exist, then the proposition *Truth does not exist* is true: and if there is anything true, there must be truth. But God is truth itself: *I am the way, the truth, and the life (Jo.* xiv. 6). There- fore *God exists* is self-evident.

On the contrary, No one can mentally admit the opposite of what is self- evident, as the Philosopher states concerning the first principles of demonstration.

But the opposite of the proposition *God is* can be mentally admitted: *The fool said in his heart, There is no God* (*Ps.* lii. 1). Therefore, that God exists is not self-evident.

I answer that, A thing can be self-evident in either of two ways: on the one hand, self-evident in itself, though not to us; on the other, self-evident in itself, and to us. A proposition is self-evident because the predicate is included in the essence of the subject: *e.g., Man is an animal,* for animal is contained in the essence of man. If, therefore, the essence of the predicate and subject be known to all, the proposition will be self-evident to all; as is clear with regard to the first principles of demonstration, the terms of which are certain common notions that no one is ignorant of, such as being and non-being, whole and part, and the like. If, however, there are some to whom the essence of the predicate and subject is unknown, the proposition will be self-evident in itself, but not to those who do not know the meaning of the predicate and subject of the proposition. Therefore, it happens, as Boethius says, that there are some notions of the mind which are common and self-evident only to the learned, as that incorporeal substances are not in space. Therefore I say that this proposition, *God exists,* of itself is self-evident, for the predicate is the same as the subject, because God is His own existence as will be hereafter shown. Now because we do not know the essence of God, the proposition is not self-evident to us, but needs to be demonstrated by things that are more known to us, though less known in their nature—namely, by His effects.

Reply Obj. 1.   To know that God exists in a general and confused way is implanted in us by nature, inasmuch as God is man's beatitude. For man naturally desires happiness, and what is naturally desired by man is naturally known by him. This, however, is not to know absolutely that God exists; just as to know that someone is approaching is not the same as to know that Peter is approaching, even though it is Peter who is approaching; for there are many who imagine that man's perfect good, which is happiness, consists in riches, and others in pleasures, and others in something else.

Reply Obj. 2.   Perhaps not everyone who hears this name *God* understands it to signify something than which nothing greater can be thought, seeing that some have believed God to be a body. Yet, granted that everyone understands that by this name *God* is signified something than which nothing greater can be thought, nevertheless, it does not therefore follow that he understands that what the name signifies exists actually, but only that it exists mentally. Nor can it be argued that it actually exists, unless it be admitted that there actually exists something than which nothing greater can be thought; and this precisely is not admitted by those who hold that God does not exist.

Reply Obj. 3.   The existence of truth in general is self-evident, but the existence of a Primal Truth is not self-evident to us.

Whether God Exists?

Objection 1.   It seems that God does not exist; because if one of two contraries be infinite, the other would be altogether destroyed. But the name *God* means that He is infinite goodness. If, therefore, God existed, there would be no evil discoverable; but there is evil in the world. Therefore God does not exist.

Obj. 2.   Further, it is superfluous to suppose that what can be accounted for by a few principles has been produced by many. But it seems that everything we see in the world can be accounted for by other principles, supposing God did not exist. For all natural things can be reduced to one principle, which is nature; and all voluntary things can be reduced to one principle, which is human reason or will. Therefore there is no need to suppose God's existence.

On the Contrary, It is said in the person of God: *I am Who am* (Exod. iii. 14).

I answer that, The existence of God can be proved in five ways.

The first and more manifest way is the argument from motion. It is certain, and evident to our senses, that in the world some things are in motion. Now whatever is moved is moved by another, for nothing can be moved except it is in potentiality to that towards which it is moved; whereas a thing moves inasmuch as it is in the act. For motion is nothing else than the reduction of something from potentiality to actuality. But nothing can be reduced from potentiality to actuality, except by something in a state of actuality. Thus that which is actually hot, as fire, makes wood, which is potentially hot, to be actually hot, and thereby moves and changes it. Now it is not possible that the same thing should be at once in actuality and potentiality in the same respect, but only in different respects. For what is actually hot cannot simultaneously be potentially hot; but it is simultaneously potentially cold. It is therefore impossible that in the same respect and in the same way a thing should be both mover and moved, *i.e.,* that it should move itself. Therefore, whatever is moved must be moved by another. If that by which it is moved be itself moved, then this also must needs be moved by another, and that by another again. But this cannot go on to infinity because then there would be no first mover, and, consequently, no other mover, seeing that subsequent movers move only inasmuch as they are moved by the first mover; as the staff moves only because it is moved by the hand. Therefore it is necessary to arrive at a first mover, moved by no other; and this everyone understands to be God.

The second way is from the nature of efficient cause.[1] In the world of sensible things we find there is an order of efficient causes. There is no case known (neither is it, indeed, possible) in which a thing is found to be the efficient cause of itself; for so it would be prior to itself, which is impossible. Now in efficient causes it is not possible to go on to infinity, because in all efficient causes following in order, the first is the cause of the intermediate cause, and the intermediate is the cause of the ultimate cause, whether the intermediate cause be several, or one only. Now to take away the cause is to take away the effect. Therefore, if there be no first cause among efficient causes, there will be no ultimate, nor any intermediate, cause. But if in efficient causes it is possible to go on to infinity, there will be no first efficient cause, neither will there be an ultimate effect, nor any intermediate efficient causes; all of which is plainly false. Therefore it is necessary to admit a first efficient cause, to which everyone gives the name of God.

---

[1] *Efficient cause:* The entity which immediately brings the effect, such as one billiard ball striking another. [ED.]

The third way is taken from possibility and necessity, and runs thus. We find in nature things that are possible to be and not to be, since they are found to be generated, and to be corrupted, and consequently, it is possible for them to be and not to be. But it is impossible for these always to exist, for that which cannot-be at some time is not. Therefore, if everything cannot-be, then at one time there was nothing in existence. Now if this were true, even now there would be nothing in existence, because that which does not exist begins to exist only through something already existing. Therefore, if at one time nothing was in existence, it would have been impossible for anything to have begun to exist; and thus even now nothing would be in existence—which is absurd. Therefore, not all beings are merely possible but there must exist something the existence of which is necessary. But every necessary thing either has its necessity caused by another, or not. Now it is impossible to go on to infinity in necessary things which have their necessity caused by another, as has been already proved in regard to efficient causes. Therefore we cannot but admit the existence of some being having of itself its own necessity, and not receiving it from another, but rather causing in others their necessity. This all men speak of as God.

The fourth way is taken from the gradation to be found in things. Among beings there are some more and some less good, true, noble, and the like. But *more* and *less* are predicated of different things according as they resemble in their different ways something which is the maximum, as a thing is said to be hotter according as it more nearly resembles that which is hottest; so that there is something which is truest, something best, something noblest, and, consequently, something which is most being, for those things that are greatest in truth are greatest in being, as it is written in [Aristotle's] *Metaphysics* ii. Now the maximum in any genus is the cause of all in that genus, as fire, which is the maximum of heat, is the cause of all hot things, as is said in the same book. Therefore there must also be something which is to all beings the cause of their being, goodness, and every other perfection; and this we call God.

The fifth way is taken from the governance of the world. We see that things which lack knowledge, such as natural bodies, act for an end, and this is evident from their acting always, or nearly always, in the same way, so as to obtain the best result. Hence it is plain that they achieve their end, not fortuitously, but designedly. Now whatever lacks knowledge cannot move towards an end, unless it be directed by some being endowed with knowledge and intelligence; as the arrow is directed by the archer. Therefore some intelligent being exists by whom all natural things are directed to their end: and this being we call God.

Reply Obj. 1.   As Augustine says: *Since God is the highest good, He would not allow any evil to exist in His works; unless His omnipotence and goodness were such as to bring good even out of evil.* This is part of the infinite goodness of God, that He should allow evil to exist, and out of it produce good.

Reply Obj. 2.   Since nature works for a determinate end under the direction of a higher agent, whatever is done by nature must be traced back to God as to its first cause. So likewise whatever is done voluntarily must be traced back to some higher cause other than human reason and will, since these can change and fail; for all things that are changeable and capable of defect must be traced back to an immovable and self-necessary first principle as has been shown.

To Think About

1. "A church is a community that keeps alive the dangerous memories of its classics. The memory of Jesus, for example, disconcerts all present reality, including that of the church, because He essentially afflicts the comfortable and comforts the afflicted. So theology makes religious institutions aware of their true spiritual resources and of their explicitly religious character. And it makes the wider culture aware of the religious dimensions of life by seeking better ways to ask *the* religious questions. This is a dangerous occupation. . . . This voice threatens those in the establishment who want religion to endorse comfortable, white, middle-class values. That is also a factor working against one person's assuming a truly prophetic role in our culture." ***Paul Tillich***

2. "Monotheism seems to me to be quite strongly associated, as both cause and effect, with intolerance." ***George Santayana***

3. "Protestantism acknowledges the paradox that sin is necessary because of the human condition, but unnecessary if man remains strong in his faith in God." ***Arthur Smith***

4. "Our religions—with their Crusades, their crucifixions, and their bloodshed of various sorts (depending on which religion you happen to be concerned with)—find their own excuses for having this kind of relationship to cruelty that kids have when they're looking at a scene that they want to see but don't want to see, so they put their hands over their eyes and then they spread their fingers, in order to see and yet not see the horror." ***Arnold Toynbee***

5. "Modern man is, as Sartre has presented him to us, man torn from his traditional group, traditional religion, his traditional metaphysics or ethic. He is the spiritually unaccommodated man, and nothing is impermissible for him. He must decide himself just what it is he forbids himself to do." ***Phillip Thody***

6. ". . . those in whom the sense of dread is so acute that they turn to extreme and doomed commitments; I know something about dread myself, and appreciate the elaborate systems with which some people manage to fill the void, appreciate all the opiates of the people, whether they are as accessible as alcohol and heroin and promiscuity or as hard to come by as faith in God or History." ***Joan Didion,*** in *Slouching Towards Bethlehem*

7. "Primitive religion is not believed. It is danced." ***Arthur Darby Nock***

8. "[W]e turn our attention to the psychical origin of religious ideas. These, which are given out as teachings, are not precipitates of experience or end-results of

thinking: they are illusions, fulfilments of the oldest, strongest and most urgent wishes of mankind. The secret of their strength lies in the strength of those wishes. As we already know, the terrifying impression of helplessness in childhood aroused the need for protection—for protection through love—which was provided by the father; and the recognition that this helplessness lasts throughout life made it necessary to cling to the existence of a father, but this time a more powerful one. Thus the benevolent rule of a divine Providence allays our fear of the dangers of life; the establishment of a moral world-order ensures the fulfilment of the demands of justice, which have so often remained unfulfilled in human civilization; and the prolongation of earthly existence in a future life provides the local and temporal framework in which these wish-fulfilments shall take place. Answers to the riddles that tempt the curiosity of man, such as how the universe began or what the relation is between body and mind, are developed in conformity with the underlying assumptions of this system."

Sigmund Freud

9. "After Russell, many philosophers in the analytic tradition began to argue that the standards of rationality in science are no more than human habits which are open to empirical and historical study like any other natural phenomena; and these habits could have no ultimate and permanent justification in timeless philosophy."

Unknown

Readings

BURILL, D., ed. *The Cosmological Arguments.* New York: Doubleday, 1967.

CRAIG, WILLIAM LANE. *The Cosmological Argument from Plato to Leibniz.* New York: Macmillan, 1980.

HICK, JOHN. *Arguments for the Existence of God.* New York: Macmillan, 1970.

MACKIE, J. L. *The Miracle of Theism.* Oxford: Clarendon Press, 1982.

MEYNELL, HUGO. *The Intelligible Universe.* New York: Barnes & Noble, 1971.

REICHENBACH, BRUCE. *The Cosmological Argument: A Reassessment.* Springfield, IL: Charles C. Thomas, 1972.

8

The Teleological Argument

William Paley (1743–1805), English philosopher and theologian, wrote a number of apologetic works; the two most famous are Evidences of Christianity *(1794) and* Natural Theology, or Evidences of the Existences and Attributes of the Deity Collected from the Appearances of Nature *(1802). He is best known for stating the argument from design for the existence of God.*

The third great argument for God's existence, like the cosmological argument, draws on experience. But here the experience is the order, design, and apparent purposefulness of the physical universe. This argument, usually called the *teleological* argument, or the argument from *design,* contends that God's existence is proven from a single experience. This is illustrated with an analogy that compares the world to machines—just as machines have makers, the world has a maker, who is God. Paley's well-known book *Natural Theology* argues from analogy by comparing a watch to the world. Just as no one would claim that a watch came into existence by chance, no one should make such a claim about the natural world. It, too, exhibits design and intelligent purpose, just as much as any object of human invention. Therefore a divine designer must exist to account for the order and purposefulness of natural objects.

This argument has always had great emotional and aesthetic force. Everyone has been deeply moved at one time or another by the order of natural processes. Acorns always, or almost always, grow to be oaks. The sun rises in the east at a precisely predictable time each day. Water boils at 100 degrees Celsius, not a degree less. This order extends from individual objects in nature to great interacting systems of things in the physical and biological realms. Since, unlike human beings, physical objects have no intelligence to design their own goals and means to achieve them, it appears necessary to assume that some external force, perhaps outside nature as a whole, has "programmed" them to act as they do. Such a designing force must be God.

From William Paley, *Natural Theology* (London: Longmans, Green & Co., 1838), 211–16.

At the same time you will want to consider certain problems. First of all, natural processes are not always uniformly perfect; many work to our disadvantage, even causing great pain and suffering. Could God's designs fail to be perfect? Another problem with this argument may be its anthropomorphism, or tendency to assign human qualities to nature. Just because we design and plan our activities does not mean that nature itself exhibits design. Allied with this difficulty is the structure of the argument itself. It is clearly an argument from analogy, an analogy with the skill of a craftsman. But there is an old saying that "every analogy limps," or fails to make its case with deductive necessity. Is there some hidden "limp" in this analogy, too?

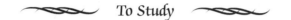

To Study

1. What is the analogical argument stated by Paley? Structure the argument carefully.
2. State Paley's answers to possible arguments against his analogy.
3. Why couldn't the watch simply be the result of laws of metallic nature?

STATEMENT OF THE ARGUMENT

In crossing a heath, suppose I pitched my foot against a *stone,* and were asked how the stone came to be there, I might possibly answer, that, for anything I knew to the contrary, it had lain there forever; nor would it, perhaps, be very easy to show the absurdity of this answer. But suppose I found a *watch* upon the ground, and it should be inquired how the watch happened to be in that place, I should hardly think of the answer which I had before given—that, for anything I knew, the watch might have always been there. Yet why should not this answer serve for the watch as well as for the stone? Why is it not as admissible in the second case as in the first? For this reason, and for no other, viz., that, when we come to inspect the watch, we perceive . . . that its several parts are framed and put together for a purpose, e.g., that they are so formed and adjusted as to produce motion, and that motion so regulated as to point out the hour of the day; that, if the different parts had been differently shaped from what they are, if a different size from what they are, or placed after any other manner, or in any other order than that in which they are placed, either no motion at all would have been carried on in the machine, or none which would have answered the use that is now served by it. To reckon up a few of the plainest of these parts, and of their offices, all tending to one result: We see a cylindrical box containing a coiled elastic spring, which, by its endeavor to relax itself, turns round the box. We next observe a flexible chain (artificially wrought for the sake of flexure) communicating the action of the spring from the box to the fuse. We then find a series of wheels, the teeth of which catch in, and apply to, each other, conducting the motion from the fuse to the balance, and from the balance to the pointer, and, at the same time, by the size and shape of those wheels, so regulating that motion as to terminate in causing an index, by an equable and measured progression, to pass over a given space in a given time.

We take notice that the wheels are made of brass, in order to keep them from rust; the springs of steel, no other metal being so elastic; that over the face of the watch there is placed a glass, a material employed in no other part of the work, but in the room of which, if there had been any other than a transparent substance, the hour could not be seen without opening the case. This mechanism being observed . . . the inference, we think, is inevitable, that the watch must have had a maker; that there must have existed, at some place or other, an artificer or artificers who formed it for the purpose which we find it actually to answer; who comprehended its construction, and designed its use.

I. Nor would it, I apprehend, weaken the conclusion that we had never seen a watch made; that we had never known an artist capable of making one; that we were altogether incapable of executing such a piece of workmanship ourselves, or of understanding in what manner it was performed; all this being no more than what is true of some exquisite remains of ancient art, of some lost arts, and, to the generality of mankind, of the more curious productions of modern manufacture. Does one man in a million know how oval frames are turned? Ignorance of this kind exalts our opinion of the unseen and unknown artist's skill, if he be unseen and unknown, but raises no doubt in our minds of the existence and agency of such an artist, at some former time, and in some place or other. Nor can I perceive that it varies at all the inference whether the question arise concerning a human agent, or concerning an agent of a different species, or an agent possessing, in some respect, a different nature.

II. Neither, secondly, would it invalidate our conclusion, that the watch sometimes went wrong, or that it seldom went exactly right. The purpose of the machinery, the design, and the designer, might be evident, and, in the case supposed, would be evident, in whatever way we accounted for the irregularity of the movement, or whether we could account for it or not. It is not necessary that a machine be perfect in order to show with what design it was made; still less necessary where the only question is whether it were made with any design at all.

III. Nor, thirdly, would it bring any uncertainty into the argument if there were a few parts of the watch concerning which we could not discover, or had not yet discovered, in what manner they conduced to the general effect; or even some parts concerning which we could not ascertain whether they conducted to that effect in any manner whatever. For, as to the first branch of the case, if by the loss, or disorder, or decay of the parts in question, the movement of the watch were found in fact to be stopped, or disturbed, or retarded, no doubt would remain in our minds as to the utility or intention of these parts, although we should be unable to investigate the manner according to which, or the connection by which, the ultimate effect depended upon their action or assistance; and the more complex is the machine, the more likely is this obscurity to arise. Then, as to the second thing supposed, namely, that there were parts which might be spared without prejudice to the movement of the watch, and that he had proved this by experiment, these superfluous parts, even if we were completely assured that they were such, would not vacate the reasoning which we had instituted concerning other parts. The indication of contrivance remained, with respect to them, nearly as it was before.

IV.   Nor, fourthly, would any man in his senses think the existence of the watch, with its various machinery, accounted for by being told that it was one out of possible combinations of material forms; that whatever he had found in the place where he found the watch must have contained some internal configuration or other; and that this configuration might be the structure exhibited, viz., of the works of a watch, as well as a different structure.

V.   Nor, fifthly, would it yield his inquiry more satisfaction, to be answered, that there existed in things a principle of order, which had disposed the parts of the watch into their present form and situation. He never knew a watch made by the principle of order; nor can he even form to himself an idea of what is meant by a principle of order, distinct from the intelligence of the watchmaker.

VI.   Sixthly, he would be surprised to hear that the mechanism of the watch was no proof of contrivance, only a motion to induce the mind to think so:

VII.   And not less surprised to be informed, that the watch in his hand was nothing more than the result of the laws of *metallic* nature. It is a perversion of language to assign any law as the efficient, operative cause of anything. A law presupposes as an agent, for it is only the mode according to which an agent proceeds; it implies a power; for it is the order according to which that power acts. Without this agent, without this power, which are both distinct from itself the *law* does nothing, is nothing. The expression, "the law of metallic nature," may sound strange and harsh to a philosophic ear; but it seems quite as justifiable as some others which are more familiar to him such as "the law of vegetable nature," "the law of animal nature," or, indeed, as "the law of nature" in general, when assigned as the cause of phenomena in exclusion of agency and power, or when it is substituted into the place of these.

VIII.   Neither, lastly, would our observer be driven out of his conclusion, or from his confidence in its truth, by being told that he knew nothing at all about the matter. He knows enough for his argument: he knows the utility of the end: he knows the subserviency and adaptation of the means to the end. These points being known, his ignorance of other points, his doubts concerning other points, affect not the certainty of his reasoning. The consciousness of knowing little need not beget a distrust of that which he does know. . . .

APPLICATION OF THE ARGUMENT

Every indication of contrivance, every manifestation of design, which existed in the watch, exists in the works of nature; with the difference, on the side of nature, of being greater and more, and that in a degree which exceeds all computation. I mean that the contrivances of nature surpass the contrivances of art in the complexity, subtlety, and curiosity of the mechanism; and still more, if possible, do they go beyond them in number and variety; yet in a multitude of cases, are not less evidently mechanical, not less evidently contrivances, not less evidently accommodated to their end or suited to their office than are the most perfect productions of human ingenuity. . . .

To Think About

1. "For the usual denial of God's existence tended to encourage people to expect a rationality in human affairs experience is likely to contradict. Religious belief, as Lichtheim saw it, had been a protection against a too-great expectation of reasonableness, a protection men in the past had benefited from, and which contemporary man, insofar as he has lost his traditional faith, has had to do without."   **W. T. Stace**

2. "That some form of religion is indispensable to any society seems no longer an open question. It has been long debated whether a society could get along without any religious organization of its life. Recent experience has made clear that if a traditional religion disintegrates, men will not calmly proceed to live without any religion at all. A new religion, or, if we prefer, a new substitute for religion, will spring up to fill the vacuum and to perform the historic functions of a religion. And this new 'religion' will be much worse than the old one it supplants. For it will inevitably express some need of the moment: it will be onesided and fanatical."   **Paul Tillich**

3. "The most ordinary misinterpretation of faith is to consider it an act of knowledge that has a low degree of evidence. . . . If this is meant, one is speaking of belief rather than of faith."   **Paul Tillich**

4. Relevant evidence to cite for the teleological argument:

    a. "The world is intelligible in a very high degree. The world, somehow or other, is capable of being understood by means of the logical and mathematical categories of the human mind.

    b. "The evolutionary process . . . has operated *as if* it were intended to produce variety, beauty, mind, and intelligence.

    c. "The inorganic world . . . is remarkably well adapted—physically, chemically, thermally, and so on—to the maintenance of life.

    d. "Nature has developed in such a way that there are numerous phenomena which elicit in human beings a sense of beauty.

    e. "The conditions of human life have developed in such a way that man is able to postulate, pursue, and, to a high degree, achieve moral ideals."
                                                    William H. Halverson

5. "God is the fundamental symbol for what concerns us ultimately. . . . Where there is ultimate concern, God can be denied only in the name of God."
                                                    Paul Tillich

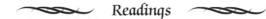 Readings

DAWKINS, RICHARD. *The Blind Watchmaker.* New York: Norton, 1986.

MCPHERSON, THOMAS. *The Design Argument.* New York: Macmillan, 1972.

SCHLESINGER, GEORGE. "Theism and Confirmation." *Pacific Philosophical Quarterly* 64 (1983): 27–35.

SWINBURNE, RICHARD. "The Argument from Design." *Philosophy* 43 (1968): 1–18.

9

It Is Better to Believe in God's Existence Than to Deny It

Blaise Pascal (1623–62) was one of the most important scientific, philosophical, and religious figures of seventeenth-century France. He made important contributions to mathematics and physics and is generally regarded as the founder of modern probability theory. But Pascal is perhaps best known for his writings in spirituality and religious controversy. He came under the influence of a radically conservative Catholic movement known as Jansenism and defended it in a series of satirical publications called Provincial Letters. *A powerful religious experience in 1654 colored his entire outlook on the relation of faith and philosophy, leading to a collection of notes on a projected defense of the Christian religion. These notes, found after his death, were published in 1670 under the title* Thoughts of M. Pascal on Religion and Several Other Subjects *and are usually referred to under their French title,* Pensées.

We have considered three major arguments for God's existence. They are drawn from widely disparate sources, some Christian like St. Anselm, others ultimately from non-religious sources. The cosmological and teleological arguments in fact are found in Aristotle and Plato, for instance, hundreds of years before the birth of Christ. Each argument has its special appeal. The ontological argument has always fascinated philosophers of a mathematical or logical turn of mind. The cosmological and teleological arguments hold great interest for philosophers who insist on the senses as origins of whatever knowledge we can have. And the teleological argument appeals to the poet in us, and to our sense of order and beauty.

But, as we said at the beginning of Part 3, philosophy and religion do not always intersect. Some great believing religionists have insisted that access to God transcends the human mind utterly. No argument for God's existence is satisfactory, and belief alone is necessary for religious life. Pascal is a great example of such a position. There is, for him, no rational proof for or against God's existence. Nonetheless, one must choose to

From Blaise Pascal, *Pensées,* trans. W. Trotter (London: Dent & Co., 1908).

believe or not. The option is unavoidable. We are forced to wager. Now consider the alternatives: either God exists or he does not exist. If he does not exist, we lose nothing for believing that he does exist. If he does exist, however, we lose everything if we choose not to believe. The rational choice must be to believe in God's existence; we have everything to gain, infinite happiness and immortality, and nothing to lose.

Interestingly, Pascal's argument is not one in support of the existence of God, but one that supports the reasonability of a natural tendency to believe in God. It supports religion, but not philosophical arguments in behalf of religion. The traditional arguments for God's existence lead to skepticism, according to Pascal, and we must change the playing field from reason to emotion. However vulgar it may seem to talk of religion as though it were a matter of betting on the horses, it is a fact of human nature that some choice is forced upon us. Either we choose to believe or we don't. Pascal asks us to consider the likely consequences of each choice. The choice for him is clear: whether or not God really exists, it makes more sense to believe than not to.

 To Study

1. On what basis does Pascal argue that we can't know God's existence?
2. Discuss Pascal's "wager."
3. How can one come to faith in God?
4. Why is it reasonable to believe God exists even though it is uncertain?
5. What is the role of custom in proof?
6. Discuss: "The heart has its reasons, which reason does not know."

Let us now speak according to natural lights.

If there is a God, He is infinitely incomprehensible, since, having neither parts nor limits, He has no affinity to us. We are then incapable of knowing either what He is or if He is. This being so, who will dare to undertake the decision of the question? Not we, who have no affinity to Him.

Who then will blame Christians for not being able to give a reason for their belief, since they profess a religion for which they cannot give a reason? They declare, in expounding it to the world, that it is a foolishness . . . ; and then you complain that they do not prove it! If they proved it, they would not keep their word; it is in lacking proofs that they are not lacking in sense. "Yes, but although this excuses those who offer it as such, and takes away from them the blame of putting it forward without reason, it does not excuse those who receive it." Let us then examine this point, and say, "God is, or He is not." But to which side shall we incline? Reason can decide nothing here. There is an infinite chaos which separates us. A game is being played at the extremity of this infinite distance where heads or tails will turn up. What will you wager? According to reason, you can do neither the one thing nor the other; according to reason, you can defend neither of the propositions.

Do not then reprove for error those who have made a choice; for you know nothing about it. "No, but I blame them for having made, not this choice, but a choice; for again both he who chooses heads and he who chooses tails are equally at fault, they are both in the wrong. The true course is not to wager at all."

Yes; but you must wager. It is not optional. You are embarked. Which will you choose then? Let us see. Since you must choose, let us see which interests you least. You have two things to lose, the true and the good; and two things to stake, your reason and your will, your knowledge and your happiness; and your nature has two things to shun, error and misery. Your reason is no more shocked in choosing one rather than the other, since you must of necessity choose. This is one point settled. But your happiness? Let us weigh the gain and the loss in wagering that God is. Let us estimate these two chances. If you gain, you gain all; if you lose, you lose nothing. Wager, then, without hesitation that He is. "That is very fine. Yes, I must wager; but I may perhaps wager too much." Let us see. Since there is an equal risk of gain and of loss, if you had only to gain two lives, instead of one, you might still wager. But if there were three lives to gain, you would have to play (since you are under the necessity of playing), and you would be imprudent, when you are forced to play, not to chance your life to gain three at a game where there is an equal risk of loss and gain. But there is an eternity of life and happiness. And this being so, if there were an infinity of chances, of which one only would be for you, you would still be right in wagering one to win two, and you would act stupidly, being obliged to play, by refusing to stake one life against three at a game in which out of an infinity of chances there is one for you, if there were an infinity of infinitely happy life to gain. But there is here an infinity of an infinitely happy life to gain, a chance of gain against an finite number of chances of loss, and what you stake is finite. It is all divided; wherever the infinite is and there is not an infinity of chances of loss against that of gain, there is no time to hesitate, you must give all. And thus, when one is forced to play, he must renounce reason to preserve his life, rather than risk it for infinite gain, as likely to happen as the loss of nothingness.

For it is no use to say it is uncertain if we will gain, and it is certain that we risk, and that the infinite distance between the *certainty* of what is staked and the *uncertainty* of what will be gained, equals the finite good which is certainly staked against the uncertain infinite. It is not so, as every player stakes a certainty to gain an uncertainty, and yet he stakes a finite certainty to gain a finite uncertainty, without transgressing against reason. There is not an infinite distance between the certainty staked and the uncertainty of the gain; that is untrue. In truth, there is an infinity between the certainty of gain and the certainty of loss. But the uncertainty of the gain is proportioned to the certainty of the stake according to the proportion of the chances of gain and loss. Hence it comes that, if there are as many risks on one side as on the other, the course is to play even; and then the certainty of the stake is equal to the uncertainty of the gain, so far is it from fact that there is an infinite distance between them. And so our proposition is of infinite force, when there is the finite to stake in a game where there are equal risks of gain and of loss and the infinite to gain. This is demonstrable; and if men are capable of any truths, this is one.

"I confess it, I admit it. But, still, is there no means of seeing the faces of the cards?" Yes, Scripture and the rest, etc. "Yes, but I have my hands tied and my mouth closed; I am forced to wager, and am not free. I am not released and am so made that I cannot believe. What, then, would you have me do?"

True. But at least learn your inability to believe, since reason brings you to this, and yet you cannot believe. Endeavour then to convince yourself, not by increase in proofs of God, but by the abatement of your passions. You would like to attain faith, and do not know the way; you would like to cure yourself of unbelief, and ask the remedy for it. Learn of those who have been bound like you, and who now stake all their possessions. These are people who know the way which you would follow, and who are cured of all ill of which you would be cured. Follow the way by which they began; by acting as if they believed, taking the holy water, having masses said, etc. Even this will naturally make you believe, and deaden your acuteness. "But this is what I am afraid of." And why? What have you to lose?

But to show you that this leads you there, it is this which will lessen the passions, which are your stumbling-blocks.

The end of this discourse. Now, what harm will befall you in taking this side? You will be faithful, honest, humble, grateful, generous, a sincere friend, truthful. Certainly you will not have those poisonous pleasures, glory and luxury; but will you not have others? I will tell you that you will thereby gain in this life, and that, at each step you take on this road, you will see so great certainty of gain, so much nothingness in what you risk, that you will at last recognise that you have wagered for something certain and infinite, for which you have given nothing.

234

If we must not act save on a certainty, we ought not to act on religion, for it is not certain. But how many things we do on an uncertainty, sea voyages, battles! I say then we must do nothing at all, for nothing is certain, and that there is more certainty in religion than there is as to whether we may see to-morrow; for it is not certain that we may see to-morrow, and it is certainly possible that we may not see it. We cannot say as much about religion. It is not certain that it is; but who will venture to say that it is certainly possible that it is not? Now when we work for to-morrow, and so on an uncertainty, we act reasonably; for we ought to work for an uncertainty according to the doctrine of chance which was demonstrated above.

Saint Augustine has seen that we work for an uncertainty, on sea, in battle, etc. But he has not seen the doctrine of chance which proves that we should do so. Montaigne has seen that we are shocked at a fool, and that habit is all-powerful; but he has not seen the reason of this effect.

All these persons have seen the effects, but they have not seen the causes. They are, in comparison with those who have discovered the causes, as those who have only eyes are in comparison with those who have intellect. For the effects are perceptible by sense, and the causes are visible only to the intellect. And although these effects are seen by the mind, this mind is, in comparison with the mind which sees the causes, as the bodily senses are in comparison with the intellect.

252

For we must not misunderstand ourselves; we are as much automatic as intellectual; and hence it comes that the instrument by which conviction is attained is not demonstration alone. How few things are demonstrated! Proofs only convince the mind. Custom is the source of our strongest and most believed proofs. It bends the automaton, which persuades the mind without its thinking about the matter. Who has demonstrated that there will be a tomorrow, and that we shall die? And what is more believed? It is then custom which persuades us of it; it is custom that makes so many men Christians; custom that makes them Turks, heathens, artisans, soldiers, etc. (Faith in baptism is more received among Christians than among Turks.) Finally, we must have recourse to it when once the mind has seen where the truth is, in order to quench our thirst, and steep ourselves in that belief, which escapes us at every hour; for always to have proofs ready is too much trouble. We must get an easier belief, which is that of custom, which, without violence, without art, without argument, makes us believe things, and inclines all our powers to this belief, so that our soul falls naturally into it.

277

The heart has its reasons, which reason does not know. We feel it in a thousand things. I say that the heart naturally loves the Universal Being, and also itself naturally, according as it gives itself to them; and it hardens itself against one or the other at its will. You have rejected the one and kept the other. Is it by reason that you love yourself?

347

Man is but a reed, the most feeble thing in nature, but he is a thinking reed. The entire universe need not arm itself to crush him. A vapour, a drop of water suffices to kill him. But, if the universe were to crush him, man would still be more noble than that which killed him, because he knows that he dies and the advantage which the universe has over him; the universe knows nothing of this.

All our dignity consists then in thought.

365

Thought.—All the dignity of man consists in thought. Thought is therefore by its nature a wonderful and incomparable thing. It must have strange defects to be contemptible. But it has such, so that nothing is more ridiculous. How great it is in its nature! How vile it is in its defects! . . . There is no permanence for man: it is a condition which is at once natural to mankind, yet most contrary to his inclinations. . . . We burn with the desire of finding a secure abode, an ultimate firm base on which to build a tower which might rise to infinity; but our very foundation crumbles completely, and earth opens before us unto the very abyss.

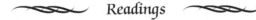

To Think About

1. Does Pascal's theory provide grounds for belief in the existence of many gods as well as only one? A female or a male God?

2. In what situation is religious belief a waste of effort? Never?

3. "There remains one fundamental hurdle which no form of Christianity can overcome: the fact that it demands of man a morally repugnant attitude towards the universe. It is now very widely held that the basic element of the Christian religion is an attitude of worship towards a being supremely worthy of being worshipped and that it is religious feelings and experiences which apprise their owner of such a being and which inspire in him the knowledge or the feeling of complete dependence, awe, worship, mystery, and self-abasement."   ***Kurt Baier***

4. "Christianity thus demands of men an attitude inconsistent with one of the presuppositions of morality: that man is not wholly dependent on something else, that man has free will, that man is in principle capable of responsibility."   ***Kurt Baier***

5. "On the surface the Christians practised an austere sexual morality, easily recognizable and acclaimed by outsiders: total sexual renunciation by the few; marital concord between the spouses; strong disapproval of remarriage. This surface was presented openly to outsiders. Lacking the clear ritual boundaries provided in Judaism by circumcision and dietary laws, Christians tended to make their exceptional sexual discipline bear the full burden of expressing the difference between themselves and the pagan world."   ***Peter Brown***

6. "Asceticism and intolerance are the two main contributions that Christianity has made to European culture."   ***W. Liebaschuetz***

7. "If only God would give me some clear sign! Like making a large deposit in my name at a Swiss bank."   ***Woody Allen***

8. "If God is male, then the male is God."   ***Mary Daly***

9. Does Pascal argue for either monotheism or polytheism?

Readings

BROOME, J. H. *Pascal.* New York: Barnes & Noble, 1965.

DAVIDSON, HUGH. *Blaise Pascal.* Boston: Twayne, 1983.

JORDAN, JEFF, ed. *Gambling on God: Essays on Pascal's Wager.* Lanham, MD: Rowman & Littlefield, 1994.

MESNARD, JEAN. *Pascal, His Life and Works.* London: Harrill Press, 1952.

RESCHER, NICHOLAS. *Pascal's Wager: A Study of Practical Reasoning in Philosophical Theology.* Notre Dame, IN: University of Notre Dame Press, 1985.

Can We Prove That God Exists?

10
Faith, Not Logic,
Is the Basis of Belief

Søren Kierkegaard (1813–55), Danish father of modern existentialism, has had a deep influence on the widespread twentieth-century theological movement associated with Karl Barth. In his Philosophical Fragments *(1836) and* Concluding Unscientific Postscript *(1842), Kierkegaard attacked the rationalist desire for proofs as an evasion of the claim of revelation.*

We turn now to a second alternative to classic arguments for God's existence. Like Pascal, Søren Kierkegaard believes that attempts to prove God's existence from reason and experience are impossible. Kierkegaard argues that knowledge of God's existence must rely on faith and not philosophical reasoning. He uses the vivid metaphor of a "leap" to characterize this position. Religious belief is not a form of knowledge, but a "leap" of faith. Philosophical "proofs" of existence provide only a conception of God. They are not arguments for God's existence. In words reminiscent of those of skeptics like David Hume, Kierkegaard insists that it is hard to prove anything exists. Reason moves *from* existence and not *toward* it. It "collides with the Unknown," a name that we can give God in our futile efforts to demonstrate God's existence.

To develop his position, Kierkegaard gives the example of the teleological argument for God's existence. We have already seen this argument in Thomas Aquinas's "fifth way" and in the essay of William Paley. It involves proving the existence of God from the fact of order and design in the universe. But, Kierkegaard asks, isn't this argument fraught with "the most terrible temptations to doubt"? Certainly it depends upon assuming at least a future free of disorder. But one overwhelming catastrophe could shake this belief. Such a "proof" then presupposes

From Søren Kierkegaard, *Philosophical Fragments.* © 1936 Princeton University Press, 1962, 1990 renewed. Reprinted by permission of Princeton University Press.

the existence of God and does not lead us to it. Reason never uncovers the Unknown. The Unknown is the limit of reason's powers. Since this is a problem with all so-called proofs, we must conclude that the Unknown is radically different from our rational expectations and is beyond human comprehension. Efforts to manage and control this inconceivable difference between Reason and the Unknown explain some forms of religious experience, such as the polytheism of paganism. Reason, for Kierkegaard, brings God "as near as possible, and yet he is as far away as ever."

At the same time, faith in God is a profoundly personal matter. Kierkegaard does not reduce it to a kind of game of chance, as Pascal seems to do. He stresses instead the subjective, intuitive, emotional, and lived dimensions of religious faith. A "religious existentialist," Kierkegaard places his emphasis on faith as a personal commitment rather than a logical inference.

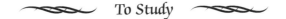

To Study

1. What is Kierkegaard's argument relating God's existence to proof?
2. Explain: "I reason from existence, not towards existence." Is the example of Napoleon and his deeds a good one?
3. According to Kierkegaard, where are the works of God?
4. Why doesn't the existence of God come out of proof?
5. How could the proof of God's existence be discredited?
6. What is "the leap"?
7. Explain the statement "The Reason has brought God as near as possible, and yet he is as far away as ever."

But what is this unknown something with which the Reason collides when inspired by its paradoxical passion, with the result of unsettling even man's knowledge of himself? It is the Unknown. It is not a human being, insofar as we know what man is; nor is it any other known thing. So let us call this unknown something: *God.* It is nothing more than a name we assign to it. The idea of demonstrating that this unknown something (God) exists could scarcely suggest itself to the Reason. For if God does not exist it would of course be impossible to prove it; and if he does exist it would be folly to attempt it. For at the very outset, in beginning my proof, I will have presupposed it, not as doubtful but as certain (a presupposition is never doubtful, for the very reason that it is a presupposition), since otherwise I would not begin, readily understanding that the whole would be impossible if he did not exist. But if when I speak of proving God's existence I mean that I propose to prove that the Unknown, which exists, is God, then I express myself unfortunately. For in that case I do not prove anything, least of all an existence, but merely develop the content of a conception. Generally speaking, it is a difficult matter to prove that anything exists; and what is still worse for the intrepid souls who undertake the venture, the difficulty is such that fame scarcely awaits those who concern themselves with it. The entire demonstration always turns into something very different from what it assumes to be, and becomes an additional development of the consequences that flow from [our] having assumed that the object in question exists. Thus I always reason from existence, not toward existence, whether I move in the sphere of palpable sensible fact or in the realm of thought. I do not, for example, prove that a stone exists, but that some existing thing is a stone. The procedure in a court of justice does not prove that a criminal exists, but that the accused, whose existence is given, is a criminal. . . . Let us take ample time for consideration. We have no such reason for haste as have those who from concern for themselves or for God or for some other thing, must make haste to get its existence demonstrated. Under such circumstances there may indeed be need for haste, especially if the prover sincerely seeks to appreciate the danger that he himself, or the thing in question, may be nonexistent unless the proof is finished; and does not surreptitiously entertain the thought that it exists whether he succeeds in proving it or not.

If it were proposed to prove Napoleon's existence from Napoleon's deeds, would it not be a most curious proceeding? His existence does indeed explain his deeds, but the deeds do not prove his existence, unless I have already understood the word "his" so as thereby to have assumed his existence. But Napoleon is only an individual, and insofar there exists no absolute relationship between him and his deeds; some other person might have performed the same deeds. Perhaps this is the reason why I cannot pass from the deeds to existence. If I call these deeds the deeds of Napoleon, the proof becomes superfluous, since I have already named him; if I ignore this, I can never prove from the deeds that they are Napoleon's, but only in a purely ideal manner that such deeds are the deeds of a great general, and so forth. But between God and his works there exists an absolute relationship; God is not a name but a concept. Is this perhaps the reason that his [essence involves existence]? The works of God are such that only God can perform them. Just so, but where then are the works of God? The works from which I would deduce his existence are not immediately given. The wisdom of God in nature, his goodness, his wisdom in the governance of the world—are all these manifest, perhaps, upon the very face of things? Are we not here confronted with the most terrible temptations to doubt, and is it not impossible finally to dispose of all these doubts? But from such an order of things I will surely not attempt to prove God's existence; and even if I began I would never finish, and would in addition have to live constantly in suspense, lest something so terrible should suddenly happen that my bit of proof would be demolished. From what works then do I propose to derive the proof? From the works as apprehended through an ideal interpretation, i.e., such as they do not immediately reveal themselves. But in that case it is not from the works that I prove God's existence. I merely develop the ideality I have presupposed, and because of my confidence in *this* I make so bold as to defy all objections, even those that have not yet been made. In beginning my proof I presuppose the ideal interpretation, and also that I will be successful in carrying it through; but what else is this but to presuppose that God exists, so that I really begin by virtue of confidence in him?

And how does God's existence emerge from the proof? Does it follow straightway, without any breach of continuity? Or have we not here an analogy to the behaviour of these toys, the little Cartesian dolls? As soon as I let go of the doll it stands on its head.

As soon as I let it go—I must therefore let it go. So also with the proof for God's existence. As long as I keep my hold on the proof, i.e., continue to demonstrate, the existence does not come out, if for no reason than that I am engaged in proving it; but when I let the proof go, the existence is there. But this act of letting go is surely also something; it is indeed a contribution of mine. Must not this also be taken into the account, this little moment, brief as it may be—it need not be long, for it is a *leap.* However brief this moment, if only an instantaneous now, this "now" must be included in the reckoning. . . .

Whoever therefore attempts to demonstrate the existence of God except in the sense of clarifying the concept . . . proves in lieu thereof something else, something which at times perhaps does not need a proof, and in any case needs none better; for the fool says in his heart that there is no God, but whoever says in his heart or to men: "Wait just a little and I will prove it"—what a rare man of wisdom is he! If in the moment of beginning his proof it is not absolutely undetermined whether God exists or not, he does not prove it; and if it is thus undetermined in the beginning he will never come to begin, partly from fear of failure, since God perhaps does not exist, and partly because he has nothing with which to begin. A project of this kind would scarcely have been undertaken by the ancients. Socrates at least, who is credited with having put forth the physicoteleological proof for God's existence, did not go about it in any such manner. He always presupposes God's existence, and under this presupposition seeks to interpenetrate nature with the idea of purpose. Had he been asked why he pursued this method, he would doubtless have explained that he lacked the courage to venture out upon so perilous a voyage of discovery without having made sure of God's existence behind him. At the word of God he casts his net as if to catch the idea of purpose; for nature herself finds many means of frightening the inquirer, and distracts him by many a digression.

The paradoxical passion of the Reason thus comes repeatedly into collision with the Unknown, which does indeed exist, but is unknown, and insofar does not exist. The Reason cannot advance beyond this point, and yet it cannot refrain in its paradoxicalness from arriving at this limit and occupying itself therewith. It will not serve to dismiss its relation to it simply by asserting that the Unknown does not exist, since this itself involves a relationship. But what then is the Unknown, since the designation of it as God merely signifies for us that it is unknown? To say that it is the Unknown because it cannot be known, and even if it were capable of being known, it could not be expressed, does not satisfy the demands of passion, though it correctly interprets the Unknown as a limit; but a limit is precisely a torment for passion, though it also serves as an incitement. And yet the Reason can come no further, whether it risks an issue *via negationis* or *via eminentia.*[1]

What then is the Unknown? It is the limit to which the Reason repeatedly comes, and insofar, substituting a static form of conception for the dynamic, it is the different, the absolutely different. But because it is absolutely different, there is no mark by which it could be distinguished. When qualified as absolutely different it seems on the verge of disclosure, but this is not the case; for the Reason cannot even conceive an absolute unlikeness. The Reason cannot negate itself absolutely, but uses itself for the

[1] By the method of making negative statements about God or by the method of attributing known qualities to God in a higher degree. [ED.]

purpose, and thus conceives only such an unlikeness within itself as it can conceive by means of itself; it cannot absolutely transcend itself, and hence conceives only such a superiority over itself as it can conceive by means of itself. Unless the Unknown (God) remains a mere limiting conception, the single idea of difference will be thrown into a state of confusion, and become many ideas of differences. The Unknown is then in a condition of dispersion . . . and the Reason may choose at pleasure from what is at hand and the imagination may suggest (the monstrous, the ludicrous, etc.).

But it is impossible to hold fast to a difference of this nature. Every time this is done it is essentially an arbitrary act, and deepest down in the heart of piety lurks the mad caprice which knows that it has itself produced its God. If no specific determination of difference can be held fast, because there is no distinguishing mark, like and unlike finally become identified with one another, thus sharing the fate of all such dialectical opposites. The unlikeness clings to the Reason and confounds it, so that the Reason no longer knows itself and quite consistently confuses itself with the unlikeness. On this point paganism has been sufficiently prolific in fantastic inventions. As for the last-named supposition, the self-irony of the Reason, I shall attempt to delineate it merely by a stroke or two, without raising any question of its being historical. There lives an individual whose appearance is precisely like that of other men; he grows up to manhood like others, he marries, he has an occupation by which he earns his livelihood, and he makes provision for the future as befits a man. For though it may be beautiful to live like the birds of the air, it is not lawful, and may lead to the sorriest of consequences: either starvation if one has enough persistence, or dependence on the bounty of others. This man is also God. How do I know? I cannot know it, for in order to know it I would have to know God, and the nature of the difference between God and man; and this I cannot know, because the Reason has reduced it to likeness with that from which it was unlike. Thus God becomes the most terrible of deceivers, because the Reason has deceived itself. The Reason has brought God as near as possible, and yet he is as far away as ever.

To Think About

1. "If God did not exist it would be necessary to invent him." *Voltaire*

2. "It seems as though the conception of a human soul . . . served as a type or model on which [a human being] framed not only his ideas of other souls of lower grade, but also his ideas of spiritual beings in general, from the tiniest elf that sports in the long grass up to the heavenly Creator and Ruler of the world, the Great Spirit." *E. B. Taylor*

3. "The idea of a God so perfect that he eternally realizes all possible values is fatal to religion, for it makes human choice of no significance whatever. . . . In my opinion Dewey gives here an unanswerable objection to the theism of Aquinas." *Charles Hartshorne*

4. "Faith is a species of belief, a belief is defined 'an assent to a proposition upon rational grounds.' Without rational grounds there is no belief, and consequently no faith." *John Wesley*

5. "Most intellectual people do not believe in God, but they fear him just the same." **Wilhelm Reich**

6. "The rash assertion that 'God made man in His own image' is ticking like a time bomb at the foundations of many faiths, and as the hierarchy of the universe is disclosed to us, we may have to recognize this chilling truth: if there are any gods whose chief concern is man, they cannot be very important gods." **Arthur C. Clarke**

7. "To be a man is to strive to be God." **Jean-Paul Sartre**

8. "Religion . . . shall mean for us the feelings, acts, and experiences of individual men in their solitude, so far as they apprehend themselves to stand in relation to whatever they may consider the divine." **William James**

9. "Religion is the aspect of depth in the totality of the human spirit. . . . What does the metaphor *depth* mean? It means that the religious aspect points to that which is ultimate, infinite, unconditional in man's spiritual life. Religion, in the largest and most basic sense of the word, is ultimate concern. And ultimate concern is manifest in all creative functions of the human spirit." **Paul Tillich**

10. "Depth is what the word God means, the source of your being, of your ultimate concern, of what you take seriously without any reservation. 'Life has no depth. Life is shallow. Being itself is surface only.' If you could say this in complete seriousness, you would be an atheist; but otherwise you are not. He who knows the depth knows about God." **Paul Tillich**

11. Because poverty and depression make people desperate, Martin Marty initially approaches fundamentalists "with empathy," but, he adds: "I'm nettled by them. They have a Manichaean view of life as a struggle between the forces of light and the forces of darkness. I think the drama of life and faith is about being poised between light and dark, between faith and doubt. Fundamentalism misses the drama of life."

12. "Whenever we remove from the wall that was designed to separate religion and government, we increase the risk of religious strife and weaken the foundation of our democracy." **Justice J. Stevens**

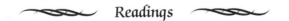

Readings

COLLINS, JAMES. *The Mind of Kierkegaard.* Chicago: Regnery, 1953.

MACKEY, LOUIS. *Kierkegaard.* Philadelphia: University of Pennsylvania Press, 1971.

MOONEY, EDWARD F. *Selves in Discord and Resolve.* New York: Routledge, 1996.

RUDD, ANTHONY. *Kierkegaard and the Limits of the Ethical.* New York: Oxford University Press, 1993.

11

A Good God
Would Exclude Evil

David Hume (1711–76), an outstanding British empiricist, not only wrote about philosophical subjects but also became famous as a historian. Among his major works are A Treatise of Human Nature *(1739–40),* Essays, Moral and Political *(1741–42), and* The History of England *(1754–62).*

The second major issue philosophy of religion considers (the first was considering arguments for God's existence) is the question of God's nature. In one sense this issue has already been raised in the ontological argument, where a definition of God as a "perfect being" was a key premise to the argument. But what does "perfect" mean? What does God's nature really consist in? One great theory is that God is an absolutely, or infinitely, powerful, wise, and good being. That is to say, God is all-powerful or omnipotent, all-knowing or omniscient, and all-good, or infinitely loving. These qualities have been fundamental elements of religion for centuries. But what if they cannot be consistently attributed to God? Especially given the existence of suffering and moral evil in the universe, how can God be thought to be powerful, wise, and loving in an absolute way? Many philosophers have raised this question, from Epicurus in the ancient world to David Hume in the modern. In fact, Hume quotes Epicurus's dilemma in a passage just a few pages before the essay we are about to read: "Epicurus's old questions are yet unanswered. Is he (God) willing to prevent evil, but not able? then is he impotent. Is he able, but not willing? then is he malevolent. Is he both able and willing? whence then is evil?" This great puzzle is commonly called "the problem of evil," and efforts to solve it are generally called "theodicy," the justification of God's nature in the face of evil. In his *Dialogues Concerning Natural Religion,* Hume argues that a very good, wise, and powerful Being, even if not infinite, would not produce a world so full of vice, misery, and disorder as our own. These ills are the result of four conditions, or circumstances, of humans

From David Hume, *Dialogues Concerning Natural Religion* (Edinburgh, Scotland, 1779).

and nature: the striving for survival and self-preservation; the limited powers of all creatures to confront their problems; the laws of nature, whose results in general bring about these miseries; and, finally, the aberrant, bizarre events in nature itself that result in disorder. Hume's solution is a skeptical one: that the human mind is incapable of understanding the nature of God. But there is a more disturbing possibility: perhaps God cannot be infinitely perfect, and some of his perfections logically contradict others. If so, then the problem of evil suggests not skepticism, but atheism, that God as traditionally defined cannot, and therefore does not, exist.

To Study

1. Why would a person not antecedently convinced of the existence of a Supreme Being not infer the goodness of such a creature upon examining the facts of nature?
2. Explain the first circumstance, which results in the ills of sensible creatures.
3. Explain the second circumstance, which results in the ills of all creatures.
4. Explain the third circumstance, which brings about the misery of all creatures.
5. Explain the fourth circumstance, which results in the ills of humans.
6. What does "the whole" of "blind nature" present to us to conclude?

If a very limited intelligence whom we shall suppose utterly unacquainted with the universe were assured that it were the production of a very good, wise, and powerful Being, however finite, he would, from his conjectures, form *beforehand* a different notion of it from what we find it to be by experience; nor would he ever imagine, merely from these attributes of the cause of which he is informed, that the effect could be so full of vice and misery and disorder, as it appears in this life. Supposing now that this person were brought into the world, still assured that it was the workmanship of such a sublime and benevolent Being, he might, perhaps, be surprised at the disappointment, but would never retract his former belief if founded on any very solid argument, since such a limited intelligence must be sensible of his own blindness and ignorance, and must allow that there may be many solutions of those phenomena which will forever escape his comprehension. But supposing, which is the real case with regard to man, that this creature is not antecedently convinced of a supreme intelligence, benevolent, and powerful, but is left to gather such a belief from the appearances of things— this entirely alters the case, nor will he ever find any reason for such a conclusion. He may be fully convinced of the narrow limits of his understanding, but this will not help him in forming an inference concerning the goodness of superior powers, since he must form that inference from what he knows, not from what he is ignorant of. The more you exaggerate his weakness and ignorance, the more diffident you render him, and give him the greater suspicion that such subjects are beyond the reach of his faculties. You are obliged, therefore, to reason with him merely from the known phenomena, and to drop every arbitrary supposition or conjecture.

Did I show you a house or palace where there was not one apartment convenient or agreeable, where the windows, doors, fires, passages, stairs, and the whole economy of the building were the source of noise, confusion, fatigue, darkness, and the extremes of heat and cold, you would certainly blame the contrivance, without any further examination. The architect would in vain display his subtilty, and prove to you that, if this door or that window were altered, greater ills would ensue. What he says may be strictly true: the alteration of one particular, while the other parts of the building remain, may only augment the inconveniences. But still you would assert in general that, if the architect had had skill and good intentions, he might have formed such a plan of the whole, and might have adjusted the parts in such a manner as would have remedied all or most of these inconveniences. His ignorance, or even your own ignorance of such a plan, will never convince you of the impossibility of it. If you find any inconveniences and deformities in the building, you will always without entering into any detail, condemn the architect.

In short, I repeat the question: Is the world, considered in general and as it appears to us in this life, different from what a man or such a limited being would, *beforehand,* expect from a very powerful, wise, and benevolent Deity? It must be strange prejudice to assert the contrary. And from thence I conclude that, however consistent the world may be, allowing certain suppositions and conjectures with the idea of such a Deity, it can never afford us an inference concerning his existence. The consistency is not absolutely denied, only the inference. Conjectures, especially where infinity is excluded from the Divine attributes, may perhaps be sufficient to prove a consistency, but can never be foundations for any inference.

There seem to be *four* circumstances on which depend all or the greatest part of the ills that molest sensible creatures; and it is not impossible but all these circumstances may be necessary and unavoidable. We know so little beyond common life, or even of common life, that, with regard to the economy of a universe, there is no conjecture, however wild, which may not be just, nor any one, however plausible, which may not be erroneous. All that belongs to human understanding, in this deep ignorance and obscurity, is to be sceptical or at least cautious, and not to admit of any hypothesis whatever, much less of any which is supported by no appearance of probability. Now this I assert to be the case with regard to all the causes of evil and the circumstances on which it depends. None of them appear to human reason in the least degree necessary or unavoidable, nor can we suppose them such, without the utmost license of imagination.

The *first* circumstance which introduces evil is that contrivance or economy of the animal creation by which pains, as well as pleasures, are employed to excite all creatures to action, and make them vigilant in the great work of self-preservation. Now pleasure alone, in its various degrees, seems to human understanding sufficient for this purpose. All animals might be constantly in a state of enjoyment; but when urged by any of the necessities of nature, such as thirst, hunger, weariness instead of pain, they might feel a diminution of pleasure by which they might be prompted to seek that object which is necessary to their subsistence. Men pursue pleasure as eagerly as they avoid pain; at least, they might have been so constituted. It seems, therefore, plainly possible to carry on the business of life without any pain. Why then is any animal ever rendered susceptible of such a sensation? If animals can be free from it an hour, they might enjoy a perpetual exemption from it, and it required as particular a contrivance of their organs to produce that feeling as to endow them with sight, hearing, or any of the senses. Shall we conjecture that such a contrivance was necessary, without any appearance of reason, and shall we build on that conjecture as on the most certain truth?

But a capacity of pain would not alone produce pain were it not for the *second* circumstance, viz., the conducting of the world by general laws; and this seems nowise necessary to a very perfect Being. It is true, if everything were conducted by particular volitions, the course of nature would be perpetually broken, and no man could employ his reason in the conduct of life. But might not other particular volitions remedy this inconvenience? In short, might not the Deity exterminate all ill, wherever it were to be found, and produce all good, without any preparation or long progress of causes and effects?

Besides, we must consider that, according to the present economy of the world, the course of nature, though supposed exactly regular, yet to us appears not so, and many events are uncertain, and many disappoint our expectations. Health and sickness, calm and tempest, with an infinite number of other accidents whose causes are unknown and variable, have a great influence both on the fortunes of particular persons and on the prosperity of public societies; and indeed all human life, in a manner, depends on such accidents. A being, therefore, who knows the secret springs of the universe might easily, by particular volitions, turn all these accidents to the good of mankind and render the whole world happy, without discovering himself in any operation. A fleet whose purposes were salutary to society might always meet with a fair wind. Good princes enjoy sound health and long life. Persons born to power and authority be framed with good tempers and virtuous dispositions. A few such events as these, regularly and wisely conducted, would change the face of the world, and yet would no more seem to disturb the course of nature or confound human conduct than the present economy of things where the causes are secret and variable and compounded. Some small touches given to Caligula's brain in his infancy might have converted him into a Trajan. One wave, a little higher than the rest, by burying Caesar and his fortune in the bottom of the ocean, might have restored liberty to a considerable part of mankind. There may, for aught we know, be good reasons why Providence interposes not in this manner, but they are unknown to us; and, though the mere supposition that such reasons exist may be sufficient to *save* the conclusion concerning the Divine attributes, yet surely it can never be sufficient to *establish* that conclusion.

If everything in the universe be conducted by general laws, and if animals be rendered susceptible of pain, it scarcely seems possible but some ill must arise in the various shocks of matter and the various concurrence and opposition of general laws; but this ill would be very rare were it not for the *third* circumstance which I proposed to mention, viz., the great frugality with which all powers and faculties are distributed to every particular being. So well adjusted are the organs and capacities of all animals, and so well fitted to their preservation, that, as far as history or tradition reaches, there appears not to be any single species which has yet been extinguished in the universe. Every animal has the requisite endowments, but these endowments are bestowed with so scrupulous an economy that any considerable diminution must entirely destroy the creature. Wherever one power is increased, there is a proportional abatement in the others. Animals which excel in swiftness are commonly defective in force. Those which possess both are either imperfect in some of their senses or are oppressed with the most craving wants. The human species, whose chief excellence is reason and sagacity, is of all others the most necessitous, and the most deficient in bodily advantages, without clothes, without arms, without food, without lodging, without any convenience of life, except what they owe to their own skill and industry. In short, nature seems to have formed an exact calculation of the necessities of her creatures, and, like a *rigid master,* has afforded them little more powers or endowments than what are strictly sufficient to supply those necessities. An *indulgent* parent would have bestowed a large stock in order to guard against accidents, and secure the happiness and welfare of the creature in the most unfortunate concurrence of circumstances. Every course of life would not have been so surrounded with precipices that the least departure from the true path, by mistake or necessity, must involve us in misery and ruin. Some reserve, some fund, would have been provided to ensure happiness, nor would the powers and the necessities have been adjusted with so rigid an economy. The Author of nature is inconceivably powerful; his force is supposed great, if not altogether inexhaustible, nor is there any reason, as far as we can judge, to make him observe this strict frugality in his dealings with his creatures. It would have been better, were his power extremely limited, to have created fewer animals, and to have endowed these with more faculties for their happiness and preservation. A builder is never esteemed prudent who undertakes a plan beyond what his stock will enable him to finish.

In order to cure most of the ills of human life, I require not that man should have the wings of the eagle, the swiftness of the stag, the force of the ox, the arms of the lion, the scales of the crocodile or rhinoceros; much less do I demand the sagacity of an angel or cherubim. I am contented to take an increase in one single power or faculty of his soul. Let him be endowed with a greater propensity to industry and labour, a more vigorous spring and activity of mind, a more constant bent to business and application. Let the whole species possess naturally an equal diligence with that which many individuals are able to attain by habit and reflection, and the most beneficial consequences, without any allay of ill, is the immediate and necessary result of this endowment. Almost all the moral as well as natural evils of human life arise from idleness; and were our species, by the original constitution of their frame, exempt from this vice or infirmity, the perfect cultivation of land, the improvement of arts and manufactures, the exact execution of every office and duty, immediately follow; and men at once may fully reach the state of society which is so imperfectly attained by the best regulated government. But as industry is a power, and the most valuable of any, nature seems determined, suitably to her usual maxims, to bestow it on men with a very sparing hand, and rather to punish him severely for his deficiency in it than to reward him for his attainments. She has so contrived his frame that nothing but the most violent necessity can oblige him to labour; and she employs all his other wants to overcome, at least in part, the want of diligence, and to endow him with some share of a faculty of which she has thought fit naturally to bereave him. Here our demands may be allowed very humble, and therefore the more reasonable. If we required the endowments of superior penetration and judgment, of a more delicate taste of beauty, of a nicer sensibility to benevolence and friendship, we might be told that we impiously pretend to break the order of nature, that we want to exalt ourselves into a higher rank of being, that the presents which we require, not being suitable to our state and condition, would only be pernicious to us. But it is hard, I dare to repeat it, it is hard that, being placed in a world so full of wants and necessities, where almost every being and element is either our foe or refuses its assistance . . . we should also have our own temper to struggle with, and should be deprived of that faculty which can alone fence against these multiplied evils.

The *fourth* circumstance whence arises the misery and ill of the universe is the inaccurate workmanship of all the springs and principles of the great machine of nature. It must be acknowledged that there are few parts of the universe which seem not to serve some purpose, and whose removal would not produce a visible defect and disorder in the whole. The parts hang all together, nor can one be touched without affecting the rest, in a greater or less degree. But at the same time, it must be observed that none of these parts or principles, however useful, are so accurately adjusted as to keep precisely within those bounds in which their utility consists; but they are, all of them, apt, on every occasion, to run into the one extreme or the other. One would imagine that this grand production had not received the last hand of the maker—so little finished is every part, and so coarse are the strokes with which it is executed. Thus the winds are requisite to convey the vapours along the surface of the globe, and to assist men in navigation; but how often, rising up to tempests and hurricanes, do they become pernicious? Rains are necessary to nourish all the plants and animals of the earth; but how often are they defective? how often excessive? Heat is a requisite of all life and vegetation, but is not always found in the due proportion. On the mixture and secretion of the humours and juices of the body depend the health and prosperity of the animal; but the parts perform not regularly their proper function. What more useful than all the passions of the mind, ambition, vanity, love, anger? But how often do they break their bounds and cause the greatest convulsions in society? There is nothing so advantageous in the universe but what frequently becomes pernicious, by its excess or defect; nor has nature guarded, with the requisite accuracy, against all disorder or confusion. The irregularity is never perhaps so great as to destroy any species, but is often sufficient to involve the individuals in ruin and misery.

On the concurrence, then, of these *four* circumstances does all or the greatest part of natural evil depend. Were all living creatures incapable of pain, or were the world administered by particular volitions, evil never could have found access into the universe; and were animals endowed with a large stock of powers and faculties, beyond what strict necessity requires, or were the several springs and principles of the universe so accurately framed as to preserve always the just temperament and medium, there must have been very little ill in comparison of what we feel at present. What then shall we pronounce on this occasion? Shall we say that these circumstances are not necessary, and that they might easily have been altered in the contrivance of the universe? This decision seems too presumptuous for creatures so blind and ignorant. Let us be more modest in our conclusions. Let us allow that, if the goodness of the Deity (I mean a goodness like the human) could be established on any tolerable reasons *a priori,* these phenomena, however untoward, would not be sufficient to subvert that principle, but might easily, in some unknown manner, be reconcilable to it. But let us still assert that, as this goodness is not antecedently established but must be inferred from the phenomena, there can be no grounds for such an inference while there are so many ills in the universe, and while these ills might so easily have been remedied, as far as human understanding can be allowed to judge on such a subject. I am sceptic enough to allow that the bad appearances, notwithstanding all my reasonings, may be compatible with such attributes as you suppose, but surely they can never prove these attributes. Such a conclusion cannot result from scepticism, but must arise from the phenomena, and from our confidence in the reasonings which we deduce from these phenomena.

Look round this universe. What an immense profusion of beings, animated and organized, sensible and active! You admire this prodigious variety and fecundity. But inspect a little more narrowly these living existences, the only beings worth regarding. How hostile and destructive to each other! How insufficient all of them for their own happiness! How contemptible or odious to the spectator! The whole presents nothing but the idea of a blind nature, impregnated by a great vivifying principle, and pouring forth from her lap, without discernment or parental care, her maimed and abortive children!

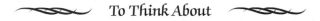

To Think About

1. "When a speculative philosopher believes he has comprehended the world once and for all in his system, he is deceiving himself; he has merely comprehended himself and then naively projected that view upon the world."   *C. G. Jung*

2. "The essence of religion is the feeling of utter dependence upon the infinite reality, that is, upon God."   *F. Schleiermacher*

3. "Any activity pursued in behalf of an ideal and against obstacles and in spite of threats of personal loss because of conviction of its general and enduring value is religious in quality."   *John Dewey*

4. "Faith brings us to truth; philosophy makes us grasp it; ethics makes us practice it; and ritual makes us one with it."   *Jagmanderlal Jaini*

5. "The true meaning of a term is to be found by observing what a man does with it, not by what he says about it."   *P. W. Bridgman*

6. "If there is no God, then God is incalculably the greatest single creation of the human imagination. No other creation of the imagination has been so fertile of ideas, so great an inspiration to philosophy, to literature, to painting, sculpture, architecture, and drama. Set beside the idea of God, the most original inventions of mathematicians and the most unforgettable characters in drama are minor products of the imagination: Hamlet and the square root of minus one pale into insignificance by comparison."   *Anthony Kenny*

7. "*Bill Moyers:* Somehow there is a reluctance on the part of an optimistic people like the Americans to acknowledge the real presence of evil and its solid state of being."

"*William Shirer:* I think so. The theologian Reinhold Niebuhr said that a people without a sense of tragedy have difficulty meeting the evils of the day. I think that's true. I don't think we as a people have it. We have our problems and our troubles and our sorrows, but no real sense of life as a tragedy."
                                                Joseph Campbell in *The Power of Myth*

8. "So that, upon the whole, we may conclude that the *Christian Religion* not only was at first attended with miracles, but even at this day cannot be believed by any reasonable person without one. And whoever is moved by *Faith* to assent to it, is conscious of a continued miracle in his own person, which subverts all the principles of his understanding, and gives him a determination to believe what is most contrary to custom and experience."

                    David Hume, in the *Treatise, Section X, "Of Miracles"*

9. "I want to see with my own eyes the hind lie down with the lion and the victim rise up and embrace his murderer. I want to be there when every one suddenly understands what it has all been for. All the religions of the world are built on this longing, and I am a believer. But then there are the children, and what am I to do about them? That's a question I can't answer. For the hundredth time I repeat, there are numbers of questions, but I've only taken the children, because in their case what I mean is so unanswerably clear. Listen! If all must suffer to pay for the eternal harmony, what have children to do with it, tell me, please? It's beyond all comprehension why they should suffer, and why they should pay for the harmony. Why should they, too, furnish material to enrich the soil for the harmony of the future? I understand solidarity in sin among men. I understand solidarity in retribution, too; but there can be no such solidarity with children. And if it is really true that they must share responsibility for all their fathers' crimes, such a truth is not of this world and is beyond my comprehension. Some jester will say, perhaps, that the child would have grown up and have sinned, but you see he didn't grow up, he was torn to pieces by the dogs, at eight years old."   *Fyodor Dostoevski,* in *The Brothers Karamazov*

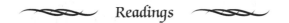

Readings

GASKIN, J. C. A. *Hume's Philosophy of Religion.* London: Macmillan, 1978, 1988.

LARRIMORE, MARK, ed. *The Problem of Evil: A Reader.* Oxford: Blackwell, 2001.

MOSSNER, K. C. *The Life of David Hume.* Oxford: Clarendon Press, 1954, 1970.

NORTON, DAVID FATE. *David Hume: Common Sense Moralist, Skeptical Metaphysician.* Princeton, NJ: Princeton University Press, 1982.

_____(ED.). *The Cambridge Companion to Hume.* Cambridge, 1993.

SMITH, N. KEMP. *The Philosophy of David Hume.* London: Macmillan, 1947.

STROUD, BARRY. *Hume.* London: Routledge and Kegan Paul, 1977.

12
God Can Allow Some Evil

John Hick (1922–), *lecturer in divinity at Cambridge University, was formerly Professor of Christian Philosophy at Princeton Theological Seminary. He received his M.A. degree from the University of Edinburgh and his Ph.D. from Oxford University. Dr. Hick is the author of* Faith and Knowledge *(1966) and* Philosophy of Religion *(1963) and the editor of* The Existence of God *(1964) and* Faith and the Philosophers *(1964).*

Solutions to the problem of evil have been a mainstay of philosophical theology for centuries. In the following essay, some of these are discussed, notably theories that evil is an illusion, or at least that good and evil are human concepts, and not attributable to nature or things as they really are. Another theory takes the dilemma's bull by the horns and simply denies that God is infinitely perfect but finite, though remaining far more perfect than any creature. Perhaps the most popular theory is a "permissive" one, namely, that God allows evil to exist in order to derive greater good from it. This was Thomas Aquinas's solution at the end of his "five ways." There are still other solutions: Some have argued that there is a kind of logical necessity built into the concept of evil. Without it, goodness would be meaningless. Similarly, beauty without ugliness and pleasure without pain would be incoherent concepts. A version of this argument holds that if God is infinitely perfect, anything else in the world, including his creation, must be only finitely perfect. Therefore, at least imperfection, if not evil itself, is necessary if the world is to be thought of as created by God and not in some way identical to him. In the following essay, John Hick suggests yet other alternatives. Distinguishing moral evil from the evil of suffering, he argues that moral evil is a necessary condition of human freedom. Without it our free acts are illusions and all our choices are determined by fixed and changeless laws of nature. And pain is necessary in a world where "soul-building," or

From John Hick, *Philosophy of Religion,* © 1963. Reprinted by permission of Prentice Hall, Inc., Upper Saddle River, NJ.

courage in the face of suffering, is a desirable human quality. If the world were only a scene of endless pleasure, there would be no value in patience, endurance, or overcoming temptation. Such a world would be morally poorer. It would exclude the possibility of moral progress and growth.

Hick offers attractive solutions to both the problem of moral evil and that of human suffering. But you may wish to consider whether human actions really are free, an issue to which we turn next in this anthology. As for pain, soul-building seems irrelevant to the pain of animals and small children. Could not a perfect God create a world without these two kinds of suffering? And wouldn't it be better than one, like our own, where these two forms of pain are so widespread?

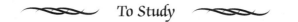

To Study

1. According to Hick, what is the most powerful positive objection to the belief in God?
2. On what ground does he refute the Christian Science solution to the problem of evil?
3. How does he refute the Personalist school solution? The Augustinian solution?
4. What objections have been raised to the traditional Christian position concerning moral evil? How does Hick reply to these?
5. What objection has been raised to the traditional Christian position concerning nonmoral evil? What is Hick's reply?
6. What is Hick's ultimate answer to the problem of evil?

To many, the most powerful positive objection to belief in God is the fact of evil. Probably for most agnostics it is the appalling depth and extent of human suffering, more than anything else, that makes the idea of a loving Creator seem so implausible and disposes them toward one or another of the various naturalistic theories of religion.

As a challenge to theism, the problem of evil has traditionally been posed in the form of a dilemma; if God is perfectly loving, he must wish to abolish evil; and if he is all-powerful, he must be able to abolish evil. But evil exists; therefore God cannot be both omnipotent and perfectly loving.

Certain solutions, which at once suggest themselves, have to be ruled out so far as the Judaic-Christian faith is concerned.

To say, for example (with contemporary Christian Science), that evil is an illusion of the human mind, is impossible within a religion based upon the stark realism of the Bible. Its pages faithfully reflect the characteristic mixture of good and evil in human experience. They record every kind of sorrow and suffering, every mode of man's inhumanity to man and of his painfully insecure existence in the world. There is no attempt to regard evil as anything but dark, menacingly ugly, heart-rending, and crushing. In the Christian scriptures, the climax of this history of evil is the crucifixion of

Jesus, which is presented not only as a case of utterly unjust suffering, but as the violent and murderous rejection of God's Messiah. There can be no doubt, then, that for biblical faith, evil is unambiguously evil, and stands in direct opposition to God's will.

Again, to solve the problem of evil by means of the theory (sponsored, for example, by the Boston "Personalist" School)[1] of a finite deity who does the best he can with a material, intractable and coeternal with himself, is to have abandoned the basic premise of Hebrew-Christian monotheism; for the theory amounts to rejecting belief in the infinity and sovereignty of God.

Indeed, any theory which would avoid the problem of the origin of evil by depicting it as an ultimate constituent of the universe, coordinate with good, has been repudiated in advance by the classic Christian teaching, first developed by Augustine, that evil represents the going wrong of something which in itself is good.[2] Augustine holds firmly to the Hebrew-Christian conviction that the universe is *good*—that is to say, it is the creation of a good God for a good purpose. He completely rejects the ancient prejudice, widespread in his day, that matter is evil. There are, according to Augustine, higher and lower, greater and lesser goods in immense abundance and variety; but everything which has being is good in its own way and degree, except in so far as it may have become spoiled or corrupted. Evil—whether it be an evil will, an instance of pain, or some disorder or decay in nature—has not been set there by God, but represents the distortion of something that is inherently valuable. Whatever exists is, as such, and in its proper place, good; evil is essentially parasitic upon good, being disorder and perversion in a fundamentally good creation. This understanding of evil as something negative means that it is not willed and created by God; but it does not mean (as some have supposed) that evil is unreal and can be disregarded. Clearly, the first effect of this doctrine is to accentuate even more the question of the origin of evil.

Theodicy,[3] as many modern Christian thinkers see it, is a modest enterprise, negative rather than positive in its conclusions. It does not claim to explain, nor to explain away, every instance of evil in human experience, but only to point to certain considerations which prevent the fact of evil (largely incomprehensible though it remains) from constituting a final and insuperable bar to rational belief in God.

In indicating these considerations it will be useful to follow the traditional division of the subject. There is the problem of *moral evil* or wickedness; why does an all-good and all-powerful God permit this? And there is the problem of the *nonmoral evil* of suffering or pain, both physical and mental: why has an all-good and all-powerful God created a world in which this occurs?

Christian thought has always considered moral evil in its relation to human freedom and responsibility. To be a person is to be a finite center of freedom, a (relatively) free and self-directing agent responsible for one's own decisions. This in-

---

[1] Edgar Brightman's *A Philosophy of Religion* (Upper Saddle River, NJ: Prentice Hall. Inc., 1940). Chapters 8–10 are a classic exposition of one form of this view.

[2] See Augustine's *Confessions,* Book VII, Chapter 12; *City of God,* Book XII, Chapter 3; *Enchiridion,* Chapter 4.

[3] The word "theodicy" from the Greek *theos* (God) and *dike* (righteous) means the justification of God's goodness in face of the fact of evil.

volves being free to act wrongly as well as to act rightly. The idea of a person who can be infallibly guaranteed always to act rightly is self-contradictory. There can be no guarantee in advance that a genuinely free moral agent will never choose amiss. Consequently, the possibility of wrongdoing or sin is logically inseparable from the creation of finite persons, and to say that God should not have created beings who might sin amounts to saying that he should not have created people.

This thesis has been challenged in some recent philosophical discussions of the problem of evil, in which it is claimed that no contradiction is involved in saying that God might have made people who would be genuinely free and who could yet be guaranteed always to act rightly. A quotation from one of these discussions follows:

> *If there is no logical impossibility in a man's freely choosing the good on one, or on several occasions, there cannot be a logical impossibility in his freely choosing the good on every occasion. God was not, then, faced with a choice between making innocent automata and making beings, who, in acting freely, would sometimes go wrong: there was open to him the obviously better possibility of making beings who would act freely but always go right. Clearly, his failure to avail himself of this possibility is inconsistent with his being both omnipotent and wholly good.*[4]

A reply to this argument is suggested in another recent contribution to the discussion.[5] If by a free action we mean an action which is not externally compelled but which flows from the nature of the agent as he reacts to the circumstances in which he finds himself, there is, indeed, no contradiction between our being free and our actions being "caused" (by our own nature), and therefore, being in principle predictable. There is a contradiction, however, in saying that God is the cause of our acting as we do but that we are free beings in relation to God. There is, in other words, a contradiction in saying that God has made us so that we shall of necessity act in a certain way, and that we are genuinely independent persons in relation to him. If all our thoughts and actions are divinely predestined, however free and morally responsible we may seem to be ourselves, we cannot be free and morally responsible in the sight of God, but must instead be his helpless puppets. Such "freedom" is like that of a patient acting out a series of posthypnotic suggestions: he appears, even to himself, to be free, but his volitions have actually been predetermined by another will, that of the hypnotist, in relation to whom the patient is not a free agent.

A different objector might raise the question of whether or not we deny God's omnipotence if we admit that he is unable to create persons who are free from the risks inherent in personal freedom. The answer that has always been given is that to create such beings is logically impossible. It is no limitation upon God's power that he cannot accomplish the logically impossible, since there is nothing here to

---

[4] J. L. Mackie, "Evil and Omnipotence," *Mind* (April, 1955), p. 209. A similar point is made by Antony Flew in "Divine Omnipotence and Human Freedom," *New Essays in Philosophical Theology.* An important critical comment on these arguments is offered by Ninian Smart in "Omnipotence, Evil and Supermen," *Philosophy* (April, 1961), with replies by Flew (January, 1962) and Mackie (April, 1962).

[5] Flew, in *New Essays in Philosophical Theology.*

accomplish, but only a meaningless conjunction of words[6]—in this case "person who is not a person." God is able to create beings of any and every conceivable kind; but creatures who lack moral freedom, however superior they might be to human beings in other respects, would not be what we mean by persons. They would constitute a different form of life which God might have brought into existence instead of persons. When we ask why God did not create such beings in place of persons, the traditional answer is that only persons could, in any meaningful sense, become "children of God," capable of entering into a personal relationship with their Creator by a free and uncompelled response to his love.

When we turn from the possibility of moral evil as a correlate of man's personal freedom to its actuality, we face something which must remain inexplicable even when it can be seen to be possible. For we can never provide a complete causal explanation of a free act; if we could, it would not be a free act. The origin of moral evil lies forever concealed within the mystery of human freedom.

The necessary connection between moral freedom and the possibility, now actualized, of sin throws light upon a great deal of the suffering which afflicts mankind. For an enormous amount of human pain arises either from the inhumanity or the culpable incompetence of mankind. This includes such major scourges as poverty, oppression and persecution, war, and all the injustice, indignity, and inequity which occur even in the most advanced societies. These evils are manifestations of human sin. Even disease is fostered to an extent, the limits of which have not yet been determined by psychosomatic medicine, by moral and emotional factors seated both in the individual and in his social environment. To the extent that all of these evils stem from human failures and wrong decisions, their possibility is inherent in the creation of free persons inhabiting a world which presents them with real choices which are followed by real consequences.

We may now turn more directly to the problem of suffering. Even though the major bulk of actual human pain is traceable to man's misused freedom as a sole or part cause, there remain other sources of pain which are entirely independent of the human will, for example, earthquake, hurricane, storm, flood, drought, and blight. In practice, it is often impossible to trace a boundary between the suffering which results from human wickedness and folly and that which falls upon mankind from without. Both kinds of suffering are inextricably mingled together in human experience. For our present purpose, however, it is important to note that the latter category does exist and that it seems to be built into the very structure of our world. In response to it, theodicy, if it is wisely conducted, follows a negative path. It is not possible to show positively that each item of human pain serves the divine purpose of good; but, on the other hand, it does seem possible to show that the divine purpose as it is understood in Judaism and Christianity could not be forwarded in a world which was designed as a permanent hedonistic paradise.

An essential premise of this argument concerns the nature of the divine purpose in creating the world. The skeptic's assumption is that man is to be viewed as

---

[6] As Aquinas said, ". . . nothing that implies a contradiction falls under the scope of God's omnipotence." *Summa Theologica,* Part 1. Question 25, article 4.

a completed creation and that God's purpose in making the world was to provide a suitable dwelling place for this fully formed creature. Since God is good and loving, the environment which he has created for human life to inhabit is naturally as pleasant and comfortable as possible. The problem is essentially similar to that of a man who builds a cage for some pet animal. Since our world, in fact, contains sources of hardship, inconvenience, and danger of innumerable kinds, the conclusion follows that this world cannot have been created by a perfectly benevolent and all-powerful deity.[7]

Christianity, however, has never supposed that God's purpose in the creation of the world was to construct a paradise whose inhabitants would experience a maximum of pleasure and a minimum of pain. The world is seen, instead, as a place of "soul-making" in which free beings grappling with the tasks and challenges of their existence in a common environment, may become "children of God" and "heirs of eternal life." A way of thinking theologically of God's continuing creative purpose for man was suggested by some of the early Hellenistic Fathers of the Christian Church, especially Irenaeus. Following hints from St. Paul, Irenaeus taught that a man has been made as a person in the image of God but has not yet been brought as a free and responsible agent into the finite likeness of God, which is revealed in Christ.[8] Our world, with all its rough edges, is the sphere in which this second and harder stage of the creative process is taking place.

This conception of the world (whether or not set in Irenaeus's theological framework) can be supported by the method of negative theodicy. Suppose, contrary to fact, that this world were a paradise from which all possibility of pain and suffering were excluded. The consequences would be very far-reaching. For example, no one could ever injure anyone else: the murderer's knife would turn to paper or his bullets to thin air; the bank safe, robbed of a million of dollars, would miraculously become filled with another million dollars (without this device, on however large a scale, proving inflationary); fraud, deceit, conspiracy, and treason would somehow always leave the fabric of society undamaged. Again, no one would ever be injured by accident: the mountain-climber, steeplejack, or playing child falling from a height would float unharmed to the ground; the reckless driver would never meet with disaster. There would be no need to work, since no harm could result from avoiding work; there would be no call to be concerned for others in time of need or danger, for in such a world there could be no real needs or dangers.

To make possible this continual series of individual adjustments, nature would have to work by "special providences" instead of running according to general laws which men must learn to respect on penalty of pain or death. The laws of nature would have to be extremely flexible: sometimes gravity would operate, sometimes not; sometimes an object would be hard and solid, sometimes soft. There could be no sciences, for there would be no enduring world structure to investigate. In eliminating the problems and hardships of an objective environment, with its own laws, life

[7] This is the nature of David Hume's argument in his discussion of the problem of evil in his *Dialogues,* Part XI.

[8] See Irenaeus's *Against Heresies,* Book IV, Chapters 37 and 38.

would become like a dream in which, delightfully but aimlessly, we would float and drift at ease.

One can at least begin to imagine such a world. It is evident that our present ethical concepts would have no meaning in it. If, for example, the notion of harming someone is an essential element in the concept of a wrong action, in our hedonistic paradise there could be no wrong actions—nor any right actions in distinction from wrong. Courage and fortitude would have no point in an environment in which there is, by definition, no danger or difficulty. Generosity, kindness, the *agape* aspect of love, prudence, unselfishness, and all other ethical notions which presuppose life in a stable environment, could not even be formed. Consequently, such a world, however well it might promote pleasure, would be very ill adapted for the development of the moral qualities of human personality. In relation to this purpose it would be the worst of all possible worlds.

It would seem, then, that an environment intended to make possible the growth in free beings of the finest characteristics of personal life, must have a good deal in common with our present world. It must operate according to general and dependable laws; and it must involve real dangers, difficulties, problems, obstacles, and possibilities of pain, failure, sorrow, frustration, and defeat. If it did not contain the particular trials and perils which—subtracting man's own very considerable contribution—our world contains, it would have to contain others instead.

To realize this is not, by any means, to be in possession of a detailed theodicy. It is to understand that this world, with all its "heartaches and the thousand natural shocks that flesh is heir to," an environment so manifestly not designed for the maximization of human pleasure and the minimization of human pain, may be rather well adapted to the quite different purpose of "soul-making."[9]

These considerations are related to theism as such. Specifically, Christian theism goes further in the light of the death of Christ, which is seen paradoxically both (as the murder of the divine Son) as the worst thing that has ever happened and (as the occasion of Man's salvation) as the best thing that has ever happened. As the supreme evil turned to supreme good, it provides the paradigm for the distinctively Christian reaction to evil. Viewed from the standpoint of Christian faith, evils do not cease to be evils; and certainly, in view of Christ's healing work, they cannot be said to have been sent by God. Yet, it has been the persistent claim of those seriously and wholeheartedly committed to Christian discipleship that tragedy, though truly tragic, may nevertheless be turned, through a man's reaction to it, from a cause of despair and alienation from God to a stage in the fulfillment of God's loving purpose for that individual. As the greatest of all evils, the crucifixion of Christ, was made the occasion of man's redemption, so good can be won from other evils. As Jesus saw his execution by the Romans as an experience which God desired him to accept, an experience which was to be brought within the

---

[9] This brief discussion has been confined to the problem of human suffering. The large and intractable problem of animal pain is not taken up here. For a discussion of it, see, for example, Nels Ferré, *Evil and the Christian Faith* (New York: Harper & Row, 1947), Chapter 7; and Austin Farrer, *Love Almighty and Ills Unlimited* (New York: Doubleday, 1961), Chapter 5.

sphere of the divine purpose and made to serve the divine ends, so the Christian response to calamity is to accept the adversities, pains, and afflictions which life brings, in order that they can be turned to a positive spiritual use.[10]

At this point, theodicy points forward in two ways to the subject of life after death.

First, although there are many striking instances of good being triumphantly brought out of evil through a man's or a woman's reaction to it, there are many other cases in which the opposite has happened. Sometimes obstacles breed strength of character, dangers evoke courage and unselfishness, and calamities produce patience and moral steadfastness. But sometimes they lead, instead, to resentment, fear, grasping selfishness, and disintegration of character. Therefore, it would seem that any divine purpose of soul-making which is at work in earthly history must continue beyond this life if it is ever to achieve more than a very partial and fragmentary success.

Second, if we ask whether the business of soul-making is worth all the toil and sorrow of human life, the Christian answer must be in terms of a future good which is great enough to justify all that has happened on the way to it.

To Think About

1. Name some famous people who have been broken by the obstacles they faced. Name some who have been made by them. What evidence can you provide?

2. Since God himself is the greatest possible good, he need not have created at all in order for the greatest possible good to exist. Discuss.

3. Some evils are such that no greater good can justify or compensate for them. The particular intrinsic evil is utterly irredeemable. Discuss.

4. "The maintenance of man's epistemic distance from God (i.e., the context in which the existence of God is not strongly impressed upon man's consciousness and in which it may even appear as if there is no God) does not require the existence of severe moral and physical evils since there are other ways God can conceal his presence. Furthermore epistemic distance makes intelligent moral choice impossible since one's duty is not discernible."   ***G. Stanley Kane***

5. "There is an inconsistency between Hick's soul making theory and his salvation belief. Soul making emphasizes human freedom while Hick's theodicy assures mankind that God will bring about human salvation."   ***G. Stanley Kane***

6. "Let us confess it: evil strides the world."   ***Voltaire***

7. "The world has always been ruled by Lucifer. The world is evil. Call his name, my love. Call the name of Lucifer."   NBC-TV's ***Ritual of Evil***

8. "The world's a failure, you know. Someone, somewhere, made a terrible mistake."   CBS-TV's ***Mission Impossible***

---

[10] This conception of providence is stated more fully in John Hick, *Faith and Knowledge* (Ithaca, NY: Cornell University Press, 1957), Chapter 7, from which some sentences are incorporated in this paragraph.

9. "If you want to accept life, you have to accept the whole bloody universe."

Alexei Panshin,

10. "Those who have suffered much become very bitter or very gentle."

Will Durant

Readings

ADAMS, MARILYN MCCORD, and ROBERT MERRIHEW ADAMS, eds. *The Problem of Evil.* Oxford: Oxford University Press, 1990.

The Bible. Book of Job. A dramatic presentation that deals with the problem of evil and the omnipotence of God.

HICK, JOHN. *Evil and the God of Love.* New York: Harper & Row, 1966. A careful analysis of the problem of pain and of moral evil.

LEWIS, C. S. *The Problem of Pain.* New York: Macmillan, 1962.

PATTERSON, MICHAEL L., ed. *The Problem of Evil.* Notre Dame, IN: Notre Dame University Press, 1992.

~~~~

Are Humans Free?

13
Humans Are Determined

Paul Henri Thiry, Baron d'Holbach (1723–89), *a French philosopher, was one of the Encylopedists. His book* The System of Nature *was called by his enemies "the Bible of Atheists."*

Nearly all of us believe that we have the free will to choose to do what we wish. One can freely choose to come to school or stay home. Thus, the belief that humans have free will is an immediate and a pervasive belief. Yet, if one raises a question about what reasons a person would give for avoiding school, then one's will doesn't seem to be so free. One might stay home if one were ill or one's mother died. But if these events *didn't* occur, then given the events that *did* occur (one has an exam at school, one hates to miss a class, and so on), one couldn't have done otherwise. This denial of free will is called the belief in *determinism*. Determinism is the belief that all acts are caused by past events, and given enough knowledge, one could predict what a person will do. A major question is, Can one be morally blamed if all of one's acts are determined?

In contrast, the *indeterminist* says that some of our acts are not determined by past conditions. This is the position of the believer in free will (William James). He holds that some acts of the will are exempt from causal determination. Each of these, determinism and indeterminism, must be distinguished from *predeterminism,* which is the belief that events (either all or some) throughout eternity have been foreordained by some supernatural power (usually God).

James contends that because there is no evidence that is deciding for determinism or indeterminism, we have the option of holding to that position to which we are temperamentally suited. In James's case, it is the belief in indeterminism. In this

From Baron Holbach, *The System of Nature,* Vol. 1, Chaps. 11 and 12, trans. H. D. Robinson (1853).

case it is argued that we are responsible for our acts, for we have the freedom to do otherwise. Hence it is claimed that only indeterminism is compatible with morality.

 To Study

1. How does Holbach describe a person's life on earth?
2. Why does society reject the idea that all of the actions of humans are necessary?
3. What is the relation between the brain and the will?
4. What have been the errors of philosophers on the free agency of man? What are the sources of actions of humans?
5. Why is not a person free when there is an absence of obstacles?
6. Does not acting against one's inclinations show that a person is free?
7. What renders it extremely difficult for a person to recur to the true principles of one's own peculiar actions?

Motives and the Determination of the Will.   In whatever manner man is considered, he is connected to universal nature, and submitted to the necessary and immutable laws that she imposes on all the beings she contains, according to their peculiar essences or to the respective properties with which, without consulting them, she endows each particular species. Man's life is a line that nature commands him to describe upon the surface of the earth, without his ever being able to swerve from it, even for an instant. He is born without his own consent; his organization does in nowise depend upon himself; his ideas come to him involuntarily; his habits are in the power of those who cause him to contract them; he is unceasingly modified by causes, whether visible or concealed, over which he has no control, which necessarily regulate his mode of existence, give the hue to his way of thinking, and determine his manner of acting. He is good or bad, happy or miserable, wise or foolish, reasonable or irrational, without his will being for anything in these various states. Nevertheless, in spite of the shackles by which he is bound, it is pretended he is a free agent, or that independent of the causes by which he is moved, he determines his own will, and regulates his own condition.

However slender the foundation of this opinion, of which everything ought to point out to him the error, it is current at this day and passes for an incontestable truth with a great number of people, otherwise extremely enlightened; it is the basis of religion, which, supposing relations between man and the unknown being she has placed above nature, has been incapable of imagining how man could merit reward or deserve punishment from this being, if he was not a free agent. Society has been believed interested in this system; because an idea has gone abroad, that if all the actions of man were to be contemplated as necessary, the right of punishing those who injure their associates would no longer exist. At length human vanity accommodated itself to a hypothesis which, unquestionably, appears to distinguish man from all other physical beings, by assigning to him the special privilege of a total independence of all other causes, but of which a very little reflection would have shown him the impossibility. . . .

The will, as we have elsewhere said, is a modification of the brain, by which it is disposed to action, or prepared to give play to the organs. This will is necessarily determined by the qualities, good or bad, agreeable or painful, of the object or the motive that acts upon his senses, or of which the idea remains with him, and is resuscitated by his memory. In consequence, he acts necessarily, his action is the result of the impulse he receives either from the motive, from the object, or from the idea which has modified his brain, or disposed his will. When he does not act according to this impulse, it is because there comes some new cause, some new motive, some new idea, which modifies his brain in a different manner, gives him a new impulse, determines his will in another way, by which the action of the former impulse is suspended: thus, the sight of an agreeable object, or its idea, determines his will to set him in action to procure it; but if a new object or a new idea more powerfully attracts him, it gives a new direction to his will, annihilates the effect of the former, and prevents the action by which it was to be procured. This is the mode in which reflection, experience, reason, necessarily arrests or suspends the action of man's will: without this he would of necessity have followed the anterior impulse which carried him towards a then desirable object. In all this he always acts according to necessary laws from which he has no means of emancipating himself.

If when tormented with violent thirst, he figures to himself in idea, or really perceives a fountain, whose limpid streams might cool his feverish want, is he sufficient master of himself to desire or not to desire the object competent to satisfy so lively a want? It will no doubt be conceded, that it is impossible he should not be desirous to satisfy it; but it will be said—if at this moment it is announced to him that the water he so ardently desires is poisoned, he will, notwithstanding his vehement thirst, abstain from drinking it: and it has, therefore, been falsely concluded that he is a free agent. The fact, however, is, that the motive in either case is exactly the same: his own conservation. The same necessity that determined him to drink before he knew the water was deleterious upon this new discovery equally determined him not to drink; the desire of conserving himself either annihilates or suspends the former impulse; the second motive becomes stronger than the preceding, that is, the fear of death, or the desire of preserving himself, necessarily prevails over the painful sensation caused by his eagerness to drink: but, it will be said, if the thirst is very parching, an inconsiderate man without regarding the danger will risk swallowing the water. Nothing is gained by this remark: in this case, the anterior impulse only regains the ascendency; he is persuaded that life may possibly be longer preserved, or that he shall derive a greater good by drinking the poisoned water than by enduring the torment, which, to his mind, threatens instant dissolution; thus the first becomes the strongest and necessarily urges him on to action. Nevertheless, in either case, whether he partakes of the water, or whether he does not, the two actions will be equally necessary; they will be the effect of that motive which finds itself most puissant; which consequently acts in the most coercive manner upon his will.

This example will serve to explain the whole phenomena of the human will. This will, or rather the brain, finds itself in the same situation as a bowl, which, although it has received an impulse that drives it forward in a straight line, is deranged in its course whenever a force superior to the first obliges it to change its direction. The man who drinks the poisoned water appears a madman; but the actions of fools are as necessary as those of the most prudent individuals. The motives that determine the voluptuary and the debauchee to risk their health are as powerful, and their actions are as necessary, as those which decide the wise man to manage his. But, it will be insisted, the debauchee may be prevailed on to change his conduct: this does not imply that he is a free agent; but that motives may be found sufficiently powerful to annihilate the effect of those that previously acted upon him; then these new motives determine his will to the new mode of conduct he may adopt as necessarily as the former did to the old mode. . . .

The errors of philosophers on the free agency of man, have arisen from their regarding his will as the *primum mobile,* the original motive of his actions; for want of recurring back, they have not perceived the multiplied, the complicated causes which, independently of him, give motion to the will itself; or which dispose and modify his brain, whilst he himself is purely passive in the motion he receives. Is he the master of desiring or not desiring an object that appears desirable to him? Without doubt it will be answered, no: but he is the master of resisting his desire, if he reflects on the consequences. But, I ask, is he capable of reflecting on these consequences, when his soul is hurried along by a very lively passion, which entirely depends upon his natural organization, and the causes by which he is modified? Is it in his power to add to these consequences all the weight necessary to counterbalance his desire? Is he the master of preventing the qualities which render an object desirable from residing in it? I shall be told: he ought to have learned to resist his passions; to contract a habit of putting a curb on his desires. I agree to it without any difficulty. But in reply, I again ask, is his nature susceptible of this modification? Does his boiling blood, his unruly imagination, the igneous fluid that circulates in his veins, permit him to make, enable him to apply true experience in the moment when it is wanted? And even when his temperament has capacitated him, has his education, the examples set before him, the ideas with which he has been inspired in early life, been suitable to make him contract this habit of repressing his desires? Have not all these things rather contributed to induce him to seek with avidity, to make him actually desire those objects which you say he ought to resist?

The Ambitious Man Cries Out.   You will have me resist my passion; but have they not unceasingly repeated to me that rank, honours, power, are the most desirable advantages in life? Have I not seen my fellow citizens envy them, the nobles of my country sacrifice every thing to obtain them? In the society in which I live, am I not obliged to feel, that if I am deprived of these advantages, I must expect to languish in contempt; to cringe under the rod of oppression?

The Miser Says.   You forbid me to love money, to seek after the means of acquiring it: alas, does not every thing tell me that, in this world, money is the greatest blessing; that it is amply sufficient to render me happy? In the country I inhabit, do I not see all my fellow citizens covetous of riches? but do I not also witness that they are little scrupulous in the means of obtaining wealth? As soon as they are enriched by the means which you censure, are they not cherished, considered and respected? By what authority, then, do you defend me from amassing treasure? What right have you to prevent my using means, which, although you call them sordid and criminal, I see approved by the sovereign? Will you have me renounce my happiness?

The Voluptuary Argues.   You pretend that I should resist my desires; but was I the maker of my own temperament, which unceasingly invites me to pleasure? You call my pleasures disgraceful; but in the country in which I live, do I not witness the most dissipated men enjoying the most distinguished rank? Do I not behold that no one is ashamed of adultery but the husband it has outraged? Do not I see men making trophies of their debaucheries, boasting of their libertinism, rewarded with applause?

The Choleric Man Vociferates.   You advise me to put a curb on my passions, and to resist the desire of avenging myself: but can I conquer my nature? Can I alter the received opinions of the world? Shall I not be forever disgraced, infallibly dishonoured in society, if I do not wash out in the blood of my fellow creatures the injuries I have received?

The Zealous Enthusiast Exclaims.   You recommend me mildness; you advise me to be tolerant; to be indulgent to the opinions of my fellow men; but is not my temperament violent? Do I not ardently love my God? Do they not assure me, that zeal is pleasing to him; that sanguinary inhuman persecutors have been his friends? As I wish to render myself acceptable in his sight, I therefore adopt the same means.

In short, the actions of man are never free; they are always the necessary consequence of his temperament, of the received ideas, and of the notions, either true or false, which he has formed to himself of happiness; of his opinions, strengthened by example, by education, and by daily experience. So many crimes are witnessed on the earth only because every thing conspires to render man vicious and criminal; the religion he has adopted, his government, his education, the examples set before him, irresistibly drive him on to evil: under these circumstances, morality preaches virtue to him in vain. In those societies where vice is esteemed, where crime is crowned, where venality is constantly recompensed, where the most dreadful disorders are punished only in those who are too weak to enjoy the privilege of committing them with impunity, the practice of virtue is considered nothing more than a painful sacrifice of happiness. Such societies chastise, in the lower orders, those excesses which they respect in the higher ranks; and frequently have the injustice to condemn those in the penalty of death, whom public prejudices, maintained by constant example, have rendered criminal.

Man, then, is not a free agent in any one instant of his life; he is necessarily guided in each step by those advantages, whether real or fictitious, that he attaches to the objects by which his passions are roused: these passions themselves are necessary in a being who unceasingly tends towards his own happiness; their energy is necessary, since that depends on his temperament; his temperament is necessary, because it depends on the physical elements which enter into his composition; the modification of this temperament is necessary, as it is the infallible and inevitable consequence of the impulse he receives from the incessant action of moral and physical beings.

Choice Does Not Prove Freedom.   In spite of these proofs of the want of free agency in man, so clear to unprejudiced minds, it will, perhaps be insisted upon with no small feeling of triumph, that if it be proposed to any one, to move or not to move his hand, an action in the number of those called indifferent, he evidently appears to be the master of choosing; from which it is concluded that evidence has been offered of free agency. The reply is, this example is perfectly simple; man in performing some action which he is resolved on doing, does not by any means prove his free agency; the very desire of displaying this quality, excited by the dispute, becomes a necessary motive, which decides his will either for the one or the other of these actions: What deludes him in this instance, or that which persuades him he is a free agent at this moment, is, that he does not discern the true motive which sets him in action, namely, the desire of convincing his opponent: if in the heat of the dispute he insists and asks, "Am I not the master of throwing myself out of the window?" I shall answer him, no; that whilst he preserves his reason there is no probability that the desire of proving his free agency, will become a motive sufficiently powerful to make him sacrifice his life to the attempt: if, notwithstanding this, to prove he is a free agent, he should actually precipitate himself from the window, it would not be a sufficient warranty to conclude he acted freely, but rather that it was the violence of his temperament which spurred him on to this folly. Madness is a state, that depends upon the heat of the blood, not upon the will. A fanatic or a hero, braves death as necessarily as a more phlegmatic man or coward flies from it.

There is, in point of fact, no difference between the man that is cast out of the window by another, and the man who throws himself out of it, except that the impulse in the first instance comes immediately from without whilst that which determines the fall in the second case, springs from within his own peculiar machine, having its more remote cause also exterior. When Mutius Scaevola held his hand in the fire, he was as much acting under the influence of necessity (caused by interior motives) that urged him to this strange action, as if his arm had been held by strong men: pride, despair, the desire of braving his enemy, a wish to astonish him, and anxiety to intimidate him, etc., were the invisible chains that held his hand bound to the fire. The love of glory, enthusiasm for their country, in like manner caused Codrus and Decius to devote themselves for their fellow citizens. The Indian Colánus and the philosopher Peregrinus were equally obliged to burn themselves, by desire of exciting the astonishment of the Grecian assembly.

It is said that free agency is the absence of those obstacles competent to oppose themselves to the actions of man, or to the exercise of his faculties: it is pretended that he is a free agent whenever, making use of these faculties, he produces the effect he has proposed to himself. In reply to this reasoning, it is sufficient to consider that it in nowise depends upon himself to place or remove the obstacles that either determine or resist him. The motive that causes his action is no more in his own power than the obstacle that impedes him, whether this obstacle or motive be within his own machine or exterior of his person. He is not master of the thought presented to his mind, which determines his will; this thought is excited by some cause independent of himself.

To be undeceived on the system of his free agency, man has simply to recur to the motive by which his will is determined; he will always find this motive is out of his own control. It is said: that in consequence of an idea to which the mind gives birth, man acts freely if he encounters no obstacle. But the question is, what gives birth to this idea in his brain? Was he the master either to prevent it from presenting itself, or from renewing itself in his brain? Does not this idea depend either upon objects that strike him exteriorly and in despite of himself, or upon causes, that without his knowledge, act within himself and modify his brain? Can he prevent his eyes, cast without design upon any object whatever, from giving him an idea of this object, and from moving his brain? He is not more master of the obstacles; they are the necessary effects of either interior or exterior causes, which always act according to their given properties. A man insults a coward; this necessarily irritates him against his insulter; but his will cannot vanquish the obstacle that cowardice places to the object of his desire, because his natural conformation, which does not depend upon himself, prevents his having courage. In this case, the coward is insulted in spite of himself; and against his will is obliged patiently to brook the insult he has received.

Absence of Restraint Is Not Absence of Necessity.   The partisans of the system of free agency appear ever to have confounded constraint with necessity. Man believes he acts as a free agent, every time he does not see any thing that places obstacles to his actions; he does not perceive that the motive which causes him to will, is always necessary and independent of himself. A prisoner loaded with chains is compelled to remain in prison; but he is not a free agent in the desire to emancipate himself; his chains prevent him from acting, but they do not prevent him from willing; he would save himself if they would loose his fetters; but he would not save himself as a free agent; fear or the idea of punishment would be sufficient motives for his action.

Man may, therefore, cease to be restrained, without, for that reason, becoming a free agent. In whatever manner he acts, he will act necessarily, according to motives by which he shall be determined. He may be compared to a heavy body that finds itself arrested in its descent by any obstacle whatever. Take away this obstacle, it will gravitate or continue to fall; but who shall say this dense body is free to fall or not? Is not its descent the necessary effect of its own specific gravity? The virtuous Socrates submitted to the laws of his country, although they were unjust; and though the doors of his jail were left open to him, he would not save himself; but in this he did not act as a free agent. The invisible chains of opinion, the secret love of decorum, the inward respect for the laws, even when they were iniquitous, the fear of tarnishing his glory, kept him in his prison; they were motives sufficiently powerful with this enthusiast for virtue, to induce him to wait death with tranquility; it was not in his power to save himself, because he could find no potential motive to bring him to depart, even for an instant, from those principles to which his mind was accustomed.

Man, it is said, frequently acts against his inclination, from whence it is falsely concluded he is a free agent; but when he appears to act contrary to his inclination, he is always determined to it by some motive sufficiently efficacious to vanquish this inclination. A sick man, with a view to his cure, arrives at conquering his repugnance to the most disgusting remedies. The fear of pain, or the dread of death, then become necessary motives; consequently this sick man cannot be said to act freely.

When it is said, that man is not a free agent, it is not pretended to compare him to a body moved by a simple impulsive cause. He contains within himself causes inherent to his existence; he is moved by an interior organ, which has its own peculiar laws, and is itself necessarily determined in consequence of ideas formed from perception resulting from sensation which it receives from exterior objects. As the mechanism of these sensations, of these perceptions, and the manner they engrave ideas on the brain of man, are not known to him; because he is unable to unravel all these motions; because he cannot perceive the chain of operations in his soul, or the motive principle that acts within him, he supposes himself a free agent; which literally translated, signifies, that he moves himself by himself; that he determines himself without cause. When he rather ought to say, that he is ignorant how or why he acts in the manner he does. It is true the soul enjoys an activity peculiar to itself, but it is equally certain that this activity would never be displayed, if some motive or some cause did not put it in a condition to exercise itself. At least it will not be pretended that the soul is able either to love or to hate without being moved, without knowing the objects, without having some idea of their qualities. Gunpowder has unquestionably a particular activity, but this activity will never display itself, unless fire be applied to it; this, however, immediately sets it in motion.

The Complexity of Human Conduct and the Illusion of Free Agency. It is the great complication of motion in man, it is the variety of his action, it is the multiplicity of causes that move him, whether simultaneously or in continual succession, that persuades him he is a free agent. If all his motions were simple, if the causes that move him did not confound themselves with each other, if they were distinct, if his machine were less complicated, he would perceive that all his actions were necessary, because he would be enabled to recur instantly to the cause that made him act. A man who should be always obliged to go towards the west, would always go on that side; but he would feel that, in so going, he was not a free agent. If he had another sense, as his actions or his motion, augmented by a sixth, would be still more varied and much more complicated, he would believe himself still more a free agent than he does with his five senses.

It is, then, for want of recurring to the causes that move him; for want of being able to analyze, from not being competent to decompose the complicated motion of his machine, that man believes himself a free agent. It is only upon his own ignorance that he founds the profound yet deceitful notion he has of his free agency; that he builds those opinions which he brings forward as a striking proof of his pretended freedom of action. If, for a short time, each man was willing to examine his own peculiar actions, search out their true motives to discover their concatenation, he would remain convinced that the sentiment he has of his natural free agency, is a chimera that must speedily be destroyed by experience.

Nevertheless it must be acknowledged that the multiplicity and diversity of the causes which continually act upon man, frequently without even his knowledge, render it impossible, or at least extremely difficult for him to recur to the true principles of his own peculiar actions, much less the actions of others. They frequently depend upon causes so fugitive, so remote from their effects, and which, superficially examined, appear to have so little analogy, so slender a relation with them, that it requires singular sagacity to bring them into light. This is what renders the study of the moral man a task of such difficulty; this is the reason why his heart is an abyss, of which it is frequently impossible for him to fathom the depth. . . .

If he understood the play of his organs, if he were able to recall to himself all the impulsions they have received, all the modifications they have undergone, all the effects they have produced, he would perceive that all his actions are submitted to the fatality, which regulates his own particular system, as it does the entire system of the universe. No one effect in him, any more than in nature, produces itself by chance; this, as has been before proved, is word void of sense. All that passes in him; all that is done by him; as well as all that happens in nature, or that is attributed to her, is derived from necessary causes, which act according to necessary laws, and which produce necessary effects from whence necessarily flow others.

Fatality, is the eternal, the immutable, the necessary order, established in nature; or the indispensable connexion of causes that act, with the effects they operate. Conforming to this order, heavy bodies fall, light bodies rise; that which is analogous in matter reciprocally attracts; that which is heterogeneous mutually repels; man congregates himself in society, modifies each his fellow; becomes either virtuous or wicked; either contributes to his mutual happiness, or reciprocates his misery; either loves his neighbour, or hates his companion necessarily, according to the manner in which the one acts upon the other. From whence it may be seen, that the same necessity which regulates the physical, also regulates the moral world, in which every thing is in consequence submitted to fatality. Man, in running over, frequently without his own knowledge, often in spite of himself, the route which nature has marked out for him, resembles a swimmer who is obliged to follow the current that carries him along. He believes himself a free agent, because he sometimes consents, sometimes does not consent, to glide with the stream, which notwithstanding, always hurries him forward; he believes himself the master of his condition, because he is obliged to use his arms under the fear of sinking. . . .

To Think About

1. "I cannot forbear adding to these reasonings an observation, which may perhaps, be found of some importance. In every system of morality which I have hitherto met with, I have always remarked, that the author proceeds for some time in the ordinary way of reasoning, and establishes the being of a God, or makes observations concerning human affairs; when of a sudden I am surprised to find, that instead of the usual copulations of propositions, *is,* and *is not,* I meet with no proposition that is not connected with an *ought,* or an *ought not.* This change is imperceptible; but is, however, of the last consequence. For as this *ought,* or *ought not,* expresses some new relation or affirmation, it is necessary that it should be observed and explained; and at the same time that a reason should be given, for what seems altogether inconceivable, how this new relation can be a deduction from others, which are entirely different from it. But as authors do not commonly use this precaution, I shall presume to recommend it to the readers; and am persuaded, that this small attention would subvert all the vulgar systems of morality, and let us see that the distinction of vice and virtue is not founded merely on the relations of objects, nor is perceived by reason."   ***David Hume***

2. ". . . that all the particular moral judgments we intuitively make are likely to derive from discarded religious systems, from warped views of sex and bodily functions, or from customs necessary for the survival of the group in social and economic circumstances that now lie in the distant past?"   ***Unknown***

3. "I experience free will when I wrestle between duty and desire." ***C. A. Campbell***

4. "We are a great deal more certain that our will is free than that everything that happens is bound to have a cause. This being the case, could we not for once in a way reverse the argument, and say: our ideas of cause and effect must be very inaccurate, for were they right, our will could not be free?" ***Georg Lichtenberg***

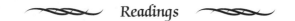 Readings

CAMPBELL, C. A. "Is 'Free Will' a Pseudo-Problem?" *Mind* 60 (1951): 446–65. Criticizes the reconciliationist position, especially in the way it is put forward by Nowell-Smith, Schlick, and Stevenson.

D'ANGELO, EDWARD. *The Problem of Freedom and Determinism.* Columbia: University of Missouri Press, 1968. A good, clear discussion of the three major positions.

HONDERICH, TED. *How Free Are You?: The Determinism Problem.* Oxford: Oxford University Press, 2002.

PEREBOOM, DERK. *Living without Free Will.* New York: Cambridge University Press, 2001.

SLOTE, MICHAEL. "Ethics without Free Will." *Social Theory and Practice* 16.3 (Fall 1990): 369–83.

TAYLOR, RICHARD. *Metaphysics.* 3rd ed. Upper Saddle River, NJ: Prentice Hall, 1983, Ch. 5.

THORTON, MARK. *Do We Have Free Will?* New York: St. Martin's Press, 1989. An introductory account of the major positions on the free will versus determinism controversy.

TRUSTED, JENNIFER. *Free Will and Responsibility.* Oxford: Oxford University Press, 1984.

14
Humans Are Free

William James (1842–1910), American philosopher and psychologist, received his M.D. from Harvard in 1869. He lectured there on anatomy and physiology until 1880, when he joined the Department of Psychology and Philosophy. He amended and popularized Peirce's pragmatism in a series of books that includes The Will to Believe and Other Essays in Popular Philosophy *(1897),* The Varieties of Religious Experience *(1902),* Pragmatism *(1907), and* Essays in Radical Empiricism *(1912).*

James has little respect for the position he refers to (with unconcealed contempt) as "a *soft* determinism which abhors harsh words, and, repudiating fatality, necessity, and even predetermination, says that its real name is freedom." You must choose, James says, between *hard* determinism, which accepts the unpalatable consequences of the determinist hypothesis, and *indeterminism,* which frankly rejects determinism.

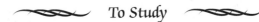 To Study

1. What is a *genuine* option?
2. According to James, what ought to be our first act if we are free?
3. Distinguish between hard and soft determinism.
4. How does James define indeterminism?
5. What role do facts play as to the determinism/indeterminism issue?
6. What is it that a deterministic world implies? As a corollary, what does an indeterministic world imply? What is James's position?
7. Can you apply the genuine option theory to the free will problem?

From William James, *The Will to Believe.* Reprinted from the Dover Publications edition published in 1960.

. . . I have long defended to my own students the lawfulness of voluntarily adopted faith; but as soon as they have got well imbued with the logical spirit, they have as a rule refused to admit my contention to be lawful philosophically, even though in point of fact they were personally all the time chock-full of some faith or other themselves. I am all the while, however, so profoundly convinced that my own position is correct, that your invitation has seemed to me a good occasion to make my statements more clear. Perhaps your minds will be more open than those with which I have hitherto had to deal. I will be as little technical as I can, though I must begin by setting up some technical distinctions that will help us in the end.

Let us give the name of *hypothesis* to anything that may be proposed to our belief; and just as the electricians speak of live and dead wires, let us speak of any hypothesis as either *live* or *dead*. A live hypothesis is one which appeals as a real possibility to him to whom it is proposed. If I ask you to believe in the Mahdi, the notion makes no electric connection with your nature,—it refuses to scintillate with any credibility at all. As an hypothesis it is completely dead. To an Arab, however (even if he be not one of the Mahdi's followers), the hypothesis is among the mind's possibilities: it is alive. This shows that deadness and liveness in an hypothesis are not intrinsic properties, but relations to the individual thinker. They are measured by his willingness to act. The maximum of liveness in an hypothesis means willingness to act irrevocably. Practically, that means belief; but there is some believing tendency wherever there is willingness to act at all.

Next, let us call the decision between two hypotheses an *option*. Options may be of several kinds. They may be—1, *living* or *dead;* 2, *forced* or *avoidable;* 3, *momentous* or *trivial;* and for our purposes we may call an option a *genuine* option when it is of the forced, living, and momentous kind.

1. A living option is one in which both hypotheses are live ones. If I say to you: "Be a theosophist or be a Mohammedan," it is probably a dead option, because for you neither hypothesis is likely to be alive. But if I say: "Be an agnostic or be a Christian," it is otherwise: trained as you are, each hypothesis makes some appeal, however small, to your belief.

2. Next, if I say to you: "Choose between going out with your umbrella or without it," I do not offer you a genuine opinion, for it is not forced. You can easily avoid it by not going out at all. Similarly, if I say, "Either love me or hate me," "Either call my theory true or call it false," your option is avoidable. You may remain indifferent to me, neither loving nor hating, and you may decline to offer any judgment as to my theory. But if I say, "Either accept this truth or go without it," I put on you a forced option, for there is no standing place outside of the alternative. Every dilemma based on a complete logical disjunction, with no possibility of not choosing, is an option of this forced kind.

3. Finally, if I were Dr. Nansen and proposed to you to join my North Pole expedition, your option would be momentous; for this would probably be your only similar opportunity, and your choice now would either exclude you from the North Pole sort of immortality altogether or put at least the chance of it into your hands. He who refuses to embrace a unique opportunity loses the prize as surely as if he tried

and failed. *Per contra,* the option is trivial when the opportunity is not unique, when the stake is insignificant, or when the decision is reversible if it later prove unwise. Such trivial options abound in the scientific life. A chemist finds an hypothesis live enough to spend a year in its verification: he believes in it to that extent. But if his experiments prove inconclusive either way, he is quit for his loss of time, no vital harm being done.

It will facilitate our discussion if we keep all these distinctions well in mind. . . .

The thesis I defend is, briefly stated, this: *Our passional nature not only lawfully may, but must, decide an option between propositions, whenever it is a genuine option that cannot by its nature be decided on intellectual grounds; for to say, under such circumstances, "Do not decide, but leave the question open," is itself a passional decision,—just like deciding yes or no,—and is attended with the same risk of losing the truth.* . . .

A common opinion prevails that the juice has ages ago been pressed out of the free-will controversy, and that no new champion can do more than warm up stale arguments which everyone has heard. This is a radical mistake. I know of no subject less worn out, or in which inventive genius has a better chance of breaking open new ground,—not, perhaps, of forcing a conclusion or of coercing assent, but of deepening our sense of what the issue between the two parties really is, of what the ideas of fate and of free-will imply. . . . [O]ur first act of freedom, if we are free, ought in all inward propriety to be to affirm that we are free. . . .

With this much understood at the outset, we can advance. But not without one more point understood as well. The arguments I am about to urge all proceed on two suppositions: first, when we make theories about the world and discuss them with one another, we do so in order to attain a conception of things which shall give us subjective satisfaction; and, second, if there be two conceptions, and the one seems to us, on the whole, more rational than the other, we are entitled to suppose that the more rational one is the truer of the two. . . .

To begin, then, I must suppose you acquainted with all the usual arguments on the subject. I cannot stop to take up the old proofs from causation, from statistics, from the certainty with which we can foretell one another's conduct, from the fixity of character, and all the rest. . . . Old-fashioned determinism was what we may call *hard* determinism.[1] It did not shrink from such words as fatality, bondage of the will, necessitation, and the like. Nowadays, we have a *soft* determinism[2] which abhors harsh words, and, repudiating fatality, necessity, and even predetermination, says that its real name is freedom; for freedom is only necessity understood, and bondage to the highest is identical with true freedom. . . .

[Determinism] professes that those parts of the universe already laid down absolutely appoint and decree what the other parts shall be. The future has no ambiguous possibilities hidden in its womb: the part we call the present is compatible with

---

[1] *Hard determinism:* All events are caused. [ED.]

[2] *Soft determinism:* Humans are free when their choices are effective, even though their choices are caused. [ED.]

only one totality. Any other future complement than the one fixed from eternity is impossible. The whole is in each and every part, and welds it with the rest into an absolute unity, an iron block, in which there can be no equivocation or shadow of turning.

> *With earth's first clay they did the last man knead,*
> *And there of the last harvest sowed the seed.*
> *And the first morning of creation wrote*
> *What the last dawn of reckoning shall read.*

Indeterminism, on the contrary, says that the parts have a certain amount of loose play on one another, so that the laying down of one of them does not necessarily determine what the others shall be. It admits that possibilities may be in excess of actualities, and that things not yet revealed to our knowledge may really in themselves be ambiguous. Of two alternative futures which we conceive, both may now be really possible; and the one become impossible only at the very moment when the other excludes it by becoming real itself. Indeterminism thus denies the world to be one unbending unit of fact. It says there is a certain ultimate pluralism in it; and, so saying, it corroborates our ordinary unsophisticated view of things. To that view, actualities seem to float in a wider sea of possibilities from out of which they are chosen; and, *somewhere,* indeterminism says, such possibilities exist, and form a part of truth.

Determinism, on the contrary, says they exist *nowhere,* and that necessity on the one hand and impossibility on the other are the sole categories of the real. Possibilities that fail to get realized are, for determinism, pure illusions: they never were possibilities at all. There is nothing inchoate, it says, about this universe of ours, all that was or is or shall be actual in it having been from eternity virtually there. The cloud of alternatives our minds escort this mass of actuality withal is a cloud of sheer deception, to which "impossibilities" is the only name that rightfully belongs.

The issue, it will be seen, is a perfectly sharp one, which no eulogistic terminology can smear over or wipe out. The truth *must* lie with one side or the other, and its lying with one side makes the other false.

The question relates solely to the existence of possibilities, in the strict sense of the term, as things that may, but need not, be. Both sides admit that a volition, for instance, has occurred. The indeterminists say another volition might have occurred in its place: the determinists swear that nothing could possibly have occurred in its place. Now, can science be called in to tell us which of these two point-blank contradicters of each other is right? Science professes to draw no conclusions but such as are based on matters of fact, things that have actually happened; but how can any amount of assurance that something actually happened give us the least grain of information as to whether another thing might or might not have happened in its place? Only facts can be proved by other facts. With things that are possibilities and not facts, facts have no concern. If we have no other evidence than the evidence of existing facts, the possibility-question must remain a mystery never to be cleared up.

And the truth is that facts practically have hardly anything to do with making us either determinists or indeterminists. Sure enough, we make a flourish of quoting facts this way or that; and if we are determinists, we talk about the infallibility with which we can predict one another's conduct; while if we are indeterminists, we lay great stress on the fact that it is just because we cannot foretell one another's conduct, either in war or statecraft or in any of the great and small intrigues and business of men, that life is so intensely anxious and hazardous a game. But who does not see the wretched insufficiency of this so-called objective testimony on both sides? What fills up the gaps in our minds is something not objective, not external. What divides us into possibility men and anti-possibility men is different faiths or postulates,—postulates of rationality. To this man the world seems more rational with possibilities in it,—to that man more rational with possibilities excluded; and talk as we will about having to yield to evidence, what makes us monists or pluralists, determinists or indeterminists, is at bottom always some sentiment like this. . . .

Nevertheless, many persons talk as if the minutest dose of disconnectedness of one part with another, the smallest modicum of independence, the faintest tremor of ambiguity about the future, for example, would ruin everything, and turn this goodly universe into a sort of insane sand-heap or nulliverse, no universe at all. Since future human volitions are as a matter of fact the only ambiguous things we are tempted to believe in, let us stop for a moment to make ourselves sure whether their independent and accidental character need be fraught with such direful consequences to the universe as these.

What is meant by saying that my choice of which way to walk home after the lecture is ambiguous and matter of chance as far as the present moment is concerned? It means that both Divinity Avenue and Oxford Street are called; but that only one, and that one *either* one, shall be chosen. Now, I ask you seriously to suppose that this ambiguity of my choice is real; and then to make the impossible hypothesis that the choice is made twice over, and each time falls on a different street. In other words, imagine that I first walk through Divinity Avenue, and then imagine that the powers governing the universe annihilate ten minutes of time with all that it contained, and set me back at the door of this hall just as I was before the choice was made. Imagine then that, everything else being the same, I now make a different choice and traverse Oxford Street. You, as passive spectators, look on and see the two alternative universes,—one of them with me walking through Divinity Avenue in it, the other with the same me walking through Oxford Street. Now, if you are determinists you believe one of these universes to have been from eternity impossible: you believe it to have been impossible because of the intrinsic irrationality or accidentality somewhere involved in it. But looking outwardly at these universes, can you say which is the impossible and accidental one, and which the rational and necessary one? I doubt if the most ironclad determinist among you could have the slightest glimmer of light on this point. In other words, either universe *after the fact* and once there would, to our means of observation and understanding, appear just as rational as the other. There would be absolutely no criterion by which we might judge one necessary and the other matter of chance. Suppose now we relieve the gods of their hypothetical task and assume my choice, once made, to be made forever. I go through Divinity Avenue for good and all. If, as good determinists, you now begin to affirm, what all good determinists punctually do affirm, that in the nature of things I *couldn't* have gone through Oxford Street,—had I done so it would have been chance, irrationality, insanity, a horrid gap in nature,—I simply call your attention to this, that your affirmation is what the Germans call a *Machtspruch,* a mere conception fulminated as a dogma and based on no insight into details. Before my choice, either street seemed as natural to you as to me. Had I happened to take Oxford Street, Divinity Avenue would have figured in your philosophy as the gap in nature; and you would have so proclaimed it with the best deterministic conscience in the world. . . .

And this at last brings us within sight of our subject. We have seen what determinism means: we have seen that indeterminism is rightly described as meaning chance; and we have seen that chance, the very name of which we are urged to shrink from as from a metaphysical pestilence, means only the negative fact that no part of the world, however big, can claim to control absolutely the destinies of the whole. But although, in discussing the word "chance," I may at moments have seemed to be arguing for its real existence, I have not meant to do so yet. We have not yet ascertained whether this be a world of chance or no; at most, we have agreed that it seems so. And I now repeat what I said at the outset, that, from any strict theoretical point of view, the question is insoluble. To deepen our theoretic sense of the *difference* between a world with chances in it and a deterministic world is the most I can hope to do; and this I may now at last begin upon, after all our tedious clearing of the way.

I wish first of all to show you just what the notion that this is a deterministic world implies. The implications I call your attention to are all bound up with the fact that it is a world in which we constantly have to make what I shall, with your permission, call judgments of regret. Hardly an hour passes in which we do not wish that something might be otherwise; and happy indeed are those of us whose hearts have never echoed the wish of Omar Khayyám—

> *That we might clasp, ere closed, the book of fate,*
> *And make the writer on a fairer leaf*
> *Inscribe our names, or quite obliterate.*

> *Ah! Love, could you and I with fate conspire*
> *To mend this sorry scheme of things entire,*
> *Would we not shatter it to bits, and then*
> *Remould it nearer to the heart's desire?*

Now, it is undeniable that most of these regrets are foolish, and quite on a par in point of philosophic value with the criticisms on the universe of that friend of our infancy, the hero of the fable The Atheist and the Acorn,—

> *Fool! had that bough a pumpkin bore,*
> *Thy whimsies would have worked no more, etc.*

Even from the point of view of our own ends, we should probably make a botch of remodelling the universe. How much more then from the point of view of ends we cannot see! Wise men therefore regret as little as they can. But still some regrets are pretty obstinate and hard to stifle,—regrets for acts of wanton cruelty or treachery, for example, whether performed by others or by ourselves. Hardly any one can remain *entirely* optimistic after reading the confession of the murderer at Brockton the other day: how, to get rid of the wife whose continued existence bored him, he inveigled her into a desert spot, shot her four times, and then, as she lay on the ground and said to him, "You didn't do it on purpose, did you, dear?" replied, "No, I didn't do it on purpose," as he raised a rock and smashed her skull. Such an occurrence, with the mild sentence and self-satisfaction of the prisoner, is a field for a crop of regrets, which one need not take up in detail. We feel that, although a perfect mechanical fit to the rest of the universe, it is a bad moral fit, and that something else would really have been better in its place.

But for the deterministic philosophy the murder, the sentence, and the prisoner's optimism were all necessary from eternity; and nothing else for a moment had a ghost of a chance of being put into their place. To admit such a chance, the determinists tell us, would be to make a suicide of reason; so we must steel our hearts against the thought. And here our plot thickens, for we see the first of those difficult implications of determinism and monism which it is my purpose to make you feel. If this Brockton murder was called for by the rest of the universe, if it had to come at its preappointed hour, and if nothing else would have been consistent with the sense of the whole, what are we to think of the universe? Are we stubbornly to stick to our judgment of regret, and say, though it *couldn't* be, yet it *would* have been a better universe with something different from this Brockton murder in it? That, of course, seems the natural and spontaneous thing for us to do; and yet it is nothing short of deliberately espousing a kind of pessimism. The judgment of regret calls the murder bad. Calling a thing bad means, if it mean anything at all, that the thing ought not to be, that something else ought to be in its stead. Determinism, in denying that anything else can be in its stead, virtually defines the universe as a place in which what ought to be is impossible,—in other words, as an organism whose constitution is afflicted with an incurable taint, an irremediable flaw. The pessimism of a Schopenhauer says no more than this,—that the murder is a symptom; and that it is a vicious symptom because it belongs to a vicious whole, which can express its nature no otherwise than by bringing forth just such a symptom as that at this particular spot. Regret for the murder must transform itself, if we are determinists and wise, into a larger regret. It is absurd to regret the murder alone. Other things being what they are, *it* could not be different. What we should regret is that whole frame of things of which the murder is one member. I see no escape whatever from this pessimistic conclusion, if, being determinists, our judgment of regret is to be allowed to stand at all.

The only deterministic escape from pessimism is everywhere to abandon the judgment of regret. That this can be done, history shows to be not impossible. The devil, *quoad existentiam,*[3] may be good. That is, although he be a *principle* of evil, yet the universe, with such a principle in it, may practically be a better universe than it could have been without. On every hand in a small way, we find that a certain amount of evil is a condition by which a higher form of good is bought. There is nothing to prevent anybody from generalizing this view, and trusting that if we could but see things in the largest of all ways, even such matters as this Brockton murder would appear to be paid for by the uses that follow in their train. An optimism *quand même,*[4]

---

[3] *quoad existentiam*—as regards existence [ED.]

[4] *quand même*—all the same [ED.]

a systematic and infatuated optimism like that ridiculed by Voltaire in his Candide, is one of the possible ideal ways in which a man may train himself to look on life. Bereft of dogmatic hardness and lit up with the expression of a tender and pathetic hope, such an optimism has been the grace of some of the most religious characters that ever lived.

> *Throb thine with Nature's throbbing breast,*
> *And all is clear from east to west.*

Even cruelty and treachery may be among the absolutely blessed fruits of time, and to quarrel with any of their details may be blasphemy. The only real blasphemy, in short, may be that pessimistic temper of the soul which lets it give way to such things as regrets, remorse, and grief.

Thus, our deterministic pessimism may become a deterministic optimism at the price of extinguishing our judgments of regret.

But does not this immediately bring us into a curious logical predicament? Our determinism leads us to call our judgments of regret wrong, because they are pessimistic in implying that what is impossible yet ought to be. But how then about the judgments of regret themselves? If they are wrong, other judgments, judgments of approval presumably, ought to be in their place. But as they are necessitated, nothing else *can* be in their place; and the universe is just what it was before,—namely, a place in which what ought to be appears impossible. We have got one foot out of the pessimistic bog, but the other one sinks all the deeper. We have rescued our actions from the bonds of evil, but our judgments are now held fast. When murders and treacheries cease to be sins, regrets are theoretic absurdities and errors. The theoretic and the active life thus play a kind of seesaw with each other on the ground of evil. The rise of either sends the other down. Murder and treachery cannot be good without regret being bad: regret cannot be good without treachery and murder being bad. Both, however, are supposed to have been foredoomed: so something must be fatally unreasonable, absurd, and wrong in the world. It must be a place of which either sin or error forms a necessary part.

But this brings us right back, to the question of indeterminism. . . . For the only consistent way of representing a pluralism and a world whose parts may affect one another through their conduct being either good or bad is the indeterministic way. What interest, zest, or excitement can there be in achieving the right way, unless we are enabled to feel that the wrong way is also a possible and a natural way—nay, more, a menacing and an imminent way? And what sense can there be in condemning ourselves for taking the wrong way, unless we need have done nothing of the sort, unless the right way was open to us as well? I cannot understand the belief that an act is bad, without regret at its happening. I cannot understand regret without the admission of real, genuine possibilities in the world. Only *then* is it other than a mockery to feel, after we have failed to do our best, that an irreparable opportunity is gone from the universe, the loss of which it must forever after mourn. The indeterminism I defend, the free-will theory of popular sense based on the judgment of regret, represents that world as vulnerable, and liable to be injured by certain of its parts if they act wrong. And it represents their acting wrong as a matter of possibility or accident, neither inevitable nor yet to be infallibly warded off. In all this, it is a theory devoid either of transparency or of stability. It gives us a pluralistic, restless universe, in which no single point of view can ever take in the whole scene; and to a mind possessed of the love of unity at any cost, it will, no doubt, remain forever inacceptable. . . . The great point is that the possibilities are really *here.* Whether it be we who solve them or he working through us, at those soul-trying moments when fate's scales seem to quiver, and good snatches the victory from evil or shrinks nerveless from the fight, is of small account, so long as we admit that the issue is decided nowhere else than *here* and *now. That* is what gives the palpitating reality to our moral life and makes it tingle, as Mr. Mallock says, with so strange and elaborate an excitement. This reality, this excitement, are what the determinists, hard and soft alike, suppress by their denial that *anything* is decided here and now, and their dogma that all things were foredoomed and settled long ago.

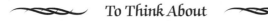

To Think About

1. Have you ever chosen the weaker of two desires? How could you prove it?

2. Can you think of any act which was not completely determined by past events?

3. The soft determinist says that "I am free insofar as my actions aren't constrained, even though they are caused by past events." Do you agree that you are free under such circumstances?

4. Are there any indetermined events in nature?

5. "This is one of man's oldest riddles. How can the independence of human volition be harmonized with the fact that we are integral parts of a universe which is subject to the rigid order of Nature's laws?"   ***Sir Arthur Eddington***

6. "There is no doubt that Sartre finds it impossible to make a distinction between freedom and free acts. The free man is not distinguished by his beliefs, but by the quality of his actions."   ***Norman H. Greene***

7. "I don't live in the past. The past lives in me."   ***Tom Osborne***

8. "Men are freest when they are most unconscious of freedom."
   D. H. Lawrence

9. "All theory is against freedom of the will; all experience for it."
   James Boswell quoting Samuel Johnson in his biography

10. "One's ability to move his hand at will is more directly and certainly known than are Newton's laws. If these laws deny one's ability to move his hand at will, the preferable conclusion is that Newton's laws require modification."
    Arthur Compton

11. "The hypothesis that man is not free is essential to the application of scientific method to the study of human behavior."   ***B. F. Skinner***

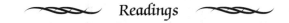 *Readings*

BOK, HILARY. *Freedom and Responsibility.* Princeton, NJ: Princeton University Press, 1998.

KANE, ROBERT. *The Significance of Free Will.* New York: Oxford University Press, 1996.

———, ed. *The Oxford Handbook of Free Will.* Oxford: Oxford University Press, 2002.

LEHRER, KEITH. "Can We Know That We Have Free Will by Introspection?" *Journal of Philosophy* 56 (1960): 145–57. Lehrer argues that we can know that we have free will by introspection.

MACHAN, TIBOR R. *Initiative: Human Agency and Society.* Stanford, CA: Hoover Institution Press, 2000.

TOMBERLIN, JAMES E., ed. *Action and Freedom, 2000.* Boston: Blackwell, 2000.

15
Ethics Are Relative

Ruth Benedict (1887–1948) was one of the best-known U.S. anthropologists. Her Patterns of Cultures *(1935) is considered a classic.*

Benedict claims that *morality* is just a term for socially approved customs (mores). It is not unusual for one society to approve of an act that is held to be immoral by another. Hence, morality is culturally relative. Homosexuality, for example, is considered abnormal in our society but was praised in some ancient ones. The accumulation of property is a desired goal for some societies but rejected as a value by others.

To Study

1. Why does Benedict believe that it is more valuable for anthropology to study the customs of primitive cultures than those of advanced cultures?
2. What does she illustrate by the phenomena of trance, homosexuality, and catalepsy?
3. On what basis is normality defined? Who are the deviants?
4. With what phrase is "morally good" synonymous?
5. What type of society amasses property?

Modern social anthropology has become more and more a study of the varieties and common elements of cultural environment and the consequences of these in human behavior. For such a study of diverse social orders primitive peoples fortunately provide

From Ruth Benedict, "Anthropology and the Abnormal," *The Journal of General Psychology* 10 (1934): 59–82. Reprinted with the permission of the Helen Dwight Reid Educational Foundation. Published by Heldref Publications, 1319 Eighteenth St. N.W., Washington, DC 20036-1802. Copyright © 1934.

a laboratory not yet entirely vitiated by the spread of a standardized world-wide civilization. Dyaks and Hopis, Fijians and Yakuts are significant for psychological and sociological study because only among these simpler peoples has there been sufficient isolation to give opportunity for the development of localized social forms. In the higher cultures the standardization of custom and belief over a couple of continents has given a false sense of the inevitability of the particular forms that have gained currency, and we need to turn to a wider survey in order to check the conclusions we hastily base upon this near-universality of familiar customs. Most of the simpler cultures did not gain the wide currency of the one which, out of our experience, we identify with human nature, but this was for various historical reasons, and certainly not for any that gives us as its carriers a monopoly of social good or of social sanity. Modern civilization, from this point of view, becomes not a necessary pinnacle of human achievement but one entry in a long series of possible adjustments.

These adjustments, whether they are in mannerisms like the ways of showing anger, or joy, or grief in any society, or in major human drives like those of sex, prove to be far more variable than experience in any one culture would suggest. In certain fields, such as that of religion or of formal marriage arrangements, these wide limits of variability are well known and can be fairly described. In others it is not yet possible to give a generalized account, but that does not absolve us of the task of indicating the significance of the work that has been done and of the problems that have arisen.

One of these problems relates to the customary modern normal-abnormal categories and our conclusions regarding them. In how far are such categories culturally determined, or in how far can we with assurance regard them as absolute? In how far can we regard inability to function socially as diagnostic of abnormality, or in how far is it necessary to regard this as a function of the culture?

As a matter of fact, one of the most striking facts that emerge from a study of widely varying cultures is the ease with which our abnormals function in other cultures. It does not matter what kind of "abnormality" we choose for illustration, those which indicate extreme instability, or those which are more in the nature of character traits like sadism or delusions of grandeur or of persecution, there are well-described cultures in which these abnormals function at ease and with honor, and apparently without danger or difficulty to the society.

The most notorious of these is trance and catalepsy. Even a very mild mystic is aberrant in our culture. But most peoples have regarded even extreme psychic manifestations not only as normal and desirable, but even as characteristic of highly valued and gifted individuals. This was true even in our own cultural background in that period when Catholicism made the ecstatic experience the mark of sainthood. It is hard for us, born and brought up in a culture that makes no use of the experience, to realize how important a role it may play and how many individuals are capable of it, once it has been given an honorable place in any society. . . .

Cataleptic and trance phenomena are, of course, only one illustration of the fact that those whom we regard as abnormals may function adequately in other cultures. Many of our culturally discarded traits are selected for elaboration in different societies. Homosexuality is an excellent example, for in this case our attention is not constantly diverted, as in the consideration of trance, to the interruption of routine activity which it implies. Homosexuality poses the problem very simply. A tendency toward this trait in our culture exposes an individual to all the conflicts to which all aberrants are always exposed, and we tend to identify the consequences of this conflict with homosexuality. But these consequences are obviously local and cultural. Homosexuals in many societies are not incompetent, but they may be if the culture asks adjustments of them that would strain any man's vitality. Wherever homosexuality has been given an honorable place in any society, those to whom it is congenital have filled adequately the honorable roles society assigns to them. Plato's *Republic* is, of course, the most convincing statement of such a reading of homosexuality. It is presented as one of the major means to the good life, and it was generally so regarded in Greece at that time.

The cultural attitude toward homosexuals has not always been on such a high ethical plane, but it has been very varied. Among many American Indian tribes there exists the institution of the berdache, as the French called them. These men-women were men who at puberty or thereafter took the dress and the occupations of women. Sometimes they married other men and lived with them. Sometimes they were men with no inversion, persons of weak sexual endowment who chose this role to avoid the jeers of the women. The berdaches were never regarded as of first-rate supernatural power, as similar men-women were in Siberia, but rather as leaders in women's occupations, good healers in certain diseases, or, among certain tribes, as the genial organizers of social affairs. In any case, they were socially placed. They were not left exposed to the conflicts that visit the deviant who is excluded from participation in the recognized patterns of his society.

The most spectacular illustrations of the extent to which normality may be culturally defined are those cultures where an abnormality of our culture is the cornerstone of their social structure. It is not possible to do justice to these possibilities in a short discussion. A recent study of an island of northwest Melanesia by Fortune describes a society built upon traits which we regard as beyond the border of paranoia. In this tribe the exogamic groups look upon each other as prime manipulators of black magic, so that one marries always into an enemy group which remains for life one's deadly and unappeasable foes. They look upon a good garden crop as a confession of theft, for everyone is engaged in making magic to induce into his garden the productiveness of his neighbors'; therefore no secrecy in the island is so rigidly insisted upon as the secrecy of a man's harvesting of his yams. Their polite phrase at the acceptance of a gift is, "And if you now poison me, how shall I repay you this present?" Their preoccupation with poisoning is constant; no woman ever leaves her cooking pot for a moment untended. Even the great affinal economic exchanges that are characteristic of this Melanesian culture area are quite altered in Dobu since they are incompatible with this fear and distrust that pervades the culture. They go farther and people the whole world outside their own quarters with such malignant spirits that all-night feasts and ceremonials simply do not occur here. They have even rigorous religiously enforced customs that forbid the sharing of seed even in one family group. Anyone else's food is deadly poison to you, so that communality of stores is out of the question. For some months before harvest the whole society is on the verge of starvation, but if one falls to the temptation and eats up one's seed yams, one is an outcast and a beachcomber for life. There is no coming back. It involves, as a matter of course, divorce and the breaking of all social ties.

Now in this society where no one may work with another and no one may share with another, Fortune describes the individual who was regarded by all his fellows as crazy. He was not one of those who periodically ran amok and, beside himself and frothing at the mouth, fell with a knife upon anyone he could reach. Such behavior they did not regard as putting anyone outside the pale. They did not even put the individuals who were known to be liable to these attacks under any kind of control. They merely fled when they saw the attack coming on and kept out of the way. "He would be all right tomorrow." But there was one man of sunny, kindly disposition who liked work and liked to be helpful. The compulsion was too strong for him to repress it in favor of the opposite tendencies of his culture. Men and women never spoke of him without laughing; he was silly and simple and definitely crazy. Nevertheless, to the ethnologist used to a culture that has, in Christianity, made his type the model of all virtue, he seemed a pleasant fellow. . . .

. . . Among the Kwakiutl it did not matter whether a relative had died in bed of disease, or by the hand of any enemy, in either case death was an affront to be wiped out by the death of another person. The fact that one had been caused to mourn was proof that one had been put upon. A chief's sister and her daughter had gone up to Victoria, and either because they drank bad whiskey or because their boat capsized they never came back. The chief called together his warriors. "Now I ask you, tribes, who shall wail? Shall I do it or shall another?" The spokesman answered, of course, "Not you, Chief. Let some other of the tribes." Immediately they set up the war pole to announce their intention of wiping out the injury, and gathered a war party. They set out, and found seven men and two children asleep and killed them. "Then they felt good when they arrived at Sebaa in the evening."

The point which is of interest to us is that in our society those who on that occasion would feel good when they arrived at Sebaa that evening would be the definitely abnormal. There would be some, even in our society, but it is not a recognized and approved mood under the circumstances. On the Northwest Coast those are favored and fortunate to whom that mood under those circumstances is congenial, and those to whom it is repugnant are unlucky. This latter minority can register in their own culture only by doing violence to their congenial responses and acquiring others that are difficult for them. The person, for instance, who, like a Plains Indian whose wife has been taken from him, is too proud to fight, can deal with the Northwest Coast civilization only by ignoring its strongest bents. If he cannot achieve it, he is the deviant in that culture, their instance of abnormality.

This head-hunting that takes place on the Northwest Coast after a death is no matter of blood revenge or of organized vengeance. There is no effort to tie up the subsequent killing with any responsibility on the part of the victim for the death of the person who is being mourned. A chief whose son has died goes visiting wherever his fancy dictates, and he says to his host, "My prince has died today, and you go with him." Then he kills him. In this, according to their interpretation, he acts nobly because he has not been downed. He has thrust back in return. The whole procedure is meaningless without the fundamental paranoid reading of bereavement. Death, like all the other untoward accidents of existence, confounds man's pride and can only be handled in the category of insults.

Behavior honored upon the Northwest Coast is one which is recognized as abnormal in our civilization, and yet it is sufficiently close to the attitudes of our own culture to be intelligible to us and to have a definite vocabulary with which we may discuss it. The megalomaniac paranoid trend is a definite danger in our society. It is encouraged by some of our major preoccupations, and it confronts us with a choice of two possible attitudes. One is to brand it as abnormal and reprehensible, and is the attitude we have chosen in our civilization. The other is to make it an essential attribute of ideal man, and this is the solution in the culture of the Northwest Coast.

These illustrations, which it has been possible to indicate only in the briefest manner, force upon us the fact that normality is culturally defined. An adult shaped to the drives and standards of either of these cultures, if he were transported into our civilization, would fall into our categories of abnormality. He would be faced with the psychic dilemmas of the socially unavailable. In his own culture, however, he is the pillar of society, the end result of socially inculcated mores, and the problem of personal instability in his case simply does not arise.

No one civilization can possibly utilize in its mores the whole potential range of human behavior. Just as there are great numbers of possible phonetic articulations, and the possibility of language depends on a selection and standardization of a few of these in order that speech communication may be possible at all, so the possibility of organized behavior of every sort, from the fashions of local dress and houses to the dicta of a people's ethics and religion, depends upon a similar selection among the possible behavior traits. In the field of recognized economic obligations or sex tabus this selection is as nonrational and subconscious a process as it is in the field of phonetics. It is a process which goes on in the group for long periods of time and is historically conditioned by innumerable accidents of isolation or of contact of peoples. In any comprehensive study of psychology, the selection that different cultures have made in the course of history within the great circumference of potential behavior is of great significance.

Every society, beginning with some slight inclination in one direction or another, carries its preference farther and farther, integrating itself more and more completely upon its chosen basis, and discarding those types of behavior that are uncongenial. Most of those organizations of personality that seem to us most uncontrovertibly abnormal have been used by different civilizations in the very foundations of their institutional life. Conversely the most valued traits of normal individuals have been looked on in differently organized cultures as aberrant. Normality, in short, within a very wide range, is culturally defined. It is primarily a term for the socially elaborated segment of human behavior in any culture; and abnormality, a term for the segment that that particular civilization does not use. The very eyes with which we see the problem are conditioned by the long traditional habits of our own society.

It is a point that has been made more often in relation to ethics than in relation to psychiatry. We do not any longer make the mistake of deriving the morality of our locality and decade directly from the inevitable constitution of human nature. We do not elevate it to the dignity of a first principle. We recognize that morality differs in every society, and is a convenient term for socially approved habits. Mankind has always preferred to say, "It is morally good," rather than "It is habitual," and the fact of this preference is matter enough for a critical science of ethics. But historically the two phrases are synonymous.

The concept of the normal is properly a variant of the concept of the good. It is that which society has approved. A normal action is one which falls well within the limits of expected behavior for a particular society. Its variability among different peoples is essentially a function of the variability of the behavior patterns that different societies have created for themselves, and can never be wholly divorced from a consideration of culturally institutionalized types of behavior.

Each culture is a more or less elaborate working-out of the potentialities of the segment it has chosen. In so far as a civilization is well integrated and consistent within itself, it will tend to carry farther and farther, accorded to its nature, its initial impulse toward a particular type of action, and from the point of view of any other culture those elaborations will include more and more extreme and aberrant traits.

Each of these traits, in proportion as it reinforces the chosen behavior patterns of that culture, is for that culture normal. Those individuals to whom it is congenial either congenitally, or as the result of childhood sets, are accorded prestige in that culture, and are not visited with the social contempt or disapproval which their traits would call down upon them in a society that was differently organized. On the other hand, those individuals whose characteristics are not congenial to the selected type of human behavior in that community are the deviants, no matter how valued their personality traits may be in a contrasted civilization.

The Dobuan who is not easily susceptible to fear of treachery, who enjoys work and likes to be helpful, is their neurotic and regarded as silly. On the Northwest Coast the person who finds it difficult to read life in terms of an insult contest will be the person upon whom fall all the difficulties of the culturally unprovided for. The person who does not find it easy to humiliate a neighbor, nor to see humiliation in his own experience, who is genial and loving, may, of course, find some unstandardized way of achieving satisfactions in his society, but not in the major patterned responses that his culture requires of him. If he is born to play an important role in a family with many hereditary privileges, he can succeed only by doing violence to his whole personality. If he does not succeed, he has betrayed his culture; that is, he is abnormal.

I have spoken of individuals as having sets toward certain types of behavior, and of these sets as running sometimes counter to the types of behavior which are institutionalized in the culture to which they belong. From all that we know of contrasting cultures it seems clear that differences of temperament occur in every society. The matter has never been made the subject of investigation, but from the available material it would appear that these temperament types are very likely of universal recurrence. That is, there is an ascertainable range of human behavior that is found wherever a sufficiently large series of individuals is observed. But the proportion in which behavior types stand to one another in different societies is not universal. The vast majority of the individuals in any group are shaped to the fashion of that culture. In other words, most individuals are plastic to the moulding force of the society into which they are born. In a society that values trance, as in India, they will have supernormal experience. In a society that institutionalizes homosexuality, they will be homosexual. In a society that sets the gathering of possessions as the chief human objective, they will amass property. The deviants, whatever the type of behavior the culture has institutionalized, will remain few in number, and there seems no more difficulty in moulding that vast malleable majority to the "normality" of what we consider an aberrant trait, such as delusions of reference, than to the normality of such accepted behavior patterns as acquisitiveness. The small proportion of the number of the deviants in any culture is not a function of the sure instinct with which that society has built itself upon the fundamental sanities, but of the universal fact that, happily, the majority of mankind quite readily take any shape that is presented to them. . . .

To Think About

1. "Ultimately, these differences were rooted in the contrasting political cultures of Germany and Italy. Steinberg rejects the simplistic image of Italian saints confounding the German satan. Instead, he develops a fascinating paradox. All the vices of Italian political life—disorder, disobedience, nonchalance, corruption, slyness, intrigue—favoured those who wanted the State not to act. The 'matrix of secondary vice' in Italian public life in this particular instance made possible the 'primary virtue' of saving human life. In contrast, German political culture was permeated by 'secondary virtues'—efficiency, duty, incorruptibility, and obedience—which made truly virtuous and humane behaviour literally 'unthinkable' to men who were 'in no ordinary sense criminals' but who none the less committed mass murder."

    Jonathan Steinberg in *All or Nothing,* writing of the fact that the Germans nearly always brutally treated Jews, while the Italians often protected them.

2. "Modern morality consists in accepting the standard of one's age." *Oscar Wilde*

3. Is relativism self-contradictory? It claims to have the absolute truth.

4. "Huckleberry Finn is in a quandary whether to help the runaway slave to freedom or to take action that will send the slave to his owner. He hesitates and starts to think. He likes Jim, the slave. He tears up his note to the owner and says, 'All right . . . I'll go to hell.' Later we hear him saying, 'It don't make no difference whether you do right or wrong, a person's conscience ain't got no sense, and just goes for him *anyway.* . . . It takes up more room than all the rest of a person's insides, and yet ain't no good nohow.' "   ***Ruth Bennett***

5. "There is nothing that the relativist, qua relativist, can say either for or against tolerance from a moral point of view. The moment he does this, he ceases to be an observer of morality and becomes a user of a moral system. . . . There is no such thing as a moral judgment made from a morally neutral or 'extramoral' position."   ***Geoffrey Harrison***

6. "The most barbarous and the most fantastic rites and the strangest myths translate some human need, some aspect of life, either individual or dual. . . . In reality, then, there are no religions which are false. All are true in their own fashion; all answer, though in different ways, to the conditions of human existence."   *Émile Durkheim*

7. "How often have we not heard people say, 'Unless values are shown to be objective, it will be *right* for everybody to do whatever he *thinks* right'? I hope that by this time I have made clear to you the confusions which lie behind this argument. The first confusion is that of supposing that there is anything to be understood by 'showing values to be objective' (or for that matter 'subjective'). The second is that of thinking that a view, of whatever sort, about the logical nature or status or meaning or use of moral concepts, necessarily commits us to a moral position about what *is* right or wrong; and in particular, to a moral position as patently absurd and pernicious as relativism is."   *Peter Hare*

16
Ethics Are Not Relative

W. T. Stace (1886–1967), an Anglo-American empirical philosopher, was born in London and studied at Trinity College, Dublin. From 1910 to 1932 he served in the British civil service in Ceylon. While in Ceylon, he published A Critical History of Greek Philosophy *(1920) and* The Philosophy of Hegel *(1924). In 1932, he resigned from the civil service and accepted a teaching position at Princeton University, where he remained until his retirement in 1955. His other works include* The Theory of Knowledge and Existence *(1932),* The Concept of Morals *(1937),* Time and Eternity *(1952), and* Mysticism and Philosophy *(1960).*

In contrast to the view of the cultural relativist, Stace argues that one cannot conclude that all moral actions are relative. He argues that if we believe that morals are relative, then we cannot judge which is best, we cannot argue that there is moral progress, and we cannot even define the limits of given groups or societies between which there are these variable morals.

To Study

1. How does Stace characterize the position of the absolutist?
2. How does Stace define ethical relativity? Is it a platitude?
3. Summarize his explanation of the difference between the relativist and the absolutist.
4. What is the argument that uses multiple standards for ethical relativity? What is Stace's refutation?
5. What is the argument in favor of ethical relativity based on the lack of a universally binding code? How does Stace refute it?

6. What is the argument against ethical relativity based on comparing different ideals? What is the argument based on the notion of moral progress?
7. What is the ultimate consequence of the position of the ethical relativist?

There is an opinion widely current nowadays in philosophical circles which passes under the name of "ethical relativity." Exactly what this phrase means or implies is certainly far from clear. But unquestionably it stands as a label for the opinions of a group of ethical philosophers whose position is roughly on the extreme left wing among the moral theorizers of the day. And perhaps one may best understand it by placing it in contrast with the opposite kind of extreme view against which, undoubtedly, it has arisen as a protest. For among moral philosophers one may clearly distinguish a left and a right wing. Those of the left wing are the ethical relativists. They are the revolutionaries, the clever young men, the up to date. Those of the right wing we may call the ethical absolutists. They are the conservatives and the old-fashioned.

ETHICAL ABSOLUTISM

According to the absolutists there is but one eternally true and valid moral code. This moral code applies with rigid impartiality to all men. What is a duty for me must likewise be a duty for you. And this will be true whether you are an Englishman, a Chinaman, or a Hottentot. If cannibalism is an abomination in England or America, it is an abomination in central Africa, notwithstanding that the African may think otherwise. The fact that he sees nothing wrong in his cannibal practices does not make them for him morally right. They are as much contrary to morality for him as they are for us. The only difference is that he is an ignorant savage who does not know this. There is not one law for one man or race of men, another for another. There is not one moral standard for Europeans, another for Indians, another for Chinese. There is but one law, one standard, one morality, for all men. And this standard, this law, is absolute and unvarying.

Moreover, as the one moral law extends its dominion over all the corners of the earth, so too it is not limited in its application by any considerations of time or period. That which is right now was right in the centuries of Greece and Rome, nay, in the very ages of the cave man. That which is evil now was evil then. If slavery is morally wicked today, it was morally wicked among the ancient Athenians, notwithstanding that their greatest men accepted it as a necessary condition of human society. Their opinion did not make slavery a moral good for them. It only showed that they were, in spite of their otherwise noble conceptions, ignorant of what is truly right and good in this matter.

The ethical absolutist recognizes as a fact that moral customs and moral ideas differ from country to country and from age to age. This indeed seems manifest and not to be disrupted. We think slavery morally wrong, the Greeks thought it morally unobjectionable. The inhabitants of New Guinea certainly have very different moral ideas from ours. But the fact that the Greeks or the inhabitants of New Guinea think something right does not make it right, even for them. Nor does the fact that we think the same things wrong make them wrong. They are *in themselves* either right or wrong. What we have to do is to discover which they are. What anyone thinks makes no difference. It is here just as it is in matters of physical science. We believe the earth to be a globe. Our ancestors may have thought it flat. This does not show that it *was* flat, and is *now* a globe. What it shows is that men having in other ages been ignorant about the shape of the earth have now learned the truth. So if the Greeks thought slavery morally legitimate, this does not indicate that it was for them and in that age morally legitimate, but rather that they were ignorant of the truth of the matter.

The ethical absolutist is not indeed committed to the opinion that his own, or our own, moral code is the true one. Theoretically at least he might hold that slavery is ethically justifiable, that the Greeks knew better than we do about this, that ignorance of the true morality lies with us and not with them. All that he is actually committed to is the opinion that, whatever the true moral code may be, it is always the same for all men in all ages. His view is not at all inconsistent with the belief that humanity has still much to learn in moral matters. If anyone were to assert that in five hundred years the moral conceptions of the present day will appear as barbarous to the people of that age as the moral conceptions of the middle ages appear to us now, he need not deny it. If anyone were to assert that the ethics of Christianity are by no means final, and will be superseded in future ages by vastly nobler moral ideals, he need not deny this either. For it is of the essence of his creed to believe that morality is in some sense objective, not man-made, not produced by human opinion; that its principles are real truths about which men have to learn— just as they have to learn about the shape of the world—about which they may have been ignorant in the past, and about which therefore they may well be ignorant now.

Thus although absolutism is conservative in the sense that it is regarded by the more daring spirits as an out of date opinion, it is not necessarily conservative in the sense of being committed to the blind support of existing moral ideas and institutions. If ethical absolutists are sometimes conservative in this sense too, that is their personal affair. Such conservatism is accidental, not essential to the absolutist's creed. There is no logical reason, in the nature of the case, why an absolutist should not be a communist, an anarchist, a surrealist, or an upholder of free love. The fact that he is usually none of these things may be accounted for in various ways. But it has nothing to do with the sheer logic of his ethical position. The sole opinion to which he is committed is that whatever is morally right (or wrong)—be it free love or monogamy or slavery or cannibalism or vegetarianism—is morally right (or wrong) for all men at all times.

Usually the absolutist goes further than this. He often maintains, not merely that the moral law is the same for all the men on this planet—which is, after all, a tiny speck in space—but that in some way or in some sense it has application everywhere in the universe. He may express himself by saying that it applies to all "rational beings"—which would apparently include angels and the men on Mars (if they are rational). He is apt to think that the moral law is a part of the fundamental structure of the universe. But with this aspect of absolutism we need not, at the moment, concern ourselves. At present we may think of it as being simply the opinion that there is a single moral standard for all human beings. . . .

ETHICAL RELATIVISM

We can now turn to the consideration of ethical relativity. . . . The revolt of the relativists against absolutism is, I believe, part and parcel of the general revolutionary tendency of our times. In particular it is a result of the decay of belief in the dogmas of orthodox religion. Belief in absolutism was supported, as we have seen, by belief in Christian monotheism. And now that, in an age of widespread religious scepticism, that support is withdrawn, absolutism tends to collapse. Revolutionary movements are as a rule, at any rate in their first onset, purely negative. They attack and destroy. And ethical relativity is, in its essence, a purely negative creed. It is simply a denial of ethical absolutism. That is why the best way of explaining it is to begin by explaining ethical absolutism. If we understand that what the latter asserts the former denies, then we understand ethical relativity.

Any ethical position which denies that there is a single moral standard which is equally applicable to all men at all times may fairly be called a species of ethical relativity. There is not, the relativist asserts, merely one moral law, one code, one standard. There are many moral laws, codes, standards. What morality ordains in one place or age may be quite different from what morality ordains in another place or age. The moral code of Chinamen is quite different from that of Europeans, that of African savages quite different from both. Any morality, therefore, is relative to the age, the place, and the circumstances in which it is found. It is in no sense absolute.

This does not mean merely—as one might at first sight be inclined to suppose—that the very same kind of action which is *thought* right in one country and period may be *thought* wrong in another. This would be a mere platitude, the truth of which everyone would have to admit. Even the absolutist would admit this—would even wish to emphasize it—since he is well aware that different peoples have different sets of moral ideas, and his whole point is that some of these sets of ideas are false. What the relativist means to assert is, not this platitude, but that the very same kind of action which *is* right in one country and period may *be* wrong in another. And this, far from being a platitude, is a very startling assertion.

It is very important to grasp thoroughly the difference between the two ideas. For there is reason to think that many minds tend to find ethical relativity attractive because they fail to keep them clearly apart. It is so very obvious that moral ideas differ from country to country and from age to age. And it is so very easy, if you are mentally lazy, to suppose that to say this means the same as to say that no universal moral standard exists—or in other words that it implies ethical relativity. We fail to see that the word "standard" is used in two different senses. It is perfectly true that, in one sense, there are many variable moral standards. We speak of judging a man by the standard of his time. And this implies that different times have different standards. And this, of course, is quite true. But when the word "standard" is used in this sense it means simply the set of moral ideas current during the period in question. It means what people *think* right, whether as a matter of fact *is* right or not. On the other hand when the absolutist asserts that there exists a single universal moral "standard," he is not using the word in this sense at all. He means by "standard" what *is* right as distinct from what people merely think right. His point is that although what people think right varies in different countries and periods, yet what actually is right is everywhere and always the same. And it follows that when the ethical relativist disputes the position of the absolutist and denies that any universal moral standard exists he too means by "standard" what actually is right. But it is exceedingly easy, if we are not careful, to slip loosely from using the word in the first sense to using it in the second sense and to suppose that the variability of moral beliefs is the same thing as the variability of what really is moral. And unless we keep the two senses of the word "standard" distinct, we are likely to think the creed of ethical relativity much more plausible than it actually is.

The genuine relativist, then, does not merely mean that Chinamen may think right what Frenchmen think wrong. He means that what is wrong for the Frenchman may *be* right for the Chinaman. And if one enquires how, in those circumstances, one is to know what actually is right in China or in France, the answer comes quite glibly. What is right in China is the same as what people think right in China; and what is right in France is the same as what people think right in France. So that, if you want to know what is moral in any particular country or age all you have to do is to ascertain what are the moral ideas current in that age or country. Those ideas are, *for that age or country,* right. Thus what is morally right is identified with what is thought to be morally right, and the distinction which we made above between these two is simply denied. To put the same thing in another way, it is denied that there can be or ought to be any distinction between the two senses of the word "standard." There is only one kind of standard of right and wrong, namely, the moral ideas current in any particular age or country.

Moral right *means* what people think morally right. It has no other meaning. What Frenchmen think right is, therefore, right *for Frenchmen.* And evidently one must conclude—though I am not aware that relativists are anxious to draw one's attention to such unsavoury but yet absolutely necessary conclusions from their creed—that cannibalism is right for people who believe in it, that human sacrifice is right for those races which practice it, and that burning widows alive was right for Hindus until the British stepped in and compelled the Hindus to behave immorally by allowing their widows to remain alive.

When it is said that, according to the ethical relativist, what is thought right in any social group is right for that group, one must be careful not to misinterpret this. The relativist does not, of course, mean that there actually is an objective moral standard in France and a different objective standard in England, and that French and British opinions respectively give us correct information about these different standards. His point is rather that there are no objectively true moral standards at all. There is no single universal objective standard. Nor are there a variety of local objective standards. All standards are subjective. People's subjective feelings about morality are the only standards which exist.

To sum up. The ethical relativist consistently denies, it would seem, whatever the ethical absolutist asserts. For the absolutist there is a single universal moral standard. For the relativist there is no such standard. There are only local, ephemeral, and variable standards. For the absolutist there are two senses of the word "standard." Standards in the sense of sets of current moral ideas are relative and changeable. But the standard in the sense of what is actually morally right is absolute and unchanging. For the relativist no such distinction can be made. There is only one meaning of the word standard, namely, that which refers to local and variable sets of moral ideas.

Or if it is insisted that the word must be allowed two meanings, then the relativist will say that there is at any rate no actual example of a standard in the absolute sense, and that the word as thus used is an empty name to which nothing in reality corresponds; so that the distinction between the two meanings becomes empty and useless. Finally—though this is merely saying the same thing in another way—the absolutist makes a distinction between what actually is right and what is thought right. The relativist rejects this distinction and identifies what is moral with what is thought moral by certain human beings or groups of human beings. . . .

Arguments in Favour of Ethical Relativity.   . . . The first [argument] is that which relies upon the actual varieties of moral "standards" found in the world. It was easy enough to believe in a single absolute morality in older times when there was no anthropology, when all humanity was divided clearly into two groups, Christian peoples and the "heathen." . . . Greater knowledge has brought greater tolerance. We can no longer exalt our own morality as alone true, while dismissing all other moralities as false or inferior. The investigations of anthropologists have shown that there exist side by side in the world a bewildering variety of moral codes. On this topic endless volumes have been written, masses of evidence piled up. Anthropologists have ransacked the Melanesian Islands, the jungles of New Guinea, the steppes of Siberia, the deserts of Australia, the forests of central Africa, and have brought back with them countless examples of weird, extravagant, and fantastic "moral" customs with which to confound us. We learn that all kinds of horrible practices are, in this, that, or the other place, regarded as essential to virtue. We find that there is nothing, or next to nothing, which has always and everywhere been regarded as morally good by all men. Where then is our universal morality? Can we, in face of all this evidence, deny that it is nothing but an empty dream?

This argument, taken by itself, is a very weak one. It relies upon a single set of facts—the variable moral customs of the world. But this variability of moral ideas is admitted by both parties to the dispute, and is capable of ready explanation upon the hypothesis of either party. The relativist says that the facts are to be explained by the non-existence of any absolute moral standard. The absolutist says that they are to be explained by human ignorance of what the absolute moral standard is. And he can truly point out that men have differed widely in their opinions about all manners of topics including the subject-matters of the physical sciences—just as much as they differ about morals. And if the various different opinions which men have held about the shape of the earth do not prove that it has no one real shape, neither do the various opinions which they have held about morality prove that there is no one true morality.

Thus the facts can be explained equally plausibly on either hypothesis. There is nothing in the facts themselves which compels us to prefer the relativistic hypothesis to that of the absolutist. And therefore the argument fails to prove the relativist conclusion. If that conclusion is to be established, it must be by means of other considerations.

This is the essential point. But I will add some supplementary remarks. The work of the anthropologists, upon which ethical relativists seem to rely so heavily, has as a matter of fact added absolutely nothing *in principle* to what has always been known about the variability of moral ideas. Educated people have known all along that the Greeks tolerated sodomy, which in modern times has been regarded in some countries as an abominable crime; that the Hindus thought it a sacred duty to burn their widows; that trickery, now thought despicable, was once believed to be a virtue; that terrible torture was thought by our own ancestors only a few centuries ago to be a justifiable weapon of justice; that it was only yesterday that western peoples came to believe that slavery is immoral. Even the ancients knew very well that moral customs and ideas vary—witness the writings of Herodotus. Thus the principle of the variability of moral ideas was well understood long before modern anthropology was ever heard of. Anthropology has added nothing to the knowledge of this principle except a mass of new and extreme examples of it drawn from very remote sources. But to multiply examples of a principle already well known and universally admitted adds nothing to the argument which is built upon that principle. The discoveries of the anthropologists have no doubt been of the highest importance in their own sphere. But in my considered opinion they have thrown no new light upon the special problems of the moral philosopher.

Although the multiplication of examples has no logical bearing on the argument, it does have an immense *psychological* effect upon people's minds. These masses of anthropological learning are impressive. They are propounded in the sacred name of "science." If they are quoted in support of ethical relativity—as they often are—people *think* that they must prove something important. They bewilder and over-awe the simple-minded, batter down their resistance, make them ready to receive humbly the doctrine of ethical relativity from those who have acquired a reputation by their immense learning and their claims to be "scientific." Perhaps this is why so much ado is made by ethical relativists regarding the anthropological evidence. But we must refuse to be impressed. We must discount all this mass of evidence about the extraordinary moral customs of remote peoples. Once we have admitted—as everyone who is instructed must have admitted these last two thousand years without any anthropology at all—the principle that moral ideas vary, all this new evidence adds nothing to the argument. And the argument itself proves nothing for the reasons already given. . . .

[Another] argument in favour of ethical relativity . . . consists in alleging that no one has ever been able to discover upon what foundation an absolute morality could rest, or from what source a universally binding moral code could derive its authority.

If, for example, it is an absolute and unalterable moral rule that all men ought to be unselfish, from whence does this *command* issue? For a command it certainly is, phrase it how you please. There is no difference in meaning between the sentence "You ought to be unselfish" and the sentence "Be unselfish." Now a command implies a commander. An obligation implies some authority which obliges. Who is this commander, what this authority? Thus the vastly difficult question is raised of *the basis of moral obligation.* Now the argument of the relativist would be that it is impossible to find any basis for a universally binding moral law; but that it is quite easy to discover a basis for morality if moral codes are admitted to be variable, ephemeral, and relative to time, place, and circumstance.

. . . I am assuming that it is no longer possible to solve this difficulty by saying naively that the universal moral law is based upon the uniform commands of God to all men. There will be many, no doubt, who will dispute this. But I am not writing for them. I am writing for those who feel the necessity of finding for morality a basis independent of particular religious dogmas. And I shall therefore make no attempt to argue the matter.

The problem which the absolutist has to face, then, is this. The religious basis of the one absolute morality having disappeared, can there be found for it any other, any secular, basis? If not, then it would seem that we cannot any longer believe in absolutism. We shall have to fall back upon belief in a variety of perhaps mutually inconsistent moral codes operating over restricted areas and limited periods. No one of these will be better, or more true, than any other. Each will be good and true for those living in those areas and periods. We shall have to fall back, in a word, on ethical relativity. . . .

Arguments Against Ethical Relativity.   . . . Ethical relativity, in asserting that the moral standards of particular social groups are the only standards which exist, renders meaningless all propositions which attempt to compare these standards with one another in respect of their moral worth. And this is a very serious matter indeed. We are accustomed to think that the moral ideas of one nation or social group may be "higher" or "lower" than those of another. We believe, for example, that Christian ethical ideals are nobler than those of the savage races of central Africa. Probably most of us would think that the Chinese moral standards are higher than those of the inhabitants of New Guinea. In short we habitually compare one civilization with another and judge the sets of ethical ideas to be found in them to be some better, some worse. The fact that such judgments are very difficult to make with any justice, and that they are frequently made on very superficial and prejudiced grounds, has no bearing on the question now at issue. The question is whether such judgments have any *meaning*. We habitually assume that they have.

But on the basis of ethical relativity they can have none whatever. For the relativist must hold that there is no *common* standard which can be applied to the various civilizations judged. Any such comparison of moral standards implies the existence of some superior standard which is applicable to both. And the existence of any such standard is precisely what the relativist denies. According to him the Christian standard is applicable only to Christians, the Chinese standard only to Chinese, the New Guinea standard only to the inhabitants of New Guinea.

What is true of comparisons between the moral standards of different races will also be true of comparisons between those of different ages. It is not unusual to ask such questions as whether the standard of our own day is superior to that which existed among our ancestors five hundred years ago. And when we remember that our ancestors employed slaves, practiced barbaric physical tortures, and burnt people alive, we may be inclined to think that it is. At any rate we assume that the question is one which has meaning and is capable of rational discussion. But if the ethical relativist is right, whatever we assert on this subject must be totally meaningless. For here again there is no common standard which could form the basis of any such judgments.

This in its turn implies that the whole notion of moral *progress* is a sheer delusion. Progress means an advance from lower to higher, from worse to better. But on the basis of ethical relativity it has no meaning to say that the standards of this age are better (or worse) than those of a previous age. For there is no common standard by which both can be measured. . . .

If these arguments are valid, the ethical relativist cannot really maintain that there is anywhere to be found a moral standard binding upon anybody against his will. And he cannot maintain that, even within the social group, there is a common standard as between individuals. And if that is so, then even judgments to the effect that one man is morally better than another become meaningless. All moral valuation thus vanishes. There is nothing to prevent each man from being a rule unto himself. The result will be moral chaos and the collapse of all effective standards. . . .

But even if we assume that the difficulty about defining moral groups has been surmounted, a further difficulty presents itself. Suppose that we have not definitely decided what are the exact boundaries of the social group within which a moral standard is to be operative. And we will assume—as is invariably done by relativists themselves—that this group is to be some actually existing social community such as a tribe or nation. How are we to know, even then, what actually *is* the moral standard within that group? How is anyone to know? How is even a member of the group to know? For there are certain to be within the group—at least this will be true among advanced peoples—wide differences of opinion as to what is right, what wrong. Whose opinion, then, is to be taken as representing *the* moral standard of the group? Either we must take the opinion of the majority within the group, or the opinion of some minority. If we rely upon the ideas of the majority, the results will be disastrous. Wherever there is found among a people a small band of select spirits, or perhaps one man, working for the establishment of higher and nobler ideals than those commonly accepted by the group, we shall be compelled to hold that, for that people at that time, the majority are right, and that the reformers are wrong and are preaching what is immoral. We shall have to maintain, for example, that Jesus was preaching immoral doctrines to the Jews. Moral goodness will have to be equated always with the mediocre and sometimes with the definitely base and ignoble. If on the other hand we say that the moral standard of the group is to be identified with the moral opinions of some minority, then what minority is this to be? We cannot answer that it is to be the minority composed of the best and most enlightened individuals of the group. This would involve us in a palpably vicious circle. For by what standard are these individuals to be judged the best and the most enlightened? There is no principle by which we could select the right minority. And therefore we should have to consider every minority as good as every other. And this means that we should have no logical right whatever to resist the claim of the gangsters of Chicago—if such a claim were made—that their practices represent the highest standards of American morality. It means in the end that every individual is to be bound by no standard save his own.

The ethical relativists are great empiricists. *What* is the actual moral standard of any group can only be discovered, they tell us, by an examination on the ground of the moral opinions and customs of that group. But will they tell us how they propose to decide, when they get to the ground, which of the many moral opinions they are sure to find there is *the* right one in that group? To some extent they will be able to do this for the Melanesian Islanders—from whom apparently all lessons in the nature of morality are in future to be taken. But it is certain that they cannot do it for advanced peoples whose members have learnt to think for themselves and to entertain among themselves a wide variety of opinions. They cannot do it unless they accept the calamitous view that the ethical opinion of the majority is always right. We are left therefore once more with the conclusion that, even within a particular social group, anybody's moral opinion is as good as anybody else's, and that every man is entitled to be judged by his own standards.

Finally, not only is ethical relativity disastrous in its consequences for moral theory. It cannot be doubted that it must tend to be equally disastrous in its impact upon practical conduct. If men come really to believe that one moral standard is as good as another, they will conclude that their own moral standard has nothing special to recommend it. They might as well then slip down to some lower and easier standard. It is true that, for a time, it may be possible to hold one view in theory and to act practically upon another. But ideas, even philosophical ideas, are not so ineffectual that they can remain for ever idle in the upper chambers of the intellect. In the end they seep down to the level of practice. They get themselves acted on. . . .

These, then, are the main arguments which the anti-relativist will urge against ethical relativity. And perhaps finally he will attempt a diagnosis of the social, intellectual, and psychological conditions of our time to which the emergence of ethical relativism is to be attributed. His diagnosis will be somewhat as follows.

We have abandoned, perhaps with good reason, the oracles of the past. Every age, of course, does this. But in our case it seems that none of us knows any more whither to turn. We do not know what to put in the place of that which has gone. What ought we, supposedly civilized peoples, to aim at? What are to be our ideals? What is right? What is wrong? What is beautiful? What is ugly? No man knows. We drift helplessly in this direction and that. We know not where we stand nor whither we are going.

There are, of course, thousands of voices frantically shouting directions. But they shout one another down, they contradict one another, and the upshot is mere uproar. And because of this confusion there creeps upon us an insidious scepticism and despair. Since no one knows what the truth is, we will deny that there is any truth. Since no one knows what right is, we will deny that there is any right. Since no one knows what the beautiful is, we will deny that there is any beauty. Or at least we will say—what comes to the same thing—that what people (the people of any particular age, region, society)—think to be true is true *for them;* that what people think morally right is morally right *for them;* that what people think beautiful is beautiful *for them.* There is no common and objective standard in any of these matters. Since all the voices contradict one another, they must be all equally right (or equally wrong, for it makes no difference which we say). It is from the practical confusion of our time that these doctrines issue. When all the despair and defeatism of our distracted age are expressed in abstract concepts, are erected into a philosophy, it is then called relativism—ethical relativism, aesthetic relativism, relativity of truth. Ethical relativity is simply defeatism in morals.

And the diagnosis will proceed. Perhaps, it will say, the current pessimism as to our future is unjustified. But there is undoubtedly a wide spread feeling that our civilization is rushing downwards to the abyss. If this should be true, and if nothing should check the headlong descent, then perhaps some historian of the future will seek to disentangle the causes. The causes will, of course, be found to be multitudinous and enormously complicated. And one must not exaggerate the relative importance of any of them. But it can hardly be doubted that our future

historian will include somewhere in his list the failure of the men of our generation to hold steadfastly before themselves the notion of an (even comparatively)
unchanging moral idea. He will cite that feebleness of intellectual and moral grasp
which has led them weakly to harbour the belief that no one moral aim is really
any better than any other, that each is good and true for those who entertain it. This
meant, he will surely say, that men had given up in despair the struggle to attain
moral truth. Civilization lives in and through its upward struggle. Whoever de-
spairs and gives up the struggle, whether it be an individual or a whole civilization, is already inwardly dead.

To Think About

1. Are the Western religions relativist in any sense?

2. "The great fault of all ethics hitherto has been that they believed themselves to
   have to deal only with the relations of man to man. In reality, however, the
   question is what is his attitude to the world and all life that comes within his
   reach. A man is ethical only when life, as such, is sacred to him, that of plants
   and animals as that of his fellow men, and when he devotes himself helpfully
   to all life that is in need of help."   ***Albert Schweitzer***

3. When asked if he had but a single gift to bequeath to the next generation what
   it would be, Ray Bradbury replied: "The gift to see that not all Republicans are
   evil, that not all Democrats are evil, that not all Communists are evil, that not
   all Negroes are evil, that not all whites are evil, that not all anything is evil. The
   ability to see the paradox in every person."

4. Discuss this comment on the sexual freedom of the 1960s: "There can seldom
   have been a clearer demonstration of the old truth that freedom is not just a matter of multiplying your options."   ***James Gould***

5. "The history of morality and moral philosophy is the history of successive challenges to some preexisting moral order."   ***Arnold Toynbee***

6. Do you think that certain kinds of behavior (e.g., incest, cannibalism, or selling opium) are wrong in whatever society they occur? Explain your answer.

7. "If only it was all so simple! If only there were evil people somewhere insidiously committing evil deeds, and it were necessary only to separate them from
   the rest of us and destroy them. But the line dividing good and evil cuts
   through the heart of every human being. And who is willing to destroy a part
   of his own heart?

   "During the life of any heart this line keeps changing place: sometimes it is
   squeezed one way to exuberant evil and sometimes it shifts to allow enough
   space for good to flourish. One and the same human being is, at various ages,
   under various circumstances, a totally different human being. At times he is
   close to being a devil, at times to sainthood. But his name doesn't change and
   to that name we ascribe the whole to good and evil." ***Aleksandr Solzhenitsyn***

8. "As we look for the causes of our behavior, so we take attention away from the act itself, fencing it round with excuses, isolating it from judgment and making inaccessible the only ground in which the seeds of morality can be sown: the ground of individual responsibility."   ***Roger Scruton***

9. "Kant postulates God, since without this hypothesis morality is unintelligible. We postulate a society specifically distinct from individuals, since otherwise morality has no object and duty no roots."   ***Émile Durkheim***

 Readings

BRANDT, RICHARD. "Ethical Relativism." In *Ethical Theory.* Upper Saddle River, NJ: Prentice Hall, 1959, chs. 5, 6, and 12.

HARMAN, GILBERT. "Moral Relativism Defended." *Philosophical Review* 84 (January 1975): 3–22.

HERSKOVITS, MORRIS. "A Defense by an Anthropologist." In *Man and His Works.* New York: Macmillan, 1948.

HOWARD, ABE V. "Do Anthropologists Become Moral Relativists by Mistake?" *Inquiry* 11 (1968): 175–89.

LADD, JOHN. *Ethical Relativism.* Belmont, CA: Wadsworth, 1973.

McCLINTOCK, THOMAS. "The Definition of Ethical Relativism." *Personalist* 50 (1969): 435–47.

ROBERTS, GEORGE W. "Some Refutations of Private Subjectivism in Ethics." *Journal of Value Inquiry* 5 (1971): 292–309.

_____. *The Nature of Morality.* New York: Oxford, 1977.

WELLMAN, CARL. "The Ethical Implications of Cultural Relativity." *Journal of Philosophy* 60 (1963): 169–84.

WONG, DAVID. *Moral Relativity.* Berkeley and Los Angeles: University of California Press, 1985.

_____. "Relativism." In *A Companion to Ethics,* ed. Peter Singer, 442–50. Cambridge: Cambridge University Press, 1991.

17

Humans Are Always Selfish: Glaucon's Challenge to Socrates

Plato (428–348 B.C.) was a student of Socrates and was present at his trial. In 388 Plato founded his school, the Academy, which is sometimes called the first European university. At the Academy he produced his famous dialogues on nearly every topic. He died in 348 B.C., sometime after a pupil named Aristotle enrolled.

Some sophisticated college students, as well as many others, believe that individuals always seek their own interests. This belief, called *psychological egoism,* refers to the fact that every time people do something they do it in order to promote what they conceive to be their own happiness. Some people go further and believe that even if this weren't true, all people ought to seek their own interests. This is called *ethical egoism.*

In his famous Myth of Gyges, Plato sets forth the argument that all people would, if possible, do exactly as they please. They would take from anyone anything they wished, they would sleep with any women they chose, they would kill whomever they desired to have dead, and so on. Is this true? Glaucon argues this, and his position is close to psychological egoism in that he believes people are motivated to seek their own pleasures whenever possible. Plato himself was not a psychological egoist.

Abridged and reprinted from *The Republic of Plato.* Translated by F. M. Cornford (1941). By permission of Oxford University Press.

~~~ **To Study** ~~~

1. What is the nature of justice and how did it originate?
2. Why do humans practice justice?
3. Why does the just person as well as the unjust believe that wrongdoing pays better?

First, Glaucon said, I will state what is commonly held about the nature of justice and its origin; secondly, I shall maintain that it is always practiced with reluctance, not as good in itself, but as a thing one cannot do without; and thirdly, that this reluctance is reasonable, because the life of injustice is much the better life of the two—so people say. . . . Accordingly, I shall set you an example by glorifying the life of injustice with all the energy that I hope you will show later in denouncing it and exalting justice in its stead. Will that plan suit you?

Nothing could be better, Socrates replied. Of all subjects this is one on which a sensible man must always be glad to exchange ideas.

Good, said Glaucon. Listen then, and I will begin with my first point: the nature and origin of justice.

What people say is that to do wrong is, in itself, a desirable thing; on the other hand, it is not at all desirable to suffer wrong, and the harm to the sufferer outweighs the advantage to the doer. Consequently, when men have had a taste of both, those who have not the power to seize the advantage and escape the harm decide that they would be better off if they made a compact neither to do wrong nor to suffer it. Hence they began to make laws and covenants with one another; and whatever the law prescribed they called lawful and right. This is what right or justice is and how it came into existence; it stands half-way between the best thing of all—to do wrong with impunity—and the worst, which is to suffer wrong without the power to retaliate. So justice is accepted as a compromise, and valued, not as good in itself, but for lack of power to do wrong; no man worthy of the name, who had that power, would ever enter into such a compact with anyone; he would be mad if he did. That, Socrates, is the nature of justice according to this account, and such the circumstances in which it arose.

The next point is that men practice it against the grain, for lack of power to do wrong. How true that is, we shall best see if we imagine two men, one just, the other unjust, given full license to do whatever they like, and then follow them to observe where each will be led by his desires. We shall catch the just man taking the same road as the unjust; he will be moved by self-interest, the end which it is natural to every creature to pursue as good, until forcibly turned aside by law and custom to respect the principle of equality.

Now, the easiest way to give them that complete liberty of action would be to imagine them possessed of the talisman found by Gyges, the ancestor of the famous

Lydian. The story tells how he was a shepherd in the King's service. One day there was a great storm, and the ground where his flock was feeding was rent by an earthquake. Astonished at the sight, he went down into the chasm and saw, among other wonders of which the story tells, a brazen horse, hollow, with windows in its sides. Peering in, he saw a dead body, which seemed to be of more than human size. It was naked save for a gold ring, which he took from the finger and made his way out. When the shepherds met, as they did every month, to send an account to the King of the state of his flocks, Gyges came wearing the ring. As he was sitting with the others, he happened to turn the bezel of the ring inside his hand. At once he became invisible, and his companions, to his surprise, began to speak of him as if he had left them. Then, as he was fingering the ring, he turned the bezel outwards and became visible again. With that, he set about testing the ring to see if it really had this power, and always with the same result: according as he turned the bezel inside or out he vanished and reappeared. After this discovery he contrived to be one of the messengers sent to the court. There he seduced the Queen, and with her help murdered the King and seized the throne.

Now suppose there were two such magic rings, and one were given to the just man, the other to the unjust. No one, it is commonly believed, would have such iron strength of mind as to stand fast in doing right or keep his hands off other men's goods, when he could go to the market-place and fearlessly help himself to anything he wanted, enter houses and sleep with any woman he chose, set prisoners free and kill men at his pleasure, and in a word go about among men with the powers of a god. He would behave no better than the other; both would take the same course. Surely this would be strong proof that men do right only under compulsion; no individual thinks of it as good for him personally, since he does wrong whenever he finds he has the power. Every man believes that wrongdoing pays him personally much better, and, according to this theory, that is the truth. Granted full license to do as he liked, people would think him a miserable fool if they found him refusing to wrong his neighbors, or to touch their belongings, though in public they would keep up a pretence of praising his conduct, for fear of being wronged themselves. So much for that. . . .

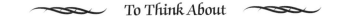

To Think About

1. a. "The perfection of one's abilities in a state of happiness is the highest goal for humans. We have a moral duty to attempt to reach this goal.

    b. "The ethics of altruism prescribes that we sacrifice our interests and lives for the good of others.

    c. "Therefore, the ethics of altruism is incompatible with the goal of happiness.

    d. "Ethical egoism prescribes that we seek our own happiness exclusively, and as such it is consistent with the happiness goal.

    e. "Therefore, ethical egoism is the correct moral theory."

    Ayn Rand, as paraphrased by ***Louis Pojman***

2.   "So did the Greeks and Romans keep all their sadnesses and gladnesses unmin-
gled and entire. Instinctively good they did not reckon sin; nor had they any such
desire to save the credit of the universe as to make them insist, as so many of *us*
insist, that what immediately appears as evil must be 'good in the making,' or
something equally ingenious. Good was good, and bad just bad, for the earlier
Greeks. They neither denied the ills of nature . . . nor did they, in order to escape
from those ills, invent 'another and a better world' of the imagination, in which,
along with the ills, the innocent goods of sense would also find no place. This
integrity of the instinctive reactions, this freedom from all moral sophistry and
strain, gives a pathetic dignity to ancient pagan feeling."   **William James**

18

Humans Are
Not Always Selfish

James Rachels (1941–2003) *was a professor of philosophy at the University of Alabama–Birmingham in the areas of ethics and philosophy of action. Among his publications is* Moral Problems *(1972).*

Rachels argues against theories of selfishness as described by psychological egoists such as de Mandeville. He first challenges the view that everyone always does what he or she wants by showing that we often do unpleasant tasks for future pleasures or from feelings of obligation. Next he repeats Bishop Butler's famous argument that what we often seek is not pleasure but objects such as food, drink, or other people's pain. The final part of his essay clears up confusions such as the belief that selfishness means the same as self-interest.

Rachels then examines *ethical egoism,* the view that people *ought* to seek their own pleasure. He concludes that such a position ultimately entails that the advocate feel no compassion for others. This, Rachels contends, is indefensible.

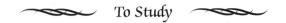 To Study

1. Distinguish psychological egoism from ethical egoism.
2. What are Rachels's arguments against the view that all acts are done for self-interest?
3. If one derives satisfaction from helping others, does it make one selfish? Why or why not?
4. What are the three common confusions about psychological egoism?

5. State the argument against ethical egoism relating to its inability to be universalized.
6. Is there any telling argument against ethical egoism?

---

1. Our ordinary thinking about morality is full of assumptions that we almost never question. We assume, for example, that we have an obligation to consider the welfare of other people when we decide what actions to perform or what rules to obey; we think that we must refrain from acting in ways harmful to others, and that we must respect their rights and interests as well as our own. We also assume that people are in fact capable of being motivated by such considerations, that is, that people are not wholly selfish and that they do sometimes act in the interests of others.

Both of these assumptions have come under attack by moral sceptics, as long ago as by Glaucon in Book II of Plato's *Republic.* Glaucon recalls the legend of Gyges, a shepherd who was said to have found a magic ring in a fissure opened by an earthquake. The ring would make its wearer invisible and thus would enable him to go anywhere and do anything undetected. Gyges used the power of the ring to gain entry to the Royal Palace where he seduced the Queen, murdered the King, and subsequently seized the throne. Now Glaucon asks us to determine that there are two such rings, one given to a man of virtue and one given to a rogue. The rogue, of course, will use his ring unscrupulously and do anything necessary to increase his own wealth and power. He will recognize no moral constraints on his conduct, and, since the cloak of invisibility will protect him from discovery, he can do anything he pleases without fear of reprisal. So, there will be no end to the mischief he will do. But how will the so-called virtuous man behave? Glaucon suggests that he will behave no better than the rogue: "No one, it is commonly believed, would have such iron strength of mind as to stand fast in doing right or keep his hands off other men's goods, when he could go to the market-place and fearlessly help himself to anything he wanted, enter houses and sleep with any woman he chose, set prisoners free and kill men at his pleasure, and in a word go among men with the powers of a god. He would behave no better than the other; both would take the same course."[1] Moreover, why shouldn't he? Once he is freed from the fear of reprisal, why shouldn't a man simply do what he pleases, or what he thinks is best for himself? What reason is there for him to continue being "moral" when it is clearly not to his own advantage to do so?

These sceptical views suggested by Glaucon have come to be known as *psychological egoism* and *ethical egoism,* respectively. Psychological egoism is the view that all men are selfish in everything that they do, that is, that the only motive from which anyone ever acts is self-interest. On this view, even when men are acting in ways apparently calculated to benefit others, they are actually motivated by the belief that acting in this way is to their own advantage, and if they did not believe this, they would not be doing that action. Ethical egoism is, by contrast, a normative view about how men *ought* to act. It is the view that, regardless of how men do in fact

[1] *The Republic of Plato,* translated by F. M. Cornford (Oxford, 1941), p. 45.

behave, they have no obligation to do anything except what is in their own interests. According to the ethical egoist, a person is always justified in doing whatever is in his own interests, regardless of the effect on others.

Clearly, if either of these views is correct, then "the moral institution of life" (to use Butler's well-turned phrase) is very different from what we normally think. The majority of mankind is grossly deceived about what is, or ought to be, the case, where morals are concerned.

2. Psychological egoism seems to fly in the face of the facts. We are tempted to say: "Of course people act unselfishly all the time. For example, Smith gives up a trip to the country, which he would have enjoyed very much, in order to stay behind and help a friend with his studies, which is a miserable way to pass the time. This is a perfectly clear case of unselfish behavior, and if the psychological egoist thinks that such cases do not occur, then he is just mistaken." Given such obvious instances of "unselfish behavior," what reply can the egoist make? There are two general arguments by which he might try to show that all actions, including those such as the one just outlined, are in fact motivated by self-interest. Let us examine these in turn:

a. The first argument goes as follows. If we describe one person's action as selfish, and another person's action as unselfish, we are overlooking the crucial fact that in both cases, assuming that the action is done voluntarily, *the agent is merely doing what he most wants to do.* If Smith stays behind to help his friend, that only shows that he wanted to help his friend more than he wanted to go to the country. And why should he be praised for his "unselfishness" when he is only doing what he most wants to do? So, since Smith is only doing what he wants to do, he cannot be said to be acting unselfishly.

This argument is so bad that it would not deserve to be taken seriously except for the fact that so many otherwise intelligent people have been taken in by it. First, the argument rests on the premise that people never voluntarily do anything except what they want to do. But this is patently false; there are at least two classes of actions that are exceptions to this generalization. One is the set of actions which we may not want to do, but which we do anyway as a means to an end which we want to achieve; for example, going to the dentist in order to stop a toothache, or going to work every day in order to be able to draw our pay at the end of the month. These cases may be regarded as consistent with the spirit of the egoist argument, however, since the ends mentioned are wanted by the agent. But the other set of actions are those which we do, not because we want to, nor even because there is an end which we want to achieve, but because we feel ourselves *under an obligation* to do them. For example, someone may do something because he has promised to do it, and thus feels obligated, even though he does not want to do it. It is sometimes suggested that in such cases we do the action because, after all, we want to keep our promises; so, even here, we are doing what we want. However, this dodge will not work: if I have promised to do something, and if I do not want to do it then it is simply false to say that I want to keep my promise. In such cases we feel a conflict precisely because we do *not* want to do what we feel obligated to do. It is reasonable to think that Smith's action falls roughly into this second category: he might stay behind, not because he wants to, but because he feels that his friend needs help.

But suppose we were to concede, for the sake of the argument, that all voluntary action is motivated by the agent's wants, or at least that Smith is so motivated. Even if this were granted, it would not follow that Smith is acting selfishly or from self-interest. For if Smith wants to do something that will help his friend, even when it means forgoing his own enjoyments, that is precisely what makes him *un*selfish. What else could unselfishness be, if not wanting to help others? Another way to put the same point is to say that it is the *object* of a want that determines whether it is selfish or not. The mere fact that I am acting on *my* wants does not mean that I am acting selfishly; that depends on *what it is* that I want. If I want only my own good, and care nothing for others, then I am selfish; but if I also want other people to be well-off and happy, and if I act on *that* desire, then my action is not selfish. So much for this argument.

b. The second argument for psychological egoism is this. Since so-called unselfish actions always produce a sense of self-satisfaction in the agent,[2] and since this sense of satisfaction is a pleasant state of consciousness, it follows that the point of the action is really to achieve a pleasant state of consciousness, rather than to bring about any good for others. Therefore, the action is "unselfish" only at a superficial level of analysis. Smith will feel much better with himself for having stayed to help his friend—if he had gone to the country, he would have felt terrible about it—and that is the real point of the action. According to a well-known story, this argument was once expressed by Abraham Lincoln:

> *Mr. Lincoln once remarked to a fellow-passenger on an old-time, mud-coach that all men were prompted by selfishness in doing good. His fellow-passenger was antagonizing this position when they were passing over a corduroy bridge that spanned a slough. As they crossed this bridge they espied an old razor-backed sow on the bank making a terrible noise because her pigs had got into the slough and were in danger of drowning. As the old coach began to climb the hill, Mr. Lincoln called out, "Driver, can't you stop just a moment?" Then Mr. Lincoln jumped out, ran back, and lifted the little pigs out of the mud and water and placed them on the bank. When he returned, his companion remarked: "Now, Abe, where does selfishness come in on this little episode?" "Why, bless your soul, Ed, that was the very essence of selfishness. I should have had no peace of mind all day had I gone on and left that suffering old sow worrying over those pigs. I did it to get peace of mind, don't you see?"[3]*

This argument suffers from defects similar to the previous one. Why should we think that merely because someone derives satisfaction from helping others this makes him selfish? Isn't the unselfish man precisely the one who *does* derive satisfaction from helping others, while the selfish man does not? If Lincoln "got peace of mind" from rescuing the piglets, does this show him to be selfish, or, on the contrary, doesn't it show him to be compassionate and good-hearted? (If a man were truly selfish, why should it bother his conscience that *others* suffer—much less pigs?) Similarly, it is nothing more than shabby sophistry to say, because Smith takes satisfaction

---

[2] Or, as it is sometimes said, "It gives him a clear conscience," or "He couldn't sleep at night if he had done otherwise," or "He would have been ashamed of himself for not doing it," and so on.

[3] Frank C. Sharp, *Ethics* (New York, 1928), pp 74–75. Quoted from the Springfield (Ill.) *Monitor* in the *Outlook,* vol. 56, p. 1059.

in helping his friend, that he is behaving selfishly. If we say this rapidly, while thinking about something else, perhaps it will sound all right; but if we speak slowly, and pay attention to what we are saying, it sounds plain silly.

Moreover, suppose we ask *why* Smith derives satisfaction from helping his friend. The answer will be, it is because Smith cares for him and wants him to succeed. If Smith did not have these concerns, then he would take no pleasure in assisting him; and these concerns, as we have already seen, are the marks of unselfishness, not selfishness. To put the point more generally: if we have a positive attitude toward the attainment of some goal, then we may derive satisfaction from attaining that goal. But the *object* of our attitude is *the attainment of that goal;* and we must want to attain the goal *before* we can find any satisfaction in it. We do not, in other words, desire some sort of "pleasurable consciousness" and then try to figure out how to achieve it; rather, we desire all sorts of different things—money, a new fishing-boat, to be a better chess-player, to get a promotion in our work, etc.—and because we desire these things, we derive satisfaction from attaining them. And so, if someone desires the welfare and happiness of another person, he will derive satisfaction from that; but this does not mean that this satisfaction is the object of his desire, or that he is in any way selfish on account of it.

It is a measure of the weakness of psychological egoism that these insupportable arguments are the ones most often advanced in its favor. Why, then, should anyone ever have thought it a true view? Perhaps because of a desire for theoretical simplicity: In thinking about human conduct, it would be nice if there were some simple formula that would unite the diverse phenomena of human behavior under a single explanatory principle, just as simple formulae in physics bring together a great many apparently different phenomena. And since it is obvious that self-regard is an overwhelmingly important factor in motivation, it is only natural to wonder whether all motivation might not be explained in these terms. But the answer is clearly No; while a great many human actions are motivated entirely or in part by self-interest, only by a deliberate distortion of the facts can we say that all conduct is so motivated. This will be clear, I think, if we correct three confusions which are commonplace. The exposure of these confusions will remove the last traces of plausibility from the psychological egoist thesis.

The first is the confusion of selfishness with self-interest. The two are clearly not the same. If I see a physician when I am feeling poorly, I am acting in my own interest but no one would think of calling me "selfish" on account of it. Similarly, brushing my teeth, working hard at my job, and obeying the law are all in my self-interest but none of these are examples of selfish conduct. This is because selfish behavior is behavior that ignores the interests of others, in circumstances in which their interests ought not to be ignored. This concept has a definite evaluative flavor; to call someone "selfish" is not just to describe his action but to condemn it. Thus, you would not call me selfish for eating a normal meal in normal circumstances (although it may surely be in my self-interest); but you would call me selfish for hoarding food while others about are starving.

The second confusion is the assumption that every action is done *either* from self-interest or from other-regarding motives. Thus, the egoist concludes that if there is no such thing as genuine altruism then all actions must be done from self-interest. But this is certainly a false dichotomy. The man who continues to smoke cigarettes, even after learning about the connection between smoking and cancer, is surely not acting from self-interest, not even by his own standards—self-interest would dictate that he quit smoking at once—and he is not acting altruistically either. He *is,* no doubt, smoking for the pleasure of it, but all that this shows is that undisciplined pleasure-seeking and acting from self-interest are very different. This is what led Butler to remark that "The thing to be lamented is, not that men have so great regard to their own good or interest in the present world, for they have not enough."[4]

The last two paragraphs show *(a)* that it is false that all actions are selfish, and *(b)* that it is false that all actions are done out of self-interest. And it should be noted that these two points can be made, and were, without any appeal to putative examples of altruism.

The third confusion is the common but false assumption that a concern for one's own welfare is incompatible with any genuine concern for the welfare of others. Thus, since it is obvious that everyone (or very nearly everyone) does desire his own well-being, it might be thought that no one can really be concerned with others. But again, this is false. There is no inconsistency in desiring that everyone, including oneself *and* others, be well-off and happy. To be sure, it may happen on occasion that our own interests conflict with the interests of others, and in these cases we will have to make hard choices. But even in these cases we might sometimes opt for the interests of others, especially when the others involved are our family or friends. But more importantly, not all cases are like this: sometimes we are able to promote the welfare of others when our own interests are not involved at all. In these cases not even the strongest self-regard need prevent us from acting considerately toward others.

Once these confusions are cleared away, it seems to me obvious enough that there is no reason whatever to accept psychological egoism. On the contrary, if we simply observe people's behavior with an open mind, we may find that a great deal of it is motivated by self-regard, but by no means all of it; and that there is no reason to deny that "the moral institution of life" can include a place for the virtue of beneficence.[5]

3. The ethical egoist would say at this point, "Of course it is possible for people to act altruistically, and perhaps many people do act that way—but there is no reason why they *should* do so. A person is under no obligation to do anything except what is in his own interests."[6] This is really quite a radical doctrine. Suppose I have an urge to set fire to some public building (say, a department store) just for the fascination of watching the spectacular blaze: according to this view, the fact that several people might be burned to death provides no reason whatever why I should not do it. After all, this only concerns *their* welfare, not my own, and according to the ethical egoist the only person I need think of is myself.

Some might deny that ethical egoism has any such monstrous consequences. They would point out that it is really to my own advantage not to set fire—for, if I do that I may be caught and put into prison (unlike Gyges, I have no magic ring for pro-

---

[4] *The Works of Joseph Butler,* edited by W. E. Gladstone (Oxford, 1896), vol. II, p 26. It should be noted that most of the points I am making against psychological egoism were first made by Butler. Butler made all the important points; all that is left for us is to remember them.

[5] The capacity for altruistic behavior is not unique to human beings. Some interesting experiments with rhesus monkeys have shown that these animals will refrain from operating a device for securing food if this causes other animals to suffer pain. See Masserman, Wechkin, and Terris, " 'Altruistic' Behavior in Rhesus Monkeys," *The American Journal of Psychiatry,* vol. 121 (1964); 584–585.

[6] I take this to be the view of Ayn Rand, in so far as I understand her confusing doctrine.

tection). Moreover, even if I could avoid being caught it is still to my advantage to respect the rights and interests of others, for it is to my advantage to live in a society in which people's rights and interests are respected. Only in such a society can I live a happy and secure life; so, in acting kindly toward others, I would merely be doing my part to create and maintain the sort of society which it is to my advantage to have.[7] Therefore, it is said, the egoist would not be such a bad man; he would be as kindly and considerate as anyone else, because he would see that it is to his own advantage to be kindly and considerate.

This is a seductive line of thought, but it seems to me mistaken. Certainly it is to everyone's advantage (including the egoist's) to preserve a stable society where people's interests are generally protected. But there is no reason for the egoist to think that merely because *he* will not honor the rules of the social game, decent society will collapse. For the vast majority of people are not egoists, and there is no reason to think that they will be converted by his example—especially if he is discreet and does not unduly flaunt his style of life. What this line of reasoning shows is not that the egoist himself must act benevolently, but that he must encourage *others* to do so. He must take care to conceal from public view his own self-centered method of decision-making, and urge others to act on precepts very different from those on which he is willing to act.

The rational egoist, then, cannot advocate that egoism be universally adopted by everyone. For he wants a world in which his own interests are maximized; and if other people adopted the egoistic policy of pursuing their own interests to the exclusion of his interests, as he pursues his interests to the exclusion of theirs, then such a world would be impossible. So he himself will be an egoist, but he will want others to be altruists.

This brings us to what is perhaps the most popular "refutation" of ethical egoism current among philosophical writers—the argument that ethical egoism is at bottom inconsistent because it cannot be universalized.[8] The argument goes like this:

To say that any action or policy of action is *right* (or that it *ought* to be adopted) entails that it is right for *anyone* in the same sort of circumstances. I cannot, for example, say that it is right for me to lie to you, and yet object when you lie to me (provided, of course, that the circumstances are the same). I cannot hold that it is all right for me to drink your beer and then complain when you drink mine. This is just the requirement that we be consistent in our evaluations; it is a requirement of logic. Now it is said that ethical egoism cannot meet this requirement because, as we have already seen, the egoist would not want others to act in the same way that he acts. Moreover, suppose he *did* advocate the universal adoption of egoistic policies: he would be saying to Peter, "You ought to pursue your own interests even if it means destroying Paul"; and he would be saying to Paul, "You ought to pursue your own interests even if it means destroying Peter." The attitudes expressed in these two recommendations seem clearly inconsistent—he is urging the advancement of Peter's interests at one moment, and countenancing their defeat at the next. Therefore, the argument goes,

---

[7] Cf. Thomas Hobbes, *Leviathan* (London, 1651), chap. 17.

[8] See, for example, Brian Medlin, "Ultimate Principles and Ethical Egoism," *Australasian Journal of Philosophy,* vol. 35 (1957), 111–118; and D. H. Monro, *Empiricism and Ethics* (Cambridge, 1967), chap. 16.

there is no way to maintain the doctrine of ethical egoism as a consistent view about how we ought to act. We will fall into inconsistency whenever we try.

What are we to make of this argument? Are we to conclude that ethical egoism has been refuted? Such a conclusion, I think, would be unwarranted; for I think that we can show, contrary to this argument, how ethical egoism can be maintained consistently. We need only to interpret the egoist's position in a sympathetic way: we should say that he has in mind a certain kind of world which he would prefer over all others; it would be a world in which his own interests were maximized, regardless of the effects on other people. The egoist's primary policy of action, then, would be to act in such a way as to bring about, as nearly as possible, this sort of world. Regardless of however morally reprehensible we might find it, there is nothing *inconsistent* in someone's adopting this as his ideal and acting in a way calculated to bring it about. And if someone did adopt this as his ideal, then he would not advocate universal egoism; as we have already seen, he would want other people to be altruists. So, if he advocates any principles of conduct for the general public, they will be altruistic principles. This would not be inconsistent; on the contrary, it would be perfectly consistent with his goal of creating a world in which his own interests are maximized. To be sure, he would have to be deceitful; in order to secure the good will of others, and a favorable hearing for his exhortations to altruism, he would have to pretend that he was himself prepared to accept altruistic principles. But again, that would be all right; from the egoist's point of view, this would merely be a matter of adopting the necessary means to the achievement of his goal—and while we might not approve of this, there is nothing inconsistent about it. Again, it might be said: "He advocates one thing, but does another. Surely *that's* inconsistent." But it is not; for what he advocates and what he does are both calculated as means to an end (the *same* end, we might note); and as such, he is doing what is rationally required in each case. Therefore, contrary to the previous argument, there is nothing inconsistent in the ethical egoist's view. He cannot be refuted by the claim that he contradicts himself.

Is there, then, no way to refute the ethical egoist? If by "refute" we mean show that he has made some *logical* error, the answer is that there is not. However, there is something more that can be said. The egoist challenge to our ordinary moral convictions amounts to a demand for an explanation of why we should adopt certain policies of action, namely policies in which the good of others is given importance. We can give an answer to this demand, albeit an indirect one. The reason one ought not to do actions that would hurt other people is: other people would be hurt. The reason one ought to do actions that would benefit other people is: other people would be benefited. This may at first seem like a piece of philosophical sleight-of-hand, but it is not. The point is that the welfare of human beings is something that most of us value *for its own sake,* and not merely for the sake of something else. Therefore, when *further* reasons are demanded for valuing the welfare of human beings, we cannot point to anything further to satisfy this demand. It is not that we have no reason for pursuing these policies, but that our reason *is* that these policies are for the good of human beings.

So: if we are asked "Why shouldn't I set fire to this department store?" one answer would be "Because if you do, people may be burned to death." This is a complete, sufficient reason which does not require qualification or supplementation of any sort. If someone seriously wants to know why this action shouldn't be done, that's the reason. If we are pressed further and asked the sceptical question "But why shouldn't I do actions that will harm others?" we may not know what to say—but this is because the questioner has included in his question the very answer we would like to give: "Why shouldn't you do actions that will harm others? Because doing those actions would harm others."

The egoist, no doubt, will not be happy with this. He will protest that *we* may accept this as a reason, but *he* does not. And here the argument stops: there are limits to what can be accomplished by argument, and if the egoist really doesn't care about other people—if he honestly doesn't care whether they are helped or hurt by his actions—then we have reached those limits. If we want to persuade him to act decently toward his fellow humans, we will have to make our appeal to such other attitudes as he does possess, by threats, bribes, or other cajolery. That is all that we can do.

Though some may find this situation distressing (we would like to be able to show that the egoist is just *wrong*), it holds no embarrassment for common morality. What we have come up against is simply a fundamental requirement of rational action, namely, that the existence of reasons for action always depends on the prior existence of certain attitudes in the agent. For example, the fact that a certain course of action would make the agent a lot of money is a reason for doing it only if the agent wants to make money; the fact that practicing at chess makes one a better player is a reason for practicing only if one wants to be a better player; and so on. Similarly, the fact that a certain action would help the agent is a reason for doing the action only if the agent cares about his own welfare, and the fact that an action would help others is a reason for doing it only if the agent cares about others. In this respect ethical egoism and what we might call ethical altruism are in exactly the same fix: both require that the agent *care* about himself, or about other people, before they can get started.

So a nonegoist will accept "It would harm another person" as a reason not to do an action simply because he cares about what happens to that other person. When the egoist says that he does *not* accept that as a reason, he is saying something quite extraordinary. He is saying that he has no affection for friends or family, that he never feels pity or compassion, that he is the sort of person who can look on scenes of human misery with complete indifference, so long as he is not the one suffering. Genuine egoists, people who really don't care at all about anyone other than themselves, are rare. It is important to keep this in mind when thinking about ethical egoism; it is easy to forget just how fundamental to human psychological makeup the feeling of sympathy is. Indeed, a man without any sympathy at all would scarely be recognizable as a man; and that is what makes ethical egoism such a disturbing doctrine in the first place.

4. There are, of course, many different ways in which the sceptic might challenge the assumptions underlying our moral practice. In this essay I have discussed only two of them, the two put forward by Glaucon in the passage that I cited from Plato's *Republic*. It is important that the assumptions underlying our moral practice should not be confused with particular judgments made within that practice. To defend one is not to defend the other. We may assume—quite properly, if my analysis has been correct—that the virtue of beneficence does, and indeed should, occupy an important place in "the moral institution of life"; and yet we may make constant and miserable errors when it comes to judging when and in what ways this virtue is to be exercised.

Even worse, we may often be able to make accurate moral judgments, and know what we ought to do, but not do it. For these ills, philosophy alone is not the cure.

To Think About

1. The essential egoism of the hedonist has been stated with devastating frankness by *George Jean Nathan,* noted literary critic of our day:
    "To me, pleasure and my own personal happiness—only infrequently collaborating with that of others—are all I deem worth a hoot. It would make me out a much finer and nobler person, I duly appreciate, to say that the happiness and welfare of all mankind were close to my heart, that nothing gave me more soulful happiness than to make others happy and that I would gladly sacrifice every cent I have in the world, together with maybe a leg, to bring a little joy to the impoverished and impaired survivors of the late floods in India, but I have difficulty in being a hypocrite. That I am selfish and to a very considerable degree possibly offensive is thus more or less regrettably obvious. All that I am able to offer in extenuation is that so are most other men if you dig down into them and, paying no attention to their altruistic pretensions, get at the hearts of them. In all my experience I have yet to find and know intimately a man worth his salt in any direction who did not think of himself first and foremost. He may drop a quarter into the hat of a beggar (when somebody is looking); he may have gracious manners; he may obey the punctilio on every occasion; he may be genial and liberal and hearty; he may buy the drinks when it comes his turn; he may be scrupulously polite, considerate and superficially lovable. But under it all his first interest, his first consideration and his first admiration are reserved for himself."

2. "That all particular appetites and passions are towards *external things themselves,* distinct from the *pleasure arising from them,* is manifested from hence, that there could not be this pleasure, were it not for that prior suitableness between the object and the passion: there could be no enjoyment or delight for one thing more than another, from eating food more than from swallowing a stone, if there were not an affection or appetite to one thing more than another."   *Joseph Butler*

3. "Selfishness is not living as one wishes to live. It is asking others to live as one wishes to live."   *Oscar Wilde*

4. "The most dreaded Chinese curse is 'I wish you an interesting life.' For an interesting life you must pay the price."   *Mary de Barchgrave*

5. "Are there any harmless immoralities? According to the utilitarian conception of ethics, harmfulness is the very ground and essential nature of immorality; but there is no doubt that our moral code is not (yet) wholly utilitarian. Certain actions are still widely held to be immoral even though they harm no one or, at most, only the actor himself. The question is whether the law should be used to force people to refrain from such conduct.

"The central problem cases are those criminal actions generally called morals offenses. Offenses against morality and decency have long constituted a category of crimes (as distinct from offenses against the person, offenses against property, etc.). These have included mainly sex offenses—adultery, fornication, sodomy, incest, and prostitution, but also a miscellany of nonsexual offenses including cruelty to animals, desecration of the flag or other venerated symbols, and mistreatment of corpses.

"In a very useful article, Louis Schwartz maintains that what sets these crimes off as a class is not their special relation to morality (after all, murder is also an offense against morality, but it is not a 'morals offense') but rather the lack of an essential connection between them and social harm. In particular, their suppression is not required by the public security. Some morals offenses may harm the perpetrators themselves, but there is rarely harm of this sort the risk of which was not consented to in advance by the actors. Offense to other parties, when it occurs, is a consequence of the perpetration of the offending deeds *in public* and can be prevented by 'public nuisance' laws or by statutes against 'open lewdness' or 'solicitation' in public places. That still leaves 'morals offenses' when committed by consenting adults in private: should they really be crimes?"   ***Joel Feinberg***

6. "One of the great drawbacks to self-centered passions is that they afford so little variety in life. The man who loves only himself cannot, it is true, be accused of promiscuity in his affections, but he is bound in the end to suffer intolerable boredom from the inevitable sameness of the object of his devotion."

    Bertrand Russell

 Readings

ALLEN, R. E. "The Speech of Glaucon in Plato's *Republic.*" *Journal of the History of Philosophy* 25 (January 1987): 3–11.

BROAD, C. D. "Egoism as a Theory of Human Motives." In *Ethics and the History of Philosophy.* London: Routledge & Kegan Paul, 1952.

DUNCAN-JONES, AUSTIN. *Butler's Moral Philosophy.* Harmondsworth, England: Penguin Books, 1952.

EPSTEIN, RICHARD. "The Varieties of Self-Interest." *Social and Political Philosophy* 8.1 (Autumn 1990): 102–20.

JACKSON, R. "Bishop Butler's Refutation of Psychological Hedonism." *Philosophy* 18 (July 1943): 114–39.

MACHAN, TIBOR. "Recent Work in Ethical Egoism." *American Philosophical Quarterly* 16 (January 1979): 1–15.

McCLINTOCK, T. "The Egotist's Psychological Argument." *American Philosophical Quarterly* 8 (January 1971): 79–85.

MEDLIN, BRIAN. "Ultimate Principles and Ethical Egoism." *Australasian Journal of Philosophy* 35 (1957): 111–18.

19

Happiness Is Living Virtuously

Aristotle (384–322 B.C.), son of a physician, studied in Plato's Academy for twenty years before founding his own more empirical school, the Lyceum. He tutored Alexander the Great. He wrote on logic, ethics, aesthetics, metaphysics, biology, physics, psychology, and politics. Further, he had an enormous influence on medieval Hebrew, Arabic, and Christian philosophers, especially St. Thomas Aquinas and his later Scholastic followers.

An individual deals with a problem in one of two ways: a solution based on principle or a solution based on consequence. For example, one woman might avoid ending a bad marriage because divorce conflicts with her religious beliefs or other principles. However, another woman might decide to seek a divorce because of the emotional pain she has suffered in her marriage and the consequent happiness she might find alone or married to another person. The first woman would be following *deontological rules* to solve her problem, that is, making decisions based on principles or sense of duty. This is Kant's approach. The second woman, basing her decision on consequences, is following a *teleological approach.* But there are two fundamentally different forms of teleological ethics, one that may be called *hedonistic,* the other *eudaimonistic.* A hedonist identifies happiness with pleasure; a eudaimonist identifies happiness with general human perfection and well-being, or what some writers call *flourishing.* Jeremy Bentham represents the former of these approaches, and Aristotle represents the latter. If we are using teleological ethics, we must question whether we should measure all action by consequence or whether there are some actions, such as promise keeping, that should be decided on the basis of principle. On the other hand, the deontologist must question whether his or her rules are adequate for all situations.

From *The Nicomachean Ethics of Aristotle,* trans. J. E. C. Weldon (London: Macmillan, 1892).

Aristotle's position is sometimes called *virtue ethics,* because he contends that happiness is achieved by living virtuously within a suitable society. Ethics is a branch of politics.

ARISTOTELIAN VIRTUES AND VICES

Deficiency/Vice	Mean/Virtue	Excess/Vice
Cowardice	Courage	Foolhardiness
Anorexia	Moderation	Gluttony
Stinginess	Generosity	Profligacy
Standoffishness	Friendliness	Obsequiousness
Shyness	Pride	Vanity
Pessimism	Realism	Optimism
Celibacy	Monogamy	Promiscuity
Dullness	Well-roundedness	Wildness

The two kinds of virtue are intellectual and moral. To increase one's intellectual virtue, one must develop one's understanding of the universe and humans' institutions. Moral virtues are learned through developing the right habits to ensure that one is courageous, temperate, just, and so on. One must seek the mean, "the Golden Mean," between the extremes, which is not the middle, but the right way at the right time for the right cause.

To Study

1. Why should we seek happiness rather than honor?
2. What is the good for humans?
3. What is Aristotle's argument that the "good of man is an activity of the soul in accordance with virtue"?
4. Define *moral virtue.* What is "the mean"? Discuss some means.
5. Explain the role of habit in the achievement of moral virtue.
6. What is the best method of hitting the mean?

We speak of that which is sought after for its own sake as more final than that which is sought after as a means to something else; we speak of that which is never desired as a means to something else as more final than the things which are desired both in themselves and as means to something else; and we speak of a thing as absolutely final if it is always desired in itself and never as a means to something else.

It seems that happiness pre-eminently answers to this description, as we always desire happiness for its own sake and never as a means to something else, whereas we desire honor, pleasure, intellect, and every virtue, partly for their own sakes (for we should desire them independently of what might result from them) but partly also as being means to happiness, because we suppose they will prove the instruments of happiness. Happiness, on the other hand, nobody desires for the sake of these things, nor indeed as a means to anything else at all. If we define the function of Man as a kind of life, and this life as an activity of soul, or a course of action in conformity with reason, if the function of a good man is such activity or action of a good and noble kind, and if everything is successfully performed when it is performed in accordance with its proper excellence, it follows that the good of Man is an activity of the soul in accordance with virtue or, if there are more virtues than one, in accordance with the best and most complete virtue. But it is necessary to add the words "in a complete life." For as one swallow or one day does not make a spring, so one day or a short time does not make a fortunate or happy man.

Inasmuch as happiness is an activity of the soul in accordance with complete or perfect virtue, it is necessary to consider virtue, as this will perhaps be the best way of studying happiness. . . .

Virtue or excellence being twofold, partly intellectual and partly moral, intellectual virtue is both originated and fostered mainly by teaching; it therefore demands experience and time. Moral virtue, on the other hand, is the outcome of habit, and accordingly its name is derived by a slight deflexion from habit. From this fact it is clear that no moral virtue is implanted in us by nature; a law of nature cannot be altered by habituation. . . . It is neither by nature then nor in defiance of nature that virtues are implanted in us. Nature gives us the capacity of receiving them, and that capacity is perfected by habit. . . . But the virtues we acquire by first exercising them, as is the case with all the arts, for it is by doing what we ought to do when we have learnt the arts that we learn the arts themselves; we become, for example, builders by building and harpists by playing the harp. Similarly it is by doing just acts that we become just, by doing temperate acts that we become temperate, by doing courageous acts that we become courageous. . . . It is by acting in such transactions as take place between man and man that we become either just or unjust. It is by acting in the face of danger and by habituating ourselves to fear or courage that we become either cowardly or courageous. It is much the same with our desires and angry passions. Some people become temperate and gentle, others become licentious and passionate, according as they conduct themselves in one way or another way in particular circumstances. In a word moral states are the results of activities corresponding to the moral states themselves. It is our duty therefore to give a certain character to the activities, as the moral states depend upon the differences of the activities. Accordingly the difference between one training of the habits and another from early days is not a light matter, but is serious or rather all-important. . . .

But it may be asked what we mean by saying that people must become just by doing what is just and temperate by doing what is temperate. For if they do what is just and temperate, they are *ipso facto* proved, it will be said, to be just and temperate in the same way as, if they practice grammar and music, they are proved to be grammarians and musicians. . . .

But actions in accordance with virtue are not, for example, justly or temperately performed [merely] because they are in themselves just or temperate. It is necessary that the agent at the time of performing them should satisfy certain conditions, that is, in the first place that he should know what he is doing, secondly that he should deliberately choose to do it and to do it for its own sake, and thirdly that he should do it as an instance of a settled and immutable moral state. If it be a question whether a person possesses any art, these conditions, except indeed the condition of knowledge, are not taken into account; but if it be a question of possessing the virtues, the mere knowledge is of little or no avail, and it is the other conditions, which are the results of frequently performing just and temperate actions, that are not of slight but of absolute importance. Accordingly deeds are said to be just and temperate, when they are such as a just or temperate person would do, and a just and temperate person is not merely one who does these deeds but one who does them in the spirit of the just and the temperate. . . .

. . . [T]he virtues are neither emotions nor faculties [but] moral states. . . . But it is not enough to state merely that virtue is a moral state, we must also describe the character of that moral state.

It must be laid down then that every virtue or excellence has the effect of producing a good condition of that of which it is a virtue or excellence, and of enabling it to perform its function well. Thus, the excellence of the eye makes the eye good and its function good, as it is by the excellence of the eye that we see well. Similarly, the excellence of the horse makes a horse excellent and good at racing, at carrying its rider and at facing the enemy.

If then this is universally true, the virtue or excellence of man will be such a moral state as makes a man good and able to perform his proper function well. We have already explained how this will be the case, but another way of making it clear will be to study the nature or character of this virtue.

Now in everything, whether it be continuous or discrete, it is possible to take a greater, a smaller, or an equal amount, and this either absolutely or in relation to ourselves, the equal being a mean between excess and deficiency. By the mean in respect of the thing itself, or the absolute mean, I understand that which is equally distinct from both extremes; and this is one and the same thing for everybody. By the mean considered relatively to ourselves I understand that which is neither too much nor too little; but this is not one thing, nor is it the same for everybody. Thus, if 10 be too much and 2 too little we take 6 as a mean in respect of the thing itself; for 6 is as much greater than 2 as it is less than 10, and this is a mean in arithmetical proportion. But the mean considered relatively to ourselves must not be ascertained in this way. It does not follow that if 10 pounds of meat be too much and 2 be too little for a man to eat, a trainer will order him 6 pounds, as this may itself be too much or too little for the person who is to take it; it will be too little, for example, for Milo, but too much for a beginner in gymnastics. It will be the same with running and wrestling; the right amount will vary with the individual. This being so, everybody who understands his business avoids alike excess and deficiency; he seeks and chooses the mean, not the absolute mean, but the mean considered relatively to ourselves.

Every science then performs its function well, if it regards the mean and refers the works which it produces to the mean. This is the reason why it is usually said of successful works that it is impossible to take anything from them or to add anything to them, which implies that excess or deficiency is fatal to excellence but that the mean state ensures it. Good artists too, as we say, have an eye to the mean in their works. But virtue, like Nature herself, is more accurate and better than any art; virtue therefore will aim at the mean;—I speak of moral virtue, as it is moral virtue which is concerned with emotions and actions, and it is these which admit of excess and deficiency and the mean. Thus, it is possible to go too far, or not to go far enough, in respect of fear, courage, desire, anger, pity, and pleasure and pain generally, and the excess and the deficiency are alike wrong; but to experience these emotions at the right times and on the right occasions and towards the right persons and for the right causes and in the right manner is the mean or the supreme good, which is characteristic of virtue. Similarly there may be excess, deficiency, or the mean, in regard to actions. But virtue is concerned with emotions and actions, and here excess is an error and deficiency a fault, whereas the mean is successful and laudable, and success and merit are both characteristics of virtue.

It appears then that virtue is a mean state, so far at least as it aims at the mean.

Again, there are many different ways of going wrong; for evil is in its nature infinite, to use the Pythagorean figure, but good is finite. But there is only one possible way of going right. Accordingly, the former is easy and the latter difficult; it is easy to miss the mark but difficult to hit it. This again is a reason why excess and deficiency are characteristics of vice and the mean state a characteristic of virtue.

For good is simple, evil manifold.

Virtue then is a state of deliberate moral purpose consisting in a mean that is relative to ourselves, the mean being determined by reason, or as a prudent man would determine it.[1] It is a mean state firstly as lying between two vices, the vice of excess on the one hand, and the vice of deficiency on the other, and secondly because, whereas the vices either fall short of or go beyond what is proper in the emotions and actions, virtue not only discovers but embraces the mean.

Accordingly, virtue, if regarded in its essence or theoretical conception, is a mean state, but, if regarded from the point of view of the highest good, or of excellence, it is an extreme.

But it is not every action or every emotion that admits of a mean state. There are some whose very name implies wickedness, as for example, malice, shamelessness, and envy, among emotions, or adultery, theft, and murder, among actions. All these, and others like them, are censured as being intrinsically wicked, not merely the excesses or deficiencies of them. It is never possible then to be right in respect of them; they are always sinful. Right or wrong in such actions as adultery does not depend on our committing them with the right person, at the right time or in the right manner; on the contrary it is sinful to do anything of the kind at all. It would be equally wrong then to

---

[1] That is, moral virtue is a state of character consisting of a disposition to choose the mean relative to oneself in matters of action and feeling, the mean being determined by reason, or as a person of practical wisdom would determine it. [ED.]

suppose that there can be a mean state or an excess or deficiency in unjust, cowardly or licentious conduct; for, if it were so, there would be a mean state of an excess or of a deficiency, an excess of an excess and a deficiency of a deficiency. But as in temperance and courage there can be no excess or deficiency because the mean is, in a sense, an extreme, so too in these cases there cannot be a mean or an excess or deficiency, but, however the acts may be done, they are wrong. For it is a general rule that an excess or deficiency does not admit of a mean state, nor a mean state of an excess or deficiency.

But it is not enough to lay down this as a general rule; it is necessary to apply it to particular cases, as in reasonings upon actions general statements, although they are broader, are less exact than particular statements. For all action refers to particulars, and it is essential that our theories should harmonize with the particular cases to which they apply. We must take particular virtues then from the catalogue of virtues.

In regard to feelings of fear and confidence, courage is a mean state. On the side of excess, he whose fearlessness is excessive has no name, as often happens, but he whose confidence is excessive is foolhardy, while he whose timidity is excessive and whose confidence is deficient is a coward.

In respect of pleasures and pains, although not indeed of all pleasures and pains, and to a less extent in respect of pains than of pleasures, the mean state is temperance, the excess is licentiousness. We never find people who are deficient in regard to pleasures; accordingly such people again have not received a name, but we may call them insensible.

As regards the giving and taking of money, the mean state is liberality, the excess and deficiency are prodigality and illiberality. Here the excess and deficiency take opposite forms; for while the prodigal man is excessive in spending and deficient in taking, the illiberal man is excessive in taking and deficient in spending.

(For the present we are giving only a rough and summary account of the virtues, and that is sufficient for our purpose; we will hereafter determine their character more exactly.)

In respect of money there are other dispositions as well. There is the mean state which is magnificence; for the magnificent man, has having to do with large sums of money, differs from the liberal man who has to do only with small sums; and the excess corresponding to it is bad taste or vulgarity, the deficiency is meanness. These are different from the excess and deficiency of liberality; what the difference is will be explained hereafter.

In respect of honour and dishonour the mean state is highmindedness, the excess is what is called vanity, the deficiency littlemindedness. Corresponding to liberality, which, as we said, differs from magnificence as having to do not with great but with small sums of money, there is a moral state which has to do with petty honour and is related to highmindedness which has to do with great honour; for it is possible to aspire to honour in the right way, or in a way which is excessive or insufficient, and if a person's aspirations are excessive, he is called ambitious, if they are deficient, he is called unambitious, while if they are between the two, he has no name. The dispositions too are nameless, except that the disposition of the ambitious person is called ambition. The consequence is that the extremes lay claim to the mean or intermediate place. We ourselves speak of one who observes the mean sometimes as ambitious, and at other times as unambitious; we sometimes praise an ambitious, and at other times an unambitious person. The reason for our doing so will be stated in due course, but let us now discuss the other virtues in accordance with the method which we have followed hitherto.

Anger, like other emotions, has its excess, its deficiency, and its mean state. It may be said that they have no names, but as we call one who observes the mean gentle, we will call the mean state gentleness. Among the extremes, if a person errs on the side of excess, he may be called passionate and his vice passionateness, if on that of deficiency, he may be called impassive and his deficiency impassivity. . . .

In the matter of truth then, he who observes the mean may be called truthful, and the mean state truthfulness. Pretence, if it takes the form of exaggeration, is boastfulness, and one who is guilty of pretence is a boaster; but if it takes the form of depreciation it is irony, and he who is guilty of it is ironical.

As regards pleasantness in amusement, he who observes the mean is witty, and his disposition wittiness; the excess is buffoonery, and he who is guilty of it a buffoon, whereas he who is deficient in wit may be called a boor and his moral state boorishness.

As to the other kind of pleasantness, viz. pleasantness in life, he who is pleasant in a proper way is friendly, and his mean state friendliness; but he who goes too far, if he has no ulterior object in view, is obsequious, while if his object is self interest, he is a flatterer, and he who does not go far enough and always makes himself unpleasant is a quarrelsome and morose sort of person.

There are also mean states in the emotions and in the expression of the emotions. For although modesty is not a virtue, yet a modest person is praised as if he were virtuous; for here too one person is said to observe the mean and another to exceed it, as for example, the bashful man who is never anything but modest, whereas a person who has insufficient modesty or no modesty at all is called shameless, and one who observes the mean modest.

Righteous indignation, again, is a mean state between envy and malice. They are all concerned with the pain and pleasure which we feel at the fortunes of our neighbours. A person who is righteously indignant is pained at the prosperity of the undeserving; but the envious person goes further and is pained at anybody's prosperity, and the malicious person is so far from being pained that he actually rejoices at misfortunes. . . .

It is in some cases the deficiency and in others the excess which is the more opposed to the mean. Thus it is not foolhardiness the excess, but cowardice the deficiency which is the more opposed to courage, nor is it insensibility the deficiency, but licentiousness the excess which is the more opposed to temperance. There are two reasons why this should be so. One lies in the nature of the thing itself; for as one of the two extremes is the nearer and more similar to the mean, it is not this extreme, but its opposite, that we chiefly set against the mean. For instance, as it appears that foolhardiness is more similar and nearer to courage than cowardice, it is cowardice that we chiefly set against courage; for things which are further removed from the mean seem to be more opposite to it. This being one reason which lies in the nature of the thing itself, there is a second which lies in our own nature. It is the things to which we ourselves are naturally more inclined that appear more opposed to the mean. Thus, we are ourselves naturally more inclined to pleasures than to their opposites, and are more prone therefore to licentiousness than to decorum. Accordingly, we speak of those things, in which we are more likely to run to great lengths, as being more opposed to the mean. Hence it follows that licentiousness which is an excess is more opposed to temperance than insensibility.

It has now been sufficiently shown that moral virtue is a mean state, and in what sense it is a mean state; it is a mean state as lying between two vices, a vice of excess on the one side and a vice of deficiency on the other, and as aiming at the mean in the emotions and actions.

That is the reason why it is so hard to be virtuous; for it is always hard work to find the mean in anything, for example, it is not everybody, but only a man of science, who can find the mean or centre of a circle. So too anybody can get angry—that is an easy matter—and anybody can give or spend money, but to give it to the right persons, to give the right amount of it and to give it at the right time and for the right cause and in the right way, this is not what anybody can do, nor is it easy. That is the reason why it is rare and laudable and noble to do well. Accordingly one who aims at the mean must begin by departing from that extreme which is the more contrary to the mean; he must act in the spirit of Calypso's advice,

Far from this smoke and swell keep thou thy bark,

for of the two extremes one is more sinful than the other. As it is difficult then to hit the mean exactly, we must take the second best course, as the saying is, and choose the lesser of two evils, and this we shall best do in the way that we have described, that is, by steering clear of the evil which is further from the mean. We must also observe the things to which we are ourselves particularly prone, as different natures have different inclinations, and we may ascertain what these are by a consideration of our feelings of pleasure and pain. And then we must drag ourselves in the direction opposite to them; for it is by removing ourselves as far as possible from what is wrong that we shall arrive at the mean, as we do when we pull a crooked stick straight.

But in all cases we must especially be on our guard against what is pleasant and against pleasure, as we are not impartial judges of pleasure. Hence, our attitude towards pleasure must be like that of the elders of the people in the *Iliad* towards Helen, and we must never be afraid of applying the words they use; for if we dismiss pleasure as they dismissed Helen, we shall be less likely to go wrong. It is by action of this kind, to put it summarily, that we shall best succeed in hitting the mean.

It may be admitted that this is a difficult task, especially in particular cases. It is not easy to determine, for example, the right manner, objects, occasions, and duration of anger. There are times when we ourselves praise people who are deficient in anger, and call them gentle, and there are other times when we speak of people who exhibit a savage temper as spirited. It is not however one who deviates a little from what is right, but one who deviates a great deal, whether on the side of excess or of deficiency, that is censured; for he is sure to be found out. Again, it is not easy to decide theoretically how far and to what extent a man may go before he becomes censurable, but neither is it easy to define theoretically anything else within the region of perception . . .

So much then is plain, that the mean state is everywhere laudable, but that we ought to incline at one time towards the excess and at another towards the deficiency; for this will be our easiest manner of hitting the mean, or in other words of attaining excellence.

To Think About

1. "The highest good for man is neither enjoyment nor passive contentment but rather a dynamic power of growth and self-realization."   ***John Dewey***

2. "Happiness is a pig's philosophy."   ***Friedrich Nietzsche***

3. "Selfishness is a virtue."   ***Ayn Rand***

4. "If we have a case where the term unjust applies purely in virtue of a factual description, can't one raise the question whether one sometimes conceivably ought to do injustice?"   ***E. Anscombe***

5. "A philosophy is an expression of a man's character."   ***William James***

6. "The human being has within him a pressure (among other pressures) toward unity of personality, toward spontaneous expressiveness, toward full individuality and identity, toward seeing the truth rather than being blind, toward being creative, toward being good, and a lot else. That is, the human being is so constructed that he presses toward fuller and fuller being.

   "[There is] a single ultimate value for mankind, a far goal toward which all men strive. This is called variously by different authors self-actualization, self-realization, integration, psychological health, individuation, autonomy, creativity, productivity, but they all agree that this amounts to realizing the potentialities of the person, that is to say, becoming fully human, everything that the person *can* become."   ***Abraham Maslow***

7. "Does the rich man's help to the needy, on which he so readily prides himself as something meritorious, really deserve to be called beneficence at all?"   ***Unknown***

8. "There is no doubt that in one form or another, Socrates and Buddha, Jesus and St. Paul, Plotinus and Spinoza, taught that . . . without renunciation of many of the ordinary appetites, no man can really live well."   ***Walter Lippmann***

9. "Morality is internal. The moral law . . . has to be expressed in the form, 'be this,' not in the form 'do this.' . . . [T]he true moral law says 'hate not,' instead of 'kill not.' . . . [T]he only mode of stating the moral law must be as a rule of character."   ***Leslie Stephens***

10. "[T]his must be agreed upon beforehand, that the whole account of matters of conduct must be given in outline and not precisely, as we said at the very beginning that the accounts we demand must be in accordance with the subject-matter; matters concerned with conduct and questions of what is good for us have no fixity, any more than matters of health."   ***Aristotle***

11. "One great difficulty must remain unsolved. Rather, I assert that it is intrinsically insoluble. There is no absolute coincidence between virtue and happiness. I cannot prove that it is always prudent to act rightly or that it is always happiest to be virtuous. My inability to prove those propositions arises, as I hold, from the fact that they are not true. This admission does nothing to diminish our belief in the surpassing importance of morality and of its essential connection with social welfare; and further, it does not diminish the intrinsic motives to virtue, inasmuch as those motives are not really based upon prudence. But I cannot go further."   ***Leslie Stephens***

12. "I have not been afraid of excess: excess on occasion is exhilarating. It prevents moderation from acquiring the deadening effect of a habit."   ***W. Somerset Maugham***

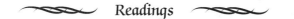 ## Readings

COMTE-SPONVILLE, ANDRÉ. *A Short Treatise on the Great Virtues: The Uses of Philosophy in Everyday Life.* London: Heinemann, 2002.

FOOT, PHILIPPA. *Virtues and Vices.* Cambridge: Blackwell, 1978.

GEWIRTH, ALAN. "Rights and Virtues." *Review of Metaphysics* 38 (1985): 739–62.

HARDIE, W. F. R. *Aristotle's Ethical Theory.* Oxford: Clarendon Press, 1968.

HILL, THOMAS. "Servility and Self-Respect." *Monist* 57 (1973): 1–21.

KRUSCHWITZ, ROBERT, and ROBERT ROBERTS, eds. *The Virtues.* Belmont, CA: Wadsworth, 1987, 1–21.

LOUDEN, ROBERT. "Some Vices of Virtue Ethics." *American Philosophical Quarterly* 21 (1984): 227–36.

MACINTYRE, ALASDAIR. *After Virtue,* rev. ed. Notre Dame, IN: University of Notre Dame Press, 1981.

MAYO, BERNARD. *Ethics and the Moral Life.* New York: Macmillan, 1938.

MURDOCH, IRIS. *The Sovereignty of Good.* New York: Schocken Books, 1971.

ROSS, W. D. *Aristotle.* London: Oxford University Press, 1955.

20
Happiness Is Seeking the Greatest Pleasure for the Greatest Number of People

Jeremy Bentham (1748–1832) was the leading figure in the early phase of the British utilitarian movement in philosophy and politics. He was primarily interested in legal reform and constantly sought a philosophic basis for the reforms he advocated. In connection with this, he wrote his highly influential works on the theory of law and ethics.

Bentham is a teleologist regarding ethical theory. He believes that not only do people seek pleasure, but that they ought to seek it both for themselves and for the wider community. This is the *principle of utility.* The particular ends that we seek, either pleasures or avoidance of pains, should be evaluated through a series of calculations that Bentham calls the *hedonistic calculus.*

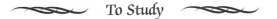 To Study

1. What does Bentham mean by the term *principle of utility?* Discuss it in terms of the interest of the individual and the community.
2. Explain the principle of asceticism and the principle of sympathy and antipathy. Why does Bentham find them lacking?
3. Is Bentham's hedonistic calculus practical? Why or why not?
4. Why doesn't Bentham believe motives to be an exception to his theory?

From Jeremy Bentham, *An Introduction to the Principles of Morals and Legislation* (London: Wilson & Pickering, 1823), chaps. 1, 2, 4, and 10.

THE PRINCIPLE OF UTILITY

Nature has placed mankind under the governance of two sovereign masters, *pain* and *pleasure.* It is for them alone to point out what we ought to do, as well as to determine what we shall do. On the one hand the standard of right and wrong, on the other the chain of causes and effects, are fastened to their throne. They govern us in all we do, in all we say, in all we think; every effort we can make to throw off our subjection will serve but to demonstrate and confirm it. In words a man may pretend to abjure their empire: but in reality he will remain subject to it all the while. The *principle of utility* recognizes the subjection, and assumes it for the foundation of that system, the object of which is to tear the fabric of felicity by the hands of reason and of law. Systems which attempt to question it, deal in sounds instead of sense, in caprice instead of reason, in darkness instead of light.

But enough of metaphor and declamation: it is not by such means that moral science is to be improved.

The principle of utility is the foundation of the present work; it will be proper, therefore, at the outset to give an explicit and determinate account of what is meant by it. By the principle of utility is meant that principle which approves or disapproves of every action whatsoever, according to the tendency which it appears to have to augment or diminish the happiness of the party whose interest is in question; or what is the same thing in other words, to promote or to oppose that happiness. I say of every action whatsoever; and therefore not only of every action of a private individual, but of every measure of government.

By utility is meant that property in any object, whereby it tends to produce benefit, advantage, pleasure, good, or happiness (all this in the present case comes to the same thing) or (what comes again to the same thing) to prevent the happening of mischief, pain, evil, or unhappiness to the party whose interest is considered: if that party be the community in general, then the happiness of the community: if a particular individual, then the happiness of that individual.

The interest of the community is one of the most general expressions that can occur in the phraseology of morals: no wonder that the meaning is often lost. When it has a meaning, it is this. The community is a fictitious *body,* composed of the individual persons who are considered as constituting as it were its *members.* The interest of the community then is, what?—the sum of the interests of the several members who compose it.

It is in vain to talk of the interest of the community, without understanding what is the interest of the individual. A thing is said to promote the interest, or to be *for* the interest, of an individual, when it tends to add to the sum total of his pleasures: or, what comes to the same thing, to diminish the sum total of his pains.

An action then may be said to be conformable to the principle of utility, or, for shortness' sake, to utility (meaning with respect to the community at large) when the tendency it has to augment the happiness of the community is greater than any it has to diminish it.

A measure of government (which is but a particular kind of action, performed by a particular person or persons) may be said to be conformable to or dictated by the principle of utility, when in like manner the tendency which it has to augment the happiness of the community is greater than any which it has to diminish it. . . .

Of an action that is conformable to the principle of utility, one may always say either that it is one that ought to be done, or at least that it is not one that ought not to be done. One may also say, that it is right it should be done; at least that it is not wrong it should be done: that it is a right action; at least that it is not a wrong action. When thus interpreted, the words *ought,* and *right* and *wrong,* and others of that stamp, have a meaning: when otherwise, they have none.

PRINCIPLES ADVERSE TO THAT OF UTILITY

If the principle of utility be a right principle to be governed by, and that in all cases, it follows from what has been just observed that whatever principle differs from it in any case must necessarily be a wrong one. To prove any other principle, therefore, to be a wrong one, there needs no more than just to show it to be what it is, a principle of which the dictates are in some point or other different from those of the principle of utility: to state it is to confute it.

A principle may be different from that of utility in two ways: (1) By being constantly opposed to it: this is the case with a principle which may be termed the principle of *asceticism.* (2) By being sometimes opposed to it and sometimes not, as it may happen: this is the case with another, which may be termed the principle of *sympathy* and *antipathy.*

By the principle of asceticism I mean that principle, which, like the principle of utility, approves or disapproves of any action, according to the tendency which it appears to have to augment or diminish the happiness of the party whose interest is in question; but in an inverse manner: approving of actions in as far as they tend to diminish his happiness; disapproving of them in as far as they tend to augment it. . . .

The principle of asceticism seems originally to have been the reverie of certain hasty speculators, who having perceived, or fancied, that certain pleasures, when reaped in certain circumstances, have, at the long run, been attended with pains more than equivalent to them, took occasion to quarrel with everything that offered itself under the name of pleasure. Having then got thus far, and having forgot the point which they set out from, they pushed on, and went so much further as to think it meritorious to fall in love with pain. Even this, we see, is at bottom but the principle of utility misapplied.

The principle of utility is capable of being consistently pursued; and it is but tautology to say that the more consistently it is pursued, the better it must ever be for humankind. The principle of asceticism never was, nor never can be, consistently pursued by any living creature. Let but one tenth part of the inhabitants of this earth pursue it consistently, and in a day's time they will have turned it into a hell.

Among principles adverse to that of utility, that which at this day seems to have most influence in matters of government, is what may be called the principle of sympathy and antipathy. By the principle of sympathy and antipathy I mean that principle which approves or disapproves of certain actions, not on account of their tending to augment the happiness, nor yet on account of their tending to diminish the happiness of the party whose interest is in question, but merely because a man finds himself disposed to approve or disapprove of them: holding up that approbation or disapprobation as a sufficient reason for itself, and disclaiming the necessity of looking out for any extrinsic ground. Thus, far in the general department of morals; and in the particular department of politics, measuring out the quantum (as well as determining the ground) of punishment, by the degree of the disapprobation.

It is manifest, that this is rather a principle in name than in reality; it is not a positive principle of itself, so much as a term employed to signify the negation of all principle. What one expects to find in a principle is something that points out some external consideration, as a means of warranting and guiding the internal sentiments of approbation and disapprobation; this expectation is but ill fulfilled by a proposition, which does neither more nor less than hold up each of those sentiments as a ground and standard for itself.

In looking over the catalogue of human actions (says a partisan of this principle) in order to determine which of them are to be marked with the seal of disapprobation you need to take counsel of your own feelings: whatever you find in yourself a propensity to condemn is wrong for that very reason. For the same reason it is also meet for punishment: in what proportion it is adverse to utility, or whether it be adverse to utility at all, is a matter that makes no difference. In that same *proportion* also it is meet for punishment; if you hate much, punish much; if you hate little, punish little; punish as you hate. If you hate not at all; punish not at all; the fine feelings of the soul are not to be overborne and tyrannized by the harsh and rugged dictates of political utility.

The various systems that have been formed concerning the standard of right and wrong, may all be reduced to the principle of sympathy and antipathy. One account may serve for all of them. They consist all of them in so many contrivances for avoiding the obligation of appealing to any external standard, and for prevailing upon the reader to accept of the author's sentiment or opinion as a reason for itself. . . .

THE HEDONISTIC CALCULUS

Pleasures, then, and the avoidance of pains, are the *ends,* which the legislator has in view: it behooves him therefore to understand their *value.* Pleasures and pains are the *instruments* he has to work with: it behooves him therefore to understand their force, which is again, in other words, their value.

To a person considered *by himself,* the value of a pleasure or pain considered *by itself,* will be greater or less, according to the four following circumstances:

1. Its *intensity.*
2. Its *duration.*
3. Its *certainty* or *uncertainty.*
4. Its *propinquity* or *remoteness.*

These are the circumstances which are to be considered in estimating a pleasure or a pain considered each of them by itself. But when the value of any pleasure or pain is considered for the purpose of estimating the tendency of any *act* by which it is produced, there are two other circumstances to be taken into the account; these are,

5.   Its *fecundity,* or the chance it has of being followed by sensations of the *same* kind: that is, pleasures, if it be a pleasure: pains, if it be a pain.
6.   Its *purity,* or the chance it has of *not* being followed by sensations of the *opposite* kind: that is, pains, if it be a pleasure: pleasures, if it be a pain.

These two last, however, are in strictness scarcely to be deemed properties of the pleasures or the pain itself; they are not, therefore, in strictness to be taken into the account of the value of that pleasure or that pain. They are in strictness to be deemed properties only of the act, or other event, by which such pleasure or pain has been produced; and accordingly are only to be taken into the account of the tendency of such act or such event.

To a *number* of persons, with reference to each of whom the value of a pleasure or a pain is considered, it will be greater or less, according to seven circumstances: to wit, the six preceding ones: viz.

1.   Its *intensity.*
2.   Its *duration.*
3.   Its *certainty* or *uncertainty.*
4.   Its *propinquity* or *remoteness.*
5.   Its *fecundity.*
6.   Its *purity.*

And one other; to wit:

7.   Its *extent;* that is, the number of persons to whom it *extends;* or (in other words) who are affected by it.

To take an exact account then of the general tendency of any act, by which the interests of a community are affected, proceed as follows. Begin with any one person of those whose interests seem most immediately to be affected by it: and take an account,

1.   Of the value of each distinguishable *pleasure* which appears to be produced by it in the *first* instance.
2.   Of the value of each *pain* which appears to be produced by it in the *first* instance.
3.   Of the value of each *pleasure* which appears to be produced by it *after* the first. This constitutes the *fecundity* of the first *pleasure* and the *impurity* of the first *pain.*
4.   Of the value of each *pain* which appears to be produced by it after the first. This constitutes the *fecundity* of the first *pain,* and the *impurity* of the first *pleasure.*

5. Sum up all the values of all the *pleasures* on the one side, and those of all the *pains* on the other. The balance, if it be on the side of pleasure, will give the *good* tendency of the act upon the whole, with respect to the interests of that *individual* person; if on the side of pain, the *bad* tendency of it upon the whole.

6. Take an account of the *number* of persons whose interests appear to be concerned; and repeat the above process with respect to each. *Sum up* the numbers expressive of the degrees of *good* tendency, which the act has, with respect to each individual, in regard to whom the tendency of it is *good* upon the whole: do this again with respect to each individual, in regard to whom tendency of it is *bad* upon the whole. Take the *balance;* which, if on the side of *pleasure,* will give the general *good tendency* of the act, with respect to the total number or community of individuals concerned; if on the side of *pain,* the general *evil tendency,* with respect to the same community.

It is not to be expected that this process should be strictly pursued previously to every moral judgment, or to every legislative or judicial operation. It may, however, be always kept in view: and as near as the process actually pursued on these occasions approaches to it, so near will such process approach to the character of an exact one.

MOTIVES

With respect to goodness and badness, as it is with everything else that is not itself either pain or pleasure, so is it with motives. If they are good or bad, it is only on account of their effects: good, on account of their tendency to produce pleasure, or avert pain: bad, on account of their tendency to produce pain, or avert pleasure. Now the case is, that from one and the same motive, and from every kind of motive, may proceed actions that are good, others that are bad, and others that are indifferent. . . .

It appears then that there is no such thing as a sort of motive which is a bad one in itself: nor, consequently, any such thing as a sort of motive which in itself is exclusively a good one. And as to their effects, it appears too that these are sometimes bad, at other times either indifferent or good, and this appears to be the case with every sort of motive. *If any sort of motive then is either good or bad on the score of its effects, this is the case only on individual occasions, and with individual motives;* and this is the case with one sort of motive as well as with another. *If any sort of motive then can, in consideration of its effects, be termed with any propriety a bad one,* it can only be with reference to the balance of all the effects it may have had of both kinds within a given period, that is, of its most usual tendency.

What then? (it will be said) are not lust, cruelty, avarice, bad motives? Is there so much as any one individual occasion, in which motives like these can be otherwise than bad? No, certainly: and yet the proposition that there is no one *sort* of motive but what will on many occasions be a good one, is nevertheless true. The fact is, that these are names which, if properly applied, are never applied but in the cases where the motives they signify happen to be bad. The names of these motives, considered apart from their effects, are sexual desire, displeasure, and pecuniary interest. To sexual desire, when the effects of it are looked upon as bad, is given the name of lust. Now lust is always a bad motive. Why? Because if the case be such that the effects of the motive are not bad, it does not go, or at least ought not to go, by the name of lust. The case is, then, that when I say, "Lust is a bad motive," it is a proposition that merely concerns the import of the word lust; and which would be false if transferred to the other word used for the same motive, sexual desire. Hence we see the emptiness of all those rhapsodies of commonplace morality, which consist in the taking of such names as lust, cruelty, and avarice, and branding them with marks of reprobation: applied to the *thing,* they are false; applied to the *name,* they are true indeed, but nugatory. Would you do a real service to mankind, show them the cases in which sexual desire *merits* the name of lust; displeasure, that of cruelty, and pecuniary interest, that of avarice.

To Think About

1. "Think of our attempts to live responsibly when we cannot prove why we should be ethical at all, or of what we believe in a fundamental order is reality which allows scientific inquiry. Or of the nature of the universe open to us by the new astronomies and cosmologies, stranger than we imagine and stranger than we can imagine. And how do we understand the oppression endured by so many of the living? What is the meaning in the profound love and joy we experience?"
   James Gould

2. "The white man has no real home. He is lost in a world that he doesn't understand. He has ceased to communicate with the spirits of the earth and the forest, the river and air, so he is alone. Unhappy, he searches for happiness and when he sees happiness in others he becomes angry and wants to destroy it because inside he is empty. I am not a politician, I am only a singer, but many people listen to me. I promise you that whenever I can speak on your behalf I will do so. I shall tell your story to whomever I can because you are the only protectors of the forest and if the forest dies then so does the earth. Even a white man can understand this."
   Sting, to Chief Raoni

3. "Behind the short prohibition 'Thou shalt not kill' lie as many tacitly understood qualifications and cultural and legal discriminations as lie behind 'Thou shalt not love thy neighbour's wife.' Just as the latter presupposes determinate institutions of marriage, determining individual marital rights, so 'Thou shalt not murder' presupposes a complex set of culturally specific rights, powers, and prerogatives. . . . [A]ny popular version of a short set of moral don'ts, such as 'don't kill,' 'don't steal,' 'don't break promises,' 'unless you are an official don't coerce,' brings with it a very rich cultural baggage, if it is to have any content at all. Either it is a purely formal moral code, not yet prohibiting or enjoining anything, or else the form gets its determinate filling, in which case we are committed not merely to these 'negative' rules but to the rules of background institutions and ways of life that supply the determinate content to these prohibitions."
   Unknown

4. "You have no more right to consume happiness without producing it than to consume wealth without producing it."   ***Bernard Shaw***

5. "[T]he central question the individual needs to ask is: 'How did I come to be as I presently am?' There are four categories I have found particularly fruitful to investigate. What *wounds* or hurts do you resent having suffered? What *gifts* were you given for which you are grateful? Who were your important *heroes* and models? What were the crucial *decisions* for which you were responsible?"   ***S. Keen***

6. "[T]he doctrine that Universal Happiness is the ultimate *standard* must not be understood to imply that Universal Benevolence is the only right or always best *motive* of action. . . . [I]t is not necessary that the end which gives the criterion of rightness should always be the end at which we consciously aim: and if experience shows that the general happiness will be more satisfactorily attained if men frequently act from other motives than pure universal philanthropy, it is obvious that these other motives are reasonably to be preferred on Utilitarian principles."   ***Henry Sidgwick***

7. "[T]he Utilitarian conclusion, carefully stated, would seem to be this; that the opinion that secrecy may render an action right which would not otherwise be so should itself be kept comparatively secret; and similarly it seems expedient that the doctrine that esoteric morality is expedient should itself be kept esoteric. . . . thus a Utilitarian may reasonably desire, on Utilitarian principles, that some of his conclusions should be rejected by mankind generally."   ***Henry Sidgwick***

8. "When we say that pleasure is the goal we do not mean the pleasures of the dissipated and those which consist in the process of enjoyment . . . but freedom from pain in the body and from disturbance in the mind. For it is not drinking and continuous parties nor sexual pleasures nor the enjoyment of fish and other delicacies of a wealthy table which produce the pleasant life, but sober reasoning which searches out the causes of every act of choice and refusal and which banishes the opinions that give rise to the greatest mental confusion."   ***Epictetus***

9. "If consequentialism is correct there are no limits of the first kind for, in principle, any sort of act at all might be permissible in the right circumstances, provided only that it leads to the best consequences overall. And there are no limits of the second kind, for there is simply no limit to the sacrifices that an agent might be required to make in the pursuit of the greater good. . . .

    "Most discussion of consequentialism has focused on the first objection, that is, that it permits too much. This is somewhat surprising, for in practical terms consequentialism may not differ in this area all that much from ordinary morality. Killing the innocent, for example, will generally not have the best results overall, and so consequentialism and ordinary morality will typically be alike in forbidding it. And in many complex cases it is often unclear what act will lead to the best results, and so unclear whether consequentialism actually diverges in that case from ordinary morality. In contrast, the second objection—which turns on whether there is a limit to the sacrifices that morality can demand of an agent—indicates an area in which consequentialism and ordinary morality diverge sharply and undeniably. For consequentialism is *far* more demanding than ordinary morality in terms of the sacrifices that must be made for the greater good."   ***Shelly Kagan***

10. "A person who utters words, or does acts, of admiration, gratitude, or appreciation only on utilitarian grounds becomes a person without admiration, gratitude, or appreciation. If utilitarianism has no place for desert, desert has no place for utilitarianism either."   ***James Griffin***

11. "It is better to be a human being dissatisfied than a pig satisfied; better to be Socrates dissatisfied than a fool satisfied. And if the fool, or the pig, is of a different opinion, it is because they only know their own side of the question."   ***John Stuart Mill***

12. "There is nothing better than my station and its duties, nor anything more truly beautiful. It holds and will hold its own against the wishes of the 'individual,' whatever form that may take."   ***Henry Sidgwick***

13. "The extreme utilitarian regards moral rules as rules of thumb and as sociological facts that have to be taken into account when deciding what to do, just as facts of any other sort have to be taken into account. But in themselves they do not justify any action."   ***John Smart***

14. "Utilitarianism is concerned with maximisation of expected utility, and is not concerned with distribution of utility."   ***John Smart***

15. "The physicist **Steven Weinberg,** in the January issue of the The Atlantic Monthly, dismisses five current ideas he thinks are misguidedly utopian: belief in the free market, in a governing elite, in the powers of religion, in ecological consciousness and in technological innovation."

16. "One persistent strand in utopian thinking is the feeling that there is some set of principles obvious enough to be accepted by all men of good will, precise enough to give unambiguous guidance in particular situations, clear enough so that all will realize its dictates, and complete enough to cover all problems which actually arise."   ***Robert Nozick***

17. Schadenfreude includes pleasure in another's comeuppance, but also shame at having felt the pleasure. It is savored in private, without public display, but it is also a reaction to the public sphere. The historian **Peter Gay**—who felt Schadenfreude as a Jewish child in Nazi-era Berlin, watching the Germans lose coveted gold medals in the 1936 Olympics—has said that it "can be one of the great joys of life."

18. "He said, It is a very hard thing to find happiness. Hundreds and thousands of examples exist of how to be miserable, and they are everywhere you look for you to copy. It is easy to be miserable, he said, millions can show you the way. It requires no thought or creativity of your own, just following. To be happy is hard, because no one can show you, it is something you have to work out, create for yourself. No one can give you a model to copy, though many will volunteer,

because happiness is not off the rack, one size fits all, it is something each of us has to tailor-make for himself or herself." ***Margaret Salinger***

19. "It is easier to love humanity as a whole than to love one's neighbor."
  Eric Hoffer

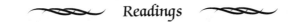

Readings

BRANDT, RICHARD. *Ethical Theory.* Upper Saddle River, NJ: Prentice Hall, 1960.

BROCK, DAN. "Recent Work in Utilitarianism." *American Philosophical Quarterly* 10 (October 1973): 241–76.

GAUTHIER, DAVID. *Morality by Agreement.* Oxford: Clarendon Press, 1986.

LYONS, D. *Forms and Limits of Utilitarianism.* Oxford: Clarendon Press, 1965.

SCHEFFLER, S. *Consequentialism and Its Critics.* Oxford: Clarendon Press, 1988.

SMART, J., AND B. WILLIAMS. *Utilitarianism: For and Against.* Cambridge: Cambridge University Press, 1973.

STEPHEN, LESLIE. *The English Utilitarians.* London: London School of Economics, 1950.

21
Duty Is Prior to Happiness

Immanuel Kant (1724–1804) was an immensely innovative and influential philosopher. His Critique of Pure Reason *(1781) introduced a revolution in thinking that set the tone for all nineteenth-century philosophy and that is still felt today. Kant lived most of his life in obscurity in Königsberg, East Prussia, teaching at the University of Königsberg.*

Kant says that the only good thing in the world is a good will. By this, he does not mean good intentions, but rather a rational will, that is, one that out of duty wills consistently. This is expressed in terms of the *categorical imperative:* "Act only according to that maxim by which you can at the same time will that it should become a universal law." Kant believes this is quite different from the Golden Rule.

~~~~~ *To Study* ~~~~~

1. According to Kant, what is the only good without qualification?
2. Why are character, gifts of fortune, and happiness not good without qualification?
3. What is an imperative? By what word are imperatives expressed?
4. Distinguish between hypothetical and categorical imperatives.
5. What is the one categorical imperative?
6. Why can't suicide be advocated as a universal law?
7. What are the consequences of making a promise when one doesn't intend to keep it?
8. Why should people necessarily develop their talents?
9. Why should one assist the poor?

From Immanuel Kant, *Fundamental Principles of the Metaphysics of Morals,* 6th ed., trans. T. K. Abbott (London: Longmans, Green, 1907).

10. Why can't the basic principle be deduced from the particular attributes of human nature?
11. State the practical imperative. Apply it to the four previous examples.
12. How did we arrive at the principle? What is the problem of innocence?
13. What are Kant's criticisms of the Golden Rule?

Nothing can possibly be conceived in the world, or even out of it, which can be called good without qualification, except a Good Will. Intelligence, wit, judgment, and the other *talents* of the mind, however they may be named, or courage, resolution, perseverance, as qualities of temperament, are undoubtedly good and desirable in many respects; but these gifts of nature may also become extremely bad and mischievous if the will which is to make use of them, and which, therefore, constitutes what is called *character,* is not good. It is the same with the *gifts of fortune.* Power, riches, honor, even health, and the general well-being and contentment with one's condition which is called *happiness,* inspire pride, and often presumption, if there is not a good will to correct the influence of these on the mind, and with this also to rectify the whole principle of acting, and adapt it to its end. The sight of a being who is not adorned with a single feature of a pure and good will, enjoying unbroken prosperity, can never give pleasure to an impartial rational spectator. Thus, a good will appears to constitute the indispensable condition even of being worthy of happiness.

There are even some qualities which are of service to this good will itself, and may facilitate its action, yet which have no intrinsic unconditional value, but always presuppose a good will, and this qualifies the esteem that we justly have for them, and does not permit us to regard them as absolutely good. Moderation in the affections and passions, self-control and calm deliberation are not only good in many respects, but even seem to constitute part of the intrinsic worth of the person; but they are far from deserving to be called good without qualification, although they have been so unconditionally praised by the ancients. For without the principles of a good will, they may become extremely bad, and the coolness of a villain not only makes him far more dangerous, but also directly makes him more abominable in our eyes than he would have been without it.

A good will is good, not because of what it performs or effects, not by its aptness for the attainment of some proposed end, but simply by virtue of the volition; that is, it is good in itself, and considered by itself is to be esteemed much higher than all that can be brought about by it in favor of any inclination, nay even of the sum total of all inclinations. Even if it should happen that, owing to special disfavor of fortune, or the niggardly provision of a stepmotherly nature, this will should wholly lack power to accomplish its purpose, if with its greatest efforts it should yet achieve nothing, and there should remain only the good will (not, to be sure, a mere wish, but the summoning of all means in our power), then, like a jewel, it would still shine by its own light, as a thing which has its whole value in itself. Its usefulness or fruitlessness can neither add to nor take away anything from this value. It would be, as it were, only the setting to enable us to handle it the more conveniently in common commerce or to attract to it the attention of those who are not yet connoisseurs, but not to recommend it to true connoisseurs, or to determine its value.

There is, however, something so strange in this idea of the absolute value of the mere will, in which no account is taken of its utility, that notwithstanding the thorough assent of even common reason to the idea, yet a suspicion must arise that it may perhaps really be the product of mere high-flown fancy, and that we may have misunderstood the purpose of nature in assigning reason as the governor of our will. Therefore, we will examine this idea from this point of view.

. . . The will is a faculty to choose *that only* which reason independent of inclination recognizes as practically necessary, that is, as good. But if reason of itself does not sufficiently determine the will, if the latter is subject also to subjective conditions (particular impulses) which do not always coincide with the objective conditions, in a word, if the will does not *in itself* completely accord with reason (which is actually the case with men), then the actions which objectively are recognized as necessary are subjectively contingent, and the determination of such a will according to objective laws is *obligation,* that is to say, the relation of the objective laws to a will that is not thoroughly good is conceived as the determination of the will of a rational being by principles of reason, but which the will from its nature does not of necessity follow.

The conception of an objective principle, in so far as it is obligatory for a will, is called a command (of reason), and the formula of the command is called an Imperative.

All imperatives are expressed by the word *ought [or shall],* and thereby indicate the relation of an objective law of reason to a will which from its subjective constitution is not necessarily determined by it (an obligation). They say that something would be good to do or to forbear, but they say it to a will which does not always do a thing because it is conceived to be good to do it. That is practically *good,* however, which determines the will by means of the conceptions of reason, and consequently not from subjective causes, but objectively, that is, on principles which are valid for every rational being as such. It is distinguished from the *pleasant* as that which influences the will only by means of sensation from merely subjective causes, valid only for the sense of this or that one, and not as a principle of reason which holds for every one.

Now all *imperatives* command either *hypothetically* or *categorically.* The former represent the practical necessity of a possible action as means to something else that is willed (or at least which one might possibly will). The categorical imperative would be that which represented an action as necessary of itself without reference to another end, that is, as objectively necessary.

Since every practical law represents a possible action as good, and on this account, for a subject who is practically determinable by reason as necessary, all imperatives are formulae determining an action which is necessary according to the principle of a will good in some respects. If now the action is good only as a means *to something else,* then the imperative is *hypothetical;* if it is conceived as good *in itself* and consequently as being necessarily the principle of a will which of itself conforms to reason, then it is *categorical.*

Thus, the imperative declares what action possible by me would be good, and presents the practical rule in relation to a will which does not forthwith perform an action simply because it is good, whether because the subject does not always know that it is good, or because, even if it know this, yet its maxims might be opposed to the objective principles of practical reason.

Accordingly the hypothetical imperative only says that the action is good for some purpose, *possible or actual.* In the first case it is a *problematical,* in the second an *assertorial* practical principle. The categorical imperative which declares an action to be objectively necessary in itself without reference to any purpose, that is, without any other end, is valid as an *apodictic* (practical) principle.

Whatever is possible only by the power of some rational being may also be conceived as a possible purpose of some will; and therefore the principles of action as regards the means necessary to attain some possible purpose are in fact infinitely numerous. All sciences have a practical part consisting of problems expressing that some end is possible for us, and of imperatives directing how it may be attained. These may, therefore, be called in general imperatives of *skill.* Here there is no question whether the end is rational and good, but only what one must do in order to attain it. The precepts for the physician to make his patient thoroughly healthy, and for a poisoner to ensure certain death, are of equal value in this respect, that each serves to effect its purpose perfectly. Since in early youth it cannot be known what ends are likely to occur to us in the course of life, parents seek to have their children taught a *great many things,* and provide for their *skill* in the use of means for all sorts of arbitrary ends, of none of which can they determine whether it may not perhaps hereafter be an object to their pupil, but which it is at all events *possible* that he might aim at; and this anxiety is so great that they commonly neglect to form and correct their judgment on the value of the things which may be chosen as ends.

There is *one* end, however, which may be assumed to be actually such to all rational beings (so far as imperatives apply to them, viz., as dependent beings), and, therefore, one purpose which they not merely *may* have, but which we may with certainty assume that they all actually *have* by a natural necessity, and this is *happiness.* The hypothetical imperative which expresses the practical necessity of an action as means to the advancement of happiness is *assertorial.* We are not to present it as necessary for an uncertain and merely possible purpose, but for a purpose which we may presuppose with certainty and *a priori* in every man, because it belongs to his being. Now skill in the choice of means to his own greatest well-being may be called *prudence,* in the narrowest sense. And thus, the imperative which refers to the choice of means to one's own happiness, that is, the precept of prudence, is still always *hypothetical;* the action is not commanded absolutely, but only as means to another purpose.

Finally, there is an imperative which commands a certain conduct immediately, without having as its condition any other purpose to be attained by it. This imperative is *categorical.* It concerns not the matter of the action, or its intended result, but its form and the principle of which it is itself a result; and what is essentially good in it consists in the mental disposition, let the consequence be what it may. This imperative may be called that of *morality. . . .*

When I conceive a hypothetical imperative, in general I do not know beforehand what it will contain until I am given the condition. But when I conceive a categorical imperative, I know at once what it contains. For as the imperative contains besides the law only the necessity that the maxims[1] shall conform to this law, while the law contains no conditions restricting it, there remains nothing but the general statement that the maxim of the action should conform to a universal law, and it is this conformity alone that the imperative properly represents as necessary.

There is therefore but one categorical imperative, namely, this: *Act only on that maxim whereby thou canst at the same time will that it should become a universal law.*

Now if all imperatives of duty can be deduced from this one imperative as from their principle, then, although it should remain undecided whether what is called duty is not merely a vain notion, yet at least we shall be able to show what we understand by it and what this notion means.

Since the universality of the law according to which effects are produced constitutes what is properly called *nature* in the most general sense (as to form)—that is, the existence of things so far as it is determined by general laws—the imperative of duty may be expressed thus: *Act as if the maxim of thy action were to become by thy will a universal law of nature.*

We will now enumerate a few duties, adopting the usual division of them into duties to ourselves and to others, and into perfect and imperfect duties.

1. A man reduced to despair by a series of misfortunes feels wearied of life, but is still so far in possession of his reason that he can ask himself whether it would not be contrary to his duty to himself to take his own life. Now he inquires whether the maxim of his action could become a universal law of nature. His maxim is: From self-love I adopt it as a principle to shorten my life when its longer duration is likely to bring more evil than satisfaction. It is asked then simply whether this principle founded on self-love can become a universal law of nature. Now we see at once that a system of nature of which it should be a law to destroy life by means of the very feeling whose special nature it is to impel to the improvement of life would contradict itself, and therefore could not exist as a system of nature; hence that maxim cannot possibly exist as a universal law of nature, and consequently would be wholly inconsistent with the supreme principle of all duty.

2. Another finds himself forced by necessity to borrow money. He knows that he will not be able to repay it, but sees also that nothing will be lent to him unless he promises stoutly to repay it in a definite time. He desires to make this promise, but he has still so much conscience as to ask himself: Is it not unlawful and inconsistent with duty to get out of a difficulty in this way? Suppose, however, that he resolves to do so, then the maxim of his action would be expressed thus: When I think myself in want of money, I will borrow money and promise to repay it, although I know that I never can do so. Now this principle of self-love or of one's own advantage may perhaps be consistent with my whole future welfare; but the question now is, Is it right?

---

[1] A "maxim" is a subjective principle of action, and must be distinguished from the *objective principle,* namely, practical law. The former contains the practical rule set by reason according to the conditions of the subject (often its ignorance or its inclinations), so that it is the principle on which the subject *acts;* but the law is the objective principle valid for every rational being, and is the principle on which it *ought to act*—that is, an imperative.

I change then the suggestion of self-love into a universal law, and state the question thus: How would it be if my maxim were a universal law? Then I see at once that it could never hold as a universal law of nature, but would necessarily contradict itself. For supposing it to be a universal law that everyone when he thinks himself in a difficulty should be able to promise whatever he pleases, with the purpose of not keeping his promise, the promise itself would become impossible, as well as the end that one might have in view in it, since no one would consider that anything was promised to him, but would ridicule all such statements as vain pretenses.

3. A third finds in himself a talent which with the help of some culture might make him a useful man in many respects. But he finds himself in comfortable circumstances and prefers to indulge in pleasure rather than to take pains in enlarging and improving his happy natural capacities. He asks, however, whether his maxim of neglect of his natural gifts, besides agreeing with his inclination to indulgence, agrees also with what is called duty. He sees then that a system of nature could indeed subsist with such a universal law, although men (like the South Sea islanders) should let their talents rest and resolve to devote their lives merely to idleness, amusement, and propagation of their species—in a word, to enjoyment; but he cannot possibly *will* that this should be a universal law of nature, or be implanted in us as such by a natural instinct. For, as a rational being, he necessarily wills that his faculties be developed, since they serve him, and have been given him, for all sorts of possible purposes.

4. A fourth, who is in prosperity, while he sees that others have to contend with great wretchedness and that he could help them, thinks: What concern is it of mine? Let everyone be as happy as Heaven pleases, or as he can make himself; I will take nothing from him nor even envy him, only I do not wish to contribute anything to his welfare or to his assistance in distress! Now no doubt, if such a mode of thinking were a universal law, the human race might very well subsist, and doubtless even better than in a state in which everyone talks of sympathy and good-will, or even takes care occasionally to put it into practice, but, on the other side, also cheats when he can, betrays the rights of men, or otherwise violates them. But although it is possible that a universal law of nature might exist in accordance with that maxim, it is impossible to *will* that such a principle should have the universal validity of a law of nature. For a will which resolved this would contradict itself, inasmuch as many cases might occur in which one would have need of the love and sympathy of others, and in which, by such a law of nature, sprung from his own will, he would deprive himself of all hope of the aid he desires.

These are a few of the many actual duties, or at least what we regard as such, which obviously fall into two classes on the one principle that we have laid down. We must be *able to will* that a maxim of our action should be a universal law. This is the canon of the moral appreciation of the action generally. Some actions are of such a character that their maxim cannot without contradiction be even *conceived* as a universal law of nature, far from it being possible that we should *will* that it *should* be so. In others, this intrinsic impossibility is not found, but still it is impossible to *will* that their maxim should be raised to the universality of a law of nature, since such a will would contradict itself. It is easily seen that the former violate strict or rigorous (inflexible) duty; the latter only laxer (meritorious) duty. Thus it has been completely shown by these examples how all duties depend as regards the nature of the obligation (not the object of the action) on the same principle.

If now we attend to ourselves on occasion of any transgression of duty, we shall find that we in fact do not will that our maxim should be a universal law, for that is impossible for us; on the contrary, we will that the opposite should remain a universal law, only we assume the liberty of making an *exception* in our own favor or (just for this time only) in favor of our inclination. Consequently, if we considered all cases from one and the same point of view, namely, that of reason, we should find a contradiction in our own will, namely, that a certain principle should be objectively necessary as a universal law, and yet subjectively should not be universal, but admit of exceptions. As, however, we at one moment regard our action from the point of view of a will wholly conformed to reason, and then again look at the same action from the point of view of a will affected by inclination, there is not really any contradiction, but an antagonism of inclination to the precept of reason, whereby the universality of the principle is changed into a mere generality, so that the practical principle of reason shall meet the maxim half way. Now, although this cannot be justified in our own impartial judgment, yet it proves that we do really recognize the validity of the categorical imperative and (with all respect for it) only allow ourselves a few exceptions which we think unimportant and forced from us.

We have thus established at least this much—that if duty is a conception which is to have any import and real legislative authority for our actions, it can only be expressed in categorical, and not at all in hypothetical, imperatives. We have also, which is of great importance, exhibited clearly and definitely for every practical application the content of the categorical imperative, which must contain the principle of all duty if there is such a thing at all. We have not yet, however, advanced so far as to prove *a priori* that there actually is such an imperative, that there is a practical law which commands absolutely of itself and without any other impulse, and that the following of this law is duty.

With the view of attaining to this it is of extreme importance to remember that we must not allow ourselves to think of deducing the reality of this principle from the *particular attributes of human nature.* For duty is to be a practical, unconditional necessity of action; it must therefore hold for all rational beings (to whom an imperative can apply at all), and *for this reason only* be also a law for all human wills. On the contrary, whatever is deduced from the particular natural characteristics of humanity, from certain feelings and propensions, nay, even, if possible, from any particular tendency proper to human reason, and which need not necessarily hold for the will of every rational being—this may indeed supply us with a maxim but not with a law; with a subjective principle on which we may have a propension and inclination to act, but not with an objective principle on which we should be *enjoined* to act, even though all our propensions, inclinations, and natural dispositions were opposed to it. In fact, the sublimity and intrinsic dignity of the command in duty are so much the more evident, the less the subjective impulses favor it and the more they oppose it, without being able in the slightest degree to weaken the obligation of the law or to diminish its validity.

Here then we see philosophy brought to a critical position, since it has to be firmly fixed, notwithstanding that it has nothing to support it in heaven or earth. Here it must show its purity as absolute director of its own laws, not the herald of those which are whispered to it by an implanted sense or who knows what tutelary nature. Although these may be better than nothing, yet they can never afford principles dictated by reason, which must have their source wholly *a priori* and thence their commanding authority, expecting everything from the supremacy of the law and the due respect for it, nothing from inclination, or else condemning the man to self-contempt and inward abhorrence.

Thus every empirical element is not only quite incapable of being an aid to the principle of morality, but is even highly prejudicial to the purity of morals; for the proper and inestimable worth of an absolutely good will consists just in this that the principle of action is free from all influence of contingent grounds, which alone experience can furnish. We cannot too much or too often repeat our warning against this lax and even mean habit of thought which seeks for its principle among empirical motives and laws; for human reason in its weariness is glad to rest on this pillow, and in a dream of sweet illusions (in which, instead of Juno, it embraces a cloud) it substitutes for morality a bastard patched up from limbs of various derivation, which looks like anything one chooses to see in it; only not like virtue to one who has once beheld her in her true form.[2]

The question then is this: Is it a necessary law *for all rational beings* that they should always judge of their actions by maxims of which they can themselves will that they should serve as universal laws? If it is so, then it must be connected (altogether *a priori*) with the very conception of the will of a rational being generally. . . .

The will is conceived as a faculty of determining oneself to action *in accordance with the conception of certain laws.* And such a faculty can be found only in rational beings. Now that which serves the will as the objective ground of its self-determination is the *end,* and if this is assigned by reason alone, it must hold for all rational beings. On the other hand, that which merely contains the ground of possibility of the action of which the effect is the end, this is called the *means.* The subjective ground of the desire is the *spring,* the objective ground of the volition is the *motive;* hence the distinction between subjective ends which rest on springs, and objective ends which depend on motives valid for every rational being. Practical principles are *formal* when they abstract from all subjective ends; they are *material* when they assume these, and therefore particular, springs of action. The ends which a rational being proposes to himself at pleasure as *effects* of his actions (material ends) are all only relative, for it is only their relation to the particular desires of the subject that gives them their worth, which therefore cannot furnish principles universal and necessary for all rational beings and for every volition, that is to say, practical laws. Hence, all these relative ends can give rise only to hypothetical imperatives.

---

[2] To behold virtue in her proper form is nothing else but to contemplate morality stripped of all admixture of sensible things and of every spurious ornament of reward or self-love. How much she then eclipses everything else that appears charming to the affections, every one may readily perceive with the least exertion of his reason, if it be not wholly spoiled for abstraction.

Supposing, however, that there were something *whose existence* has *in itself* an absolute worth, something which, being *an end in itself,* could be a source of definite laws, then in this and this alone would lie the source of a possible categorical imperative, that is, a practical law.

Now I say: man and generally any rational being *exists* as an end in himself, *not merely as a means* to be arbitrarily used by this or that will, but in all his actions, whether they concern himself or other rational beings, must be always regarded at the same time as an end. All objects of the inclinations have only a conditional worth; for if the inclinations and the wants founded on them did not exist, then their object would be without value. But the inclinations themselves, being sources of want, are so far from having an absolute worth for which they should be desired that, on the contrary, it must be the universal wish of every rational being to be wholly free from them. Thus, the worth of any object which is *to be acquired* by our action is always conditional. Beings whose existence depends not on our will but on nature's, have nevertheless, if they are irrational beings, only a relative value as means, and are therefore called *things;* rational beings, on the contrary, are called *persons,* because their very nature points them out as ends in themselves, that is, as something which must not be used merely as means, and so far therefore restricts freedom of action (and is an object of respect). These, therefore, are not merely subjective ends whose existence has a worth *for us* as an effect of our action, but *objective ends,* that is, things whose existence is an end in itself—an end, moreover, for which no other can be substituted, which they should subserve *merely* as means, for otherwise nothing whatever would possess *absolute worth;* but if all worth were conditioned and therefore contingent, then there would be no supreme practical principle of reason whatever.

If then there is a supreme practical principle or, in respect of the human will, a categorical imperative, it must be one which, being drawn from the conception of that which is necessarily an end for everyone because it is *an end in itself,* constitutes an *objective* principle of will, and can therefore serve as a universal practical law. The foundation of this principle is: *rational nature exists as an end in itself.* Man necessarily conceives his own existence as being so; so far then this is a *subjective* principle of human actions. But every other rational being regards its existence similarly, just on the same rational principle that holds for me; so that it is at the same time an objective principle from which as a supreme practical law all laws of the will must be capable of being deduced. Accordingly the practical imperative will be as follows: *So act as to treat humanity, whether in thine own person or in that of any other, in every case as an end withal, never as means only.* We will now inquire whether this can be practically carried out.

To abide by the previous examples:

First, under the head of necessary duty to oneself: He who contemplates suicide should ask himself whether his action can be consistent with the idea of humanity *as an end in itself.* If he destroys himself in order to escape from painful circumstances, he uses a person merely as *a mean* to maintain a tolerable condition up to the end of life. But a man is not a thing, that is to say, something which can be used merely as means, but must in all his actions be always considered as an end in himself. I cannot, therefore, dispose in any way of a man in my own person so as to mutilate him, to damage or kill him. (It belongs to ethics proper to define this principle more precisely, so as to avoid all misunderstanding, for example, as to the amputation of the limbs in order to preserve myself; as to exposing my life to danger with a view to preserve it, etc. This question is therefore omitted here.)

Secondly, as regards necessary duties, or those of strict obligation, towards others: He who is thinking of making a lying promise to others will see at once that he would be using another man *merely as a mean,* without the latter containing at the same time the end in himself. For he whom I propose by such a promise to use for my own purposes cannot possibly assent to my mode of acting towards him, and therefore cannot himself contain the end of this action. This violation of the principle of humanity in other men is more obvious if we take in examples of attacks on the freedom and property of others. For then it is clear that he who transgresses the rights of men intends to use the person of others merely as means, without considering that as rational beings they ought always to be esteemed also as ends, that is, as beings who must be capable of containing in themselves the end of the very same action.

Thirdly, as regards contingent (meritorious) duties to oneself: It is not enough that the action does not violate humanity in our own person as an end in itself, it must also *harmonize with it.* Now there are in humanity capacities of greater perfection which belong to the end that nature has in view in regard to humanity in ourselves as the subject; to neglect these might perhaps be consistent with the *maintenance* of humanity as an end in itself, but not with the *advancement of* this end.

Fourthly, as regards meritorious duties towards others: The natural end which all men have is their own happiness. Now humanity might indeed subsist although no one should contribute anything to the happiness of others, provided he did not intentionally withdraw anything from it; but after all, this would only harmonize negatively, not positively, with *humanity as an end in itself,* if everyone does not also endeavor, as far as in him lies, to forward the ends of others. For the ends of any subject which is an end in himself ought as far as possible to be *my* ends also, if that conception is to have its *full* effect with me.

This principle that humanity and generally every rational nature is *an end in itself* (which is the supreme limiting condition of every man's freedom of action), is not borrowed from experience, *first,* because it is universal, applying as it does to all rational beings whatever, and experience is not capable of determining anything about them; *secondly,* because it does not present humanity as an end to men (subjectively), that is, as an object which men do of themselves actually adopt as an end; but as an objective end which must as a law constitute the supreme limiting condition of all our subjective ends, let them be what we will; it must therefore spring from pure reason. In fact the objective principle of all practical legislation lies (according to the first principle) in *the rule* and its form of universality which makes it capable of being a law (say, for example, a law of nature); but the *subjective* principle is in the *end;* now by the second principle, the subject of all ends is each rational being inasmuch as it is an end in itself. Hence follows the third practical principle of the will, which is the ultimate condition of its harmony with the universal practical reason, viz., the idea of *the will of every rational being as a universally legislative will.*

On this principle all maxims are rejected which are inconsistent with the will being itself universal legislator. Thus the will is not subject to the law, but so subject that it must be regarded *as itself giving the law,* and on this ground only subject to the law (of which it can regard itself as the author).

Thus, then, without quitting the moral knowledge of common human reason, we have arrived at its principle. And although, no doubt, common men do not conceive it in such an abstract and universal form, yet they always have it really before their eyes, and use it as the standard of their decision. Here it would be easy to show how, with this compass in hand, men are well able to distinguish, in every case that occurs, what is good, what bad, conformably to duty or inconsistent with it, if, without in the least teaching them anything new, we only, like Socrates, direct their attention to the principle they themselves employ; and that, therefore, we do not need science and philosophy to know what we should do to be honest and good, yea, even wise and virtuous. Indeed, we might well have conjectured beforehand that the knowledge of what every man is bound to do, and therefore also to know, would be within the reach of every man, even the commonest. Here we cannot forbear admiration when we see how great an advantage the practical judgment has over the theoretical in the common understanding of men. In the latter, if common reason ventures to depart from the laws of experience and from the perceptions of the senses it falls into mere inconceivabilities and self-contradictions, at least into a chaos of uncertainty, obscurity, and instability. But in the practical sphere, it is just when the common understanding excludes all sensible springs from practical laws that its power of judgment begins to show itself to advantage. It then becomes even subtle, whether it be that it chicanes with its own conscience or with other claims respecting what is to be called right, or whether it desires for its own instruction to determine honestly the worth of actions; and, in the latter case, it may even have as good a hope of hitting the mark as any philosopher whatever can promise himself. Nay, it is almost more sure of doing so, because the philosopher cannot have any other principle, while he may easily perplex his judgment by a multitude of considerations foreign to the matter, and so turn aside from the right way. Would it not, therefore, be wiser in moral concerns to acquiesce in the judgment of common reason, or at most, only to call in philosophy for the purpose of rendering the system of morals more complete and intelligible, and its rules more convenient for use (especially for disputation), but not so as to draw off the common understanding from its happy simplicity, or to bring it by means of philosophy into a new path of inquiry and instruction?

Innocence is indeed a glorious thing, only, on the other hand, it is very sad that it cannot well maintain itself, and is easily seduced. On this account even wisdom—which otherwise consists more in conduct than in knowledge—yet has need of science, not in order to learn from it, but to secure for its precepts admission and permanence. Against all the commands of duty which reason represents to man as so deserving of respect, he feels in himself a powerful counterpoise in his wants and inclinations, the entire satisfaction of which he sums up under the name of happiness. Now reason issues its commands unyieldingly, without promising anything to the inclinations, and, as it were, with disregard and contempt for these claims, which are so impetuous, and at the same time so plausible, and which will not allow themselves to be suppressed by any command. Hence there arises a natural *dialectic,* that is, a disposition to argue against these strict laws of duty and to question their validity, or at least their purity and strictness; and, if possible, to make them more accordant with our wishes and inclinations, that is to say, to corrupt them at their very source, and entirely to destroy their worth—a thing which even common practical reason cannot ultimately call good.

Thus is the *common reason of man* compelled to go out of its sphere, and to take a step into the field of a *practical philosophy,* not to satisfy any speculative want (which never occurs to it as long as it is content to be mere sound reason), but even on practical grounds, in order to attain in it information and clear instruction respecting the source of its principle, and the correct determination of it in opposition to the maxims which are based on wants and inclinations, so that it may escape from the perplexity of opposite claims, and not run the risk of losing all genuine moral principles through the equivocation into which it easily falls. Thus, when practical reason cultivates itself, there insensibly arises in it a dialectic which forces it to seek aid in philosophy, just as happens to it in its theoretic use; and in this case, therefore, as well as in the other, it will find rest nowhere but in a thorough critical examination of our reason.

KANT'S CRITICISM OF THE GOLDEN RULE

Let it not be thought that the common: *quod tibi non vis fieri,*[3] etc. could serve here as the rule of principle . . . it cannot be a universal law, for it does not contain the principle of duties to oneself, nor of the duties of benevolence to others (for many a one would gladly consent that others should not benefit him, provided only that they might be excused from showing benevolence to them), nor finally that of duties of strict obligation to one another, for on this principle the criminal might argue against the judge who punishes him, etc.[4]

To Think About

1. "Kantian ethics leave little room for friendship, fellow-feeling, loyalty, a sense of community, personal attachment, and, indeed, personality."   ***Unknown***
2. "Don't think me arrogant for saying this, but the commandments of morality are too trifling for me; for I should gladly do twice as much as they command. . . . I console myself often with the thought that since the practice of morality is so bound up with sensuality, it can only count for this world, and with that thought I could still hope not to have to live another life of empty vegetating and of so few and easy moral demands after this life."   ***Unknown***

[3] "Do not do unto others what you would not have them do to you."
[4] T. K. Abbott, *Kant's Critique of Practical Reason,* 6th ed. (London: Longmans, Green, 1909): 48.

3. "To have a *law* conception of ethics is to hold that what is needed for conformity with the virtues—failure in which is the mark of being bad *qua* man (and not merely, say, *qua* craftsman or logician)—that what is needed for *this,* is required by divine law. Naturally it is not possible to have such a conception unless you believe in God as a law-giver, like Jews, Stoics, and Christians. But if such a conception is dominant for many centuries, and then is given up, it is a natural result that the concepts of 'obligation,' of being bound or required as by a law, should remain though they had lost their root; and if the word 'ought' has become invested in certain contexts with the sense of 'obligation' it too will remain to be spoken with a special emphasis and a special feeling in these contexts. . . . It is as if the notion 'criminal' were to remain when criminal law and criminal courts had been abolished and forgotten."   ***E. Anscombe***

4. "I take it that the central feature of a morality is not that there are some (self-evident) beliefs about obligations but that there is in an individual, or group, a system of intrinsic aversions to types of actions."   ***Richard Brandt***

5. "Even if it should happen that, owing to special disfavor of fortune, or the niggardly provision of a stepmotherly nature, this [Good] will should wholly lack power to accomplish its purpose, if with its greatest efforts it should yet achieve nothing, and there should remain only the good will . . . , then, like a jewel, it would still shine by its own light, as a thing which has its whole value in itself. Its usefulness or fruitfulness can neither add to nor take away anything from this value."   ***Immanuel Kant***

6. "If I were ever to find, as I luckily never have, a man who assured me that he really *believed* Kant's metaphysical morals, and that he modeled his own conduct and his relations with others after those principles, then my incredulity and distrust of him as a human being could not be greater than if he told me he regularly drowned children just to see them squirm."   ***Richard Taylor***

7. "Kant abolished God and made man God in His stead. We are still living in the age of the Kantian man, or Kantian man-god."   ***E. Anscombe***

8. "Think of our attempts to live responsibly when we cannot prove why we should be ethical at all, or of what we believe in a fundamental order is reality which allows scientific inquiry. Or of the nature of the universe open to us by the new astronomies and cosmologies, stranger than we imagine and stranger than we can imagine."   ***E. Anscombe***

9. "Just as what Kant took to be the principles and presuppositions of natural science as such turned out after all to be the principles and presuppositions specific to Newtonian physics, so what Kant took to be the principles and presuppositions of morality as such turned out to be the principles and presuppositions of one highly specific morality, a secularized version of Protestantism which furnished modern liberal individualism with one of its founding charters. Thus the claim to universality foundered."   ***Unknown***

10. "Was Gauguin 'justified' in deserting his family in order to paint in the South Pacific? After all, we think his paintings a great addition to human well-being."   ***James Gould***

11. "Power and separation secure the man in an identity achieved through work. . . . Women define their identity through relationships of intimacy and care [home], the moral problems they encounter pertain to issues of a different sort. . . . One is the morality of rights, while the other is the ethics of responsibility."

      Carol Gilligan

12. "Morality is not properly the doctrine how we should make ourselves happy, but how we should become worthy of happiness."   ***Immanuel Kant***

13. "It is, most fundamentally, because moral judgements are universalizable that we can speak of moral thought as rational (to universalize is to give the reason); and their prescriptivity is very intimately connected with our freedom to form our own moral opinions (only those free to think and act need a prescriptive language)."   ***Peter Hare***

14. "The majesty of duty has nothing to do with the enjoyment of life."

      Immanuel Kant

15. "True morality is a sort of unesoteric mysticism, having its source in an austere and unconsoled love of the Good."   ***Iris Murdoch***

Readings

ACTON, HARRY. *Kant's Moral Philosophy.* New York: Macmillan, 1970.

BROAD, C. D. *Five Types of Ethical Theory.* New York: Harcourt, Brace, 1930, ch. 5.

NELL, ONORA. *Acting on Principle: An Essay on Kantian Ethics.* New York: Columbia University Press, 1975.

PATON, H. J. *The Categorical Imperative.* Chicago: University of Chicago Press, 1948.

RAPHAEL, D. D. *Moral Philosophy.* Oxford: Oxford University Press, 1981, ch. 6.

ROSS, W. D. *Kant's Ethical Theory.* Oxford: Clarendon Press, 1954.

WARD, KEITH. *The Development of Kant's Views on Ethics.* Oxford: Basil Blackwell, 1972.

22

Power Is the Highest Value

Friedrich W. Nietzsche (1844–1900), a German Romantic philosopher, was born in Rocken, a Prussian province of Saxony. His academic training was in theology, classical languages, and literature at the University of Bonn. The influence of Schopenhauer's philosophy led him away from both theological studies and traditional Christianity. Granted a professorship at Basle, he resigned in 1879 because of poor health. He wrote The Birth of Tragedy *(1872),* Thus Spoke Zarathustra *(1883ff.),* Beyond Good and Evil *(1886), and* The Genealogy of Morals *(1887).*

Nietzsche believes that the uncorrupt aristocratic class provides the meaning and justification of a society. This master group determines what is good. It creates values, particularly the value of power. The values of the common people, the slave society, are usually pity, humility, friendship, and patience. If they are allowed to dominate, society will decay. Nietzsche sought a new basis for ethics and civilization in what he regarded as the most basic of human drives: the will to power.

~~~~~ To Study ~~~~~

1. According to Nietzsche, how do societies advance? What causes the corruption of a society?
2. What is the "essential characteristic of a good and healthy aristocracy"?
3. What is life "essentially"?
4. Explain the difference between the master morality and the slave morality.
5. Why did the early equality of humanity disappear? What followed the destruction of equality?

257

Every enhancement of the type "man" has so far been the work of an aristocratic society—and it will be so again and again—a society that believes in the long ladder of an order of rank and differences in value between man and man, and that needs slavery in some sense or other. Without the *pathos of distance* which grows out of the ingrained difference between strata—when the ruling caste constantly looks afar and looks down upon subjects and instruments and just as constantly practices obedience and command, keeping down and keeping at a distance—that other, more mysterious pathos could not have grown up either—the craving for an ever new widening of distances within the soul itself, the development of ever higher, rarer, more remote, further stretching, more comprehensive states—in brief, simply the enhancement of the type "man," the continual "self-overcoming of man," to use a moral formula in a supramoral sense.

To be sure, one should not yield to humanitarian illusions about the origins of an aristocratic society (and thus of the presupposition of this enhancement of the type "man"): truth is hard. Let us admit to ourselves, without trying to be considerate, how every higher culture on earth so far has *begun*. Human beings whose nature was still natural, barbarians in every terrible sense of the word, men of prey who were still in possession of unbroken strength of will and lust for power, hurled themselves upon weaker, more civilized, more peaceful races, perhaps traders or cattle raisers, or upon mellow old cultures whose last vitality was even then flaring up in splendid fireworks of spirit and corruption. In the beginning, the noble caste was always the barbarian caste: their predominance did not lie mainly in physical strength but in strength of the soul—they were more *whole* human beings (which also means, at every level, "more whole beasts").

258

Corruption as the expression of a threatening anarchy among the instincts and of the fact that the foundation of the affects, which is called "life," has been shaken: corruption is something totally different depending on the organism in which it appears. When, for example, an aristocracy, like that of France at the beginning of the Revolution, throws away its privileges with a sublime disgust and sacrifices itself to an extravagance of its own moral feelings, that is corruption; it was really only the last act of that centuries-old corruption which had led them to surrender, step by step, their governmental prerogatives, demoting themselves to a mere *function* of the monarchy (finally even to a mere ornament and showpiece). The essential characteristic of a good and healthy aristocrat, however, is that it experiences itself *not* as a function (whether of the monarchy or the commonwealth) but as their *meaning* and highest justification—that it therefore accepts with a good conscience the sacrifice of untold human beings who, *for its sake,* must be reduced and lowered to incomplete human beings, to slaves, to instruments. Their fundamental faith simply has to be that society must *not* exist for society's sake but only as the foundation and scaffolding on which a choice type of being is able to raise itself to its higher task and to a higher state of *being*—comparable to those sunseeking vines of Java—they are called *Sipo*

Matador—that so long and so often enclasp an oak tree with their tendrils until eventually, high above it but supported by it, they can unfold their crowns in the open light and display their happiness.

259

Refraining mutually from injury, violence, and exploitation and placing one's will on a par with that of someone else—this may become, in a certain rough sense, good manners among individuals if the appropriate conditions are present (namely, if these men are actually similar in strength and value standards and belong together in *one* body). But as soon as this principle is extended, and possibly even accepted as the *fundamental principle of society,* it immediately proves to be what it really is—a will to the *denial* of life, a principle of disintegration and decay.

Here we must beware of superficiality and get to the bottom of the matter, resisting all sentimental weakness: life itself is *essentially* appropriation, injury, overpowering of what is alien and weaker; suppression, hardness, imposition of one's own forms, incorporation and at least, at its mildest, exploitation—but why should one always use those words in which a slanderous intent has been imprinted for ages?

Even the body within which individuals treat each other as equals, as suggested before—and this happens in every healthy aristocracy—if it is a living and not a dying body, has to do to other bodies what the individuals within it refrain from doing to each other: it will have to be an incarnate will to power, it will strive to grow, spread, seize, become predominant—not from any morality or immorality but because it is *living* and because life simply *is* will to power. But there is no point on which the ordinary consciousness of Europeans resists instruction as on this: everywhere people are now raving, even under scientific disguises, about coming conditions of society in which "the exploitative aspect" will be removed—which sounds to me as if they promised to invent a way of life that would dispense with all organic functions. "Exploitation" does not belong to a corrupt or imperfect and primitive society: it belongs to the *essence* of what lives, as a basic organic function; it is a consequence of the will to power, which is after all the will of life.

If this should be an innovation as a theory—as a reality it is the *primordial fact* of all history: people ought to be honest with themselves at least that far.

260

Wandering through the many subtler and coarser moralities which have so far been prevalent on earth, or still are prevalent, I found that certain features recurred regularly together and were closely associated—until I finally discovered two basic types and one basic difference.

There are *master morality* and *slave morality*—I add immediately that in all the higher and more mixed cultures there also appear attempts at mediation between these two moralities, and yet more often the interpretation and mutual misunderstanding of both, and at times they occur directly alongside each other—even in the same human being, with a *single* soul. The moral discrimination of values has origi-nated either among a ruling group whose consciousness of its difference from the ruled group was accompanied by delight—or among the ruled, the slaves and de-pendents of every degree.

In the first case, when the ruling group determines what is "good," the exalted, proud states of the soul are experienced as conferring distinction and determining the order of rank. The noble human being separates from himself those in whom the op-posite of such exalted, proud states finds expression: he despises them. It should be noted immediately that in this first type of morality the opposition of "good" and "bad" means approximately the same as "noble" and "contemptible." (The opposi-tion of "good" and "evil" has a different origin.) One feels contempt for the cowardly, the anxious, the petty, those intent on narrow utility; also for the suspicious with their unfree glances, those who humble themselves, the doglike people who allow them-selves to be maltreated, the begging flatterers, above all the liars: it is part of the fun-damental faith of all aristocrats that the common people lie. "We truthful ones"—thus, the nobility of ancient Greece referred to itself.

It is obvious that moral designations were everywhere first applied to *human be-ings* and only later, derivatively, to actions. Therefore it is a gross mistake when his-torians of morality start from such questions as: why was the compassionate act praised? The noble type of man experiences *itself* as determining values; it does not need approval; it judges, "what is harmful to me is harmful in itself"; it knows itself to be that which first accords honor to things; it is *value-creating*. Everything it knows as part of itself it honors: such a morality is self-glorification. In the foreground there is the feeling of fullness, of power that seeks to overflow, the happiness of high ten-sion, the consciousness of wealth that would give and bestow: the noble human being, too, helps the unfortunate, but not, or almost not, from pity, but prompted more by an urge begotten by excess of power. The noble human being honors himself as one who is powerful, also as one who has power over himself, who knows how to speak and be silent, who delights in being severe and hard with himself and respects all severity and hardness. "A hard heart Wotan put into my breast," says an old Scandinavian saga: a fitting poetic expression, seeing that it comes from the soul of a proud Viking. Such a type of man is actually proud of the fact that he is *not* made for pity, and the hero of the saga therefore adds as a warning. "If the heart is not hard in youth it will never harden." Noble and courageous human beings who think that way are furthest re-moved from that morality which finds the distinction of morality precisely in pity, or in acting for others, or in *désintéressement;* faith in oneself, a fundamental hostility and irony against "selflessness" belong just as definitely to noble morality as does a slight disdain and caution regarding compassionate feelings and a "warm heart."

It is the powerful who *understand* how to honor; this is their art, their realm of invention. The profound reverence for age and tradition—all law rests on this double reverence—the faith and prejudice in favor of ancestors and disfavor of those yet to come are typical of the morality of the powerful; and when the men of "modern ideas," conversely, believe almost instinctively in "progress" and "the future" and more and more lack respect for age, this in itself would sufficiently betray the igno-ble origin of these "ideas."

A morality of the ruling group, however, is most alien and embarrassing to the present taste in the severity of its principle that one has duties only to one's peers; that against beings of a lower rank, against everything alien, one may behave as one pleases or "as the heart desires," and in any case "beyond good and evil"—here pity and like feelings may find their place. The capacity for, and the duty of, long gratitude and long revenge—both only among one's peers—refinement in repaying, the sophisticated concept of friendship, a certain necessity for having enemies (as it were, as drainage ditches for the affects of envy, quarrelsomeness, exuberance—at bottom, in order to be capable of being good *friends*): all these are typical characteristics of noble morality which, as suggested, is not the morality of "modern ideas" and therefore is hard to empathize with today, also hard to dig up and uncover.[1]

It is different with the second type of morality, *slave morality*. Suppose the violated, oppressed, suffering, unfree, who are uncertain of themselves and weary, moralize: what will their moral valuations have in common? Probably, a pessimistic suspicion about the whole condition of man will find expression, perhaps a condemnation of man along with his condition. The slave's eye is not favorable to the virtues of the powerful: he is skeptical and suspicious, *subtly* suspicious, of all the "good" honored there—he would like to persuade himself that even their happiness is not genuine. Conversely, those qualities are brought out and flooded with light which serve to ease existence for those who suffer: here pity, the complaisant and obliging hand, the warm heart, patience, industry, humility, and friendliness are honored—for here these are the most useful qualities and almost the only means for enduring the pressure of existence. Slave morality is essentially a morality of utility.

Here is the place for the origin of that famous opposition of "good" and "evil": into evil one's feelings project power and dangerousness, a certain terribleness, subtlety, and strength that does not permit contempt to develop. According to slave morality, those who are "evil" thus inspire fear; according to master morality it is precisely those who are "good" that inspire, and wish to inspire, fear, while the "bad" are felt to be contemptible.

The opposition reaches its climax when, as a logical consequence of slave morality, a touch of disdain is associated also with the "good" of this morality—this may be slight and benevolent—because the good human being has to be *undangerous* in the slaves' way of thinking: he is good-natured, easy to deceive, a little stupid perhaps, *un bonhomme*.[2] Wherever slave morality becomes preponderant, language tends to bring the words "good" and "stupid" closer together.

One last fundamental difference: the longing for *freedom,* the instinct for happiness and the subtleties of the feeling of freedom belong just as necessarily to slave morality and morals as artful and enthusiastic reverence and devotion are the regular symptom of an aristocratic way of thinking and evaluating.

---

[1] Clearly master morality cannot be discovered by introspection nor by the observation of individuals who are "masters" rather than "slaves." Both of these misunderstandings are widespread. What is called for is rather a rereading of, say, the *Iliad* and, to illustrate "slave morality," the New Testament.—[W. Kaufmann]

[2] Literally "a good human being," the term is used for precisely the type described here.—[W. Kaufmann]

This makes plain why love *as passion*—which is our European specialty—simply must be of noble origin: as is well known, its invention must be credited to the Provençal knight-poets, those magnificent and inventive human beings of the *"gai saber"*[3] to whom Europe owes so many things and almost owes itself.

261

Among the things that may be hardest to understand for a noble human being is vanity: he will be tempted to deny it, where another type of human being could not find it more palpable. The problem for him is to imagine people who seek to create a good opinion of themselves which they do not have of themselves—and thus also do not "deserve"—and who nevertheless end up *believing* this good opinion themselves. This strikes him half as such bad taste and lack of self-respect, and half as so baroquely irrational, that he would like to consider vanity as exceptional, and in most cases when it is spoken of he doubts it.

He will say, for example: "I may be mistaken about my value and nevertheless demand that my value, exactly as I define it, should be acknowledged by others as well—but this is no vanity (but conceit or, more frequently, what is called 'humility' or 'modest')." Or: "For many reasons I may take pleasure in the good opinion of others: perhaps because I honor and love them and all their pleasures give me pleasure; perhaps also because their good opinion confirms and strengthens my faith in my own good opinion; perhaps because the good opinion of others, even in cases where I do not share it, is still useful to me or promises to become so—but all that is not vanity."

The noble human being must force himself, with the aid of history, to recognize that, since time immemorial, in all somehow dependent social strata the common man *was* only what he was *considered:* not at all used to positing values himself, he also attached no other value to himself than his masters attached to him (it is the characteristic *right of masters* to create values).

It may be understood as the consequence of an immense atavism that even now the ordinary man still always *waits* for an opinion about himself and then instinctively submits to that—but by no means only a "good" opinion; also a bad and unfair one (consider, for example, the great majority of the self-estimates and self-underestimates that believing women accept from their father confessors, and believing Christians quite generally from their church).

In accordance with the slowly arising democratic order of things (and its cause, the intermarriage of masters and slaves), the originally noble and rare urge to ascribe value to oneself on one's own and to "think well" of oneself will actually be encouraged and spread more and more now; but it is always opposed by an older, ampler, and more deeply ingrained propensity—and in the phenomenon of "vanity" this older

---

[3] "Gay science": in the early fourteenth century the term was used to designate the art of the troubadours, codified in *Leys d'amors*. Nietzsche subtitled his own *Fröhliche Wissenschaft* (1882), *"la gaya scienza,"* placed a quatrain on the title page, began the book with a fifteen-page "Prelude in German Rhymes," and in the second edition (1887) added, besides a Preface and Book V, an "Appendix" of further verses.—[W. Kaufmann]

propensity masters the younger one. The vain person is delighted by *every* good opinion he hears of himself (quite apart from all considerations of its utility, and also apart from truth or falsehood), just as every bad opinion of him pains him: for he submits to both, he *feels* subjected to them in accordance with that oldest instinct of submission that breaks out in him.

It is "the slave" in the blood of the vain person, a residue of the slave's craftiness—and how much "slave" is still residual in woman, for example—that seeks to *seduce* him to good opinions about himself; it is also the slave who afterwards immediately prostrates himself before these opinions as if he had not called them forth.

To Think About

1. "Morality, said Jesus, is kindness to the weak; morality, said Nietzsche, is the bravery of the strong; morality, said Plato, is the effective harmony of the whole. Probably all three doctrines must be combined to find a perfect ethic; but can we doubt which of the elements is fundamental?"   ***Will Durant***

2. "Reason is the slave of the passions."   ***David Hume***

3. "Again, look back to see how the huge expanse of time past, before we are born, has been nothing to us. Nature shows us that it is the mirror-image of the time that is to come after we are dead. Is anything there terrifying, does anything there seem gloomy? Is it not more peaceful than any sleep?"
    Friedrich Nietzsche

4. "For one thing is needful: that a human being should attain satisfaction with himself, whether it be by means of this or that poetry and art; only then is a human being at all tolerable to behold. Whoever is dissatisfied with himself is continually ready for revenge, and we others will be his victims."
    Friedrich Nietzsche

5. "We do not want a thing because we reason; we find reasons for anything because we want it."   ***G. W. F. Hegel***

6. "By his infamous remark that God is dead, Friedrich Nietzsche did not mean that God once existed and now no longer does. He meant that all people with an ounce of intelligence would now perceive that there is no intelligent plan to the universe or rational order in it: they would now understand that there is no reason why things happen one way and not another and that the harmony and order we imagine to exist in the universe is merely pasted on by the human mind."   ***Brudu***

7. "What are man's truths ultimately? Merely his *irrefutable* errors."
    Friedrich Nietzsche

8. "The weaker are always anxious for justice and equality. The strong pay no heed to either."   ***Aristotle***

Readings

CLARK, MAUDEMARIE. *Nietzsche on Truth and Philosophy.* Cambridge: Cambridge University Press, 1990.

DANTO, ARTHUR. *Nietzsche as Philosopher.* New York: Columbia University Press, 1980.

HAYMAN, RONALD. *Nietzsche: A Critical Life.* London: Weidenfeld and Nicolson, 1980.

KAUFMANN, WALTER. *Nietzsche: Philosopher, Psychologist, Antichrist.* 4th ed. Princeton, NJ: Princeton University Press, 1974.

NEHAMAS, ALEXANDER. *Nietzsche: Life as Literature.* Cambridge, MA: Harvard University Press, 1985.

SCHACHT, RICHARD. *Nietzsche.* London: Routledge & Kegan Paul, 1983.

23

Existentialist Ethics

Jean-Paul Sartre (1905–80), a French philosopher, Resistance fighter, novelist, and playwright, is generally considered the dean of contemporary existentialism. His massive Being and Nothingness *(1943) presents a definitive account of his meta-physics, while his literary works, such as* No Exit, Nausea, *and* The Wall, *dramatize various aspects of the existentialist ethic, especially the belief in human freedom.*

Sartre's famous essay *Existentialism* sets forth the basic tenets of atheistic existentialism: that we are nothing but what we make of ourselves. We exist first and then our essence is developed. Hence, I choose myself and, in so doing, I create an image for all people. This necessity of choosing creates anguish, forlornness, and despair in us all. Furthermore, because existence precedes essence, there is no determinism and hence, one is free. In this sense, one is condemned to be free.

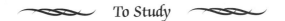 To Study

1. Explain what "existence precedes essence" means.
2. What is the significance of the statement that "man is a being who hurls himself toward a future"?
3. Explain why existentialists believe that "in choosing myself, I choose man"?
4. What causes anguish in humans? In what ways do we deny this anguish?
5. Why is forlornness a result of the human condition?
6. In what sense is humanity "condemned to be free"?
7. How does Sartre define *despair?* Give an example showing this concept.

From Jean-Paul Sartre, *Existentialism,* trans. Bernard Frechtman (New York: Philosophical Library, 1947), 14–18, 34–39, 45–46. Reprinted by permission of the publisher.

There are two kinds of existentialist; first, those who are Christian, among whom I would include Jaspers and Gabriel Marcel, both Catholic; and on the other hand the atheistic existentialists, among whom I class Heidegger, and then the French existentialists and myself. What they have in common is that they think that existence precedes essence, or, if you prefer, that subjectivity must be the starting point.

Just what does that mean? Let us consider some object that is manufactured, for example, a book or a paper-cutter: here is an object which has been made by an artisan whose inspiration came from a concept. He referred to the concept of what a paper-cutter is and likewise to a known method of production, which is part of the concept, something which is, by and large, a routine. Thus, the paper-cutter is at once an object produced in a certain way and, on the other hand, one having a specific use; and one can not postulate a man who produces a paper-cutter but does not know what it is used for. Therefore, let us say that, for the paper-cutter, essence—that is, the ensemble of both the production routines and the properties which enable it to be both produced and defined—precedes existence. Thus, the presence of the paper-cutter or book in front of me is determined. Therefore, we have here a technical view of the world whereby it can be said that production precedes existence.

When we conceive God as the Creator, He is generally thought of as a superior sort of artisan. Whatever doctrine we may be considering, whether one like that of Descartes or that of Leibnitz, we always grant that will more or less follows understanding or, at the very least, accompanies it, and that when God creates He knows exactly what He is creating. Thus, the concept of man in the mind of God is comparable to the concept of paper-cutter in the mind of the manufacturer, and, following certain techniques and a conception, God produces man, just as the artisan, following a definition and a technique, makes a paper-cutter. Thus, the individual man is the realization of a certain concept in the divine intelligence.

In the eighteenth century, the atheism of the *philosophes* discarded the idea of God, but not so much for the notion that essence precedes existence. To a certain extent, this idea is found everywhere; we find it in Diderot, in Voltaire, and even in Kant. Man has a human nature; this human nature, which is the concept of the human, is found in all men, which means that each man is a particular example of a universal concept, man. In Kant, the result of this universality is that the wildman, the natural man, as well as the bourgeois, are circumscribed by the same definition and have the same basic qualities. Thus, here too the essence of man precedes the historical existence that we find in nature.

Atheistic existentialism, which I represent, is more coherent. It states that if God does not exist, there is at least one being in whom existence precedes essence, a being who exists before he can be defined by any concept, and that this being is man, or, as Heidegger says, human reality. What is meant here by saying that existence precedes essence? It means that, first of all, man exists, turns up, appears on the scene, and, only afterwards, defines himself. If man, as the existentialist conceives him, is indefinable, it is because at first he is nothing. Only afterward will he be something, and he himself will have made what he will be. Thus, there is no human nature, since there is no God to conceive it. Not only is man what he conceives himself to be, but he is also only what he wills himself to be after this thrust toward existence.

Man is nothing else but what he makes of himself. Such is the first principle of existentialism. It is also what is called subjectivity, the name we are labeled with when charges are brought against us. But what do we mean by this, if not that man has a greater dignity than a stone or table? For we mean that man first exists, that is, that man first of all is the being who hurls himself toward a future and who is conscious of imagining himself as being in the future. Man is at the start a plan which is aware of itself, rather than a patch of moss, a piece of garbage, or a cauliflower; nothing exists prior to this plan; there is nothing in heaven; man will be what he will have planned to be. Not what he will want to be. Because by the word "will" we generally mean a conscious decision, which is subsequent to what we have already made of ourselves. I may want to belong to a political party, write a book, get married; but all that is only a manifestation of an earlier, more spontaneous choice that is called "will." But if existence really does precede essence, man is responsible for what he is. Thus, existentialism's first move is to make every man aware of what he is and to make the full responsibility of his existence rest on him. And when we say that a man is responsible for himself, we do not only mean that he is responsible for his own individuality, but that he is responsible for all men.

The word subjectivism has two meanings, and our opponents play on the two. Subjectivism means, on the one hand, that an individual chooses and makes himself; and, on the other, that it is impossible for man to transcend human subjectivity. The second of these is the essential meaning of existentialism. When we say that man chooses his own self, we mean that every one of us does likewise; but we also mean by that that in making this choice he also chooses all men. In fact, in creating the man that we want to be, there is not a single one of our acts which does not at the same time create an image of man as we think he ought to be. To choose to be this or that is to affirm at the same time the value of what we choose, because we can never choose evil. We always choose the good, and nothing can be good for us without being good for all.

If, on the other hand, existence precedes essence, and if we grant that we exist and fashion our image at one and the same time, the image is valid for everybody and for our whole age. Thus, our responsibility is much greater than we might have supposed, because it involves all mankind. If I am a working man and choose to join a Christian trade-union rather than be a communist, and if by being a member I want to show that the best thing for man is resignation, that the kingdom of man is not of this world, I am not only involving my own case—I want to be resigned for everyone. As a result, my action has involved all humanity. To take a more individual matter, if I want to marry, to have children; even if this marriage depends solely on my own circumstances or passion or wish, I am involving all humanity in monogamy and not merely myself. Therefore, I am responsible for myself and for everyone else. I am creating a certain image of man of my own choosing. In choosing myself, I choose man.

This helps us understand what the actual content is of such rather grandiloquent words as anguish, forlornness, despair. As you will see, it's all quite simple.

First, what is meant by anguish? The existentialists say at once that man is anguish. What that means is this: the man who involves himself and who realizes that he is not only the person he chooses to be, but also a law-maker who is, at the same time, choosing all mankind as well as himself, cannot help escape the feeling of his total and deep responsibility. Of course, there are many people who are not anxious; but we claim that they are hiding their anxiety, that they are fleeing from it. Certainly, many people believe that when they do something, they themselves are the only ones involved, and when someone says to them, "What if everyone acted that way?" they shrug their shoulders and answer, "Everyone doesn't act that way." But really, one should always ask himself, "What would happen if everybody looked at things that way?" There is no escaping this disturbing thought except by a kind of double-dealing. A man who lies and makes excuses for himself by saying "not everybody does that," is someone with an uneasy conscience, because the act of lying implies that a universal value is conferred upon the lie.

Anguish is evident even when it conceals itself. This is the anguish that Kierkegaard called the anguish of Abraham. You know the story: an angel has ordered Abraham to sacrifice his son; if it really were an angel who has come and said, "You are Abraham, you shall sacrifice your son," everything would be all right. But everyone might first wonder, "Is it really an angel, and am I really Abraham? What proof do I have?"

There was a madwoman who had hallucinations; someone used to speak to her on the telephone and give her orders. Her doctor asked her, "Who is it who talks to you?" She answered, "He says it's God." What proof did she really have that it was God? If an angel comes to me, what proof is there that it's an angel? And if I hear voices, what proof is there that they come from heaven and not from hell, or from the subconscious or a pathological condition? What proves that they are addressed to me? What proof is there that I have been appointed to impose my choice and my conception of man on humanity? I'll never find any proof or sign to convince me of that. If a voice addresses me, it is always for me to decide that this is the angel's voice; if I consider that such an act is a good one, it is I who will choose to say that it is good rather than bad.

Now, I'm not being singled out as an Abraham, and yet at every moment I'm obliged to perform exemplary acts. For every man, everything happens as if all mankind had its eyes fixed on him and were guiding itself by what he does. And every man ought to say to himself, "Am I really the kind of man who has the right to act in such a way that humanity might guide itself by my actions?" And if he does not say that to himself, he is masking his anguish.

There is no question here of the kind of anguish which would lead to quietism, to inaction. It is a matter of a simple sort of anguish that anybody who has had responsibilities is familiar with. For example, when a military officer takes the responsibility for an attack and sends a certain number of men to death, he chooses to do so, and in the main he alone makes the choice. Doubtless, orders come from above, but they are too broad; he interprets them, and on this interpretation depend the lives of ten or fourteen or twenty men. In making a decision he can not help having a certain anguish. All leaders know this anguish. That doesn't keep them from acting; on the contrary, it is the very condition of their action. For it implies that they envisage a number of possibilities, and when they choose one, they realize that it has value only because it is chosen. We shall see this kind of anguish, which is the kind that existentialism describes, is explained, in addition, by a direct responsibility to the other men whom it involves. It is not a curtain separating us from action, but is part of action itself.

When we speak of forlornness, a term Heidegger was fond of, we mean only that God does not exist and that we have to face all the consequences of this. The existentialist is strongly opposed to a certain kind of secular ethics which would like to abolish God with the least possible expense. About 1880, some French teachers tried to set up a secular ethics which went something like this: God is a useless and costly hypothesis; we are discarding it; but, meanwhile, in order for there to be an ethics, a society, a civilization, it is essential that certain values be taken seriously and that they be considered as having an *a priori* existence. It must be obligatory, *a priori,* to be honest, not to lie, not to beat your wife, to have children, etc., etc. So we're going to try a little device which will make it possible to show that values exist all the same, inscribed in a heaven of ideas, though otherwise God does not exist. In other words— and this, I believe, is the tendency of everything called reformism in France— nothing will be changed if God does not exist. We shall find ourselves with the same norms of honesty, progress, and humanism, and we shall have made of God an outdated hypothesis which will peacefully die off by itself.

The existentialist, on the contrary, thinks it very distressing that God does not exist, because all possibility of finding values in a heaven of ideas disappears along with Him; there can no longer be an *a priori* Good, since there is no infinite and perfect consciousness to think it. Nowhere is it written that the Good exists, that we must be honest, that we must not lie; because the fact is we are on a plane where there are only men. Dostoevski said, "If God didn't exist, everything would be possible." That is the very starting point of existentialism. Indeed, everything is permissible if God does not exist, and as a result man is forlorn, because neither within him nor without does he find anything to cling to. He can't start making excuses for himself.

If existence really does precede essence, there is no explaining things away by reference to a fixed and given human nature. In other words, there is no determinism, man is free, man is freedom. On the other hand, if God does not exist, we find no values or commands to turn to which legitimize our conduct. So, in the bright realm of values, we have no excuse behind us, nor justification before us. We are alone, with no excuses.

That is the idea I shall try to convey when I say that man is condemned to be free. Condemned, because he did not create himself, yet, in other respects is free; because, once thrown into the world, he is responsible for everything he does. The existentialist does not believe in the power of passion. He will never agree that a sweeping passion is a ravaging torrent which fatally leads a man to certain acts and is therefore an excuse. He thinks that man is responsible for his passion.

The existentialist does not think that man is going to help himself by finding in the world some omen by which to orient himself. Because he thinks that man will interpret the omen to suit himself. Therefore, he thinks that man, with no support and no aid, is condemned every moment to invent man. Ponge, in a very fine article, has said, "Man is the future of man." That's exactly it. But if it is taken to mean that this future is recorded in heaven, that God sees it, then it is false, because it would really no longer be a future. If it is taken to mean that, whatever a man may be, there is a future to be forged, a virgin future before him, then this remark is sound. But then we are forlorn.

To give you an example which will enable you to understand forlornness better, I shall cite the case of one of my students who came to see me under the following circumstances: his father was on bad terms with his mother, and, moreover, was inclined to be a collaborationist; his older brother had been killed in the German offensive of 1940, and the young man, with somewhat immature but generous feelings, wanted to avenge him. His mother lived alone with him, very much upset by the half-treason of her husband and the death of her older son; the boy was her only consolation.

The boy was faced with the choice of leaving for England and joining the Free French Forces—that is, leaving his mother behind—or remaining with his mother and helping her to carry on. He was fully aware that the woman lived only for him and that his going-off—and perhaps his death—would plunge her into despair. He was also aware that every act that he did for his mother's sake was a sure thing, in the sense that it was helping her to carry on, whereas every effort he made toward going off and fighting was an uncertain move which might run aground and prove completely useless; for example, on his way to England he might, while passing through Spain, be detained indefinitely in a Spanish camp; he might reach England or Algiers and be stuck in an office at a desk job. As a result, he was faced with two very different kinds of action: one, concrete, immediate, but concerning only one individual; the other concerned an incomparably vaster group, a national collectivity, but for that very reason was dubious, and might be interrupted en route. And, at the same time, he was wavering between two kinds of ethics. On the one hand, an ethics of sympathy, of personal devotion; on the other, a broader ethics, but one whose efficacy was more dubious. He had to choose between the two.

Who could help him choose? Christian doctrine? No. Christian doctrine says, "Be charitable, love your neighbor, take the more rugged path, etc., etc." But which is the more rugged path? Whom should he love as a brother? The fighting man or his mother? Which does the greater good, the vague act of fighting in a group, or the concrete one of helping a particular human being to go on living? Who can decide *a priori*? Nobody. No book of ethics can tell him. The Kantian ethics says, "Never treat any person as a means, but as an end." Very well, if I stay with my mother, I'll treat her as an end and not as a means; but by virtue of this very fact, I'm running the risk of treating the people around me who are fighting, as means; and, conversely, if I go to join those who are fighting, I'll be treating them as an end, and, by doing that, I run the risk of treating my mother as a means.

If values are vague, and if they are always too broad for the concrete and specific case that we are considering, the only thing left for us is to trust our instincts. That's what this young man tried to do; and when I saw him, he said, "In the end, feeling is what counts. I ought to choose whichever pushes me in one direction. If I feel that I love my mother enough to sacrifice everything else for her—my desire for vengeance, for action, for adventure—then I'll stay with her. If, on the contrary, I feel that my love for my mother isn't enough, I'll leave."

But how is the value of a feeling determined? What gives his feeling for his mother value? Precisely the fact that he remained with her. I may say that I like so-and-so well enough to sacrifice a certain amount of money for him, but I may say so only if I've done it. I may say "I love my mother well enough to remain with her" if I have remained with her. The only way to determine the value of this affection is, precisely, to perform an act which confirms and defines it. But, since I require this affection to justify my act, I find myself caught in a vicious circle.

On the other hand, Gide has well said that a mock feeling and a true feeling are almost indistinguishable; to decide that I love my mother and will remain with her, or to remain with her by putting on an act, amount somewhat to the same thing. In other words, the feeling is formed by the acts one performs; so, I can not refer to it in order to act upon it. Which means that I can neither seek within myself the true condition which will impel me to act, nor apply to a system of ethics for concepts which will permit me to act. You will say, "At least, he did go to a teacher for advice." But if you seek advice from a priest, for example, you have chosen this priest; you already knew, more or less, just about what advice he was going to give you. In other words, choosing your adviser is involving yourself. The proof of this is that if you are a Christian, you will say, "Consult a priest." But some priests are collaborating, some are just marking time, some are resisting. Which to choose? If the young man chooses a priest who is resisting or collaborating, he has already decided on the kind of advice he's going to get. Therefore, in coming to see me he knew the answer I was going to give him, and I had only one answer to give: "You're free, choose, that is, invent." No general ethics can show you what is to be done, there are no omens in the world. The Catholics will reply, "But there are." Granted—but, in any case, I myself choose the meaning they have.

As for despair, the term has a very simple meaning. It means that we shall confine ourselves to reckoning only with what depends upon our will, or on the ensemble of probabilities which make our action possible. When we want something, we always have to reckon with probabilities. I may be counting on the arrival of a friend. The friend is coming by rail or street-car; this supposes that the train will arrive on schedule, or that the street-car will not jump the track. I am left in the realm of possibility; but possibilities are to be reckoned with only to the point where my action comports with the ensemble of these possibilities, and no further. The moment the possibilities I am considering are not rigorously involved by my action, I ought to disengage myself from them, because no God, no scheme, can adapt the world and its possibilities to my will. When Descartes said, "Conquer yourself rather than the world," he meant essentially the same thing.

The Marxists to whom I have spoken reply, "You can rely on the support of others in your notion, which obviously has certain limits because you're not going to live forever. That means: rely on both what others are doing elsewhere to help you, in China, in Russia, and what they will do later on, after your death, to carry on the action and lead it to its fulfillment, which will be the revolution. You even *have* to rely upon that, otherwise you're immoral." I reply at once that I will always rely on fellow-fighters insofar as these comrades are involved with me in a common struggle, in the unity of a party or a group in which I can more or less make my weight felt; that is, one whose ranks I am in as a fighter and whose movements I am aware of at every movement. In such a situation, relying on the unity and will of the party is exactly like counting on the fact that the train will arrive on time or that the car won't jump the track. But, given that man is free and that there is no human nature for me to depend on, I can not count on men whom I do not know by relying on human goodness or man's concern for the good of society. I don't know what will become of the Russian revolution; I may make an example of it to the extent that at the present time it is apparent that the proletariat plays a part in Russia that it plays in no other nation. But I can't swear that this will inevitably lead to a triumph of the proletariat. I've got to limit myself to what I see.

Given that men are free and that tomorrow they will freely decide what man will be, I can not be sure that, after my death, fellow-fighters will carry on my work to bring it to its maximum perfection. Tomorrow, after my death, some men may decide to set up Fascism, and the others may be cowardly and muddled enough to let them do it. Fascism will then be the human reality, so much the worse for us.

Actually, things will be as man will have decided they are to be. Does that mean that I should abandon myself to quietism? No. First, I should involve myself; then, act on the old saw, "Nothing ventured, nothing gained." Nor does it mean that I shouldn't belong to a party, but rather that I shall have no illusions and shall do what I can. For example, suppose I ask myself, "Will socialization, as such, ever come about?" I know nothing about it. All I know is that I'm going to do everything in my power to bring it about. Beyond that, I can't count on anything. Quietism is the attitude of people who say, "Let others do what I can't do." The doctrine I am presenting is the very opposite of quietism, since it declares, "There is no reality except in action." Moreover, it goes further, since it adds, "Man is nothing else than his plan; he exists only to the extent that he fulfills himself; he is therefore nothing else than the ensemble of his acts, nothing else than his life."

According to this, we can understand why our doctrine horrifies certain people. Because often the only way they can bear their wretchedness is to think, "Circumstances have been against me. What I've been and done doesn't show my true worth. To be sure, I've had no great love, no great friendship, but that's because I haven't met a man or woman who was worthy. The books I've written haven't been very good because I haven't had the proper leisure. I haven't had children to devote myself to because I didn't find a man with whom I could have spent my life. So there remains within me, unused and quite viable, a host of propensities, inclinations, possibilities, that one wouldn't guess from the mere series of things I've done."

Now, for the existentialist there is really no love other than one which manifests itself in a person's being in love. There is no genius other than one which is expressed in works of art; the genius of Proust is the sum of Proust's works; the genius of Racine is his series of tragedies. Outside of that, there is nothing. Why say that Racine could have written another tragedy, when he didn't write it? A man is involved in life, leaves his impress on it, and outside of that there is nothing. To be sure, this may seem a harsh thought to someone whose life hasn't been a success. But, on the other hand, it prompts people to understand that reality alone is what counts, that dreams, expectations, and hopes warrant no more than to define a man as a disappointed dream, as miscarried hopes, as vain expectations. In other words, to define him negatively and not positively. However, when we say "You are nothing else than your life," that does not imply that the artist will be judged solely on the basis of his works of art; a thousand other things will contribute toward summing him up. What we mean is that a man is nothing else than a series of undertakings, that he is the sum, the organization, the ensemble of the relationships which make up these undertakings.

To Think About

1. "The God of each man is the God whom he has chosen to serve." **F. Jeanson**

2. "To exist is tantamount to being a problem for oneself." **F. Jeanson**

3. "There cannot be any hierarchy with regard to freedom. There is nothing above freedom." **Jean-Paul Sartre**

4. "Modern man is, as Sartre has presented him to us, man torn from his traditional group, traditional religion, his traditional metaphysics or ethic. He is the spiritually unaccommodated man, and nothing is impermissible for him. He must decide himself just what it is he forbids himself to do." **Walter Kaufmann**

5. "That moral theories are unnecessary for answering moral questions is proved in that moral dilemmas have been getting settled all through history without moral theories." **Unknown**

6. "[E]thical theory is essentially a modern invention. . . . [T]he structures known as ethical theories are more threats to moral sanity and balance than instruments for their attainment." **Edmund Pincoffs**

7. Do you have an ultimate ethical principle? What is it? Do you have several? Do they ever conflict? How do you decide which is the most important?

8. Are religious ethics teleological or deontological? Which are Sartre's ethics?

9. Do you agree with the following statements? Why or why not?

   "Goodness without knowledge is blind; knowledge without goodness is dangerous." **Phillips Academy**

   "There are no ethical truths; there are just justifications of particular ethical problems." **Mortimer Kalish**

   "For whoever would save his life will lose it; and whoever loses his life for my sake, he will save it." **Luke 9:24**

   "People are to be loved, and things are to be used. . . . Immorality occurs when things are loved and people are used." **Unknown**

10. "I have thus arrived at the conclusion that neither the attempts of moral philosophers or theologians to prove the objective validity of moral values, nor the common sense assumption to the same effect, gives us any right at all to accept such a validity as a fact. . . . In my opinion the predicates of all moral judgments, all moral concepts, are ultimately based on emotions, and, as is very commonly admitted, no objectivity can come from emotions." **Edward Westermarck**

11.   "Reading *Buddenbrooks* (Thomas Mann), this *Forsyte Saga* of old Lübeck, I cannot help but regret that I did not live fifty or a hundred years sooner. Life is too full in these times to be comprehensible. We know too many cities to be able to grow into any of them, and our arrivals and departures are no longer matters for emotional debauches—they are too common. Similarly, we have too many friends to have any friendships, too many books to know any of them well; and the quality of our impressions gives way to the quantity, so that life begins to seem like a movie, with hundreds of kaleidoscopic senses flashing on and off our field of perception—gone before we have time to consider them.

"I should like to have lived in the days when a visit was a matter of months, when political and social problems were regarded from simple standpoints called 'liberal' and 'conservative,' when foreign countries were still foreign, when a vast part of the world always bore the glamour of the great unknown, when there were still wars worth fighting and gods worth worshipping."   ***George Kennan***

Readings

GOLOMB, JACOB. *In Search of Authenticity: From Kierkegaard to Camus.* New York: Routledge, 1995.

HOWELLS, CHRISTINA, ed. *The Cambridge Companion to Sartre.* New York: Cambridge University Press, 1992.

KERNER, GEORGE C. *Three Philosophical Moralists: Mill, Kant, and Sartre: An Introduction to Ethics.* Oxford: Oxford University Press, 1990.

MCBRIDE, WILLIAM L., ed. *Existentialist Ethics.* New York: Garland, 1997.

SCHILPP, PAUL ARTHUR, ed. *The Philosophy of Jean-Paul Sartre.* La Salle, IL: Open Court, 1981.

24
Feminist Ethics Are Different

Virginia Held (1929–) is Distinguished Professor of Philosophy at the City University of New York Graduate School and Professor Emerita at Hunter College. She has taught at Yale, Dartmouth, the University of California at Los Angeles, and Hamilton College and has been a fellow at the Center for Advanced Study in the Behavioral Sciences. In 2001–2 she was President of the American Philosophical Association (Eastern Division). She has held Fulbright and Rockefeller fellowships. Among her many publications are The Public Interest and Individual Interests *(1970),* Rights and Goods: Justifying Social Action *(1984),* Feminist Morality: Transforming Culture, Society, and Politics *(1993), an edition entitled* Justice and Care: Essential Readings in Feminist Ethics *(1995), and* The Ethics of Care: Personal, Political and Global *(2005).*

Most of the ethical theories presented in this text concern general moral principles, as represented, for example, by Kant's theory of the categorical imperative. However, during the late twentieth century, feminists raised a challenge to many of these systems, arguing that they are either explicitly male-centered or contain hidden biases in favor of a male interpretation of obligation and the good life. Held argues in the following reading that concepts of rationality, privacy, and even the supposedly gender-neutral notion of the *self* obscure a male orientation that needs revision. She insists that an urgent task for moral theorists is to balance the claims of justice and care as primary moral values. Along with this must likewise come some effort at transforming modern society and culture to reflect a wider sense of democratic ideals, one including a larger place for women and families and a greater sense of social and institutional equality.

From Virginia Held, "Feminist Reconceptualizations in Ethics," in Kourany, Janet, *Philosophy in a Feminist Voice*. Copyright 1998 Princeton University Press. Reprinted by permission of Princeton University Press.

~~~~~ To Study ~~~~~

1. What three concepts does Held believe feminism is transforming?
2. In modern moral theory, what two forms does the priority of reason take?
3. Explain the two ways in which feminists are reevaluating the place of emotion in morality.
4. What criticism of nature underlies Held's position on the public and private spheres of morality and life?
5. How does Held critique the two extremes of individualism and abstract universalism in her theory of the relational self?
6. Why are Marxism and communitarianism inadequate responses to these extremes?
7. According to Held's theory, how will the integration of care and justice transform society?

When feminist perspectives are brought to bear in ethics, they may at first suggest topics overlooked or neglected by the philosophical field of inquiry known as "moral philosophy" or "ethics." Such topics include discrimination against women and justifiable remedies, abortion and reproductive technologies and the moral problems involved, violence against women, and many others.

Soon attention may be turned to the moral theory appealed to in any discussion of ethical problems. And it will be seen that moral theory, like other philosophical theory, has a long history of gender bias.[1] Ethics, like most of philosophy, has been built on assumptions, and constructed with concepts, that are by no means gender-neutral.

In comparison with nonfeminist approaches, feminists characteristically begin with different concerns and give different emphases to the issues we consider. Far from merely providing additional insights that can be incorporated into traditional theory, feminist explorations often require radical transformations of existing fields of inquiry and theory.[2] From a feminist point of view, moral theory, along with almost all theory, will have to be transformed to take adequate account of the experience of women.

I will begin this essay with a brief examination of how various fundamental aspects of the history of ethics have not been gender-neutral. I will discuss three issues where feminist rethinking is transforming moral concepts and theories: the split between reason and emotion, and the devaluation of emotion; the public-private distinction and the relegation of the private to the natural; and the concept of the self as constructed from a male point of view. . . .

REASON AND EMOTION

In the area of moral theory in the modern era, the priority accorded to reason has taken two major forms. On the one hand has been the Kantian, or Kantian-inspired, search for very general, abstract, deontological, universal moral principles by which rational beings should be guided. Kant's Categorical Imperative is a prime example. It suggests that all moral problems can be handled by applying an impartial, pure, rational principle to particular cases. It requires that we try to see what the general features of the problem before us are and that we apply to the problem an abstract principle or rules derivable from it. This procedure, it is said, should be adequate for all moral decisions. We should thus be able to act as reason recommends, and resist yielding to emotional inclinations and desires in conflict with our rational wills.

On the other hand, the priority accorded to reason in the modern era has taken a Utilitarian form. The Utilitarian approach, reflected in rational choice theory, recognizes that persons have desires and interests, and it suggests rules of rational choice for maximizing the satisfaction of these desires and interests. While some philosophers in the tradition espouse egoism, especially of an intelligent and long-term kind, many do not. They begin, however, with assumptions that what is morally relevant are the gains and losses of utility to theoretically isolable individuals and that morality should aim to maximize the satisfaction of individuals. Rational calculation about such an outcome will, in this view, provide moral recommendations to guide all our choices. Like the Kantian approach, the Utilitarian approach relies on abstract general principles or rules to be applied to particular cases. And it holds that although emotion is, in fact, the source of our desires for certain objectives, the task of morality should be to instruct us on how to pursue those objectives most rationally. Emotional attitudes toward moral issues themselves interfere with rationality and should be disregarded.

Although the conceptions of what the judgments of morality should be based on and how reason should guide moral decisions are different in Kantian and Utilitarian approaches, they share a reliance on a highly abstract, universal principle as the appropriate source of moral guidance, and they share the view that moral problems are to be solved by the application of such an abstract principle to particular cases. Both admire the rules of reason to be appealed to in moral contexts, and both denigrate emotional responses to moral issues.

Many feminist philosophers have questioned whether the reliance on abstract rules, rather than the adoption of more context-respectful approaches, can possibly be adequate for dealing with moral problems, especially as women experience them. Though Kantians may hold that complex rules can be elaborated for specific contexts, there is nevertheless an assumption in this approach that the more abstract the reasoning applied to a moral problem, the more satisfactory. And Utilitarians suppose that one highly abstract principle, the Principle of Utility, can be applied to every moral problem no matter what the context.

A genuinely universal or gender-neutral moral theory would be one that would take account of the experience and concerns of women as fully as it does the experience and concerns of men. When we focus on women's experience of moral problems, however, we find that they are often especially concerned with actual relationships between embodied persons and with what these relationships seem to require. Women are often inclined to attend to rather than to dismiss the particularities of the context in which a moral problem arises. And many of us pay attention to feelings of empathy and caring to help us decide what to do rather than relying as fully as possible on abstract rules of reason. . .

Feminist philosophers are in the process of reevaluating the place of emotion in morality in at least two respects. First, many think morality requires the development of the moral emotions, in contrast to moral theories emphasizing the primacy of reason. As Annette Baier observes, the rationalism typical of traditional moral theory will be challenged when we pay attention to the role of parent:

> It might be important for father figures to have rational control over their violent urges to beat to death the children whose screams enrage them, but more than control of such nasty passions seems needed in the mother or primary parent, or parent-substitute, by most psychological theories. They need to love their children, not just to control their irritation.[3]

So the emphasis in traditional theories on rational control over the emotions, rather than on cultivating desirable forms of emotion, is challenged by feminist approaches to ethics.

Second, emotions will be respected rather than dismissed by many feminist moral philosophers in the process of gaining moral understanding. The experience and practice out of which we can expect to develop feminist moral theory will include embodied feeling as well as thought. In an overview of a vast amount of writing, Kathryn Morgan states that "feminist theorists begin ethical theorizing with embodied, gendered subjects who have particular histories, particular communities, particular allegiances, and particular visions of human flourishing. The starting point involves valorizing what has frequently been most mistrusted and despised in the western philosophical tradition."[4] Foremost among the elements being reevaluated are women's emotions. The "care" of the alternative feminist approach to morality appreciates rather than rejects emotion, and such caring relationships cannot be understood in terms of abstract rules or moral reasoning. And the "weighing" so often needed between the conflicting claims of some relationships and others cannot be settled by deduction or rational calculation. A feminist ethic will not just acknowledge emotion, as do Utilitarians, as giving us the objectives toward which moral rationality can direct us; it will embrace emotion as providing at least a partial basis for morality itself and certainly for moral understanding.

Trust is essential for at least some segments of morality.[5] Achieving and maintaining trusting, caring relationships is quite different from acting in accord with rational principles or satisfying the individual desires of either self or other. Caring, empathy, feeling for others, being sensitive to each other's feelings—all may be better guides to what morality requires in actual contexts than may abstract rules of reason, or rational calculation.

The fear that a feminist ethic will be a relativistic "situation ethic" is misplaced. Some feelings can be as widely shared as are rational beliefs, and feminists do not see their views as reducible to "just another attitude." In her discussion of the differences between feminist and nonfeminist medical ethics, Susan Sherwin shows why feminists reject the mere case-by-case approach that prevails in nonfeminist medical ethics. The latter also rejects the excessive reliance on abstract rules characteristic of standard ethics, and in this way resembles feminist ethics. But the very focus on cases in isolation makes it difficult to attend to general features in the institutions and practices of medicine that, among other faults, systematically contribute to the oppression of women.[6] The difference of approach can be seen in the treatment of issues in the new reproductive technologies that may further decrease the control of women over reproduction.

This difference is not one of substance alone; Sherwin shows its implications for method as well. With respect to reproductive technologies, one can see clearly the deficiencies of the case-by-case approach: what needs to be considered is not only choice as seen in the purely individualistic terms of the focus on cases but control at a more general level and how such control affects the structure of gender in society. Thus, a feminist perspective does not always counsel attention to specific case versus appeal to general considerations, as some sort of methodological rule. But the general considerations are often not the purely abstract ones of traditional and standard moral theory; they are the general features and judgments to be made about cases in actual (which means, so far, male-dominated) societies. A feminist evaluation of a moral problem should never omit the political elements involved; and it is likely to recognize that political issues cannot be dealt with adequately in purely abstract terms any more than can moral issues.

The liberal tradition in social and moral philosophy argues that in a pluralistic society, and even more clearly in a pluralistic world, we cannot agree on our visions of the good life, on what is the best kind of life for human beings, but we can hope to agree on the minimal conditions for justice, for coexistence within a framework allowing us to pursue our visions of the good life.[7] Many feminists contend that the commitment to justice needed for agreement in actual conditions on even minimal requirements of justice is as likely to demand relational feelings as a rational recognition of abstract principles. Human beings can and do care—and are capable of caring far more than most do at present—about the suffering of children quite distant from them, about the prospects for future generations, and about the well-being of the globe. The mutually disinterested rational individualists of the liberal tradition would seem unlikely to care enough to take the actions needed to achieve moral decency at a global level, or environmental sanity for decades hence, just as they seem unable to represent caring relationships within the family and among friends. Annette Baier puts it thus:

> *A moral theory, it can plausibly be claimed, cannot regard concern for new and future persons as an optional charity left for those with a taste for it. If the morality the theory endorses is to sustain itself, it must provide for its own continuers, not just take out a loan on a carefully encouraged maternal instinct or on the enthusiasm of a self-selected group of environmentalists, who make it their business or hobby to be concerned with what we are doing to mother earth.*[8]

The possibilities, as well as the problems (and we are well aware of some of them), in a feminist reenvisioning of emotion and reason need to be further developed, but we can already see that the views of nonfeminist moral theory are unsatisfactory.

THE PUBLIC AND THE PRIVATE

A second questionable aspect of the history of ethics is its conception of the distinction between the public and the private. As with the split between reason and emotion, feminists are showing how gender bias has distorted previous conceptions of these spheres, and we are trying to offer more appropriate understandings of "private" morality and "public" life.

Feminists reject the implication that what occurs in the household occurs as if on an island beyond politics. In fact, the personal is highly affected by the political power beyond, from legislation about abortion to the greater earning power of men, to the interconnected division of labor by gender both within and beyond the household, to the lack of adequate social protection for women against domestic violence.[9] Of course we recognize that the family is not identical with the state, and we still need concepts for thinking about the private and the personal, the public and the political; but we do know they will have to be very different from the traditional concepts.

Feminists have also criticized deeper assumptions about what is distinctively human and what is "natural" in the public and private aspects of human life, and what is meant by "natural" in connection with women.[10] Consider the associations that have traditionally been built up: the public realm is seen as the distinctively human realm in which man transcends his animal nature, while the private realm of the household is seen as the natural region in which women merely reproduce the species. These associations are extraordinarily pervasive in standard concepts and theories, in art and thought and cultural ideals, and especially in politics. So entrenched is this way of thinking that it was reflected even in Simone de Beauvoir's path-breaking feminist text, *The Second Sex,* published in 1949.[11] In thinking about the household and about politics, as about many other topics, feminists need to transcend our own early searches for our own perspectives.

Dominant patterns of thought have seen women as primarily mothers, and mothering as the performance of a primarily biological function. Then it has been supposed that while engaging in political life is a specifically human activity, women are engaged in an activity that is not specifically human. Women accordingly have been thought to be closer to nature than men, to be enmeshed in a biological function involving processes more like those in which other animals are involved than like the rational discussion of the citizen in the polis, or the glorious battles of noble soldiers, or the trading and rational contracting of "economic man."[12] The total or relative exclusion of women from the domain of public life has thus been seen as either fitting or inevitable.

The view that women are more determined by biology than are men is still extraordinarily prevalent. From a feminist perspective it is highly questionable. Human mothering is a different activity from the mothering engaged in by other animals, as different as the work and speech of men is from what might be thought of as the "work" and "speech" of other animals. Of course, all human beings are animal as well as human. But to whatever extent it is appropriate to recognize a difference between "man" and other animals, so is it appropriate to recognize a comparable difference between "woman" and other animals, and between the activities—including mothering—engaged in by women and the behavior of other animals.

Human mothering shapes language and culture, it forms human social personhood, it develops morality. Animal behavior can be highly complex, but it does not have built into it any of the consciously chosen aims of morality. In creating human social persons, human mothering is different in kind from merely propagating a species. And human mothering can be fully as creative an activity as those activities traditionally thought of as distinctively human, because to create new persons and new types of persons can surely be as creative as to make new objects, products, or institutions. Human mothering is no more "natural" or "primarily biological" than is any human activity.

Consider nursing an infant, often thought of as the epitome of a biological process with which mothering is associated and women are identified. There is no more reason to think of human nursing as simply biological than there is to think this way of, say, a businessmen's lunch. Eating is a biological process, but what and how and with whom we eat are thoroughly cultural. Whether and how long and with whom a woman nurses an infant are also human, cultural matters. If men transcend the natural by conquering new territory and trading with their neighbors and making deals over lunch to do so, women can transcend the natural by choosing not to nurse their children when they could, or choosing to nurse them when their culture tells them not to, or singing songs to their infants as they nurse, or nursing in restaurants to overcome the prejudices against doing so, or thinking human thoughts as they nurse, and so forth. Human culture surrounds and characterizes the activity of nursing as it does the activities of eating or governing or writing or thinking.

We are continually being presented with images of the humanly new and creative as occurring in the public realm of the polis or in the realms of the marketplace or of art and science outside the household. The very term "reproduction" suggests mere repetition, the bringing into existence of repeated instances of the same human animal. But human reproduction is not repetition. This is not to suggest that bringing up children in the interstices of patriarchal families, in society structured by institutions supporting male dominance, can achieve the potential of transformation latent in the activity of human mothering. But the activity of creating new social persons and new kinds of persons is potentially the most transformative human activity of all. And it suggests that morality should concern itself first of all with this activity, with what its norms and practices ought to be, and with how the institutions and arrangements throughout society and the world ought to be structured to facilitate the right kinds of development of the best kinds of new persons. The flourishing of children ought to be at the very center of moral, social, political, economic, and legal thought, rather than, as at present, at the periphery, if attended to at all.

Revised conceptions of public and private have significant implications for our conceptions of human beings and relationships between them. Some feminists suggest that instead of interpreting human relationships on the model of the impersonal "public" sphere, as standard political and moral theory has so often done, we might consider interpreting them on the model of the "private," or of what these relationships could be imagined to be like in postpatriarchal society. The traditional approach is illustrated by those who generalize, to regions of human life other than the economic, assumptions about "economic man" in contractual relations with other men. It sees such impersonal, contractual relations as paradigmatic, even, on some views, for moral theory. Many feminists, in contrast, consider the realm of what has been misconstrued as the "private" as offering guidance to what human beings and their relationships should be like in regions beyond those of family and friendship, as well as in more intimate contexts. Sara Ruddick looks at the implications of the practice of mothering for the conduct of peace politics. Marilyn Friedman and Lorraine Code consider friendship, especially as women understand it, as a possible model for human relationships.[13] Others see society as noncontractual rather than contractual.

Clearly, a reconceptualization is needed of the ways in which every human life is entwined with both personal and social components. Feminist theorists are rethinking and reorganizing the private and the public, the personal and the political, and thus morality.

THE CONCEPT OF SELF

Let me turn now to the third aspect of the history of ethics that is being reenvisioned by feminists: the concept of self. A major emphasis in a feminist approach to morality is the recognition that more attention must be paid to the domain between the self as ego, as self-interested individual, and the universal, everyone, others in general. Traditionally, ethics has dealt with these poles of individual self and universal all. Often it has called for impartiality against the partiality of the egoistic self; sometimes it has defended egoism against claims for a universal perspective. But most standard moral theory has hardly noticed as morally significant the intermediate realm of family relations and relations of friendship, of group ties and neighborhood concerns, especially from the point of view of women.

When it has noticed this intermediate realm, it has often seen its attachments as threatening to the aspirations of the man of reason or as subversive of "true" morality. In seeing the problems of ethics as problems of reconciling the interests of the self with what would be right or best for "everyone," standard ethics has neglected the moral aspects of the concern and sympathy that people actually feel for particular others, and what moral experience in this intermediate realm suggests for an adequate morality.

The region of "particular others" is a distinct domain, where what can be seen to be artificial and problematic are the very egoistic "self" and the universal "all others" of standard moral theory. In the domain of particular others, the self is already constituted to an important degree by relations with others, and these relations may be much more salient and significant than the interests of any individual self in isolation.[14] The "others" in the picture, however, are not the "all others," or "everyone," of traditional moral theory; they are not what a universal point of view or a view from nowhere could provide.[15] They are, characteristically, actual flesh-and-blood other human beings for whom we have actual feelings and with whom we have real ties.

From the point of view of much feminist theory, the individualistic assumptions of liberal theory and of most standard moral theory are suspect.[16] Even if we were freed from the debilitating aspects of dominating male power to "be ourselves" and to pursue our own interests, we would, as persons, still have ties to other persons, and we would at least in part be constituted by such ties. Such ties would be part of what we inherently are. We are, for instance, the daughter or son of given parents or the mother or father of given children, and we carry with us at least some ties to the racial or ethnic or national group within which we developed into the persons we are.

If we look at the realities of the relation between mothering person (who can be female or male) and child, we can see that what we value in the relation cannot be broken down into individual gains and losses for the individual members in the relation. Nor can it be understood in universalistic terms. Self-development apart from the relation may be much less important than the satisfactory development of the relation. What matters may often be the health, growth, and development of the relation-and-its-members in ways that cannot be understood in the individualistic terms of standard moral theories designed to maximize the satisfaction of self-interest. Neither can the universalistic terms of moral theories grounded in what would be right for "all rational beings" or "everyone" handle what has moral value in the relations between mothering person and child.

Feminism is, of course, not the only locus of criticism of the individualistic and abstractly universalistic features of liberalism and standard moral theory. Marxists and communitarians also see the self as constituted by its social relations. But in their usual form Marxist and communitarian criticisms pay no more attention than liberalism and standard moral theory to the experience of women, to the context of mothering, or to friendship as women experience it.[17] Some nonfeminist criticisms, such as offered by Bernard Williams, of the impartiality required by standard moral theory, stress how a person's identity may be formed by personal projects in ways that do not satisfy universal norms yet ought to be admired. Such views still interpret morality from the point of view of an individual and his project, not a social relationship such as that between mothering person and child. And nonfeminist criticisms in terms of traditional communities and their moral practices, as seen, for instance, in the work of Alasdair MacIntyre, often take traditional gender roles as given or else provide no basis for a radical critique of them.[18] There is no substitute, then, for feminist exploration of the area between ego and universal, as women experience this area, or for the development of a refocused concept of relational self that could be acceptable from a feminist point of view.

Relationships can be evaluated as trusting or mistrustful, mutually considerate or selfish, harmonious or stressful, and so forth. Where trust and consideration are appropriate, which is not always, we can find ways to foster them. But to understand and evaluate relationships and to encourage them to be what they can be at their best require us to look at relationships between actual persons and to see what both standard moral theories and their nonfeminist critics often miss. To be adequate, moral theories must pay attention to the neglected realm of particular others in the actual relationships and actual contexts of women's experience. In doing so, problems of individual self-interest versus universal rules may recede to a region more like background, out-of-focus insolubility, or relative unimportance. The salient problems may then be seen to be how we ought best to guide or maintain or reshape the relationships, both close and more distant, that we have, or might have, with actual other human beings. Particular others can be actual children in need on distant continents or the anticipated children of generations not yet even close to being born. But they are not "all rational beings" or "the greatest number," and the self that is in relationships with particular others and is shaped to a significant degree by such relations is not a self whose ego must be pitted against abstract, universal claims.

The concept of a relational self is evolving within feminist thought. Among the interesting inquiries it is leading to is the work done at the Stone Center at Wellesley College.[19] Psychologists there have posited a self-in-relation theory and have conducted empirical inquiries to try to establish how the female self develops. In working with a theory that a female relational self develops through a mutually empathetic mother-daughter bond, they have been influenced by Jean Baker Miller's reevaluation of women's psychological qualities as strengths rather than weaknesses. In the mid-1970s, Miller identified women's "great desire for affiliation" as one such strength. Nancy Chodorow's *Reproduction of Mothering* has also influenced the work done at the Stone Center.[20] Chodorow argued that a female sense of self is reproduced by a structure of parenting in which mothers are the primary caretakers and that sons and daughters develop differently in relation to a parent of the same sex, or a parent of different sex, as primary caretaker. Daughters come to define themselves as connected to or in relation with others. Sons, in contrast, come to define themselves as separate from or less connected with others. An implication often drawn from Chodorow's work is that parenting should be shared equally by fathers and mothers so that children of either sex can develop with caretakers of both the same and different sex.

In the early 1980s, Carol Gilligan offered her view of the "different voice" with which girls and women express their understanding of moral problems.[21] Like Miller and Chodorow, Gilligan valued tendencies found especially in women to affiliate with others and to interpret their moral responsibilities in terms of their relationships with others. In all, to value autonomy and individual independence over care and concern for relationships was seen as an expression of male bias. Psychologists at the Stone Center have tried to elaborate on and to study a feminist conception of the relational self. In a series of working papers, researchers and clinicians have explored the implications of the conception of the relational self for various issues in women's psychology (for example, power, anger, work inhibitions, violence, eating patterns) and for therapy.

The self as conceptualized in these studies is seen as having both a need for recognition and a need to understand the other, and these needs are seen as compatible. They are created in the context of mother-child interaction and are satisfied in a mutually empathetic relationship. This requires not a loss of self but a relationship of mutuality in which self and other both express an understanding of each other's subjectivity. Both give and take in a way that not only contributes to the satisfaction of their needs as individuals but also affirms the "larger relational unit" they compose.[22] Maintaining this larger relational unit then becomes a goal, and maturity is seen not in terms of individual autonomy but in terms of competence in creating and sustaining relations of empathy and mutual intersubjectivity.

The Stone Center psychologists contend that the goal of mutuality is rarely achieved in adult male-female relationships because of the traditional gender system, which leads men to seek autonomy and power over others and to undervalue the caring and relational connectedness that is expected of women. Women rarely receive the nurturing and empathetic support they provide. Accordingly, these psychologists look to the interaction that occurs in mother-daughter relationships as the best source of insight into the promotion of the healthy relational self. This research provides an example of exploration into a refocused, feminist conception of the self and into empirical questions about its development. . .

To argue for a view of the self as relational does not mean that women need to remain enmeshed in the ties by which we are constituted. Increasingly, women are breaking free from oppressive relationships with parents, with the communities in which we grew up, and with men—relationships in which we defined our selves through the traditional and often stifling expectations of others.[23] These quests for self have often involved wrenching instability and painful insecurity. But the quest has been for a new and more satisfactory relational self, not for the self-sufficient individual of liberal theory. Many might share the concerns expressed by Alison Jaggar that disconnecting ourselves from particular others, as ideals of individual autonomy seem to presuppose we should, might render us incapable of morality, rather than capable of it if, as so many feminists think, "an ineliminable part of morality consists in responding emotionally to particular others."[24]

I have examined three topics on which feminist philosophers and feminists in other fields are thinking anew about where we should start and how we should focus our attention in ethics. Feminist reconceptualizations and recommendations concerning the relation between reason and emotion, the distinction between public and private, and the concept of the self are providing insights that are deeply challenging to standard moral theory. The implications of this work are that we need an almost total reconstruction of social, political, economic, and legal theory in all their traditional forms, as well as a reconstruction of moral theory and practice at more comprehensive, or fundamental, levels.

TRANSFORMATIONS OF SOCIETY

As we look ahead, we can see some of the directions in which feminist rethinking of the basic assumptions and concepts of standard moral theorizing is leading.

One is toward the view that any moral theory likely to be found satisfactory will have to combine aspects of an ethic of care with aspects of an ethic of justice. An ethic of care is indisputably important for a context in which we feel concern for and engage in the actual care of particular others, and we must insist that this context be recognized as one that is as relevant to moral theory as any of the contexts traditionally attended to. The ethics of care can and should be extended far beyond the household, encouraging more sensitive public policies and greater empathy for those distant from us and unlike ourselves. Still, an ethic of care alone may not be able to ground the criticism that is needed of social inequality and global injustice. Aspects of an ethic of justice continue to be needed, and not only for public or global contexts. Overcoming unjust inequalities in the way work is divided between women and men, in the household and elsewhere, requires clarity concerning what justice demands. And ending unjust violence and coercion against women and children in private as well as public spaces calls for an extension of the ethics of justice. At the same time, justice alone is unable to provide a full and nuanced morality of good lives, trusting relationships, successful families, and healthy communities. An ethic we can accept will need to weave together the moral concerns of care and justice.

Another discernible direction in feminist thought concerns the reshaping of society. We try to envision what society might be like if male dominance were to be overcome. Just because the gender structure is so fundamental, transforming it is likely to transform everything else. We wonder what all the different segments of society would be like, and what the relations between them would be like. How they fit together would almost certainly be transformed, as would each domain.

In a feminist society, some segments might remain relatively intact and distinguishable from other segments—a democratic political system, say, with true equality for women at all levels. But if all such segments are infused with feminist values, and if all are embedded in a society hospitable to feminism, then the relative positions of the segments might change in fundamental ways, as well as many of their internal characteristics.

A feminist society would be fundamentally different from a society composed of individuals each pursuing his own interest, especially his own economic interest, and evaluating public institutions by how well they facilitate or contribute to his own advancement—the traditional model of liberal and pluralistic society. It would be different as well from Marxist conceptions of society, with their neglect of the issues of women and the family, and different as well from conservative communitarian views, with their upholding of patriarchy.

Feminist society might be seen as having various relatively independent and distinct segments, with some not traditionally thought of as especially central and influential now being so, and with all such segments embedded in a wider network of social relations characterized by social caring and trust. Certainly the levels of caring and trust appropriate for the relations of all members of society with all others will be different from the levels appropriate for the members of a family with one another. But social relations in what can be thought of as society as a whole will not be characterized by indifference to the well-being of others, or an absence of trust, as they are in many nonfeminist conceptions. What kinds and amounts of caring and trust might characterize the relations of the most general kind in society should be decided on the basis of experience and practice with institutions that have overcome male dominance.

From the point of view of the self-interested head of household, the individual's interest in his own family may be at odds with the wider political and public interest. And aspects of mothering in patriarchal society have contributed to parochialism and racism. But from a satisfactorily worked-out feminist and moral point of view, the picture of the particularistic family in conflict with the good of society is distorted. The postpatriarchal family can express universal emotions and can be guided by universally shared concerns. A content and healthy child eager to learn and to love can elicit general approval. A child whose distress can be prevented or alleviated should elicit universal efforts to deal with the distress and prevent its recurrence. Any feminist society can be expected to cherish new persons, seeing in the face and body of a child both the specialness of a unique person and the universal features of a child's wonder and curiosity and hope. Feminist society should seek to build institutions and practices and a world worthy of each particular child. But no particular child can flourish in isolation; feminist society should reflect the awareness that for each to do well, children must flourish together in an appropriate global environment.

Although feminist society would have democratic political processes, an independent judicial system to handle the recalcitrant, and probably markets to organize some economic activity, these and other institutions would be evaluated in terms of how well they work to achieve feminist goals. And other segments of society might be recognized as far more central in doing so. Cultural expression would continually evaluate imaginative alternatives for consideration. It would provide entertainment not primarily to serve commercial interests or to relieve for a few hours the distress of persons caught in demeaning and exploitative jobs or with no jobs at all but to enrich the lives of respected members of cultural and social communities.

A society organized along feminist lines would be likely to put the proper care and suitable development of all children at the very center of its concerns. Instead of allowing, as so often at present, family policies and arrangements for child care and for the education and health of children to be marginal concerns, vastly less important than military strength and corporate profits, a feminist society might understand the future of children to be its highest priority. Its practices might then be guided by the fundamental considerations—global and local and in between—needed for all children, as for our own, to begin to lead the lives of their hopes.

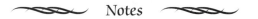 Notes

1. See, e.g., Cheshire Calhoun, "Justice, Care, Gender Bias," *Journal of Philosophy* 85 (September 1988): 451–63.
2. See, e.g., Sue Rosenberg Zalk and Janice Gordon-Kelter, eds., *Revolutions in Knowledge: Feminism in the Social Sciences* (Boulder, Colo.: Westview Press, 1992).
3. Annette Baier, "The Need for More Than Justice," in *Science, Morality and Feminist Theory,* ed. M. Hanen and K. Nielsen (Calgary, Alberta: University of Calgary Press, 1987), 55.
4. Kathryn Pauly Morgan, "Strangers in a Strange Land: Feminists Visit Relativists," in *Perspectives on Relativism,* ed. D. Odegaard and C. Stewart (Toronto: Agathon Press, 1990), 2.
5. See Baier, "Trust and Anti-Trust," *Ethics 96* (January 1986): 231–60; and Laurence Thomas, "Trust, Affirmation, and Moral Character: A Critique of Kantian Morality," in *Identity, Character, and Morality: Essays in Moral Psychology,* ed. Owen Flanagan and Amelie Oksenberg Rorty (Cambridge, Mass.: MIT Press, 1990).
6. Susan Sherwin, "Feminist and Medical Ethics: Two Different Approaches to Contextual Ethics," *Hypatia* 4 (Summer 1989): 57–72.
7. See John Rawls, "Justice as Fairness: Political Not Metaphysical," *Philosophy and Public Affairs* 14 (Summer 1985): 251–75; Rawls, "The Priority of Right and Ideas of the Good," *Philosophy and Public Affairs* 17 (Fall 1988): 251–76; Rawls, "The Idea of Overlapping Consensus," *Oxford Journal of Legal Studies* 7 (Spring 1987): 1–25; and Ronald Dworkin, "Liberalism," in *Public and Private Morality,* ed. Stuart Hampshire (Cambridge: Cambridge University Press, 1978). See also Charles Larmore, *Patterns of Moral Complexity* (Cambridge: Cambridge University Press, 1987).

8. Baier, "The Need for More Than Justice," 53–54.
9. See Linda Nicholson, *Gender and History: The Limits of Social Theory in the Age of the Family* (New York: Columbia University Press, 1986); and Jean Bethke Elshtain, *Public Man, Private Woman* (Princeton, N.J.: Princeton University Press, 1981). See also Carole Pateman, *The Sexual Contract* (Stanford, Calif.: Stanford University Press, 1988).
10. Susan Moller Okin, *Women in Western Political Thought* (Princeton, N.J.: Princeton University Press, 1979); and Alison M. Jaggar, *Feminist Politics and Human Nature* (Totowa, N.J.: Rowman and Allanheld, 1983).
11. Simone de Beauvoir, *The Second Sex,* trans. H. Parshley (New York: Bantam, 1953).
12. See Sherry B. Ortner "Is Female to Male as Nature Is to Culture?" in *Woman, Culture, and Society,* ed. Michelle Z. Rosaldo and Louise Lamphere (Stanford, Calif.: Stanford University Press, 1974).
13. See Marilyn Friedman, "Feminism and Modern Friendship: Dislocating the Community," *Ethics* 99 (January 1989): 275–90; and Lorraine Code, "Second Persons," in *Science, Morality and Feminist Theory,* ed. Marsha Hanen and Kai Nielsen (Calgary: University of Calgary Press, 1987), 357–82.
14. See Seyla Benhabib, "The Generalized and the Concrete Other: The Kohlberg-Gilligan Controversy and Moral Theory," in *Women and Moral Theory,* ed. E. Kittay and D. Meyers; (Totowa, NJ: Rowman & Littlefield, 1987); Caroline Whitbeck, "Feminist Ontology: A Different Reality," in *Beyond Domination: New Perspectives on Women and Philosophy,* ed. Carol C. Gould (Totowa, N.J.: Rowman and Allanheld, 1983); Janice Raymond, *A Passion for Friends: Towards a Philosophy of Female Affection* (Boston: Beacon Press, 1986); and Marilyn Friedman, "Individuality without Individualism: Review of Janice Raymond's *A Passion for Friends,*" *Hypatia* 3 (Summer 1988): 13.
15. See Thomas Nagel, *The View from Nowhere* (New York: Oxford University Press, 1986). For a feminist critique, see Susan Bordo, "Feminism, Postmodernism, and Gender-Skepticism," in *Feminism/Postmodernism*, ed. Linda J. Nicholson (New York: Routledge, 1990).
16. See Naomi Scheman, "Individualism and the Objects of Psychology," in *Discovering Reality: Feminist Perspectives on Epistemology, Metaphysics, Methodology and Philosophy of Science*, ed. Sandra Harding and Merrill B. Hintikka (Dordrecht: Reidel, 1983).
17. On Marxist theory, see Lydia Sargent, ed., *Women and Revolution* (Boston: South End Press, 1981).
18. Bernard Williams, *Moral Luck: Philosophical Papers 1973–1980* (Cambridge: Cambridge University Press, 1981); Hampshire, *Public and Private Morality;* and Alasdair MacIntyre, *After Virtue: A Study in Moral Theory* (Notre Dame, Ind.: University of Notre Dame Press, 1981). For discussion, see Susan Moller Okin, *Justice, Gender, and the Family* (New York: Basic Books, 1989).
19. On the Stone Center concept of self, see especially the following working papers from the center, in Wellesley, Massachusetts: Jean Baker Miller, "The Development of Women's Sense of Self," Working Paper no. 12 (1984); Janet Surrey, "The 'Self-in-Relation': A Theory of Women's Development," Working Paper no. 13 (1985); and Judith Jordan, "The Meaning of Mutuality," Working Paper no. 23 (1986). For a feminist but critical view of this work, see Marcia Westkott, "Female Relationality and the Idealized Self," *American Journal of Psychoanalysis* 49 (September 1989): 239–50.

20. Jean Baker Miller, *Toward a New Psychology of Women* (Boston: Beacon Press, 1976); Nancy Chodorow, *The Reproduction of Mothering: Psychoanalysis and the Sociology of Gender* (Berkeley and Los Angeles: University of California Press, 1978).

21. See Carol Gilligan, *In a Different Voice: Psychological Theory and Women's Development* (Cambridge, Mass.: Harvard University Press, 1982).

22. Jordan, "The Meaning of Mutuality," 2.

23. See Mary Field Belenky, Blythe McVicker Clinchy, Nancy Rule Goldberger, and Jill Mattuck Tarule, *Women's Ways of Knowing: The Development of Self, Voice, and Mind* (New York: Basic Books, 1986).

24. Alison M. Jaggar, "Feminist Ethics: Projects, Problems, Prospects," in *Feminist Ethics*, ed. Claudia Card (Lawrence: University Press of Kansas, 1991), 11.

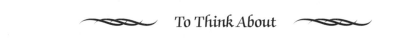

To Think About

1. "People are to be loved, and things are to be used. . . . Immorality occurs when things are loved and people are used."   ***Unknown***

2. "The need for sexual repression increases with the complexity of the society, since a large amount of the psychical energy which [civilization] uses for its own purposes has to be drawn from sexuality."   ***Unknown***

3. "The most common female escape (from their imprisonment in the female role and the denial of their humanity) is the psychopathological condition of love. It is a euphoric state of fantasy in which the victim transforms her oppressor into her redeemer: she turns her natural hostility towards the aggressor against the remnants of herself—her Consciousness—and sees her counterpart in contrast to herself as all powerful (as he is by now at her expense). The combination of his power, her self-hatred, and the hope for a life that is self-justifying—the goal of all living creatures—results in a yearning for her stolen life—her Self—that is the delusion and poignancy of love. 'Love' is the natural response of the victim to the rapist."   ***T. G. Atkinson***

4. "What disturbs us here is well put by Sartre in relation to love. The beloved is often called *the chosen one*. But this choice must not be relative and contingent. The lover is irritated and feels himself cheapened when he thinks that the beloved has chosen him *from among others*. Characteristics that critics of every epoch have brought up against women—that they show less sense of justice than men, that they are less ready to submit to the exigencies of life, that they are more often influenced in their judgments by feelings, affection, or hostility—all these would be amply accounted for by the modifications in the formation in their superego."   ***Unknown***

5. "Rooted in desire and pleasure love reigns between the two borders of narcissism and idealization."   ***Unknown***

6. "Does what it takes to become a person destroy one as a person?"

   Wendy Wasserstein

7. "Goodness without knowledge is blind; knowledge without goodness is dangerous."   ***Phillips Academy***

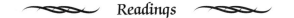 **Readings**

GILLIGAN, CAROL. *In a Different Voice: Psychological Theory and Women's Development.* Cambridge, MA: Harvard University Press, 1982.

HOLVECK, ELEANORE. *Simone de Beauvoir's Philosophy of Lived Experience: Literature and Metaphysics.* Lanham, MD: Rowman & Littlefield, 2002.

KOEHN, DARYL. *Rethinking Feminist Ethics: Care, Trust and Empathy.* New York: Routledge, 1998.

STERBA, JAMES P. *Three Challenges to Ethics: Environmentalism, Feminism, and Multiculturalism.* New York: Oxford University Press, 2001.

What Is Knowledge?

25
Knowledge Is "Warranted, True Belief"

Plato (427?–347 B.C.), one of the great Greek philosophers, has exerted more influence on the development of Western philosophy than any other writer, with the possible exception of Aristotle, his student. Plato established the Academy in Athens, the first of the major schools of ancient Greece. His works, written in dialogue form and featuring his teacher Socrates as the principal figure, have continued to be widely read not only for their intellectual content, but also for their literary merit. Among his writings are Euthyphro, Apology, Crito, Phaedo, Republic, Protagoras, Gorgias, *and* Philebus.

The word *philosophy* comes from a Greek term meaning "the love of wisdom." The love of wisdom, of course, can mean many things, perhaps especially a deep desire for knowledge. But what is knowledge? And can we really attain it, no matter how much we may want to? Questions like these emerge in the minds of most reflective people at some point in their lives. They may be especially important when great discoveries are made, for instance in the sciences. So, when the new astronomy emerged four hundred years ago and the belief that the earth was the center of the universe was shaken, people began to question many more of their assumptions about the nature and extent of their knowledge. But even at a much simpler level, questions about the certainty of our opinions emerge as we grow out of childhood—when we begin to question the existence of Santa Claus, for example. We like to think that a mark of developing intelligence is a willingness to question our beliefs, to ask for evidence for them, and to develop what we may call a "healthy skepticism."

From *Plato's Theory of Knowledge: The Theaetetus and the Sophist of Plato,* trans. F. M. Cornford (New York: Harcourt, Brace and Co., 1935).

In the following readings, we begin with a famous effort at defining knowledge as "warranted, true belief." Plato, who developed this definition for the first time, was also its first critic, finding difficulties with each of the three parts included in his definition. It nevertheless survived and forms a typical definition of knowledge even today. We shall explore two of the three elements of this definition, truth and warrant, or, as Plato calls it, an *account*.

~~~~~ To Study ~~~~~

1. Why does Socrates think it is important to define "knowledge"?
2. Why does Theaetetus himself reject a definition of knowledge as simply consisting of judgment "as a whole"?
3. Is there a difference between "thinking falsely" and "not thinking at all"?
4. How does Socrates characterize the skill or art of orators? Why are "true beliefs" insufficient for real knowledge?
5. Socrates gives three possible meanings to the word *account*. What are they?
6. Why isn't a complete list of the elements or parts of an object a sufficient account of it?
7. What circular reasoning is involved in defining an account in terms of a distinguishing characteristic of an object?
8. If all these analyses of an *account* fail, why is the definition of knowledge as true judgment with an account still valuable?

Socrates. I am puzzled about one small matter which you and our friends must help me to think out. Tell me: is it not true that learning about something means becoming wiser in that matter?

Theaetetus. Of course.

Socr. And what makes people wise is wisdom, I suppose.

Theaet. Yes.

Socr. And is that in any way different from knowledge?

Theaet. Is what different?

Socr. Wisdom. Are not people wise in the things of which they have knowledge?

Theaet. Certainly.

Socr. Then knowledge and wisdom are the same thing?

Theaet. Yes.

Socr. Well, that is precisely what I am puzzled about: I cannot make out to my own satisfaction what knowledge is. Can we answer that question? What do you all say? Which of us will speak first. . . .

Theaet. I cannot say it is judgment as a whole, because there is false judgment; but perhaps true judgment is knowledge. You may take that as my answer. If, as we go further, it turns out to be less convincing than it seems now, I will try to find another.

Socr. Good, Theaetetus; this promptness is much better than hanging back as you did at first. If we go on like this, either we shall find what we are after, or we shall be less inclined to imagine we know something of which we know nothing whatever; and that surely is a reward not to be despised. And now, what is this you say: that there are two sorts of judgment, one true, the other false, and you define knowledge as judgment that is true?

Theaet.   Yes; that is the view I have come to now. . . .

Socr.   Instead of "knowing or not knowing", let us take "being or not being".

Theaet.   How do you mean?

Socr.   May it not simply be that one who thinks *what is not* about anything cannot but be thinking what is false, whatever his state of mind may be in other respects?

Theaet.   There is some likelihood in that, Socrates.

Socr.   Then what shall we say, Theaetetus, if we are asked: "But is what you describe possible for anyone? Can any man think what is not, either about something that is or absolutely?" I suppose we must answer to that: "Yes, when he believes something and what he believes is not true." Or what are we to say?

Theaet.   We must say that.

Socr.   Then is the same sort of thing possible in any other case?

Theaet.   What sort of thing?

Socr.   That a man should see something, and yet what he sees should be nothing.

Theaet.   No. How could that be?

Socr.   Yet surely if what he sees is something, it must be a thing that is. Or do you suppose that "something" can be reckoned among things that have no being at all?

Theaet.   No, I don't.

Socr.   Then, if he sees something, he sees a thing that is.

Theaet.   Evidently.

Socr.   And if he hears a thing, he hears something and hears a thing that is.

Theaet.   Yes.

Socr.   And if he touches a thing, he touches something, and if something, then a thing that is.

Theaet.   That also is true.

Socr.   And if he thinks, he thinks something, doesn't he?

Theaet.   Necessarily.

Socr.   And when he thinks something, he thinks a thing that is?

Theaet.   I agree.

Socr.   So to think what is not is to think nothing.

Theaet.   Clearly.

Socr.   But surely to think nothing is the same as not to think at all.

Theaet.   That seems plain.

Socr.   If so, it is impossible to think what is not, either about anything that is, or absolutely.

Theaet.   Evidently.

Socr. Then thinking falsely must be something different from thinking what is not.

Theaet. So it seems.

Socr. False judgment, then, is no more possible for us on these lines than on those we were following just now.

Theaet. No, it certainly is not. . . .

Socr. To start all over again, then: what is one to say that knowledge is? For surely we are not going to give up yet.

Theaet. Not unless you do so.

Socr. Then tell me: what definition can we give with the least risk of contradicting ourselves?

Theaet. The one we tried before, Socrates. I have nothing else to suggest.

Socr. What was that?

Theaet. That true belief is knowledge. Surely there can at least be no mistake in believing what is true and the consequences are always satisfactory.

Socr. Try, and you will see, Theaetetus, as the man said when he was asked if the river was too deep to ford. So here, if we go forward on our search, we may stumble upon something that will reveal the thing we are looking for. We shall make nothing out, if we stay where we are.

Theaet. True; let us go forward and see.

Socr. Well, we need not go far to see this much: you will find a whole profession to prove that true belief is not knowledge.

Theaet. How so? What profession?

Socr. The profession of those paragons of intellect known as orators and lawyers. There you have men who use their skill to produce conviction, not by instruction, but by making people believe whatever they want them to believe. You can hardly imagine teachers so clever as to be able, in the short time allowed by the clock, to instruct their hearers thoroughly in the true facts of a case of robbery or other violence which those hearers had not witnessed.

Theaet. No, I cannot imagine that; but they can convince them.

Socr. And by convincing you mean making them believe something.

Theaet. Of course.

Socr. And when a jury is rightly convinced of facts which can be known only by an eye-witness, then, judging by hearsay and accepting a true belief, they are judging without knowledge, although, if they find the right verdict, their conviction is correct?

Theaet. Certainly.

Socr. But if true belief and knowledge were the same thing, the best of jurymen could never have a correct belief without knowledge. It now appears that they must be different things.

Theaet. Yes, Socrates, I have heard someone make the distinction. I had forgotten, but now it comes back to me. He said that true belief with the addition of an account (*logos*) was knowledge, while belief without an account was outside its range. Where no account could be given of a thing, it was not "knowable"—that was the word he used—where it could, it was knowable. . . .

Socr.   Well then, what is this term "account" intended to convey to us? I think it must mean one of three things.

Theaet.   What are they?

Socr.   The first will be giving overt expression to one's thought by means of vocal sound with names and verbs, casting an image of one's notion on the stream that flows through the lips, like a reflection in a mirror or in water. Do you agree that expression of that sort is an "account"?

Theaet.   I do. We certainly call that expressing ourselves in speech.

Socr.   On the other hand, that is a thing that anyone can do more or less readily. If a man is not born deaf or dumb, he can signify what he thinks on any subject. So in this sense anyone whatever who has a correct notion evidently will have it "with an account", and there will be no place left anywhere for a correct notion apart from knowledge.

Theaet.   True.

Socr.   Then we must not be too ready to charge the author of the definition of knowledge now before us with talking nonsense. Perhaps that is not what he meant. He may have meant: being able to reply to the question, what any given thing is, by enumerating its elements.

Theaet.   For example, Socrates?

Socr.   For example, Hesiod says about a wagon, "In a wagon are a hundred pieces of wood." I could not name them all; no more, I imagine, could you. If we were asked what a wagon is, we should be content if we could mention wheels, axle, body, rails, yoke.

Theaet.   Certainly.

Socr.   But I dare say he would think us just as ridiculous as if we replied to the question about your own name by telling the syllables. We might think and express ourselves correctly, but we should be absurd if we fancied ourselves to be grammarians and able to give such an account of the name Theaetetus as a grammarian would offer. He would say it is impossible to give a scientific account of anything, short of adding to your true notion a complete catalogue of the elements, as, I think, was said earlier.

Theaet.   Yes, it was.

Socr.   In the same way, he would say, we may have a correct notion of the wagon, but the man who can give a complete statement of its nature by going through those hundred parts has thereby added an account to his correct notion and, in place of mere belief, has arrived at a technical knowledge of the wagon's nature, by going through all the elements in the whole.

Theaet.   Don't you approve, Socrates?

Socr.   Tell me if you approve, my friend, and whether you accept the view that the complete enumeration of elements is an account of any given thing, whereas description in terms of syllables or of any larger unit still leaves it unaccounted for. Then we can look into the matter further.

Theaet.   Well, I do accept that.

Socr.   Do you think, then, that anyone has knowledge of whatever it may be, when he thinks that one and the same thing is a part sometimes of one thing, sometimes of a different thing; or again when he believes now one and now another thing to be part of one and the same thing?

Theaet.   Certainly not.

Socr.   Have you forgotten, then, that when you first began learning to read and write, that was what you and your schoolfellows did?

Theaet.   Do you mean, when we thought that now one letter and now another was part of the same syllable, and when we put the same letter sometimes into the proper syllable, sometimes into another?

Socr.   That is what I mean.

Theaet.   Then I have certainly not forgotten; and I do not think that one has reached knowledge so long as one is in that condition.

Socr.   Well then, if at that stage you are writing "Theaetetus" and you think you ought to write T and H and E and do so, and again when you are trying to write "Theodorus", you think you ought to write T and E and do so, can we say that you know the first syllable of your two names?

Theaet.   No; we have just agreed that one has not knowledge so long as one is in that condition.

Socr.   And there is no reason why a person should not be in the same condition with respect to the second, third, and fourth syllables as well?

Theaet.   None whatever.

Socr.   Can we, then, say that whenever in writing "Theaetetus" he puts down all the letters in order, then he is in possession of the complete catalogue of elements together with correct belief?

Theaet.   Obviously.

Socr.   Being still, as we agree, without knowledge, though his beliefs are correct?

Theaet.   Yes.

Socr.   Although he possesses the "account" in addition to right belief. For when he wrote he was in possession of the catalogue of the elements, which we agreed was the "account".

Theaet.   True.

Socr.   So, my friend, there is such a thing as right belief together with an account, which is not yet entitled to be called knowledge.

Theaet.   I am afraid so.

Socr.   Then, apparently, our idea that we had found the perfectly true definition of knowledge was no better than a golden dream. Or shall we not condemn the theory yet? Perhaps the meaning to be given to "account" is not this, but the remaining one of the three, one of which we said must be intended by anyone who defines knowledge as correct belief together with an account.

Theaet.   A good reminder; there is still one meaning left. The first was what might be called the image of thought in spoken sound; and the one we have just discussed was going all through the elements to arrive at the whole. What is the third?

Socr.   The meaning most people would give: being able to name some mark by which the thing one is asked about differs from everything else.

Theaet.   Could you give me an example of such an account of a thing?

Socr.   Take the sun as an example. I dare say you will be satisfied with the account of it as the brightest of the heavenly bodies that go round the earth.

Theaet.   Certainly.

Socr.   Let me explain the point of this example. It is to illustrate what we were just saying: that if you get hold of the difference distinguishing any given thing from all others, then, so some people say, you will have an "account" of it; whereas, so long as you fix upon something common to other things, your account will embrace all the things that share it.

Theaet.   I understand. I agree that what you describe may fairly be called an "account".

Socr.   And if, besides a right notion about a thing, whatever it may be, you also grasp its difference from all other things, you will have arrived at knowledge of what, till then, you had only a notion of.

Theaet.   We do say that, certainly.

Socr.   Really, Theaetetus, now I come to look at this statement at close quarters, it is like a scene-painting: I cannot make it out at all, though, so long as I kept at a distance, there seemed to be some sense in it.

Theaet.   What do you mean? Why so?

Socr.   I will explain, if I can. Suppose I have a correct notion about you; if I add to that the account of you, then, we are to understand, I know you. Otherwise I have only a notion.

Theaet.   Yes.

Socr.   And "account" means putting your differentness into words.

Theaet.   Yes.

Socr.   So, at the time when I had only a notion, my mind did not grasp any of the points in which you differ from others?

Theaet.   Apparently not.

Socr.   Then I must have had before my mind one of those common things which belong to another person as much as to you.

Theaet.   That follows.

Socr.   But look here! If that was so, how could I possibly be having a notion of you rather than of anyone else? Suppose I was thinking: Theaetetus is one who is a man and has a nose and eyes and a mouth and so forth, enumerating every part of the body. Will thinking in that way result in my thinking of Theaetetus rather than of Theodorus or, as they say, of the man in the street?

Theaet.   How should it?

Socr.   Well, now suppose I think not merely of a man with a nose and eyes, but of one with a snub nose and prominent eyes, once more shall I be having a notion of you any more than of myself or anyone else of that description?

Theaet. No.

Socr. In fact, there will be no notion of Theaetetus in my mind, I suppose, until this particular snubness has stamped and registered within me a record distinct from all the other cases of snubness that I have seen; and so with every other part of you. Then, if I meet you tomorrow, that trait will revive my memory and give me a correct notion about you.

Theaet. Quite true.

Socr. If that is so, the correct notion of anything must itself include the differentness of that thing.

Theaet. Evidently.

Socr. Then what meaning is left for getting hold of an "account" in addition to the correct notion? If, on the one hand, it means adding the notion of how a thing differs from other things, such an injunction is simply absurd.

Theaet. How so?

Socr. When we have a correct notion of the way in which certain things differ from other things, it tells us to add a correct notion of the way in which they differ from other things. On this showing, the most vicious of circles would be nothing to this injunction. It might better deserve to be called the sort of direction a blind man might give: to tell us to get hold of something we already have, in order to get to know something we are already thinking of, suggests a state of the most absolute darkness.

Theaet. Whereas, if ——? The supposition you made just now implied that you would state some alternative: what was it?

Socr. If the direction to add an "account" means that we are to get to *know* the differentness, as opposed to merely having a notion of it, this most admirable of all definitions of knowledge will be a pretty business; because "getting to know" means acquiring knowledge, doesn't it?

Theaet. Yes.

Socr. So, apparently, to the question, What is knowledge? our definition will reply: "Correct belief together with knowledge of a differentness"; for, according to it, "adding an account" will come to that.

Theaet. So it seems.

Socr. Yes; and when we are inquiring after the nature of knowledge, nothing could be sillier than to say that it is correct belief together with a *knowledge* of differentness or of anything whatever.

So, Theaetetus, neither true belief, nor the addition of an "account" to true belief can be knowledge.

Theaet. Apparently not.

Socr. Are we in labour, then, with any further child, my friend, or have we brought to birth all we have to say about knowledge?

Theaet. Indeed we have; and for my part I have already, thanks to you, given utterance to more than I had in me.

Socr. All of which our midwife's skill pronounces to be mere wind-eggs and not worth the rearing?

Theaet. Undoubtedly.

Socr.   Then supposing you should ever henceforth try to conceive afresh, Theaetetus, if you succeed, your embryo thoughts will be the better as a consequence of to-day's scrutiny; and if you remain barren, you will be gentler and more agreeable to your companions, having the good sense not to fancy you know what you do not know. For that, and no more, is all that my art can effect; nor have I any of that knowledge possessed by all the great and admirable men of our own day or of the past. But this midwife's art is a gift from heaven; my mother had it for women, and I for young men of a generous spirit and for all in whom beauty dwells.

Now I must go to the portico of the King Archon to meet the indictment which Meletus has drawn up against me. But to-morrow morning, Theodorus, let us meet here again.

To Think About

1. "Knowledge is power, but only wisdom is liberty."   ***Will Durant***

2. "From Plato until the present, with a few notable exceptions, reason rather than emotion has been regarded as the indispensable faculty for acquiring knowledge. . . . [Objective] testability became accepted as the hallmark of natural science; this, in turn, was viewed as the paradigm of genuine knowledge. . . . Because values and emotions had been identified as variable and idiosyncratic, [the objective standard] stipulated that trustworthy knowledge could be established only by methods that neutralized the values and emotions of individual [thinkers]."   ***A. Jaggar***

3. "There are no whole truths; all truths are half-truths. It is trying to treat them as whole truths that plays the devil."   ***Alfred North Whitehead***

Readings

BOSTOCK, DAVID. *Plato's Theaetetus.* Oxford: Clarendon Press, 1998.

BURNYEAT, MYLES. *The Theaetetus of Plato.* Indianapolis: Hackett, 1990.

CHISHOLM, RODERICK M. *Theory of Knowledge.* 3d ed. Upper Saddle River, NJ: Prentice Hall, 1989.

GETTIER, EDMUND. "Is Justified True Belief Knowledge?" *Analysis* 23 (1963): 121–23.

POLANSKY, RONALD M. *Philosophy and Knowledge: A Commentary on Plato's Theaetetus.* Lewisburg, PA: Bucknell University Press, 1992.

SCHEFFLER, ISRAEL. *Conditions of Knowledge.* Glenview, IL: Scott, Foresman, 1965.

WELBOURNE, MICHAEL. *Knowledge.* Montreal: McGill-Queen's University Press, 2001.

26
Knowledge Is Not Ultimately Sense Knowledge

René Descartes (1596–1650), French philosopher, mathematician, and scientist, is often called the father of modern philosophy because of his criticism of earlier philosophical thought and his advocacy of methodical doubt as a first step in the discovery of truth. As a young man he became disillusioned with the formal education he had been receiving, but was greatly impressed by the elegance and certainty of mathematics. Inspired by this model, he sought to introduce the same rigorous use of reason into other areas of our thinking. His most important works are Discourse on Method, Meditations, *and* Principles of Philosophy.

We turn now to a consideration of warrant or evidence for our knowledge, or, to use Plato's term, an *account*. What are our ultimate grounds for knowing something? If I say that "two plus two equals four," or that "all copper conducts electricity," how are these statements ultimately established? One might reply to the question "how do you know it?" by saying "seeing is believing," but obviously this is insufficient because there is a great deal that we claim to know and have never seen. What, then, is our ultimate basis of knowledge? Descartes was a rationalist. He did not think sense knowledge was the ultimate basis of knowledge, but rather maintained that "whatever is clearly and distinctly perceived is true" is the best general rule for knowledge. This means that an idea is "clear" if its content includes the nature and essence of it. Similarly, an idea is "distinct" if nothing contradictory to the essence of an object is included within it. For example,

From *The Philosophical Works of Descartes,* "Meditation I" and "Meditation II," trans. E. S. Haldane and G. R. T. Ross (Cambridge: Cambridge University Press, 1931). Reprinted by permission of the publisher.

your idea of humans is clear if you know the nature and essence of humans, and your idea of humans is distinct if your idea of humans is not contradictory. That sense knowledge is not the ultimate criterion for Descartes is brought out by the example of "the piece of wax" in "Meditation II." With this example Descartes concludes that it is not by sense perception that he understands the nature of the wax, but by the intellect itself.

 To Study

1. Why did Descartes undertake the method of doubt? What is it?
2. On what grounds can we doubt our senses?
3. What remains true, even if one is now dreaming?
4. On what grounds is even mathematics possibly false?
5. What is necessarily true each time it is expressed by a person?
6. What is a person? What is the nature of the mind?
7. What is the nature of material bodies?
8. What important conclusion about the mind does Descartes draw from the example of the piece of wax?

MEDITATION I

Of the Things Which May Be Brought Within the Sphere of the Doubtful

It is now some years since I detected how many were the false beliefs that I had from my earliest youth admitted as true, and how doubtful was everything I had since constructed on this basis; and from that time I was convinced that I must once for all seriously undertake to rid myself of all the opinions which I had formerly accepted, and commence to build anew from the foundation, if I wanted to establish any firm and permanent structure in the sciences. But as this enterprise appeared to be a very great one, I waited until I had attained an age so mature that I could not hope that at any later date I should be better fitted to execute my design. This reason caused me to delay so long that I should feel that I was doing wrong were I to occupy in deliberation the time that yet remains to me for action. Today, then, since very opportunely for the plan I have in view I have delivered my mind from every care [and am happily agitated by no passions] and since I have procured for myself an assured leisure in a peaceable retirement, I shall at last seriously and freely address myself to the general upheaval of all my former opinions.

Now for this object it is not necessary that I should show that all of these are false—I shall perhaps never arrive at this end. But in as much as reason already persuades me that I ought no less carefully to withhold my assent from matters which are not entirely certain and indubitable than from those which appear to me manifestly to be false, if I am able to find in each one some reason to doubt, this will suffice to justify my rejecting the whole. And for that end it will not be requisite that I should examine each in particular, which would be an endless undertaking; for owing to the fact that the destruction of the foundations of necessity brings with it the downfall of the rest of the edifice, I shall only in the first place attack those principles upon which all my former opinions rested.

All that up to the present time I have accepted as most true and certain I have learned either from the senses or through the senses; but it is sometimes proved to me that these senses are deceptive, and it is wiser not to trust entirely to any thing by which we have once been deceived.

But it may be that although the senses sometimes deceive us concerning things which are hardly perceptible, or very far away, there are yet many others to be met with as to which we cannot reasonably have any doubt, although we recognise them by their means. For example, there is the fact that I am here, seated by the fire, attired in a dressing gown, having this paper in my hands and other similar matters. And how could I deny that these hands and this body are mine, were it not perhaps that I compare myself to certain persons, devoid of sense, whose cerebella are so troubled and clouded by the violent vapours of black bile, that they constantly assure us that they think they are kings when they are really quite poor, or that they are clothed in purple when they are really without covering, or who imagine that they have an earthenware head or are nothing but pumpkins or are made of glass. But they are mad, and I should not be any the less insane were I to follow examples so extravagant.

At the same time I must remember that I am a man, and that consequently I am in the habit of sleeping, and in my dreams representing to myself the same things or sometimes even less probable things, than do those who are insane in their waking moments. How often has it happened to me that in the night I dreamt that I found myself in this particular place, that I was dressed and seated near the fire, whilst in reality I was lying undressed in bed! At this moment it does indeed seem to me that it is with eyes awake that I am looking at this paper, that this head which I move is not asleep, that it is deliberately and of set purpose that I extend my hand and perceive it; what happens in sleep does not appear so clear nor so distinct as does all this. But in thinking over this I remind myself that on many occasions I have in sleep been deceived by similar illusions, and in dwelling carefully on this reflection I see so manifestly that there are no certain indications by which we may clearly distinguish wakefulness from sleep that I am lost in astonishment. And my astonishment is such that it is almost capable of persuading me that I now dream.

Now let us assume that we are asleep and that all these particulars, for example, that we open our eyes, shake our head, extend our hands, and so on, are but false delusions; and let us reflect that possibly neither our hands nor our whole body are such as they appear to us to be. At the same time we must at least confess that the things which are represented to us in sleep are like painted representations which can only have been formed as the counterparts of something real and true, and that in this way those general things at least, that is, eyes, a head, hands, and a whole body, are not imaginary things, but things really existent. For, as a matter of fact, painters, even when they study with the greatest skill to represent sirens and satyrs by forms the most strange and extraordinary, cannot give them natures which are entirely new, but merely make a certain medley of the members of different animals; or if their imagination is extravagant enough to invent something so novel that nothing similar has ever before been seen, and that their work represents a thing purely fictitious and absolutely false, it is certain all the same that the colours of which this is composed are necessarily real. And for the same reason, although these general things, to wit, [a body], eyes, a head, hands, and such like, may be imaginary, we are bound at the same time to confess that there are at least some other objects yet more simple and more universal, which are real and true; and of these just in the same way as with certain real colours, all these images of things which dwell in our thoughts, whether true and real or false and fantastic, are formed.

To such a class of things pertains corporeal nature in general, and its extension, the figure of extended things, their quantity or magnitude and number, as also the place in which they are, the time which measures their duration, and so on.

That is possibly why our reasoning is not unjust when we conclude from this that Physics, Astronomy, Medicine and all other sciences which have as their end the consideration of composite things are very dubious and uncertain; but that Arithmetic, Geometry and other sciences of that kind which only treat of things that are very simple and very general, without taking great trouble to ascertain whether they are actually existent or not, contain some measure of certainty and an element of the indubitable. For whether I am awake or asleep, two and three together always form five, and the square can never have more than four sides, and it does not seem possible that truths so clear and apparent can be suspected of any falsity [or uncertainty].

Nevertheless I have long had fixed in my mind the belief that an all-powerful God existed by whom I have been created such as I am. But how do I know that He has not brought it to pass that there is no earth, no heaven, no extended body, no magnitude, no place, and that nevertheless [I possess the perceptions of all these things and that] they seem to me to exist just exactly as I now see them? And, besides, as I sometimes imagine that others deceive themselves in the things which they think they know best, how do I know that I am not deceived every time that I add two and three, or count the sides of a square, or judge of things yet simpler, if anything simpler can be imagined? But possibly God has not desired that I should be thus deceived, for He is said to be supremely good. If, however, it is contrary to His goodness to have made me such that I constantly deceive myself, it would also appear to be contrary to His goodness to permit me to be sometimes deceived, and nevertheless I cannot doubt that He does permit this.

There may indeed be those who would prefer to deny the existence of a God so powerful, rather than believe that all other things are uncertain. But let us not oppose them for the present, and grant that all that is here said of a God is a fable; nevertheless in whatever way they suppose that I have arrived at the state of being that I have reached—whether they attribute it to fate or to accident, or make out that it is by a continual succession of antecedents, or by some other method—since to err and

deceive oneself is a defect, it is clear that the greater will be the probability of my being so imperfect as to deceive myself ever, as is the Author to whom they assign my
origin the less powerful. To these reasons I have certainly nothing to reply, but at the
end I feel constrained to confess that there is nothing in all that I formerly believed
to be true, of which I cannot in some measure doubt, and that not merely through want
of thought or through levity, but for reasons which are very powerful and maturely
considered; so that henceforth I ought not the less carefully to refrain from giving credence to these opinions than to that which is manifestly false, if I desire to arrive at
any certainty [in the sciences].

But it is not sufficient to have made these remarks, we must also be careful to
keep them in mind. For these ancient and commonly held opinions still revert frequently to my mind, long and familiar custom having given them the right to occupy
my mind against my inclination and rendered them almost masters of my belief; nor
will I ever lose the habit of deferring to them or of placing my confidence in them, so
long as I consider them as they really are, i.e. opinions in some measure doubtful, as
I have just shown, and at the same time highly probable, so that there is much more
reason to believe in than to deny them. That is why I consider that I shall not be acting amiss, if, taking of set purpose a contrary belief, I allow myself to be deceived,
and for a certain time pretend that all these opinions are entirely false and imaginary,
until at least, having thus balanced my former prejudices with my latter [so that they
cannot divert my opinions more to one side than to the other], my judgment will no
longer be dominated by bad usage or turned away from the right knowledge of the
truth. For I am assured that there can be neither peril nor error in this course, and that
I cannot at present yield too much to distrust, since I am not considering the question
of action, but only of knowledge.

I shall then suppose, not that God who is supremely good and the fountain of
truth, but some evil genius not less powerful than deceitful, has employed his whole
energies deceiving me; I shall consider that the heavens, the earth, colours, figures,
sound, and all other external things are nought but the illusions and dreams of which
this genius has availed himself in order to lay traps for my credulity; I shall consider
myself as having no hands, no eyes, no flesh, no blood, nor any senses, yet falsely
believing myself to possess all these things; I shall remain obstinately attached to this
idea, and if by this means it is not in my power to arrive at the knowledge of any truth,
I may at least do what is in my power [i.e., suspend my judgment] and with firm purpose avoid giving credence to any false thing, or being imposed upon by this arch
deceiver, however powerful and deceptive he may be. But this task is a laborious one,
and insensibly a certain lassitude leads me into the course of my ordinary life. And
just as a captive who in sleep enjoys an imaginary liberty, when he begins to suspect
that his liberty is but a dream, fears to awaken, and conspires with these agreeable
illusions that the deception may be prolonged, so insensibly of my own accord I fall
back into my former opinions, and I dread awakening from this slumber, lest the
laborious wakefulness which would follow the tranquility of this repose should have
to be spent not in daylight, but in the excessive darkness of the difficulties which have
just been discussed.

MEDITATION II

Of the Nature of the Human Mind, and That It Is More Easily Known Than the Body

The Meditation of yesterday filled my mind with so many doubts that it is no longer in my power to forget them. And yet I do not see in what manner I can resolve them; and, just as if I had all of a sudden fallen into very deep water, I am so disconcerted that I can neither make certain of setting my feet on the bottom, nor can I swim and so support myself on the surface. I shall nevertheless make an effort and follow anew the same path as that on which I yesterday entered, that is, I shall proceed by setting aside all that in which the least doubt could be supposed to exist, just as if I had discovered that it was absolutely false; and I shall ever follow in this road until I have met with something which is certain, or at least, if I can do nothing else, until I have learned for certain that there is nothing in the world that is certain. Archimedes, in order that he might draw the terrestrial globe out of its place, and transport it elsewhere, demanded only that one point should be fixed and immoveable; in the same way I shall have the right to conceive high hopes if I am happy enough to discover one thing only which is certain and indubitable.

I suppose, then, that all the things that I see are false; I persuade myself that nothing has ever existed of all that my fallacious memory represents to me. I consider that I possess no senses; I imagine that body, figure, extension, movement and place are but the fiction of my mind. What, then, can be esteemed as true? Perhaps nothing at all, unless that there is nothing in the world that is certain.

But how can I know there is not something different from those things that I have just considered, of which one cannot have the slightest doubt? Is there not some God, or some other being by whatever name we call it, who puts these reflections into my mind? That is not necessary, for is it not possible that I am capable of producing them myself? I myself, am I not at least something? But I have already denied that I had senses and body. Yet I hesitate, for what follows from that? Am I so dependent on body and senses that I cannot exist without these? But I was persuaded that there were no minds, nor any bodies: was I not then likewise persuaded that I did not exist? Not at all; of a surety I myself did exist since I persuaded myself of something [or merely because I thought of something]. But there is some deceiver or other, very powerful and very cunning, who ever employs his ingenuity in deceiving me. Then without doubt I exist also if he deceives me, and let him deceive me as much as he will, he can never cause me to be nothing so long as I think that I am something. So that after having reflected well and carefully examined all things, we must come to the definite conclusion that this proposition: I am, I exist, is necessarily true each time that I pronounce it, or that I mentally conceive it.

But I do not yet know clearly enough what I am, I who am certain that I am; and hence I must be careful to see that I do not imprudently take some other object in place of myself, and thus that I do not go astray in respect of this knowledge that I hold to be the most evident of all that I have formerly learned. That is why I shall now consider anew what I believed myself to be before I embarked upon these last reflections; and of my former opinions I shall withdraw all that might even in a small

degree be invalidated by the reasons which I have just brought forward, in order that
there may be nothing at all left beyond what is absolutely certain and indubitable.

What then did I formerly believe myself to be? Undoubtedly I believed myself
to be a man. But what is a man? Shall I say a reasonable animal? Certainly not; for
then I should have to inquire what an animal is, and what is reasonable; and thus from
a single question I should insensibly fall into an infinitude of others more difficult; and
I should not wish to waste the little time and leisure remaining to me in trying to unravel subtleties like these. But I shall rather stop here to consider the thoughts which
of themselves spring up in my mind, and which were not inspired by anything beyond
my own nature alone when I applied myself to the consideration of my being. In the
first place, then, I considered myself as having a face, hands, arms, and all that system
of members composed of bones and flesh as seen in a corpse which I designated by
the name of body. In addition to this I considered that I was nourished, that I walked,
that I felt, and that I thought, and I referred all these actions to the soul: but I did not
stop to consider what the soul was, or if I did stop, I imagined that it was something
extremely rare and subtle like a wind, a flame, or an ether, which was spread throughout my grosser parts. As to body I had no manner of doubt about its nature, but thought
I had a very clear knowledge of it; and if I had desired to explain it according to the
notions that I had then formed of it, I should have described it thus: By the body I understand all that which can be defined by a certain figure: something which can be confined in a certain place, and which can fill a space in such a way that every other body
will be excluded from it; which can be perceived either by touch, or by sight, or by
hearing, or by taste, or by smell: which can be moved in many ways not, in truth, by
itself but by something which is foreign to it, by which it is touched [and from which
it receives impressions]: for to have the power of self-movement, as also of feeling or
of thinking, I did not consider to appertain to the nature of body: on the contrary, I was
rather astonished to find that faculties similar to them existed in some bodies.

But what am I, now that I suppose that there is a certain genius which is extremely powerful, and, if I may say so, malicious, who employs all his powers in deceiving me? Can I affirm that I possess the least of all those things which I have just
said pertain to the nature of body? I pause to consider, I revolve all these things in my
mind, and I find none of which I can say that it pertains to me. It would be tedious to
stop to enumerate them. Let us pass to the attributes of soul and see if there is any one
which is in me. What of nutrition or walking [the first mentioned]? But if it is so that
I have no body it is also true that I can neither walk nor take nourishment. Another
attribute is sensation. But one cannot feel without body, and besides I have thought I
perceived many things during sleep that I recognized in my waking moments as not
having been experienced at all. What of thinking? I find here that thought is an attributable that belongs to me; it alone cannot be separated from me. I am, I exist, that
is certain. But how often? Just when I think; for it might possibly be the case if I
ceased entirely to think, that I should likewise cease altogether to exist. I do not now
admit anything which is not necessarily true: to speak accurately I am not more than
a thing which thinks, that is to say a mind or a soul, or an understanding, or a reason,
which are terms whose significance was formerly unknown to me. I am, however, a
real thing and really exist; but what thing? I have answered: a thing which thinks.

And what more? I shall exercise my imagination [in order to see if I am not something more]. I am not a collection of members which we call the human body: I am not a subtle air distributed through these members, I am not a wind, a fire, a vapour, a breath, nor anything at all which I can imagine or conceive; because I have assumed that all these were nothing. Without changing that supposition I find that I only leave myself certain of the fact that I am somewhat. But perhaps it is true that these same things which I supposed were non-existent because they are unknown to me, are really not different from the self which I know. I am not sure about this, I shall not dispute about it now; I can only give judgment on things that are known to me. I know that I exist, and I inquire what I am, I whom I know to exist. But it is very certain that the knowledge of my existence taken in its precise significance does not depend on things whose existence is not yet known to me; consequently it does not depend on those which I can feign in imagination. And indeed the very term *feign* in imagination proves to me my error, for I really do this if I image myself a something, since to imagine is nothing else than to contemplate the figure or image of a corporeal thing. But I already know for certain that I am, and that it may be that all these images, and, speaking generally, all things that relate to the nature of body are nothing but dreams [and chimeras]. For this reason I see clearly that I have as little reason to say, "I shall stimulate my imagination in order to know more distinctly what I am," than if I were to say, "I am now awake, and I perceive somewhat that is real and true: but because I do not yet perceive it distinctly enough, I shall go to sleep of express purpose, so that my dreams may represent the perception with greatest truth and evidence." And, thus, I know for certain that nothing of all that I can understand by means of my imagination belongs to this knowledge which I have of myself, and that it is necessary to recall the mind from this mode of thought with the utmost diligence in order that it may be able to know its own nature with perfect distinctness.

But what then am I? A thing which thinks. What is a thing which thinks? It is a thing which doubts, understands, [conceives], affirms, denies, wills, refuses, which also imagines and feels. . . .

Certainly it is no small matter if all these things pertain to my nature. But why should they not so pertain? Am I not that being who now doubts nearly everything, who nevertheless understands certain things, who affirms that one only is true, who denies all the others, who desires to know more, is averse from being deceived, who imagines many things, sometimes indeed despite his will, and who perceives many likewise, as by the intervention of the bodily organs? Is there nothing in all this which is as true as it is certain that I exist, even though I should always sleep and though he who has given me being employed all his ingenuity in deceiving me? Is there likewise any one of these attributes which can be distinguished from my thought, or which might be said to be separated from myself? For it is so evident of itself that it is I who doubts, who understands, and who desires, that there is no reason here to add anything to explain it. And I have certainly the power of imagining likewise; for although it may happen (as I formerly supposed) that none of the things which I imagine are true, nevertheless this power of imagining does not cease to be really in use, and it forms part of my thought. Finally, I am the same who feels, that is to say, who perceives certain things, as by the organs of sense, since in truth I see light, I hear noise, I feel heat. But it will be said that these phenomena are false and that I am dreaming. Let it be so; still it is at least quite certain that it seems to me that I see light, that I hear noise and that I feel heat. That cannot be false; properly speaking it is what is in me called feeling; and used in this precise sense that is no other thing than thinking.

From this time I begin to know what I am with a little more clearness and distinction than before; but nevertheless it still seems to me, and I cannot prevent myself from thinking, that corporeal things, whose images are framed by thought, which are tested by the senses, are much more distinctly known than that obscure part of me which does not come under the imagination. Although really it is very strange to say that I know and understand more distinctly these things whose existence seems to me dubious, which are unknown to me, and which do not belong to me, than others of the truth of which I am convinced, which are known to me and which pertain to my real nature, in a word, than myself. But I see clearly how the case stands: my mind loves to wander, and cannot yet suffer itself to be retained within the just limits of truth. Very good, let us once more give it the freest rein, so that, when afterwards we seize the proper occasion for pulling up, it may the more easily be regulated and controlled.

Let us begin by considering the commonest matters, those which we believe to be the most distinctly comprehended, to wit, the bodies which we touch and see; not indeed bodies in general, for these general ideas are usually a little more confused, but let us consider one body in particular. Let us take, for example, this piece of wax: it has been taken quite freshly from the hive, and it has not yet lost the sweetness of the honey which it contains; it still retains somewhat of the odour of the flowers from which it has been culled; its colour, its figure, its size are apparent; it is hard, cold, easily handled, and if you strike it with the finger, it will emit a sound. Finally all the things which are requisite to cause us distinctly to recognise a body, are met within it. But notice that while I speak and approach the fire what remained of the taste is exhaled, the smell evaporates, the colour alters, the figure is destroyed, the size increases, it becomes liquid, it heats, scarcely can one handle it, and when one strikes it, no sound is emitted. Does the same wax remain after this change? We must confess that it remains; none would judge otherwise. What then did I know so distinctly in this piece of wax? It could certainly be nothing of all that the senses brought to my notice, since all these things which fall under taste, smell, sight, touch, and hearing are found to be changed, and yet the same wax remains.

Perhaps it was what I now think, viz. that this wax was not that sweetness of honey, nor that agreeable scent of flowers, nor that particular whiteness, nor that figure, nor that sound, but simply a body which a little while before appeared to me as perceptible under these forms, and which is now perceptible under others. But what, precisely, is it that I imagine when I form such conceptions? Let us attentively consider this, and, abstracting from all that does not belong to the wax, let us see what remains. Certainly nothing remains excepting a certain extended thing which is flexible and movable. But what is the meaning of flexible and movable? Is it not that I imagine that this piece of wax being round is capable of becoming square and of passing from a square to a triangular figure? No, certainly it is not that, since I imagine it admits of an infinitude of similar changes, and I nevertheless do not know how to compass the infinitude by my imagination, and consequently this conception which I have of the wax is not brought about by the faculty of imagination. What now is this extension? Is it not also unknown? For it becomes greater when the wax is melted, greater when it is boiled, and greater still when the heat increases; and I should not conceive [clearly] according to truth what wax is, if I did not think that even this piece that we are considering is capable of receiving more variations in extension than I have ever imagined. We must then grant that I could not even understand through the imagination what this piece of wax is, and that it is my mind alone which perceives it. I say this piece of wax in particular, for as to wax in general it is yet clearer. But what is this piece of wax which cannot be understood excepting by the [understanding or] mind? It is certainly the same that I see, touch, imagine, and finally it is the same which I have always believed it to be from the beginning. But what must particularly be observed is that its perception is neither an act of vision, nor of touch, nor of imagination, and has never been such although it may have appeared formerly to be so, but only an intuition of the mind, which may be imperfect and confused as it was formerly, or clear and distinct as it is at present, according as my attention is more or less directed to the elements which are found in it, and of which it is composed.

Yet in the meantime I am greatly astonished when I consider [the great feebleness of mind] and its proneness to fall [insensibly] into error; for although without giving expression to my thoughts I consider all this in my own mind, words often impede me and I am almost deceived by the terms of ordinary language. For we say that we see the same wax, if it is present, and not that we simply judge that it is the same from its having the same colour and figure. From this I should conclude that I knew the wax by means of vision and not simply by the intuition of the mind; unless by chance I remember that, when looking from a window and saying I see men who pass in the street, I really do not see them, but infer that what I see is men, just as I say that I see wax. And yet what do I see from the window but hats and coats which may cover automatic machines? Yet I judge these to be men. And similarly solely by the faculty of judgment which rests in my mind, I comprehend that which I believed I saw with my eyes.

A man who makes it his aim to raise his knowledge above the common should be ashamed to derive the occasion for doubting from the forms of speech invented by the vulgar; I prefer to pass on and consider whether I had a more evident and perfect conception of what the wax was when I first perceived it, and when I believed I knew it by means of the external senses or at least by the common sense as it is called, that is to say by the imaginative faculty, or whether my present conception is clearer now that I have most carefully examined what it is, and in what way it can be known. It would certainly be absurd to doubt as to this. For what was there in this first perception which was distinct? What was there which might not as well have been perceived by any of the animals? But when I distinguish the wax from its external forms, and when, just as if I had taken from it its vestments, I consider it quite naked, it is certain that although some error may still be found in my judgment, I can nevertheless not perceive it thus without a human mind.

But finally what shall I say of this mind, that is, of myself, for up to this point I do not admit in myself anything but mind? What then, I who seem to perceive this piece of wax so distinctly, do I not know myself, not only with much more truth and certainty, but also with much more distinctiveness and clearness? For if I judge that the wax is or exists from the fact that I see it, it certainly follows much more clearly that I am or that I exist myself from the fact that I see it. For it may be that what I see is not really wax, it may also be that I do not possess eyes with which to see anything; but it cannot be that when I see, or (for I no longer take account of the distinction) when I think I see, that I myself who think am nought. So if I judge that the wax exists from the fact that I touch it, the same thing will follow, to wit, that I am; and if I judge that my imagination, or some other cause, whatever it is, persuades me that the wax exists, I shall still conclude the same. And what I have here remarked of wax may be applied to all other things which are external to me [and which are met with outside of me]. And further, if the [notion or] perception of wax has seemed to me clearer and more distinct, not only after the sight or the touch, but also after many other causes have rendered it quite manifest to me, with how much more [evidence] and distinctness must it be said that I now know myself, since all the reasons which contribute to the knowledge of wax, or any other body whatever, are yet better proofs of the nature of my mind! And there are so many other things in the mind itself which may contribute to the elucidation of its nature, that those which depend on body such as these just mentioned, hardly merit being taken into account.

But finally here I am, having insensibly reverted to the point I desired, for, since it is now manifest to me that even bodies are not properly speaking known by the senses or by the faculty of imagination, but by the understanding only, and since they are not known from the fact that they are seen or touched, but only because they are understood, I see clearly that there is nothing which is easier for me to know than my mind. But because it is difficult to rid oneself so promptly of an opinion to which one was accustomed for so long, it will be well that I should halt a little at this point, so that by the length of my meditation I may more deeply imprint on my memory this new knowledge.

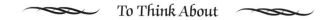

To Think About

1. "Good sense is the best distributed thing in the world: for everyone thinks himself so well endowed with it that even those who are the hardest to please in everything else do not usually desire more of it than they possess. In this it is unlikely that everyone is mistaken. It indicates rather that the power of judging well and of distinguishing the true from the false—which is what we properly call 'good sense' or 'reason'—is naturally equal in all men."   ***René Descartes***

2. "On the one hand I have a clear and distinct idea of myself, in so far as I am simply a thinking nonextended thing; and on the other hand I have a distinct

idea of body, in so far as this is simply an extended, nonthinking thing. And accordingly, it is certain that I am really distinct from my body, and can exist without it." ***René Descartes***

3. It "does not seem to me that the human mind is capable of conceiving at the same time the distinction and the union between body and soul, because for this it is necessary to conceive them as a single thing and at the same time to conceive them as two things; and this is absurd. . . . Everyone feels that he is a single person with both body and thought so related by nature that the thought can move the body and feel the things which happen to it." ***René Descartes***

4. "Descartes for the first time defined thought as the absolutely unextended, and later philosophers have accepted the description as correct. But what possible meaning has it to say that, when we think of a foot-rule or a square yard, extension is not attributable to our thought? Of every extended object the adequate mental picture must have all the extension of the object itself." ***G. Hempel***

5. "Descartes . . . arrives at the *cogito ergo sum,* which St. Augustine had already anticipated; but the *ego* implicit in this enthymeme, *ego cogito, ergo ego sum,* is an unreal—that is, an ideal—*ego* or I, and its *sum,* its existence, something unreal also. 'I think, therefore I am' can only mean 'I think, therefore I am a thinker'; the being of the 'I am', which is deduced from 'I think', is merely a knowing; that being is knowledge, but not life. And the primary reality is not that I think, but that I live, for those also live who do not think." ***Miguel De Unamuno***

6. "Our problem is that once we have accepted an irreducible distinction between mental and physical facts and properties, and have allowed that physical facts and properties constitute sufficient causes of actions, we seem to be forced to admit that mental facts and properties are epiphenomenal, causally idle; yet this conclusion is itself implausible." ***G. Hempel***

7. "Could it be that I am now dreaming? Not only does the right answer seem to me to be 'Yes' but, more importantly, it seems to me that the possibility continues to make sense even if I go on to imagine that no one on the face of the earth or anywhere else could ever know that I *am* dreaming because they too could never know whether they were awake or dreaming. Adding the further thought that the truth about my state is unknown or even unknowable to everyone does not seem to me to affect the possibility I originally tried to imagine at all. Of course, I might be wrong about this, but how is one to tell?" ***Barry Stroud***

8. Are these statements absolutely certain?

    a. "I am, I exist, that is certain." ***René Descartes***

    b. "I know I am not you." ***Jean-Paul Sartre***

    c. "It seems (appears, etc.) to me that I am seeing *pink.*" ***James Gould***

    d. "Cogito, ergo sum." ***René Descartes***

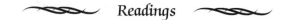 Readings

BECK, L. J. *The Method of Descartes: A Study of the Regulae.* Oxford: Clarendon Press, 1952.

BROUGHTON, JANET. *Descartes's Method of Doubt.* Princeton, NJ: Princeton University Press, 2002.

COTTINGHAM, J. *Descartes.* New York: B. Blackwell, 1986.

———, ed. *The Cambridge Companion to Descartes.* Cambridge: Cambridge University Press, 1992.

SCHOULS, PETER A. *Descartes and the Possibility of Science.* Ithaca, NY: Cornell University Press, 2000.

WEINTRAUB, RUTH. *The Sceptical Challenge.* New York: Routledge, 1997.

27
Knowledge Is Ultimately Sensed

John Locke (1632–1704), English empiricist and political philosopher, wrote two major works regarded as classics, Two Treatises of Government *(1689) and* An Essay Concerning Human Understanding *(1690).*

John Locke is an empiricist. He believes that sense perceptions ultimately give us warrant for all knowledge, that they alone are clear and distinct. First he argues that there are no innate ideas because, if there were, they would not depend upon experience. All knowledge is founded on and ultimately derives from experience. There are two sources for our ideas: sensation, through which the mind is furnished with sense qualities, and reflection, which supplies the mind with ideas of its own operation. The mind itself is a blank page upon which the ideas of experience are written.

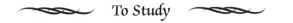 To Study

1. What is the purpose of Locke's essay? What method does he indicate he will pursue?
2. What does Locke mean by the word *idea?*
3. What are innate principles?
4. What is the universal consent argument regarding innate principles? How does Locke refute this argument?
5. What is the argument by use of reason? What is Locke's refutation?
6. How does the mind form abstract ideas?
7. By what analogy does Locke describe the mind? Where does the mind get its materials?
8. What are the two general classes of the mind's contents?
9. How does Locke distinguish between simple and complex ideas?

From John Locke, *An Essay Concerning Human Understanding* (London: E. Holt, 1690).

INTRODUCTION

1. Since it is the *understanding* that sets man above the rest of sensible beings, and gives him all the advantage and dominion which he has over them, it is certainly a subject, even for its nobleness, worth our labour to inquire into. The understanding, like the eye, whilst it makes us see and perceive all other things, takes no notice of itself; and it requires art and pains to set it at a distance and make it its own object. But whatever be the difficulties that lie in the way of this inquiry, whatever it be that keeps us so much in the dark to ourselves, sure I am that all the light we can let in upon our minds, all the acquaintances we can make with our own understandings, will not only be very pleasant, but bring us great advantage in directing our thoughts in the search of other things.

2. This, therefore, being my purpose—to inquire into the original, certainty, and extent of *human knowledge,* together with the grounds and degrees of *belief, opinion,* and *assent*—I shall not at present meddle with the physical consideration of the mind, or trouble myself to examine wherein its essence consists, or by what motions of our spirits or alterations of our bodies we come to have any *sensation* by our organs, or any *ideas* in our understandings, and whether those ideas do in their formation, any or all of them, depend on matter or not. These are speculations which, however curious and entertaining, I shall decline, as lying out of my way in the design I am now upon. It shall suffice to my present purpose to consider the discerning faculties of a man, as they are employed about the objects which they have to do with. And I shall imagine I have not wholly misemployed myself in the thoughts I shall have on this occasion, if, in this historical, plain method, I can give any account of the ways whereby our understandings come to attain those notions of things we have, and can set down any measures of the certainty of our knowledge, or the grounds of those persuasions which are to be found amongst men, so various, different, and wholly contradictory and yet asserted somewhere or other with such assurance and confidence that he shall take a view of the opinions of mankind, observe their opposition, and at the same time consider the fondness and devotion wherewith they are embraced, the resolution and eagerness wherewith they are maintained may perhaps have reason to suspect that either there is no such thing as truth at all, or that mankind hath no sufficient means to attain a certain knowledge of it.

3. It is therefore worthwhile to search out the bounds between opinion and knowledge; and examine by what measures, in things whereof we have no certain knowledge, we ought to regulate our assent and moderate our persuasion. In order whereunto I shall pursue this following method.

First, I shall inquire into the original of those *ideas,* notions, or whatever else you please to call them, which a man observes, and is conscious to himself he has in his mind; and the ways whereby the understanding comes to be furnished with them.

Secondly, I shall endeavour to show what *knowledge* the understanding hath by those ideas; and the certainty, evidence, and extent of it.

Thirdly, I shall make some inquiry into the nature and grounds of *faith* or *opinion:* whereby I mean that assent which we give to any proposition as true, of whose truth yet we have not certain knowledge. And here we shall have occasion to examine the reasons and degrees of *assent*.

4. If by this inquiry into the nature of the understanding, I can discover the powers thereof; how far they reach; to what things they are in any degree proportionate; and where they fail us, I suppose it may be of use to prevail with the busy mind of man to be more cautious in meddling with things exceeding its comprehension; to stop when it is at the utmost extent of its tether; and to sit down in a quiet ignorance of those things which, upon examination, are found to be beyond the reach of our capacities. We should not then perhaps be so forward, out of an affectation of an universal knowledge, to raise questions, and perplex ourselves and others with disputes about things to which our understandings are not suited, and of which we cannot frame in our minds any clear or distinct perceptions, or whereof (as it has perhaps too often happened) we have not any notions at all. If we can find out how far the understanding can extend its view; how far it has faculties to attain certainty, and in what cases it can only judge and guess, we may learn to content ourselves with what is attainable by us in this state.

5. For though the comprehension of our understandings comes exceeding short of the vast extent of things, yet we shall have cause enough to magnify the bountiful Author of our being for that proportion and degree of knowledge he has bestowed on us, so far above all the rest of the inhabitants of this our mansion. Men have reason to be well satisfied with what God hath thought fit for them, since he hath given them . . . whatsoever is necessary for the conveniences of life and information of virtue; and has put within the reach of their discovery the comfortable provision for this life, and the way that leads to a better. How short soever their knowledge may come of an universal or perfect comprehension of whatsoever is, it yet secures their great concernments that they have light enough to lead them to the knowledge of their Maker and the sight of their own duties. Men may find matter sufficient to busy their heads and employ their hands with variety, delight, and satisfaction, if they will not boldly quarrel with their own constitution, and throw away the blessings their hands are filled with because they are not big enough to grasp everything. We shall not have much reason to complain of the narrowness of our minds if we will but employ them about what may be of use to us, for of that they are very capable. And it will be an unpardonable, as well as childish, peevishness if we undervalue the advantages of our knowledge, and neglect to improve it to the ends for which it was given us because there are some things that are set out of the reach of it. It will be no excuse to an idle and untoward servant who would not attend his business by candle light to plead that he had not broad sunshine. The Candle that is set up in us shines bright enough for all our purposes. The discoveries we can make with this ought to satisfy us; and we shall then use our understandings right, when we entertain all objects in that way and proportion that they are suited to our faculties, and upon those grounds they are capable of being proposed to us; and not peremptorily or intemperately require demonstration, and demand certainty, where probability only is to be had, and which is sufficient to govern all our concernments. If we will disbelieve everything, because we cannot certainly know all things, we shall do much what as wisely as he who would not use his legs, but sit still and perish, because he had no wings to fly.

6. When we know our own strength, we shall the better know what to undertake with hopes of success; and when we have well surveyed the *powers* of our own minds, and made some estimate what we may expect from them, we shall not be inclined either to sit still, and not set our thoughts on work at all, in despair of knowing anything; nor on the other side, question everything, and disclaim all knowledge, because some things are not to be understood. It is of great use to the sailor to know the length of his line, though he cannot with it fathom all the depths of the ocean. It is well he knows that it is long enough to reach the bottom at such places as are necessary to direct his voyage, and caution him against running upon shoals that may ruin him. Our business here is not to know all things, but those which concern our conduct. If we can find out those measures, whereby a rational creature, put in that state in which man is in this world, may and ought to govern his opinions, and actions depending thereon, we need not to be troubled that some other things escape our knowledge.

7. This was that which gave the first rise to this *Essay* concerning the understanding. For I thought that the first step towards satisfying several inquiries the mind of man was very apt to run into was to take a survey of our own understandings, examine our own powers, and see to what things they were adapted. Till that was done I suspected we began at the wrong end, and in vain sought for satisfaction in a quiet and sure possession of truths that most concerned us, whilst we let loose our thoughts into the vast ocean of Being; as if all that boundless extent were the natural and undoubted possession of our understandings wherein there was nothing exempt from its decisions, or that escaped its comprehension. Thus men, extending their inquiries beyond their capacities, and letting their thoughts wander into those depths where they can find no sure footing, it is no wonder that they raise questions and multiply disputes, which, never coming to any clear resolution, are proper only to continue and increase their doubts, and to confirm them at last in perfect scepticism. Whereas, were the capacities of our understandings well considered, the extent of our knowledge once discovered, and the horizon found which sets the bounds between the enlightened and dark parts of things, between what is and what is not comprehensible by us, men would perhaps with less scruple acquiesce in the avowed ignorance of the one, and employ their thoughts and discourse with more advantage and satisfaction in the other.

8. Thus much I thought necessary to say concerning the occasion of this Inquiry into human Understanding. But, before I proceed on to what I have thought on this subject, I must here in the entrance beg pardon of my reader for the frequent use of the word *idea,* which he will find in the following treatise. It being that term which, I think, serves best to stand for whatsoever is the *object* of the understanding when a man thinks, I have used it to express whatever is meant by *phantasm, notion, species,* or *whatever it is which the mind can be employed about in thinking,* and I could not avoid frequently using it.

I presume it will be easily granted me, that there are such *ideas* in men's minds: everyone is conscious of them in himself; and men's words and actions will satisfy him that they are in others.

Our first inquiry then shall be how they come into the mind.

No Innate Speculative Principles

I, ii.

1. It is an established opinion amongst some men, that there are in the understanding certain *innate principles;* some primary notions, characters, as it were stamped upon the mind of man, which the soul receives in its very first being, and brings into the world with it. It would be sufficient to convince unprejudiced readers of the falseness of this supposition, if I should only show (as I hope I shall in the following parts of this Discourse) how men, barely by the use of their natural faculties, may attain to all the knowledge they have, without the help of any innate impressions; and may arrive at certainty, without any such original notions or principles. For I imagine any one will easily grant that it would be impertinent to suppose the ideas of colours innate in a creature to whom God hath given sight, and a power to receive them by the eyes from external objects: and no less unreasonable would it be to attribute several truths to the impressions of nature, and innate characters, when we may observe in ourselves faculties fit to attain as easy and certain knowledge of them as if they were originally imprinted on the mind.

But because a man is not permitted without censure to follow his own thoughts in the search of truth when they lead him ever so little out of the common road, I shall set down the reasons that made me doubt of the truth of that opinion, as an excuse for my mistake, if I be in one, which I leave to be considered by those who, with me, dispose themselves to embrace truth wherever they find it.

2. There is nothing more commonly taken for granted than that there are certain *principles,* both *speculative* and *practical* (for they speak of both), universally agreed upon by all mankind: which therefore, they argue, must needs be the constant impressions which the souls of men receive in their first beings, and which they bring into the world with them, as necessarily and really as they do any of their inherent faculties.

3. This argument, drawn from universal consent, has this misfortune in it, that if it were true in matter of fact that there were certain truths wherein all mankind agreed, it would not prove them innate, if there can be any other way shown how men may come to that universal agreement in the things they do consent in, which I presume may be done.

4. But, which is worse, this argument of universal consent, which is made use of to prove innate principles, seems to me a demonstration that there are none such: because there are none to which all mankind give an universal assent. I shall begin with the speculative, and instance in those magnified principles of demonstration, "Whatsoever is, is," and "It is impossible for the same thing to be and not to be," which, of all others, I think have the most allowed title to innate. These have so settled a reputation of maxims universally received that it will no doubt be thought strange if any one should seem to question it. But yet I take liberty to say, that these propositions are so far from having an universal assent, that there are a great part of mankind to whom they are not so much as known.

5. For, first, it is evident, that all children and idiots have not the least apprehension or thought of them. And the want of that is enough to destroy that universal

assent which must needs be the necessary concomitant of all innate truths. It seems to me near a contradiction to say, that there are truths imprinted on the soul which it perceives or understands not: imprinting, if it signify anything, being nothing else but the making of certain truths to be perceived. For to imprint anything on the mind without the mind's perceiving it seems to me hardly intelligible. If therefore children and idiots have souls, have minds, with those impressions upon them, *they* must unavoidably perceive them, and necessarily know and assent to these truths; which since they do not, it is evident that there are no such impressions. For if they are not notions naturally imprinted, how can they be innate? And if they are notions imprinted, how can they be unknown? To say a notion is imprinted on the mind, and yet at the same time to say, that the mind is ignorant of it, and never yet took notice of it, is to make this impression nothing. No proposition can be said to be in the mind which it never yet knew, which it was never yet conscious of. For if any one may, then, by the same reason, all propositions that are true, and the mind is capable ever of assenting to, may be said to be in the mind, and to be imprinted: since, if any one can be said to be in the mind, which it never yet knew, it must be only because it is capable of knowing it; and so the mind is of all truths it ever shall know. Nay, thus truths may be imprinted on the mind which it never did, nor ever shall know; for a man may live long, and die at last in ignorance of many truths which his mind was capable of knowing, and that with certainty. So that if the capacity of knowing be the natural impression contended for, all the truths a man ever comes to know will, by this account, be every one of them innate; and this great point will amount to no more, but only to a very improper way of speaking; which, whilst it pretends to assert the contrary, says nothing different from those who deny innate principles. For nobody, I think, ever denied that the mind was capable of knowing several truths. The capacity, they say, is innate; the knowledge acquired. But then to what end such contest for certain innate maxims? If truths can be imprinted on the understanding without being perceived, I can see no difference there can be between any truths the mind is *capable* of knowing in respect of their original: they must all be innate or all adventitious: in vain shall a man go about to distinguish them. He therefore that talks of innate notions in the understanding cannot (if he intend thereby any distinct sort of truths) mean such truths to be in the understanding as it never perceived, and is yet wholly ignorant of. For if these words "to be in the understanding" have any propriety, they signify to be understood. So that to be in the understanding, and not to be understood, to be in the mind and never to be perceived, is all one as to say anything is and is not in the mind or understanding. If therefore these two propositions, "Whatsoever is, is," and "It is impossible for the same thing to be and not to be," are by nature imprinted, children cannot be ignorant of them: infants, and all that have souls, must necessarily have them in their understandings, know the truth of them, and assent to it.

6. To avoid this it is usually answered that all men know and assent to them *when they come to the use of reason,* and this is enough to prove them innate. I answer:

7. Doubtful expressions, that have scarce any significance, go for clear reasons to those who, being prepossessed, take not the pains to examine even what they themselves say. For, to apply this answer with any tolerable sense to our present purpose,

it must signify one of these two things: either that as soon as men come to the use of reason these supposed native inscriptions come to be known and observed by them, or else, that the use and exercise of men's reason assists them in the discovery of these principles, and certainly makes them known to them.

8. If they mean that by the use of reason men may discover these principles, and that this is sufficient to prove them innate, their way of arguing will stand thus, viz. that whatever truths reason can certainly discover to us, and make us firmly assent to, those are all naturally imprinted on the mind, since that universal assent, which is made the mark of them amounts to no more but this—that by the use of reason we are capable to come to a certain knowledge of and assent to them, and, by this means, there will be no difference between the maxims of the mathematicians and theorems they deduce from them: all must be equally allowed innate; they being all discoveries made by the use of reason, and truths that a rational creature may certainly come to know, if he apply his thoughts rightly that way.

9. But how can these men think the use of reason necessary to discover principles that are supposed innate, when reason (if we may believe them) is nothing else but the faculty of deducing unknown truths from principles of propositions that are already known? That certainly can never be thought innate which we have need of reason to discover, unless as I have said, we will have all the certain truths that reason ever teaches us to be innate. We may as well think the use of reason necessary to make our eyes discover visible objects, as that there should be need of reason, or the exercise thereof, to make the understanding see what is originally engraven on it, and cannot be in the understanding before it be perceived by it. So that to make reason discover those truths thus imprinted is to say that the use of reason discovers to a man what he knew before; and if men have those innate impressed truths originally, and before the use of reason, and yet are always ignorant of them till they come to the use of reason, it is in effect to say that men know and know them not at the same time.

10. It will here perhaps be said that mathematical demonstrations, and other truths that are not innate, are not assented to as soon as proposed, wherein they are distinguished from these maxims and other innate truths. I shall have occasion to speak of assent upon the first proposing more particularly by and by. I shall here only, and that very readily, allow that these maxims and mathematical demonstrations are in this different: that the one have need of reason, using of proofs, to make them out and to gain our assent; but the other, as soon as understood, are, without any the least reasoning, embraced and assented to. But I withal beg leave to observe, that it lays open the weakness of this subterfuge, which requires the use of reason for the discovery of these general truths: since it must be confessed that in their discovery there is no use made of reasoning at all. And I think those who give this answer will not be forward to affirm that the knowledge of this maxim, "That it is impossible for the same thing to be and not to be," is a deduction of our reason. For this would be to destroy that bounty of nature they seem so fond of, whilst they make the knowledge of those principles to depend on the labour of our thoughts. For all reasoning is search, and casting about, and requires pains and application. And how can it with any tolerable sense be supposed, that what was imprinted by nature, as the foundation and guide of our reason, should need the use of reason to discover it?

11. Those who will take the pains to reflect with a little attention on the operations of the understanding will find that this ready assent of the mind to some truths depends not either on native inscription or the use of reason, but on a faculty of the mind quite distinct from both of them, as we shall see hereafter. Reason, therefore, having nothing to do in procuring our assent to these maxims, if by saying, that "men know and assent to them when they come to the use of reason," be meant, that the use of reason assists us in the knowledge of these maxims, it is utterly false; and were it true, would prove them not to be innate.

12. If by knowing and assenting to them "when we come to the use of reason," be meant, that this is the time when they come to be taken notice of by the mind, and that as soon as children come to the use of reason they come also to know and assent to these maxims, this also is false and frivolous. First, it is false because it is evident these maxims are not in the mind so early as the use of reason; and therefore the coming to the use of reason is falsely assigned as the time of their discovery. How many instances of the use of reason may we observe in children a long time before they have any knowledge of this maxim, "That it is impossible for the same thing to be and not to be"? And a great part of illiterate people and savages pass many years, even of their rational age, without ever thinking on this and the like general propositions. I grant, men come not to the knowledge of these general and more abstract truths, which are thought innate, till they come to the use of reason; and I add, nor then neither. Which is so because till after they come to the use of reason, those general abstract ideas are not framed in the mind, about which those general maxims are, which are mistaken for innate principles, but are indeed discoveries made and verities introduced and brought into the mind by the same way, and discovered by the same steps, as several other propositions, which nobody was ever so extravagant as to suppose innate. This I hope to make plain in the sequel of this Discourse. I allow therefore, a necessity that men should come to the use of reason before they get the knowledge of those general truths; but deny that men's coming to the use of reason is the time of their discovery.

13. In the mean time it is observable, that this saying, that men know and assent to these maxims "when they come to the use of reason," amounts in reality of fact to no more but this—that they are never known nor taken notice of before the use of reason, but may possibly be assented to some time after, during a man's life; but when is uncertain. And so may all other knowable truths, as well as these; which therefore have no advantage nor distinction from others by this note of being known when we come to the use of reason; nor are thereby proved to be innate, but quite the contrary.

14. But, secondly, were it true that the precise time of their being known and assented to were when men come to the use of reason, neither would that prove them innate. This way of arguing is as frivolous as the supposition itself is false. For, by what kind of logic will it appear that any notion is originally by nature imprinted in the mind in its first constitution, because it comes first to be observed and assented to when a faculty of the mind, which has quite a distinct province, begins to exert itself? And therefore the coming to the use of speech, if it were supposed the time that these maxims are first assented to, (which it may be with as much truth

as the time when men come to the use of reason) would be as good a proof that they were innate, as to say they are innate because men assent to them when they come to the use of reason. I agree then with these men of innate principles, that there is no knowledge of these general and self-evident maxims in the mind, till it comes to the exercise of reason: but I deny that the coming to the use of reason is the precise time when they are first taken notice of; and if that were the precise time, I deny that it would prove them innate. All that can with any truth be meant by this proposition, that men "assent to them when they come to the use of reason," is no more but this—that the making of general abstract ideas and the understanding of general names being a concomitant of the rational faculty, and growing up with it, children commonly get not those general ideas, nor learn the names that stand for them, till, having for a good while exercised their reason about familiar and more particular ideas, they are, by their ordinary discourse and actions with others, acknowledged to be capable of rational conversation. If assenting to these maxims, when men come to the use of reason, can be true in any other sense, I desire it may be shown; or at least, how in this, or any other sense, it proves them innate.

15. The senses at first let in *particular* ideas, and furnish the yet empty cabinet, and the mind by degrees growing familiar with some of them, they are lodged in the memory, and names go to them. Afterwards, the mind proceeding further, abstracts them, and by degrees learns the use of general names. In this manner the mind comes to be furnished with ideas and language, the *materials* about which to exercise its discursive faculty. And the use of reason becomes daily more visible, as these materials that give it employment increase. But though the having of general ideas and the use of general words and reason usually grow together, yet I see not how this any way proves them innate. The knowledge of some truths, I confess, is very early in the mind; but in a way that shows them not to be innate. For, if we will observe, we shall find it to be about ideas, not innate, but acquired; it being about those first which are imprinted by external things, with which infants have earliest to do, which make the most frequent impressions on their senses. In ideas thus got, the mind discovers that some agree and others differ, probably as soon as it has any use of memory; as soon as it is able to retain and perceive distinct ideas. But whether it be then or no, this is certain, it does so long before it has the use of words; or comes to that which we commonly call "the use of reason." For a child knows as certainly before it can speak the difference between the ideas of sweet and bitter (i.e., that sweet is not bitter), as it knows afterwards (when it comes to speak) that wormwood and sugarplums are not the same thing. . . .

OF IDEAS IN GENERAL, AND THEIR ORIGIN

II, i.

1. Every man being conscious to himself that he thinks, and that which his mind is applied about whilst thinking being the *ideas* that are there, it is past doubt that men have in their minds several ideas—such as are those expressed by the words

whiteness, hardness, sweetness, thinking, motion, man, elephant, army, drunkenness, and others: it is in the first place then to be inquired, *How he comes by them?*

I know it is a received doctrine that men have native ideas and original characters stamped upon their minds in their very first being. This opinion I have at large examined already, and I suppose what I have said in the foregoing Book will be much more easily admitted when I have shown whence the understanding may get all the ideas it has; and by what ways and degrees they may come into the mind—for which I shall appeal to every one's own observation and experience.

2. Let us then suppose the mind to be, as we say, white paper, void of all characters, without any ideas—How comes it to be furnished? Whence comes it by that vast store which the busy and boundless fancy of man has painted on it with an almost endless variety? Whence has it all the *materials* of reason and knowledge? To this I answer, in one word, from *experience.* In that all our knowledge is founded; and from that it ultimately derives itself. Our observation employed either about external sensible objects or about the internal operations of our minds perceived and reflected on by ourselves, is that which supplies our understandings with all the *materials* of thinking. These two are the fountains of knowledge from whence all the ideas we have, or can naturally have, do spring.

3. First, our Senses, conversant about particular sensible objects, do convey into the mind several distinct perceptions of things, according to those various ways wherein those objects do affect them. And thus we come by those *ideas* we have of *yellow, white, heat, cold, soft, hard, bitter, sweet,* and all those which we call sensible qualities; which when I say the senses convey into the mind, I mean, they from external objects convey into the mind what produces there those perceptions. This great source of most of the ideas we have, depending wholly upon our senses, and derived by them to the understanding, I call *sensation.*

4. Secondly, the other fountain from which experience furnisheth the understanding with ideas is the perception of the operations of our own mind within us, as it is employed about the ideas it has got; which operations, when the soul comes to reflect on and consider, do furnish the understanding with another set of ideas, which could not be had from things without. And such are *perception, thinking, doubting, believing, reasoning, knowing, willing,* and all the different actings of our own minds—which we being conscious of, and observing in ourselves, do from these receive into our understandings as distinct ideas as we do from bodies affecting our senses. This source of ideas every man has wholly in himself; and though it be not sense, as having nothing to do with external objects, yet it is very like it, and might properly enough be called *internal sense.* But as I call the other Sensation, so I call this *reflection,* the ideas it affords being such only as the mind gets by reflecting on its own operations within itself. By reflection then, in the following part of this discourse, I would be understood to mean, that notice which the mind takes of its own operations, and the manner or not; and the operations of our minds will not let us be without, at least, some obscure notions of them. No man can be wholly ignorant of what he does when he thinks. These simple ideas, when offered to the

mind, the understanding can no more refuse to have, nor alter when they are imprinted, nor blot them out and make new ones itself, than a mirror can refuse, alter or obliterate the images or ideas which the objects set before it do therein produce. As the bodies that surround us do diversely affect our organs, the mind is forced to receive the impressions, and cannot avoid the perception of those ideas that are annexed to them.

OF SIMPLE IDEAS

II, ii.

1. The better to understand the nature, manner, and extent of our knowledge, one thing is carefully to be observed concerning the ideas we have, and that is, that some of them are *simple* and some *complex*.

Though the qualities that affect our senses are, in the things themselves, so united and blended that there is no separation, no distance between them, yet it is plain that the ideas they produce in the mind enter by the senses simple and unmixed. For, though the sight and touch often take in from the same object, at the same time, different ideas—as a man sees at once motion and colour [and] the hand feels softness and warmth in the same piece of wax—yet the simple ideas thus united in the same subject are as perfectly distinct as those that come in by differing senses. The coldness and hardness which a man feels in a piece of ice being as distinct ideas in the mind as the smell and whiteness of a lily, or as the taste of sugar and the smell of a rose. And there is nothing can be plainer to a man than the clear and distinct perception he has of those simple ideas; which, being each in itself uncompounded, contains in it nothing but *one uniform appearance or conception in the mind,* and is not distinguishable into different ideas.

2. These simple ideas, the materials of all our knowledge, are suggested and furnished to the mind only by those two ways above mentioned, viz. sensation and reflection. When the understanding is once stored with these simple ideas, it has the power to repeat, compare, and unite them, even to an almost infinite variety, and so can make at pleasure new complex ideas. But if it is not in the power of the most exalted wit, or enlarged understanding, by any quickness or variety of thought, to *invent* or *frame* one new simple idea in the mind, not taken in by the ways before mentioned: nor can any force of the understanding *destroy* those that are there. The dominion of man, in this little world of his own understanding being much what the same as it is in the great world of visible things, wherein his power, however managed by art and skill, reaches no farther than to compound and divide the materials that are made to his hand, but can do nothing towards the making the least particle of new matter, or destroying one atom of what is already in being. The same inability will every one find in himself, who shall go about to fashion in his understanding one simple idea, not received in by his senses from external objects, or by reflection from the operations of his own mind about them. I would have any one try to fancy any taste which had never affected his palate, or

frame the idea of a scent he had never smelt: and when he can do this, I will also conclude that a blind man hath ideas of colours, and a deaf man true distinct notions of sounds.

3. This is the reason why—though we cannot believe it impossible to God to make a creature with other organs, and more ways to convey into the understanding the notice of corporeal things than those five, as they are usually counted, which he has given to man—yet I think it is not possible for any *man* to imagine any other qualities in bodies, howsoever constituted, whereby they can be taken notice of, besides sounds, tastes, smells, visible and tangible qualities. And had mankind been made but with four senses, the qualities then which are the objects of the fifth sense had been as far from our notice, imagination, and conception, as now any belonging to a sixth, seventh, or eighth sense can possibly be—which, whether yet some other creatures, in some other parts of this vast and stupendous universe, may not have, will be a great presumption to deny. He that will not set himself proudly at the top of all things, but will consider the immensity of this fabric, and the great variety that is to be found in this little and inconsiderable part of it which he has to do with, may be apt to think that, in other mansions of it, there may be other and different intelligent beings of whose faculties he has as little knowledge or apprehension as a worm shut up in one drawer of a cabinet hath of the senses or understanding of a man; such variety and excellency being suitable to the wisdom and power of the Maker. I have here followed the common opinion of man's having but five senses, though, perhaps, there may be justly counted more—but either supposition serves equally to my present purpose.

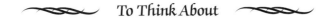

To Think About

1. "It is impossible to explain . . . qualities of matter except by tracing these back to the behavior of entities which themselves no longer possess these qualities. If atoms are really to explain the origin of color and smell of visible material bodies, then they cannot possess properties like color and smell. . . . Atomic theory consistently denies the atom any such perceptible qualities."   ***Werner Heisenberg***

2. "I have one longing only: to grasp what is hidden behind appearances, to ferret out that mystery which brings me to birth and then kills me, to discover if behind the visible and unceasing stream of the world an invisible and immutable presence is hiding."   ***Nikos Kazantzakis***

3. "It's funny how the colors of the real world only seem real when you viddy them on the screen."   ***Anthony Burgess,*** *A Clockwork Orange*

4. "The dichotomy between the soul and the body, elaborated by Plato and other Greeks, has rightly been described by ***E. R. Dodds*** as 'the most far-reaching and perhaps the most questionable . . . of all [Greece's] gifts to human culture.' But it was an idea so powerful that it is still alive and well in the West over 2,300 years later."

5. "For since the mind, in all its thoughts and reasonings, hath no other immediate objects but its own ideas, it is evident that our knowledge is only conversant about them."
   John Locke

6. "From Plato until the present, with a few notable exceptions, reason rather than emotion has been regarded as the indispensable faculty for acquiring knowledge. . . . [Objective] testability became accepted as the hallmark of natural science; this, in turn, was viewed as the paradigm of genuine knowledge. . . . Because values and emotions had been identified as variable and idiosyncratic, [the objective standard] stipulated that trustworthy knowledge could be established only by methods that neutralized the values and emotions of individual [thinkers]."
   A. Jaggar

7. "If the facts of experience—facts about what it is like *for* the experiencing organism—are accessible only from one point of view, then it is a mystery how the true character of experiences could be revealed in the physical operation of that organism. The latter is a domain of objective facts *par excellence*—the kind that can be observed and understood from many points of view and by individuals with differing perceptual systems."
   Ernest Nagel

8. "Thus he who has raised himself above the alms-basket, and, not content to live lazily on scraps of begged opinions, sets his own thoughts on work, to find and follow truth, will (whatever he lights on) not miss the hunter's satisfaction; every moment of his pursuit will reward his pains with some delight; and he will have reason to think his time not ill spent, even when he cannot much boast of any great acquisition."
   John Locke

~~~~ Readings ~~~~

AYERS, MICHAEL. *Locke,* 2 vols. New York: Routledge, 1991.

BONJOUR, LAWRENCE. *The Structure of Empirical Knowledge.* Cambridge, MA: Harvard University Press, 1985.

DUNN, JOHN. *John Locke.* Oxford: Oxford University Press, 1984.

LEHRER, KEITH. *Theory of Knowledge.* Boulder, CO: Westview Press, 1990.

MOSER, PAUL. *Empirical Justifications.* Dordrecht, the Netherlands: D. Reidel, 1986.

PITCHER, GEORGE. *A Theory of Perception.* Princeton, NJ: Princeton University Press, 1971.

POLLOCK, JOHN. *Contemporary Theories of Knowledge.* Totowa, NJ: Rowman & Littlefield, 1986.

SMART, J. J. C. "Sensations and Brain Processes." *Philosophical Review* 68 (1959): 141–56.

WOOLHOUSE, R. S. *Locke.* Minneapolis: University of Minnesota Press, 1983.

YOLTON, J. W. *Locke and the Compass of the Human Understanding.* Cambridge: Cambridge University Press, 1970.

28
Knowledge Is Both
Rational and Empirical

Immanuel Kant (1724–1804) was a renowned German philosopher who sought to reconcile the Continental rational philosophies with those of the British empirical philosophers. One of his students wrote:

> *I have had the good fortune to know a philosopher who was my teacher. In the prime of his life he possessed the joyous courage of youth, and this also, as I believe, attended him to extreme old age. His open, thoughtful brow was the seat of untroubled cheerfulness and joy, his conversation was full of ideas most suggestive. He had at his service jest, witticism, and humorous fancy, and his lectures were at once instructive and most entertaining. . . . No cabal or sect, no prejudice or reverence for a name, had the slightest influence with him in opposition to the extension and promotion of truth. He encouraged and gently compelled his hearers to think for themselves. . . . This man, whom I name with the greatest gratitude and reverence, is Immanuel Kant; his image stands before me, and is dear to me. (Johann Gottfried Herder, 1744–1803)* [*]

The rationalist philosophers, such as Descartes, believed that the fundamental source of all knowledge was not simply observation, but that some knowledge was *a priori,* that is, independent of experience. This knowledge was to be distinguished from *a posteriori,* or experiential knowledge, which the British empiricists claimed was the source of all knowledge. Kant sought to reconcile these two views and thereby develop a thorough epistemology.

---

[*]Quoted by Will and Ariel Durant in *Rousseau and Revolution,* vol. 10 of *The Story of Civilization* (New York: Simon & Schuster, 1967), 532.

From Immanuel Kant, *Critique of Pure Reason,* trans. Norman Kemp Smith (London: Macmillan, 1929), 41–45, 48–51, 189–91.

A posteriori knowledge is contingent, and the truth or falsity of statements depends upon the particular conditions at a given time. A sunset, for example, could be either pink or gray. *A priori* knowledge is necessarily always true, and it is manifest in certain concepts, such as space and substance, as well as in judgments. *A priori* judgments are called *analytic,* while *a posteriori* judgments are designated as *synthetic.* There is, according to Kant, a third type of judgment, *synthetic a priori.* These judgments are necessary and also have an empirical element. If, for example, one says, "A cube has six sides," one can realize that it is necessarily true, and at the same time image the cube (an empirical act) to count these sides. Kant believes it is also true of the statement "Everything has a cause." As a result of these distinctions, Kant created grounds for debate that continues to this day.

To Study

1. Explain the statement "Though all of our knowledge begins with experience, it does not follow that it all arises out of experience."
2. Distinguish and give examples of *a priori* and *a posteriori* knowledge.
3. Name an *a priori* concept.
4. Distinguish analytic judgments from synthetic judgments and synthetic *a priori* judgments.
5. Explain why mathematical and geometric judgments are synthetic *a priori.*
6. State the highest principle of all analytic judgments. Give an example.

THE DISTINCTION BETWEEN PURE AND EMPIRICAL KNOWLEDGE

There can be no doubt that all our knowledge begins with experience. For how should our faculty of knowledge be awakened into action did not objects affecting our senses partly of themselves produce representations, partly arouse the activity of our understanding to compare these representations, and, by combining or separating them, work up the raw material of the sensible impressions into that knowledge of objects which is entitled experience? In the order of time, therefore, we have no knowledge antecedent to experience, and with experience all our knowledge begins.

But though all our knowledge begins with experience, it does not follow that it all arises out of experience. For it may well be that even our empirical knowledge is made up of what we receive through impressions and of what our own faculty of knowledge (sensible impressions serving merely as the occasion) supplies from itself. If our faculty of knowledge makes any such addition, it may be that we are not in a position to distinguish it from the raw material, until with long practice of attention we have become skilled in separating it.

This, then, is a question which at least calls for closer examination, and does not allow of any off-hand answer:—whether there is any knowledge that is thus independent of experience and even of all impressions of the senses. Such knowledge is entitled *a priori,* and distinguished from the *empirical,* which has its sources *a posteriori,* that is, in experience.

The expression "*a priori*" does not, however, indicate with sufficient precision the full meaning of our question. For it has been customary to say, even of much knowledge that is derived from empirical sources, that we have it or are capable of having it *a priori,* meaning thereby that we do not derive it immediately from experience, but from a universal rule—a rule which is itself, however, borrowed by us from experience. Thus we would say of a man who undermined the foundations of his house, that he might have known *a priori* that it would fall, that he need not have waited for the experience of its actual falling. But still he could not know this completely *a priori.* For he had first to learn through experience that bodies are heavy, and therefore fall when their supports are withdrawn.

In what follows, therefore, we shall understand by *a priori* knowledge, not knowledge independent of this or that experience, but knowledge absolutely independent of all experience. Opposed to it is empirical knowledge, which is knowledge possible only *a posteriori,* that is, through experience. *A priori* modes of knowledge are entitled pure when there is no admixture of anything empirical. Thus, for instance, the proposition, "every alteration has its cause," while an *a priori* proposition, is not a pure proposition, because alteration is a concept which can be derived only from experience.

WE ARE IN POSSESSION OF CERTAIN MODES OF *A PRIORI* KNOWLEDGE, AND EVEN THE COMMON UNDERSTANDING IS NEVER WITHOUT THEM

What we here require is a criterion by which to distinguish with certainty between pure and empirical knowledge. Experience teaches us that a thing is so and so, but not that it cannot be otherwise. First, then, if we have a proposition which in being thought is thought as *necessary,* it is an *a priori* judgment; and if, besides, it is not derived from any proposition except one which also has the validity of a necessary judgment, it is an absolutely *a priori* judgment. Secondly, experience never confers on its judgments true or strict, but only assumed and comparative *universality,* through induction. We can properly only say, therefore, that, so far as we have hitherto observed, there is no exception to this or that rule. If then, a judgment is thought with strict universality, that is, in such manner that no exception is allowed as possible, it is not derived from experience, but is valid absolutely *a priori.* Empirical universality is only an arbitrary extension of a validity holding in most cases to one which holds in all, for instance, in the proposition, "all bodies are heavy." When, on the other hand, strict universality is essential to a judgment, this indicates a special source of knowledge, namely, a faculty of *a priori* knowledge. Necessity and strict universality are thus sure criteria of *a priori* knowledge, and are inseparable from one another. But since in the employment of these criteria the contingency of judgments is sometimes more easily shown than their empirical limitation, or, as sometimes also happens, their unlimited universality can be more convincingly proved than their necessity, it is advisable to use the two criteria separately, each by itself being infallible.

Now it is easy to show that there actually are in human knowledge judgments which are necessary and in the strictest sense universal, and which are therefore pure *a priori* judgments. If an example from the sciences be desired, we have only to look to any of the propositions of mathematics; if we seek an example from the understanding in its quite ordinary employment, the proposition, "every alteration must have a cause," will serve our purpose. In the latter case, indeed, the very concept of a cause so manifestly contains the concept of a necessity of connection with an effect and of the strict universality of the rule, that the concept would be altogether lost if we attempted to derive it, as Hume has done, from a repeated association of that which happens with that which precedes, and from a custom of connecting representations, a custom originating in this repeated association, and constituting therefore a merely subjective necessity. Even without appealing to such examples, it is possible to show that pure *a priori* principles are indispensable for the possibility of experience, and so to prove their existence *a priori*. For whence could experience derive its certainty, if all the rules, according to which it proceeds, were always themselves empirical, and therefore contingent? Such rules could hardly be regarded as first principles. At present, however, we may be content to have established the fact that our faculty of knowledge does have a pure employment, and to have shown what are the criteria of such an employment.

Such *a priori* origin is manifest in certain concepts, no less than in judgments. If we remove from our empirical concept of a body, one by one, every feature in it which is [merely] empirical, the colour, the hardness or softness, the weight, even the impenetrability, there still remains the space which the body (now entirely vanished) occupied, and this cannot be removed. Again, if we remove from our empirical concept of any object, corporeal or incorporeal, all properties which experience has taught us, we yet cannot take away that property through which the object is thought as substance or as inhering in a substance (although this concept of substance is more determinate than that of an object in general). Owing, therefore, to the necessity with which this concept of substance forces itself upon us, we have no option save to admit that it has its seat in our faculty of *a priori* knowledge.

THE DISTINCTION BETWEEN ANALYTIC AND SYNTHETIC JUDGMENTS

In all judgments in which the relation of a subject to the predicate is thought (I take into consideration affirmative judgments only, the subsequent application to negative judgments being easily made), this relation is possible in two different ways. Either the predicate B belongs to the subject A, as something which is (covertly) contained in this concept A; or B lies outside the concept A, although it does indeed stand in connection with it. In the one case I entitle the judgment analytic, in the other synthetic. Analytic judgments (affirmative) are therefore those in which the connection of the predicate with the subject is thought through identity; those in which this connection is thought without identity should be entitled synthetic. The former, as adding nothing through the predicate to the concept of the subject, but merely breaking it up into those constituent concepts that have all along been thought in it, although confusedly, can also be entitled explicative. The latter, on the other hand, add to the concept of the subject a predicate which has not been in any wise thought in it, and which no analysis could possibly extract from it; and they may therefore be entitled ampliative. If I say, for instance, "All bodies are extended," this is an analytic judgment. For I do not require to go beyond the concept which I connect with "body" in order to find extension as bound up with it. To meet with this predicate, I have merely to analyze the concept, that is, to become conscious to myself of the manifold which I always think in that concept. The judgment is therefore analytic. But when I say, "All bodies are heavy," the predicate is something quite different from anything that I think in the mere concept of body in general; and the addition of such a predicate therefore yields a synthetic judgment.

Judgments of experience, as such, are one and all synthetic. For it would be absurd to found an analytic judgment on experience. Since, in framing the judgment, I must not go outside my concept, there is no need to appeal to the testimony of experience in its support. That a body is extended is a proposition that holds *a priori* and is not empirical. For, before appealing to experience, I have already in the concept of body all the conditions required for my judgment. I have only to extract from it, in accordance with the principle of contradiction, the required predicate, and in so doing can at the same time become conscious of the necessity of the judgment—and that is what experience could never have taught me. On the other hand, though I do not include in the concept of a body in general the predicate "weight," none the less this concept indicates an object of experience through one of its parts, and I can add to that part other parts of this same experience, as in this way belonging together with the concept. From the start I can apprehend the concept of body analytically through the characters of extension, impenetrability, figure, etc., all of which are thought in the concept. Now, however, looking back on the experience from which I have derived this concept of body, and finding weight to be invariably connected with the above characters, I attach it as a predicate to the concept; and in doing so I attach it synthetically, and am therefore extending my knowledge. The possibility of the synthesis of the predicate "weight" with the concept of "body" thus rests upon experience. While the one concept is not contained in the other, they yet belong to one another, though only contingently, as parts of a whole, namely, of an experience which is itself a synthetic combination of intuitions.

But in *a priori* synthetic judgments this help is entirely lacking: [I do not here have the advantage of looking around in the field of experience.] Upon what, then, am I to rely, when I seek to go beyond the concept A, and to know that another concept B is connected with it? Through what is the synthesis made possible? Let us take the proposition, "Everything which happens has its cause." In the concept of "something which happens," I do indeed think an existence which is preceded by a time, etc., and from this concept analytic judgments may be obtained. But the concept of a "cause" lies entirely outside the other concept, and signifies something different from "that which happens," and is not therefore in any way contained in this latter representation. How come I then to predicate of that which happens something quite different, and to apprehend that the concept of cause, though not contained in it, yet belongs, and indeed necessarily belongs, to it? What is here the unknown = X which gives support to the understanding when it believes that it can discover outside the concept A a predicate B foreign to this concept, which it yet at the same time considers to be connected with it? It cannot be experience, because the suggested principle has connected the second representation with the first, not only with greater universality, but also with the character of necessity, and therefore completely *a priori* and on the basis of mere concepts. Upon such synthetic, that is, ampliative principles, all our *a priori* speculative knowledge must ultimately rest; analytic judgments are very important, and indeed necessary, but only for obtaining that clearness in the concepts which is requisite for such a sure and wide synthesis as will lead to a genuinely new addition to all previous knowledge.

IN ALL THEORETICAL SCIENCES OF REASON SYNTHETIC *A PRIORI* JUDGMENTS ARE CONTAINED AS PRINCIPLES

1. *All mathematical judgments, without exception, are synthetic.* This fact, though incontestably certain and in its consequences very important, has hitherto escaped the notice of those who are engaged in the analysis of human reason, and is, indeed, directly opposed to all their conjectures. For as it was found that all mathematical inferences proceed in accordance with the principle of contradiction (which the nature of all apodeictic certainty requires), it was supposed that the fundamental propositions of the science can themselves be known to be true through that principle. This is an erroneous view. For though a synthetic proposition can indeed be discerned in accordance with the principle of contradiction, this can only be if another synthetic proposition is presupposed, and if it can then be apprehended as following from this other proposition; it can never be so discerned in and by itself.

First of all, it has to be noted that mathematical propositions, strictly so called, are always judgments *a priori,* not empirical; because they carry with them necessity, which cannot be derived from experience. If this be demurred to, I am willing to limit my statement to *pure* mathematics, the very concept of which implies that it does not contain empirical, but only pure *a priori* knowledge.

We might, indeed, at first suppose that the proposition $7 + 5 = 12$ is a merely analytic proposition, and follows by the principle of contradiction from the concept of a sum of 7 and 5. But if we look more closely we find that the concept of the sum of 7 and 5 contains nothing save the union of the two numbers into one, and in this no thought is being taken as to what that single number may be which combines both. The concept of 12 is by no means already thought in merely thinking this union of 7 and 5; and I may analyse my concept of such a possible sum as long as I please, still I shall never find the 12 in it. We have to go outside these concepts, and call in the aid of the intuition which corresponds to one of them, our five fingers, for instance, or, as Segner does in his *Arithmetic,* five points, adding to the concept of 7, unit by unit, the five given in intuition. For starting with the number 7, and for the concept of 5 calling in the aid of the fingers of my hand as intuition, I now add one by one to the number 7 the units which I previously took together to form the number 5, and with the aid of that figure [the hand] see the number 12 coming into being. That 5 should be added to 7, I have indeed already thought in the concept of a sum = 7 + 5, but not that this sum is equivalent to the number 12. Arithmetical propositions are therefore always synthetic. This is still more evident if we take larger numbers. For it is then obvious that, however, we might turn and twist our concepts, we could never, by the mere analysis of them, and without the aid of intuition, discover what [the number is that] is the sum.

Just as little is any fundamental proposition of pure geometry analytic. That the straight line between two points is the shortest, is a synthetic proposition. For my concept of *straight* contains nothing of quantity, but only of quality. The concept of the shortest is wholly an addition, and cannot be derived, through any process of analysis, from the concept of the straight line. Intuition, therefore, must here be called in; only by its aid is the synthesis possible. What here causes us commonly to believe that the predicate of such apodeictic judgments is already contained in our concept, and that the judgment is therefore analytic, is merely an ambiguous character of the terms used. We are required to join in thought a certain predicate to a given concept, and this necessity is inherent in the concepts themselves. But the question is not what we *ought* to join in thought to the given concept, but what we *actually* think in it, even if only obscurely; and it is then manifest that, while the predicate is indeed attached necessarily to the concept, it is so in virtue of an intuition which must be added to the concept, not as thought in the concept itself.

Some few fundamental propositions, presupposed by the geometrician, are, indeed, really analytic, and rest on the principle of contradiction. But, as identical propositions, they serve only as links in the chain of method and not as principles; for instance, $a = a$; the whole is equal to itself; or $(a + b) > a$, that is, the whole is greater than its part. And even these propositions, though they are valid according to pure concepts, are only admitted in mathematics because they can be exhibited in intuition.

2. *Natural science (physics) contains* a priori *synthetic judgments as principles.* I need cite only two such judgments: that in all changes of the material world the quantity of matter remains unchanged; and that in all communication of motion, action and reaction must always be equal. Both propositions, it is evident, are not only necessary, and therefore in their origin *a priori,* but also synthetic. For in the concept of matter I do not think its permanence, but only its presence in the space which it occupies. I go outside and beyond the concept of matter, joining to it *a priori* in thought something which I have not thought *in* it. The proposition is not, therefore, analytic,

but synthetic, and yet is thought *a priori;* and so likewise are the other propositions of the pure part of natural science.

3. *Metaphysics,* even if we look upon it as having hitherto failed in all its endeavours, is yet, owing to the nature of human reason, a quite indispensable science, and *ought to contain* a priori *synthetic knowledge.* For its business is not merely to analyse concepts which we make for ourselves *a priori* of things, and thereby to clarify them analytically, but to extend our *a priori* knowledge. And for this purpose we must employ principles which add to the given concept of something that was not contained in it, and through *a priori* synthetic judgments venture out so far that experience is quite unable to follow us, as, for instance, in the proposition, that the world must have a first beginning, and such like. Thus metaphysics consists, at least *in intention,* entirely of *a priori* synthetic propositions.

THE HIGHEST PRINCIPLE OF ALL ANALYTIC JUDGMENTS

The universal, though merely negative, condition of all our judgments in general, whatever be the content of our knowledge, and however it may relate to the object is that they be not self-contradictory; for if self-contradictory, these judgments are in themselves, even without reference to the object, null and void. But even if our judgment contains no contradiction, it may connect concepts in a manner not borne out by the object, or else in a manner for which no ground is given, either *a priori* or *a posteriori,* sufficient to justify such judgment, and so may still, in spite of being free from all inner contradiction, be either false or groundless.

The proposition that no predicate contradictory of a thing can belong to it, is entitled the principle of contradiction, and is a universal, though merely negative, criterion of all truth. For this reason it belongs only to logic. It holds of knowledge, merely as knowledge in general, irrespective of content; and asserts that the contradiction completely cancels and invalidates it.

But it also allows of a positive employment, not merely, that is, to dispel falsehood and error (so far as they rest on contradiction), but also for the knowing of truth. For, *if the judgment is analytic,* whether negative or affirmative, its truth can always be adequately known in accordance with the principle of contradiction. The reverse of that which as concept is contained and is thought in the knowledge of the object, is always rightly denied. But since the opposite of the concept would contradict the object, the concept itself must necessarily be affirmed of it.

The principle of contradiction must therefore be recognized as being the universal and completely sufficient *principle of all analytic knowledge;* but beyond the sphere of analytic knowledge it has, as a *sufficient* criterion of truth, no authority and no field of application. The fact that no knowledge can be contrary to it without self-nullification, makes this principle a *conditio sine qua non,* but not a determining ground, of the truth of our [nonanalytic] knowledge. Now in our critical enquiry it is only with the synthetic portion of our knowledge that we are concerned; and in regard to the truth of this kind of knowledge we can never look to the above principle for any positive information, though, of course, since it is inviolable, we must always be careful to conform to it.

Although this famous principle is thus without content and merely formal, it has sometimes been carelessly formulated in a manner which involves the quite unnecessary admixture of a synthetic element. The formula runs: It is impossible that something should *at one and the same time* both be and not be. Apart from the fact that the apodeictic certainty, expressed through the word "impossible," is superfluously added—since it is evident of itself from the [very nature of the] proposition—the proposition is modified by the condition of time. It then, as it were, asserts: A thing = A, which is something = B, cannot at the same time be not-B, but may very well in succession be both B and not-B. For instance, a man who is young cannot at the same time be old, but may very well at one time be young and at another time not-young, that is, old. The principle of contradiction, however, as a merely logical principle, must not in any way limit its assertions to time-relations. The above formula is therefore completely contrary to the intention of the principle. The misunderstanding results from our first of all separating a predicate of a thing from the concept of that thing, and afterwards connecting this predicate with its opposite—a procedure which never occasions a contradiction with the subject but only with the predicate which has been synthetically connected with that subject, and even then only when both predicates are affirmed at one and the same time. If I say that a man who is unlearned is not learned, the condition, *at one and the same time,* must be added; for he who is at one time unlearned can very well at another be learned. But if I say, no unlearned man is learned, the proposition is analytic, since the property, unlearnedness, now goes to make up the concept of the subject, and the truth of the negative judgment then becomes evident as an immediate consequence of the principle of contradiction, without requiring the supplementary condition, *at one and the same time.* This, then, is the reason why I have altered its formulation, namely, in order that the nature of an analytic proposition be clearly expressed through it.

To Think About

1. "The universe is not to be narrowed down to the limits of the Understanding—but the Understanding must be stretched and enlarged to take in the image of the Universe as it is discovered." *Francis Bacon*

2. "In trying to distinguish appearance from reality and lay bare the fundamental structure of the universe, science has had to transcend the 'rabble of the senses'." *Lincoln Barnett*

3. "Kant said that the old assumption that our ideas to be true must conform to objects outside the mind must be replaced with a new assumption that objects outside the mind must conform to that which the mind imposes on them in experiencing them." *Broder*

~~~ Readings ~~~

CHADWICK, RUTH, ed. *Immanuel Kant, Critical Assessments.* New York: Routledge, 1992.

GARDNER, SEBASTIAN. *Routledge Philosophy Guidebook to Kant and the Critique of Pure Reason.* New York: Routledge, 1999.

GUYER, PAUL, ed. *The Cambridge Companion to Kant.* New York: Cambridge University Press, 1992.

KÖRNER, STEPHAN. *Kant.* Harmondsworth: Penguin Books, 1955.

SCRUTON, ROGER. *Kant.* Oxford: Oxford University Press, 1982.

29

Truth Is Established by Correspondence

Bertrand Russell (1872–1970), the grandson of Lord John Russell, a prime minister under Queen Victoria, was born in Wales. He studied mathematics and philosophy at Trinity College, Cambridge, from 1890 to 1894. He was a fellow at Trinity from 1895 to 1901, and a lecturer in philosophy there from 1910 to 1916. In 1916, Russell was dismissed from his position because of his pacifist activities. Then, in 1918, he was sentenced to six months in prison because of an allegedly libelous article in which he expressed his opposition to World War I and his desire for peace. Russell was a fellow of the Royal Society, an honorary fellow of the British Academy, and a recipient of the Order of Merit. He was awarded the Nobel Prize for literature in 1950. In the area of logic, Russell has written Principles of Mathematics *(1903),* Principia Mathematica *(with A. N. Whitehead; three volumes, 1910–13), and* Introduction to Mathematical Philosophy *(1919). His works in epistemology and metaphysics include* Our Knowledge of the External World *(1914),* The Analysis of Matter *(1927), and* Human Knowledge, Its Scope and Limits *(1948). Among his books on social issues are* Marriage and Morals *(1929) and* Education and the Social Order *(1932).*

Having discussed warrant, we turn now to a consideration of truth. Philosophers from the time of Jesus Christ to the present day have sought an answer to the question, What is truth? Three theories have emerged as answers to this question: the pragmatic theory, which states that truths are what work; the coherence theory, which argues that truths are necessarily part of a consistent system; and the correspondence theory, which contends that truths correspond to facts. Russell holds to the correspondence theory of truth. He believes that what we say is true if it corresponds to reality. There is a realm of *facts* independent of any of us ("San Francisco is in California," "my mother is alive," etc.), and our beliefs are *true* if they correspond with these facts.

From Bertrand Russell, *The Problems of Philosophy* (Oxford: Oxford University Press, 1912).

~~~~~ To Study ~~~~~

1. According to Russell, what is the difference between our knowledge of things and our knowledge of truth?
2. Explain each of the three requisites of any theory of truth.
3. What are Russell's criticisms of the coherence theory of truth?
4. According to Russell, what distinguishes a true judgment from a false one?

Our knowledge of truths, unlike our knowledge of things, has an opposite, namely *error.* So far as things are concerned, we may know them or not know them, but there is no positive state of mind which can be described as erroneous knowledge of things, so long, at any rate, as we confine ourselves to knowledge by acquaintance. Whatever we are acquainted with must be something: we may draw wrong inference from our acquaintance, but the acquaintance itself cannot be deceptive. Thus there is no dualism as regards acquaintance. But as regards knowledge of truths, there is a dualism. We may believe what is false as well as what is true. We know that on very many subjects different people hold different and incompatible opinions: hence some beliefs must be erroneous. Since erroneous beliefs are often held just as strongly as true beliefs, it becomes a difficult question how they are to be distinguished from true beliefs. How are we to know, in a given case, that our belief is not erroneous? That is a question of the very greatest difficulty, to which no completely satisfactory answer is possible. There is, however, a preliminary question which is rather less difficult, and that is: What do we *mean* by truth and falsehood? It is this preliminary question which is to be considered in this chapter.

  . . . We are not asking how we can know whether a belief is true or false: we are asking what is meant by the question whether a belief is true or false. It is to be hoped that a clear answer to this question may help us to obtain an answer to the question what beliefs are true, but for the present we ask only "What is truth?" and "What is falsehood?" not "What beliefs are true?" and "What beliefs are false?" It is very important to keep these different questions entirely separate, since any confusion between them is sure to produce an answer which is not really applicable to either.

  There are three points to observe in the attempt to discover the nature of truth, three requisites which any theory must fulfill.

  1. Our theory of truth must be such as to admit of its opposite, falsehood. A good many philosophers have failed adequately to satisfy this condition: they have constructed theories according to which all our thinking ought to have been true, and have then had the greatest difficulty in finding a place for falsehood. In this respect our theory of belief must differ from our theory of acquaintance, since in the case of acquaintance it was not necessary to take account of any opposite.

  2. It seems fairly evident that if there were no beliefs there could be no falsehood, and no truth either, in the sense in which truth is correlative to falsehood. If we imagine a world of mere matter, there would be no room for falsehood in such a world, and although it would contain what may be called "facts," it would not contain any truths,

in the sense in which truths are things of the same kind as falsehoods. In fact, truth and falsehood are properties of beliefs and statements: hence a world of mere matter, since it would contain no beliefs or statements, would also contain no truth or falsehood.

3. But, as against what we have just said, it is to be observed that the truth or falsehood of a belief always depends upon something which lies outside the belief itself. If I believe that Charles I died on the scaffold, I believe truly, not because of any intrinsic quality of my belief, which could be discovered by merely examining the belief, but because of an historical event which happened two and a half centuries ago. If I believe that Charles I died in his bed, I believe falsely: no degree of vividness in my belief, or of care in arriving at it, prevents it from being false, again because of what happened long ago, and not because of any intrinsic property of my belief. Hence, although truth and falsehood are properties of beliefs, they are properties dependent upon the relations of the beliefs to other things, not upon any internal quality of the beliefs.

The third of the above requisites leads us to adopt the view—which has on the whole been commonest among philosophers—that truth consists in some form of correspondence between belief and fact. It is, however, by no means an easy matter to discover a form of correspondence to which there are no irrefutable objections. By this partly—and partly by the feeling that, if truth consists in a correspondence of thought with something outside thought, thought can never know when truth has been attained—many philosophers have been led to try to find some definition of truth which shall not consist in relation to something wholly outside belief. The most important attempt at a definition of this sort is the theory that truth consists in *coherence.* It is said that the mark of falsehood is failure to cohere in the body of our beliefs, and that it is the essence of a truth to form part of the completely rounded system which is The Truth.

There is, however, a great difficulty in this view, or rather two great difficulties. The first is that there is no reason to suppose that only *one* coherent body of beliefs is possible. It may be that, with sufficient imagination, a novelist might invent a past for the world that would perfectly fit on to what we know, and yet be quite different from the real past. In more scientific matters, it is certain that there are often two or more hypotheses which account for all the known facts on some subject, and although, in such cases, men of science endeavor to find facts which will rule out all the hypotheses except one, there is no reason why they should always succeed.

In philosophy, again, it seems not uncommon for two rival hypotheses to be both able to account for all the facts. Thus, for example, it is possible that life is one long dream, and that the outer world has only that degree of reality that the objects of dreams have; but although such a view does not seem inconsistent with known facts, there is no reason to prefer it to the common-sense view, according to which other people and things do really exist. Thus, coherence as the definition of truth fails because there is no proof that there can be only one coherent system.

The other objection to this definition of truth is that it assumes the meaning of "coherence" known, whereas, in fact, "coherence" presupposes the truth of the laws of logic. Two propositions are coherent when both may be true, and are incoherent when one at least must be false. Now in order to know whether two propositions can both be true, we must know such truths as the law of contradiction. For example, the two propositions "this tree is a beech" and "this tree is not a beech," are not coherent, because of the law of contradiction. But if the law of contradiction itself were subjected to the test of coherence, we should find that, if we choose to suppose it false, nothing will any longer be incoherent with anything else. Thus, the laws of logic supply the skeleton or framework within which the test of coherence applies, and they themselves cannot be established by this test.

For the above two reasons, coherence cannot be accepted as giving the *meaning* of truth, though it is often a most important *test* of truth after a certain amount of truth has become known.

Hence we are driven back to *correspondence with fact* as constituting the nature of truth. It remains to define precisely what we mean by "fact," and what is the nature of the correspondence which must subsist between belief and fact, in order that belief may be true.

In accordance with our three requisites, we have to seek a theory of truth which (1) allows truth to have an opposite, namely falsehood, (2) makes truth a property of beliefs, but (3) makes it a property wholly dependent upon the relation of the beliefs to outside things.

The necessity of allowing for falsehood makes it impossible to regard belief as a relation of the mind to a single object, which could be said to be what is believed. If belief were so regarded, we should find that, like acquaintance, it would not admit of the opposition of truth and falsehood, but would have to be always true. This may be made clear by examples. Othello believes falsely that Desdemona loves Cassio. We cannot say that this belief consists in a relation to a single object, "Desdemona's love for Cassio," for if there were such an object, the belief would be true. There is in fact no such object, and therefore Othello cannot have any relation to such an object. Hence his belief cannot possibly consist in a relation to this object.

It might be said that his belief is a relation to a different object, namely "that Desdemona loves Cassio"; but it is almost as difficult to suppose that there is such an object as this, when Desdemona does not love Cassio, as it was to suppose that there is "Desdemona's love for Cassio." Hence it will be better to seek for a theory of belief which does not make it consist in a relation of the mind to a single object.

It is common to think of relations as though they always held between *two* terms, but in fact this is not always the case. Some relations demand three terms, some four, and so on. Take, for instance, the relation "between." So long as only two terms come in, the relation "between" is impossible: three terms are the smallest number that render it possible. York is between London and Edinburgh; but if London and Edinburgh were the only places in the world, there could be nothing which was between one place and another. Similarly, *jealousy* requires three people: there can be no such relation that does not involve three at least. Such a proposition as "A wishes B to promote C's marriage with D" involves a relation of four terms; that is to say, A and B and C and D all come in, and the relation involved cannot be expressed otherwise than in a form involving all four. Instances might be multiplied indefinitely, but enough has been said to show that there are relations which require more than two terms before they can occur.

The relation involved in *judging* or *believing* must, if falsehood is to be duly allowed for, be taken to be a relation between several terms, not between two. When Othello believes that Desdemona loves Cassio, he must not have before his mind a single object, "Desdemona's love for Cassio," or "that Desdemona loves Cassio," for that would require that there should be objective falsehoods, which subsist independently of any minds; and this, though not logically refutable, is a theory to be avoided if possible. Thus it is easier to account for falsehood if we take judgment to be a relation in which the mind and the various objects concerned all occur severally; that is to say, Desdemona and loving and Cassio must all be terms in the relation which subsists when Othello believes that Desdemona loves Cassio. This relation, therefore, is a relation of four terms, since Othello also is one of the terms of the relation. When we say that it is a relation of four terms, we do not mean that Othello has a certain relation to Desdemona, and has the same relation to loving and also to Cassio. This may be true of some other relation than believing; but believing, plainly, is not a relation which Othello has to *each* of the three terms concerned, but to *all* of them together: there is only one example of the relation of believing involved, but this one example knits together four terms. Thus, the actual occurrence, at the moment when Othello is entertaining his belief, is that the relation called "believing" is knitting together into one complex whole the four terms Othello, Desdemona, loving, and Cassio. What is called belief or judgment is nothing but this relation of believing or judging, which relates a mind to several things other than itself. An *act* of belief or of judgment in the occurrence between certain terms at some particular time, of the relation of believing or judging.

We are now in a position to understand what it is that distinguishes a true judgment from a false one. For this purpose we will adopt certain definitions. In every act of judgment there is a mind which judges, and there are terms concerning which it judges. We will call the mind the *subject* in the judgment, and the remaining terms the *objects*. Thus, when Othello judges that Desdemona loves Cassio, Othello is the subject, while the objects are Desdemona and loving and Cassio. The subject and the objects together are called the *constituents* of the judgment. It will be observed that the relation of judging has what is called a "sense" or "direction." We may say, metaphorically, that it puts its objects in a certain *order*, which we may indicate by means of the order of the words in the sentence. (In an inflected language, the same thing will be indicated by inflections, for example, by the difference between nominative and accusative.) Othello's judgment that Cassio loves Desdemona differs from his judgment that Desdemona loves Cassio, in spite of the fact that it consists of the same constituents, because the relation of judging places the constituents in a different order in the two cases. Similarly, if Cassio judges that Desdemona loves Othello, the constituents of the judgment are still the same, but their order is different. This property of having a "sense" or "direction" is one which the relation of judging shares with all other relations. The "sense" of relations is the ultimate source of order and series and a host of mathematical concepts; but we need not concern ourselves further with this aspect.

We spoke of the relation called "judging" or "believing" as knitting together into one complex whole the subject and the objects. In this respect, judging is exactly like every other relation. Whenever a relation holds between two or more terms, it unites the terms into a complex whole. If Othello loves Desdemona, there is such a complex whole as "Othello's love for Desdemona." The terms united by the relation may be themselves complex, or may be simple, but the whole which results from their being united must be complex. Wherever there is a relation which relates certain terms, there is a complex object formed of the union of those terms; and conversely, wherever there is a complex object, there is a relation which relates its constituents. When an act of believing occurs, there is a complex, in which "believing" is the uniting relation, and subject and objects are arranged in a certain order by the "sense" of the relation of believing. Among the objects, as we saw in considering "Othello believes that Desdemona loves Cassio," one must be a relation—in this instance, the relation "loving." But this relation, as it occurs in the act of believing, is not the relation which creates the unity of the complex whole consisting of the subject and the objects. The relation "loving," as it occurs in the act of believing, is one of the objects— it is a brick in the structure, not the cement. The cement is the relation "believing." When the belief is *true,* there is another complex unity, in which the relation which was one of the objects of the belief relates the other objects. Thus, for example, if Othello believes *truly* that Desdemona loves Cassio, then there is a complex unity, "Desdemona's love for Cassio," which is composed exclusively of the *objects* of the belief, in the same order as they had in the belief, with the relation which was one of the objects occurring now as the cement that binds together the other objects of the belief. On the other hand, when a belief is *false,* there is no such complex unity composed only of the objects of the belief. If Othello believes *falsely* that Desdemona loves Cassio, then there is no such complex unity as "Desdemona's love for Cassio."

Thus a belief is *true* when it *corresponds* to a certain associated complex, and *false* when it does not. Assuming, for the sake of definiteness, that the objects of the belief are two terms and a relation, the terms being put in a certain order by the "sense" of the believing, then if the two terms in that order are united by the relation into a complex, the belief is true; if not, it is false. This constitutes the definition of truth and falsehood that we were in search of. Judging or believing is a certain complex unity of which a mind is a constituent; if the remaining constituents, taken in the order which they have in the belief, form a complex unity, then the belief is true; if not, it is false.

Thus, although truth and falsehood are properties of beliefs, yet they are in a sense extrinsic properties, for the condition of the truth of a belief is something not involving beliefs, or (in general) any mind at all, but only the *objects* of the belief. A mind, which believes, believes truly when there is a *corresponding* complex not involving the mind, but only its objects. This correspondence ensures truth, and its absence entails falsehood. Hence, we account simultaneously for the two facts that beliefs (*a*) depend on minds for their *existence,* (*b*) do not depend on minds for their *truth.*

We may restate our theory as follows: If we take such a belief as "Othello believes that Desdemona loves Cassio," we will call Desdemona and Cassio the *object-terms,* and loving the *object-relation.* If there is a complex unity "Desdemona's love for Cassio," consisting of the object-terms related by the object relation in the same order as they have in the belief, then this complex unity is called the *fact corresponding to the belief.* Thus a belief is true when there is a corresponding fact, and is false when there is no corresponding fact.

. . . Minds do not *create* truth or falsehood. They create beliefs, but when once the beliefs are created, the mind cannot make them true or false, except in the special case where they concern future things which are within the power of the person believing, such as catching trains. What makes a belief true is a *fact,* and this fact does not (except in exceptional cases) in any way involve the mind of the person who has the belief.

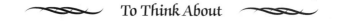

To Think About

1. In court, witnesses are asked to swear "to tell the truth, the whole truth, and nothing but the truth." What assumptions underlie this oath? Are you able to accept these assumptions?

2. "What everybody echoes as true today, may turn out to be falsehood tomorrow, mere smoke of opinion."   ***Henry David Thoreau***

3. "The greatest friend of truth is Time, her greatest enemy is Prejudice, and her constant companion is Humility."   ***C. C. Colton***

4. "Can it not be laid down that truth exists when there is correspondence in certain respect? But in which? For what would we then have to do to decide whether something were true? We should have to inquire whether it were true that an idea and a reality, perhaps, corresponded in the laid down respect. And then we should be confronted by a question of the same kind and the game could begin again. So the attempt to explain truth as correspondence collapses. And every other attempt to define truth collapses too. For in a definition certain characteristics would have to be stated. And in application to any particular case the question would always arise whether it were true that the characteristics were present. So one goes round in a circle. Consequently, it is probable that the content of the word 'true' is unique and indefinable."   ***Edward Parfit***

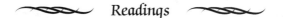

Readings

KÜNNE, WOLFGANG. *Conceptions of Truth.* Oxford: Clarendon Press, 2003.

LYNCH, MICHAEL P., ed. *The Nature of Truth.* Cambridge, MA: MIT Press, 2001.

WILLIAMS, BERNARD. *Truth and Truthfulness: An Essay in Genealogy.* Princeton, NJ: Princeton University Press, 2002.

30
Truth Is Established by Coherence

Francis H. Bradley (1846–1924) *was the most distinguished of the British absolute idealists who dominated Anglo-American philosophy in the late nineteenth century.*

Bradley holds to the coherence theory of truth and believes that the correspondence theory is inadequate. He contends that our judgments are not like the physical things to which they refer. We cannot know the "reality" to which our beliefs correspond. Bradley argues that the coherence theory of truth is better because the consistency and comprehensiveness of our ideas are the only ways of testing truth.

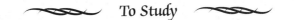 To Study

1. According to Bradley, what is the test of the truth we apply to facts of perception and memory?
2. Consider the statement "Perception gives us infallible truth." In what sense is this doctrine sound? In what sense is it defective?
3. On what grounds is one's experience solid? Why does no fact possess an absolute right?
4. How do we establish facts of memory and of history?
5. What are the characteristics of Bradley's own theory of truth?

. . . What I maintain is that in the case of facts of perception and memory the test [of truth] which we do apply, and which we must apply, is that of system. I contend that this test works satisfactorily, and that no other test will work. And I argue in consequence that there are no judgements of sense which are in principle infallible. . . .

From Francis Herbert Bradley, *Essays on Truth and Reality* (Oxford: Oxford University Press, 1914), 202–18.

The reason for maintaining independent facts and infallible judgements, as I understand it, is twofold. (1) Such data, it may be said, can be actually shown. And (2) in any case they must exist, since without them the intelligence cannot work. . . .

1. I doubt my ability to do justice to the position of the man who claims to show ultimate given facts exempt from all possible error. In the case of any datum of sensation or feeling, to prove that we have this wholly unmodified by what is called "apperception" seems a hopeless undertaking. And how far it is supposed that such a negative can be proved I do not know. What, however, is meant must be this, that we somehow and somewhere have verifiable facts of perception and memory, and also judgements, free from all chance of error. I will begin hereby recalling a truth familiar but often forgotten. . . . In your search for independent facts and for infallible truths you may go so low that, when you have descended beyond the level of error, you find yourself below the level of any fact or of any truth which you can use. What you seek is particular facts of perception or memory, but what you get may be something not answering to that character. I will go on to give instances of what I mean, and I think that in every case we shall do well to ask this question, "What on the strength of our ultimate fact are we able to contradict?"

    a.   If we take the instance of simple unrelated sensations or feelings, *a, b, c*— supposing that there are such things—what judgement would such a fact enable us to deny? We could on the strength of this fact deny the denial that *a, b,* and *c* exist in any way, manner or sense. But surely this is not the kind of independent fact of which we are in search.

    b.   From this let us pass to the case of a complex feeling containing, at once and together, both *a* and *b.* On the ground of this we can deny the statement that *a* and *b* cannot or do not ever anyhow co-exist in feeling. This is an advance, but it surely leaves us far short of our goal.

    c.   What we want, I presume, is something that at once is infallible and that also can be called a particular fact of perception or memory. And we want, in the case of perception, something that would be called a fact for observation. We do not seem to reach this fact until we arrive somewhere about the level of "I am here and now having a sensation or complex of sensations of such or such a kind." The goal is reached; but at this point, unfortunately, the judgement has become fallible, so far at least as it really states particular truth.

        (α)   In such a judgement it is in the first place hard to say what is meant by the "I." If, however, we go beyond feeling far enough to mean a self with such or such a real existence in time, then memory is involved, and the judgement at once, I should urge, becomes fallible. . . . Thus the statement made in the judgement is liable to error, or else the statement does not convey particular truth.

        (β)   And this fatal dilemma holds good when applied to the "now" and "here." If these words mean a certain special place in a certain special series or order, they are liable to mistake. But, if they fall short of this meaning, then they fail to state individual fact. My feeling is, I agree, not subject to error in the proper sense of that term, but on the other side my feeling does not of itself deliver truth. And the process which gets from it a deliverance as to individual fact is fallible.

Everywhere such fact depends on construction. And we have here to face not only the possibility of what would commonly be called mistaken interpretation. We have in addition the chance of actual sense-hallucination. And, worse than this, we have the far-reaching influence of abnormal suggestion and morbid fixed idea. This influence may stop short of hallucination, and yet may vitiate the memory and the judgement to such an extent that there remains no practical difference between idea and perceived fact. And, in the face of these possibilities, it seems idle to speak of perceptions and memories secure from all chance of error. Or on the other side banish the chance of error, and with what are you left? You then have something which (as we have seen) goes no further than to warrant the assertion that such and such elements can and do co-exist—somehow and somewhere, or again that such or such a judgement happens—without any regard to its truth and without any specification of its psychical context. And no one surely will contend that with this we have particular fact.

The doctrine that perception gives us infallible truth rests on a foundation which in part is sound and in part fatally defective. That what is felt is felt, and cannot, so far as felt, be mistaken—so much as this must be accepted. But the view that, when I say "this," "now," "here," or "my," what I feel, when so speaking, is carried over intact into my judgement, and that my judgement in consequence is exempt from error, seems wholly indefensible. It survives, I venture to think, only because it never has understood its complete refutation. That which I designate is not and cannot be carried over into my judgement. The judgement may in a sense answer to that which I feel, but none the less it fails to contain and to convey my feeling. And on the other hand, so far as it succeeds in expressing my meaning, the judgement does this in a way which makes it liable to error. Or, to put it otherwise, the perceived truth, to be of any use, must be particularized. So far as it is stated in a general form, it contains not only that which you meant to say but also, and just as much, the opposite of that which you meant. And to contend for the infallibility of such a truth seems futile. On the other side so far as your truth really is individualized, so far as it is placed in a special construction and vitally related to its context, to the same extent the element of interpretation or implication is added. And, with this element obviously comes the possibility of mistake. As we have seen above that, viewed psychologically, particular judgements of perception immune from all chance of error seem hardly tenable.

2.   I pass now to the second reason for accepting infallible data of perception. Even if we cannot show these (it is urged) we are bound to assume them. For in their

absence our knowledge has nothing on which to stand, and this want of support results in total scepticism.

It is possible of course here to embrace both premises and conclusion, and to argue that scepticism is to be preferred to an untrue assumption. And such a position I would press on the notice of those who uphold infallible judgements of sense and memory. But personally I am hardly concerned in this issue, for I reject both the conclusion and the premises together. Such infallible and incorrigible judgements are really not required for our knowledge, and, since they cannot be shown, we must not say that they exist. . . .

I agree that we depend vitally on the sense-world, that our material comes from it, and that apart from it knowledge could not begin. To this world, I agree, we have for ever to return, not only to gain new matter but to confirm and maintain the old. I agree that to impose order from without on sheer disorder would be wholly impracticable, and that, if my sense-world were disorderly beyond a certain point, my intelligence would not exist. And further I agree that we cannot suppose it possible that *all* the judgements of perception and memory which for me come first, could in fact for me be corrected. I cannot, that is, imagine the world of my experience to be so modified that in the end none of these accepted facts should be left standing. But so far, I hasten to add, we have not yet come to the real issue. There is still a chasm between such admissions and the conclusion that there are judgements of sense which possess truth absolute and infallible.

We meet here a false doctrine largely due to a misleading metaphor. My known world is taken to be a construction built upon such and such foundations. It is argued, therefore, to be in principle a superstructure which rests upon these supports. You can go on adding to it no doubt, but only so long as the supports remain; and, unless they remain, the whole building comes down. But the doctrine, I have to contend, is untenable, and the metaphor ruinously inapplicable. The foundation in truth is provisional merely. In order to begin my construction I take the foundation as absolute—so much certainly is true. But that my construction continues to rest on the beginnings of my knowledge is a conclusion which does not follow. It does not follow that, if these are allowed to be fallible, the whole building collapses. For it is in another sense that my world rests upon the data of perception.

My experience is solid, not so far as it is a superstructure but so far as in short it is a system. My object is to have a world as comprehensive and coherent as possible, and, in order to attain this object, I have not only to reflect but perpetually to have recourse to the materials of sense. I must go to this source both to verify the matter which is old and also to increase it by what is new. And in this way I must depend upon the judgements of perception. Now it is agreed that, if I am to have an orderly world, I cannot possibly accept all "facts." Some of these must be relegated, as they are, to the world of error, whether we succeed or fail in modifying and correcting them. And the view which I advocate takes them all as in principle fallible. On the other hand, that view denies that there is any necessity for absolute facts of sense. Facts for it are true, we may say, just so far as they work, just so far as they contribute to the order of experience. If by taking certain judgements of perception as true, I can get more system into my world, then these "facts" are so far true, and if by taking certain "facts" as errors I can order my experience better, then so far these "facts" are errors. And there is no "fact" which possesses an absolute right. Certainly there are truths with which I begin and which I personally never have to discard, and which therefore remain in fact as members of my known world. And of some of these certainly it may be said that without them I should not know how to order my knowledge. But it is quite another thing to maintain that every single one of these judgements is in principle infallible. The absolute indispensable fact is in my view the mere creature of false theory. Facts are valid so far as, when taken otherwise than as "real," they bring disorder into my world. And there are today for me facts such that, if I take them as mistakes, my known world is damaged and, it is possible, ruined. But how does it follow that I cannot tomorrow on the strength of new facts gain a wider order in which these old facts can take a place as errors? The supposition may be improbable, but what you have got to show is that it is in principle impossible. A foundation used at the beginning does not in short mean something fundamental at the end, and there is no single "fact" which in the end can be called fundamental absolutely. It is all a question of relative contribution to my known world-order.

"Then no judgement of perception will be more than probable?" Certainly that is my contention. "Facts" are justified because and as far as, while taking them as real, I am better able to deal with the incoming new "facts" and in general to make my world wider and more harmonious. The higher and wider my structure, and the more that any particular fact or set of facts is implied in that structure, the more certain are the structure and the facts. And, if we could reach an all-embracing ordered whole, then our certainty would be absolute. But, since we cannot do this, we have to remain content with relative probability. Why is this or that fact of observation taken as practically certain? It is so taken just so far as it is *not* taken in its own right. (i) Its validity is due to such and such a person perceiving it under such and such conditions. This means that a certain intellectual order in the person is necessary as a basis, and again that nothing in the way of sensible or mental distortion intervenes between this order and what is given. And (ii) the observed fact must agree with our world as already arranged, or at least must not upset this. If the fact is too much contrary to our arranged world we provisionally reject it. We eventually accept the fact only when after confirmation the hypothesis of its error becomes still more ruinous. We are forced then more or less to rearrange our world, and more or less perhaps to reject some previous "facts." The question throughout is as to what is better or worse for our order as a whole.

Why again to me is a remembered fact certain, supposing that it is so? Assuredly not because it is infallibly delivered by the faculty of Memory, but because I do not see how to reconcile the fact of its error with my accepted world. Unless I go on the principle of trusting my memory, apart from any special reason to the contrary, I cannot order my world so well, if indeed I can order it at all. The principle here again is system. . . .

The same account holds with regard to the facts of history. For instance, the guillotining of Louis XVI is practically certain because to take this as error would entail too much disturbance of my world. Error is possible here of course. Fresh facts conceivably might come before me such as would compel me to modify in part my knowledge as so far arranged. And in this modified arrangement the execution of Louis would find its place as an error. But the reason for such a modification would have to be considerable, while, as things are, no reason exists. . . . To take memory as in general trustworthy, where I have no special reason for doubt, and to take the testimony of those persons, whom I suppose to view the world as I view it, as being true, apart from special reason on the other side—these are principles by which I construct my ordered world, such as it is. And because by any other method the result is worse, therefore for me these principles are true. On the other hand to suppose that any "fact" or perception or memory is so certain that no possible experience could justify me in taking it as error seems to me injurious if not ruinous. On such a principle my world of knowledge would be ordered worse, if indeed it could be ordered at all. For to accept all the "facts," as they offer themselves, seems obviously impossible; and, if it is we who have to decide as to which facts are infallible, then I ask how we are to decide. The ground of validity, I maintain, consists in successful contribution. That is a principle of order, while any other principle, so far as I see, leads to chaos.

"But," it may still be objected, "my fancy is unlimited. I can therefore invent an imaginary world even more orderly than my known world. And further this fanciful arrangement might possibly be made so wide that the world of perception would become for me in comparison small and inconsiderable. Hence, my perceived world, so far as not supporting my fancied arrangement, might be included within it as *error*. Such a consequence would or might lead to confusion in theory and to disaster in practice. And yet the result follows from your view inevitably, unless after all you fall back upon the certainty of perception."

To this possible objection, I should reply first, that it has probably failed to understand rightly the criterion which I defend. The aspect of comprehensiveness has not received here its due emphasis. The idea of system demands the inclusion of all possible material. Not only must you include everything to be gained from immediate experience and perception, but you must also be ready to act on the same principle with regard to fancy. But this means that you cannot confine yourself within the limits of this or that fancied world, as suits your pleasure or private convenience. You are bound also, so far as is possible, to recognize and to include the opposite fancy.

This consideration to my mind ruins the above hypothesis on which the objection was based. The fancied arrangement not only has opposed to it the world of perception. It also has against it any opposite arrangement and any contrary fact which I can fancy. And, so far as I can judge, these contrary fancies will balance the first. Nothing, therefore, will be left to outweigh the world as perceived, and the imaginary hypothesis will be condemned by our criterion.

. . . I may state the view which has commended itself to my mind. Truth is an ideal expression of the Universe, at once coherent and comprehensive. It must not conflict with itself, and there must be no suggestion which fails to fall inside it. Perfect truth in short must realize the idea of a systematic whole. And such a whole . . . possesses essentially the two characters of coherence and comprehensiveness.

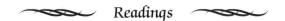

To Think About

1. "A judgment of fact can be verified only by the sort of apprehension that can present us with a fact, and this must be a further judgment. And an agreement between judgments is best described not as a correspondence, but as coherence."   ***Brand Blanshard***

2. "What can give us more sure knowledge than our senses? How else can we distinguish between the true and the false?"   ***Lucretius***

3. "Any judgment is true if it is both self-consistent and coherently connected with our system of judgments as a whole."   ***Edgar S. Brightman***

Readings

BLANSHARD, BRAND. "The Test of the Truth," ch. 25; "Coherence," ch. 26. In *The Nature of Thought,* vol. 2. New York: Macmillan, 1939.

KHATCHADOURIAN, HAIG. *The Coherence Theory of Truth.* Beirut: American University Press, 1961.

WHITE, A. R. *Truth.* Garden City, NY: Doubleday (Anchor Books), 1970. A small paperback that carefully analyzes the different meanings of truth and discusses important theories of truth.

31
Truth Is Established
on Pragmatic Grounds

William James (1842–1910), *American philosopher and psychologist, received his medical degree from Harvard in 1869. He lectured there on anatomy and physiology until 1880, when he joined the Department of Psychology and Philosophy. He amended and popularized Peirce's pragmatism in a series of books that include* The Will to Believe and Other Essays in Popular Philosophy *(1897),* The Varieties of Religious Experience *(1902),* Pragmatism *(1907), and* Essays in Radical Empiricism *(1912).*

William James holds to the pragmatic theory of truth. He believes that because the coherence theory cannot distinguish between consistent truth and consistent error, the best way to define truth is in terms of beliefs that "work." For the pragmatist the test of truth is utility, workability, or satisfactory consequences. There is no such thing as static or absolute truth; rather, truth is made in the processes of human adjustment. What works in practice will decide which of our alternative beliefs are true.

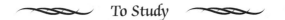 To Study

1. According to James, what are the classic stages of a theory's career?
2. What is James's argument against the correspondence theory?
3. What are the processes of validation and verification? How do they relate to our idea of truth?
4. How does James define true and false ideas?
5. According to James, what is the value of the possession of true thoughts?
6. In what way is truth "on a credit system"?

From William James, *Pragmatism* (New York: Longmans, Green, 1970), 75–78, 198–209, 218–23.

7. What does James mean when he says "Truth is made"? What is the rationalist's argument against this? What is James's reply?
8. According to James, what is the "absolutely" true?
9. According to James, what is the relationship between the good and the true?

I

. . . I fully expect to see the pragmatist view of truth run through the classic stages of a theory's career. First, you know, a new theory is attacked as absurd; then it is admitted to be true, but obvious and insignificant; finally it is seen to be so important that its adversaries claim that they themselves discovered it. Our doctrine of truth is at present in the first of these three stages, with symptoms of the second stage having begun in certain quarters. I wish that this lecture might help it beyond the first stage in the eyes of many of you.

Truth, as any dictionary will tell you, is a property of certain of our ideas. It means their "agreement," as falsity means their disagreement, with "reality." Pragmatists and intellectualists both accept this definition as a matter of course. They begin to quarrel only after the question is raised as to what may precisely be meant by the term "agreement," and what by the term "reality," when reality is taken as something for our ideas to agree with.

In answering these questions the pragmatists are more analytic and painstaking, the intellectualists more offhand and irreflective. The popular notion is that a true idea must copy its reality. Like other popular views, this one follows the analogy of the most usual experience. Our true ideas of sensible things do indeed copy them. Shut your eyes and think of yonder clock on the wall, and you get just such a true picture or copy of its dial. But your idea of its "works" (unless you are a clock-maker) is much less of a copy, yet it passes muster, for it in no way clashes with the reality. Even though it should shrink to the mere word "works," that word still serves you truly; and when you speak of the "time-keeping function" of the clock, or of its spring's "elasticity," it is hard to see exactly what your ideas can copy.

You perceive that there is a problem here. Where our ideas cannot copy definitely their object, what does agreement with that object mean? Some idealists seem to say that they are true whenever they are what God means that we ought to think about that object. Others hold the copy-view all through, and speak as if our ideas possessed truth just in proportion as they approach to being copies of the Absolute's eternal way of thinking.

These views, you see, invite pragmatistic discussion. But the great assumption of the intellectualists is that truth means essentially an inert static relation. When you've got your true idea of anything, there's an end of the matter. You're in possession; you *know;* you have fulfilled your thinking destiny. You are where you ought to be mentally; you have obeyed your categorical imperative; and nothing more need follow on that climax of your rational destiny. Epistemologically you are in stable equilibrium.

Pragmatism, on the other hand, asks its usual question. "Grant an idea or belief to be true," it says, "what concrete difference will its being true make in anyone's actual life? How will the truth be realized? What experiences will be different from those which would obtain if the belief were false? What, in short, is the truth's cash-value in experiential terms?"

The moment pragmatism asks this question, it sees the answer: *True ideas are those that we can assimilate, validate, corroborate and verify. False ideas are those that we cannot.* That is the practical difference it makes to us to have true ideas; that, therefore, is the meaning of truth, for it is all that truth is known as.

This thesis is what I have to defend. The truth of an idea is not a stagnant property inherent in it. Truth *happens* to an idea. It *becomes* true, is *made* true by events. Its verity *is* in fact an event, a process: the process namely of its verifying itself, its veri-*fication*. Its validity is the process of its valid-*ation*.

But what do the words verification and validation themselves pragmatically mean? They again signify certain practical consequences of the verified and validated idea. It is hard to find any one phrase that characterized these consequences better than the ordinary agreement-formula—just such consequences being what we have in mind whenever we say that our ideas "agree" with reality. They lead us, namely, through the acts and other ideas which they instigate, into or up to, or towards, other parts of experience with which we feel all the while—such feeling being among our potentialities—that the original ideas remain in agreement. The connections and transitions come to use from point to point as being progressive, harmonious, satisfactory. This function of agreeable leading is what we mean by an idea's verification. . . .

. . . The possession of true thoughts means everywhere the possession of invaluable instruments of action; and . . . our duty to gain truth, so far from being a blank command from out of the blue, or a "stunt" self-imposed by our intellect, can account for itself by excellent practical reasons.

The importance to human life of having true beliefs about matters of fact is a thing too notorious. We live in a world of realities that can be infinitely useful or infinitely harmful. Ideas that tell us which of them to expect count as the true ideas in all this primary sphere of verification, and the pursuit of such ideas is a primary human duty. The possession of truth, so far from being here an end in itself, is only a preliminary means towards other vital satisfactions. If I am lost in the woods and starved, and find what looks like a cow-path, it is of the utmost importance that I should think of a human habitation at the end of it, for if I do so and follow it, I save myself. The true thought is useful here because the house which is its object is useful. The practical value of true ideas is thus primarily derived from the practical importance of their objects to us. Their objects are, indeed, not important at all times. I may on another occasion have no use for the house; and then my idea of it, however verifiable, will be practically irrelevant, and had better remain latent. Yet since almost any object may some day become temporarily important, the advantage of having a general stock of *extra* truths, of ideas that shall be true of merely possible situations, is obvious. We store such extra truths away in our memories, and with the overflow we fill our books of reference. Whenever such an extra truth becomes practically relevant to one of our emergencies, it passes from cold-storage to do work in the world and our belief in it grows active. You can say of it then either that "it is useful because it is true" or that "it is true because it is useful." Both these phrases mean exactly the same thing, namely that here is an idea that gets fulfilled and can be verified. True is the name for whatever idea starts the verification-process, useful is the name for its completed function in experience. True ideas would never have been singled out as such, would never have acquired a class-name, least of all a name suggesting value, unless they had been useful from the outset in this way.

From this simple cue pragmatism gets her general notion of truth as something essentially bound up with the way in which one moment in our experience may lead us towards other moments which it will be worthwhile to have been led to. Primarily, and on the common-sense level, the truth of a state of mind means this function of *a leading that is worthwhile.* When a moment in our experience, of any kind whatever, inspires us with a thought that is true, that means that sooner or later we dip by that thought's guidance into the particulars of experience again and make advantageous connection with them. This is a vague enough statement, but I beg you to retain it, for it is essential.

Our experience meanwhile is all shot through with regularities. One bit of it can warn us to get ready for another bit, can "intend" or be "significant of" that remoter object. The object's advent is the significance's verification. Truth, in these cases, meaning nothing but eventual verification, is manifestly incompatible with waywardness on our part. Woe to him whose beliefs play fast and loose with the order which realities follow in his experience; they will lead him nowhere or else make false connections.

By "realities" or "objects" here, we mean either things of common sense, sensibly present, or else common-sense relations, such as dates, places, distances, kinds, activities. Following our mental image of a house along the cow-path, we actually come to see the house; we get the image's full verification. *Such simply and fully verified leadings are certainly the originals and prototypes of the truth-process.* Experience offers indeed other forms of truth-process, but they are all conceivable as being primary verifications arrested, multiplied or substituted one for another.

Take, for instance, yonder object on the wall. You and I consider it to be a "clock," altho no one of us has seen the hidden works that make it one. We let our notion pass for true without attempting to verify. If truths mean verification-process essentially, ought we then to call such unverified truths as this abortive? No, for they form the overwhelmingly large number of the truths we live by. Indirect as well as direct verifications pass muster. Where circumstantial evidence is sufficient, we can go without eye-witnessing. Just as we here assume Japan to exist without ever having been there, because it *works* to do so, everything we know conspiring with the belief, and nothing interfering, so we assume that thing to be a clock. We *use* it as a clock, regulating the length of our lecture by it. The verification of the assumption here means its leading to no frustration or contradiction. Verifi-*ability* of wheels and weights and pendulum is as good as verification. For one truth-process completed there are a million in our lives that function in this state of nascency. They turn us *towards* direct verification; lead us into the *surroundings* of the objects they envisage; and then, if everything runs on harmoniously, we are so sure that verification is possible that we omit it, and are usually justified by all that happens.

Truth lives, in fact, for the most part on a credit system. Our thoughts and beliefs "pass," so long as nothing challenges them, just as bank-notes pass so long as nobody refuses them. But this all points to direct face-to-face verifications somewhere, without which the fabric of truth collapses like a financial system with no cash-basis whatever. You accept my verification of one thing, I yours of another. We trade on each other's truth. But beliefs verified concretely by *somebody* are the posts of the whole superstructure.

Another great reason—beside economy of time—for waiving complete verification in the usual business of life is that all things exist in kinds and not singly. Our world is found once for all to have that peculiarity. So that when we have once directly verified our ideas about one specimen of a kind, we consider ourselves free to apply them to other specimens without verification. A mind that habitually discerns the kind of thing before it, and acts by the law of the kind immediately, without pausing to verify, will be a "true" mind in ninety-nine out of a hundred emergencies, proved so by its conduct fitting everything it meets, and getting no refutation.

Indirectly or only potentially verifying processes may thus be true as well as full verification-processes. They work as true processes would work, give us the same advantages, and claim our recognition for the same reasons. . . .

II

Our account of truth is an account of truths in the plural, of processes of leading, realized *in rebus,*[1] and having only this quality in common, that they *pay.* They pay by guiding us into or towards some part of a system that dips at numerous points into sense-percepts, which we may copy mentally or not, but with which at any rate we are now in the kind of commerce vaguely designated as verification. Truth for us is simply a collective name for verification-processes, just as health, wealth, strength, etc., are names for other processes connected with life, and also pursued because it pays to pursue them. Truth is made, just as health, wealth and strength are *made,* in the course of experience.

Here rationalism is instantaneously up in arms against us. I can imagine a rationalist to talk as follows:

"Truth is not made," he will say; "it absolutely obtains, being a unique relation that does not wait upon any process, but shoots straight over the head of experience, and hits its reality every time. Our belief that yon thing on the wall is a clock is true already, altho no one in the whole history of the world should verify it. The bare quality of standing in that transcendent relation is what makes any thought true that possesses it, whether or not there be verification. You pragmatists put the cart before the horse in making truth's being reside in verification-processes. These are merely signs of its being, merely our lame ways of ascertaining after the fact which of our ideas already has possessed the wondrous quality. The quality itself is timeless, like all essences and natures. Thoughts partake of it directly, as they partake of falsity or of irrelevancy. It can't be analyzed away into pragmatic consequences."

[1] In things. [ED.]

The whole plausibility of this rationalist tirade is due to the fact to which we have already paid so much attention. In our world, namely, abounding as it does in things of similar kinds and similarly associated, one verification serves for others of its kind, and one great use of knowing things is to be led not so much to them as to their associates, especially to human talk about them. The quality of truth, obtaining *ante rem,*[2] pragmatically means, then, the fact that in such a world innumerable ideas work better by their indirect or possible than by their direct and actual verification. Truth *ante rem* means only verifiability, then; or else it is a case of the stock rationalist trick of treating the *name* of a concrete phenomenal reality as an independent prior entity, and placing it behind the reality as its explanation. . . .

In the case of "wealth" we all see the fallacy. We know that wealth is but a name for concrete processes that certain men's lives play a part in, and not a natural excellence found in Messrs. Rockefeller and Carnegie, but not in the rest of us.

Like wealth, health also lives *in rebus.* It is a name for processes, as digestion, circulation, sleep, etc., that go on happily, tho in this instance we are more inclined to think of it as a principle and to say that man digests and sleeps so well *because* he is so healthy.

With "strength" we are, I think, more rationalistic still, and decidedly inclined to treat it as an excellence pre-existing in the man and explanatory of the herculean performances of his muscles.

With "truth" most people go over the border entirely, and treat the rationalistic account as self-evident. But really all these words in *truth* are exactly similar. Truth exists *ante rem* just as much and as little as the other things do.

The scholastics, following Aristotle, made much of the distinction between habit and act. Health *in actu*[3] means, among other things, good sleeping and digesting. But a healthy man need not always be sleeping, or always digesting, any more than a wealthy man need be always handling money, or a strong man always lifting weights. All such qualities sink to the status of "habits" between their times of exercise; and similarly truth becomes a habit of certain of our ideas and beliefs in their intervals of rest from their verifying activities. But those activities are the root of the whole matter, and the condition of there being any habit to exist in the intervals.

"The true," to put it very briefly, is only the expedient in the way of our thinking, just as "the right" is only the expedient in the way of our behaving. Expedient in almost any fashion; and expedient in the long run and on the whole of course; for what meets expediently all the experience in sight won't necessarily meet all farther experiences equally satisfactorily. Experience, as we know, has ways of *boiling over,* and making us correct our present formulas.

The "absolutely" true, meaning what no farther experience will ever alter, is that ideal vanishing-point towards which we imagine that all our temporary truths will some day converge. It runs on all fours with the perfectly wise man, and with the absolutely complete experience; and, if these ideals are ever realized, they will all be

---

[2] Before the thing. [ED.]

[3] In actuality. [ED.]

realized together. Meanwhile we have to live today by what truth we can get today, and be ready tomorrow to call it falsehood. Ptolemaic astronomy, Euclidean space, Aristotelian logic, scholastic metaphysics, were expedient for centuries, but human experience has boiled over those limits, and we now call these things only relatively true, or true within those borders of experience. "Absolutely" they are false; for we know that those limits were causal, and might have been transcended by past theorists just as they are by present thinkers. . . .

III

. . . Truth is *one species of good,* and not, as is usually supposed, a category distinct from good, and coordinate with it. *The true is the name of whatever prove itself to be good in the way of belief, and good, too, for definite, assignable reasons.* Surely you must admit this, that if there were *no* good for life in true ideas, or if the knowledge of them were positively disadvantageous and false ideas the only useful ones, then the current notion that truth is divine and precious, and its pursuit a duty, could never have grown up or become a dogma. In a world like that, our duty would be to *shun* truth, rather. But in this world, just as certain foods are not only agreeable to our taste, but good for our teeth, our stomach, and our tissues; so certain ideas are not only agreeable to think about, or agreeable as supporting other ideas that we are fond of, but they are also helpful in life's practical struggles. If there be any life that it is really better we should lead, and if there be any idea which, if believed in, would help us to lead that life, then it would be really *better for us* to believe in that idea, *unless, indeed, belief in it incidentally clashed with other greater vital benefits.*

"What would be better for us to believe!" This sounds very like a definition of truth. It comes very near to saying "what we *ought* to believe": and in *that* definition none of you would find any oddity. Ought we ever not to believe what it is *better for us* to believe? And can we then keep the notion of what is better for us, and what is true for us, permanently apart?

Pragmatism says no, and I fully agree with her. Probably you also agree so far as the abstract statement goes, but with a suspicion that if we practically did believe everything that made for good in our own personal lives, we should be found indulging all kinds of fancies about this world's affairs, and all kinds of sentimental superstitions about a world hereafter. Your suspicion here is undoubtedly well founded, and it is evident that something happens when you pass from the abstract to the concrete that complicates the situation.

I said just now that what is better for us to believe is true *unless the belief incidentally clashes with some other vital benefit.* Now in real life what vital benefits is any particular belief of ours most liable to clash with? What indeed except the vital benefits yielded by *other beliefs* when these *prove* incompatible with the first ones? In other words, the greatest enemy of any one of our truths may be the rest of our truths. Truths have once for all this desperate instinct of self-preservation and of desire to extinguish whatever contradicts them. . . .

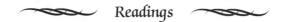

To Think About

1. "We do not want a thing because we reason; we find reasons for a thing because we want it. Mind invents logic for the whims of the will."   ***G. W. F. Hegel***

2. "You will never succeed in getting at the truth if you think you know, ahead of time, what the truth ought to be."   ***Marchette Chute***

3. "What is Truth but to live for an idea? . . . It is a question of discovering a truth which is truth *for me,* of finding the idea for which I am willing to live and die."   ***Søren Kierkegaard***

4. "When men have realized that time has upset many fighting faiths, they may come to believe even more than they believe the very foundations of their own conduct that the ultimate good desired is better reached by free trade in ideas— that the best test of truth is the power of the thought to get itself accepted in the competition of the market."   ***Oliver Wendell Holmes, Jr.***

Readings

Dummett, Michael. "Truth." *Proceedings of the Aristotelian Society* 45 (1958–59): 141–62.

Ezorsky, Gertrude. "Truth in Context." *Journal of Philosophy* 60 (1963): 113–35.

Kaufmann, Felix. "Three Meanings of 'Truth.' " *Journal of Philosophy* 45 (1948): 337–50.

Murphy, Arthur E. "The Pragmatic Theory of Truth." In *The Uses of Reason,* 85–95. New York: Macmillan, 1943.

Pepper, Stephen. "The Utter Skeptic," ch. 1; "Dogmatists," ch. 2. In *World Hypotheses: A Study in Evidence.* Los Angeles: University of California Press, 1942.

Russell, Bertrand. "Fact, Belief, Truth, and Knowledge." In *Human Knowledge: Its Scope and Limits, Part II.* New York: Simon & Schuster, 1948.

32
Cause Means Regular Association

David Hume (1711–72) was a British philosopher, historian, and essayist whose views on causality stimulated Kant to construct his "critical philosophy." Noted for his development of the empiricism of Locke and Berkeley and for his skepticism, he wrote Treatise on Human Nature *(1739).*

There are many views concerning the relationship of cause and effect. One of the most famous, represented by Hume, states that two events are causally related if the three following conditions are satisfied: (1) the two events are spatially contiguous; (2) one event precedes the other; (3) these two events have been associated in such spatial and temporal conditions many times. Thus if one says that smoking causes cancer, one means that smoking and cancer are spatially contiguous, that smoking precedes cancer, and that there are many cases of smoking being associated with cancer. Given such an example, Hume would deny that there is any necessary connection between smoking and cancer and that there is an impression of any necessary connection between the two events. Hence, the ordinary belief that one event necessarily causes the second is false.

 To Study

1. What is Hume trying to illustrate by the example of the billiard balls?
2. What is the difference between the "will" and the example of the billiard balls?
3. What three arguments does Hume give against the idea of "willing" proving the idea of power or necessary connection?
4. How does Hume believe the idea of necessary connection arises among events?
5. How does he define *cause*?

From David Hume, *An Enquiry Concerning Human Understanding* (Oxford: Clarendon Press, 1748), sections 7 and 5.

Part I

There are no ideas which occur in metaphysics more obscure and uncertain than those of *power, force, energy or necessary connexion,* of which it is every moment necessary for us to treat in all our disquisitions. We shall, therefore, endeavor in this section to fix, if possible, the precise meaning of these terms, and thereby remove some part of that obscurity which is so much complained of in this species of philosophy.

It seems a proposition which will not admit of much dispute, that all our ideas are nothing but copies of our impressions, or, in other words, that it is impossible for us to *think* of any thing, which we have not antecedently *felt,* either by our external or internal senses. . . . To be fully acquainted, therefore, with the idea of power or necessary connexion, let us examine its impression with greater certainty, let us search for it in all the sources, from which it may possibly be derived.

When we look about us towards external objects, and consider the operation of causes, we are never able, in a single instance, to discover any power or necessary connexion; [that is,] any quality which binds the effect to the cause and renders the one an infallible consequence of the other. We only find that the one does actually, in fact, follow the other. The impulse of one billiard-ball is attended with motion in the second. This is the whole that appears to the *outward* senses. The mind feels no sentiment or *inward* impression from this succession of objects: Consequently, there is not, in any single, particular instance of cause and effect, any thing which can suggest the idea of power or necessary connexion.

From the first appearance of an object, we never can conjecture what effect will result from it. But were the power or energy of any cause discoverable by the mind, we could foresee the effect even without experience, and might, at first, pronounce with certainty concerning it, by mere dint of thought and reasoning.

In reality, there is no part of matter that does ever, by its sensible qualities, discover any power or energy, or give us ground to imagine, that it could produce any thing, or be followed by any other object, which we could denominate its effect. Solidity, extension, motion; these qualities are all complete in themselves, and never point out any other event which may result from them. The scenes of the universe are continually shifting, and one object follows another in an uninterrupted succession; but the power or force which actuates the whole machine is entirely concealed from us, and never discovers itself in any of the sensible qualities of body. We know, that, in fact, heat is a constant attendant of flame; but what is the connexion between them, we have no room so much as to conjecture or imagine. It is impossible, therefore, that the idea of power can be derived from the contemplation of bodies, in single instances of their operation; because no bodies ever discover any power which can be the original of this idea.

Since, therefore, external objects as they appear to the senses give us no idea of power or necessary connexion by their operation in particular instances, let us see whether this idea be derived from reflection on the operations of our own minds, and be copied from any internal impression. It may be said that we are every moment conscious of internal power; while we feel, that, by the simple command of our will, we can move the organs of our body, or direct the faculties of our mind. An act of volition produces motion in our limbs, or raises a new idea in our imagination. This influence of the will we know by consciousness. Hence we acquire the idea of power or energy, and are certain that we ourselves and all other intelligent beings are possessed of power. . . .

We shall proceed to examine this pretension; and first with regard to the influence of volition over the organs of the body. This influence, we may observe, is a fact, which, like all other natural events, can be known only by experience, and can never be foreseen from any apparent energy or power in the cause, which connects it with the effect, and renders the one an infallible consequence of the other. The motion of our body follows upon the command of our will. Of this we are every moment conscious. But the means by which this is effected, the energy by which the will performs so extraordinary an operation, of this we are so far from being immediately conscious that it must for ever escape our most diligent enquiry.

For *first,* is there any principle in all nature more mysterious than the union of soul with body, by which a supposed spiritual substance acquires such an influence over a material one that the most refined thought is able to actuate the grossest matter? Were we empowered, by a secret wish, to remove mountains, or control the planets in their orbit; this extensive authority would not be more extraordinary, nor more beyond our comprehension. But if by consciousness we perceived any power or energy in the will, we must know this power; we must know its connexion with the effect; we must know the secret union of soul and body, and the nature of both these substances, by which the one is able to operate, in so many instances, upon the other.

Secondly, We are not able to move all the organs of the body with a like authority; though we cannot assign any reason besides experience for so remarkable a difference between one and the other. Why has the will an influence over the tongue and fingers, not over the heart or liver? This question would never embarrass us were we conscious of a power in the former case, not in the latter. . . .

Thirdly, We learn from anatomy that the immediate object of power in voluntary motion is not the member itself which is moved, but certain muscles, and nerves, and animal spirits, and, perhaps, something still more minute and more unknown, through which the motion is successively propagated, ere it reach the member itself whose motion is the immediate object of volition. Can there be a more certain proof that the power by which this whole operation is performed, so far from being directly and fully known by an inward sentiment or consciousness, is, to the last degree, mysterious and unintelligible? Here the mind wills a certain event: Immediately another event, unknown to ourselves, and totally different from the one intended, is produced: This event produces another, equally unknown: Till at last, through a long succession, the desired event is produced. But if the original power were felt, it must be known: Were it known, its effect also must be known; since all power is relative to its effect. And *vice versa,* if the effect be not known, the power cannot be known nor felt. How indeed can we be conscious of a power to move our limbs when we have no such power; but only that to move certain animal spirits, which, though they produce at last the motion of our limbs, yet operate in such a manner as is wholly beyond our comprehension?

We may, therefore, conclude . . . that our idea of power is not copied from any sentiment or consciousness of power within ourselves, when we give rise to animal motion, or apply our limbs to their proper use and office. That their motion follows the command of the will is a matter of common experience, like other natural events: But the power or energy by which this is effected, like that in other natural events, is unknown and inconceivable. . . .

The generality of mankind never finds any difficulty in accounting for the more common and familiar operations of nature—such as the descent of heavy bodies, the growth of plants, the generation of animals, or the nourishment of bodies by food: But suppose that, in all these cases, they perceive the very force or energy of the cause, by which it is connected with its effect, and is for ever infallible in its operation. They acquire, by long habit such a turn of mind that, upon the appearance of the cause, they immediately expect with assurance its usual attendant, and hardly conceive it possible that any other event could result from it. It is only on the discovery of extraordinary phenomena, such as earthquakes, pestilence, and prodigies of any kind, that they find themselves at a loss to assign a proper cause, and to explain the manner in which the effect is produced by it. It is usual for men, in such difficulties, to have recourse to some invisible intelligent principle as the immediate cause of that event which surprises them, and which, they think, cannot be accounted for from the common powers of nature. But philosophers, who carry their scrutiny a little farther, immediately perceive that, even, in the most familiar events, the energy of the cause is as unintelligible as in the most unusual, and that we only learn by experience the frequent *Conjunction* of objects, without being ever able to comprehend anything like *Connexion* between them. . . .

PART II

But to hasten a conclusion of this argument, which is already drawn out to too great a length: We have sought in vain for an idea of power or necessary connexion in all the sources from which we could suppose it to be derived. It appears that, in single instances of the operation of bodies, we never can, by our utmost scrutiny, discover any thing but one event following another, without being able to comprehend any force or power by which the cause operates, or any connexion between it and its supposed effect. The same difficulty occurs in contemplating the operations of mind on body— where we observe the motion of the latter to follow upon the volition of the former, but are not able to observe or conceive the tie which binds together the motion and volition, or the energy by which the mind produces this effect. The authority of the will over its own faculties and ideas is not a whit more comprehensible: So that, upon the whole, there appears not, throughout all nature, any one instance of connexion which is conceivable by us. All events seem entirely loose and separate. One event follows another; but we never can observe any tie between them. They seem *conjoined,* but never *connected.* And as we can have no idea of anything which never appeared to our outward sense or inward sentiment, the necessary conclusion *seems* to be that we have no idea of connexion or power at all, and that these words are absolutely nothing without any meaning, when employed either in philosophical reasonings or common life.

But there still remains one method of avoiding this conclusion, and one source which we have not yet examined. When any natural object or event is presented, it is impossible for us, by any sagacity or penetration, to discover, or even conjecture, without experience, what event will result from it, or to carry our foresight beyond that object which is immediately present to the memory and senses. Even after one instance or experiment where we have observed a particular event to follow upon another, we are not entitled to form a general rule, or foretell what will happen in like cases; it being justly esteemed an unpardonable temerity to judge of the whole course of nature from one single experiment, however accurate or certain. But when one particular species of event has always, in all instances, been conjoined with another, we make no longer any scruple of foretelling one upon the appearance of the other, and of employing that reasoning, which can alone assure us of any matter of fact or existence. We then call the one object, *Cause;* the other, *Effect.* We suppose that there is some connexion between them; some power in the one, by which it infallibly produces the other, and operates with the greatest certainty and strongest necessity.

It appears, then, that this idea of a necessary connexion among events arises from a number of similar instances which occur of the constant conjunction of these events; nor can that idea ever be suggested by any one of these instances, surveyed in all possible lights and positions. But there is nothing in a number of instances different from every single instance which is supposed to be exactly similar, except only that after a repetition of similar instances, the mind is carried by habit, upon the appearance of one event, to expect its usual attendant, and to believe that it will exist. This connexion, therefore, which we *feel* in the mind, this customary transition of the imagination from one object to its usual attendant, is the sentiment or impression from which we form the idea of power or necessary connexion. Nothing farther is in the case. Contemplate the subject on all sides; you will never find any other origin of that idea. This is the sole difference between one instance, from which we can never receive the idea of connexion, and a number of similar instances, by which it is suggested. The first time a man saw the communication of motion by impulse, as by the shock of two billiard balls, he could not pronounce that the one event was *connected:* but only that it was *conjoined* with the other. After he has observed several instances of this nature, he then pronounces them to be *connected.* What alteration has happened to give rise to this new idea of *connexion?* Nothing but that he now *feels* these events to be *connected* in his imagination, and can readily foretell the existence of one from the appearance of the other. When we say, therefore, that one object is connected with another, we mean only that they have acquired a connexion in our thought, and give rise to this inference, by which they become proofs of each other's existence: A conclusion which is somewhat extraordinary, but which seems founded on sufficient evidence. Nor will its evidence be weakened by any general diffidence on the understanding, or sceptical suspicion concerning every conclusion which is new and extraordinary. No conclusions can be more agreeable to scepticism than such as make discoveries concerning the weakness and narrow limits of human reason and capacity.

And what stronger instance can be produced of the surprising ignorance and weakness of the understanding than the present? For surely, if there be any relation among objects which it imports to us to know perfectly, it is that of cause and effect.

On this are founded all our reasonings concerning matter of fact or existence. By means of it alone we attain any assurance concerning objects which are removed from the present testimony of our memory and senses. The only immediate utility of all sciences, is to teach us how to control and regulate future events by their causes. Our thoughts and enquiries are, therefore, every moment employed about this relation: Yet so imperfect are the ideas which we form concerning it that it is impossible to give any just definition of cause, except what is drawn from something extraneous and foreign to it. Similar objects are always conjoined with similar. Of this we have experience. Suitably to this experience, therefore, we may define a cause to be *an object, followed by another, and where all the objects similar to the first are followed by objects similar to the second.* Or in other words, *where, if the first object had not been, the second never had existed.* The appearance of a cause always conveys the mind, by a customary transition, to the idea of the effect. Of this also we have experience. We may, therefore, suitably to this experience, form another definition of cause, and call it *an object followed by another, and whose appearance always conveys the thought to that other.* But though both these definitions be drawn from circumstances foreign to the cause, we cannot remedy this inconvenience, or attain any more perfect definition, which may point out that circumstance in the cause which gives it a connexion with its effect. We have no idea of this connexion, nor even any distinct notion what it is we desire to know, where we endeavor at a conception of it. We say, for instance, that the vibration of this string is the cause of this particular sound. But what do we mean by that affirmation? We either mean *that this vibration is followed by this sound, and that all similar vibrations have been followed by similar sounds: Or, that this vibration is followed by this sound, and that upon the appearance of one the mind anticipates the senses, and forms immediately an idea of the other.* We may consider the relation of cause and effect in either of these two lights; but beyond these, we have no idea of it.

To recapitulate, therefore, the reasonings of this section: Every idea is copied from some preceding impression or sentiment; and where we cannot find any impression, we may be certain that there is no idea at all. In all single instances of the operation of bodies or minds, there is nothing that produces any impression, nor consequently can suggest any idea of power or necessary connexion. But when many uniform instances appear, and the same object is always followed by the same event, we then begin to entertain the notion of cause and connexion. We then *feel* a new sentiment or impression, to wit, a customary connexion in the thought or imagination between one object and its usual attendant; and this sentiment is the original of that idea which we seek for. For as this idea arises from a number of similar instances, and not from any single instance, it must arise from that circumstance in which the number of instances differ from every individual instance. But this customary connexion or transition of the imagination is the only circumstance in which they differ. In every other particular they are alike. The first instance which we saw of motion communicated by the shock of two billiard balls (to return to this obvious illustration) is exactly similar to any instance that may, at present, occur to us; except only that we could not, at first, *infer* one event from the other; which we enabled to do at present after so long a course of uniform experience.

1. "In contrast to Hume, Whitehead claims that we have many daily experiences in which we are directly aware of causal connection. He uses the famous example of the reflex action in which an electric light is suddenly turned on and a person's eyes blink. The person is directly aware that the flash caused the blink; a necessary relationship exists between the light and the blink. With this doctrine, Whitehead directly attacks Hume's influential theory of causation."

    James Gould

2. "Whoever has taken the pains to refute the cavils of this *total* scepticism, has really disputed without an antagonist, and endeavour'd by arguments to establish a faculty, which nature has antecedently implanted in the mind, and renders unavoidable."   ***David Hume***

3. "The supposition of recurrence is thus wholly irrelevant to the meaning of cause; that supposition is relevant only to the meaning of law. And recurrence becomes related at all to causation only when a law is considered which happens to be a generalization of facts themselves individually causal to begin with. A general proposition concerning such facts is, indeed, a causal law, but it is not causal because general. It is general, that is, a law, only because it is about a class of resembling facts; and it is causal only because each of them already happens to be a causal fact individually and in its own right (instead of, as Hume would have it, by right of its co-membership with others in a class of pairs of successive events)."   ***Curt Ducasse***

33
There Are No Possible Grounds for Induction

David Hume (1711–76) was a British philosopher, historian, and essayist whose views on causality stimulated Kant to construct his "critical philosophy."

The problem of induction is related to the consideration of causality. Causality involves the definition of *cause,* while induction involves the presence of a causal relationship. For example, when we say that smoking causes cancer, how do we know? How can we prove it? The usual reply is that because smoking has been accompanied by cancer in the past, we can assume that it will be accompanied by cancer in the future. We thus presuppose that *nature is uniform.* Hume would argue that a causal relationship between events can never be proved because there is no way to establish the uniformity of nature. According to Hume, such proof is nothing but the *habit* of expecting what has happened in the past to happen again in similar circumstances.

⁓⁓ To Study ⁓⁓

1. Into what two types are all objects of human reason divided? How are they distinguished from one another?
2. What then is the subject of Hume's inquiry?
3. On what are all reasonings concerning fact based?
4. What is the significance of the example of the two smooth pieces of marble?
5. Explain: "The mind can never possibly find the effect in the supposed cause."
6. What are the two kinds of reasonings?
7. Upon what are all arguments from experience founded?
8. On what do we base belief in cause-and-effect relations?
9. What is Hume's conclusion concerning the whole matter?

From David Hume, *An Enquiry Concerning Human Understanding* (Oxford: Clarendon Press, 1748).

SECTION IV
SCEPTICAL DOUBTS CONCERNING THE OPERATIONS OF THE UNDERSTANDING

Part I

All the objects of human reason or inquiry may naturally be divided into two kinds, to wit, *Relations of Ideas,* and *Matters of Fact.* Of the first kind are the sciences of Geometry, Algebra, and Arithmetic; and in short, every affirmation which is either intuitively or demonstratively certain. *That the square of the hypothenuse is equal to the square of the two sides,* is a proposition which expresses a relation between these figures. *That three times five is equal to the half of thirty,* expresses a relation between these numbers. Propositions of this kind are discoverable by the mere operation of thought, without dependence on what is anywhere existent in the universe. Though there never were a circle or triangle in nature, the truths demonstrated by Euclid would forever retain their certainty and evidence.

Matters of fact, which are the second objects of human reason, are not ascertained in the same manner; nor is our evidence of their truth, however great, of a like nature with the foregoing. The contrary of every matter of fact is still possible because it can never imply a contradiction, and is conceived by the mind with the same facility and distinctness as if ever so conformable to reality. *That the sun will not rise tomorrow* is no less intelligible a proposition, and implies no more contradiction than the affirmation *that it will rise.* We should in vain, therefore, attempt to demonstrate its falsehood. Were it demonstratively false, it would imply a contradiction and could never be distinctly conceived by the mind.

It may, therefore, be a subject worthy of curiosity to inquire what is the nature of that evidence which assures us of any real existence and matter of fact beyond the present testimony of our senses or the records of our memory. This part of philosophy, it is observable, has been little cultivated, either by the ancients or moderns; and, therefore, our doubts and errors in the prosecution of so important an inquiry may be the more excusable, while we march through such difficult paths without any guide or direction. They may even prove useful by exciting curiosity and destroying that implicit faith and security which is the bane of all reasoning and free inquiry. The discovery of defects in the common philosophy, if any such there be, will not, I presume, be a discouragement, but rather an incitement, as is usual, to attempt something more full and satisfactory than has yet been proposed to the public.

All reasonings concerning matter of fact seem to be founded on the relation of *Cause and Effect.* By means of that relation alone we can go beyond the evidence of our memory and senses. If you were to ask a man why he believes any matter of fact which is absent, for instance, that his friend is in the country or in France, he would give you a reason; and this reason would be some other fact; as a letter received from him, or the knowledge of his former resolutions and promises. A man finding a watch or any other machine in a desert island would conclude that there had once been men on that island. All our reasonings concerning fact are of the same nature. And here it is constantly supposed that there is a connection between the present fact and that which is inferred from it. Were there nothing to bind them together, the inference would be entirely precarious. The hearing of an articulate voice and rational discourse in the dark assures us of the presence of some person: Why? because these are the effects of the human make and fabric, and closely connected with it. If we anatomize all the other reasonings of this nature, we shall find that they are founded on the relation of cause and effect, and that this relation is either near or remote, direct or collateral. Heat and light are collateral effects of fire, and the one effect may justly be inferred from the other.

If we would satisfy ourselves, therefore, concerning the nature of that evidence which assures us of matters of fact we must inquire how we arrive at the knowledge of cause and effect.

I shall venture to affirm, as a general proposition, which admits of no exception, that the knowledge of this relation is not, in any instance, attained by reasonings *a priori;* but arises entirely from experience, when we find that any particular objects are constantly conjoined with each other. Let an object be presented to a man of ever so strong natural reason and abilities; if that object be entirely new to him, he will not be able, by the most accurate examination of its sensible qualities, to discover any of its causes or effects. Adam, though his rational faculties be supposed, at the very first, entirely perfect, could not have inferred from the fluidity and transparency of water that it would suffocate him, or from the light and warmth of fire that it would consume him. No object ever discovers, by the qualities which appear to the senses, either the causes which produced it, or the effects which will arise from it; nor can our reason, unassisted by experience, ever draw any inference concerning real existence and matter of fact.

This proposition, *that causes and effects are discoverable, not by reason but by experience,* will readily be admitted with regard to such objects as we remember to have once been altogether unknown to us, since we must be conscious of the utter inability, which we then lay under, of foretelling what would arise from them. Present two smooth pieces of marble to a man who has no tincture of natural philosophy; he will never discover that they will adhere together in such a manner as to require great force to separate them in a direct line, while they make so small a resistance to a lateral pressure. Such events, as bear little analogy to the common course of nature, are also readily confessed to be known only by experience; nor does any man imagine that the explosion of gun-powder, or the attraction of a loadstone, could ever be discovered by arguments *a priori*. In like manner, when an effect is supposed to depend upon an intricate machinery or secret structure of parts, we make no difficulty in attributing all our knowledge of it to experience. Who will assert that he can give the ultimate reason why milk or bread is proper nourishment for a man, not for a lion or a tiger?

But the same truth may not appear, at first sight, to have the same evidence with regard to events, which have become familiar to us from our first appearance in the world, which bear a close analogy to the whole course of nature, and which are supposed to depend on the simple qualities of objects, without any secret structure of parts. We are apt to imagine that we could discover these effects by the mere operation of our reason, without experience. We fancy, that were we brought on a sudden into this world, we could at first have inferred that one billiard ball would communicate motion to another upon impulse; and that we needed not to have waited for the event, in order to pronounce with certainty concerning it. Such is the influence of custom, that, where it is strongest, it not only covers our natural ignorance, but even conceals itself, and seems not to take place, merely because it is found in the highest degree.

But to convince us that all the laws of nature, and all the operations of bodies without exception, are known only by experience, the following reflections may, perhaps, suffice. Were any object presented to us, and were we required to pronounce concerning the effect which will result from it, without consulting past observation, after what manner, I beseech you, must the mind proceed in this operation? It must invent or imagine some event, which it ascribes to the object as its effect; and it is plain that this invention must be entirely arbitrary. The mind can never possibly find the effect in the supposed cause, by the most accurate scrutiny and examination. For the effect is totally different from the cause, and consequently can never be discovered in it. Motion in the second billiard ball is a quite distinct event from motion in the first; nor is there anything in the one to suggest the smallest hint of the other. A stone or piece of metal raised into the air, and left without any support, immediately falls: but to consider the matter *a priori,* is there anything we discover in this situation which can beget the idea of a downward, rather than an upward, or any other motion, in the stone or metal?

And as the first imagination or invention of a particular effect, in all natural operations, is arbitrary, where we consult not experience; so must we also esteem the supposed tie or connection between the cause and effect, which binds them together, and renders it impossible that any other effect could result from the operation of that cause. When I see, for instance, a billiard ball moving in a straight line towards another: even suppose motion in the second ball should by accident be suggested to me, as the result of their contact or impulse; may I not conceive, that a hundred different events might as well follow from that cause? May not both these balls remain at absolute rest? May not the first ball return in a straight line, or leap off from the second in any line or direction? All these suppositions are consistent and conceivable. Why then should we give preference to one, which is no more consistent or conceivable than the rest? All our reasonings *a priori* will never be able to show us any foundation for this preference.

In a word, then, every effect is a distinct event from its cause. It could not, therefore, be discovered in the cause, and the first invention or conception of it, *a priori,* must be entirely arbitrary. And even after it is suggested, the conjunction of it with the cause must appear equally arbitrary; since there are always many other effects, which, to reason, must seem fully as consistent and natural. In vain, therefore, should we pretend to determine any single event, or infer any cause or effect, without the assistance of observation and experience.

Hence, we may discover the reason why no philosopher, who is rational and modest, has ever pretended to assign the ultimate cause of any natural operation, or to show distinctly the action of that power, which produces any single effect in the universe. It is confessed that the utmost effort of human reason is to reduce the principles, productive of natural phenomena, to a greater simplicity, and to resolve the many particular effects into a few general causes by means of reasonings from analogy, experience, and observation. But as to the causes of these general causes, we should in vain attempt their discovery; nor shall we ever be able to satisfy ourselves by any particular explication of them. These ultimate springs and principles are totally shut up from human curiosity and inquiry. Elasticity, gravity, cohesion of parts, communication of motion by impulse—these are probably the ultimate causes and principles which we shall ever discover in nature; and we may esteem ourselves sufficiently happy, if, by accurate inquiry and reasoning, we can trace up the particular phenomena to, or near to, these general principles. The most perfect philosophy of the natural kind only staves off our ignorance a little longer: as perhaps the most perfect philosophy of the moral or metaphysical kind serves only to discover larger portions of it. Thus the observation of human blindness and weakness is the result of all philosophy, and meets us at every turn, in spite of our endeavors to elude or avoid it.

Part II

But we have not yet attained any tolerable satisfaction with regard to the question first proposed. Each solution still gives rise to a new question as difficult as the foregoing, and leads us on to farther inquiries. When it is asked, *What is the nature of all our reasonings concerning matter of fact?* the proper answer seems to be, that they are founded on the relation of cause and effect. When again it is asked, *What is the foundation of all our reasonings and conclusions concerning that relation?* it may be replied in one word, Experience. But if we still carry on our sifting humor, and ask, *What is the foundation of all conclusions from experience?* this implies a new question, which may be of more difficult solution and explication. Philosophers, that give themselves airs of superior wisdom and sufficiency, have a hard task when they encounter persons of inquisitive dispositions, who push them from every corner to which they retreat, and who are sure at last to bring them to some dangerous dilemma. The best expedient to prevent this confusion is to be modest in our pretensions; and even to discover the difficulty ourselves before it is objected to us. By this means, we may make a kind of merit of our very ignorance.

I shall content myself, in this section, with an easy task, and shall pretend only to give a negative answer to the question here proposed. I say then, that, even after we have experience of the operations of cause and effect, our conclusions from that experience are *not* founded on reasoning, or any process of the understanding. This answer we must endeavor both to explain and to defend.

It must certainly be allowed that nature has kept us at a great distance from all her secrets, and has afforded us only the knowledge of a few superficial qualities of objects, while she conceals from us those powers and principles on which the influence of those objects entirely depends. Our senses inform us of the color, weight, and consistence of bread; but neither sense nor reason can ever inform us of those qualities which fit it for the nourishment and support of a human body. Sight or feeling conveys an idea of the actual motion of bodies; but as to that wonderful force or power, which would carry on a moving body forever in a continued change of place, and which bodies never lose but by communicating it to others; of this we cannot form the most distant conception. But notwithstanding this ignorance of natural powers and principles, we always presume, when we see like sensible qualities, that they have like secret powers, and expect that effects, similar to those which we have experienced, will follow from them. If a body of like color and consistence with that bread, which we have formerly eaten, be presented to us, we make no scruple of repeating the experiment, and foresee, with certainty, like nourishment and support. Now this is a process of the mind or thought, of which I would willingly know the foundation. It is allowed on all hands that there is no known connection between the sensible qualities and the secret powers; and consequently, that the mind is not led to form such a conclusion concerning their constant and regular conjunction, by anything which it knows of their nature. As to past *Experience,* it can be allowed to give *direct* and *certain* information of those precise objects only, and that precise period of time, which fell under its cognizance: but why this experience should be extended to future times, and to other objects, which for aught we know, may be only in appearance similar; this is the main question on which I would insist. The bread, which I formerly ate, nourished me; that is, a body of such sensible qualities was, at that time, endued with such secret powers: but does it follow, that other bread must also nourish me at another time, and that like sensible qualities must always be attended with like secret powers? The consequence seems nowise necessary. At least, it must be acknowledged that there is here a consequence drawn by the mind; that there is a certain step taken; a process of thought, and an inference, which wants to be explained. These two propositions are far from being the same; *I have found that such an object has always been attended with such an effect,* and *I forsee, that other objects, which are, in appearance, similar, will be attended with similar effects.* I shall allow, if you please, that the one proposition may justly be inferred from the other: I know, in fact, that it always is inferred. But if you insist that the inference is made by a chain of reasoning, I desire you to produce that reasoning. The connection between these propositions is not intuitive. There is required a medium, which may enable the mind to draw such an inference, if indeed it be drawn by reasoning and argument. What that medium is, I must confess, passes my comprehension; and it is incumbent on those to produce it, who assert that it really exists, and is the origin of all our conclusions concerning matter of fact.

This negative argument must certainly, in process of time, become altogether convincing, if many penetrating and able philosophers shall turn their inquiries this way and no one be ever able to discover any connecting proposition or intermediate step which supports the understanding in this conclusion. But as the question is yet new, every reader may not trust so far to his own penetration as to conclude, because an argument escapes his inquiry, that therefore it does not really exist. For this reason it may be requisite to venture upon a more difficult task; and, enumerating all the branches of human knowledge, endeavor to show that none of them can afford such an argument.

All reasonings may be divided into two kinds, namely, demonstrative reasoning, or that concerning relations of ideas, and moral reasoning, or that concerning matter of fact and existence. That there are no demonstrative arguments in the case seems evident; since it implies no contradiction that the course of nature may change, and that an object, seemingly like those which we have experienced, may be attended with different or contrary effects. May I not clearly and distinctly conceive that a body, falling from the clouds, and which, in all other respects, resembles snow, has yet the taste of salt or feeling of fire? Is there any more intelligible proposition than to affirm that all trees will flourish in December and January, and decay in May and June? Now whatever is intelligible, and can be distinctly conceived, implies no contradiction, and can never be proved false by any demonstrative argument or abstract reasoning *a priori.*

If we be, therefore, engaged by arguments to put trust in past experience, and make it the standard of our future judgment, these arguments must be probable only, or such as regard matter of fact and real existence, according to the division above mentioned. But, that there is no argument of this kind, must appear, if our explication of that species of reasoning be admitted as solid and satisfactory. We have said that all arguments concerning existence are founded on the relation of cause and effect; that our knowledge of that relation is derived entirely from experience; and that all our experimental conclusions proceed upon the supposition that the future will be conformable to the past. To endeavor, therefore, the proof of this last supposition by probable arguments, or arguments regarding existence, must be evidently going in a circle, and taking that for granted which is the very point in question.

In reality, all arguments from experience are founded on the similarity which we discover among natural objects, and by which we are induced to expect effects similar to those which we have found to follow from such objects. And though none but a fool or madman will ever pretend to dispute the authority of experience, or to reject that great guide of human life, it may surely be allowed a philosopher to have so much curiosity at least as to examine the principle of human nature, which gives this mighty authority to experience, and makes us draw advantage from that similarity which nature has placed among different objects. From causes which appear *similar* we expect similar effects. This is the sum of all our experimental conclusions. Now it seems evident that if this conclusion were formed by reason, it would be as perfect at first, and upon one instance, as after ever so long a course of experience. But the case is far otherwise. Nothing so like as eggs; yet no one, on account of this appearing similarity, expects the same taste and relish in all of them. It is only after a long course of uniform experiments in any kind, that we attain a firm reliance and security with regard to a particular event. Now where is that process of reasoning which, from one instance, draws a conclusion so different from that which it infers from a hundred instances that are nowise different from that single one? This question I propose as much for the sake of information, as with an intention of raising difficulties. I cannot find, I cannot imagine any such reasoning. But I keep my mind still open to instruction, if anyone will vouchsafe to bestow it on me.

Should it be said that from a number of uniform experiments, we *infer* a connection between the sensible qualities and the secret powers; this, I must confess, seems the same difficulty, couched in different terms. The question still recurs, on what process of argument this *inference* is founded? Where is the medium, the interposing ideas, which join propositions so very wide of each other? It is confessed that the color, consistence, and other sensible qualities of bread appear not, of themselves, to have any connection with the secret powers of nourishment and support. For otherwise we could infer these secret powers from the first appearance of these sensible qualities, without the aid of experience; contrary to the sentiment of all philosophers, and contrary to plain matter of fact. Here, then, is our natural state of ignorance with regard to the powers and influence of all objects. How is this remedied by experience?

It only shows us a number of uniform effects resulting from certain objects, and teaches us that those particular objects, at that particular time, were endowed with such powers and forces. When a new object, endowed with similar sensible qualities, is produced, we expect similar powers and forces, and look for a like effect. From a body of like color and consistence with bread we expect like nourishment and support. But this surely is a step or progress of the mind, which wants to be explained. When a man says, *I have found, in all-past instances, such sensible qualities conjoined with such secret powers:* and when he says, *Similar sensible qualities will always be conjoined with similar secret powers,* he is not guilty of a tautology, nor are these propositions in any respect the same. You say that the one proposition is an inference from the other. But you must confess that the inference is not intuitive; neither is it demonstrative: of what nature is it, then? To say it is experimental, is begging the question. For all inferences from experience suppose, as their foundation, that the future will resemble the past, and that similar powers will be conjoined with similar sensible qualities. If there be any suspicion that the course of nature may change, and that the past may be no rule for the future, all experience becomes useless, and can give rise to no inference or conclusion. It is impossible, therefore, that any arguments from experience can prove this resemblance of the past to the future; since all these arguments are founded on the supposition of that resemblance. Let the course of things be allowed hitherto ever so regular; that alone, without some new argument or inference, proves not that, for the future, it will continue so. In vain do you pretend to have learned the nature of bodies from your past experience. Their secret nature, and consequently all their effects and influence, may change, without any change in their sensible qualities. This happens sometimes, and with regard to some objects: why may it not happen always, and with regard to all objects? What logic, what process of argument secures you against this supposition? My practice, you say, refutes my doubts. But you mistake the purport of my question. As an agent, I am quite satisfied in the point; but as a philosopher, who has some share of curiosity, I will not say scepticism, I want to learn the foundation of this inference. No reading, no inquiry has yet been able to remove my difficulty, or give me satisfaction in a matter of such importance. Can I do better than propose the difficulty to the public, even though, perhaps, I have small hopes of obtaining a solution? We shall at least, by this means, be sensible of our ignorance, if we do not augment our knowledge.

SECTION V
SCEPTICAL SOLUTION OF THESE DOUBTS

Part I

Nature will always maintain her rights, and prevail in the end over any abstract reasoning whatsoever. Though we should conclude, for instance, as in the foregoing section, that, in all reasonings from experience, there is a step taken by the mind which is not supported by any argument or process of the understanding; there is no danger that these reasonings, on which almost all knowledge depends, will ever be affected by such a discovery. If the mind be not engaged by argument to make this step, it must be induced by some other principle of equal weight and authority, and that principle will preserve its influence as long as human nature remains the same. What that principle is may well be worth the pains of inquiry.

Suppose a person, though endowed with the strongest faculties of reason and reflection, to be brought on a sudden into this world; he would, indeed, immediately observe a continual succession of objects, and one event following another; but he would not be able to discover anything farther. He would not, at first, by any reasoning, be able to reach the idea of cause and effect; since the particular powers, by which all natural operations are performed, never appear to the senses, nor is it reasonable to conclude, merely because one event, in one instance, precedes another, that therefore the one is the cause, the other the effect. Their conjunction may be arbitrary and casual. There may be no reason to infer the existence of one from the appearance of the other. And in a word, such a person, without more experience, could never employ his conjecture or reasoning concerning any matter of fact, or be assured of anything beyond what was immediately present to his memory and senses.

Suppose, again, that he has acquired more experience, and has lived so long in the world as to have observed familiar objects or events to be constantly conjoined together; what is the consequence of this experience? He immediately infers the existence of the other. Yet he has not, by all his experience, acquired any idea or knowledge of the secret power by which the one object produces the other; nor is it, by any process of reasoning, he is engaged to draw this inference. But still he finds himself determined to draw it: and though he should be convinced that his understanding has no part in the operation, he would nevertheless continue in the same course of thinking. There is some other principle which determines him to form such a conclusion.

This principle is Custom or Habit. For wherever the repetition of any particular act or operation produces a propensity to renew the same act of operation, without being impelled by any reasoning or process of the understanding, we always say that this propensity is the effect of *Custom*. By employing that word, we pretend not to have given the ultimate reason of such a propensity. We only point out a principle of human nature, which is universally acknowledged, and which is well known by its effects. Perhaps we can push our inquiries no farther, or pretend to give the cause of this cause; but must rest contented with it as the ultimate principle, which we can assign, of all our conclusions from experience. It is sufficient satisfaction that we can go so far, without repining at the narrowness of our faculties because they will carry us no farther. And it is certain we here advance a very intelligible proposition at least, if not a true one, when we assert that, after the constant conjunction of two objects—heat and flame, for instance, weight and solidity—we are determined by custom alone to expect the one from the appearance of the other. This hypothesis seems even the only one which explains the difficulty, why we draw, from a thousand instances, an inference which we are not able to draw from one instance that is, in no respect, different from them. Reason is incapable of any such variation. The conclusions which it draws from considering one circle are the same which it would form upon surveying all the circles in the universe. But no man, having seen only one body move after being impelled by another, could infer that every other body will move after a like impulse. All inferences from experience, therefore, are effects of custom, not of reasoning.

Custom, then, is the great guide of human life. It is that principle alone which renders our experience useful to us, and makes us expect, for the future, a similar train of events with those which have appeared in the past. Without the influence of custom, we should be entirely ignorant of every matter of fact beyond what is immediately present to the memory and senses. We should never know how to adjust means to ends, or to employ our natural powers in the production of any effect. There would be an end at once of all action, as well as of the chief part of speculation.

But here it may be proper to remark that, though our conclusions from experience carry us beyond our memory and senses, and assure us of matters of fact which happened in the most distant places and most remote ages, yet some fact must always be present to the senses or memory, from which we may first proceed in drawing these conclusions. A man, who should find in a desert country the remains of pompous buildings, would conclude that the country had, in ancient times, been cultivated by civilized inhabitants; but did nothing of this nature occur to him, he could never form such an inference. We learn the events of former ages from history; but then we must peruse the volumes in which this instruction is contained, and thence carry up our inferences from one testimony to another, till we arrive at the eyewitnesses and spectators of these distant events. In a word, if we proceed not upon some fact, present to the memory or senses, our reasonings would be merely hypothetical; and however the particular links might be connected with each other, the whole chain of inferences would have nothing to support it, nor could we ever, by its means, arrive at the knowledge of any real existence. If I ask why you believe any particular matter of fact which you relate, you must tell me some reason; and this reason will be some other fact connected with it. But as you cannot proceed after this manner, *in infinitum,* you must at last terminate in some fact which is present to your memory or senses; or must allow that your belief is entirely without foundation.

What, then, is the conclusion of the whole matter? A simple one; though, it must be confessed, pretty remote from the common theories of philosophy. All belief of matter of fact or real existence is derived merely from some object, present to the memory or senses, and a customary conjunction between that and some other object. Or in other words; having found, in many instances, that any two kinds of objects—flame and heat, snow and cold—have always been conjoined together; if flame or snow be presented anew to the senses, the mind is carried by custom to expect heat or cold, and to *believe* that such a quality does exist and will discover itself upon a nearer approach. This belief is the necessary result of placing the mind in such circumstances. It is an operation of the soul, when we are so situated, as unavoidable as to feel the passion of love, when we receive benefits; or hatred, when we meet with injuries. All these operations are a species of natural instincts, which no reasoning or process of the thought and understanding is able either to produce or to prevent.

To Think About

1. "Hitherto people have looked upon the Principle of Causality as a proposition which would in the course of years admit of experimental proof with an ever-increasing exactitude. . . .

    "Now Heisenberg has discovered a flaw in the proposition. . . . The principle of causality loses its significance as an empirical proposition.

    "Causality is thus only conceivable as a *Form of the theoretical system.*"
    Albert Einstein

2. "The issue is whether causality is an ultimate principle or merely a substitute for statistical regularity."
    Hans Reichenbach

3. "The connection between cause and effect is evidently seen as *logical* connection of some sort, that was overthrown by Hume, the most influential of all philosophers on this subject in the English-speaking and allied schools. For he made us see that, given any particular cause—or 'total causal situation' for that matter—and its effect, there is not in general any contradiction in supposing the one to occur and the other not to occur."
    Unknown

4. "The high success of Newton's astronomy was in one way an intellectual disaster: it produced an illusion from which we tend still to suffer. This illusion was created by the circumstance that Newton's mechanics *had a good model in the solar system.* For this gave the impression that we had here an ideal of scientific explanation; whereas the truth was, it was mere obligingness on the part of the solar system, by having had so peaceful a history in recorded time, to provide such a model. For suppose that some planet had at some time erupted with such violence that its shell was propelled rocket-like out of the solar system. Such an event would not have violated Newton's laws; on the contrary, it would have illustrated them."
    Unknown

5. "Socrates' death is not a cause of Xantippe's widowhood. What then is the cause? The death was caused by Socrates' drinking of hemlock. Could this event be a cause of Xantippe's widowhood? . . . by what causal mechanism does the ingestion of hemlock lead to the widowhood? We can trace the causal chain from the hemlock drinking to the death, but no farther; the connection between the death and Xantippe's becoming a widow isn't causal. . . .

    "To rule out Socrates' drinking as a cause of Xantippe's widowhood is to rule out, by implication, any other event that is a cause of the death as a cause of the widowhood. And if neither Socrates' death nor any of its causes is a cause of Xantippe's widowhood, we can only conclude, I think, that this event has no cause."
    Jon Kim

PART 6

METAPHYSICS

Why Is There Something Rather Than Nothing?

34
Being Is Uncaused

Parmenides (515 B.C.–?) Little is known with certainty of Parmenides's life. He was born in the Greek colony of Elea in southern Italy around 515 B.C., and he studied the works of a number of ancient pre-Socratic Greek philosophers, particularly Xenophanes and Pythagoras. Parmenides's name constitutes the title of one of Plato's dialogues, and he may have actually conversed with Socrates, since he visited Athens as an old man in 450 B.C. or so. Only fragments of Parmenides's writing survive. They are written in verse and seem to have been part of a long poem on nature.

The word *metaphysics* suggests many things. For some it brings to mind bookstores carrying "metaphysical" literature, everything from astrology to tarot cards and various "new age" books and magazines. Others will think of a kind of problem having no solution, unlike physics, which is a science and proceeds mathematically and experimentally. Finally some will think of metaphysics as concerned with the nature of ultimate reality, an inquiry into the most general qualities of things in themselves, or the nature of being itself. It is this third sense that many philosophers focus on. In the following selection we consider four issues found in ancient and modern metaphysics: What is the nature of being? Are universal terms in any sense real or are only particular things real? Are the things we observe in the world material entities, immaterial entities, or some combination of both? And finally, what is the nature of personal identity?

The first of these questions is itself complex. Does everything in the universe simply exist? Or is being itself produced by something else? Is reality one single thing, and are diversity and difference illusions? Is reality changeable or changeless? Is non-being itself possible? Such questions may strike you as strange, but they have been raised time and again in the history of philosophy. Here we consider two philosophers, one from ancient Greece, the other from ancient China, both of whom thought that the question of being was of primary importance in philosophy. It is extraordinary that two individuals from such a remote past and such radically different cultures should raise almost identical questions.

We begin with Parmenides, who held that all reality is one, and that diversity and multiplicity are illusions of the senses. The absolute unity of reality is generally referred to as *monism*. Parmenides approaches this issue from a strictly logical perspective. Being and non-being are contradictories. One therefore can have nothing to do with the other. Being simply "is." It cannot come from nothing, since nothing simply is not. Change and motion involve something becoming what it formerly was not. Therefore, being is changeless and at rest. Much of what we observe in nature consequently cannot be real. These paradoxical positions have led to many of the most puzzling metaphysical issues in Western philosophy. What is commonly called the problem of *the one and the many* was for the first time clearly formulated by Parmenides.

To Study

1. For Parmenides, what are the only two ways of inquiry into the nature of reality? How do they differ?
2. Why does Parmenides reject the way of inquiry into things that are not?
3. The way of "it is" has many signposts. What are some of them?
4. Why cannot being come from non-being?
5. Why is being indivisible?
6. Why is being motionless?

---

[1] The mares that carry me as far as my heart ever aspires sped me on, when they had brought and set me on the far-famed road of the god, which bears the man who knows over all cities. On that road was I borne, for that way the wise horses bore me, straining at the chariot, and maidens led the way. And the axle in the naves gave out the whistle of a pipe, blazing, for it was pressed hard on either side by the two well-turned wheels as the daughters of the Sun made haste to escort me, having left the halls of Night for the light, and having thrust the veils from their heads with their hands.

There are the gates of the paths of Night and Day, and a lintel and a stone threshold enclose them. They themselves, high in the air, are blocked with great doors, and avenging Justice holds the alternate bolts. Her the maidens beguiled with gentle words and cunningly persuaded to push back swiftly from the gates the bolted bar. And the gates created a yawning gap in the door frame when they flew open, swinging in turn in their sockets the bronze-bound pivots made fast with dowels and rivets. Straight through them, on the broad way, did the maidens keep the horses and the chariot.

And the goddess greeted me kindly, and took my right hand in hers, and addressed me with these words: "Young man, you who come to my house in the company of immortal charioteers with the mares which bear you, greetings. No ill fate has sent you to travel this road—far indeed does it lie from the steps of men—but right and justice. It is proper that you should learn all things, both the unshaken heart of well-rounded truth, and the opinions of mortals, in which there is no true reliance. But nonetheless you shall learn these things too, how what is believed would have to be assuredly, pervading all things throughout."

[2] Come now, and I will tell you (and you must carry my account away with you when you have heard it) the only ways of enquiry that are to be thought of. The one, that [it] is and that it is impossible for [it] not to be, is the path of Persuasion (for she attends upon Truth); the other, that [it] is not and that it is needful that [it] not be, that I declare to you is an altogether indiscernible track: for you could not know what is not—that cannot be done—nor indicate it.

[3] For the same thing is there both to be thought of and to be.

[4] But look at things which, though far off, are securely present to the mind; for you will not cut off for yourself what is from holding to what is, neither scattering everywhere in every way in order [i.e., cosmic order] nor drawing together.

[5] It is a common point from which I start; for there again and again I shall return.

[6] What is there to be said and thought needs must be; for it is there for being, but nothing is not. I bid you ponder that, for this is the first way of enquiry from which I hold you back, but then from that on which mortals wander knowing nothing, two-headed; for helplessness guides the wandering thought in their breasts, and they are carried along, deaf and blind at once, dazed, undiscriminating hordes, who believe that to be and not to be are the same and not the same, and the path taken by them is backward-turning.

[7] For never shall this be forcibly maintained, that things that are not are, but you must hold back your thought from this way of enquiry, nor let habit, born of much experience, force you down this way, by making you use an aimless eye or an ear and a tongue full of meaningless sound: judge by reason the strife-encompassed refutation spoken by me.

[8] Only one way remains; that it is. To this way there are very many sign-posts: that being has no coming-into-being and no destruction, for it is whole of limb, without motion, and without end. And it never was, nor will be, because it is now, a whole all together, one, continuous; for what creation of it will you look? How, whence sprung? Nor shall I allow you to speak or think of it as springing from not-being; for it is neither expressible nor thinkable that what-is-not is. Also, what necessity impelled it, if it did spring from nothing, to be produced later or earlier? Thus it must be absolutely, or not at all. Nor will the force of credibility ever admit that anything should come into being, beside being itself, out of not-being. So far as that is concerned, justice has never released (*being*) from its fetters and set it free either to come into being

or to perish, but holds it fast. The decision on these matters depends on the following: it is, or it is not. It is therefore decided, as is inevitable: ignore the one way as unthinkable and inexpressible (for it is no true way) and take the other as the way of being and reality. How could being perish? How could it come into being? If it came into being, it is not, and so too if it is about-to-be at some future time. Thus coming-into-being is quenched, and destruction also into the unseen.

Nor is being divisible, since it is all alike. Nor is there anything there which could prevent it from holding together, nor any lesser thing, but all is full of being. Therefore it is altogether continuous; for being is close to being.

But it is motionless in the limits of mighty bonds, without beginning, without cease, since becoming and destruction have been driven very far away, and true conviction has rejected them. And remaining the same in the same place, it rests by itself and thus remains there fixed; for powerful necessity holds it in the bonds of a limit, which constrains it round about, because it is decreed by divine law that being shall not be without boundary. For it is not lacking; but if it were (*spatially infinite*), it would be lacking everything.

To think is the same as the thought that it is; for you will not find thinking without being to which it refers. For nothing else either is or shall be except being, since fate has tied it down to be a whole and motionless; therefore all things that mortals have established, believing in their truth, are just a name: becoming and perishing, being and not-being, and change of position, and alteration of bright color.

But since there is a (*spatial*) limit, it is complete on every side, like the mass of a well-rounded sphere, equally balanced from its center in every direction; for it is not bound to be at all either greater or less in this direction or that; nor is there not-being which could check it from reaching to the same point, nor is it possible for being to be more in this direction, less in that, than being, because it is an inviolate whole. For, in all directions equal to itself, it reaches its limits uniformly.

At this point I cease my reliable theory (*Logos*) and thought, concerning Truth; from here onwards you must learn the opinions of mortals, listening to the deceptive order of my words.

They have established (*the custom of*) naming two forms, one of which ought not to be (*mentioned*): that is where they have gone astray. They have distinguished them as opposite in form, and have marked them off from another by giving them different signs: on one side the flaming fire in the heavens, mild, very light (*in weight*), the same as itself in every direction, and not the same as the other. This (*other*) also is by itself and opposite: dark night, a dense and heavy body. This world-order I describe to you throughout as it appears with all its phenomena, in order that no intellect of mortal men may outstrip you.

[9] But since all things are named light and night, and names have been given to each class of things according to the power of one or the other, everything is full equally of light and invisible night, as both are equal, because to neither of them belongs any share (of the other).

[10] You shall know the nature of the heavens, and all the signs in the heavens, and the destructive works of the pure bright torch of the sun, and whence they came into being. And you shall learn of the wandering works of the round-faced moon, and

its nature; and you shall know also the surrounding heaven, whence it sprang and how necessity brought and constrained it to hold the limits of the stars.

[11] (*I will describe*) how earth and sun and moon, and the aether common to all, and the milky way in the heavens, and outermost Olympus, and the hot power of the stars, hastened to come into being.

[12] For the narrower rings were filled with unmixed fire, and those next to them with night, but between (these) rushes the portion of flame. And in the center of these is the goddess who guides everything; for throughout she rules over cruel birth and mating, sending the female to mate with the male, and conversely again the male with the female.

[13] First of all the gods she devised Love.

[14] (*The moon*): Shining by night with a light not her own, wandering round the earth.

To Think About

1. "Nor is there any emptiness; for the empty is nothing; and so that which nothing cannot be. Nor does it move: for it cannot withdraw in any direction, but all is full. For if there were any empty, it would have withdrawn into the empty; but as the empty does not exist, there is nowhere for it to withdraw."

   Melissus

2. "For some of the older philosophers thought that 'what is' must of necessity be 'one' and immovable. The void, they argue, 'is not': but unless there is a void with a separate being of its own, 'what is' cannot be moved—nor again can it be 'many,' since there is nothing to keep things apart. . . . Reasoning in this way, therefore, they were led to transcend sense-perception, and to disregard it on the ground that 'one ought to follow the argument.'. . . Moreover, although these opinions appear to follow logically in a dialectical discussion, yet to believe them seems next door to madness when one considers the facts. For indeed no lunatic seems to be so afar out of his senses as to suppose that fire and ice are 'one.'. . ."   *Aristotle*

3. "How apt was the way in which God sent his servant Moses (Exod. 3:13–15)! Moses asked for the name of his sender. 'What shall I tell the children of Israel, he said, if they say to me Who sent you to us?' And he answers 'I am who I am.'. . . Is that your name, is that all you are called? If your name then is just 'To be,' it must mean that anything else compared to you is found not really to be."   *St. Augustine*

4. "Whatever we conceive as existent, we can also conceive as non-existent. There is no being, therefore, whose non-existence implies a contradiction."

   David Hume

5. "The being of every creature depends on God, so that not for a moment could it subsist, but would fall into nothingness, were it not kept in being by the operation of the divine power."   *St. Thomas Aquinas*

6. "So long as the universe had a beginning, we could suppose it had a creator. But if the universe is really completely self-contained, having no boundary or edge, it would have neither beginning nor end: it would simply be."

Stephen Hawking

7. "Nothing will come of nothing."   *Shakespeare,* in *King Lear*

8. "Academic philosophers, ever since the time of Parmenides, have believed that the world is a unity. . . . The most fundamental of my intellectual beliefs is that this is rubbish. I think the universe is all spots and jumps, without unity, without continuity, without coherence or orderliness or any of the other properties that governesses love . . . it consists of events, short, small and haphazard. Order, unity, and continuity are human inventions, just as truly as are catalogues and encyclopedias."   *Bertrand Russell*

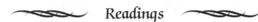

Readings

BRANN, EVA. *The Ways of Naysaying: No, Not, Nothing, and Nonbeing.* Lanham, MD: Rowman & Littlefield, 2001.

BRUNSCHWIG, JACQUES, AND GEOFFREY E. R. LLOYD, eds. *Greek Thought: A Guide to Classical Knowledge.* Cambridge, MA: Harvard University Press, 2000.

GOTTLIEB, ANTHONY. *The Dream of Reason: A History of Western Philosophy from the Greeks to the Renaissance.* New York: Norton, 2000.

RUNDLE, BEDE. *Why There Is Something Rather Than Nothing.* New York: Oxford University Press, 2004.

SORENSEN, ROY A. *A Brief History of the Paradox: Philosophy and the Labyrinths of the Mind.* New York: Oxford University Press, 2003.

Why Is There Something Rather Than Nothing?

35
Non-Being Is the Source of Being

Lao-Tzu (c. 604–531 B.C.) As we have seen, little is known of the life of Parmenides. Even less is known about the ancient Chinese philosopher Lao-Tzu. Since his name simply means "the master," he may not even have existed, and his poem may be the work of several individuals. Tradition has it, nevertheless, that he was a contemporary of Confucius (551–479 B.C.), thus making him a near-contemporary of Parmenides. It is likely, however, that he lived somewhat later. His poem, the Tao Te Ching, *usually called simply the* Tao, *is a classic of world literature.*

Taoism, as Lao-Tzu's position is commonly called, began in opposition to some forms of Confucianism and what its followers perceived as merely external conformity to moral virtue. Taoism claimed that true goodness and wise governance rested upon some immediate acquaintance with a message of nature, called the "Way" or "*Tao*," accessible to the mind in meditation and physical and spiritual discipline. Unlike Parmenides, the Way of Taoism has a clearly moral and social aim, the art of living well both individually and socially. But both share a metaphysical core, and the contrast between their starting points could not be more stark. For Parmenides, being simply is, and non-being is not. The *Tao,* in contrast, is a reality beyond being itself, unknowable, ineffable, and the source of the world of changing natural things. If so, non-being is in some sense real and the origin of being itself. Ultimate reality is multiple, and diversity is real. The ruler, either the individual ruling the self or the emperor ruling others, must come to understand the nature of this complex reality. If change is real in the moral world, it must be real in the world of metaphysics as well.

 To Study

1. Why, for Lao-Tzu, must being and non-being be complementary aspects of reality?
2. Why must the Tao be nameless?

From Wing-Tsit Chan, *The Way of Lao Tzu,* 1st edition, Copyright 1963. Reprinted by permission of Pearson Education, Inc., Upper Saddle River, NJ.

329

3. Why are tranquility and quietude goals for the Taoist?
4. How is the Tao related to the world of nature?
5. How is nature related to kingship for the Taoist?
6. What practical ethics and ideal of wisdom does Lao-Tzu recommend in his "Way"?

1

THE TAO that can be told of is not the eternal Tao;
The name that can be named is not the eternal name.
The Nameless is the origin of Heaven and Earth.
The Named is the mother of all things.

Therefore let there always be non-being, so we may see their subtlety.
And let there always be being so we may see their outcome.
The two are the same,
But after they are produced, they have different names.
They both may be called deep and profound.
Deeper and more profound,
The door of all subtleties!

2

WHEN THE people of the world all know beauty as beauty,
    There arises the recognition of ugliness.
When they all know the good as good,
    There arises the recognition of evil.
Therefore:
    Being and non-being produce each other;
    Difficult and easy complete each other;
    Long and short contrast each other;
    High and low distinguish each other;
    Sound and voice harmonize each other;
    Front and behind accompany each other.

    Therefore the sage manages affairs without action
    And spreads doctrines without words.
    All things arise, and he does not turn away from them.
    He produces them but does not take possession of them.
    He acts but does not rely on his own ability.
    He accomplishes his task but does not claim credit for it.
    It is precisely because he does not claim credit that his
        accomplishment remains with him.

11

THIRTY SPOKES are united around the hub to make a wheel,
    But it is on its non-being that the utility of the carriage depends.
Clay is molded to form a utensil,
    But it is on its non-being that the utility of the utensil depends.
Doors and windows are cut out to make a room,
    But it is on its non-being that the utility of the room depends.
Therefore turn being into advantage, and turn non-being into utility.

14

WE LOOK at it and do not see it;
   Its name is The Invisible.
We listen to it and do not hear it;
   Its name is The Inaudible.
We touch it and do not find it;
   Its name is The Subtle (formless).

These three cannot be further inquired into,
And hence merge into one.
Going up high, it is not bright, and coming down low, it is not dark.
Infinite and boundless, it cannot be given any name;
It reverts to nothingness.
This is called shape without shape,
Form without objects.
It is The Vague and Elusive.
Meet it and you will not see its head.
Follow it and you will not see its back.
Hold on to the Tao of old in order to master the things of the present.
From this one may know the primeval beginning (of the universe).
This is called the bond of Tao.

16

ATTAIN complete vacuity.
Maintain steadfast quietude.

All things come into being,
And I see thereby their return.
All things flourish,
But each one returns to its root.
This return to its root means tranquility.
It is called returning to its destiny.
To return to destiny is called the eternal (Tao).
To know the eternal is called enlightenment.
Not to know the eternal is to act blindly to result in disaster.
He who knows the eternal is all-embracing.
Being all-embracing, he is impartial.
Being impartial, he is kingly (universal).
Being kingly, he is one with Nature.
Being one with Nature, he is in accord with Tao.
Being in accord with Tao, he is everlasting
And is free from danger throughout his lifetime.

25

THERE WAS something undifferentiated and yet complete,
   Which existed before heaven and earth.
Soundless and formless, it depends on nothing and does not change.
It operates everywhere and is free from danger.

It may be considered the mother of the universe.
I do not know its name; I call it Tao.
If forced to give it a name, I shall call it Great.
Now being great means functioning everywhere.
Functioning everywhere means far-reaching.
Being far-reaching means returning to the original point.

Therefore Tao is great.
Heaven is great.
Earth is great.
And the king is also great.
There are four great things in the universe and
    the king is one of them.
Man models himself after Earth.
Earth models itself after Heaven.
Heaven models itself after Tao.
And Tao models itself after Nature.

32

TAO IS eternal and has no name.
Though its simplicity seems insignificant, none in the
    world can master it.
If kings and barons would hold on to it, all things would submit
    to them spontaneously.
Heaven and earth unite to drip sweet dew.
Without the command of men, it drips evenly over all.
As soon as there were regulations and institutions, there were
    names.
As soon as there are names, know that it is time to stop.
It is by knowing when to stop that one can be free from danger.
Analogically, Tao in the world may be compared to rivers
    and streams running into the sea.

40

REVERSION is the action of Tao.
Weakness is the function of Tao.
All things in the world come from being.
And being comes from non-being.

42

TAO PRODUCED the One.
The One produced the two.
The two produced the three.
And the three produced the ten thousand things.
The ten thousand things carry the yin and embrace the yang,
    and through the blending of the material force they
    achieve harmony.

People hate to be children without parents, lonely people without
   spouses, or men without food to eat,
And yet kings and lords call themselves by these names.
Therefore it is often the case that things gain by losing
   and lose by gaining.

What others have taught, I teach also:
"Violent and fierce people do not die a natural death."
I shall make this the father of my teaching.

70

MY DOCTRINES are very easy to understand and very easy to
   practice,
But none in the world can understand or practice them.
My doctrines have a source (Nature); my deeds have a master
   (Tao).
It is because people do not understand this that they do not
   understand me.
Few people know me, and therefore I am highly valued.
Therefore the sage wears a coarse cloth on top and carries
   jade within his bosom.

71

TO KNOW that you do not know is the best.
To pretend to know when you do not know is a disease.
Only when one recognizes this disease as a disease can one
   be free from the disease.
The sage is free from the disease.
Because he recognizes this disease to be disease, he is free
   from it.

81

TRUE WORDS are not beautiful;
   Beautiful words are not true.
A good man does not argue;
   He who argues is not a good man.
A wise man has no extensive knowledge;
   He who has extensive knowledge is not a wise man.

The sage does not accumulate for himself.
The more he uses for others, the more he has himself.
The more he gives to others, the more he possesses
   of his own.
The Way of Heaven is to benefit others and not to injure.
The Way of the sage is to act but not to compete.

<hr>

To Think About

1. "To the Chinese what is highest and the origin of things is nothing, emptiness, the altogether undetermined, the abstract universal, and this is also called Tao or reason. When the Greeks say that the absolute is one . . . all determinations are abolished, and by the merely abstract Being nothing has been expressed excepting this same negation, only in an affirmative form. But if Philosophy has got no further than to such expression, it still stands on its most elementary stage. What is there to be found in all this learning?"   ***G. W. F. Hegel***

2. "If we should wish to partake in those productions of the most exalted minds we would have to Orientalize ourselves, as the Orient is not going to approach us."   ***Johann Wolfgang von Goethe***

3. "*Tao* is the origin and goal of the world and all things, hence also of the thinker."   ***Karl Jaspers***

4. "The Great Ultimate through movement generates yang. When its activity reaches its limit, it becomes tranquil. Through tranquillity the Great Ultimate generates yin. When tranquillity reaches its limit, activity begins again. So movement and tranquillity alternate and become the root of each other, giving rise to the distinction of yin and yang, and the two modes are thus established."   ***Zhou Dunyi***

5. "Once Chuang Chou dreamt he was a butterfly, a butterfly flitting and fluttering around, happy with himself and doing as he pleased. He didn't know he was Chuang Chou. Suddenly he woke up and there he was, solid and unmistakable, Chuang Chou. But he didn't know if he was Chuang Chou who had dreamt he was a butterfly, or a butterfly dreaming he was Chuang Chou. Between Chuang Chou and a butterfly there must be *some* distinction. This is called the Transformation of Things."   ***Chuang Tzu***

6. "If all is one, can anything be said? Once it has been said that all is one, can nothing be said? Unity and speech make two; two plus one make three. . . . Therefore when you go from nonbeing to being, you thereby come to a third point."   ***Chuang Tzu***

7. "What we cannot speak about we must pass over in silence."   ***Ludwig Wittgenstein***

<hr>

Readings

BILLINGTON, RAY. *Understanding Eastern Philosophy.* London: Routledge, 1997.

CLARKE, J. J. *The Tao of the West: Western Transformations of Taoist Thought.* London and New York: Routledge, 2000.

FENG, YOULAN. *A Short History of Chinese Philosophy.* New York: Free Press, 1966.

KOHN, LIVIA AND MICHAEL LAFARGUE, eds. *Lao-tzu and the Tao-te-ching.* Albany: State University of New York Press, 1998.

SMULLYAN, RAYMOND M. *The Tao Is Silent.* San Francisco: Harper & Row, 1992.

Is Reality General or Particular?

36
Universals Are Real

Plato (427?–347 B.C.), one of the great Greek philosophers, has exerted more influence on the development of Western philosophy than any other writer, with the possible exception of his student Aristotle. He established the Academy in Athens, the first of the major schools of ancient Greece. His works, written in dialogue form and featuring his teacher Socrates as the principal speaker, have continued to be widely read not only for their intellectual content but also for their literary merit.

Of all the words we use, few of them besides proper names stand for particular things. We often use words, such as *table, red, greater,* or *strike,* to stand for types of things, or for qualities, relations, or actions that do not exist by themselves. We observe particular tables or particular reds, but never a table in general or a red in general. The problem, then, is to determine what these universal terms represent.

Plato, a realist concerning universals, says that these terms stand for what a number of particular things have in common, and it is this common element that we refer to as a *universal.* Unlike some realists, Plato believes that these universals exist eternally in a nontemporal, nonspatial realm independent of our space-time world. He argues for the unique existence of these universals, or Ideas, in the following way. We have knowledge of objects, such as perfect circles, that cannot be based on anything we have sensed. Knowledge must have an object. Therefore there must exist some other entities (the Ideas) distinct from those of the senses.

Plato expressed these thoughts in two famous works, "The Divided Line" and "Allegory of the Cave." His epistemological system is divided into four types: conjecture, practical belief, reasoning, and dialectic. This system corresponds to four degrees of reality: images, physical objects, mathematical objects, and the Forms.

The following diagrams illustrate the two allegories and their corresponding aspects to the four degrees of reality. Reference to these graphic representations will help in understanding these difficult passages, and should be referred to during reading.

From *The Republic of Plato,* trans. F. M. Cornford (Oxford: Oxford University Press, 1941).

335

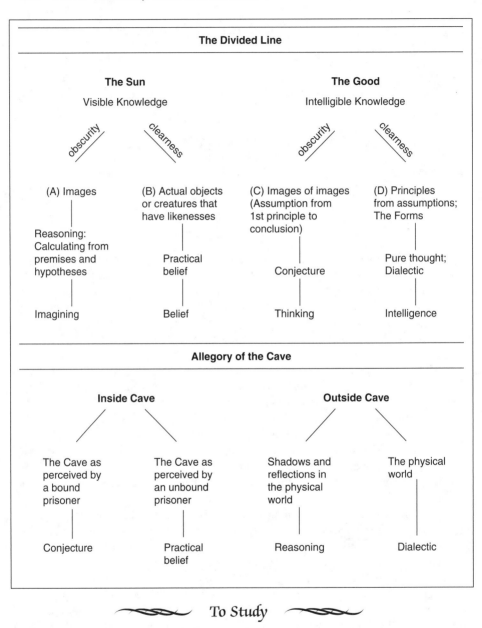

The Divided Line

The Sun	**The Good**
Visible Knowledge	Intelligible Knowledge

obscurity — clearness   obscurity — clearness

(A) Images

Reasoning:
Calculating from
premises and
hypotheses

Imagining

(B) Actual objects
or creatures that
have likenesses

Practical
belief

Belief

(C) Images of images
(Assumption from
1st principle to
conclusion)

Conjecture

Thinking

(D) Principles
from assumptions;
The Forms

Pure thought;
Dialectic

Intelligence

Allegory of the Cave

Inside Cave   **Outside Cave**

The Cave as
perceived by
a bound
prisoner

Conjecture

The Cave as
perceived by
an unbound
prisoner

Practical
belief

Shadows and
reflections in
the physical
world

Reasoning

The physical
world

Dialectic

To Study

1. Describe the nature of the Forms.
2. What is the relation between the Good and the Sun? What is the analogy between the Sun and the Good?
3. What are the four levels of reality and knowledge? Give examples. What four states of mind correspond to these?
4. Draw a sketch of the Cave allegory.

THE OBJECTS OF KNOWLEDGE

. . . Let me remind you of the distinction we drew earlier and have often drawn on other occasions between the multiplicity of things that we call good or beautiful or whatever it may be and, on the other hand, Goodness itself or Beauty itself and so on. Corresponding to each of these sets of many things, we postulate a single Form or real essence, as we call it.[1]

Yes, that is so.

Further, the many things, we say, can be seen, but are not objects of rational thought; whereas the Forms are objects of thought, but invisible.

Yes, certainly.

And we see things with our eyesight, just as we hear sounds with our ears and, to speak generally, perceive any sensible thing with our sense-faculties.

Of course.

Have you noticed, then, that the artificer who designed the senses has been exceptionally lavish of his materials in making the eyes able to see and their objects visible?

That never occurred to me.

Well, look at it in this way. Hearing and sound do not stand in need of any third thing, without which the ear will not hear nor sound be heard,[2] and I think the same is true of most, not to say all, of the other senses. Can you think of one that does require anything of the sort?

No, I cannot.

But there is this need in the case of sight and its objects. You may have the power of vision in your eyes and try to use it, and color may be there in the objects; but sight will see nothing and the colors will remain invisible in the absence of a third thing peculiarly constituted to serve this very purpose.

By which you mean—?

Naturally I mean what you call light; and if light is a thing of value, the sense of sight and the power of being visible are linked together by a very precious bond, such as unites no other sense with its object.

No one could say that light is not a precious thing.

And of all the divinities in the skies[3] is there one whose light, above all the rest, is responsible for making our eyes see perfectly and making objects perfectly visible?

There can be no two opinions: of course you mean the Sun.

And how is sight related to this deity? Neither sight nor the eye which contains it is the sun, but of all the sense-organs it is the most sun-like; and further, the power it possesses is dispensed by the Sun, like a stream flooding the eye. And again, the Sun is not vision, but it is the cause of vision and also is seen by the vision it causes.

Yes.

---

[1] Socrates is speaking to a group of people, and Glaucon is his interlocutor.

[2] Plato held that the hearing of sound is caused by blows inflicted by the air (*Timaeus,* 67 B, 80 A); but the air is hardly analogous to light.

[3] Plato held that the heavenly bodies are immortal living creatures, i.e., gods.

It was the Sun, then, that I meant when I spoke of that offspring which the Good has created in the visible world, to stand there in the same relation to vision and visible things as that which the Good itself bears in the intelligible world to intelligence and to intelligible objects.

How is that? You must explain further.

You know what happens when the colors of things are no longer irradiated by the daylight, but only by the fainter luminaries of the night: when you look at them, the eyes are dim and seem almost blind, as if there were no unclouded vision in them. But when you look at things on which the Sun is shining, the same eyes see distinctly and it becomes evident that they do contain the power of vision.

Certainly.

Apply this comparison, then, to the soul. When its gaze is fixed upon an object irradiated by truth and reality, the soul gains understanding and knowledge and is manifestly in possession of intelligence. But when it looks towards that twilight world of things that come into existence and pass away, its sight is dim and it has only opinions and beliefs which shift to and fro, and it seems like a thing that has no intelligence.

That is true.

This, then, which gives to the objects of knowledge their truth and to him who knows them his power of knowing, is the Form or essential nature of Goodness. It is the cause of knowledge and truth; and so, while you may think of it as an object of knowledge, you will do well to regard it as something beyond truth and knowledge and, precious as these both are, of still higher worth. And, just as in our analogy light and vision were to be thought of as like the Sun, but not identical with it, so here both knowledge and truth are to be regarded as like the Good, but to identify either with the Good is wrong. The Good must hold a yet higher place of honor.

You are giving it a position of extraordinary splendor, if it is the source of knowledge and truth and itself surpasses them in worth. You surely cannot mean that it is pleasure.

Heaven forbid. . . . But I want to follow up our analogy still further. You will agree that the Sun not only makes the things we see visible, but also brings them into existence and gives them growth and nourishment; yet he is not the same thing as existence. And so with the objects of knowledge: these derive from the Good not only their power of being known, but their very being and reality; and Goodness is not the same thing as being, but even beyond being, surpassing it in dignity and power.

Glaucon exclaimed with some amusement at my exalting Goodness in such extravagant terms.

It is your fault, I replied; you forced me to say what I think.

Yes, and you must stop there. At any rate, complete your comparison with the Sun, if there is any more to be said.

There is a good deal more, I answered.

Let us hear it, then; don't leave anything out.

I am afraid much must be left unspoken. However, I will not, if I can help it, leave anything that can be said on this occasion.

Please do not.

Four Stages of Cognition. The Line

Conceive, then, that there are these two powers I speak of, the Good reigning over the domain of all that is intelligible, the Sun over the visible world—or the heaven as I might call it; only you would think I was showing off my skill in etymology. At any rate have you these two orders of things clearly before your mind: the visible and the intelligible?

I have.

Now take a line divided into two unequal parts, one to represent the visible order, the other the intelligible; and divide each part again in the same proportion, symbolizing degrees of comparative clearness or obscurity. Then (*A*) one of the two sections in the visible world will stand for images. By images I mean first shadows, and then reflections in water or in close-grained, polished surfaces, and everything of that kind, if you understand.

Yes, I understand.

Let the second section (*B*) stand for the actual things of which the first are likenesses, the living creatures about us and all the works of nature or of human hands.

So be it.

Will you also take the proportion in which the visible world has been divided as corresponding to degrees of reality and truth, so that the likeness shall stand to the original in the same ratio as the sphere of appearances and belief to the sphere of knowledge?

Certainly.

Now consider how we are to divide the part which stands for the intelligible world. There are two sections. In the first (*C*) the mind uses as images those actual things which themselves had images in the visible world; and it is compelled to pursue its inquiry by starting from assumptions and traveling, not up to a principle, but down to a conclusion. In the second (*D*) the mind moves in the other direction, from an assumption up towards a principle which is not hypothetical; and it makes no use of the images employed in the other section, but only of Forms, and conducts its inquiry solely by their means.

I don't quite understand what you mean.

Then we will try again; what I have just said will help you to understand. (*C*) You know, of course, how students of subjects like geometry and arithmetic begin by postulating odd and even numbers, or the various figures and the three kinds of angle, and other such data in each subject. These data they take as known; and, having adopted them as assumptions, they do not feel called upon to give any account of them to themselves or to anyone else, but treat them as self-evident. Then, starting from these assumptions, they go on until they arrive, by a series of consistent steps, at all the conclusions they set out to investigate.

Yes, I know that.

You also know how they make use of visible figures and discourse about them, though what they really have in mind is the originals of which these figures are images: they are not reasoning, for instance, about this particular square and diagonal which they have drawn, but about *the* Square and *the* Diagonal; and so in all cases. The diagrams they draw and the models they make are actual things, which may have their shadows or images in water; but now they serve in their turn as images, while the student is seeking to behold those realities which only thought can apprehend.[4]

True.

This, then, is the class of things that I spoke of as intelligible, but with two qualifications: first, that the mind, in studying them, is compelled to employ assumptions, and, because it cannot rise above these, does not travel upwards to a first principle; and second, that it uses as images those actual things which have images of their own in the section below them and which, in comparison with those shadows and reflections, are reputed to be more palpable and valued accordingly.

I understand: you mean the procedure of geometry and of the kindred arts.

(*D*) Then by the second section of the intelligible world you may understand me to mean all that unaided reasoning apprehends by the power of dialectic, when it treats its assumptions, not as first principles, but as *hypotheses* in the literal sense, things "laid down" like a flight of steps up which it may mount all the way to something that is not hypothetical, the first principle of all; and having grasped this, may turn back and, holding on to the consequences which depend upon it, descend at last to a conclusion, never making use of any sensible object, but only of Forms, moving through Forms from one to another and ending with Forms.

I understand, he said, though not perfectly; for the procedure you describe sounds like an enormous undertaking. But I see that you mean to distinguish the field of intelligible reality studied by dialectic as having a greater certainty and truth than the subject-matter of the "arts," as they are called, which treat their assumptions as first principles. The students of these arts are, it is true, compelled to exercise thought in contemplating objects which the senses cannot perceive; but because they start from assumptions without going back to a first principle, you do not regard them as gaining true understanding about those objects, although the objects themselves, when connected with a first principle, are intelligible. And I think you would call the state of mind of the students of geometry and other such arts, not intelligence, but thinking, as being something between intelligence and mere acceptance of appearances.

You have understood me quite well enough, I replied. And now you may take, as corresponding to the four sections, these four states of mind: *intelligence* for the highest, *thinking* for the second, *belief* for the third, and for the last *imagining*. These you may arrange as the terms in a proportion, assigning to each a degree of clearness and certainty corresponding to the measure in which their objects possess truth and reality.

I understand and agree with you. I will arrange them as you say.

---

[4] Conversely, the fact that the mathematician can use visible objects as illustrations indicates that the realities and truths of mathematics are embodied, though imperfectly, in the world of visible and tangible things; whereas the counterparts of the moral Forms can only be beheld by thought.

THE ALLEGORY OF THE CAVE

. . . Here is a parable to illustrate the degrees in which our nature may be enlightened or unenlightened. Imagine the condition of men living in a sort of cavernous chamber underground, with an entrance open to the light and a long passage all down the cave. Here they have been from childhood, chained by the leg and also by the neck, so that they cannot move and can see only what is in front of them, because the chains will not let them turn their heads. At some distance higher up is the light of a fire burning behind them; and between the prisoners and the fire is a track with a parapet built along it, like the screen at a puppet-show, which hides the performers while they show their puppets over the top.

I see, said he.

Now behind this parapet imagine persons carrying along various artificial objects, including figures of men and animals in wood or stone or other materials, which project above the parapet. Naturally, some of these persons will be talking, others silent.

It is a strange picture, he said, and a strange sort of prisoners.

Like ourselves, I replied; for in the first place prisoners so confined would have seen nothing of themselves or of one another, except the shadows thrown by the firelight on the wall of the Cave facing them, would they?

Not if all their lives they had been prevented from moving their heads.

And they would have seen as little of the objects carried past.

Of course.

Now, if they could talk to one another, would they not suppose that their words referred only to those passing shadows which they saw?

Necessarily.

And suppose their prison had an echo from the wall facing them? When one of the people crossing behind them spoke, they could only suppose that the sound came from the shadow passing before their eyes.

No doubt.

In every way, then, such prisoners would recognize as reality nothing but the shadows of those artificial objects.

Inevitably.

Now consider what would happen if their release from the chains and the healing of their unwisdom should come about in this way. Suppose one of them was set free and forced suddenly to stand up, turn his head, and walk with eyes lifted to the light; all these movements would be painful, and he would be too dazzled to make out the objects whose shadows he had been used to see. What do you think he would say, if someone told him that what he had formerly seen was meaningless illusion, but now, being somewhat nearer to reality and turned towards more real objects, he was getting a truer view? Suppose further that he were shown the various objects being carried by and were made to say, in reply to questions, what each of them was. Would he not be perplexed and believe the objects now shown him to be not so real as what he formerly saw?

Yes, not nearly so real.

And if he were forced to look at the fire-light itself, would not his eyes ache, so that he would try to escape and turn back to the things which he could see distinctly, convinced that they really were clearer than these other objects now being shown to him?

Yes.

And suppose someone were to drag him away forcibly up the steep and rugged ascent and not let him go until he had hauled him out into the sunlight, would he not suffer pain and vexation at such treatment, and, when he had come out into the light, find his eyes so full of its radiance that he could not see a single one of the things that he was now told were real?

Certainly he would not see them all at once.

He would need, then, to grow accustomed before he could see things in that upper world. At first it would be easiest to make out shadows, and then the images of men and things reflected in water, and later on the things themselves. After that, it would be easier to watch the heavenly bodies and the sky itself by night, looking at the light of the moon and stars rather than the Sun and the Sun's light in the day-time.

Yes, surely.

Last of all, he would be able to look at the Sun and contemplate its nature, not as it appears when reflected in water or any alien medium, but as it is in itself in its own domain.

No doubt.

And now he would begin to draw the conclusion that it is the Sun that produces the seasons and the course of the year and controls everything in the visible world, and moreover is in a way the cause of all that he and his companions used to see.

Clearly he would come at last to that conclusion.

Then if he called to mind his fellow prisoners and what passed for wisdom in his former dwelling-place, he would surely think himself happy in the change and be sorry for them. They may have had a practice of honoring and commending one another, with prizes for the man who had the keenest eye for the passing shadows and the best memory for the order in which they followed or accompanied one another, so that he could make a good guess as to which was going to come next. Would our released prisoner be likely to covet those prizes or to envy the men exalted to honor and power in the Cave? . . .

Yes, he would prefer any fate to such a life.

Now imagine what would happen if he went down again to take his former seat in the Cave. Coming suddenly out of the sunlight, his eyes would be filled with darkness. He might be required once more to deliver his opinion on those shadows, in competition with the prisoners who had never been released, while his eyesight was still dim and unsteady; and it might take some time to become used to the darkness. They would laugh at him and say that he had gone up only to come back with his sight ruined; it was worth no one's while even to attempt the ascent. If they could lay hands on the man who was trying to set them free and lead them up, they would kill him.

Yes, they would.

Every feature in this parable, my dear Glaucon, is meant to fit our earlier analysis. The prison dwelling corresponds to the region revealed to us through the sense of sight, and the fire-light within it to the power of the Sun. The ascent to see the things in the upper world you may take as standing for the upward journey of the soul into the region of the intelligible; then you will be in possession of what I surmise, since that is what you wish to be told. Heaven knows whether it is true; but this, at any rate, is how it appears to me. In the world of knowledge, the last thing to be perceived and only with great difficulty is the essential Form of Goodness. Once it is perceived, the conclusion must follow that, for all things, this is the cause of whatever is right and good; in the visible world it gives birth to light and to the lord of light, while it is itself sovereign in the intelligible world and the parent of intelligence and truth. Without having had a vision of this Form no one can act with wisdom, either in his own life or in matters of state.

So far as I can understand, I share your belief.

Then you may also agree that it is no wonder if those who have reached this height are reluctant to manage the affairs of men. Their souls long to spend all their time in that upper world—naturally enough, if here once more our parable holds true. Nor, again, is it at all strange that one who comes from the contemplation of divine things to the miseries of human life should appear awkward and ridiculous when, with eyes still dazed and not yet accustomed to the darkness, he is compelled, in a law-court or elsewhere, to dispute about the shadows of justice or the images that cast those shadows, and to wrangle over the notions of what is right in the minds of men who have never beheld Justice itself.

It is not at all strange.

No; a sensible man will remember that the eyes may be confused in two ways— by a change from light to darkness or from darkness to light; and he will recognize that the same thing happens to the soul. When he sees it troubled and unable to discern anything clearly, instead of laughing thoughtlessly, he will ask whether, coming from a brighter existence, its unaccustomed vision is obscured by the darkness, in which case he will think its condition enviable and its life a happy one; or whether, emerging from the depths of ignorance, it is dazzled by excess of light. If so, he will rather feel sorry for it; or, if he were inclined to laugh, that would be less ridiculous than to laugh at the soul which has come down from the light.

That is a fair statement.

If this is true, then, we must conclude that education is not what it is said to be by some who profess to put knowledge into a soul which does not possess it, as if they could put sight into blind eyes. On the contrary, our own account signifies that the soul of every man does possess the power of learning the truth and the organ to see it with; and that, just as one might have to turn the whole body round in order that the eye should see light instead of darkness, so the entire soul must be turned away from this changing world, until its eye can bear to contemplate reality and that supreme splendor which we have called the Good. Hence there may well be an art whose aim would be to effect this very thing, the conversion of the soul, in the readiest way; not to put the power of sight into the soul's eye, which already has it, but to ensure that, instead of looking in the wrong direction, it is turned the way it ought to be.

Yes it may well be so.

It looks, then, as though wisdom were different from those ordinary virtues, as they are called, which are not far removed from bodily qualities, in that they can be produced by habituation and exercise in a soul which has not possessed them from the first. Wisdom, it seems, is certainly the virtue of some diviner faculty, which never loses its power, though its use for good or harm depends on the direction towards which it is turned. You must have noticed in dishonest men with a reputation for sagacity the shrewd glance of a narrow intelligence piercing the objects to which it is directed. There is nothing wrong with their power of vision, but it has been forced into the service of evil, so that the keener its sight, the more harm it works.

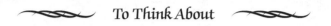 To Think About

1. "There is reality behind the world as it appears to us, possibly a many-layered reality, of which the appearances are the outermost layers. What the great scientist does is boldly to guess, daringly to conjecture, what these inner realities are like. This is akin to myth making. . . . The boldness can be gauged by the distance between the world of appearance and the conjectured reality, the explanatory hypotheses."   ***Karl Popper***

2. "It certainly seems that I can believe that reality extends beyond the reach of possible human thought, since this would be closely analogous to something which is not only possibly but actually the case. There are plenty of ordinary human beings who constitutionally lack the capacity to conceive of some of the things that others know about."   ***Ernest Nagel***

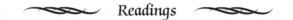 Readings

LOUX, MICHAEL J., ed. *Universals and Particulars: Readings in Ontology.* Garden City, NY: Anchor Books, 1970.

MORELAND, J. P. *Universals.* Montreal and Kingston: McGill-Queen's University Press, 2001.

STRAWSON, P. F. *Individuals.* London: Methuen, 1959.

WOLTERSTORFF, N. *On Universals.* Chicago: University of Chicago Press, 1970.

Is Reality General or Particular?

37
Particulars Are Real

David Hume (1711–76), an outstanding British empiricist, wrote on history as well as philosophy. Among his major works are A Treatise of Human Nature *(1739–40),* Essays, Moral and Political *(1741–42), and* The History of England *(1754–62).*

Hume, a nominalist regarding universals, argues that all of our ideas are ideas of particular entities, qualities, or relations. For example, we do not sense tables in general, but only particular tables. Nominalists such as Hume contend that there is nothing universal in the world, but only in the language we use to describe the world. Because many particulars resemble each other, we give the same name to these resembling objects for the sake of convenience.

~~~~~ To Study ~~~~~

1. How does Berkeley view the nature of general ideas?
2. According to Hume, how do we form most of our general ideas?
3. What is Hume's argument refuting the view that abstract ideas have no particular degree of quantity or quality?
4. What purposes of life are served by applying the same term to resembling ideas? Explain Hume's example of the triangle.
5. Explain: "Some ideas are particular in their nature, but general in their representation."
6. Explain Hume's basic principle that "All ideas, which are different, are separable."

A very material question has been stated concerning *abstract* or *general* ideas, *whether they be general or particular in the mind's conception of them.* A great

From David Hume, *An Enquiry Concerning Human Understanding* (Oxford: Clarendon Press, 1748).

philosopher[1] has disputed the received opinion in this particular, and has asserted that all general ideas are nothing but particular ones annexed to a certain term, which gives them a more extensive signification and makes them recall upon occasion other individuals which are similar to them. As I look upon this to be one of the greatest and most valuable discoveries that has been made of late years in the republic of letters, I shall here endeavor to confirm it by some arguments which I hope will put it beyond all doubt and controversy.

'Tis evident that in forming most of our general ideas, if not all of them, we abstract from every particular degree of quantity and quality, and that an object ceases not to be of any particular species on account of every small alteration in its extension, duration, and other properties. It may therefore be thought that here is a plain dilemma that decides concerning the nature of those abstract ideas which have afforded so much speculation to philosophers. The abstract idea of a man represents men of all sizes and all qualities; which 'tis concluded it cannot do, but either by representing at once all possible sizes and all possible qualities, or by representing no particular one at all. Now it having been esteemed absurd to defend the former proposition, as implying an infinite capacity in the mind, it has been commonly inferred in favor of the latter; and our abstract ideas have been supposed to represent no particular degree either of quantity or quality. But that this inference is erroneous, I shall endeavor to make appear, *first,* by proving that 'tis utterly impossible to conceive any quantity or quality without forming a precise notion of its degrees, and *secondly* by showing that though the capacity of the mind be not infinite, yet we can at once form a notion of all possible degrees of quantity and quality in such a manner at least as, however imperfect, may serve all the purposes of reflection and conversation.

To begin with the first proposition, *that the mind cannot form any notion of quantity or quality without forming a precise notion of degrees of each;* we may prove this by the three following arguments. First, we have observed that whatever objects are different are distinguishable, and that whatever objects are distinguishable are separable by the thought and imagination. And we may here add that these propositions are equally true in the *inverse,* and that whatever objects are separable are also distinguishable, and that whatever objects are distinguishable are also different. For how is it possible we can separate what is not distinguishable, or distinguish what is not different? In order therefore to know whether abstraction implies a separation, we need only consider it in this view, and examine whether all the circumstances which we abstract from in our general ideas, be such as are distinguishable and different from those which we retain as essential parts of them. But 'tis evident at first sight that the precise length of a line is not different nor distinguishable from the line itself, nor the precise degree of any quality from the quality. These ideas, therefore, admit no more of separation than they do of distinction and difference. They are consequently conjoined with each other in the conception; and the general idea of a line, notwithstanding all our abstractions and refinements has in its appearance in the mind a precise degree of quantity and quality; however it may be made to represent others which have different degrees of both.

---

[1] George Berkeley, *A Treatise Concerning the Principles of Human Knowledge* (London: J. Tanson, 1710).

Secondly, 'tis confessed that no object can appear to the senses; or in other words, that no impression can become present to the mind, without being determined in its degrees both of quantity and quality. The confusion, in which impressions are sometimes involved, proceeds only from their faintness and unsteadiness, not from any capacity in the mind to receive any impression, which in its real existence has no particular degree nor proportion. That is a contradiction in terms, and even implies the flattest of all contradictions, viz., that 'tis possible for the same thing both to be and not to be.

Now since all ideas are derived from impressions, and are nothing but copies and representations of them, whatever is true of the one must be acknowledged concerning the other. Impressions and ideas differ only in their strength and vivacity. The foregoing conclusion is not founded on any particular degree of vivacity. It cannot therefore be affected by any variation in that particular. An idea is a weaker impression; and as strong impression must necessarily have a determinate quantity and quality, the case must be the same with its copy or representative.

Thirdly, 'tis a principle generally received in philosophy that everything in nature is individual, and that 'tis utterly absurd to suppose a triangle really existent which has no precise proportion of sides and angles. If this therefore be absurd in *fact and reality,* it must also be absurd in *idea,* since nothing of which we can form a clear and distinct idea is absurd and impossible. But to form the idea of an object and to form an idea simply is the same thing; the reference of the idea to an object being an extraneous denomination of which in itself it bears no mark or character. Now as 'tis impossible to form an idea of an object that is possessed of quantity and quality, and yet is possessed of no precise degree of either, it follows that there is an equal impossibility of forming an idea that is not limited and confined in both these particulars. Abstract ideas are therefore in themselves individual, however they may become general in their representation. The image in the mind is only that of a particular object, though the application of it in our reasoning be the same, as if it were universal.

This application of ideas beyond their nature proceeds from our collecting all their possible degrees of quantity and quality in such an imperfect manner as may serve the purposes of life, which is the second proposition I proposed to explain. When we have found a resemblance among several objects that often occur to us, we apply the same name to all of them, whatever differences we may observe in the degrees of their quantity and quality, and whatever other differences may appear among them. After we have acquired a custom of this kind, the hearing of that name revives the idea of one of these objects and makes the imagination conceive it with all its particular circumstances and proportions. But as the same word is supposed to have been frequently applied to other individuals, that are different in many respects from that idea which is immediately present to the mind; the word not being able to revive the idea of all these individuals, but only touches the soul, if I may be allowed so to speak, and revives that custom which we have acquired by surveying them. They are not really and in fact present to the mind, but only in power; nor do we draw them all out distinctly in the imagination, but keep ourselves in a readiness to survey any of them, as we may be prompted by a present design or necessity. The word raises up an individual idea, along with a certain custom; and that custom produces any other individual one, for which we may have occasion. But as the production of all the ideas, to which the name may be applied, is in most cases impossible, we abridge that work by a more partial consideration, and find but few inconveniences to arise in our reasoning from that abridgment.

For this is one of the most extraordinary circumstances in the present affair, that after the mind has produced an individual idea upon which we reason the attendant custom, revived by the general or abstract term, readily suggests any other individual if by chance we form any reasoning, that agrees not with it. Thus should we mention the word *triangle,* and form the idea of a particular equilateral one to correspond to it, and should we afterwards assert, *that the three angles of a triangle are equal to each other,* the other individuals of a scalenum and isosceles, which we overlooked at first, immediately crowd in upon us, and make us perceive the falsehood of this proposition, though it be true with relation to that idea which we had formed. If the mind suggests not always these ideas upon occasion, it proceeds from some imperfection in its faculties; and such a one as is often the source of false reasoning and sophistry. But this is principally the case with those ideas which are abstruse and compounded. On other occasions the custom is more entire, and 'tis seldom we run into such errors.

Nay, so entire is the custom that the very same idea may be annexed to several different words, and may be employed in different reasonings without any danger of mistake. Thus the idea of an equilateral triangle of an inch perpendicular may serve us in talking of a figure, of a rectilineal figure, of a regular figure, of a triangle, and of an equilateral triangle. All these terms, therefore, are in this case attended with the same idea; but as they are wont to be applied in a greater or lesser compass, they excite their particular habits, and thereby keep the mind in a readiness to observe, that no conclusion be formed contrary to any ideas, which are usually comprised under them.

Before those habits have become entirely perfect, perhaps the mind may not be content with forming the idea of only one individual, but may run over several in order to make itself comprehend its own meaning, and the compass of that collection which it intends to express by the general term. That we may fix the meaning of the word *figure,* we may resolve in our mind the ideas of circles, squares, parallelograms, triangles of different sizes and proportions, and may not rest on one image or idea. However this may be, 'tis certain *that* we form the idea of individuals, whenever we use any general term; *that* we seldom or never can exhaust these individuals; and *that* those, which remain, are only represented by means of that habit, by which we recall them, whenever any present occasion requires it. This then is the nature of our abstract ideas and general terms; and 'tis after this manner we account for the foregoing paradox, *that some ideas are particular in their nature, but general in their representation.* A particular idea becomes general by being annexed to a general term; that is, to a term which from a customary conjunction has a relation to many other particular ideas, and readily recalls them in the imagination.

Before I leave this subject I shall employ the same principles to explain that *distinction of reason,* which is so much talked of and is so little understood in the schools. Of this kind is the distinction betwixt figure and the body figured; motion and the body moved. The difficulty of explaining this distinction arises from the principle above explained, *that all ideas, which are different, are separable.* For it follows from thence, that if the figure be different from the body, their ideas must be separable as well as distinguishable; if they be not different, their ideas can neither be separable nor distinguishable. What then is meant by a distinction of reason, since it implies neither a difference nor separation?

To remove this difficulty we must have recourse to the foregoing explication of abstract ideas. 'Tis certain that the mind would never have dreamed of distinguishing a figure from the body figured as being in reality neither distinguishable, nor different, nor separable; did it not observe that even in this simplicity there might be contained many different resemblances and relations. Thus when a globe of white marble is presented, we receive only the impression of a white color disposed in a certain form, nor are we able to separate and distinguish the color from the form. But observing afterwards a globe of black marble and a cube of white, and comparing them with our former object, we find two separate resemblances, in what formerly seemed, and really is, perfectly inseparable. After a little more practice of this kind, we begin to distinguish the figure from the color by a *distinction of reason;* that is, we consider the figure and color together, since they are in effect the same and undistinguishable; but still view them in different aspects, according to the resemblances, of which they are susceptible. When we would consider only the figure of the globe of white marble, we form in reality an idea both of the figure and color, but tactily carry our eye to its resemblance with the globe of black marble. And in the same manner, when we would consider its color only, we turn our view to its resemblance with the cube of white marble. By this means we accompany our ideas with a kind of reflection of which custom renders us, in a great measure insensible. A person, who desires us to consider the figure of a globe of white marble without thinking on its color desires an impossibility; but his meaning is that we should consider the figure and color together, but still keep in our eye the resemblance to the globe of black marble, or that to any other globe of whatever color or substance.

~~~~~~~~~~~~ To Think About ~~~~~~~~~~~~

1. "All substance appears to signify that which is individual."   *Aristotle*

2. Is there a general concept of a color, such as "blue," or "existence"? Can either be imaged?

3. "In trying to distinguish appearance from reality and lay bare the fundamental structure of the universe, science has had to transcend the 'rabble of the senses.'"
   Lincoln Barnett

4. "For nowhere in the call of Being is the cry of the *victim* to be heard, nowhere the plea for mercy, the summons for help. The silent peal of Being is deaf to the appeal of suffering."   *John D. Caputo*

5. "To affirm the priority of *Being* over *existents* is to already decide the essence of philosophy; it is to subordinate the relation with *someone,* who is an existent, (the ethical relation) to a relation with the *Being of existents,* which impersonal, permits the apprehension, the domination of existents (a relationship of knowing), subordinates justice to freedom."   *Emmanuel Lévinas*

6. "The difficulty that inheres in existence, with which the existing individual is con-
    fronted, is one that never really comes to expression in the language of abstract
    thought, much less receives an explanation. . . . Abstract thought . . . ignores the
    concrete and the temporal, the existential process, the predicament of the exist-
    ing individual arising from his being a synthesis of the temporal and the eternal
    situated in existence."   ***Unknown***

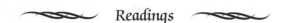 Readings

AARON, R. I. *The Theory of Universals.* Oxford: Oxford University Press, 1952.

AYER, A. J. "Particulars and Universals." *Proceedings of the Aristotelian Society* 34
    (1933–34): 51–62.

BAMBROUGH, RENFORD. "Universals and Family Resemblance." *Proceedings of the
    Aristotelian Society* 61 (1960–61): 207–22.

38
Reality Consists of Mind and Matter

René Descartes (1596–1650), French philosopher, has been discussed earlier in this volume, in the section on knowledge (see reading 26). There we saw the beginnings of his theory of mind and matter, but Descartes's impact upon the development of metaphysics is demonstrated more fully from the following essay, from the sixth part of his Meditations.

So far we have considered metaphysics in terms of very general ways of thinking about ultimate reality. Is being one or many? Are universal terms real or are only particular things real? We turn now to a consideration of ultimate reality in terms of a common distinction between minds and bodies, and ask if ultimate reality is some combination of mental and material entities, or whether reality is reducible to merely material substance or perhaps merely mental substance.

The first of these hypotheses is commonly called *dualism,* a theory that the basic constituents of the real world include (1) material entities or substances, like bodies and other physical objects, and (2) immaterial entities or substances, like minds and souls. René Descartes gave the most powerful modern expression of metaphysical dualism by focusing on human nature. Human beings had long been thought to be composites of mind and body, but the precise nature of these two dimensions of humanity had always been controversial. Descartes suggested that the human animal is in reality reducible to two separable and distinct substances, a mind having no parts or other physical characteristics and a body having shape, measurable quantity, and motion. Because he formulated his position chiefly as a theory of human nature, his position is sometimes called *psycho-physical dualism.* But it is still a general theory of reality itself. Everything in the universe, according to Descartes, is either a mind or a body. Human beings are both.

One immediate problem with this position that you may wish to consider is the nature of the relationship between minds and bodies. It is evident that we have the mental

From *The Philosophical Works of Descartes,* "Meditation VI," trans. E. S. Haldane and G. R. T. Ross (Cambridge University Press, 1931). Reprinted by permission of the publisher.

power to move our bodies, and it is equally obvious that physical events have effects on our minds. But how is this possible if bodies and minds are two completely and radically different kinds of substance? Bodies seem to be able to move other bodies, and minds appear to generate ideas. But how can they interact? How can minds move bodies and bodies produce ideas? Dualists present us with one of the most compelling theories supporting the common belief that human beings have a mind and a body, but dualists also have a very hard time accounting for the unity of these two substances.

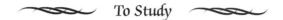 To Study

1. How does Descartes know that bodies, his own and other bodies in the world, really exist?
2. In what does Descartes think his ultimate reality or "essence" consists?
3. Why is God's existence necessary to prove to Descartes that bodies really exist?
4. Even if bodies or physical objects are real, are they necessarily the same as what we sense?
5. Are the body and mind "one" for Descartes? How does he know this?

First of all, then, I perceived that I had a head, hands, feet, and all other members of which this body—which I considered as a part, or possibly even as the whole, of myself—is composed. Further I was sensible that this body was placed amidst many others, from which it was capable of being affected in many different ways, beneficial and hurtful, and I remarked that a certain feeling of pleasure accompanied those that were beneficial, and pain those which were harmful. And in addition to this pleasure and pain, I also experienced hunger, thirst, and other similar appetites, as also certain corporeal inclinations towards joy, sadness, anger, and other similar passions. And outside myself, in addition to extension, figure, and motions of bodies, I remarked in them hardness, heat, and all other tactile qualities, and, further, light and colour, and scents and sounds, the variety of which gave me the means of distinguishing the sky, the earth, the sea, and generally all the other bodies, one from the other. And certainly, considering the ideas of all these qualities which presented themselves to my mind, and which alone I perceived properly or immediately, it was not without reason that I believed myself to perceive objects quite different from my thought, to wit, bodies from which those ideas proceeded; for I found by experience that these ideas presented themselves to me without my consent being requisite, so that I could not perceive any object, however desirous I might be, unless it were present to the organs of sense; and it was not in my power not to perceive it, when it was present. And because the ideas which I received through the senses were much more lively, more clear, and even, in their own way, more distinct than any of those which I could of myself frame in meditation, or than those I found impressed on my memory, it appeared as though they could not have proceeded from my mind, so that they must necessarily have been produced in me by some other things. And having no knowledge of those objects excepting the knowledge which the ideas themselves gave me, nothing was more likely to occur to my mind than that the objects were similar to the ideas which were caused. And because I likewise remembered that I had formerly made use of my senses rather than my reason, and recognised that the ideas which I formed of myself were not so distinct as those which I perceived through the senses, and that they were most frequently even composed of portions of these last, I persuaded myself easily that I had no idea in my mind which had not formerly come to me through the senses. Nor was it without some reason that I believed that this body (which by a certain special right I call my own) belonged to me more properly and more strictly than any other; for in fact I could never be separated from it as from other bodies; I experienced in it and on account of it all my appetites and affections, and finally I was touched by the feeling of pain and the titillation of pleasure in its parts, and not in the parts of other bodies which were separated from it.

Therefore, just because I know certainly that I exist, and that meanwhile I do not remark that any other thing necessarily pertains to my nature or essence, excepting that I am a thinking thing, I rightly conclude that my essence consists solely in the fact that I am a thinking thing [or a substance whose whole essence or nature is to think]. And although possibly (or rather certainly, as I shall say in a moment) I possess a body with which I am very intimately conjoined, yet because, on the one side, I have a clear and distinct idea of myself inasmuch as I am only a thinking and unextended thing, and as, on the other, I possess a distinct idea of body, inasmuch as it is only an extended and unthinking thing, it is certain that this I [that is to say, my soul by which I am what I am], is entirely and absolutely distinct from my body, and can exist without it.

I further find in myself faculties employing modes of thinking peculiar to themselves, to wit, the faculties of imagination and feeling, without which I can easily conceive myself clearly and distinctly as a complete being; while, on the other hand, they cannot be so conceived apart from me, that is without an intelligent substance in which they reside, for [in the notion we have of these faculties, or, to use the language of the Schools] in their formal concept, some kind of intellection is comprised, from which I infer that they are distinct from me as its modes are from a thing. I observe also in me some other faculties such as that of change of position, the assumption of different figures and such like, which cannot be conceived, any more than can the preceding, apart from some substance to which they are attached, and consequently cannot exist without it; but it is very clear that these faculties, if it be true that they exist, must be attached to some corporeal or extended substance, and not to an intelligent substance, since in the clear and distinct conception of these there is some sort of extension found to be present, but no intellection at all. There is certainly further in me a certain passive faculty of perception, that is, of receiving and recognising the ideas of sensible things, but this would be useless to me [and I could in no way avail myself of it], if there were not either in me or in some other thing another active faculty capable of forming and producing these ideas. But this active faculty cannot exist in me [inasmuch as I am a thing that thinks] seeing that it does not presuppose thought, and also that those ideas are often produced in me without my contributing in any way to the same, and often even against my will; it is thus necessarily the case that the faculty resides in some substance different from me in which all the reality which is objectively in the ideas that are produced by this faculty is formally or eminently contained, as I remarked before. And this substance is either a body, that is, a corporeal nature in which there is contained formally [and really] all that which is objectively [and by representation] in those ideas, or it is God Himself, or some other creature more noble than body in which that same is contained eminently. But, since God is no deceiver, it is very manifest that He does not communicate to me these ideas immediately and by Himself, nor yet by the intervention of some creature in which their reality is not formally, but only eminently, contained. For since He has given me no faculty to recognise that this is the case, but, on the other hand, a very great inclination to believe [that they are sent to me or] that they are conveyed to me by corporeal objects, I do not see how He could be defended from the accusation of deceit if these ideas were produced by causes other than corporeal objects. Hence we must allow that corporeal things exist. However, they are perhaps not exactly what we perceive by the senses, since this comprehension by the senses is in many instances very obscure and confused; but we must at least admit that all things which I conceive in them clearly and distinctly, that is to say, all things which, speaking generally, are comprehended in the object of pure mathematics, are truly to be recognised as external objects.

As to other things, however, which are either particular only, as, for example, that the sun is of such and such a figure, etc., or which are less clearly and distinctly conceived, such as light, sound, pain and the like, it is certain that although they are very dubious and uncertain, yet on the sole ground that God is not a deceiver, and that consequently He has not permitted any falsity to exist in my opinion which He has not likewise given me the faculty of correcting, I may assuredly hope to conclude that I have within me the means of arriving at the truth even here. And first of all there is no doubt that in all things which nature teaches me there is some truth contained; for by nature, considered in general, I now understand no other thing than either God Himself or else the order and disposition which God has established in created things; and by my nature in particular I understand no other thing than the complexus of all the things which God has given me.

But there is nothing which this nature teaches me more expressly [nor more sensibly] than that I have a body which is adversely affected when I feel pain, which has need of food or drink when I experience the feelings of hunger and thirst, and so on; nor can I doubt there being some truth in all this.

Nature also teaches me by these sensations of pain, hunger, thirst, etc., that I am not only lodged in my body as a pilot in a vessel, but that I am very closely united to it, and so to speak so intermingled with it that I seem to compose with it one whole. For if that were not the case, when my body is hurt, I, who am merely a thinking thing, should not feel pain, for I should perceive this wound by the understanding only, just as the sailor perceives by sight when something is damaged in his vessel; and when my body has need of drink or food, I should clearly understand the fact without being warned of it by confused feelings of hunger and thirst. For all these sensations of hunger, thirst, pain, etc. are in truth none other than certain confused modes of thought which are produced by the union and apparent intermingling of mind and body.

Moreover, nature teaches me that many other bodies exist around mine, of which some are to be avoided, and others sought after. And certainly from the fact that I am sensible of different sorts of colours, sounds, scents, tastes, heat, hardness, etc., I very easily conclude that there are in the bodies from which all these diverse sense-perceptions proceed certain variations which answer to them, although possibly these are not really at all similar to them. And also from the fact that amongst these different sense-perceptions some are very agreeable to me and others disagreeable, it is quite certain that my body (or rather myself in my entirety, inasmuch as I am formed of body and soul) may receive different impressions agreeable and disagreeable from the other bodies which surround it.

There is a great difference between mind and body, inasmuch as body is by nature always divisible, and the mind is entirely indivisible. For, as a matter of fact, when I consider the mind, that is to say, myself inasmuch as I am only a thinking thing, I cannot distinguish in myself any parts, but apprehend myself to be clearly one and entire; and although the whole mind seems to be united to the whole body, yet if a foot, or an arm, or some other part, is separated from my body, I am aware that nothing has been taken away from my mind. And the faculties of willing, feeling, conceiving, etc. cannot be properly speaking said to be its parts, for it is one and the same mind which employs itself in willing and in feeling and understanding. But it is quite otherwise with corporeal or extended objects, for there is not one of these imaginable by me which my mind cannot easily divide into parts, and which consequently I do not recognise as being divisible; this would be sufficient to teach me that the mind or soul of man is entirely different from the body, if I had not already learned it from other sources.

I further notice that the mind does not receive the impressions from all parts of the body immediately, but only from the brain, or perhaps even from one of its smallest parts, to wit, from that in which the common sense is said to reside, which, whenever it is disposed in the same particular way, conveys the same thing to the mind, although meanwhile the other portions of the body may be differently disposed, as is testified by innumerable experiments which it is unnecessary here to recount.

I notice, also, that the nature of body is such that none of its parts can be moved by another part a little way off which cannot also be moved in the same way by each one of the parts which are between the two, although this more remote part does not act at all. As, for example, in the cord *ABCD* [which is in tension] if we pull the last part *D*, the first part *A* will not be moved in any way differently from what would be the case if one of the intervening parts *B* or *C* were pulled, and the last part *D* were to remain unmoved. And in the same way, when I feel pain in my foot, my knowledge of physics teaches me that this sensation is communicated by means of nerves dispersed through the foot, which, being extended like cords from there to the brain, when they are contracted in the foot, at the same time contract the inmost portions of the brain which is their extremity and place of origin, and then excite a certain movement which nature has established in order to cause the mind to be affected by a sensation of pain represented as existing in the foot. But because these nerves must pass through the tibia, the thigh, the loins, the back and the neck, in order to reach from the leg to the brain, it may happen that although their extremities which are in the foot are not affected, but only certain ones of their intervening parts [which pass by the loins or the neck], this action will excite the same movement in the brain that might have been excited there by a hurt received in the foot, in consequence of which the mind will necessarily feel in the foot the same pain as if it had received a hurt. And the same holds good of all the other perceptions of our senses.

I notice finally that since each of the movements which are in the portion of the brain by which the mind is immediately affected brings about one particular sensation only, we cannot under the circumstances imagine anything more likely than that this movement, amongst all the sensations which it is capable of impressing on it, causes mind to be affected by that one which is best fitted and most generally useful for the conservation of the human body when it is in health. But experience makes us aware that all the feelings with which nature inspires us are such as I have just spoken of; and there is therefore nothing in them which does not give testimony to the power and goodness of the God [who has produced them]. Thus, for example, when the nerves which are in the feet are violently or more than usually moved, their movement, passing through the medulla of the spine to the inmost parts of the brain, gives a sign to the mind which makes it feel somewhat, to wit, pain, as though in the foot, by which the mind is excited to do its utmost to remove the cause of the evil as dangerous and hurtful to the foot. It is true that God could have constituted the nature of man in such a way that this same movement in the brain would have conveyed something quite different to the mind; for example, it might have produced consciousness of itself either in so far as it is in the brain, or as it is in the foot, or as it is in some other place between the foot and the brain, or it might finally have produced consciousness of anything else whatsoever; but none of all this would have contributed so well to the conservation of the body. Similarly, when we desire to drink, a certain dryness of the throat is produced which moves its nerves, and by their means the internal portions of the brain; and this movement causes in the mind the sensation of thirst, because in this case there is nothing more useful to us than to become aware that we have need to drink for the conservation of our health; and the same holds good in other instances.

From this it is quite clear that, notwithstanding the supreme goodness of God, the nature of man, inasmuch as it is composed of mind and body, cannot be otherwise than sometimes a source of deception. For if there is any cause which excites, not in the foot but in some part of the nerves which are extended between the foot and the brain, or even in the brain itself, the same movement which usually is produced when the foot is detrimentally affected, pain will be experienced as though it were in the foot, and the sense will thus naturally be deceived; for since the same movement in the brain is capable of causing but one sensation in the mind, and this sensation is much more frequently excited by a cause which hurts the foot than by another existing in some other quarter, it is reasonable that it should convey to the mind pain in the foot rather than in any other part of the body. And although the parchedness of the throat does not always proceed, as it usually does, from the fact that drinking is necessary for the health of the body, but sometimes comes from quite a different cause, as is the case with dropsical patients, it is yet much better that it should mislead on this occasion than if, on the other hand, it were always to deceive us when the body is in good health; and so on in similar cases.

To Think About

1. "To think of being is to make it a distinct being. If we ask what being is, we have many answers to choose from: empirical reality in space and time; dead and living matter; persons and things; tools and material; ideas that apply to reality; cogent constructions of ideal objects, as in mathematics; contents of the imagination—in a word, objectiveness. Whatever being I find in my situation is to me an object. I am different. I do not confront myself as I confront things. I am the questioner. I know that I do the asking and that those modes of objective being are offered to me as replies. Whichever way I turn, trying to make an object of myself, there is always the 'I' for which my self becomes an object. There remains a being that is I."   ***Karl Jaspers***

2. "We can never arrive at the real nature of things from the outside. However much we investigate, we can never reach anything but images and names. We are like a man who goes round a castle seeking in vain for an entrance and sometimes sketching the facades."   ***Arthur Schopenhauer***

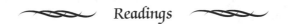

Readings

BECK, L. J. *The Metaphysics of Descartes: A Study of the Meditations.* Oxford: Clarendon Press, 1965.

CHAPPELL, VERE, ed. *Descartes's Meditations: Critical Essays.* Lanham, MD: Rowman & Littlefield, 1997.

KEELING, S. V. *Descartes.* 2nd ed. London: Oxford University Press, 1968.

RORTY, AMELIE OKSENBERG. *Essays on Descartes' Meditations.* Berkeley: University of California Press, 1986.

WILSON, MARGARET DAULER. *Descartes.* London: Routledge & Kegan Paul, 1978.

39
Reality Consists of Matter

Richard Taylor (1919–2003), *professor of philosophy at the University of Rochester, has written highly acclaimed books and articles on a variety of philosophical problems.*

There are many alternatives to Descartes's dualism. In this book we shall consider three of them. The first of these is materialism, represented in the following essay by Richard Taylor. Taylor believes there are no mental entities. He is a materialist. *Materialism,* in its philosophical meaning, is the view that all that exists is material or is completely dependent on matter for its existence. There are two aspects to this position: (1) There is only one basic kind of reality and that is material, and (2) human beings are not entities composed equally of both a material body and an immaterial soul, but are fundamentally bodily in nature. The following essay represents the statement of an extreme materialist. It is important to be aware that materialists do not deny the existence of mind, but they deny that mind is a characteristic of an immaterial soul; they believe the mind is matter, just as everything is matter.

To Study

1. On what basis does Taylor argue that there is no mind-body problem?
2. Why can't a philosophical argument prove that something does or does not exist?
3. What is the grand presupposition of the mind-body problem?
4. Explain the ambiguity of the terms *selves, people,* and *person.*
5. What are bodily and personal predicates? Why are they not interchangeable?
6. What is the mentalistic thesis?
7. What is the materialistic thesis?

From Richard Taylor, "How to Bury the Mind-Body Problem," *American Philosophical Quarterly* 6 (April 1969): 136–43. Reprinted by permission of the author and the publisher.

8. What is Taylor's refutation of the thesis that certain predicates cannot be applied to the human body?
9. What is Taylor's argument against the thesis that there are unique acts which the body cannot do?
10. What is Taylor's refutation of the thesis that we directly know the existence of mental things? What is imagination?
11. What is the fourth argument and Taylor's reply?
12. Does matter think?
13. What is the difference between the soul as life and the soul as thought?

The mind-body problem, in all its variants, is a philosophical fabrication resting on no genuine data at all. It has arisen from certain presuppositions about matter and human nature familiar to philosophy from the time of the Pythagoreans, presuppositions which have persisted just to the extent that they have been left unexamined. And they have not been questioned very much simply because they are so familiar.

There are vexing, unsolved problems of psychology and problems of mental health, but there are no mind-body problems. And there are problems of "philosophical psychology," as they are sometimes called today—problems of perception, sensation, the analysis of deliberation, of purposeful behavior, and so on—but there are no mind-body problems.

The reason why there are no mind-body problems is the most straightforward imaginable: It is because there are no such things as *minds* in the first place. There being no minds, there are in strictness no mental states or events; there are only certain familiar states, capacities, and abilities which are conventionally but misleadingly called "mental." They are so-called, partly in deference to certain philosophical presuppositions, and partly as a reflection of our lack of understanding of them, that is of our ignorance.

Men and women are not minds, nor do they "have" minds. It is not merely that they do not "have" minds the way they have arms and legs; they do not have minds in any proper sense at all. And just as no man or woman has or ever has had any mind, so also are cats, dogs, frogs, vegetables, and the rest of living creation without minds—though philosophers of the highest rank, such as Aristotle, have felt driven to say that all living things, vegetables included, must have souls (else how could they be *living* things?) just as others of similar eminence, like Descartes, have thought that men must have minds, else how could they be *thinking* things? Today, when philosophers talk about mind-body problems, and advance various claims concerning the possible relationships between "mental" and "physical" states and events, they are, of course, talking about men. But they might as well be talking about frogs, because the presuppositions that give rise to these theories apply to other animals as well as to men.

I. Philosophical Arguments for the Existence or Nonexistence of Things

There cannot be any philosophical argument proving that something does or does not exist, so long as the description or definition of it is self-consistent. Thus there cannot be a philosophical argument proving that men do or do not, as some medieval thinkers believed, have an indestructible bone in their bodies. One can only say that such a bone has never been found (which is not a philosophical argument) and then exhibit the groundlessness or falsity of the presuppositions that gave rise to the belief in the first place. (In this case it was certain presuppositions concerning the requirements of the resurrection of the body.) Similarly, there can be no philosophical argument proving that men do or do not have souls, spirits, or minds, or that there are not *sui generis*[1] mental states or events, assuming that these can be described in a self-consistent way. One can only note that such things have never been found in any man, living or dead, and then exhibit the arbitrariness and apparent falsity of the presuppositions that give rise to these opinions in the first place. Now of course, as far as *finding* them goes, many philosophers claim to find them all the time, *within themselves*. They are alleged to be *private* things, deeply hidden, discernible only by their possessors. All they really "find," however, are the most commonplace facts about themselves that are perfectly well known to anyone who knows anything at all—but of this, more later.

II. The Grand Presupposition of the Mind-Body Problem

What I must do now, then, is consider the presupposition that has given birth to the so-called "mind-body" problem, and show that there is nothing in it at all that anyone needs to believe; that, on the contrary, we have good evidence that it is false.

The presupposition can be tersely expressed by saying: *Matter cannot think.* That is the way a Cartesian would put it, but philosophers now spell it out a little better. Thus, we are apt to be told that thinking, choosing, deliberating, reasoning, perceiving, and even feeling, are not concepts of physics and chemistry, so that these terms have no application to bodies. Since, however, men do think, choose, deliberate, reason, perceive and feel, it follows that men are not "mere bodies." They are instead minds or souls or, as it is more common to say today "selves" or "persons," and such terms as "is thinking," "is choosing," "is perceiving," etc., are not physical or bodily but *personal* predications. A man may be in one clear sense a physical object, having arms and legs and so on, but a person is not just that visible and palpable object; there is more to a self or person than this. For it is the self or person that thinks, chooses, deliberates, feels, and so on, and not his body or some part of it.

Again—and this is really only another way of expressing the same presupposition—we are apt to be told that thoughts, choices, reasons, feelings, etc., are not physical things. It makes no sense to ask how large a thought is, whether it is soluble in alcohol, and so on. Yet these things do exist—any man can be aware of them, "within himself." Hence, that "self" within which such things occur

[1] Self-generated. [Ed.]

must be something more than or other than the body. It might be just the totality of all those nonphysical ("mental") things, but in any case it is mental in nature, so a self or person is not the same thing as his body.

Or again, in case one boggles at calling thoughts, feelings, and the like, "things," at least (it is said) no one can deny that they are events or states. But they are not events or states that occur or obtain in the laboratories of physicists and chemists—except in the sense that they sometimes occur in physicists and chemists themselves, who sometimes happen to be in laboratories. No one could ever truly represent whatever might be happening in a test tube or vacuum tube as the transpiring of a thought or feeling. These things just do not—indeed, obviously could not—happen in test tubes or vacuum tubes, because they are not the *kind* of event involving changes of matter. They are a kind of "mental" event. And since these things do, obviously, happen in men, then things happen in men which are nonphysical, "mental," in nature. . . .

III. "Selves" or "Persons" as Minds and Bodies

The word "self" and the plural "selves" are fairly common items of contemporary philosophical vocabulary. These words never occur outside of philosophy, except as suffixes to personal pronouns, but in philosophical contexts they are sometimes taken to denote rather extraordinary things. Selves are, indeed, about the strangest inhabitants of nature that one can imagine—except that, as sometimes described in philosophy, they are not even imaginable in the first place, being quite nonphysical. You cannot poke a self with a stick; the nearest you can come to that is to poke his body. The self that has that body is not supposed to be quite the same thing as his body—that is a (mere) physical object, a possible subject matter for physics and chemistry. *That* is not what thinks, reasons, deliberates, and so on; it is the self that does things like this.

At the same time, selves are never doubted to be the same things as *persons,* and persons are thought to be the same things as people, as men. And there is no doubt at all that men are visible, palpable objects, having arms and legs and so on: That they are in short, physical objects. So the thing becomes highly ambiguous. We do not, in contexts in which it would seem silly or embarrassing to do so, have to say that selves (men) are spirit beings (minds) which in some sense or other happen to "have" bodies. Clearly men are visible and palpable things, that is, are bodies. We can say that all right. But at the same time we need not say—indeed, *must* not say—that men are just (mere) bodies. There is, after all, a difference between a man's body, and that which thinks, perceives, feels, deliberates, and so on; and those are things that men (selves) do, not things that bodies do. Or again, there is, after all, a difference between bodily predicates (weighs 160 pounds, tall, is warm, etc.) and personal predicates (chooses, believes, loves his country, etc.). The former can be predicated of a man's body, just like any other body, but it would "make no sense" to predicate the latter of any (mere) body, and hence of any man's body. They are only predicated of persons. So even though selves are persons and persons are men and men are visible, palpable beings, we must not think that they are just nothing but physical beings. They are physical bodies with minds, or, as some would prefer, minds with physical bodies or, as most writers on this subject want to say, they are somehow *both.*

So the "mental" is discriminated from the (merely) "physical," and the mind-body problem emerges at once: What is the *connection* between them? What is the relationship between men's minds and their bodies? Or between mental and physical events? Or between personal and physical predicates? Anyone who raises this question—for these all amount to one and the same question—can see at once that it is going to be extremely difficult to answer. And this means that it is capable of nourishing a vast amount of philosophy. It has, in fact, kept philosophers on scattered continents busy for hundreds of years, and even today claims much of the time of philosophical faculties and their proteges. It seems a conceit to undertake to put an end to all this, but that is what I propose now to do.

IV. MENTALISM AND MATERIALISM

Consider the following two theses:

I.   A person is not something that has, possesses, utilizes, or contains a mind. That is, a person is not one thing and his mind another thing. A person or self and his mind are one and the same thing.

II.   A person is not something that has, possesses, utilizes, or occupies a body. That is, a person is not one thing and his body another thing. A person or self and his body are one and the same thing.

We can call these two theses "mentalism" and "materialism" respectively, since the first asserts that men are minds and not bodies, and the second that they are bodies and not minds.

Now the first thing to note about these two rather crudely stated theses is that both of them cannot be true, since each asserts what the other denies. They could, of course, both be false, since a person might be identical neither with his body nor with his mind (though it is hard to think of any other candidate for the title of "person"), or a person might somehow be identical with the two of them at once. These two simple theses are, nevertheless, a good starting point for discussion, and I am going to maintain that (II), the materialist thesis, is absolutely true.

Philosophers have tended to regard (I), or some more sophisticated version of it, as correct, and to dismiss (II) as unworthy of consideration. In fact, however—and it is hard to see how this could have been so generally overlooked—*any* philosophical argument in favor of (I) against (II) is just as good an argument for (II) against (I). This I shall illustrate shortly.

In the meantime, let us give what is due to the humble fact that there are considerations drawn from common sense, indeed from the common knowledge of mankind, which favor, without proving, (II). It is common knowledge that there are such things as human bodies, that there are men and women in the world. There is also one such body which everyone customarily, and without the least suggestion of absurdity, refers to as himself; he sees himself in the mirror, dresses himself, scratches himself, and so on. This is known, absolutely as well as anything can be known, and if any man were to profess doubt about it—if he doubted, for example, that there are such physical objects in the world as men and women, and therefore doubted the reality of his own body—then that man would have to be considered *totally* ignorant. For there is nothing more obvious than this. A man would be ignorant indeed if he did not know that there are such things as the sun, moon, earth, rivers, and lakes. I have never met anyone so ignorant as that. But a man who did not even know that there are men and women in the world, and that he—his body—was one of them, would be totally ignorant.

Now there is no such common knowledge of the existence of minds or souls. No one has ever found such a thing anywhere. Belief in such things rests either on religious persuasion or on philosophical arguments, sometimes on nothing but the connotations of familiar words. Such beliefs are opinions, easily doubted, and nothing that anyone knows. If a man denies that such things exist, as many have, then he exhibits no ignorance; he expresses only scepticism or doubt concerning certain religious or philosophical presuppositions or arguments.

If, accordingly, we are seeking some sort of thing with which to identify persons, then this is a *prima facie* consideration in favor of identifying them with their bodies, with things we know to be real, rather than with things postulated to suit the requirements of philosophical arguments or religious faith. This does not prove that men are nothing but bodies, of course, but it is enough to show that, since we know there are such things as persons, and we know there are such things as men (living human bodies), we had better regard these as the very same things *unless* there are some facts which would prohibit our doing so. And I shall maintain that there are no such facts. There are only philosophical arguments, not one of which proves anything.

The Arguments for Mentalism

I shall now consider the arguments I know, already adumbrated, in favor of what I have called mentalism. Of course not all philosophers who take seriously the mind-body problem subscribe to this simple thesis as I have formulated it, but the more sophisticated versions can be considered as we go along, and it will be seen that the arguments for these are equally inconclusive.

The First Argument.   There are certain predicates that undoubtedly apply to persons, but not to their bodies. Persons and their bodies cannot, therefore, be the same. One can sometimes truly say of a person, for example, that he is intelligent, sentimental, that he loves his country, believes in God, holds strange theories on the doctrine of universals, and so on. But it would sound very odd—indeed, not even make sense—to assert any such things of any physical object whatever and hence of any man's body. It would at best be a confusion of categories to say that a certain man's *body* loves its country, for example.

Reply.   If the foregoing is considered a good argument for the nonidentity of persons and bodies, then the following is obviously just as good an argument for not identifying them with their minds: There are certain predicates that undoubtedly apply to persons, but not to their minds. A person and his mind cannot, therefore, be the same. One can sometimes truly say of a person, for example, that he is walking, ran into a post, is feverish, or that he fell down. But it would sound very odd—indeed not even make sense—to assert such things of any mind whatever. It would at best be a confusion of categories to say, for instance, that a certain man's *mind* ran into a post.

Considerations such as these have led many philosophers to affirm that a person or the "true self" is neither a mind, nor a body. Hence, a person must be either (*a*) something else altogether or, as some would prefer to say, the term "person" must express a "primitive" concept or (*b*) both mind and body; i.e., a person must be something having both mental and physical properties.

The former of these alternatives is simply evasive. Persons are real beings, so there must be existing things which are persons. If when we bump into a man we are not bumping into a person, and if at the same time we are not referring to a person when we say of someone that he is thinking, then it is quite impossible to see what is left to fill the role of a person. The word "person" may indeed be a primitive one, but this, I think, only means that such arguments as to the two just cited are equally good and equally bad.

The second alternative, that persons are beings having both mental and physical properties, is obviously only as good as the claim that there are such things as "mental properties" to begin with. Indeed, it is not even that good, for just as a physical property can be nothing but a property of a physical thing, i.e., a body, so also a mental property can be nothing but the property of the mental thing, i.e., a mind. For something to count as a physical property of something it is sufficient, and necessary, that the thing in question is a physical object. By the same token, for something to count as a mental property it is sufficient, and necessary, that it be the property that some mind possesses. Any property whatsoever that can be truly claimed to be the property of some body, animate or inanimate, is a physical property; the assertion that some body possesses a nonphysical property is simply a contradiction. This second alternative, that persons are beings possessing both physical and mental properties, therefore amounts to saying that a person is at one and the same time *two* utterly different things—a body with its physical properties and a mind with its mental properties. These are not supposed to be two things in the same sense that a family, for instance, is a plurality of beings consisting of husband, wife, and perhaps one or more children, but two wholly disparate kinds of beings having, as Descartes put it, nothing in common. Now this is no resolution of the antithesis between what I have called mentalism and materialism. It is only a reformulation of that issue. For now we can surely ask: Which of these two is the person, the true self? The body which has a mind, or the mind which has a body? And we are then back where we started.

The Second Argument.   This argument consists of pointing out the rather remarkable things that a person can do but which, it is alleged, no physical object, of whatever complexity, can do, from which it of course follows that a person is not a physical object and hence not identical with his own body. A person, for example, can reason, deliberate about ends and means, plan for the future, draw inferences from evidence, speculate, and so on. No physical objects do such things, and even complicated machines can at best only simulate these activities. Indeed, it would not even make sense to say that a man's body was, for example, speculating on the outcome of the election, though this would not be an absurd description of some person. A person, therefore, is not the same thing as his body, and can only be described in terms of certain concepts of mind.

Reply.   This argument is not very different from the first; it only substitutes activities for properties which are baptized "mental." And one reply to it is the same as to the first argument; namely, that since persons often do things that no mind could do—for instance, they run races, go fishing, raise families, and so on—then it follows that persons are not minds.

A far better reply, however, and one that is not so question-begging as it looks, is to note that since men do reason, deliberate, plan, speculate, draw inferences, run races, go fishing, raise families, and so on, and since the men that do all such things are the visible, palpable beings that we see around us all the time, then it follows that *some* physical objects—namely, men—do all these things. All are, accordingly, the activities of physical objects; they are not activities divided between a physical object, the visible man, on the one hand, and some invisible thing, his mind, on the other.

Consider the statement: "I saw George yesterday; he was trying to figure out the best way to get from Albany to Montpelier." Now this statement obviously refers, in a normal context, to a person, and it is perfectly clear that the name "George" and the pronoun "he" refer to *one and the same* being, that person. And what they both refer to is something that was seen, a certain man's body; they do not refer to some unseen thing, of which that body is some sort of visible manifestation. If that were so, then the statement would not really be true. And in any case, it would be embarrassingly silly to suppose that a more accurate rendition of the thought expressed in this statement might be: "I saw George's body yesterday. His mind was trying to figure out how to get (how to get what?) from Albany to Montpelier." It is, accordingly, one and the same thing which (*a*) is seen, and (*b*) figures and plans, and that thing is undoubtedly the physical object George. Now if conventions incline us to describe figuring out something as a "mental" activity, then we shall have to say that some purely physical objects—namely, living men—engage in mental activities. But this is simply misleading, if not contradictory, for it suggests that we are ascribing to a physical object an activity of something that is not physical, but mental. It would, therefore, be far better to say that some physical objects, namely, men or persons, sometimes perform physical activities such as figuring and planning which are quite unlike those we are accustomed to finding in certain other physical objects such as machines and the like.

The Third Argument.   This argument, the commonest of all, is to the effect that while there may or may not be such things as "minds" (whatever that might mean), there are indisputably certain nonphysical things which are quite properly called "mental," as anyone can verify within himself. Indeed, it is sometimes claimed that nothing, not even the reality of our own bodies, is as certain as the existence of these mental things, which are perceived "directly."

Reply.   What are here referred to as mental entities are, of course, such things as thoughts, mental images, after-images, sensations, feelings, and so on. Pains are frequently mentioned in this context, being, presumably, things whose existence no one would question. Having got to this point then the next step, of course, is to speculate on the connection between these mental things and certain "physical" states of the body. They evidently are not the same, and yet it is hard to see what the connection could be. Speculation also extends to such questions as whether two or more men might have "the same" pain, or why it is impossible that they should, in view of the fact that they can hold common possession of ordinary "physical" things like clocks and books. Again, curiosity is aroused by the fact that a mental image, for instance, seems to have color, and yet it somehow can be perceived only by one person, its owner. Again, images sometimes seem to have shape—enough so that a perceiver can distinguish one from another, for instance—and yet no assignable size. Here, really, is a gold mine for philosophical speculation, and such speculations have filled, as they still fill, volumes.

Now surely there is a *better* way to express all that is known to be true in all this, and it is a way that does not even permit these odd theories to get started. What we know is true, and all we know is true, is that men think, sense, imagine, feel, etc. It is sheer redundancy to say that men think things called "thoughts," sense things called "sensations," imagine "images," and feel "feelings." There are no such things. And to say there are no such things is *not* to deny that men think, sense, imagine, and feel.

What, for instance, does it mean to say a man feels a pain in his foot? Absolutely nothing, except that his foot hurts. But this hurting, what sort of thing is it? It is not a thing at all; not a thing felt, and certainly not a mental thing that is felt *in his foot.* It is a state, and in no sense a state of his mind, but a straightforward state of his foot. But can that be a *physical* state? Well, it is assuredly a state of his foot, and that is a physical object; there is nothing else—no spirit foot, no spirit being, no spirit mind—that it can be a state of. Why, then, cannot other people have that same state? Why cannot other people feel the same pain I feel in my foot? And if it is a physical state, why cannot we open the foot and *see* it there? Or make some straightforward test of its presence in another man's foot?

To ask questions like these is just not to understand what is meant by describing an object as being in a certain state. Consider a piece of molten lead. Now this molten state, what sort of thing is it? The answer is that it is not a thing at all; it is a state or condition of a thing. Is it a physical state? Well, it is a state of the lead, and that is a physical object; there is nothing else for it to be a state of. Why, then, cannot another piece of lead have that same state? Why cannot something else have the molten state of this piece of lead? Of course something else can, in the only meaningful sense that can be attached to such a question; that is, another piece of lead, or some things which are not lead can melt the same way this piece of lead melted. To ask why another piece of lead cannot have the molten state of this piece of lead is, of course, unintelligible, unless it is interpreted the way just suggested, in which case the answer is that it can. But similarly, to ask why another man cannot have the pain that this man is feeling is also unintelligible, unless construed as the question why other men cannot suffer pain, in which case its presupposition is wrong—they can. And if the piece of lead's being melted is a "physical" state, why can we not separate the lead into drops and see that state? Simply because it is a state of the lead, and not some other thing contained in the lead. Indeed, to separate it into drops *is* to see, not its meltedness (there is no such thing), but that it is melted—that is just the test. We do not have to *ask* the lead whether it is melted, and rely upon its testimony; we can tell by its behavior. And in the same way we can sometimes—admittedly not always—see that a man is suffering, without having to ask him. That we sometimes go wrong here does not result from the fact that his suffering is something quite hidden within him, which he alone can find and then report; there is nothing hidden, and nothing for him to find. Still, there is a straightforward way of testing whether a piece of lead is melted, and there is no similarly straightforward way of testing whether a man's foot hurts—he may only be pretending it does. Does this indicate that there might be a pain, which he has found in his foot but might conceal, as he might conceal the contents of his wallet? Surely not; it shows only that men, unlike pieces of lead, are capable of dissimulating. No philosophy was needed to unearth that commonplace fact. It is easier to test for the presence of some states of properties than others, and this is true not only of the states of men's bodies, but of everything under the sun. But things that are hard to establish do not, just by virtue of that, warrant the title of "mental."

Similar remarks can be made about images, which are frequent candidates for the role of mental entities. When queried about their mental imagery, people often will describe it in colorful detail and even with pride, not unlike the regard one might have for a precious gem accessible only to himself. It turns out, though, that all one thereby describes is his power of imagination, which is, of course, sometimes quite great. To say that one has a lively imagination, even great powers of imagination, does not mean that he can create within his mind . . . things called "images" and composed of some mental, nonphysical, spiritual material. There is no material that is nonmaterial, and there are no images composed of this or anything else—except, of course, those physical objects (pictures, etc.) visible to anyone who can see, which are rightly called images of things. When someone sees something, there is (*i*) the man who sees, and (*ii*) the thing seen; for instance, some building or scene. There is not, between these, a third thing called the appearance of what is seen; philosophers are pretty much agreed on this. But similarly, when someone *imagines* something or, as it is misleadingly put, "forms an image" of it, there is (*i*) the man who imagines, and (*ii*) sometimes, but not always, something that he imagines; for instance, some building or scene, which might or might not be real. There is not, between these, a third thing called the image of what is imagined. There is just the imagining of the thing in question. And to say that a man is imagining something is to say what he is doing, or perhaps to refer to some state he is in; it is not to refer to some inner thing that he creates and, while it lasts, exclusively possesses.

It is enough, it seems to me, to point this out; that is, to point out that we can say all we want to say about men's powers of imagination without ever introducing the substantive "an image." Philosophy is robbed of nothing by the disposal of these, and there is absolutely no fact about human nature which requires us to affirm their existence. But if one does insist upon the reality of mental images, and professes, for instance, to find them right in his own mind by introspecting—and it is astonishing how eager students of philosophy seem to be to make this claim— then we can ask some very embarrassing questions. Suppose, for instance, one professes to be able to form a very clear image of, say, the campus library—he can bring if before his mind, hold it there, perhaps even turn it bottom side up, and banish it at will. We ask him, then, to hold it before his mind and count the number of steps in the image, the number of windows, the number and disposition of pigeons on the roof, and so on. He could do these things if he had a photograph of the thing before him. But he cannot do them with the image, in spite of the fact that it is supposed to be right there "before his mind," easily and "directly" inspectable. He can tell how many steps there are only if he has sometime counted the steps on the building itself (or in a photograph of it) and now *remembers*—but that is not counting the steps in the image. Or he can *imagine* that it has, say, 30 steps, and then *say* "30"—but that is not counting anything either; it is only a performance. The image he professes to "have" there, so clearly and with such detail, does not even exist. He claims to have produced in his mind an image of the library; but all he has actually done is imagine the library.

What, then, is imagining something? Is it an activity, a state, or what? It does not really matter here how we answer that; it is only *not* the producing of an entity called a "mental image." Let us suppose for this context, then, that to be imagining something is to be in a certain *state*. Is it, then, a *physical* state? Well, it is a state of a man, just as drunkenness, sleep, perspiration, obesity, etc., are sometimes states of this man or that. What is meant by asking whether these are "physical" states, other than asking whether they are states of a physical object? What shall we say of being in a state of sleep, for instance? It is the state of a man, and a man is a physical—that is, a visible and palpable—being. You cannot poke a man's state of imagining something with a stick; all you can do is poke him. That is true. But you cannot poke his somnolence with a stick either. There is nothing to poke; there is only the man sleeping, or the man imagining, or the man becoming drunk, or whatever.

How then can a man, if he is nothing but a (mere) physical object, be in such a state as this, that is, of imagining something? If he is only a body and can do this, why cannot sticks and stones be in such a state, for are they not bodies too? The answer is: For just the same reason that sticks and stones cannot be drunken, asleep, perspiring, obese, or hungry; namely, that they are sticks and stones and not men. The reason is not that they lack minds. Even if they had them, they still could not be drunken, asleep, perspiring, obese or hungry, for they would still be sticks and stones and not men.

The Fourth (and last) Argument. It is fairly common for people, including philosophers, to say that they can perfectly well imagine surviving the death of their bodies, which would be quite impossible for anyone who supposed that he and his body were one and the same thing. Admittedly no one knows whether there is any survival of death, but it is at least not necessarily false. The doctrine of metempsychosis,[2] for example, though there may be no reason for believing it, cannot be shown to be impossible just on philosophical grounds. It would be impossible, however, if a person and his body were identical, and so would any other form of survival. We

---

[2] The passing of the soul at death into another body. [ED.]

know the fate of the body: dust. If I am the same as my body, then it is logically impossible that I should not share that fate.

Reply.   All this argument shows is that not everyone, perhaps even no one, *knows* that he and his body are one and the same thing. It does not in the least show that, in fact, they are not. Some things, like the Evening Star and the Morning Star, which some are accustomed to thinking of and describing as different things, nevertheless do turn out to be the same.

Suppose a god were to promise me a life after death—promising, perhaps, to have me (the very person that I am) reborn elsewhere with a different body. Now such a promise might quicken a real hope in me, provided I am capable (as everyone is) of thinking of myself as being something different from my body. But the fact that I can think such a distinction does not show that there is one, and in case there is not—in case I happen to be identical with my body—then of course no god could fulfill such a promise. Consider this analogy: If an enemy of our country did not know that Albany is (the same thing as) the capital of New York, then he might be very interested in a proposal to bomb the one but to spare the other. It would nevertheless be a proposal that no one could carry out. The fact that someone who is ignorant of this identity can entertain the possibility of its being carried out does not show that it is possible; it shows only that he does not know that it is not.

V. THE SOUL AS LIFE AND THE SOUL AS THOUGHT

It is useful in concluding, I think, to compare the philosophical conception of the mind with what was once the philosophical conception of life. It was once pretty much taken for granted that men and other animals *possess* something which inanimate things lack, namely, life, and that it is *because* they possess this that they can do all sorts of things that inanimate things cannot do, such as move themselves, assimilate nourishment, reproduce their kind, and so on. Aristotle classified the souls of living things according to the abilities they imparted to their owners, and thought that even vegetables had souls. Indeed, an animal's *life* and *soul* were generally thought to be one and the same thing. The very word "animal" has its origin in this belief. Socrates, according to Plato, was even able to convince himself of his own immortality on the basis of this notion for, he thought, if it is only because he has a life or soul to begin with that he is a living man, then it is idle to fear the death of that very soul. Life seemed to him identical with his soul, but accidental to his body, indeed even foreign to such a thing of clay. A similar model was at work in Descartes' philosophy when he declared that the soul could never stop thinking. Thought seemed to him identical with his soul, but positively foreign to his body.

Now of course we still talk of life that way, but we no longer take such common modes of speech as descriptive of any reality. We speak of a man "losing" his life, of a man "taking" another's life, of the "gift" of life, and even of the "breath" of life which God is supposed to infuse into an otherwise *lifeless* body. But these are plainly metaphors. No one supposes that a man or animal moves, assimilates nourishment, reproduces, and so on *because* it is possessed of life. We no longer think of life as something added to an animal body, some separable thing that quickens matter. To distinguish something as a living animal is only to call attention to the very complicated way the matter of its body is organized and to a large class of capacities which result from such organization. A living body is simply one in which certain processes, some of them frightfully complex and ill understood, take place. A living body, in short, differs from a nonliving one, not in what it possesses, but in what it does, and these are facts about it that can be verified in a straightforward way.

I have been urging a similar way of speaking of the mind; not as something mysteriously *embodied* here and there, and something that is supposed to *account* for the more or less intelligent behavior of certain beings. A being capable of more or less intelligent thought and action differs from one lacking such capacities, not in something it possesses, but precisely in what it does. And this, incidentally, explains why a man tends to regard it as a deep insult to be told that he has no mind. It is not because he is thus divested in our eyes of some possession dearly prized, but rather, because such a remark is quite rightly taken to mean that he lacks certain important and distinctively human abilities and capacities. If a man is assured that his possession of certain more or less intellectual abilities is in no way in question, he feels divested of nothing upon learning that among his parts or possessions there is none that is properly denoted "a mind."

VI. DOES MATTER THINK?

Probably every philosopher has felt more or less acutely at one time or another a profound puzzlement in the idea of (mere) matter doing those various things rightly ascribable only to persons. How, it is wondered, can a body think, deliberate, imagine things, figure and plan, and so on?

This is really no proper source of bafflement, however. No one can say, *a priori,* what the highly organized material systems of one's body are or are not capable of. It was once thought incredible that matter, unquickened by any soul, could be alive, for matter seemed to inquirers to be inert or lifeless by its very nature. Yet we see around us all the time specimens of living matter—in the merest insects, for instance—so philosophical prejudice has had to yield to the fact. Similarly, I submit, we see around us all the time specimens of thinking matter; that is, material beings which deliberate, imagine, plan, and so on. For men do in fact do these things, and when we see a man, we are seeing a material being—a dreadfully complex and highly organized one, to be sure, but no less a visible and palpable object for that. In any case, the seeming mystery or incredibility that may attach to the idea of matter exercising intellectual capacities is hardly dissolved by postulating something *else* to exercise those capacities. If there is a difficulty in comprehending how a body can do such things, there is surely no less difficulty in seeing how something which is not a body can do them any better.

To Think About

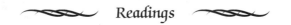

1. "Life exists in the Universe only because the carbon atom possesses certain exceptional properties."   ***Unknown***

2. "The man who is ready to prove that metaphysical knowledge is wholly impossible . . . is a brother metaphysician with a rival theory of first principles."   ***F. H. Bradley***

3. "We may accordingly define a metaphysical sentence as a sentence which purports to express a genuine proposition, but does, in fact, express neither a tautology (one meaning stated in different terms) nor an empirical hypothesis. And as tautologies and empirical hypotheses form the entire class of significant propositions, we are justified in concluding that all metaphysical assertions are nonsensical."   ***Alfred Ayer***

4. "We look not to the things that are seen but to the things that are unseen; for the things that are seen are transient, but the things that are unseen are eternal."   ***2 Corinthians 4:18, RSV***

5. "To rest in the apparent and to mistake it for the real is the one general error, root of all others and cause of all our stumbling and suffering, to which man is exposed by the nature of his mentality."   ***Sri Aurobindo***

Readings

HUDSON, HUD. *A Materialist Metaphysics of the Human Person.* Ithaca, NY: Cornell University Press, 2001.

MELNYK, ANDREW. *A Physicalist Manifesto: Thoroughly Modern Materialism.* New York: Cambridge University Press, 2003.

PAPINEAU, DAVID. *Thinking about Consciousness.* Oxford: Oxford University Press, 2002.

PUTNAM, HILARY. *Renewing Philosophy.* Cambridge, MA: Harvard University Press, 1992.

40
Reality Consists of Ideas

George Berkeley (1685–1753) was an Anglican minister and one of the most acute British philosophers. The main principles of his pluralistic idealism were fully formed before he turned twenty years old. His major works were A Treatise on the Principles of Human Knowledge *(1710) and* Three Dialogues between Hylas and Philonous *(1713). The analysis of knowledge they contain has had substantial influence on all subsequent philosophy.*

The second alternative to Descartes's dualism that we shall consider, idealism, denies the reality of material objects. George Berkeley was an *idealist,* a term ordinarily used to refer to high moral aims, but for him idealism is the opposite of materialism. Berkeley argues that there is no matter; all is mental. What we refer to as physical objects Berkeley states are simply coherent sets of ideas or sense impressions. There is no substance or substratum in which they inhere. Because a thing is but a group of ideas, it can exist only in a mind. He believes that what exists is either an idea or a perceiver of that idea. Thus his basic dictum: "to be is to be perceived or to be a perceiver."

Physical objects exist, or, rather, systematic collections of ideas exist, and they do not cease to exist when they are not perceived by beings in this world. This is because God always perceives them and causes all of us to have similar perceptions.

In the following dialogue, the character of Philonous (literally, "Friend of Mind") represents Berkeley's position. Hylas ("Matter") represents the position of his opponent.

~~~~ To Study ~~~~

1. How does Hylas define *skepticism?* Why does Philonous deny the charge that he is a skeptic?
2. What does Philonous mean by distinguishing *immediate* from *mediate* perception of sensible things?

From George Berkeley, *Three Dialogues Between Hylas and Philonous* (London: Henry Clements, 1713).

3. Why does Philonous deny that heat and color can exist in a material object external to the mind?
4. What relevance to Philonous's argument do microscopes have?
5. What does Hylas mean by *primary* and *secondary* qualities?
6. Explain Philonous's position that the same arguments against secondary qualities can also be maintained against primary qualities.
7. What does Hylas mean by *material substratum* or *substance?*
8. Why does Philonous think that material substance is inconceivable and that its existence is absurd?

Hylas   You were represented in last night's conversation as one who maintained the most extravagant opinion that ever entered into the mind of man, to wit, that there is no such thing as "material substance" in the world.

Philonous   That there is no such thing as what philosophers call "material substance," I am seriously persuaded; but if I were made to see anything absurd or skeptical in this, I should then have the same reason to renounce this that I imagine I have now to reject the contrary opinion.

Hylas   What! Can anything be more fantastical, more repugnant to common sense or a more manifest piece of skepticism than to believe there is no such thing as matter?. . .

Philonous   Pray, Hylas, what do you mean by a "skeptic?"

Hylas   I mean what all men mean, one that doubts of everything.

Philonous   He then who entertains no doubt concerning some particular point, with regard to that point cannot be thought a skeptic.

Hylas   I agree with you.

Philonous   Whether does doubting consist in embracing the affirmative or negative side of a question?

Hylas   In neither; for whoever understands English cannot but know that *doubting* signifies a suspense between both.

Philonous   He then that denies any point can no more be said to doubt of it than he who affirms it with the same degree of assurance.

Hylas   True.

Philonous   And, consequently, for such his denial is no more to be esteemed a skeptic than the other.

Hylas   I acknowledge it.

Philonous   How comes it to pass then, Hylas, that you pronounce me a skeptic because I deny what you affirm, to wit, the existence of matter? Since, for aught you can tell, I am as peremptory in my denial as you in your affirmation.

Hylas   Hold, Philonous, I have been a little out in my definition; but every false step a man makes in discourse is not to be insisted on. I said indeed that a "skeptic" was one who doubted of everything; but I should have added: or who denies the reality and truth of things.

Philonous What things? Do you mean the principles and theorems of sciences? But these you know are universal intellectual notions, and consequently independent of matter; the denial therefore of this does not imply the denying them.

Hylas I grant it. But are there no other things? What think you of distrusting the senses, of denying the real existence of sensible things, or pretending to know nothing of them. Is not this sufficient to denominate a man a skeptic?

Philonous Shall we therefore examine which of us it is that denies the reality of sensible things or professes the greatest ignorance of them, since, if I take you rightly, he is to be esteemed the greatest skeptic?

Hylas That is what I desire.

Philonous What mean you by "sensible things?"

Hylas Those things which are perceived by the senses. Can you imagine that I mean anything else?

Philonous Pardon me, Hylas, if I am desirous clearly to apprehend your notions, since this may much shorten our inquiry. Suffer me then to ask you this further question. Are those things only perceived by the senses which are perceived immediately? Or may those things properly be said to be "sensible" which are perceived mediately, or not without the intervention of others?

Hylas I do not sufficiently understand you.

Philonous In reading a book, what I immediately perceive are the letters, but mediately, or by means of these, are suggested to my mind the notions of God, virtue, truth, etc. Now, that the letters are truly sensible things, or perceived by sense, there is no doubt; but I would know whether you take the things suggested by them to be so too.

Hylas No, certainly; it were absurd to think God or virtue sensible things, though they may be signified and suggested to the mind by sensible marks with which they have an arbitrary connection.

Philonous It seems, then, that by "sensible things" you mean those only which can be perceived immediately by sense.

Hylas Right.

Philonous Does it not follow from this that, though I see one part of the sky red, and another blue, and that my reason does thence evidently conclude there must be some cause of that diversity of colors, yet that cause cannot be said to be a sensible thing or perceived by the sense of seeing?

Hylas It does.

Philonous In like manner, though I hear variety of sounds, yet I cannot be said to hear the causes of those sounds.

Hylas You cannot.

Philonous And when by my touch I perceive a thing to be hot and heavy, I cannot say, with any truth or propriety, that I feel the cause of its heat or weight.

Hylas To prevent any more questions of this kind, I tell you once for all that by "sensible things" I mean those only which are perceived by sense, and that in truth the senses perceive nothing which they do not perceive immediately, for they make no inferences. The deducing therefore of causes or occasions from effects and appearances which alone are perceived by sense, entirely relates to reason. . . .

Philonous   Heat is then a sensible thing?

Hylas   Certainly.

Philonous   Does the reality of sensible things consist in being perceived, or is it something distinct from their being perceived, and that bears no relation to the mind?

Hylas   To *exist* is one thing, and to be *perceived* is another.

Philonous   I speak with regard to sensible things only; and of these I ask, whether by their real existence you mean a subsistence exterior to the mind and distinct from their being perceived?

Hylas   I mean a real absolute being, distinct from and without any relation to their being perceived.

Philonous   Heat therefore, if it be allowed a real being, must exist without the mind?

Hylas   It must.

Philonous   Tell me, Hylas, is this real existence equally compatible to all degrees of heat, which we perceive, or is there any reason why we should attribute it to some and deny it to others? And if there be, pray let me know that reason.

Hylas   Whatever degree of heat we perceive by sense, we may be sure the same exists in the object that occasions it.

Philonous   What! the greatest as well as the least?

Hylas   I tell you, the reason is plainly the same in respect of both: they are both perceived by sense; nay, the greater degree of heat is more sensibly perceived; and consequently, if there is any difference, we are more certain of its real existence than we can be of the reality of a lesser degree.

Philonous   But is not the most vehement and intense degree of heat a very great pain?

Hylas   No one can deny it.

Philonous   And is any unperceiving thing capable of pain or pleasure?

Hylas   No, certainly.

Philonous   Is your material substance a senseless being or a being endowed with sense and perception?

Hylas   It is senseless, without doubt.

Philonous   It cannot, therefore, be the subject of pain?

Hylas   By no means.

Philonous   Nor, consequently, of the greatest heat perceived by sense, since you acknowledge this to be no small pain?

Hylas   I grant it.

Philonous   What shall we say then of your external object: is it a material substance, or no?

Hylas   It is a material substance with the sensible qualities inhering in it.

Philonous   How then can a great heat exist in it, since you own it cannot in a material substance? I desire you would clear this point.

Hylas   Hold, Philonous, I fear I was out in yielding intense heat to be a pain. It should seem rather that pain is something distinct from heat, and the consequence or effect of it.

Philonous   Upon putting your hand near the fire, do you perceive one simple uniform sensation or two distinct sensations?

Hylas   But one simple sensation.

Philonous   Is not the heat immediately perceived?

Hylas   It is.

Philonous   And the pain?

Hylas   True.

Philonous   Seeing therefore they are both immediately perceived at the same time, and the fire affects you only with one simple or uncompounded idea, it follows that this same simple idea is both the intense heat immediately perceived and the pain; and, consequently, that the intense heat immediately perceived is nothing distinct from a particular sort of pain.

Hylas   It seems so.

Philonous   Again, try in your thoughts, Hylas, if you can conceive a vehement sensation to be without pain or pleasure.

Hylas   I cannot.

Philonous   Or can you frame to yourself an idea of sensible pain or pleasure, in general, abstracted from every particular idea of heat, cold, tastes, smells, etc.?

Hylas   I do not find that I can.

Philonous   Does it not therefore follow that sensible pain is nothing distinct from those sensations or ideas—in an intense degree?

Hylas   It is undeniable; and, to speak the truth, I begin to suspect a very great heat cannot exist but in a mind perceiving it.

Philonous   What! are you then in that *skeptical* state of suspense, between affirming and denying?

Hylas   I think I may be positive in the point. A very violent and painful heat cannot exist without the mind.

Philonous   It has not therefore, according to you, any real being?

Hylas   I own it. . . .

Philonous   Can any doctrine be true that necessarily leads a man into an absurdity?

Hylas   Without doubt it cannot.

Philonous   Is it not an absurdity to think that the same thing should be at the same time both cold and warm?

Hylas   It is.

Philonous   Suppose now one of your hands hot, and the other cold, and that they are both at once put into the same vessel of water, in an intermediate state, will not the water seem cold to one hand, and warm to the other?

Hylas   It will.

Philonous   Ought we not therefore, by your principles, to conclude it is really both cold and warm at the same time, that is, according to your own concession, to believe an absurdity?

Hylas   I confess it seems so.

Philonous   Consequently, the principles themselves are false, since you have granted that no true principle leads to an absurdity.

Hylas   But, after all, can anything be more absurd than to say, *there is no heat in the fire?*

Philonous   To make the point still clearer; tell me whether, in two cases exactly alike, we ought not to make the same judgment?

Hylas   We ought.

Philonous   When a pin pricks your finger, does it not rend and divide the fibres of your flesh?

Hylas   It does.

Philonous   And when a coal burns your finger, does it any more?

Hylas   It does not.

Philonous   Since, therefore, you neither judge the sensation itself occasioned by the pin, nor anything like it to be in the pin, you should not, conformably to what you have now granted, judge the sensation occasioned by the fire, or anything like it, to be in the fire.

Hylas   Well, since it must be so, I am content to yield this point and acknowledge that heat and cold are only sensations existing in our minds. But there still remain qualities enough to secure the reality of external things. . . . The case of colors is very different. Can anything be plainer than that we see them on the objects?

Philonous   The objects you speak of are, I suppose, corporeal substances existing without the mind?

Hylas   They are.

Philonous   And have true and real colors inhering in them?

Hylas   Each visible object has that color which we see in it.

Philonous   How! is there anything visible but what we perceive by sight?

Hylas   There is not.

Philonous   And do we perceive anything by sense which we do not perceive immediately?

Hylas   How often must I be obliged to repeat the same thing? I tell you, we do not.

Philonous   Have patience, good Hylas, and tell me once more whether there is anything immediately perceived by the senses except sensible qualities. I know you asserted there was not; but I would now be informed whether you still persist in the same opinion.

Hylas   I do.

Philonous   Pray, is your corporeal substance either a sensible quality or made up of sensible qualities?

Hylas   What a question that is! Who ever thought it was?

Philonous My reason for asking was, because in saying "each visible object has that color which we see in it," you make visible objects to be corporeal substances, which implies either that corporeal substances are sensible qualities or else that there is something besides sensible qualities perceived by sight; but as this point was formerly agreed between us, and is still maintained by you, it is a clear consequence that your corporeal substance is nothing distinct from sensible qualities.

Hylas You may draw as many absurd consequences as you please and endeavor to perplex the plainest things, but you shall never persuade me out of my senses. I clearly understand my own meaning.

Philonous I wish you would make me understand it, too. But, since you are unwilling to have your notion of corporeal substance examined, I shall urge that point no further. Only be pleased to let me know whether the same colors which we see exist in external bodies or some other.

Hylas The very same.

Philonous What! are then the beautiful red and purple we see on yonder clouds really in them? Or do you imagine they have in themselves any other form than that of a dark mist or vapor?

Hylas I must own, Philonous, those colors are not really in the clouds as they seem to be at this distance. They are only apparent colors.

Philonous "Apparent" call you them? How shall we distinguish these apparent colors from real?

Hylas Very easily. Those are to be thought apparent which, appearing only at a distance, vanish upon a nearer approach.

Philonous And those, I suppose, are to be thought real which are discovered by the most near and exact survey.

Hylas Right.

Philonous Is the nearest and exactest survey made by the help of a microscope or by the naked eye?

Hylas By a microscope, doubtless.

Philonous But a microscope often discovers colors in an object different from those perceived by the unassisted sight. And, in case we had microscopes magnifying to any assigned degree, it is certain that no object whatsoever, viewed through them, would appear in the same color which it exhibits to the naked eye.

Hylas And what will you conclude from all this? You cannot argue that there are really and naturally no colors on objects because by artificial managements they may be altered or made to vanish.

Philonous I think it may evidently be concluded from your own concessions that all the colors we see with our naked eyes are only apparent as those on the clouds, since they vanish upon a more close and accurate inspection which is afforded us by a microscope. . . .

Hylas I frankly own, Philonous, that it is in vain to stand out any longer. Colors, sounds, tastes, in a word, all those termed "secondary qualities," have certainly no existence without the mind. But by this acknowledgment I must not be supposed to derogate anything from the reality of matter or external objects; seeing it is no more than several philosophers maintain, who nevertheless are the farthest imaginable from denying matter. For the clearer understanding of this you must know sensible qualities are by philosophers divided into "primary" and "secondary." The former are extension, figure, solidity, gravity, motion, and rest. And these they hold exist really in bodies. The latter are those above enumerated, or, briefly, all sensible qualities besides the primary, which they assert are only so many sensations or ideas existing nowhere but in the mind. But all this, I doubt not, you are already apprised of. For my part I have been a long time sensible there was such an opinion current among philosophers, but was never thoroughly convinced of its truth till now.

Philonous   You are still then of opinion that *extension* and *figures* are inherent in external unthinking substances?

Hylas   I am.

Philonous   But what if the same arguments which are brought against secondary qualities will hold good against these also?

Hylas   Why then I shall be obliged to think they too exist only in the mind.

Philonous   Is it your opinion the very figure and extension which you perceive by sense exist in the outward object or material substance?

Hylas   It is.

Philonous   Have all other animals as good grounds to think the same of the figure and extension which they see and feel?

Hylas   Without doubt, if they have any thought at all.

Philonous   Answer me, Hylas. Think you the senses were bestowed upon all animals for their preservation and well-being in life? Or were they given to men alone for this end?

Hylas   I make no question but they have the same use in all other animals.

Philonous   If so, is it not necessary they should be enabled by them to perceive their own limbs and those bodies which are capable of harming them?

Hylas   Certainly.

Philonous   A mite therefore must be supposed to see his own foot, and things equal or even less than it, as bodies of some considerable dimension, though at the same time they appear to you scarce discernible or at best as so many visible points?

Hylas   I cannot deny it.

Philonous   And to creatures less than the mite they will seem yet larger?

Hylas   They will.

Philonous   Insomuch that what you can hardly discern will to another extremely minute animal appear as some huge mountain?

Hylas   All this I grant.

Philonous   Can one and the same thing be at the same time in itself of different dimensions?

Hylas   That were absurd to imagine.

Philonous   But from what you have laid down it follows that both the extension by you perceived and that perceived by the mite itself, as likewise all those perceived by lesser animals, are each of them the true extension of the mite's foot; that is to say, by your own principles you are led into an absurdity.

Hylas   There seems to be some difficulty in the point.

Philonous   Again, have you not acknowledged that no real inherent property of any object can be changed without some change in the thing itself?

Hylas   I have.

Philonous   But, as we approach to or recede from an object, the visible extension varies, being at one distance ten or a hundred times greater than at another. Does it not therefore follow from hence likewise that it is not really inherent in the object?

Hylas   I own I am at a loss what to think.

Philonous   Your judgment will soon be determined if you will venture to think as freely concerning this quality as you have done concerning the rest. Was it not admitted as a good argument that neither heat nor cold was in the water because it seemed warm to one hand and cold to the other?

Hylas   It was.

Philonous   Is it not the very same reasoning to conclude there is no extension or figure in an object because to one eye it shall seem little, smooth, and round, when at the same time it appears to the other great, uneven, and angular?. . . Consequently, the very same arguments which you admitted as conclusive against the secondary qualities are without any further application of force, against the primary, too. . . .

Hylas   I acknowledge, Philonous, that, upon a fair observation of what passes in my mind, I can discover nothing else but that I am a thinking being affected with variety of sensations, neither is it possible to conceive how a sensation should exist in an unperceiving substance. But then, on the other hand, when I look on sensible things in a different view, considering them as so many modes and qualities, I find it necessary to suppose a material *substratum,* without which they cannot be conceived to exist.

Philonous   "Material substratum" call you it? Pray, by which of your senses came you acquainted with that being?

Hylas   It is not itself sensible; its modes and qualities only being perceived by the senses.

Philonous   I presume then it was by reflection and reason you obtained the idea of it?

Hylas   I do not pretend to any proper positive idea of it. However, I conclude it exists because qualities cannot be conceived to exist without a support.

Philonous   It seems then you have only a relative notion of it, or that you conceive it not otherwise than by conceiving the relation it bears to sensible qualities?

Hylas   Right.

Philonous   Be pleased, therefore, to let me know wherein that relation consists.

Hylas   Is it not sufficiently expressed in the term "substratum" or "substance?"

Philonous   If so, the word "substratum" should import that it is spread under the sensible qualities or accidents?

Hylas   True.

Philonous   And consequently under extension?

Hylas   I own it.

Philonous   It is therefore somewhat in its own nature entirely distinct from extension?

Hylas   I tell you extension is only a mode, and matter is something that supports modes. And is it not evident the thing supported is different from the thing supporting?

Philonous   So that something distinct from, and exclusive of, extension is supposed to be the *substratum* of extension?

Hylas   Just so.

Philonous   Answer me, Hylas, can a thing be spread without extension, or is not the idea of extension necessarily included in *spreading?*

Hylas   It is.

Philonous   Whatsoever therefore you suppose spread under anything must have in itself an extension distinct from the extension of that thing under which it is spread?

Hylas   It must.

Philonous   Consequently, every corporeal substance being the *substratum* of extension must have in itself another extension by which it is qualified to be a *substratum,* and so on to infinity? And I ask whether this be not absurd in itself and repugnant to what you granted just now, to wit, that the *substratum* was something distinct from and exclusive of extension?

Hylas   Aye, but, Philonous, you take me wrong. I do not mean that matter is *spread* in a gross literal sense under extension. The word "substratum" is used only to express in general the same thing with "substance."

Philonous   Well then, let us examine the relation implied in the term "substance." Is it not that it stands under accidents?

Hylas   The very same.

Philonous   But that one thing may stand under or support another, must it not be extended?

Hylas   It must.

Philonous   Is not therefore this supposition liable to the same absurdity with the former?

Hylas   You still take things in a strict literal sense; that is not fair, Philonous.

Philonous   I am not for imposing any sense on your words; you are at liberty to explain them as you please. Only, I beseech you, make me understand something by them. You tell me matter supports or stands under accidents. How! is it as your legs support your body?

Hylas No; that is the literal sense.

Philonous Pray let me know any sense, literal or not literal, that you understand it in.-- How long must I wait for an answer, Hylas?

Hylas I declare I know not what to say. I once thought I understood well enough what was meant by matter's supporting accidents. But now, the more I think on it, the less can I comprehend it; in short, I find that I know nothing of it.

Philonous It seems then you have no idea at all, neither relative nor positive, of matter; you know neither what it is in itself nor what relation it bears to accidents?

Hylas I acknowledge it.

Philonous And yet you asserted that you could not conceive how qualities or accidents should really exist without conceiving at the same time a material support of them?

Hylas I did.

Philonous That is to say, when you conceive the real existence of qualities, you do withal conceive something which you cannot conceive? . . . But neither is this all. Which are material objects in themselves—perceptible or imperceptible?

Hylas Properly and immediately nothing can be perceived but ideas. All material things, therefore, are in themselves insensible and to be perceived only by their ideas.

Philonous Ideas then are sensible, and their archetypes or originals insensible?

Hylas Right.

Philonous But how can that which is sensible be like that which is insensible? Can a real thing, in itself *invisible,* be like a *color,* or a real thing which is not *audible* be like a *sound?* In a word, can anything be like a sensation or idea, but another sensation or idea?

Hylas I must own, I think not.

Philonous Is it possible there should be any doubt on the point? Do you not perfectly know your own ideas?

Hylas I know them perfectly, since what I do not perceive or know can be no part of my idea.

Philonous Consider, therefore, and examine them, and then tell me if there be anything in them which can exist without the mind, or if you can conceive anything like them existing without the mind?

Hylas Upon inquiry I find it is impossible for me to conceive or understand how anything but an idea can be like an idea. And it is most evident that *no idea can exist without the mind.*

Philonous You are, therefore, by your principles forced to deny the reality of sensible things, since you made it to consist in an absolute existence exterior to the mind. That is to say, you are a downright skeptic. So I have gained my point, which was to show your principles led to skepticism.

Hylas For the present I am, if not entirely convinced, at least silenced. . . .

To Think About

1. "Consider this table in front of us. It is not what it seems. Leibniz tells us it is a community of souls. Bishop Berkeley tells us it is an idea in the mind of God. Sober science, scarcely less wonderful, tells us it is a vast collection of electric charges in violent motion." ***Bertrand Russell***

2. Subjective idealism has not been a very popular theory of perception in Western philosophy. Some theorists hold that science gives only knowledge of correlations among perceptions and has no need to assume the existence of external objects. But the average person believes that science has extended our knowledge and improved our lives by dealing very directly with a real world of objects. Furthermore, the world of practical affairs is conducted on the assumption of a natural universe of material things that exist in their own right and that human beings must take into account.

3. Another objection to idealistic theories of perception is raised when it comes to the problem of proof. It is argued that if there is no outside material reality to which we can refer, then we can never be sure that any two people perceive the same thing in the same way and that no common denominator can be established for assessing the accuracy or inaccuracy of our perceptions. Furthermore, if to be is to be perceived, how do we know that the mind, which does the perceiving, exists?

4. "When we do our utmost to conceive the existence of external bodies we are all the while only contemplating our own ideas." ***George Berkeley***

5. There was a young man who said, *"God*

    Must think it exceedingly odd;

    If he finds that this tree

    Continues to be

    When there's no one about in the Quad." ***Ronald Knox***

    Reply.

    "Dear Sir: Your astonishment's odd:

    I am always about in the Quad.

    And that's why the tree

    Will continue to be

    Since observed by

    —Yours faithfully,

    —God." ***Anonymous***

6. "The table I write on I say exists, that is, I see and feel it; and if I were out of my study I should say it existed—meaning thereby that if I was in my study I might perceive it, or that some other spirit actually does perceive it. There was an odour, that is, it was smelt; there was a sound, that is, it was heard; a colour or figure, and it was perceived by sight or touch. This is all that I can understand by these and

the like expressions. For as to what is said of the absolute existence of unthinking things without any relation to their being perceived, that is to me perfectly unintelligible. Their *esse* is *percipi,* nor is it possible they should have any existence out of the minds or thinking things which perceive them."   ***George Berkeley***

7.   "Many of the things he (Berkeley) writes I find correct and in agreement with my own position. But he expresses himself too paradoxically. There is no need for us to say that matter is nothing; it is enough to say that it is a phenomenon like a rainbow; not that it is a substance, but that it is a result of substances."

Gottfried Wilhelm Leibniz

8.   "After we came out of the church, we stood talking for some time together of Bishop Berkeley's ingenious sophistry to prove the non-existence of matter, and that every thing in the universe is merely ideal. I observed, that though we are satisfied his doctrine is not true, it is impossible to refute it. I never shall forget the alacrity with which Johnson answered, striking his foot with mighty force against a large stone, till he rebounded from it, 'I refute it *thus.*'"   ***James Boswell***

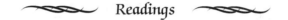

Readings

ATHERTON, MARGARET, ed. *The Empiricists: Critical Essays on Locke, Berkeley, and Hume.* Lanham, MD: Rowman & Littlefield, 1999.

CREERY, WALTER E., ed. *George Berkeley: Critical Assessments.* London: Routledge, 1991.

DANCY, JONATHAN. *Berkeley, an Introduction.* New York: Blackwell, 1987.

PITCHER, GEORGE. *Berkeley.* London: Routledge & Kegan Paul, 1977.

URMSON, J. O. *Berkeley.* Oxford: Oxford University Press, 1982.

WARNOCK, G. J. *Berkeley.* Notre Dame, IN: University of Notre Dame Press, 1983.

41

Reality Consists of Mental and Physical Qualities

John Dewey (1859–1952) was born in Burlington, Vermont. He did his undergraduate work at the University of Vermont and received his Ph.D. in 1884 at Johns Hopkins, then a new university, in Baltimore, Maryland. He taught at the Universities of Michigan, Minnesota, and Chicago until 1904, when he joined the faculty of Columbia University in New York, remaining there until his retirement in 1930. An extraordinarily prolific author, he wrote in all areas of philosophy but made his greatest impact in the philosophy of education. His Democracy and Education *(1916) is considered a seminal work in educational theory, perhaps the finest work of its kind in the English language. Dewey, along with William James and C. S. Peirce, is a central figure in American philosophy. But Dewey had greater influence in the practical areas of social and political thought and action. In this respect he stands out as a prime example of the neglected ideal of the public philosopher.*

A third alternative to Descartes's dualism involves a refusal to accept the basic assumptions of his position, that there are mental and material substances in the universe. Some critics hold that mind and body are not two kinds of substance. Rather, mind and body are properties or functions of a single entity, the natural, organic, living whole. John Dewey holds this third alternative. According to him, dualists are wrong in claiming that reality consists of two separable things, mind and body. And materialists and idealists both err in reducing one kind of substantial reality to the other. Rejecting dualisms of all kinds, philosophical, moral, social, and cultural, Dewey insists that a good empiricist (a *radical* empiricist, he is fond of saying with William James) recognizes the ultimate reality of the living individual. Mental and physical events are experiential aspects or natural properties of living persons manifested in their behavior. In an older meaning

Reprinted by permission of Open Court Publishing Company, a division of Carus Publishing Company, Peru, IL, from *Experience and Nature* by John Dewey, 2nd edition, copyright 1929 by Open Court.

of the term, Dewey's position can be called *functionalism,* meaning simply that mind and body refer to integrated mental and physical functions of the living human being. In the following reading, Dewey shows how dualism is rooted in political and social factors dominant in Western cultural history. Overcoming dualism involves simultaneously a metaphysical, social, and political critique.

To Study

1. What series of cultural facts in the history of Greek, medieval, and modern thought sets the scene for conflicting attitudes toward the relationship of mind and nature?
2. What underlying metaphysical issues are important in analyzing these attitudes toward mind and matter?
3. What role does the concept of *organization* play in Dewey's account of nature?
4. Explain what Dewey means by "substantiation of eventual functions" in his account of the differences between physical and mental accounts of nature.
5. Why may Dewey call his account either "materialism" or "idealism"?
6. Why does Dewey consider "parallelism" an inadequate account of the relation of mind and body?
7. Describe Dewey's three "fields" of interaction in nature?
8. What problems in language cause some of the difficulty in adequately explaining the relation of mind and matter?
9. Explain Dewey's concepts of *soul* and *spirit.*
10. What is the meaning and role of *continuity* in Dewey's account?

A series of cultural experiences exhibits a series of diverging conceptions of the relation of mind to nature in general and to the organic body in particular. Greek experience included affairs that rewarded without want and struggle the contemplation of free men; they enjoyed a civic life full and rich with an equable adaptation to natural surroundings. Such a life seemed to be upon the whole for those in its full possession a gracious culmination of nature; the organic body was the medium through which the culmination took place. Since any created thing is subject to natural contingency, death was not a problem; a being who is generated shares while he may in mind and eternal forms, and then piously merges with the forces which generated him. But life does not always exist in this happy equilibrium: it is onerous and devastating, civil life corrupt and harsh. Under such circumstances, a spirit which believes that it was created in the image of a divine eternal spirit, in whose everlastingness it properly shares, finds itself an alien and pilgrim in a strange and fallen world. Its presence in that world and its residence in a material body which is a part of that world are an enigma. Again the scene shifts. Nature is conceived to be wholly mechanical. The existence within nature and as part of it of a body possessed of life, manifesting thought and enjoying consciousness is a mystery.

This series of experiences with their corresponding philosophies display characteristic factors in the problem of life and mind in relation to body. . . . And these conceptions have primarily nothing to do with mind-body; they have to do with underlying metaphysical issues:—the denial of quality in general to natural events; the ignoring in particular of temporal quality and the dogma of the superior reality of "causes."

If we identify, as common speech does, the physical as such with the inanimate we need another word to denote the activity of organisms as such. Psycho-physical is an appropriate term. Thus employed, "psycho-physical" denotes the conjunctive presence in activity of need-demand-satisfaction, in the sense in which these terms have been defined. In the compound word, the prefix "psycho" denotes that physical activity has acquired additional properties, those of ability to procure a peculiar kind of interactive support of needs from surrounding media. Psycho-physical does not denote an abrogation of the physico-chemical; nor a peculiar mixture of something physical and something psychical (as a centaur is half man and half horse); it denotes the possession of certain qualities and efficacies not displayed by the inanimate.

Thus conceived there is no problem of the relation of physical *and* psychic. There are specifiable empirical events marked by distinctive qualities and efficacies. There is first of all, *organization* with all which is implied thereby. . . . Organization is an empirical trait of some events, no matter how speculative and dubious theories about it may be; especially no matter how false are certain doctrines about it which have had great vogue—namely, those doctrines which have construed it as evidence of a special force or entity called life or soul. Organization is so characteristic of the nature of some events in their sequential linkages that no theory about it can be as speculative or absurd as those which ignore or deny its genuine existence. . . .

Complex and active animals *have,* therefore, feelings which vary abundantly in quality, corresponding to distinctive directions and phases—initiating, mediating, fulfilling or frustrating—of activities, bound up in distinctive connections with environmental affairs. They *have* them, but they do not know they have them. Activity is psycho-physical, but not "mental," that is, not aware of meanings. As life is a character of events in a peculiar condition of organization, and "feeling" is a quality of life-forms marked by complexly mobile and discriminating responses, so "mind" is an added property assumed by a feeling creature, when it reaches that organized interaction with other living creatures which is language, communication. Then the qualities of feeling become significant of objective differences in external things and of episodes past and to come. This state of things in which qualitatively different feelings are not just had but are significant of objective differences, is mind. Feelings are no longer just felt. They have and they make *sense;* record and prophesy.

The distinction between physical, psycho-physical, and mental is thus one of levels of increasing complexity and intimacy of interaction among natural events. The idea that matter, life and mind represent separate kinds of Being is a doctrine that springs, as so many philosophic errors have sprung, from a substantiation of eventual functions. The fallacy converts consequences of interaction of events into causes of the occurrence of these consequences—a reduplication which is significant as to the *importance* of the functions, but which hopelessly confuses understanding of them.

"Matter," or the physical, is a character of events when they occur at a certain level of interaction. It is not itself an event or existence; the notion that while "mind" denotes essence, "matter" denotes existence is superstition. It is more than a bare essence; for it is a property of a particular field of interacting events. But as it figures in *science* it is as much an essence, as is acceleration, or the square root of minus one; which meanings also express derivative characters of events in interaction. Consequently, while the theory that life, feeling and thought are never independent of physical events may be deemed materialism, it may also be considered just the opposite. For it is reasonable to believe that the most adequate definition of the basic traits of natural existence can be had only when its properties are most fully displayed—a condition which is met in the degree of the scope and intimacy of interactions realized.

In any case, genuine objection to metaphysical materialism is neither moral nor esthetic. Historically speaking, materialism and mechanistic metaphysics—as distinct from mechanistic science—designate the doctrine that matter is the efficient cause of life and mind, and that "cause" occupies a position superior in reality to that of "effect." Both parts of this statement are contrary to fact. As far as the conception of causation is to be introduced at all, not matter but the natural events having matter as a character, "cause" life and mind. "Effects," since they mark the release of potentialities, are more adequate indications of the nature of nature than are just "causes." Control of the occurrence of the complex depends upon its analysis into the more elementary; the dependence of life, sentiency and mind upon "matter" is thus practical or instrumental. Lesser, more external fields of interaction are more manageable than are wider and more intimate ones, and only through managing the former can we direct the occurrence of the latter. Thus it is in virtue of the character of events which is termed matter that psycho-physical and intellectual affairs can be differentially determined. Every discovery of concrete dependence of life and mind upon physical events is therefore an addition to our resources. If life and mind had no mechanism, education, deliberate modification, rectification, prevention and constructive control would be impossible. To damn "matter" because of honorific interest in spirit is but another edition of the old habit of eulogizing ends and disparaging the means on which they depend.

This, then, is the significance of our introductory statement that the "solution" of the problem of mind-body is to be found in a revision of the preliminary assumptions about existence which generate the problem. . . . The notion that the universe is split into two separate and disconnected realms of existence, one psychical and the other physical, and then that these two realms of being, in spite of their total disjunction, specifically and minutely correspond to each other—as a serial order of numbered vibrations corresponds to the immediately felt qualities of vision of the prismatic spectrum—presents the acme of incredibility. The one-to-one agreement is intelligible only as a correspondence of properties and relations in one and the same world which is first taken upon a narrower and more external level of interaction, and then upon a more inclusive and intimate level. When we recall that by taking natural events on these two levels and instituting point to point correspondence (or "parallelism") between them, the richer and more complex display of characters is rendered amenable to prediction and deliberate guidance, the intelligibility of the procedure becomes concretely sensible.

Thus while modern science is correct in denying direct efficacy and position in the described sequence of events to say, red, or dry; yet Greek science was correct in its underlying naïve assumption that qualities count for something highly important.

The foregoing discussion is both too technical and not elaborately technical enough for adequate comprehension. It may be conceived as an attempt to contribute to what has come to be called an "emergent" theory of mind. But every word that we can use, organism, feeling, psycho-physical, sensation and sense, "emergence" itself, is infected by the associations of old theories, whose import is opposite to that here stated. We may, however attempt a recapitulation by premising that while there is no isolated occurrence in nature, yet interaction and connection are not wholesale and homogenous. Interacting-events have tighter and looser ties, which qualify them with certain beginnings and endings, and which mark them off from other fields of inter- action. Such relatively closed fields come into conjunction at times so as to interact with each other, and a critical alteration is effected. A new larger field is formed, in which new energies are released, and to which new qualities appertain. Regulation, conscious direction and science imply ability to smooth over the rough junctures, and to form by translation and substitution a homogenous medium. Yet these func- tions do not abrogate or deny qualitative differences and unlike fields or ranges of operation, from atoms to solar systems. They do just what they are meant to do: give facility and security in utilizing the simpler manageable field to predict and modify the course of the more complete and highly organized.

In general, three plateaus of such fields may be discriminated. The first, the scene of narrower and more external interactions, while qualitatively diversified in itself, is physical; its distinctive properties are those of the mathematical-mechanical system dis- covered by physics and which define matter as a general character. The second level is that of life. Qualitative differences, like those of plant and animal, lower and higher animal forms, are here even more conspicuous; but in spite of their variety they have qualities in common which define the psycho-physical. The third plateau is that of asso- ciation, communication, participation. This is still further internally diversified, consist- ing of individualities. It is marked throughout its diversities, however, by common properties, which define mind as intellect; possession of and response to meanings.

Body-mind designates an affair with its own properties. A large part of the dif- ficulty in its discussion—perhaps the whole of the difficulty in general apart from de- tailed questions—is due to vocabulary. Our language is so permeated with consequences of theories which have divided the body and mind from each other, making separate existential realms out of them, that we lack words to designate the actual existential fact. The circumlocutions we are compelled to resort to—exemplified in the previous discussion—thus induce us to think that analogous separations exist in nature, which can also only be got around by elaborate circuitous arrangements. But body-mind simply designates what actually takes place when a living body is im- plicated in situations of discourse, communication and participation. In the hyphen- ated phrase body-mind, "body" designates the continued and conserved, the registered and cumulative operation of factors continuous with the rest of nature, inanimate as well as animate; while "mind" designates the characters and conse- quences which are differential, indicative of features which emerge when "body" is engaged in a wider, more complex and interdependent situation. . . .

In conclusion, it may be asserted that "soul" when freed from all traces of traditional materialistic animism denotes the qualities of psycho-physical activities as far as these are organized into unity. Some bodies have souls preeminently as some conspicuously have fragrance, color, and solidity. To make this statement is to call attention to properties that characterize these bodies, not to import a mysterious non-natural entity or force. Were there not in actual existence properties of sensitivity and of marvelously comprehensive and delicate participative response characterizing living bodies, mythical notions about the nature of the soul would never have risen. The myths have lost whatever poetic quality they once had; when offered as science they are superstitious encumbrances. But the idiomatic non-doctrinal use of the word soul retains a sense of the realities concerned. To say emphatically of a particular person that he has soul or a great soul is not to utter a platitude, applicable equally to all human beings. It expresses the conviction that the man or woman in question has in marked degree qualities of sensitive, rich and coordinated participation in all the situations of life. Thus works of art, music, poetry, painting, architecture, have soul, while others are dead, mechanical.

When the organization called soul is free, moving and operative, initial as well as terminal, it is spirit. Qualities are both static, substantial, and transitive. Spirit quickens; it is not only alive, but spirit gives life. Animals are spirited, but man is a living spirit. He lives in his works and his works do follow him. Soul is form, spirit informs. It is the moving function of that of which soul is the substance. Perhaps the words soul and spirit are so heavily laden with traditional mythology and sophisticated doctrine that they must be surrendered; it may be impossible to recover for them in science and philosophy the realities designated in idiomatic speech. But the realities are there, by whatever names they be called.

Old ideas do not die when the beliefs which have been explicitly associated with them disappear; they usually only change their clothes. Present notions about the organism are largely a survival, with changed vocabulary, of old ideas about soul and body. The soul was conceived as inhabiting the body in an external way. Now the nervous system is conceived as a substitute, mysteriously within the body. But as the soul was "simple" and therefore not diffused through the body, so the nervous system as the seat of mental events is narrowed down to the brain, and then to the cortex of the brain; while many physiological inquirers would doubtless feel enormously relieved if a specific portion of the cortex could be ascertained to be *the* seat of consciousness. Those who talk most of the organism, physiologists and psychologists, are often just those who display least sense of the intimate, delicate and subtle interdependence of all organic structures and processes with one another. The world seems mad in preoccupation with what is specific, particular, disconnected in medicine, politics, science, industry, education. In terms of a conscious control of inclusive wholes, search for those links which occupy key positions and which effect critical connections is indispensable. But recovery of sanity depends upon seeing and using these specifiable things *as* links functionally significant in a process. To see the organism *in* nature, the nervous system in the organism, the brain in the nervous system, the cortex in the brain is the answer to the problems which haunt philosophy. And when thus seen they will be seen to be *in,* not as marbles are in a box but as events are in history, in a moving, growing never finished process. Until we have a procedure in actual practice which demonstrates this continuity, we shall continue to engage in appealing to some other specific thing, some other broken off affair, to restore connectedness and unity—calling the specific religion or reform or whatever specific is the fashionable cure of the period. Thus we increase the disease in the means used to cure it.[1]

In matters predominantly physical we know that all control depends upon conscious perception of relations obtaining between things, otherwise one cannot be used to affect the other. We have been marvellously successful in inventing and constructing external machines, because with respect to such things we take for granted that success occurs only upon the conscious plane—that of conscious perception of the relations which things sustain to one another. We know that locomotives and aeroplanes and telephones and power-plants do not arise from instinct or the subconscious but from deliberately ascertained perception of connections and orders of connections. Now after a period in which advance in these respects was complacently treated as proof and measure of progress, we have been forced to adopt pessimistic attitudes, and to wonder if this "progress" is to end in the deterioration of man and the possible destruction of civilization.

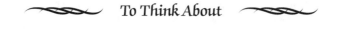 To Think About

1. "Now the philosophy by which Americans live, in contrast to the philosophies which they profess, is naturalistic. In profession they may be Fundamentalists, Catholics, or idealists, because American opinion is largely pre-American; but in their hearts and lives they are all pragmatists, and they prove it even by the spirit in which they maintain those other traditional allegiances, not out of rapt speculative sympathy, but because such allegiance seems an insurance against moral dissolution, guaranteeing social cohesion and practical success. Their real philosophy is the philosophy of enterprise."   ***George Santayana***

2. ". . . Dewey's procedure is more revealing than his words. *Experience and Nature* is not unique, but typical: again and again on every major philosophic issue he first displays the dualisms, the wrenchings apart, the messy confusions of modern thought, only to turn to the Greeks in admiration for their clarity of perception. It is their ideas he deems fruitful material for further critical development. And in contrast to the whole of modern philosophy, save where it in turn has most powerfully felt Greek influence, Dewey himself seems to be working primarily with the conceptions of Aristotle."

    John Herman Randall, Jr.

3. "Experience is a form of existence, a part of the natural history of existence. Experience is, as such, a part of a wider field of existence. The pragmatist willingly acknowledges this dualism *within* the world which the epistemological dualist mistakes usually for a dualism of mind and nature as independent substances."

    Donald A. Piatt

[1]See F. Matthias Alexander's Man's Supreme Inheritance, and Conscious Constructive Control.

4. "Dewey thinks that the mind-body question is a pseudo-problem. But the problem of (the) joinings of direct experience and the external world takes the place of the pseudo-problem. There is a double connection: perspectives are joined to physical things (as the physicist describes them) and attitudes are joined to the human organism (as the physiologist describes it). The problem has shifted; it should be solved and not shelved." ***William Savery***

5. "I have just finished reading Morris Cohen's book *Reason and Nature.* . . . The title suggests a sort of challenge to John Dewey's *Experience and Nature* to which it is much superior as a piece of writing. . . . But although Dewey's book is incredibly ill written, it seemed to me after several rereadings to have a feeling of intimacy with the inside of the cosmos that I found unequaled. So methought God would have spoken had He been inarticulate but keenly desirous to tell you how it was." ***Oliver Wendell Holmes, Jr.***

6. "The term *experience* . . . in Professor Dewey's thought is equally applicable to everything that is an object of consideration. I cannot therefore see that it serves any definite intellectual function beyond carrying the faint aroma of praise. . . . In general, when familiar words are stretched and put to new uses, confusion is bound to result. For the meaning we attach to words is based on habits which arbitrary resolutions cannot readily change, and we invariably drag the old meaning into the new context." ***Morris Cohen***

7. "If we are willing to conceive education as the process of forming fundamental dispositions, intellectual and emotional, toward nature and fellow men, philosophy may even be defined *as the general theory of education.* Unless a philosophy is to remain symbolic—or verbal—or a sentimental indulgence for a few, or else mere arbitrary dogma, its auditing of past experience and its program of values must take effect in conduct. . . . Education is the laboratory in which philosophic distinctions become concrete and are tested." ***John Dewey***

8. "As a rule we disbelieve all facts and theories for which we have no use." ***William James***

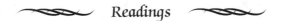 Readings

BOISVERT, RAYMOND D. *Dewey's Metaphysics.* New York: Fordham University Press, 1988.

HICKMAN, LARRY A., ed. *Reading Dewey: Interpretations for a Postmodern Generation.* Bloomington: Indiana University Press, 1998.

MARGOLIS, JOSEPH. *Reinventing Pragmatism: American Philosophy at the End of the Twentieth Century.* Ithaca, NY: Cornell University Press, 2002.

SLEEPER, R. W. *The Necessity of Pragmatism: John Dewey's Conception of Philosophy.* New Haven, CT: Yale University Press, 1986.

42

Human Beings Have an
Identical Self

John Locke (1632–1704), a major figure of the Enlightenment and founder of the empiricist tradition in Britain, wrote two major works regarded as classics, Two Treatises of Government *(1689) and* An Essay Concerning Human Understanding *(1690). His preoccupation in later years was literary, much of it concerned with a defense of his political and religious views against the attacks of the orthodox.*

Because people's personalities are so changeable, it is common to hear someone remark of a friend, "He [or she] is not the same person." But seldom, if ever, does that mean he or she is *so* changed that we no longer identify him or her with the same past acts. In considering the issue of self-identity, Locke defines a person as a "thinking intelligent being, that has reason and reflection, and can consider itself as itself, the same thinking thing, in different times and places." This self-consciousness, which is inseparable from thinking, constitutes the essence of personality. Consequently, the identity of a person is to be found in the identity of consciousness. Of course, we are not always conscious (for example, when we are sleeping). Because we are morally responsible even in cases where we are not conscious, our identity has to be established on forensic, or legal, means.

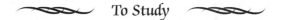 To Study

1. According to Locke, what does the word *person* stand for?
2. Of what does personal identity consist?
3. What is the problem in saying that one's consciousness proves that one is continuously the same identical substance?

From John Locke, *An Essay Concerning Human Understanding* (London: Holt, 1690), book II, chap. 27.

4. If our bodies change, do we have the same personal identity? Why? If our minds change, do we have the same personal identity?
5. Can two thinking substances be one person? Explain.
6. Can one immaterial substance be two persons? Explain.
7. Upon which does the self depend, consciousness or substance?
8. What is the object of punishment, persons or substances? Should a sleepwalker be punished for bad deeds committed while sleepwalking?
9. What is meant by the same individual *person?*
10. Is a person the same person whether sober or drunk?
11. What alone unites separate existences into the same person? Could two distinct consciousnesses occupy the same body?
12. Why is *person* a forensic term?
13. What does Locke conclude?

. . . To find wherein personal identity consists we must consider what *person* stands for—which, I think, is a thinking intelligent being, that has reason and reflection, and can consider itself as itself, the same thinking thing, in different times and places; which it does only by that consciousness which is inseparable from thinking, and, as it seems to me, essential to it: it being impossible for anyone to perceive without *perceiving* that he does perceive. When we see, hear, smell, taste, feel, mediate, or will anything, we know that we do so. Thus, it is always as to our present sensations and perceptions: and by this everyone is to himself that which he calls *self*—it not being considered, in this case, whether the same self be continued in the same or diverse substances. For, since consciousness always accompanies thinking, and it is that which makes everyone to be what he calls self, and thereby distinguishes himself from all other thinking things, in this alone consists personal identity, that is, the sameness of a rational being: and as far as this consciousness can be extended backwards to any past action or thought, so far reaches the identity of that person; it is the same self now it was then; and it is by the same self with this present one that now reflects on it, that action was done.

But it is further inquired whether it be the same identical substance. This few would think they had reason to doubt of, if these perceptions, with their consciousness, always remained present in the mind, whereby the same thinking thing would be always consciously present, and, as would be thought, evidently the same to itself. But that which seems to make the difficulty is this, that this consciousness being interrupted always by forgetfulness, there being no moment of our lives wherein we have the whole train of all our past actions before our eyes in one view, but even the best memories losing the sight of one part whilst they are viewing another; and we sometimes, and that the greatest part of our lives, not reflecting on our past selves, being intent on our present thoughts, and in sound sleep having no thoughts at all, or at least none with that consciousness which remarks our waking thoughts—I say, in all these cases, our consciousness being interrupted, and we losing the sight of our past selves, doubts are raised whether we are the same thinking thing, that is, the same *substance*[1] or no. Which, however reasonable or unreasonable, concerns not *personal* identity at all. The question being what makes the same person, and not whether it be the same identical substance which always thinks in the same person, which, in this case, matters not at all: different substances, by the same consciousness (where they do partake in it) being united into one person, as well as different bodies by the same life are united into one animal, whose identity is preserved in that change of substances by the unity of one continued life. For, it being the same consciousness that makes a man be himself to himself, personal identity depends on that only, whether it be annexed solely to one individual substance, or can be continued in a succession of several substances. For as far as any intelligent being *can* repeat the idea of any past action with the same consciousness it had of it at first, and with the same consciousness it has of any present action, so far it is the same personal self. For it is by the consciousness it has of its present thoughts and actions that it is *self to itself* now, and so will be the same self as far as the same consciousness can extend to actions past or to come; and would be by distance of time, or change of substance, no more two persons, than a man be two men by wearing other clothes to-day than he did yesterday, with a long or a short sleep between: the same consciousness uniting those distant actions into the same person, whatever substances contributed to their production.

That this is so, we have some kind of evidence in our very bodies, all whose particles, whilst vitally united to this same thinking conscious self so that *we feel* when they are touched, and are affected by, and conscious of good or harm that happens to them, are a part of ourselves, that is, of our thinking conscious self. Thus, the limbs of his body are to every one a part of himself; he sympathizes and is concerned for them. Cut off a hand, and thereby separate it from that consciousness he had of its heat, cold, and other affections, and it is then no longer a part of that which is himself, any more than the remotest part of matter. Thus, we see the *substance* whereof personal self consisted at one time may be varied at another, without the change of personal identity; there being no question about the same person, though the limbs which but now were a part of it be cut off.

But the question is, Whether if the same substance which thinks be changed, it can be the same person; or, remaining the same, it can be different persons?

And to this I answer: First, This can be no question at all to those who place thought in a purely material animal constitution, void of an immaterial substance. For, whether their supposition be true or no, it is plain they conceive personal identity preserved in something else than identity of substance; as animal identity is preserved in identity of life, and not of substance. And therefore those who place thinking in an immaterial substance only, before they can come to deal with these men, must show why personal identity cannot be preserved in the change of immaterial substances, or variety of particular immaterial substances, as well as animal identity is preserved in the change of material substances, or variety of particular bodies: unless they will say, it is one immaterial spirit that makes the same life in brutes as it is one immaterial spirit that makes the same person in men. . . .

---

[1] A mind that exists in and of itself. [ED.]

But next, as to the first part of the question, Whether, if the same thinking substance (supporting immaterial substances only to think) be changed, it can be the same person? I answer, that cannot be resolved but by those who know what kind of substances they are that do think; and whether the consciousness of past actions can be transferred from one thinking substance to another. I grant were the same consciousness the same individual action it could not: but it being a present representation of a past action, why it may not be possible that may be represented to the mind to have been which really never was, will remain to be shown. And therefore how far the consciousness of past actions is annexed to any individual agent, so that another cannot possibly have it, will be hard for us to determine till we know what kind of action it is that cannot be done without a reflex act of perception accompanying it, and how performed by thinking substances, who cannot think without being conscious of it. But that which we call the same consciousness, not being the same individual act, why one intellectual substance may not have represented to it, as done by itself, what *it* never did, and was perhaps done by some other agent—why, I say, such a representation may not possibly be without reality of matter of fact, as well as several representations in dreams are, which yet whilst dreaming we take for true—will be difficult to conclude from the nature of things. . . . But yet, to return to the question before us, it must be allowed, that, if the same consciousness . . . can be transferred from one thinking substance to another, it will be possible that two thinking substances may make but one person. For the same consciousness being preserved, whether in the same or different substances, the personal identity is preserved.

As to the second part of the question, Whether the same immaterial substance remaining, there may be two distinct persons; which question seems to me to be built on this—Whether the same immaterial being, being conscious of the action of its past duration, may be wholly stripped of all the consciousness of its past existence, and lost it beyond the power of ever retrieving it again: and so as it were beginning a new account from a new period, have a consciousness that *cannot* reach beyond this new state. All those who hold pre-existence are evidently of this mind, since they allow the soul to have no remaining consciousness of what it did in that pre-existent state, either wholly separate from body, or in forming any other body; and if they should not, it is plain experience would be against them. So that personal identity, reaching no further than consciousness reaches, a pre-existent spirit not having continued so many ages in a state of silence, must needs make different persons. . . . I once met with one, who was persuaded his had been the *soul* of Socrates . . . would any one say, that he, being not conscious of any of Socrates's actions or thoughts, could be the same *person* with Socrates? Let any one reflect upon himself, and conclude that he has in himself an immaterial spirit, which is that which thinks in him, and, in the constant change of his body keeps him the same: and is that which he calls *himself*: let him also suppose it to be the same soul that was in Nestor or Thersites, at the siege of Troy, . . . which it may have been, as well as it is now the soul of any other man: but he now having no consciousness of any of the actions either of Nestor or Thersites, does or can he conceive himself the same person with either of them? Can he be concerned in either of their actions, attribute them to himself, or think them his own, more than the actions of any other men that ever existed? So that this consciousness, not reaching to any of the actions of either of those men, he is no more one *self* with either of them than if the soul or immaterial spirit that now informs him had been created, and began to exist, when it began to inform his present body; though it were never so true, that the same *spirit* that informed Nestor's or Thersites' body were numerically the same that now informs his. For this would no more make him the same person with Nestor than if some of the particles of matter that were once a part of Nestor were now a part of this man; the same immaterial substance, without the same consciousness, no more making the same person by being united to any body than the same particle of matter, without consciousness, united to any body, makes the same person. But let him once find himself conscious of any of the actions of Nestor, he then finds himself the same person with Nestor. . . .

But though the same immaterial substance or soul does not alone, wherever it be, and in whatsoever state, make the same *man,* yet it is plain [that] consciousness, as far as ever it can be extended—should it be to ages past—unites existences and actions very remote in time into the same *person,* as well as it does the existences and actions of the immediately preceding moment: so that whatever has the consciousness of present and past actions is the same person to whom they both belong. Had I the same consciousness that I saw the ark and Noah's flood as that I saw an overflowing of the Thames last winter, or as that I write now, I could no more doubt that I who write this now, that saw the Thames overflowed last winter, and that viewed the flood at the general deluge, was the same *self*—place that self in what *substance* you please—than that I who write this am the same *myself* now whilst I write (whether I consist of all the same substance, material or immaterial, or no) that I was yesterday. For as to this point of being the same self, it matters not whether this present self be made up of the same or other substances—I being as much concerned, and as justly accountable for any action that was done a thousand years since, appropriated to me now by this self-consciousness, as I am for what I did the last moment.

Self is that conscious thinking thing—whatever substance made up of (whether spiritual or material, simple or compounded, it matters not)—which is sensible or conscious of pleasure and pain, capable of happiness or misery, and so is concerned for itself, as far as that consciousness extends. Thus everyone finds that, whilst comprehended under that consciousness, the little finger is as much a part of himself as what is most so. Upon separation of this little finger, should this consciousness go along with the little finger and leave the rest of the body, it is evident the little finger would be the person, the same person; and self then would have nothing to do with the rest of the body. As in this case it is the consciousness that goes along with the substance, when one part is separate from another, which makes the same person and constitutes this inseparable self: so it is in reference to substances remote in time. That with which the consciousness of this present thinking thing *can* join itself makes the same person, and is one self with it, and with nothing else, and so attributes to itself, and owns all the actions of that thing as its own, as far as that consciousness reaches, and no further, as every one who reflects will perceive.

In this personal identity is founded all the right and justice of reward and punishment, happiness and misery being that for which everyone is concerned for *himself,* and not mattering what becomes of any *substance,* not joined to, or affected with that consciousness. For, as it is evident in the instance I gave but now, if the consciousness went along with the little finger when it was cut off, that would be the same self which was concerned for the whole body yesterday, as making part of itself, whose actions then it cannot but admit as its own now. Though, if the same body should still live, and immediately from the separation of the little finger have its own peculiar consciousness, whereof the little finger knew nothing, it would not at all be concerned for it, as a part of itself, or could own any of its actions, or have any of them imputed to him.

This may show us wherein personal identity consists: not in the identity of substance, but, as I have said, in the identity of consciousness, wherein if Socrates and the present mayor of Queinborough agree, they are the same person: if the same Socrates waking and sleeping do not partake of the same consciousness, Socrates waking and sleeping is not the same person. And to punish Socrates waking for what sleeping Socrates thought, and waking Socrates was never conscious of, would be no more of right, than to punish one twin for what his brother-twin did, whereof he knew nothing, because their outsides were so alike, that they could not be distinguished. . . .

But yet possibly it will still be objected. Suppose I wholly lose the memory of some parts of my life, beyond a possibility of retrieving them, so that perhaps I shall never be conscious of them again; yet am I not the same person that did those actions, had those thoughts that I once was conscious of, though I have now forgot them? To which I answer that we must here take notice what the word *I* is applied to, which, in this case, is the *man* only. And the same man being presumed to be the same person, *I* is easily here supposed to stand also for the same person. But if it be possible for the same man to have distinct incommunicable consciousness at different times, it is past doubt the same man would at different times make different persons; which, we see, is the sense of mankind in the solemnest declaration of their opinions, human laws not punishing the mad man for the sober man's actions, nor the sober man for what the mad man did, thereby making them two persons: which is somewhat explained by our way of speaking in English when we say . . . one is "not himself," or is "beside himself," in which phrases it is insinuated, as if those who now, or at least first, used them thought that self was changed; the selfsame person was no longer in that man.

But yet it is hard to conceive that Socrates, the same individual man, should be two persons. To help us a little in this, we must consider what is meant by . . . the same individual *man*.

First, it must be either the same individual, immaterial, thinking substance, in short, the same numerical soul, and nothing else.

Secondly, or in the same animal, without any regard to an immaterial soul.

Thirdly, or the same immaterial spirit united to the same animal.

Now, take which of these suppositions you please, it is impossible to make personal identity to consist in anything but consciousness, or reach any further than that does.

For, by the first of them, it must be allowed possible that a man born of different women, and in distant times, may be the same man. A way of speaking which, whoever admits, must allow it possible for the same man to be two distinct persons, as any two that have lived in different ages without the knowledge of one another's thoughts.

By the second and third, Socrates, in this life and after it, cannot be the same man any way but by the same consciousness; and so making human identity to consist in the same thing wherein we place personal identity, there will be no difficulty to allow the same man to be the same person. But then they who place human identity in consciousness only, and not in something else, must consider how they will make the infant Socrates the same man with Socrates after the resurrection. But whatsoever to some men makes a man, and consequently the same individual man, wherein perhaps few are agreed, personal identity can by us be placed in nothing but consciousness (which is that alone which makes us what we call *self*) without involving us in great absurdities.

But is not a man drunk and sober the same person? Why else is he punished for the act he commits when drunk, though he be never afterwards conscious of it? Just as much the same person as a man that walks, and does other things in his sleep, is the same person, and is answerable for any mischief he shall do in it. Human laws punish both, with a justice suitable to *their* way of knowledge—because, in these cases, they cannot distinguish certainly what is real, what counterfeit: and so the ignorance of drunkenness or sleep is not admitted as a plea. [For, though punishment be annexed to personality, and personality to consciousness, and the drunkard perhaps be not conscious of what he did, yet human judicatures justly punish him because the fact is proved against him, but want of consciousness cannot be proved for him.] . . .

Nothing but consciousness can unite remote existences into the same person: the identity of substance will not do it; for whatever substance there is, however framed, without consciousness there is no person: and a carcass may be a person, as well as any sort of substance be so, without consciousness.

Could we suppose two distinct incommunicable consciousnesses acting in the same body, the one constantly by day, the other by night; and, on the other side, the same consciousness, acting by intervals, in two distinct bodies: I ask, in the first case, whether the day and night man would not be two as distinct persons as Socrates and Plato? And whether, in the second case, there would not be one person in two distinct persons' bodies, as much as one man is the same in two distinct clothings? Nor is it at all material to say, that this same and this distinct consciousness, in the cases above mentioned, is owing to the same and distinct immaterial substances, bringing it with them to those bodies, which, whether true or no, alters not the case, since it is evident [that] the personal identity would equally be determined by the consciousness whether that consciousness were annexed to some individual immaterial substance or no. For, granting that the thinking substance in man must be necessarily supposed immaterial, it is evident that [that] immaterial thinking thing may sometimes part with its past consciousness and be restored to it again, as appears in the forgetfulness men often have of their past actions; and the mind many times recovers the memory of a past consciousness which it had lost for twenty years together. Make these intervals of memory and forgetfulness to take their turns regularly by day and night and you have two persons with the same immaterial spirit, as much as in the former instance of two persons with the same body. So that self is not determined by identity or diversity of substance, which it cannot be sure of, but only by identity of consciousness.

Indeed it may conceive the substance whereof it is now made up to have existed formerly, united in the same conscious being: but, consciousness removed, that substance is no more itself, or makes no more a part of it than any other substance, as is evident in the instance we have already given of a limb cut off, of whose heat, or cold, or other affections, having no longer any consciousness, it is no more of a man's self than any other matter of the universe. In like manner it will be in reference to any immaterial substance which is void of that consciousness whereby I am myself to myself: [if there be any part of its existence which] I cannot upon recollection join with that present consciousness whereby I am now myself, it is in that part of its existence no more *myself* than any other immaterial being. For, whatsoever any substance has thought or done which I cannot recollect and by my consciousness make my own thought and action, it will no more belong to me, whether a part of me thought or did it, than if it had been thought or done by any other immaterial being anywhere existing.

I agree, the more probable opinion is that this consciousness is annexed to, and the affection of, one individual immaterial substance.

But let men, according to their diverse hypotheses, resolve of that as they please. This every intelligent being, sensible of happiness or misery, must grant— that there is something that is *himself,* that he is concerned for, and would have happy; that this self has existed in a continued duration more than one instant, and therefore it is possible may exist, as it has done, months and years to come, without any certain bounds to be set to its duration; and may be the same self, by the same consciousness continued on for the future. And thus, by this consciousness he finds himself to be the same self which did such and such an action some years since, by which he comes to be happy or miserable now. In all which account of self, the same numerical *substance* is not considered as making the same self; but the same continued consciousness, in which several substances may have been united, and again separated from it, which, whilst they continued in a vital union with that wherein this consciousness then resided, made a part of that same self. Thus any part of our bodies vitally united to that which is conscious in us makes a part of ourselves: but upon separation from the vital union by which that consciousness is communicated, that which a moment since was part of ourselves, is now no more so than a part of another man's self is a part of me: and it is not impossible but in a little time may become a real part of another person. And so we have the same numerical substance become a part of two different persons, and the same person preserved under the change of various substances. Could we suppose any spirit wholly stripped of all its memory or consciousness of past actions, as we find our minds always are of a great part of ours, and sometimes of them all, the union or separation of such a spiritual substance would make no variation of personal identity any more than that of any particle of matter does. Any substance vitally united to the present thinking being is a part of that very same self which now is; anything united to it by a consciousness of former actions, makes also a part of the same self, which is the same both then and now.

Person, as I take it, is the name for this self. Wherever a man finds what he calls himself, there, I think, another may say is the same person. It is a forensic term, appropriating actions and their merit, and so belongs only to intelligent agents capable of a law, and happiness, and misery. This personality extends itself beyond present existence to what is past only by consciousness—whereby it becomes concerned and accountable; owns and imputes to itself past actions, just upon the same ground and for the same reason as it does the present. All which is founded in a concern for happiness, the unavoidable concomitant of consciousness; that which is conscious of pleasure and pain, desiring that self that is conscious should be happy. And therefore whatever past actions it cannot reconcile or *appropriate* to that present self by consciousness, it can be no more concerned in than if they had never been done: and to receive pleasure or pain, i.e. reward or punishment, on the account of any such action is all one as to be made happy or miserable in its first being without any demerit at all. For, supposing a *man* punished now for what he had done in another life, whereof he could be made to have no consciousness at all, what difference is there between that punishment and being *created* miserable? And therefore, conformable to this, the apostle tells us, that, at the great day, when everyone shall "receive according to his doings, the secrets of all hearts shall be laid open." The sentence shall be justified by the consciousness all persons shall have, that *they themselves,* in what bodies soever they appear, or what substances soever that consciousness adheres to, are the *same* that committed those actions, and deserve that punishment for them. . . .

To conclude: Whatever substance begins to exist, it must, during its existence, necessarily be the same: whatever compositions of substances begin to exist, during the union of those substances, the concrete must be the same: whatsoever mode begins to exist, during its existence it is the same: and so if the composition be of distinct substances and different modes, the same rule holds. Whereby it will appear that the difficulty or obscurity that has been about this matter rather rises from the names ill-used than from any obscurity in things themselves. For whatever makes the specific idea to which the name is applied, if that idea be steadily kept to, the distinction of anything into the same and diverse will easily be conceived, and there can arise no doubt about it.

~~~~ To Think About ~~~~

1. In his book *Reality* (New York: Macmillan, 1926: 36) **B. H. Streeter** says that what a person really knows of the "inner quality of life" depends primarily on the following three things: "first, the depth and the range of his own personal experience; secondly, how far he has the imaginative sympathy to penetrate into the inner experience of others; thirdly, the extent to which he has reflected on the material so presented." Give reasons for agreeing or disagreeing with Streeter.

2. A woman's skull is opened, under local anesthetic, so that she remains conscious. The ridges of the whitish-gray matter (the cortex) of the brain are exposed to view. The movements or changes that take place in the brain are shown in magnifying mirrors, so that the woman is able to watch these brain changes while she perceives and thinks. Who or what is doing the watching?

3. Report on views of the self and man as found in modern literature. You may prefer to pick out one or two writers, such as Ibsen, Sartre, or others.

4. Much of a person's sense of self is related to that person's biological sex and to the sex roles assigned by society. To what extent do you feel that you define yourself in terms of your sex? What limitations do you see in this kind of personal definition?

5. "The member of a primitive clan might express his identity in the formula 'I am we'; he cannot yet conceive of himself as an 'individual,' existing apart from his group. . . . When the feudal system broke down, this sense of identity was shaken and the acute question 'who am I?' arose."   *Unknown*

6. "The supreme ideal of Greece is to save the ego from anarchy and chaos. The supreme ideal of the Orient is to dissolve the ego into the infinite and to become one with it."   *Kimon Friar*

43
Human Beings Have
No Identical Self

David Hume (1711–72), a Scottish philosopher and man of letters, lived at a time when thinkers were engaged in controversy about the nature of morals and religion. He influenced the development of skepticism in philosophy, for he distrusted philosophical speculation and asserted that all knowledge comes from experience.

Upon Hume's death Adam Smith wrote:

Thus died our most excellent and never to be forgotten friend; concerning whose philosophical opinions men will, no doubt, judge variously but concerning whose character and conduct there can scarce be a difference of opinion. His temper, indeed, seemed to be more happily balanced, if I may be allowed such an expression, than that perhaps of any other man I have ever known. Even in the lowest state of his fortune, his great and necessary frugality never hindered him from exercising, upon proper occasions, acts both of charity and generosity. It was a frugality bounded not upon avarice, but upon the love of independency. The extreme gentleness of his nature never weakened either the firmness of his mind or the steadiness of his resolutions. His constant pleasantry was the genuine effusion of good nature and good humor, tempered with delicacy and modesty, and without even the slightest tincture of malignity so frequently the disagreeable source of what is called wit in other men. It never was the meaning of his raillery to mortify; and therefore, far from offending, it seldom failed to please and delight even those who were frequently the objects of it; there was not perhaps any one of all his great and amiable qualities which contributed more to endear his conversation. And that gayety of temper, so agreeable in society, but which is so often accompanied with frivolous and superficial qualities, was in him certainly attended with the most severe application, the most extensive learning, the greatest depth of thought, and a capacity, in every respect the most comprehensive. Upon the whole, I have always considered him, both in his lifetime and since his death, as approaching as nearly to the idea of a perfectly wise and virtuous man as perhaps the nature of human frailty will permit.

From David Hume, "Of Personal Identity," *A Treatise of Human Nature* (London: Printed for J. Noon, 1739), book I, part 4.

In contrast to Locke, Hume does not believe there is an identical self. He argues that there are no constant and invariable impressions of such a self, and that introspection does not discover anything but particular perceptions. Thus we can have particular sensations and emotions, but no impression of a self. Hume says that "the identity which we ascribe to the mind of man is a fictitious one . . . (this because) it . . . is not able to run the several different perceptions into one, and make them lose their character of distinction and difference, which are essential to them."

 To Study

1. What do some philosophers believe about the self?
2. What does Hume believe about the ideas of self? Why?
3. What does Hume say occurs when he "enters most intimately into what I call myself"?
4. According to Hume, what is the self?
5. Upon what does identity depend?
6. Why do we believe there is a personal identity?

There are some philosophers who imagine we are every moment intimately conscious of what we call our Self; that we feel its existence and its continuance in existence; and are certain, beyond the evidence of a demonstration, both of its perfect identity and simplicity. The strongest sensation, the most violent passion, say they, instead of distracting us from this view, only fix it the more intensely, and make us consider their influence on *self* either by their pain or pleasure. To attempt a farther proof of this were to weaken its evidence, since no proof can be derived from any fact of which we are so intimately conscious, nor is there any thing of which we can be certain if we doubt of this.

Unluckily all these positive assertions are contrary to that very experience which is pleaded for them, nor have we any idea of *self* after the manner it is here explained. For from what impression could this idea be derived? This question it is impossible to answer without a manifest contradiction and absurdity; and yet it is a question which must necessarily be answered if we would have the idea of self pass for clear and intelligible. It must be some one impression that gives rise to every real idea. But self or person is not any one impression, but that to which our several impressions and ideas are supposed to have a reference. If any impression gives rise to the idea of self, that impression must continue invariably the same, through the whole course of our lives; since self is supposed to exist after that manner. But there is no impression constant and invariable. Pain and pleasure, grief and joy, passions and sensations succeed each other, and never all exist at the same time. It cannot, therefore, be from any of these impressions, or from any other, that the idea of self is derived; and consequently there is no such idea.

But farther, what must become of all our particular perceptions upon this hypothesis? All these are different, and distinguishable, and separable from each other, and may be separately considered, and may exist separately, and have no need of anything to support their existence. After what manner, therefore, do they belong to self; and how are they connected with it? For my part, when I enter most intimately into what I call *myself,* I always stumble on some particular perception or other, of heat or cold, light or shade, love or hatred, pain or pleasure. I never can catch *myself* at any time without a perception, and never can observe anything but the perception. When my perceptions are removed for any time, as by sound sleep, so long am I not sensible of *myself,* and may truly be said not to exist. And were all my perceptions removed by death, and could I neither think, nor feel, nor see, nor love, nor hate after the dissolution of my body, I should be entirely annihilated, nor do I conceive what is farther requisite to make me a perfect non-entity. If anyone upon serious and unprejudiced reflection thinks he has a different notion of *himself,* I must confess I can reason no longer with him. All I can allow him is that he may be in the right as well as I, and that we are essentially different in this particular. He may, perhaps, perceive something simple and continued, which he calls *himself;* though I am certain there is no such principle in me.

But setting aside some metaphysicians of this kind, I may venture to affirm of the rest of mankind that they are nothing but a bundle or collection of different perceptions which succeed each other with an inconceivable rapidity, and are in a perpetual flux and movement. Our eyes cannot turn in their sockets without varying our perceptions. Our thought is still more variable than our sight; and all our other senses and faculties contribute to this change; nor is there any single power of the soul which remains unalterably the same perhaps for one moment. The mind is a kind of theatre where several perceptions successively make their appearance, pass, repass, glide away, and mingle in an infinite variety of postures and situations. There is properly no *simplicity* in it at one time, nor *identity* in different, whatever natural propension we may have to imagine that simplicity and identity. The comparison of the theatre must not mislead us. They are the successive perceptions only that constitute the mind; nor have we the most distant notion of the place where these scenes are represented, or of the materials of which it is composed.

What then gives us so great a propension to ascribe an identity to these successive perceptions, and to suppose ourselves [possessed] of an invariable and uninterrupted existence through the whole course of our lives? . . .

We have a distinct idea of an object that remains invariable and uninterrupted through a supposed variation of time; and this idea we call that of *identity* or *sameness.* We have also a distinct idea of several different objects existing in succession, and connected together by a close relation; and this to an accurate view affords as perfect a notion of *diversity,* as if there was no manner of relation among the objects. But though these two ideas of identity, and a succession of related objects be in themselves perfectly distinct, and even contrary, yet it is certain that in our common way of thinking they are generally confounded with each other. That action of the imagination by which we consider the uninterrupted and invariable object, and that by which we reflect on the succession of related objects, are almost the same to the feeling, nor is there much more effort of thought required in the latter case than in the former. The relation facilitates the transition of the mind from one object to another, and renders its passage as smooth as if it contemplated one continued object. This resemblance is the case of the confusion and mistake, and makes us substitute the notion of identity, instead of that of related objects. However at one instant we may consider the related succession as variable or interrupted, we are sure the next to ascribe to it a perfect identity, and regard it as invariable and uninterrupted. Our propensity to this mistake is so great from the resemblance above-mentioned, that we fall into it before we are aware; and though we incessantly correct ourselves by reflection, and return to a more accurate method of thinking, yet we cannot long sustain our philosophy, or take off this bias from the imagination. Our last resource is to yield to it, and boldly assert that these different related objects are in effect the same, however interrupted and variable. In order to justify to ourselves this absurdity, we often feign some new and unintelligible principle that connects the objects together, and prevents their interruption or variation. Thus we feign the continued existence of the perceptions of our senses, to remove the interruption, and run into the notion of a *soul*, and *self*, and *substance*, to disguise the variation. But we may farther observe that where we do not give rise to such a fiction, our propension to confound identity with relation is so great that we are apt to imagine something unknown and mysterious connecting the parts beside their relation; and this I take to be the case with regard to the identity we ascribe to plants and vegetables. And even when this does not take place, we still feel a propensity to confound these ideas, though we are not able fully to satisfy ourselves in that particular, nor find anything invariable and uninterrupted to justify our notion of identity.

Thus the controversy concerning identity is not merely a dispute of words. For when we attribute identity, in an improper sense, to variable or interrupted objects, our mistake is not confined to the expression, but is commonly attended with a fiction, either of something invariable and uninterrupted, or of something mysterious and inexplicable, or at least with a propensity to such fictions. . . .

We now proceed to explain the nature of *personal identity.* . . .

It is evident, that the identity, which we attribute to the human mind, however perfect we may imagine it to be, is not able to run the several different perceptions into one, and make them lose their characters of distinction and difference, which are essential to them. It is still true, that every distinct perception, which enters in to the composition of the mind, is a distinct existence, and is different and distinguishable and separable from every other perception, either contemporary or successive. But, as, notwithstanding this distinction and separability, we suppose the whole train of perceptions to be united by identity, a question naturally arises concerning this relation of identity; whether it be something that really binds our several perceptions together, or only associates their ideas in the imagination. That is, in other words, whether in pronouncing concerning the identity of a person, we observe some real bond among his perceptions, or only feel one among the ideas we form of them. This question we might easily decide if we would recollect what has been already proved at large, that the understanding never observes any real connection among objects, and that even the union of cause and effect, when strictly examined, resolves itself into a customary association of ideas. For thence it evidently follows that identity is nothing really belonging to these different perceptions, and uniting them together; but is merely a quality, which we attribute to them because of the union of their ideas in the imagination when we reflect upon them. Now the only qualities, which can give ideas a union in the imagination are these three relations above-mentioned. These are the uniting principles in the ideal world, and without them every distinct object is separable by the mind, and may be separately considered, and appears not to have any more connection with any other object than if disjoined by the greatest difference and remoteness. It is, therefore, on some of these three relations of resemblance, contiguity and causation that identity depends; and as the very essence of these relations consists in their producing an easy transition of ideas; it follows, that our notions of personal identity proceed entirely from the smooth and uninterrupted progress of the thought along a train of connected ideas according to the principles above-explained.

The only question, therefore, which remains is by what relations this uninterrupted progress of our thought is produced when we consider the successive existence of a mind or thinking person. And here it is evident we must confine ourselves to resemblance and causation, and must drop contiguity, which has little or no influence in the present case.

To begin with *resemblance;* suppose we could see clearly into the breast of another, and observe that succession of perceptions which constitutes his mind or thinking principle, and suppose that he always preserves the memory of a considerable part of past perceptions; it is evident that nothing could more contribute to the bestowing a relation on this succession amidst all its variations. For what is the memory but a faculty by which we raise up the images of past perceptions? And as an image necessarily resembles its object, must not the frequent placing of these resembling perceptions in the chain of thought convey the imagination more easily from one link to another, and make the whole seem like the continuance of one object? In this particular, then, the memory not only discovers the identity, but also contributes to its production, by producing the relation of resemblance among the perceptions. The case is the same whether we consider ourselves or others.

As to *causation,* we may observe that the true idea of the human mind is to consider it as a system of different perceptions or different existences which are linked together by the relation of cause and effect, and mutually produce, destroy, influence, and modify each other. Our impressions give rise to their correspondent ideas; and these ideas in their turn produce other impressions. One thought chases another, and draws after it a third, by which it is expelled in its turn. In this respect, I cannot compare the soul more properly to anything than to a republic or commonwealth, in which the several members are united by the reciprocal ties of government and subordination, and give rise to other persons, who propagate the same republic in the incessant changes of its parts. And as the same individual republic may not only change its members, but also its laws and constitutions, in like manner the same person may vary his character and disposition, as well as his impressions and ideas, without losing his identity. Whatever changes he endures, his several parts are still connected by the relation of causation. And in this view our identity with regard to the passions serves to corroborate that with regard to the imagination by the making our distant perceptions influence each other, and by giving us a present concern for our past or future pains or pleasures.

As memory alone acquaints us with the continuance and extent of this succession of perceptions, it is to be considered, upon that account chiefly, as the source of personal identity. Had we no memory, we never should have any notion of causation, nor consequently of that chain of causes and effects which constitute our self or person. But having once acquired this notion of causation from the memory, we can extend the same chain of causes, and consequently the identity of our persons beyond our memory, and can comprehend times, and circumstances, and actions which we have entirely forgot, but suppose in general to have existed. . . . In this view, therefore, memory does not so much *produce* as *discover* personal identity, by showing us the relation of cause and effect among our different perceptions. It will be incumbent on those who affirm that memory produces entirely our personal identity to give a reason why we can thus extend our identity beyond our memory.

The whole of this doctrine leads us to a conclusion, which is of great importance in the present affair, *viz.,* that all the nice and subtle questions concerning personal identity can never possibly be decided.

To Think About

1. "A man's character is discernible in the mental or moral attitude in which, when it came upon him, he felt himself most deeply and intensely active and alive. At such moments there is a voice inside which speaks and says: 'This is the real me!' [Such experience always includes] . . . an element of active tension, of holding my own, as it were, and trusting outward things to perform their part so as to make it a full harmony, but without any guaranty that they will. Make it a guaranty . . . and the attitude immediately becomes to my consciousness stagnant and stingless. Take away the guaranty, and I feel . . . a sort of deep enthusiastic bliss of bitter willingness to do and suffer anything . . . and which, although it is a mere mood or emotion to which I can give no form in words, authenticates itself to me as the deepest principle of all active and theoretic determination which I possess."
   William James

2. "What bound me to Jewry was (I am ashamed to admit) neither faith nor national pride, for I have always been an unbeliever and was brought up without any religion though not without a respect for what are called the 'ethical' standards of human civilization. Whenever I felt an inclination to national enthusiasm I strove to suppress it as being harmful and wrong, alarmed by the warning examples of the peoples among whom we Jews live. But plenty of other things remained over to make the attraction of Jewry and Jews irresistible—many obscure emotional forces, which were the more powerful the less they could be expressed in words, as well as a clear consciousness of inner identity, the safe privacy of a common mental construction. And beyond this there was a perception that it was to my Jewish nature alone that I owed two characteristics that had become indispensable to me in the difficult course of my life. Because I was a Jew, I found myself free from many prejudices which restricted others in the use of their intellect; and as a Jew I was prepared to join the Opposition, and to do without agreement with the 'compact majority.'"
   Sigmund Freud

3. "I am not the person you took me to be."
   Jane Carlyle

4. "We are what we pretend to be, so we must be careful about what we pretend to be."   ***Kurt Vonnegut, Jr.***

5. "The teacher's obligation is to be patient enough to permit deliberation and decision by each of those he is trying to help. If his students do not choose, each in the light of his own contingent existence and his own limitations, they will not become ethical beings; if they are not ethical beings—in search of their own ethical reality—they are not individuals; if they are not individuals, they will not learn."   ***Søren Kierkegaard***

6. "Could it be that I am now dreaming? Not only does the right answer seem to me to be 'Yes' but, more importantly, it seems to me that the possibility continues to make sense even if I go on to imagine that no one on the face of the earth or anywhere else could ever know that I *am* dreaming because they too could never know whether they were awake or dreaming. Adding the further thought that the truth about my state is unknown or even unknowable to everyone does not seem to me to affect the possibility I originally tried to imagine at all. Of course, I might be wrong about this, but how is one to tell?"   ***Barry Stroud***

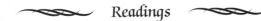

Readings

BUTCHYAROY, PANAYOT. "The Self and Perceptions: A Study in Human Philosophy." *Philosophical Quarterly* 9 (1959): 97–115.

CAPALDI, N. "The Hume Literature of the 1980s." *American Philosophical Quarterly* 28 (1991): 255–72.

ERIKSON, ERIK. *Identity, Youth, and Crisis.* New York: Norton, 1968.

FLEW, ANTONY. "Locke and the Problem of Personal Identity." *Philosophy* 26 (1951): 53–68.

GOULD, J., AND J. IORIO. *Love, Sex, and Identity.* San Francisco: Boyd & Fraser, 1972.

OGILVY, JAMES. *Self and World.* New York: Harcourt, 1973.

PENELHUM, T. "Hume on Personal Identity." *Philosophical Review* 64 (1955): 571–89.

PART 7

SOCIAL AND POLITICAL PHILOSOPHY

What Is Freedom?

44
Freedom and Authority

Fyodor Dostoevski (1822–81) was a renowned Russian novelist. Some of his famous novels are Crime and Punishment *(1866),* The Idiot *(1868), and* The Brothers Karamazov *(1880).*

Discussion of human freedom raises fundamental issues about the nature of people and their goals. Do people really wish to have freedom to choose and to determine their own lives? Would they not be happier without the burdens of such freedom? Can they be trusted to use such freedom wisely?

Fyodor Dostoevski has provided one of the most famous discussions of these basic questions. In a chapter of his novel *The Brothers Karamazov*, Dostoevski narrates a conversation between two of the central characters, Ivan Karamazov and his younger brother Alyosha. Ivan and Alyosha represent contrasting types. Ivan is an intellectual who has become skeptical of traditional beliefs and faiths, whereas Alyosha is a man of faith, training for a future career as a Christian priest. In the selection that follows, Ivan has written a story about the Grand Inquisitor, and he tells it to Alyosha.

Ivan's story takes place in sixteenth-century Spain. He imagines Christ returning to earth and meeting a cardinal of the church, the Grand Inquisitor, who has been responsible for burning a hundred heretics the day before. The Grand Inquisitor recognizes Christ, imprisons him, and then explains why Christ must also be sentenced to death by fire.

In the eyes of the Grand Inquisitor, Christ's heresy consists of the value he placed on one's freedom of choice and conscience. The Grand Inquisitor reviews

From Fyodor Dostoevski, *The Brothers Karamazov*, trans. Constance Garnett (London: Heinemann, 1912).

411

Christ's three temptations and notes that in each case Christ could have chosen to enslave people and thereby make them happy, but did not do so for the sake of leaving
them free. When Christ, in the first temptation, would not turn stones into bread, he
thwarted our desire to have someone to worship. When Christ next refused to prove
he was the son of God by flinging himself from the top of a temple and being saved
by angels, he rejected the needs for "miracle, mystery, and authority." Finally, when
Christ would not take the kingdoms of the world, he turned down the opportunity to
give people unity and peace on earth. For the Grand Inquisitor, people are weak by
nature, and the true lover of humanity must correct Christ's work by removing their
freedom and giving them "all that man seeks on earth—that is, some one to worship,
some one to keep his conscience, and some means of uniting all in one unanimous
and harmonious ant-heap."

One freedom Christ championed was different from the negative freedom from
constraint. It was the freedom experienced through living by religious ideals. We
would all say that Christ was in some sense a free man. However, he was not politically or economically free, and he lived within the guidelines of Judaic moral ideals
such as the Ten Commandments. But this was Christ's freedom, that is, living by his
ideal. Thus, Christ's freedom was his acquired freedom, the kind achieved by the man
who lives by a significant moral ideal.

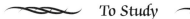

To Study

1. On what grounds can the Grand Inquisitor say to Christ, "Thou hast no right to
    add anything to what Thou hadst said of old"?
2. What does the Grand Inquisitor mean when he says Christ cannot take from
    humans the freedom he had exalted? What freedom have the people given to
    the church?
3. What is meant by "Freedom and bread enough for all are inconceivable together"?
4. What freedom is the church ready to endure that the people have found so
    dreadful?
5. What is the significance of the first question in the wilderness?
6. According to the Grand Inquisitor, why would it have been better for Christ to
    deprive humans of freedom of conscience? Discuss the three forces that could
    conquer the conscience.
7. What harm does the Grand Inquisitor imply by stating, "Instead of taking pos-
    session of men's freedom, Thou didst increase it"?
8. In what sense was Christ responsible for the destruction of his own kingdom?
9. What does the Grand Inquisitor mean when he says, "They will only become
    free when they renounce their freedom to us and submit to us"? Explain, using
    examples from the selection.

"My story is laid in Spain, in Seville, in the most terrible time of the Inquisition, when fires were lighted every day to the glory of God, and 'in the splendid *auto*

da fé[1] the wicked heretics were burnt.' Oh, of course, this was not the coming in which He will appear according to His promise at the end of time in all His heavenly glory, and which will be sudden 'as lightning flashing from east to west.' No, He visited His children only for a moment, and there where the flames were crackling round the heretics. In His infinite mercy He came once more among men in that human shape in which He walked among men for three years fifteen centuries ago. He came down to the 'hot pavement' of the southern town in which on the day before almost a hundred heretics had . . . been burnt by the cardinal, the Grand Inquisitor, in a magnificent *auto de fé,* in the presence of the king, the court, the knights, the cardinals, the most charming ladies of the court, and the whole population of Seville.

"He came softly, unobserved, and yet, strange to say, every one recognized Him. That might be one of the best passages in the poem. I mean, why they recognized Him. The people are irresistibly drawn to Him, they surround Him, they flock about Him, follow Him. He moves silently in their midst with a gentle smile of infinite compassion. The sun of love burns in His heart, light and power shine from His eyes, and their radiance, shed on the people, stirs their hearts with responsive love. He holds out His hands to them, blesses them, and a healing virtue comes from contact with Him, even with His garments. An old man in the crowd, blind from childhood, cries out, 'O Lord, heal me and I shall see Thee!' and, as it were, scales fall from his eyes and the blind man sees Him. The crowd weeps and kisses the earth under His feet. Children throw flowers before Him, sing, and cry hosannah. 'It is He—it is He!' all repeat. 'It must be He, it can be no one but Him!' He stops at the steps of the Seville cathedral at the moment when the weeping mourners are bringing in a little open white coffin. In it lies a child of seven, the only daughter of a prominent citizen. The dead child lies hidden in flowers. 'He will raise your child,' the crowd shouts to the weeping mother. The priest, coming to meet the coffin, looks perplexed, and frowns, but the mother of the dead child throws herself at His feet with a wail. 'If it is Thou, raise my child!' she cries, holding out her hands to Him. The procession halts, the coffin is laid on the steps at His feet. He looks with compassion, and His lips once more softly pronounce, 'Maiden, arise!' and the maiden arises. The little girl sits up in the coffin and looks around, smiling with wide-open wondering eyes, holding a bunch of white roses they had put in her hand.

"There are cries, sobs, confusion among the people, and at that moment the cardinal himself, the Grand Inquisitor, passes by the cathedral. He is an old man, almost ninety, tall and erect, with a withered face and sunken eyes, in which there is still a gleam of light. He is not dressed in his gorgeous cardinal's robes, as he was the day before, when he was burning the enemies of the Roman Church—at that moment he was wearing his coarse, old, monk's cassock. At a distance behind him come his gloomy assistants and slaves and the 'holy guard.' He stops at the sight of the crowd and watches it from a distance. He sees everything; he sees them set the coffin down at His feet, sees the child rise up, and his face darkens. He knits his thick grey brows and his eyes gleam with a sinister fire. He holds out his finger and bids the guards take Him. And such is his power, so completely are the people cowed into submission and trembling obedience to him, that the crowd immediately makes way for the

---

[1] "Act of Faith," but refers to burning at the stake. [ED.]

guards, and in the midst of deathlike silence they lay hands on Him and lead Him away. The crowd instantly bows down to the earth, like one man, before the old inquisitor. He blesses the people in silence and passes on. The guards lead their prisoner to the close, gloomy vaulted prison in the ancient palace of the Holy Inquisition and shut Him in it. The day passes and is followed by the dark, burning 'breathless' night of Seville. . . . In the pitch darkness the iron door of the prison is suddenly open and the Grand Inquisitor himself comes in with a light in his hand. He is alone; the door is closed at once behind him. He stands in the doorway and for a minute or two gazes into His face. At last he goes up slowly, sets the light on the table and speaks.

" 'Is it Thou? Thou?' but receiving no answer, he adds at once, 'Don't answer, be silent. What canst Thou say, indeed? I know too well what Thou wouldst say. And Thou hast no right to add anything to what Thou hadst said of old. Why, then, art Thou come to hinder us? For Thou hast come to hinder us, and Thou knowest that. But dost Thou know what will be tomorrow? I know not who Thou art and care not to know whether it is Thou or only a semblance of Him, but tomorrow I shall condemn Thee and burn Thee at the stake as the worst of heretics. And the very people who have to-day kissed Thy feet, tomorrow at the faintest sign from me will rush to heap up the embers of Thy fire. Knowest Thou that? Yes, maybe Thou knowest it,' he added with thoughtful penetration, never for a moment taking his eyes off the Prisoner."

"I don't quite understand, Ivan. What does it mean?" Alyosha, who has been listening in silence, said with a smile. "Is it simply a wild fantasy, or a mistake on the part of the old man—some impossible [mistake]?"

"Take it as the last," said Ivan, laughing, "if you are so corrupted by modern realism and can't stand anything fantastic. If you like it to be a case of mistaken identity, let it be so. It is true," he went on, laughing, "the old man was ninety; and he might well be crazy over his set idea. He might have been struck by the appearance of the Prisoner. It might, in fact, be simply his ravings, the delusion of an old man of ninety, over-excited by the *auto da fé* of a hundred heretics the day before. But does it matter to us after all whether it was a mistake of identity or a wild fantasy? All that matters is that the old man should speak out, should speak openly of what he has thought in silence for ninety years."

"And the Prisoner too is silent? Does He look at him and not say a word?"

"That's inevitable in any case," Ivan laughed again. "The old man has told Him He hasn't the right to add anything to what He has said of old. One may say it is the most fundamental feature of Roman Catholicism, in my opinion at least. 'All has been given by Thee to the Pope,' they say, 'and all, therefore, is still in the Pope's hands, and there is no need for Thee to come now at all. Thou must not meddle for the time, at least.' That's how they speak and write too—the Jesuits, at any rate, I have read it myself in the works of their theologians. 'Hast Thou the right to reveal to us one of the mysteries of that world from which thou hast come?' my old man asks Him, and answers the question for Him. 'No, Thou hast not: that Thou mayest not add to what has been said of old, and mayest not take from men the freedom which Thou didst exalt when Thou wast on earth. Whatsoever thou revealest anew will encroach on men's freedom of faith; for it will be manifest as a miracle, and the freedom of their faith was dearer to Thee than anything in those days fifteen hundred years ago. Didst Thou not often say then, "I will make you free"? But now Thou hast seen these "free" men,' the old man adds suddenly, with a pensive smile. 'Yes, we've paid dearly for it,' he goes on, looking sternly at Him, 'but at last we have completed that work in Thy name. For fifteen centuries we have been wrestling with Thy freedom, but now it is ended and over for good. Dost Thou not believe that it's over for good? Thou lookest meekly at me and deignest not even to be wroth with me. But let me tell Thee that now, today, people are more persuaded than ever that they have perfect freedom, yet they have brought their freedom to us and laid it humbly at our feet. But that has been our doing. Was this what Thou didst? Was this Thy freedom?' "

"I don't understand again," Alyosha broke in. "Is he ironical, is he jesting?"

"Not a bit of it! He claims it as a merit for himself and his Church that at last they have vanquished freedom and have done so to make men happy. 'For now' (he is speaking of the Inquisition, of course) 'for the first time it has become possible to think of the happiness of men. Man was created a rebel; and how can rebels be happy? Thou wast warned,' he says to Him. 'Thou hast had no lack of admonitions and warnings, but Thou didst not listen to those warnings: Thou didst reject the only way by which men might be made happy. But, fortunately, departing Thou didst hand on the work to us. Thou hast promised, Thou hast established Thy word. Thou hast given to us the right to bind and to unbind, and now, of course, Thou canst not think of taking it away. Why, then, hast Thou come to hinder us?' "

"And what's the meaning of 'no lack of admonitions and warnings'?" asked Alyosha.

"Why, that's the chief part of what the old man must say."

" 'The wise and dread spirit, the spirit of self-destruction and nonexistence,' the old man goes on, 'the great spirit talked with Thee in the wilderness, and we are told in the books that he "tempted" Thee. Is that so? And could anything truer be said than what he revealed to Thee in three questions and what Thou didst reject, and what in the books is called "the temptation"? And yet if there has ever been on earth a real stupendous miracle, it took place on that day, on the day of the three temptations. The statement of those three questions was itself the miracle. If it were possible to imagine simply for the sake of argument that those three questions of the dread spirit have perished utterly from the books, and that we had to restore them and to invent them anew, and to do so had gathered together all the wise men of the earth—rulers, chief priests, learned men, philosophers, poets—and had set them the task to invent three questions, such as would not only fit the occasion, but express in three words, three human phrases, the whole future history of the world and of humanity—dost Thou believe that all the wisdom of the earth united could have invented anything in depth and force equal to the three questions which were actually put to Thee then by the wise and mighty spirit in the wilderness? From those questions alone, from the miracle of their statement, we can see that we have here to do not with the fleeting human intelligence, but with the absolute and eternal. For in those three questions the whole subsequent history of mankind is, as it were, brought together into one whole, and foretold, and in them are united all the unsolved historical contradictions of human nature. At the time it could not be so clear, since the future was unknown; but now that fifteen hundred years have passed, we see that everything in those three questions was so justly divined and foretold, and has been so truly fulfilled, that nothing can be added to them or taken from them.

" 'Judge Thyself who was right—Thou or he who questioned Thee then? Remember the first question; its meaning, in other words, was this: "Thou wouldst go into the world, and art going with empty hands, with some promise of freedom which men in their simplicity and their natural unruliness cannot even understand, which they fear and dread—for nothing has ever been more insupportable for a man and a human society than freedom. But seest Thou these stones in this parched and barren wilderness. Turn them into bread, and mankind will run after Thee like a flock of sheep, grateful and obedient, Thou forever trembling, lest Thou withdraw Thy hand and deny them Thy bread." But Thou wouldst not deprive man of freedom and didst reject the offer, thinking, what is that freedom worth, if obedience is bought with bread? Thou didst reply that man lives not by bread alone. But dost Thou know that for the sake of that earthly bread the spirit of the earth will rise up against Thee and will strive with Thee and overcome Thee and all will follow him, crying, "Who can compare with this beast? He has given us fire from heaven!" Dost Thou know that the ages will pass, and humanity will proclaim by the lips of their sages that there is no crime, and therefore no sin; there is only hunger? "Feed men, and then ask of them virtue!" that's what they'll write on the banner, which they will raise against Thee, and with which they will destroy Thy temple. Where Thy temple stood will rise a new building; the terrible tower of Babel will be built again, and though, like the one of old, it will not be finished, yet Thou mightest have prevented that new tower and have cut short the sufferings of men for a thousand years; for they will come back to us after a thousand years of agony with their tower. They will seek us again, hidden underground in the catacombs, for we shall be again persecuted and tortured. They will find us and cry to us, "Feed us, for those who have promised us fire from heaven haven't given it!" And then we shall finish building their tower, for he finishes the building who feeds them. And we alone shall feed them in Thy name, declaring falsely that it is in Thy name. Oh, never, never can they feed themselves without us! No science will give them bread so long as they remain free. In the end they will lay their freedom at our feet, and say to us, "Make us your slaves, but feed us." They will understand themselves, at last, that freedom and bread enough for all are inconceivable together, for never, never will they be able to share between them! They will be convinced, too, that they can never be free, for they are weak, and vicious, worthless and rebellious. Thou didst promise them the bread of Heaven, but, I repeat again, can it compare with earthly bread in the eye of the weak, ever sinful and ignoble race of men? And if for the sake of the bread of Heaven thousands and tens of thousands shall follow Thee, what is to become of the millions and tens of thousands of millions of creatures who will not have the strength to forego the earthly bread for the sake of the heavenly? Or dost Thou care only for the tens of thousands of the great and strong, while the millions, numerous as the sands of the sea, who are weak but love Thee, must exist only for the sake of the great and strong? No, we care for the weak too. They are sinful and rebellious, but in the end they too will become obedient. They will marvel at us and look on us as gods, because we are ready to endure the freedom which they have found so dreadful and to rule over them—so awful it will seem to them to be free. But we shall tell them that we are Thy servants and rule them in Thy name. We shall deceive them again, for we will not let Thee come to us again. That deception will be our suffering for we shall be forced to lie.

" 'This is the significance of the first question in the wilderness, and this is what Thou hast rejected for the sake of that freedom which Thou hast exalted above everything. Yet in this question lies hid the great secret of this world. Choosing "bread," Thou wouldst have satisfied the universal and everlasting craving of humanity—to find someone to worship. So long as man remains free he strives for nothing so incessantly and so painfully as to find someone to worship. But man seeks to worship what is established beyond dispute, so that all men would agree at once to worship it. For these pitiful creatures are concerned not only to find what one or the other can worship, but to find something that all would believe in and worship; what is essential is that all may be *together* in it. This craving for *community* of worship is the chief misery of every man individually and of all humanity from the beginning of time. For the sake of common worship they've slain each other with the sword. They have set up gods and challenged one another, "Put away your gods and come and worship ours, or we will kill you and your gods!" And so it will be to the end of the world, even when gods disappear from the earth; they will fall down before idols just the same. Thou didst know, Thou couldst not but have known, this fundamental secret of human nature, but Thou didst reject the one infallible banner which was offered Thee to make all men bow down to Thee alone—the banner of earthly bread; and Thou hast rejected it for the sake of freedom and the bread of Heaven. Behold what Thou didst further. And all again in the name of Freedom! I tell Thee that man is tormented by no greater anxiety than to find someone quickly to whom he can hand over that gift of freedom with which the ill-fated creature is born. But only one who can appease their conscience can take over their freedom. In bread there was offered Thee an invincible banner; give bread, and man will worship Thee, for nothing is more certain than bread. But if someone else gains possession of his conscience—oh! then he will cast away Thy bread and follow after him who has ensnared his conscience. In that Thou wast right. For the secret of man's being is not only to live but to have something to live for. Without a stable conception of the object of life, man would not consent to go on living, and would rather destroy himself than remain on earth, though he had bread in abundance. That is true. But what happened? Instead of taking men's freedom from them, Thou didst make it greater than ever! Didst Thou forget that man prefers peace, and even death, to freedom of choice in the knowledge of good and evil? Nothing is more seductive for man than his freedom of conscience, but nothing is a greater cause of suffering. And behold, instead of giving a firm foundation for setting the conscience of man at rest forever, Thou didst choose all that is exceptional, vague and enigmatic; Thou didst choose what was utterly beyond the strength of men, acting as though Thou didst not love them at all—Thou who didst come to give Thy life for them! Instead of taking possession of men's freedom, Thou didst increase it, and burdened the spiritual kingdom of mankind with its sufferings for ever. Thou didst desire man's free love, that he should follow Thee freely, enticed and taken captive by Thee. In place of the rigid ancient law, man must hereafter with free heart decide for himself what is good and what is evil, having only Thy image before him as his guide. But didst Thou not know he would at last reject even Thy image and Thy truth, if he is weighed down with the fearful burden of free choice? They will cry aloud at last that the truth is not in Thee, for they could not have been left in greater confusion and suffering than Thou hast caused, laying upon them so many cares and unanswerable problems.

" 'So that, in truth, Thou didst Thyself lay the foundation for the destruction of Thy kingdom, and no one is more to blame for it. Yet what was offered Thee? There are three powers, three powers alone, able to conquer and to hold captive forever the conscience of these impotent rebels for their happiness—those forces are miracle, mystery and authority. Thou hast rejected all three and hast set the example for doing so. When the wise and dread spirit set Thee on the pinnacle of the temple and said to Thee, "If Thou wouldst know whether Thou art the Son of God then cast Thyself down, for it is written: the angels shall hold him up lest he fall and bruise himself, and Thou shalt know then whether Thou art the Son of God and shalt prove then how great is Thy faith in Thy Father." But Thou didst refuse and wouldst not cast Thyself down. Oh! of course, Thou didst proudly and well, like God; but the weak, unruly race of men, are they gods? Oh, Thou didst know then that in taking one step, in making one movement to cast Thyself down, Thou wouldst be tempting God and have lost all Thy faith in Him, and wouldst have been dashed to pieces against that earth which Thou didst come to save. And the wise spirit that tempted Thee would have rejoiced. But I ask again, are there many like Thee? And couldst Thou believe for one moment that men, too, could face such a temptation? Is the nature of men such, that they can reject miracle, and at the great moments of their life, moments of their deepest, most agonising spiritual difficulties, cling only to the free verdict of the heart? Oh, Thou didst know that Thy deed would be recorded in books, would be handed down to remote times and the utmost ends of the earth, and Thou didst hope that man, following Thee, would cling to God and not ask for a miracle. But Thou didst not know that when man rejects miracle he rejects God too; for man seeks not so much God as the miraculous. And as man cannot bear to be without the miraculous, he will create new miracles of his own for himself, and will worship deeds of sorcery and witchcraft, though he might be a hundred times over a rebel, heretic and infidel. Thou didst not come down from the Cross when they shouted to Thee; mocking and reviling Thee, "Come down from the cross and we will believe that Thou art He." Thou didst not come down, for again Thou wouldst not enslave man by a miracle, and didst crave faith given freely, not based on miracle. Thou didst crave for free love and not the base raptures of the slave before the might that has overawed him forever. But Thou didst think too highly of men therein, for they are slaves, of course, though rebellious by nature. Look round and judge; fifteen centuries have passed, look upon them. Whom hast Thou raised up to Thyself? I swear, man is weaker and baser by nature than Thou hast believed him! Can he, can he do what Thou didst? By showing him so much respect, Thou didst, as it were, cease to feel for him, for Thou didst ask far too much for him—Thou who hast loved him more than Thyself! Respecting him less, Thou wouldst have asked less of him. That would have been more like love, for his burden would have been lighter. He is weak and vile. What though he is everywhere now rebelling against our power, and proud of his rebellion? It is the pride of a child and a schoolboy. They are little children rioting and barring out the teacher at school. But their childish delight will end; it will cost them dear. They will cast down temples and drench the earth with blood. But they will see at last, the foolish children,

that, though they are rebels, they are impotent rebels, unable to keep up their own rebellion. Bathed in their foolish tears, they will recognize at last that He who created
them rebels must have meant to mock at them. They will say this in despair, and their
utterance will be a blasphemy which will make them more unhappy still, for man's
nature cannot bear blasphemy, and in the end always avenges it on itself. And so unrest, confusion and unhappiness—that is the present lot of man after Thou didst bear
so much for their freedom! Thy great prophet tells in vision and in image, that he saw
all those who took part in the first resurrection and that there were of each tribe twelve
thousand. But if there were so many of them, they must have been not men but gods.
They had borne Thy cross, they had endured scores of years in the barren, hungry
wilderness, living upon locust roots—and Thou mayest indeed point with pride at
those children of freedom, of free love, of free and splendid sacrifice for Thy name.
But remember that they were only some thousands; and what of the rest? And how
are the other weak ones to blame, because they could not endure what the strong have
endured? How is the weak soul to blame that it is unable to receive such terrible gifts?
Canst Thou have simply come to the elect and for the elect? But if so, it is a mystery
and we cannot understand it. And if it is a mystery, we too have a right to preach a
mystery, and to teach them that it's not the free judgment of their hearts, not love that
matters, but a mystery which they must follow blindly, even against their conscience.
So we have done. We have corrected Thy work and have founded it upon *miracle,
mystery and authority.* And men rejoiced that they were again led like sheep, and that
the terrible gift that had brought them such suffering, was, at last, lifted from their
hearts. Were we right teaching them this? Speak! Did we not love mankind, so
meekly acknowledging their feebleness, lovingly lightening their burden, and permitting their weak nature even sin with our sanction? Why hast Thou come now to
hinder us? And why dost Thou look silently and searchingly at me with Thy mild
eyes? Be angry. I don't want Thy love, for I love Thee not. And what use is it for me
to hide anything from Thee? Don't I know to Whom I am speaking? All that I can say
is known to Thee already. And is it for me to conceal from Thee our mystery? Perhaps it is Thy will to hear it from my lips. Listen, then. We are not working with Thee,
but with *him*—that is our mystery. It's long—eight centuries—since we have been on
his side and not on Thine. Just eight centuries ago, we took from him what Thou didst
reject with scorn, that last gift he offered Thee, showing Thee all the kingdoms of the
earth. We took from him Rome and the sword of Caesar, and proclaimed ourselves
sole rulers of the earth, though hitherto we have not been able to complete our work.
But whose fault it that? Oh, the work is only beginning, but it has begun. It has long
to await completion and the earth has yet much to suffer, but we shall triumph and
shall be Caesars, and then we shall plan the universal happiness of man. But Thou
mightest have taken even then the sword of Caesar, Why didst thou reject that last
gift? Hadst Thou accepted that last counsel of the mighty spirit, Thou wouldst have
accomplished all that man seeks on earth—that is, someone to worship, someone to
keep his conscience, and some means of uniting all in one unanimous and harmonious ant-heap, for the craving for universal unity is the third and last anguish of men.
Mankind as a whole has always striven to organize a universal state. There have been
many great nations with great histories, but the more highly they were developed the

more unhappy they were, for they felt more acutely than other people the craving for worldwide union. The great conquerors, Timours and Ghenghis-Khans, whirled like hurricanes over the face of the earth striving to subdue its people, and they too were but the unconscious expression of the same craving for universal unity. Hadst Thou taken the world and Caesar's purple, Thou wouldst have founded the universal state and have given universal peace. For who can rule men if not he who holds their conscience and their bread in his hands? We have taken the sword of Caesar, and in taking it, of course, have rejected Thee and followed *him*. Oh, ages are yet to come of the confusion of free thought, of their science and cannibalism. For having begun to build their tower of Babel without us, they will end, of course, with cannibalism. But then the beast will crawl to us and lick our feet and spatter them with tears of blood. And we shall sit upon the beast and raise the cup, and on it will be written, "Mystery." But then, and only then, the reign of peace and happiness will come for men. Thou art proud of Thine elect, but Thou hast only the elect, while we give rest to all. And besides, how many of those elect, those mighty ones who could become elect, have grown weary waiting for Thee, and have transferred and will transfer the powers of their spirit and the warmth of their heart to the other camp, and end by raising their *free* banner against Thee. Thou didst Thyself lift up that banner. But with us all will be happy and will no more rebel nor destroy one another as under Thy freedom. Oh, we shall persuade them that they will only become free when they renounce their freedom to us and submit to us. And shall we be right or shall we be lying? They will be convinced that we are right, for they will remember the horrors of slavery and confusion to which Thy freedom brought them. Freedom, free thought and science, will lead them into such straits and will bring them face to face with such marvels and insoluble mysteries, and some of them, the fierce and rebellious, will destroy themselves, others, rebellious but weak, will destroy one another, while the rest, weak and unhappy, will crawl fawning to our feet and whine to us: "Yes, you were right, you alone possess His mystery, and we come back to you, save us from ourselves!"

" 'Receiving bread from us, they will see clearly that we take the bread made by their hands from them, to give it to them, without any miracle. They will see that we do not change the stones to bread, but in truth they will be more thankful for taking it from our hands than for the bread itself! For they will remember only too well that in old days, without our help, even the bread they made turned to stones in their hands, while since they have come back to us, the very stones have turned to bread in their hands. Too, too well they know the value of complete submission! And until men know that, they will be unhappy. Who is most to blame for their not knowing it, speak? Who scattered the flock and sent it astray on unknown paths? But the flock will come together again and will submit once more, and then it will be once for all. Then we shall give them the quiet humble happiness of weak creatures such as they are by nature. Oh, we shall persuade them at last not to be proud, for Thou didst lift them up and thereby taught them to be proud. We shall show them that they are weak, that they are only pitiful children, but that childlike happiness is the sweetest of all. They will become timid and will look to us and huddle close to us in fear, as chicks to the hen. They will marvel at us and will be awestricken before us, and will be proud at our being so powerful and clever, that we have been able to subdue such a turbulent flock of thousands of millions. They will tremble impotently before our wrath, their minds will grow fearful, they will be quick to shed tears like women and children, but they will be just as ready at a sign from us to pass to laughter and rejoicing, to happy mirth and childish song. Yes, we shall set them to work, but in their leisure hours we shall make their life like a child's game, with children's songs and innocent dance. Oh, we shall allow them even sin, they are weak and helpless, and they will love us like children because we allow them to sin. We shall tell them that every sin will be expiated, if it is done with our permission, that we allow them to sin because we love them, and the punishment for these sins we take upon ourselves. And we shall take it upon ourselves, and they will adore us as their saviours, who have taken on themselves their sins before God. And they will have no secrets from us. We shall allow or forbid them to live with their wives and mistresses, to have or not to have children—according to whether they have been obedient or disobedient—and they will submit to us gladly and cheerfully. The most painful secrets of their conscience, all, all they will bring to us, and we shall have an answer for all. And they will be glad to believe our answer, for it will save them from the great anxiety and terrible agony they endure at present in making a free decision for themselves. And all will be happy, all the millions of creatures except the hundred thousand who rule over them. For only we, we who guard the mystery, shall be unhappy. There will be thousands of millions of happy babes, and a hundred thousand sufferers who have taken upon themselves the curse of the knowledge of good and evil. Peacefully they will die, peacefully they will expire in Thy name, and beyond the grave they will find nothing but death. But we shall keep the secret, and for our happiness we shall allure them with the reward of heaven and eternity. Though if there were anything in the other world, it certainly would not be for such as they. It is prophesied that Thou wilt come again in victory, Thou wilt come with Thy chosen, the proud and strong, but we will say that they have only saved themselves, but we have saved all. We are told that the harlot who sits upon the beast, and holds in her hands the *mystery* shall be put to shame, that the weak will rise up again, and will rend her royal purple and will strip naked her loathsome body. But then I will stand up and point out to Thee the thousand millions of happy children who have known no sin. And we who have taken their sins upon us for their happiness will stand up before Thee and say: "Judge us if Thou canst and darest." Know that I fear Thee not, Know that I too have been in the wilderness, I too have lived on roots and locusts, I too prized the freedom with which Thou has blessed men, and I too was striving to stand among Thy elect, among the strong and powerful, thirsting "to make up the number." But I awakened and would not serve madness. I turned back and joined the ranks of those *who have corrected Thy work.* I left the proud and went back to the humble, for the happiness of the humble. What I say to Thee will come to pass, and our dominion will be built up. I repeat, tomorrow Thou shalt see that obedient flock who at a sign from me will hasten to heap up the hot cinders about the pile on which I shall burn Thee for coming to hinder us. For if any one has ever deserved our fires, it is Thou. Tomorrow I shall burn Thee. . . .'

  ". . . When the Inquisitor ceased speaking, he waited some time for his prisoner to answer him. His silence weighed down upon him. He saw that the prisoner had listened intently all the time, looking gently in his face and evidently not wishing to reply. The old man longed for Him to say something, however bitter and terrible. But he suddenly approached the old man in silence and softly kissed him on his bloodless aged lips. That was all his answer. The old man shuddered. His lips moved. He went to the door, opened it, and said to Him: 'Go, and come no more . . . come not at all, never, never!' And he let Him out into the dark alleys of the town. The prisoner went away."

"And the old man?"

"The kiss glows in his heart, but the old man adheres to his idea."

"And you with him, you too?" cried Alyosha, mournfully.

Ivan laughed.

"Why, it's all nonsense, Alyosha. It's only a senseless poem of a senseless student, who could never write two lines of verse. Why do you take it so seriously? . . . "

To Think About

1. *Einstein* once remarked that with the arrival of the atomic age everything had changed, except our thinking. Our Western dreams of domination, mastery, and certainty are over.

2. "No matter how much debate occurs the truth is not necessarily reached."
   James Gould

3. Letter from Monticello: "God forbid, we should ever be twenty years without such a rebellion." Elsewhere he elaborated: "What country can preserve its liberties, if its rulers are not warned from time to time, that this people preserve the spirit of resistance? Let them take arms. . . . The tree of liberty must be refreshed from time to time, with the blood of patriots and tyrants."
   Thomas Jefferson

4. "Let [the child] believe that he is always in control, though it is always you [the teacher] who really controls. There is no subjugation so perfect as that which keeps the appearance of freedom, for in that way one captures volition itself."
   Jean-Jacques Rousseau

5. "Our ignorance of history causes us to slander our own times."
   Gustave Flaubert

6. "Those who ignore history are doomed to repeat it."   **George Santayana**

7. "Success makes men rigid and they tend to exalt stability over all the other virtues; tired of the effort of willing they become fanatics about conservatism."
   Walter Lippmann

Readings

BERDYAEV, NICOLAS. *Dostoevsky.* New York: Meridian Books, 1957.

EAGLETON, TERRY. *Sweet Violence: The Idea of the Tragic.* Oxford: Blackwell, 2003.

KROEKER, P. TRAVIS, AND BRUCE K. WARD. *Remembering the End: Dostoevsky as Prophet to Modernity.* Boulder, CO: Westview Press, 2001.

SCANLAN, JAMES P. *Dostoevsky the Thinker.* Ithaca, NY: Cornell University Press, 2002.

45
Freedom Is Independence
from the Majority's Tyranny

John Stuart Mill (1806–73) *was an eminent English philosopher, political thinker, and administrator. He never attended school, but received a remarkable and intensive private education from his distinguished father, James Mill. By age fourteen he had read most of the major Greek and Latin classics, as well as much history, logic, and mathematics. He became a spokesman and defender of the basic principles of nineteenth-century liberalism and utilitarianism. His writing in these fields, as well as in the field of logic, brought him great distinction in the English-speaking world.*

John Stuart Mill published his famous essay *On Liberty* in 1859. His argument for freedom for all individual thought and discussion, no matter how completely false or true the opinions, is especially relevant today when authoritarian elements abroad and in our own midst threaten to stifle hopes of realizing a democratic civilization for mankind.

In arguing against the repression of any opinion, Mill sets forth the following argument: If an opinion is suppressed, and it is true, then we lose the opportunity of exchanging truth for falsehood. If an opinion is suppressed, and it is false, then we lose the opportunity of obtaining a clearer conception of our own position. Hence, there shouldn't be any censorship of political speech.

Mill's essay, however, also raises another important problem for our own age, the problem of the tyranny of the majority. This is the tyrannical tendency of society to impose its own ideas and practices as rules of conduct on those who dissent from them. The student should consider whether the tyranny of the majority is an inseparable evil of democracy.

From John Stuart Mill, *On Liberty* (London: Henry Halb, 1859).

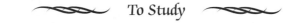

To Study

1. What is the subject of Mill's essay?
2. Describe the two ways the patriots set limits on the ruler's power.
3. Explain "the tyranny of the majority" and its dangers.
4. According to Mill, what is the relationship between intolerance and religion?
5. What is the simple principle asserted in this essay? Explain it as fully as possible.
6. Discuss Mill's position regarding the rights of speech.

The subject of this Essay is not the so-called Liberty of the Will, so unfortunately opposed to the misnamed doctrine of Philosophical Necessity; but Civil, or Social Liberty: the nature and limits of the power which can be legitimately exercised by society over the individual. A question seldom stated, and hardly ever discussed, in general terms, but which profoundly influences the practical controversies of the age by its latent presence, and is likely soon to make itself recognized as the vital question of the future. It is so far from being new, that, in a certain sense, it has divided mankind, almost from the remotest ages, but in the stage of progress into which the more civilized portions of the species have now entered, it presents itself under new conditions, and requires a different and more fundamental treatment.

The struggle between Liberty and Authority is the most conspicuous feature in the portions of history with which we are earliest familiar, particularly in that of Greece, Rome, and England. But in old times this contest was between subjects, or some classes of subjects, and the government. By liberty was meant protection against the tyranny of the political rulers. The rulers were conceived (except in some of the popular governments of Greece) as in a necessarily antagonistic position to the people whom they ruled. They consisted of a governing One, or a governing tribe or caste, who derived their authority from inheritance or conquest; who, at all events, did not hold it at the pleasure of the governed, and whose supremacy men did not venture, perhaps did not desire, to contest, whatever precautions might be taken against its oppressive exercise. Their power was regarded as necessary, but also as highly dangerous; as a weapon which they would attempt to use against their subjects, no less than against external enemies. To prevent the weaker members of the community from being preyed upon by innumerable vultures, it was needful that there should be an animal of prey stronger than the rest, commissioned to keep them down. But as the king of the vultures would be no less bent upon preying on the flock than any of the minor harpies, it was indispensable to be in a perpetual attitude of defense against his beak and claws. The aim, therefore, of patriots, was to set limits to the power which the ruler should be suffered to exercise over the community; and this limitation was what they meant by liberty. It was attempted in two ways. First, by obtaining a recognition of certain immunities, called political liberties or rights, which it was to be regarded as a breach of duty in the ruler to infringe, and which, if he did infringe, specific resistance, or general rebellion, was held to be justifiable. A second, and generally a later expedient, was the establishment of constitutional checks by which the consent of the community, or of a body of some sort supposed to represent its interests, was made a necessary condition to some of the more important acts of the governing power. To the first of these modes of limitation, the ruling power, in most European countries, was compelled, more or less, to submit. It was not so with the second; and to attain this, or when already in some degree possessed, to attain it more completely, became everywhere the principal object of the lovers of liberty. And so long as mankind were content to combat one enemy by another, and to be ruled by a master, on condition of being guaranteed more or less efficaciously against his tyranny, they did not carry their aspirations beyond this point.

A time, however, came in the progress of human affairs when men ceased to think it a necessity of nature that their governors should be an independent power, opposed in interest to themselves. It appeared to them much better that the various magistrates of the State should be their tenants or delegates, revocable at their pleasure. In that way alone, it seemed, could they have complete security that the powers of government would never be abused to their disadvantage. By degrees, this new demand for elective and temporary rulers became the prominent object of the exertions of the popular party, wherever any such party existed; and superseded, to a considerable extent, the previous efforts to limit the power of rulers. As the struggle proceeded for making the ruling power emanate from the periodical choice of the ruled, some persons began to think that too much importance had been attached to the limitation of the power itself. *That* (it might seem) was a resource against rulers whose interests were habitually opposed to those of the people. What was now wanted was that the rulers should be identified with the people; that their interest and will should be the interest and will of the nation. The nation did not need to be protected against its own will. There was no fear of its tyrannizing over itself. Let the rulers be effactually responsible to it, promptly removable by it, and could afford to trust them with power of which it could itself dictate the use to be made. Their power was but the nation's own power, concentrated, and in a form convenient for exercise. This mode of thought, or rather perhaps of feeling, was common among the last generation of European liberalism, in the Continental section of which, it still apparently predominates. Those who admit any limit to what a government may do, except in the case of such governments as they think ought not to exist, stand out as brilliant exceptions among the political thinkers of the Continent. A similar tone of sentiment might by this time have been prevalent in our own country, if the circumstances which for a time encouraged it had continued unaltered.

But, in political and philosophical theories, as well as in persons, success discloses faults and infirmities which failure might have concealed from observation. The notion that the people have no need to limit their power over themselves might seem axiomatic when popular government was a thing only dreamed about or read of as having existed at some distant period of the past. Neither was that notion necessarily disturbed by such temporary aberrations as those of the French Revolution, the worst of which were the work of an usurping few, and which, in any case, belonged, not to the permanent working of popular institutions, but to a sudden and convulsive outbreak against monarchical and aristocratic despotism. In time, however, a democratic republic came to occupy a large portion of the earth's surface, and made itself felt as one of the most powerful members of the community of nations; and elective and responsible government became subject to the observations and criticisms which wait upon a great existing fact. It was now perceived that such phrases as "self-government," and "the power of the people over themselves," do not express the true state of the case. The "people" who exercise the power, are not always the same people with those over whom it is exercised, and the "self-government" spoken of is not the government of each by himself, but of each by all the rest. The will of the people, moreover, practically means, the will of the most numerous or the most active *part* of the people; the majority, or those who succeed in making themselves accepted as the majority: the people, consequently, *may* desire to oppress a part of their number; and precautions are as much needed against this, as against any other abuse of power. The limitation, therefore, of the power of government over individuals loses none of its importance when the holders of power are regularly accountable to the community, that is, to the strongest party therein. This view of things, recommending itself equally to the intelligence of thinkers and to the inclination of those important classes in European society to whose real or supposed interests democracy is adverse, has had no difficulty in establishing itself; and in political speculations "the tyranny of the majority" is now generally included among the evils against which society requires to be on its guard.

Like other tyrannies, the tyranny of the majority was at first, and is still, vulgarly held in dread, chiefly as operating through the acts of the public authorities. But reflecting persons perceived that when society is itself the tyrant—society collectively, over the separate individuals who compose it—its means of tyrannizing are not restricted to the acts which it may do by the hands of its political functionaries. Society can and does execute its own mandates: and if it issues wrong mandates instead of right, or any mandates at all in things with which it ought not to meddle, it practices a social tyranny more formidable than many kinds of political oppression, since, though not usually upheld by such extreme penalties, it leaves fewer means of escape, penetrating much more deeply into the details of life, and enslaving the soul itself. Protection, therefore, against the tyranny of the magistrate is not enough; there needs protection also against the tyranny of the prevailing opinion and feeling; against the tendency of society to impose, by other means than civil penalties, its own ideas and practices as rules of conduct on those who dissent from them; to fetter the development, and, if possible, prevent the formation of any individuality not in harmony with its ways, and compel all characters to fashion themselves upon the model of its own. There is a limit to the legitimate interference of collective opinion with individual independence; and to find that limit, and maintain it against encroachment, is as indispensable to a good condition of human affairs, as protection against political despotism.

But though this proposition is not likely to be contested in general terms, the practical question, where to place the limit—how to make the fitting adjustment between individual independence and social control—is a subject on which nearly everything remains to be done. All that makes existence valuable to anyone depends on the enforcements of restraints upon the actions of other people. Some rules of conduct, therefore, must be imposed by law in the first place, and by opinion on many things which are not fit subjects for the operation of law. What these rules should be is the principal question in human affairs; but if we except a few of the most obvious cases, it is one of those which least progress has been made in resolving. No two ages, and scarcely any two countries, have decided it alike; and the decision of one age or country is a wonder to another. Yet the people of any given age and country no more suspect any difficulty in it than if it were a subject on which mankind had always been agreed. The rules which obtain among themselves appear to them self-evident and self-justifying. This all but universal illusion is one of the examples of the magical influence of custom, which is not only, as the proverb says, a second nature, but is continually mistaken for the first. The effect of custom, in preventing any misgiving respecting the rules of conduct which mankind impose on one another, is all the more complete because the subject is one on which it is not generally considered necessary that reasons should be given, either by one person to others, or by each to himself. People are accustomed to believe, and have been encouraged in the belief by some who aspire to the character of philosophers, that their feelings on subjects of this nature are better than reasons, and render reasons unnecessary. The practical principal which guides them to their opinions on the regulation of human conduct is the feeling in each person's mind that everybody should be required to act as he, and those with whom he sympathizes would like them to act. No one, indeed, acknowledges to himself that his standard of judgment is his own liking; but an opinion on a point of conduct, not supported by reasons, can only count as one person's preference; and if the reasons, when given, are a mere appeal to a similar preference felt by other people, it is still only many people's liking instead of one. To an ordinary man, however, his own preference, thus supported, is not only a perfectly satisfactory reason, but the only one he generally has for any of his notions of morality, taste, or propriety, which are not expressly written in his religious creed; and his chief guide in the interpretation even of that. Men's opinions, accordingly, on what is laudable or blameable, are affected by all the multifarious causes which influence their wishes in regard to the conduct of others, and which are as numerous as those which determine their wishes on any other subject. Sometimes their reason—at other times their prejudices or superstitions: often their social affections, not seldom their antisocial ones, their envy or jealousy, their arrogance or contemptuousness: but most commonly, their desires or fears for themselves—their legitimate or illegitimate self-interest. Wherever there is an ascendant class, a large portion of the morality of the country emanates from its class interests, and its feelings of class superiority. The morality between Spartans and Helots, between planters and negroes, between princes and subjects, between nobles and roturiers, between men and women, has been for the most part the creation of these class interests and feelings: and the sentiments thus generated react in turn upon the moral feelings of the members of the ascendant class in their relations among themselves. Where, on the other hand, a class, formerly ascendant, has lost its ascendency, or where its ascendency is unpopular, the prevailing moral sentiments frequently bear the impress of an impatient dislike of superiority. Another grand determining principle of the rules of conduct, both in act and forbearance which have been enforced by law or opinion, has been the servility of mankind towards the supposed preferences or aversions of their temporal masters, or of their gods. This servility, though essentially selfish, is not hypocrisy; it gives rise to perfectly genuine sentiments of abhorence; it made men burn magicians and heretics. Among so many baser influences, the general and obvious interests of society have of course had a share, and a large one, in the direction of the moral sentiments: less, however, as a matter of reason, and on their own account, than as a consequence of the sympathies and antipathies which grew out of them: and sympathies and antipathies which had little or nothing to do with the interests of society, have made themselves felt in the establishment of moralities with quite as great force.

The likings and dislikings of society or of some powerful portion of it, are thus the main thing which has practically determined the rules laid down for general observance under the penalties of law or opinion. And in general, those who have been in advance of society in thought and feeling, have left this condition of things unassailed in principle, however they may have come into conflict with it in some of its details. They have occupied themselves rather in inquiring what things society ought to like or dislike, than in questioning whether its likings or dislikings should be a law to individuals. They preferred endeavoring to alter the feelings of mankind on the particular points on which they were themselves heretical, rather than make common cause in defence of freedom, with heretics generally. The only case in which the higher ground has been taken on principle and maintained with consistency, by any but an individual here and there, is that of religious belief: a case instructive in many ways, and not least so as forming a most striking instance of the fallibility of what is called the moral sense: for the [hatred of rival theologians] in a sincere bigot is one of the most unequivocal cases of moral feeling. Those who first broke the yoke of what called itself the Universal Church, were in general as little willing to permit difference of religious opinion as that church itself. But when the heat of the conflict was over, without giving a complete victory to any party, and each church or sect was reduced to limit its hopes to retaining possession of the ground it already occupied; minorities, seeing that they had no chance of becoming majorities, were under the necessity of pleading to those whom they could not convert, for permission to differ. It is accordingly on this battle-field almost solely that the rights of the individual against society have been asserted on broad grounds of principle, and the claim of society to exercise authority over dissentients openly controverted. The great writers to whom the world owes what religious liberty it possesses have mostly asserted freedom of conscience as an indefeasible right, and denied absolutely that a human being is accountable to others for his religious belief. Yet, so natural to mankind is intolerance in whatever they really care about, that religious freedom has hardly anywhere been practically realized, except where religious indifference, which dislikes to have its peace disturbed by theological quarrels, has added its weight to the scale. In the minds of almost all religious persons, even in the most tolerant countries, the duty of toleration is admitted with tacit reserves. One person will bear with dissent in matters of church government, but not a dogma; another can tolerate everybody, short of a Papist or an Unitarian; another, everyone who believes in revealed religion; a few extend their charity a little further, but stop at the belief in a God and in a future state. Wherever the sentiment of the majority is still genuine and intense, it is found to have abated little of its claim to be obeyed.

In England, from the peculiar circumstances of our political history, though the yoke of opinion is perhaps heavier, that of law is lighter than in most other countries of Europe; and there is considerable jealousy of direct interference, by the legislative or the executive power with private conduct; not so much from any just regard for the independence of the individual, as from the still subsisting habit of looking on the government as representing an opposite interest to the public. The majority have not yet learnt to feel the power of the government their power, or its opinions their opinions. When they do so, individual liberty will probably be as much exposed to invasion from the government, as it already is from public opinion. But, as yet, there is a considerable amount of feeling ready to be called forth against any attempt of the law to control individuals in things in which they have not hitherto been accustomed to be controlled by it; and this with very little discrimination as to whether the matter is, or is not, within the legitimate sphere of legal control; insomuch that the feeling, highly salutary on the whole, is perhaps quite as often misplaced as well grounded in the particular instances of its application. There is, in fact, no recognized principle by which the propriety or impropriety of government interference is customarily tested. People decide according to their personal preferences. Some, whenever they see any good to be done, or evil to be remedied, would willingly instigate the government to undertake the business; while others prefer to bear almost any amount of social evil, rather than add one to the departments of human interests amenable to government control. And men range themselves on one or the other side in any particular case, according to this general direction of their sentiments; or according to the degree of interest which they feel in the particular thing which it is proposed that the government should do; or according to the belief they entertain that the government would, or would not, do it in the manner they prefer; but very rarely on account of any opinion to which they consistently adhere, as to what things are fit to be done by a government. And it seems to me that, in consequence of this absence of rule or principle, one side is at present as often wrong as the other; the interference of government is, with about equal frequency, improperly invoked and improperly condemned.

The object of this Essay is to assert one very simple principle as entitled to govern absolutely the dealings of society with the individual in the way of compulsion and control, whether the means used by physical force in the form of legal penalties, or the moral coercion of public opinion. That principle is, that the sole end for which mankind are warranted, individually or collectively, in interfering with the liberty of action of any of their number, is self-protection. That the only purpose for which power can be rightfully exercised over any member of a civilized community against his will is to prevent harm to others. His own good, either physical or moral, is not a sufficient warrant. He cannot rightfully be compelled to do or forbear because it will be better for him to do so, because it will make him happier, because, in the opinions of others, to do so would be wise, or even right. There are good reasons for remonstrating with him, or reasoning with him, or persuading him, or entreating him, but not for compelling him, or visiting him with any evil, in case he do otherwise. To justify that, the conduct from which it is desired to deter him must be calculated to produce evil to some one else. The only part of the conduct of anyone for which he is amenable to society is that which concerns others. In the part which merely concerns himself, his independence is, of right, absolute. Over himself, over his own body and mind, the individual is sovereign. . . .

It is proper to state that I forego any advantage which could be derived to my argument from the idea of abstract right, as a thing independent of utility. I regard utility as the ultimate appeal on all ethical questions; but it must be utility in the largest sense, grounded on the permanent interests of man as a progressive being. Those interests, I contend, authorize the subjection of individual spontaneity to external control, only in respect to those actions of each, which concern the interest of other people. If anyone does an act hurtful to others, there is a . . . case for punishing him, by law, or, where legal penalties are not safely applicable, by general disapprobation. There are also many positive acts for the benefit of others, which he may rightfully be compelled to perform; such as, to give evidence in a court of justice; to bear his fair share in the common defense, or in any other joint work necessary to the interest of the society of which he enjoys the protection; and to perform certain acts of individual beneficence, such as saving a fellow creature's life, or interposing to protect the defenseless against ill-usage, things which whenever it is obviously a man's duty to do, he may rightfully be made responsible to society for not doing. A person may cause evil to others not only by his actions but by his inaction, and in either case he is justly accountable to them for the injury. The latter case, it is true, requires a much more cautious exercise of compulsion than the former. To make anyone answerable for doing evil to others is the rule; to make him answerable for not preventing evil, is, comparatively speaking, the exception. Yet there are many cases clear enough and grave enough to justify that exception. In all things which regard the external relations of the individual, he is *de jure* amenable to those whose interests are concerned, and if need be, to society as their protector. There are often good reasons for not holding him to the responsibility; but these reasons must arise from the special expediencies of the case: either because it is a kind of case in which he is on the whole likely to act better when left to his own discretion than when controlled in any way in which society have it in their power to control him; or because the attempt to exercise control would produce other evils, greater than those which it would prevent. When such reasons as these preclude the enforcement of responsibility, the conscience of the agent himself should step into the vacant judgment-seat, and protect those interests of others which have no external protection; judging himself all the more rigidly because the case does not admit of his being made accountable to the judgment of his fellow creatures.

But there is a sphere of action in which society, as distinguished from the individual, has, if any, only an indirect interest; comprehending all that portion of a person's life and conduct which affects only himself, or, if it also affects others, only with their free, voluntary, and undeceived consent and participation. When I say only himself, I mean directly, and in the first instance: for whatever affects himself, may affect others *through* himself; and the objection which may be grounded on this contingency will receive consideration in the sequel. This, then, is the appropriate region of human liberty. It comprises, first, the inward domain of consciousness; demanding liberty of conscience, in the most comprehensive sense; liberty of thought and feeling; absolute freedom of opinion and sentiment on all subjects, practical or speculative, scientific, moral, or theological. The liberty of expressing and publishing opinions may seem to fall under a different principle, since it belongs to that part of the conduct of an individual which concerns other people; but, being almost of as much importance as the liberty of thought itself, and resting in great part on the same reasons is practically inseparable from it. Secondly, the principle requires liberty of tastes and pursuits; of framing the plan of our life to suit our own character; of doing as we like, subject to such consequences as may follow; without impediment from our fellow-creatures, so long as what we do does not harm them, even though they should think our conduct foolish, perverse, or wrong. Thirdly, from this liberty of each individual follows the liberty, within the same limits, of combination among individuals; freedom to unite, for any purpose not involving harm to others: the persons combining being supposed to be of full age, and not forced or deceived.

No society in which these liberties are not . . . respected is free whatever may be its form of government; and none is completely free in which they do not exist absolute and unqualified. The only freedom which deserves the name is that of pursuing our own good in our own way, so long as we do not attempt to deprive others of theirs, or impede their efforts to obtain it. Each is the proper guardian of his own health, whether bodily, or mental and spiritual. Mankind are greater gainers by suffering each other to live as seems good to themselves, than by compelling each to live as seems good to the rest.

Apart from the peculiar tenets of individual thinkers, there is also in the world at large an increasing inclination to stretch unduly the powers of society over the individual, both by the force of opinion and even by that of legislation: and as the tendency of all the changes taking place in the world is to strengthen society, and diminish the power of the individual, this encroachment is not one of the evils which tend spontaneously to disappear, but, on the contrary, to grow more and more formidable. The disposition of mankind, whether as rulers or as fellow-citizens, to impose their own opinions and inclinations as a rule of conduct on others, is so energetically supported by some of the best and by some of the worst feelings incident to human nature, that it is hardly ever kept under restraint by anything but want of power; and as the power is not declining, but growing, unless a strong barrier of moral conviction can be raised against the mischief, we must expect, in the present circumstances of the world, to see it increase.

We have now recognized the necessity to the mental well-being of mankind (on which all their other well-being depends) of freedom of opinion, and freedom of the expression of opinion, on four distinct grounds; which we will now briefly recapitulate.

First, if any opinion is compelled to silence, that opinion may, for aught we can certainly know, be true. To deny this is to assume our own infallibility.

Secondly, though the silenced opinion be an error, it may, and very commonly does, contain a portion of truth; and since the general or prevailing opinion on any subject is rarely or never the whole truth, it is only by the collision of adverse opinions that the remainder of the truth has any chance of being supplied.

Thirdly, even if the received opinion be not only true, but the whole truth; unless it is suffered to be, and actually is, vigorously and earnestly contested, it will, by most of those who receive it, be held in the manner of a prejudice, with little comprehension or feeling of its rational grounds. And not only this, but, fourthly, the meaning of the doctrine itself will be in danger of being lost, or enfeebled, and deprived of its vital effect on the character and conduct: the dogma becoming a mere formal profession, inefficacious for good, but cumbering the ground, and preventing the growth of any real and heartfelt conviction, from reason or personal experience.

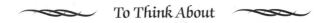

To Think About

1. "Democratic societies need free speech; only with it can citizens discover the truth, participate in their society's decisions, and better realize their endeavors. With free speech all people have the opportunity to understand and evaluate the issues they face. Free expression, in all its diversity, is guaranteed in the First Amendment of the Constitution, which states 'Congress shall make no law . . . abridging the freedom of speech.'

   "John Stuart Mill believes that opinions should never be suppressed. He grounds this belief in his famous dilemma:

   1. If you suppress an opinion and it is true, then you lose the chance of exchanging truth for falsity.

   2. If you suppress an opinion and it is false, then you lose the opportunity of obtaining a clearer view of your own position.

   "Because all opinions are either true or false, we can lose the opportunity to gain truth or to clarify our own ideas by suppressing anyone's speech. Hence, Mill concludes that *no* political speech should be suppressed. Few other writers, if any, agree with him.

   ". . . Some critics argue that certain forms of speech (slander, fraudulent advertising, and obscenity) should be illegal. They also point out that free expression must occasionally be subordinated to other values such as happiness, justice, and privacy. Mill himself notes a case in which a crowd might be incited to riot against a corn dealer they think is unjust. This example is a valid argument *against* absolute free speech because the dealer may be innocent, because he deserves a fair trial, and because the ensuing violence could hurt someone in the crowd. Even liberals would argue that, in such cases, speech should be suppressed when it creates a 'clear and present danger,' which means that the danger must be definitely probable, imminent, and of significant harm. Such famous jurists as Holmes, Brandeis, and Douglas have argued that any revolutionist who attempts to incite a large group to revolutionary action should be arrested. Some writers, such as Felix Frankfurter, argue against political free speech as an absolute:

The demands of free speech in a democratic society as well as the interest in national security are better served by candid and informed weighing of the competing interests, within the confines of the judicial process, than by announcing dogmas too inflexible for the . . . problems to be solved. (*Dennis* v. *U.S.* 341 U.S. 524)

"Cases involving crowd justice or incitement to revolt would seem to shatter Mill's belief that political free speech is an absolute. Furthermore, cases of libel, false advertising, and obscenity would seem to make the limiting of political free speech a necessity. But is this so? The answer depends on one's concept of political speech. It is clear that falsely shouting 'Fire!' in a crowded theatre isn't a political matter. The First Amendment wasn't meant to protect such irresponsible utterances. Rather it was meant to protect citizens' freedom to discuss and think about their government.

"Who then has the correct position regarding free speech? Do we accept the 'clear and present danger' theory, the 'weighing of competing interest' view, or Mill's contention that political free speech must be an absolute?"

James Gould

2. "More and more, courtwatchers are observing the growth of so called 'speech plus' or quasi speech.

"These arguments are surfacing everywhere. For example, they surface in Catharine MacKinnon's antipornography arguments at those points when she argues that pornography is not only speech but action against women. She asks:

> which is saying 'kill' to a trained guard dog, a word or an act? Which is its training? How about a sign that reads 'whites only'? Is that the idea or practice of segregation? Is a woman raped by an attitude or a behavior? . . . under conditions of male dominance, pornography hides and distorts truth while at the same time enforcing itself, imprinting itself on the world, making itself real. That's another way in which pornography is a kind of act."

Thomas Emerson

3. "There is, of course, a sphere within which the individual may assert the supremacy of his own will and rightfully dispute the authority of any human government—especially of any free government existing under a written constitution, to interfere with the exercise of that will."   *Louis Brandeis*

4. "Natural rights is simple nonsense: natural and imprescriptible rights, rhetorical nonsense,—nonsense upon stilts. . . . Right is a child of law; from real laws come real rights, but from imaginary law, from 'laws of nature,' come imaginary rights. . . . A natural right is a son that never had a father. . . ."   *Jeremy Bentham*

5. "The greatest danger to liberty lurks in the insidious encroachment by men of zeal, well-meaning but without understanding."   *Louis Brandeis*

6. "The right to be heard does not include the right to be taken seriously."

Hubert Humphrey

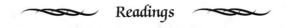 **Readings**

ADLER, MORTIMER I. *The Idea of Freedom.* 2 vols. Garden City, NY: Doubleday, 1958–61. Summarizes the results of research done by the staff of the Institute for Philosophical Research. Volume 1 examines conceptions of freedom. Volume 2 examines controversies about freedom.

CHAFEE, Z. *Free Speech in the United States.* Cambridge, MA: Harvard University Press, 1940. An excellent book on free speech and its history.

What Is Freedom?

46
Freedom and Racial Prejudice

Martin Luther King Jr. (1929–1969), the most outstanding champion of civil rights in America during the mid-twentieth century, was born in Atlanta, Georgia. He studied at Morehouse College and Boston University, where he received his Ph.D. in 1955. He served as a Baptist minister in Alabama, where he gained national recognition by leading a boycott against segregated buses in Montgomery in 1955–56. He founded the Southern Christian Leadership Conference and organized the famous march in Washington in 1963. Awarded the Nobel Peace Prize the following year, he extended his range of concerns to include international peace and the plight of the poor. In 1969, during a trip to Memphis, Tennessee, in support of striking sanitation workers, he was assassinated. Among his best-known writings and addresses are his "Letter from Birmingham Jail" (1963), his "I Have a Dream" speech (August 28, 1963), and his collection of writings Where Do We Go from Here? *(1967). His birthday, celebrated in January, is a national holiday.*

One of the greatest challenges to the value of human freedom in today's society lies in the majority's treatment of minority populations, whether these be ethnic, racial, religious, or gender minorities. In the United States particularly, racial oppression has been a feature of its public and private life since the earliest days of the country's existence, a tragic irony in a nation founded on the proposition that "all men are created equal." Even a century after the elimination of slavery, America continued to permit racial segregation in much of its institutional life, including schools, the work world, housing, legal service, and medical care, to name but a few. Among the twentieth century's most effective champions of minority rights was Martin Luther King Jr., whose powerful leadership, eloquent preaching, and campaigns of civil disobedience galvanized black and white citizens of the United States in opposition to the evils of racism. In the following address, King considers some of the philosophical themes

From "Love, Law and Civil Disobedience," published in *New South* (December, 1961). Reprinted by arrangement with the Estate of Martin Luther King, Jr., c/o Writer's House as agent for the proprietor. Copyright Martin Luther King 1963, copyright renewed 1991 Coretta Scott King.

undergirding his activism. Civil disobedience, the core strategic response to oppression, is for King founded upon a set of moral and philosophical positions, including a commitment to nonviolence, an ethic of love, and what can be called the philosophy of personalism, whereby individual human beings occupy the center of philosophical concerns. Where the law "uplifts human personality," it is just. Where it "degrades the human personality," it is unjust. But nonviolent opposition to unjust law is not to be confused with anarchy. King insists upon the highest respect for law itself and a willingness to accept the consequences of punishment for breaking the law. Basic human inclinations to goodness and perfection require a response of respect, noninjury, and even willingness to endure suffering in the challenge to unjust social practices and law. Subtle moral and even metaphysical principles underlie this ethics, including a theory of the continuity of means and ends and a critique of what King calls the "myth of time."

To Study

1. In what three ways does King say oppressed people have generally dealt with their oppression?
2. What method of protest has been employed most commonly in dealing with oppression in the United States?
3. What does King mean when he says that ends and means must "cohere" in nonviolent resistance?
4. What is meant by the *principle of noninjury*?
5. King distinguishes three types of love. What are they, and which one is relevant to the student movement?
6. The value of individual persons is at the core of King's philosophy. Explain what he means by *human nature* and *personality*.
7. How is a just law distinguished from an unjust law?
8. What does King mean by the *myth of time*?

Members of the Fellowship of the Concerned, of the Southern Regional Council, I need not pause to say how very delighted I am to be here today, and to have the opportunity of being a little part of this very significant gathering. I certainly want to express my personal appreciation to Mrs. Tilly and the members of the Committee, for giving me this opportunity. I would also like to express just a personal word of thanks and appreciation for your vital witness in this period of transition which we are facing in our Southland, and in the nation, and I am sure that as a result of this genuine concern, and your significant work in communities all across the South, we have a better South today and I am sure will have a better South tomorrow with your continued endeavor and I do want to express my personal gratitude and appreciation to you of the Fellowship of the Concerned for your significant work and for your forthright witness.

Now, I have been asked to talk about the philosophy behind the student movement. There can be no gainsaying of the fact that we confront a crisis in race relations in the United States. This crisis has been precipitated on the one hand by the determined resistance of reactionary forces in the South to the Supreme Court's decision in 1954 outlawing segregation in the public schools. And we know that at times this resistance has risen to ominous proportions. At times we find the legislative halls of the South ringing loud with such words as interposition and nullification. And all of these forces have developed into massive resistance. But we must also say that the crisis has been precipitated on the other hand by the determination of hundreds and thousands and millions of Negro people to achieve freedom and human dignity. If the Negro stayed in his place and accepted discrimination and segregation, there would be no crisis. But the Negro has a new sense of dignity, a new self-respect and new determination. He has reevaluated his own intrinsic worth. Now this new sense of dignity on the part of the Negro grows out of the same longing for freedom and human dignity on the part of the oppressed people all over the world; for we see it in Africa, we see it in Asia, and we see it all over the world. Now we must say that this struggle for freedom will not come to an automatic halt, for history reveals to us that once oppressed people rise up against that oppression, there is no stopping point short of full freedom. On the other hand, history reveals to us that those who oppose the movement for freedom are those who are in privileged positions who very seldom give up their privileges without strong resistance. And they very seldom do it voluntarily. So the sense of struggle will continue. The question is how will the struggle be waged.

Now there are three ways that oppressed people have generally dealt with their oppression. One way is the method of acquiescence, the method of surrender; that is, the individuals will somehow adjust themselves to oppression, they adjust themselves to discrimination or to segregation or colonialism or what have you. The other method that has been used in history is that of rising up against the oppressor with corroding hatred and physical violence. Now of course we know about this method in Western civilization because in a sense it has been the hallmark of its grandeur, and the inseparable twin of western materialism. But there is a weakness in this method because it ends up creating many more social problems than it solves. And I am convinced that if the Negro succumbs to the temptation of using violence in his struggle for freedom and justice, unborn generations will be the recipients of a long and desolate night of bitterness. And our chief legacy to the future will be an endless reign of meaningless chaos.

But there is another way, namely the way of nonviolent resistance. This method was popularized in our generation by a little man from India, whose name was Mohandas K. Gandhi. He used this method in a magnificent way to free his people from the economic exploitation and the political domination inflicted upon them by a foreign power.

This has been the method used by the student movement in the South and all over the United States. And naturally whenever I talk about the student movement I cannot be totally objective. I have to be somewhat subjective because of my great admiration for what the students have done. For in a real sense they have taken our deep groans and passionate yearnings for freedom, and filtered them in their own tender souls, and fashioned them into a creative protest which is an epic known all over our nation. As a result of their disciplined, nonviolent, yet courageous struggle, they have been able to do wonders in the South, and in our nation. But this movement does have an underlying philosophy, it has certain ideas that are attached to it, it has certain philosophical precepts. These are the things that I would like to discuss for the few moments left.

I would say that the first point or the first principle in the movement is the idea that means must be as pure as the end. This movement is based on the philosophy that ends and means must cohere. Now this has been one of the long struggles in history, the whole idea of means and ends. Great philosophers have grappled with it, and sometimes they have emerged with the idea, from Machiavelli on down, that the end justifies the means. There is a great system of thought in our world today, known as communism. And I think that with all of the weakness and tragedies of communism, we find its greatest tragedy right here, that it goes under the philosophy that the end justifies the means that are used in the process. So we can read or we can hear the Lenins say that lying, deceit, or violence, that many of these things justify the ends of the classless society.

This is where the student movement and the nonviolent movement that is taking place in our nation would break with communism and any other system that would argue that the end justifies the means. For in the long run, we must see that the end represents the means in process and the ideal in the making. In other words, we cannot believe, or we cannot go with the idea that the end justifies the means because the end is preexistent in the means. So the idea of nonviolent resistance, the philosophy of nonviolent resistance, is the philosophy which says that the means must be as pure as the end, that in the long run of history, immoral destructive means cannot bring about moral and constructive ends.

There is another thing about this philosophy, this method of nonviolence which is followed by the student movement. It says that those who adhere to or follow this philosophy must follow a consistent principle of noninjury. They must consistently refuse to inflict injury upon another. Sometimes you will read the literature of the student movement and see that, as they are getting ready for the sit-in or stand-in, they will read something like this, "If you are hit do not hit back, if you are cursed do not curse back." This is the whole idea, that the individual who is engaged in a nonviolent struggle must never inflict injury upon another. Now this has an external aspect and it has an internal one. From the external point of view it means that the individuals involved must avoid external physical violence. So they don't have guns, they don't retaliate with physical violence. If they are hit in the process, they avoid external physical violence at every point. But it also means that they avoid internal violence of spirit. This is why the love ethic stands so high in the student movement. We have a great deal of talk about love and nonviolence in this whole thrust.

Now when the students talk about love, certainly they are not talking about emotional bosh, they are not talking about merely a sentimental outpouring: they're talking something much deeper, and I always have to stop and try to define the meaning of love in this context. The Greek language comes to our aid in trying to deal with this. There are three words in the Greek language for love; one is the word *eros.* This is a beautiful type of love, it is an aesthetic love. Plato talks about it a great deal in his Dialogue, the yearning of the soul for the realm of the divine. It has come to us to be a sort of romantic love, and so in a sense we have read about it and experienced it. We've read about it in all the beauties of literature. I guess in a sense Edgar Allan Poe was talking about *eros* when he talked about his beautiful Annabelle Lee, with the love surrounded by the halo of eternity. In a sense Shakespeare was talking about *eros* when he said "Love is not love which alters when it alteration finds, or bends with the remover to remove; O'no! It is an ever fixed mark that looks on tempests and is never shaken, it is the star to every wandering bark." (You know, I remember that because I used to quote it to this little lady when we were courting; that's *eros.*) The Greek language talks about *philia* which was another level of love. It is an intimate affection between personal friends, it is a reciprocal love. On this level you love because you are loved. It is friendship.

Then the Greek language comes out with another word which is called the *agape. Agape* is more than romantic love, *agape* is more than friendship. *Agape* is understanding, creative, redemptive, good will to all men. It is an overflowing love which seeks nothing in return. Theologians would say that it is the love of God operating in the human heart. So that when one rises to love on this level, he loves men not because he likes them, not because their ways appeal to him, but he loves every man because God loves him. And he rises to the point of loving the person who does an evil deed while hating the deed that the person does. I think this is what Jesus meant when he said "love your enemies." I'm very happy that he didn't say like your enemies, because it is pretty difficult to like some people. Like is sentimental, and it is pretty difficult to like someone bombing your home; it is pretty difficult to like somebody threatening your children; it is difficult to like congressmen who spend all of their time trying to defeat civil rights. But Jesus says love them, and love is greater than like. Love is understanding, redemptive, creative, good will for all men. And it is this idea, it is this whole ethic of love which is the idea standing at the basis of the student movement.

There is something else: that one seeks to defeat the unjust system, rather than individuals who are caught in that system. And that one goes on believing that somehow this is the important thing, to get rid of the evil system and not the individual who happens to be misguided, who happens to be misled, who was taught wrong. The thing to do is to get rid of the system and thereby create a moral balance within society.

Another thing that stands at the center of this movement is another idea: that suffering can be a most creative and powerful social force. Suffering has certain moral attributes involved, but it can be a powerful and creative social force. Now, it is very interesting at this point to notice that both violence and nonviolence agree that suffering can be a very powerful social force. But there is this difference: violence says that suffering can be a powerful social force by inflicting the suffering on somebody else: so this is what we do in war, this is what we do in the whole violent thrust of the violent movement. It believes that you achieve some end by inflicting suffering on another. The nonviolent say that suffering becomes a powerful social force when you willingly accept that violence on yourself, so that self-suffering stands at the center of the nonviolent movement and the individuals involved are able to suffer in a creative manner, feeling that unearned suffering is redemptive, and that suffering may serve to transform the social situation.

Another thing in this movement is the idea that there is within human nature an amazing potential for goodness. There is within human nature something that can respond to goodness. I know somebody's liable to say that this is an unrealistic movement if it goes on believing that all people are good. Well, I didn't say that. I think the students are realistic enough to believe that there is a strange dichotomy of disturbing dualism within human nature. Many of the great philosophers and thinkers through the ages have seen this. It caused Ovid the Latin poet to say, "I see and approve the better things of life, but the evil things I do." It caused even Saint Augustine to say "Lord, make me pure, but not yet." So that that is in human nature. Plato, centuries ago said that the human personality is like a charioteer with two headstrong horses, each wanting to go in different directions, so that within our own individual lives we see this conflict and certainly when we come to the collective life of man, we see a strange badness. But in spite of this there is something in human nature that can respond to goodness. So that man is neither innately good nor is he innately bad; he has potentialities for both. So in this sense, Carlyle was right when he said that, "there are depths in man which go down to the lowest hell, and heights which reach the highest heaven, for are not both heaven and hell made out of him, ever-lasting miracle and mystery that he is?" Man has the capacity to be good, man has the capacity to be evil.

And so the nonviolent resister never lets this idea go, that there is something within human nature than can respond to goodness. So that a Jesus of Nazareth or a Mohandas Gandhi, can appeal to human beings and appeal to that element of goodness within them, and a Hitler can appeal to the element of evil within them. But we must never forget that there is something within human nature that can respond to goodness, that man is not totally depraved; to put it in theological terms, the image of God is never totally gone. And so the individuals who believe in this movement and who believe in nonviolence and our struggle in the South, somehow believe that even the worst segregationist can become an integrationist. Now sometimes it is hard to believe that this is what this movement says, and it believes it firmly, that there is something within human nature that can be changed, and this stands at the top of the whole philosophy of the student movement and the philosophy of nonviolence.

It says something else. It says that it is as much a moral obligation to refuse to cooperate with evil as it is to cooperate with good. Noncooperation with evil is as much a moral obligation as the cooperation with good. So that the student movement is willing to stand up courageously on the idea of civil disobedience. Now I think this is the part of the student movement that is probably misunderstood more than anything else. And it is a difficult aspect, because on the one hand the students would say, and I would say, and all the people who believe in civil rights would say, obey the Supreme Court's decision of 1954 and at the same time, we would disobey certain laws that exist on the statutes of the South today.

This brings in the whole question of how can you be logically consistent when you advocate obeying some laws and disobeying other laws. Well, I think one would have to see the whole meaning of this movement at this point by seeing that the students recognize that there are two types of laws. There are just laws and there are unjust laws. And they would be the first to say obey the just laws, they would be the first to say that men and women have a moral obligation to obey just and right laws. And they would go on to say that we must see that there are unjust laws. Now the question comes into being, what is the difference, and who determines the difference, what is the difference between a just and an unjust law?

Well, a just law is a law that squares with a moral law. It is a law that squares with that which is right, so that any law that uplifts human personality is a just law. Whereas that law which is out of harmony with the moral is a law which does not square with the moral law of the universe. It does not square with the law of God, so for that reason it is unjust and any law that degrades the human personality is an unjust law.

Well, somebody says that that does not mean anything to me; first, I don't believe in these abstract things called moral laws and I'm not too religious, so I don't believe in the law of God; you have to get a little more concrete, and more practical. What do you mean when you say that a law is unjust, and a law is just? Well, I would go on to say in more concrete terms that an unjust law is a code that the majority inflicts on the minority that is not binding on itself. So that this becomes difference made legal. Another thing that we can say is that an unjust law is a code which the majority inflicts upon the minority, which that minority had no part in enacting or creating, because that minority had no right to vote in many instances, so that the legislative bodies that made these laws were not democratically elected. Who could ever say that the legislative body of Mississippi was democratically elected, or the legislative body of Alabama was democratically elected, or the legislative body even of Georgia has been democratically elected, when there are people in Terrell County and in other counties because of the color of their skin who cannot vote? They confront reprisals and threats and all of that; so that an unjust law is a law that individuals did not have a part in creating or enacting because they were denied the right to vote.

Now the same token of just law would be just the opposite. A just law becomes saneness made legal. It is a code that the majority, who happen to believe in that code, compel the minority, who don't believe in it, to follow, because they are willing to follow it themselves, so it is saneness made legal. Therefore the individuals who stand up on the basis of civil disobedience realize that they are following something that says that there are just laws and there are unjust laws. Now, they are not anarchists. They believe that there are laws which must be followed: they do not seek to defy the law, they do not seek to evade the law. For many individuals who would call themselves segregationists and who would hold on to segregation at any cost seek to defy the law, they seek to evade the law, and their process can lead on into anarchy. They seek in the final analysis to follow a way of uncivil disobedience, not civil disobedience. And I submit that the individual who disobeys the law, whose conscience tells him it is unjust and who is willing to accept the penalty by staying in jail until that law is altered, is expressing at the moment the very highest respect for law.

This is what the students have followed in their movement. Of course there is nothing new about this; they feel that they are in good company and rightly so. We go back and read the Apology and the Crito, and you see Socrates practicing civil disobedience. And to a degree academic freedom is a reality today because Socrates practiced civil disobedience. The early Christians practiced civil disobedience in a superb manner, to a point where they were willing to be thrown to the lions. They were willing to face all kinds of suffering in order to stand up for what they knew was right even though they knew it was against the laws of the Roman Empire.

We could come up to our own day and we see it in many instances. We must never forget that everything that Hitler did in Germany was "legal." It was illegal to aid and comfort a Jew, in the days of Hitler's Germany. But I believe that if I had the same attitude then as I have now I would publicly aid and comfort my Jewish brothers in Germany if Hitler were alive today calling this an illegal process. If I lived in South Africa today in the midst of the white supremacy law in South Africa, I would join Chief Luthuli and others in saying break these unjust laws. And even let us come up to America. Our nation in a sense came into being through a massive act of civil disobedience for the Boston Tea Party was nothing but a massive act of civil disobedience. Those who stood up against the slave laws, the abolitionists, by and large practiced civil disobedience. So I think these students are in good company, and they feel that by practicing civil disobedience they are in line with men and women through the ages who have stood up for something that is morally right.

Now there are one or two other things that I want to say about this student movement, moving out of the philosophy of nonviolence, something about what it is a revolt against. On the one hand it is a revolt against the negative peace that has encompassed the South for many years. I remember when I was in Montgomery, Alabama, one of the white citizens came to me one day and said—and I think he was very sincere about this—that in Montgomery for all of these years we have been such a peaceful community, we have had so much harmony in race relations and then you people have started this movement and boycott, and it has done so much to disturb race relations, and we just don't love the Negro like we used to love them, because you have destroyed the harmony and the peace that we once had in race relations. And I said to him, in the best way I could say and I tried to say it in nonviolent terms, we have never had peace in Montgomery, Alabama, we have never had peace in the South. We have had a negative peace, which is merely the absence of tension; we've had a negative peace in which the Negro patiently accepted his situation and his plight, but we've never had true peace, we've never had positive peace, and what we're seeking now is to develop this positive peace. For we must come to see that peace is not merely the absence of some negative force, it is the presence of a positive force. True peace is not merely the absence of tension, but it is the presence of justice and brotherhood. I think this is what Jesus meant when he said, "I come not to bring peace but a sword." Now Jesus didn't mean he came to start war, to bring a physical sword, and he didn't mean, I come not to bring positive peace. But I think what Jesus was saying in substance was this, that I come not to bring an old negative peace, which makes for stagnant passivity and deadening complacency, I come to bring something different, and whenever I come, a conflict is precipitated, between the old and the new, whenever I come a struggle takes place between justice and injustice, between the forces of light and the forces of darkness. I come not to bring a negative peace, but a positive peace, which is brotherhood, which is justice, which is the Kingdom of God.

And I think this is what we are seeking to do today, and this movement is a revolt against a negative peace and a struggle to bring into being a positive peace, which makes for true brotherhood, true integration, true person-to-person relationships. This movement is also revolt against what is often called tokenism. Here again many people do not understand this, they feel that in this struggle the Negro will be satisfied with tokens of integration, just a few students and a few schools here and there and a few doors open here and there. But this isn't the meaning of the movement and I think that honesty impels me to admit it everywhere I have an opportunity, that the Negro's aim is to bring about complete integration in American life. And he has come to see that token integration is little more than token democracy, which ends up with many new evasive schemes and it ends up with new discrimination, covered up with such niceties of complexity. It is very interesting to discover that the movement has thrived in many communities that had token integration. So this reveals that the movement is based on a principle that integration must become real and complete, not just token integration.

It is also a revolt against what I often call the myth of time. We hear this quite often, that only time can solve this problem. That if we will only be patient, and only pray—which we must do, we must be patient and we must pray—but there are those who say just do these things and wait for time, and time will solve the problem. Well the people who argue this do not themselves realize that time is neutral, that it can be used constructively or destructively. At points the people of ill will, the segregationists, have used time much more effectively than the people of good will. So individuals in the struggle must come to realize that it is necessary to aid time, that without this kind of aid, time itself will become an ally of the insurgent and primitive forces of social stagnation. Therefore, this movement is a revolt against the myth of time.

There is a final thing that I would like to say to you, this movement is a movement based on faith in the future. It is a movement based on a philosophy, the possibility of the future bringing into being something real and meaningful. It is a movement based on hope. I think this is very important. The students have developed a theme song for their movement, maybe you've heard it. It goes something like this, "We shall overcome, deep in my heart, I do believe, we shall overcome," and then they go on to say another verse, "We are not afraid, we are not afraid today, deep in my heart I do believe, we shall overcome." So it is out of this deep faith in the future that they are able to move out and adjourn the councils of despair, and to bring new light in the dark chambers of pessimism. I can remember the times that we've been together, I remember that night in Montgomery, Alabama, when we had stayed up all night discussing the Freedom Rides, and that morning came to see that it was necessary to go on with the Freedom Rides, that we would not in all good conscience call an end to the Freedom Rides at that point. And I remember the first group got ready to leave, to take a bus for Jackson, Mississippi, we all joined hands and started singing together. "We shall overcome, we shall overcome." And something within me said, now how is it that these students can sing this, they are going down to Mississippi, they are going to face hostile and jeering mobs, and yet they could sing, "We shall overcome." They may even face physical death, and yet they could sing, "We shall overcome." Most of them realized that they would be thrown into jail, and yet they could sing, "We shall overcome, we are not afraid." Then something caused me to see at that moment the real meaning of the movement. That students had faith in the future. That the movement was based on hope, that this movement had something within it that says somehow even though the arc of the moral universe is long, it bends toward justice. And I think this should be a challenge to all others who are struggling to transform the dangling discords of our Southland into a beautiful symphony of brotherhood. There is something in this student movement which says to us, that we shall overcome. Before the victory is won some may have to get scarred up, but we shall overcome. Before the victory of brotherhood is achieved, some will maybe face physical death, but we shall overcome. Before the victory is won, some will lose jobs, some will be called communists, and reds, merely because they believe in brotherhood, some will be dismissed as dangerous rabblerousers and agitators merely because they're standing up for what is right, but we shall overcome. That is the basis of this movement, and as I like to say, there is something in this universe that justifies Carlyle in saying no lie can live forever. We shall overcome because there is something in this universe which justifies William Cullen Bryant in saying truth crushed to earth shall rise again. We shall overcome because there is something in this universe that justifies James Russell Lowell in saying, truth forever on the scaffold, wrong forever on the throne. Yet that scaffold sways the future, and behind the dim unknown standeth God within the shadows keeping watch above His own. With this faith in the future, with this determined struggle, we will be able to emerge from the bleak and desolate midnight of man's inhumanity to man, into the bright and glittering daybreak of freedom and justice. Thank you.

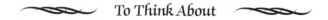

To Think About

1. "Back of the problem of race and color lies a greater problem which both obscures and implements it; and that is the fact that so many civilized persons are willing to live in comfort even if the price of this is poverty, ignorance and disease of the majority of their fellowmen; that to maintain this privilege men have waged war until today war tends to become universal and continuous, and the excuse for this war continues largely to be color and race."   ***W. E. B. Du Bois***

2. "Anthropology provides no scientific basis for discrimination against any people on the ground of racial inferiority, religious affiliation, or linguistic heritage."
   American Anthropological Association 1938 statement of resolution

3. "The existence of slavery in this country brands your republicanism as a sham, your humanity as a base pretense, and your Christianity as a lie."
   Frederick Douglass

4. "The black man who cannot let love and sympathy go out to the white man is but half free. The white man who retards his own development by opposing the black man is but half free."   ***Booker T. Washington***

5. "As I would not be a slave, so I would not be a master. This expresses my idea of democracy."   ***Abraham Lincoln***

6. "Where love rules, there is no will to power; and where power predominates, there love is lacking."   ***Carl Jung***

7. "Maya Angelou says there is the unknowing majority, 'it,' and the knowing minority, 'you.' *Victims know when they're being cruelly treated and victimizers are usually the unknowing majority.* The sword does not feel the wound. The flesh on which that sword strikes does. The empirical, skeptical authority for cruelty is the victim and the victim alone."   ***Phillip Hallie***

8. "Violent revolutions do not so much redistribute wealth as destroy it. . . . The only real revolution is in the enlightenment of the mind and the improvement of character. The only real emancipation is individual."   ***Will Durant***

9. "We must be entirely clear that law is not God. It has always been a basic Christian conviction that there are times when a Christian ought to break the law."   ***Eugene Carson Blake***

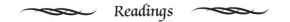

Readings

APPIAH, K. ANTHONY, AND AMY GUTTMANN. *Color Conscious: The Political Morality of Race.* Princeton, NJ: Princeton University Press, 1996.

COOK, ANTHONY E. *The Least of These: Race, Law, and Religion in American Culture.* New York: Routledge, 1997.

DAWSON, MICHAEL C. *Black Visions: The Roots of Contemporary African-American Political Ideologies.* Chicago: University of Chicago Press, 2001.

MOSES, GREG. *Revolution of Conscience: Martin Luther King, Jr. and the Philosophy of Nonviolence.* New York: Guilford Press, 1997.

47

Feminism in the New Millennium

Rosemarie Tong (1947–) is Distinguished Professor of Health Care Ethics in the Department of Philosophy and the Director of the Center for Professional and Applied Ethics at the University of North Carolina at Charlotte. She obtained her Ph.D. from Temple University and has also taught at Davidson College and at Williams College. She currently serves as an Executive Board Member of the International Association of Bioethics. She is the Chair of the American Philosophical Association's Committee on the Status of Women, a frequent panelist and judge for the National Institutes of Health, and a winner of the 1986 CASE National Professor of the Year Award. Dr. Tong has authored or coedited thirteen books, including Controlling Our Reproductive Destiny: A Technological and Philosophical Perspective *(1994),* Feminist Approaches to Bioethics *(1996),* Feminist Thought: A More Comprehensive Introduction *(1998),* Globalizing Feminist Bioethics: Crosscultural Perspectives, *with Aida Santos and Gwen Anderson (2001), and* Linking Visions: Feminist Bioethics, Human Rights, and the Developing World *with Anne Donchin and Sue Dodds (2004).*

American history presents us with a very slow and grudging acknowledgment of the political rights of minorities in general, and in particular of the rights of racial minorities and women. In the following reading, Rosemarie Tong outlines the history of feminism in the context of American social and political history, showing especially the role philosophical and cultural criticism has played in this developing story. She shows how increased educational opportunity, the right to vote, the civil rights movement, and other landmark achievements in past and current American life have led to a new, largely uncharted concept of feminist politics. This *third wave* of feminism recognizes a kind of unity in multiplicity in contemporary feminism, a view recognizing similarities as well as differences in women's self-concept, especially when played out against a global perspective. The international dimension of the women's movement and its necessary intersection with economic and cultural issues, especially poverty in

From Rosemarie Tong, "A Millennial Feminist Vision," in James Sterba, ed., *Controversies in Feminism* (Lanham, MD: Rowman & Littlefield, 2000), 173–96. © 2000. Reprinted by permission of Rowman & Littlefield.

the third world, emphasizes cultural differences among women around the world, a new focus on ecological concerns, and a renewed sense of the place of the family in the feminist struggle.

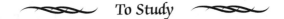

To Study

1. Describe the essential features of each of the three periods or 'waves' Tong uses to chart the history of U.S. feminism.
2. Why, according to second-wave feminists, did winning the right to vote fail to achieve equality for women?
3. What did the Civil Rights Act of 1964 achieve and fail to achieve in the liberation of women?
4. What differences exist between 'liberal' and 'radical' second-wave feminists?
5. Third-wave feminists differ among themselves in claiming identity and difference among women. Explain.
6. What global and racial concerns are developing in third-wave feminism that increasingly distinguish it as a new moment?
7. What challenges to life-style and standard of living does global feminism present to the women's movement?
8. Feminism, according to Tong, is about justice and caring. What new directions in achieving these ideals the third-wave feminism seem to be taking?

Because feminism is both a sociopolitical and cultural movement, its meaning changes depending on where, when, how, why, and in what forms it manifests itself. Since this is so, I plan to focus on feminism in the United States. I will examine U.S. feminism both as a sociopolitical movement and as a cultural movement, proceeding on the commonly held assumption that U.S. women have ridden through two waves of feminism and are now in the process of riding through a third one. The first wave of U.S. feminism began in the mid-nineteenth century and ended in approximately 1920. The second wave began in the 1960s and ended very early in the 1990s. The third wave emerged later in the 1990s. At present there is uncertainty as to whether the third wave will increase or decrease in size. In the course of describing each of these waves of U.S. feminism, I will note the differences as well as the similarities between them. My intent is to determine the degree to which U.S. feminism is progressing beyond its borders, and whether this movement signals the further development of feminism or the replacement of feminism with a perspective yet to be named.

THE FIRST WAVE OF U.S. FEMINISM

The first wave of U.S. feminism is rooted in eighteenth- and nineteenth-century liberal thought as articulated by Mary Wollstonecraft, John Stuart Mill, and Harriet Taylor Mill, in particular. According to Wollstonecraft, since men and women have the *same* capacities for rationality and morality, the key to developing these capacities equally in both sexes is to provide all individuals with the same education in the sciences and humanities. Wollstonecraft believed that if women were educated like men, women would stop acting like children—or, worse, like caged birds, hothouse plants, or decorative ornaments—and start acting like autonomous and responsible persons with meaningful life projects.[1] Although Wollstonecraft realized that women's access to men's education might depend to some degree on women's economic and political independence from men, she did not advise women to work in the public world. Nor did she urge women to fight for suffrage. Instead, Wollstonecraft envisioned properly educated women exercising their mature personhood primarily in the domestic realm—as "observant daughters," "affectionate sisters," "faithful wives," and "reasonable mothers."[2] . . .

Familiar with English liberal thought, many educated U.S. women promptly took a stand against sex discrimination. Sarah Grimké and her sister, Angelina, for example, wrote several passionate essays and letters on behalf of women's rights. Both claimed that women's inferiority is a product not of nature but of nurture; that traditional family structures and marriage contracts keep women in a subordinate position; that male-dominated institutional religions like Christianity make men into leaders and women into followers; and that men monopolize all the lucrative professions, leaving for women mostly low-paying occupations. . . .[3] As they became cognizant of the relationship between sex discrimination and race discrimination, first-wave U.S. feminists began to defend slaves' rights as well as women's rights. So eloquent were they that male abolitionists eagerly enlisted them in the cause of slaves' liberation. . . .

Believing that male abolitionists wanted men and women to be equal participants in the abolition movement, the first-wave U.S. feminists who attended the 1840 World Anti-Slavery Conference in London were sorely disappointed. No woman, not even Lucretia Mott or Elizabeth Cady Stanton, two of the most prominent leaders of the U.S. women's rights movement, was allowed to speak at the meeting. Angered by men's silencing of women, Mott and Stanton vowed to hold a women's rights convention on their return to the United States. Eight years later, in 1848, 300 women and men met in Seneca Falls, New York, and produced a Declaration of Sentiments and twelve resolutions.

Modeled on the Declaration of Independence, the Declaration of Sentiments stressed the issues that Mill and Taylor had emphasized in England, particularly the need for reforms in marriage, divorce, property, and child custody laws. The twelve resolutions emphasized women's rights to express themselves in public, to speak out on the burning issues of the day, especially "in regard to the great subjects of morals and religion,"[4] which women were thought to be more qualified to address than men. The Seneca Falls convention endorsed all the resolutions brought before it, with the notable exception of Susan B. Anthony's Woman's Suffrage Resolution, which read: "Resolved, that it is the duty of the women of this country to secure to themselves their sacred right to the elective franchise."[5] Apparently, the majority of the convention viewed Anthony's resolution as an extremely radical request that would alienate mainstream U.S. citizens otherwise sympathetic to the cause of women's rights. . . . From 1890 until 1920, when the Nineteenth Amendment to the U.S. Constitution was passed, the National American Woman Suffrage Association confined almost all of its activities to gaining the vote for women. Victorious after years of concerted struggle, most of the exhausted suffragists chose to believe that simply by gaining the vote women had indeed become men's equals. . . .

THE SECOND WAVE OF U.S. FEMINISM

As second-wave feminists saw it, suffrage had not and would never make women equal to men. Women, they said, needed the same educational, occupational, and professional opportunities men had, the same chance to succeed in a competitive public realm. These feminists, usually referred to as "liberal feminists," also stressed that women needed to control their sexual and reproductive lives to avoid being treated merely as "sex objects" or as dutiful wives and indulgent mothers confined to the domestic world of children, church, and kitchen. Already sensitized to the myriad ways in which U.S. systems, structures, and laws oppressed blacks, liberal feminists active in the Civil Rights Movement pointed to the similarities between race-based oppression and gender-based oppression.

In response to this growing interest in women's rights, President John F. Kennedy established the Commission on the Status of Women in 1961. This group produced much new data about women and resulted in the formation of the Citizens' Advisory Council, various state commissions on the status of women, and the passage of the Equal Pay Act. When Congress passed the 1964 Civil Rights Act—amended with the Title VII provision to prohibit discrimination on the basis of sex as well as race, color, religion, or national origin by private employers, employment agencies, and unions—a woman shouted from the congressional gallery: "We made it! God bless America!"[6] Unfortunately, this woman's jubilation and that of women in general was short-lived; the courts were reluctant to enforce Title VII's so-called sex amendment. Feeling betrayed by the powers that be, women's joy turned to anger, an anger that feminist activists used to energize the so-called women's liberation movement.[7]

Among these feminist activists was Betty Friedan. Reflecting on how she and some of her associates had reacted to the courts' refusal to take Title VII's sex amendment seriously, she wrote: "The absolute necessity for a civil rights movement for women had reached such a point of subterranean explosive urgency by 1966, that it only took a few of us to get together to ignite the spark—and it spread like a nuclear chain reaction."[8] The result was the founding of the National Organization for Women (NOW). It put forth an agenda that seemed both less and more demanding than the nineteenth-century Seneca Falls Convention agenda, which had been bold enough to portray "Man" as "Woman's" *chief* oppressor, and yet too timid to demand suffrage for women.[9]

Although first-wave *liberal* U.S. feminists viewed NOW's feminist agenda as *revolutionary,* second-wave *radical* U.S. feminists dismissed its proposals as overly *moderate* ones that, with the exception of abortion, paid little attention to women's need for sexual and reproductive freedom. . . .[10]

Initially, second-wave radical feminists, sometimes referred to as "radical libertarian feminists,"[11] aimed to explore what they saw as the pleasures of sex. . . . They sought to free women from the beliefs that "good" sex could be experienced only in a "love relationship," and that sex for sex's sake was somehow "bad" or promiscuous. In addition, second-wave radical libertarian feminists wished to help women avoid the burdens of human reproduction, going so far as to recommend that natural reproduction be replaced by technological reproduction. They agreed with thinkers such as Shulamith Firestone that no matter how much educational, political, and economic equality women achieve, nothing fundamental will change for women so long as their reproductive role remains the same. Natural reproduction, said Firestone, is definitely not in women's best interests. Pregnancy is "barbaric. . . ."[12]

As might be expected, the views of second-wave radical libertarian feminists troubled not only some second-wave liberal feminists but also most mainstream Americans. Although most 1960s and 1970s Americans were more sexually permissive than their parents had been, they were not ready to abandon all of their so-called sexual hang-ups. Nor were they prepared to forsake old-fashioned procreation for in vitro fertilization and ex utero gestation. But what really caused mainstream Americans, as well as some second-wave liberal feminists, the most problems with second-wave radical libertarian feminist thought was its conception of so-called androgyny. For example, Firestone claimed that as soon as men and women were truly free to engage in polymorphous, perverse sex, it would no longer be necessary for men to display only masculine identities and behaviors and for women to display only feminine ones. Freed from their gender roles at the level of biology (that is, reproduction), women would no longer have to be passive, receptive, and vulnerable, sending out "signals" to men to dominate, possess, and penetrate them to keep the wheels of human procreation spinning. . . . Furthermore, in this newly evolved androgynous culture, the categories of the technological and the aesthetic, together with the categories of the masculine and the feminine, would disappear through what Firestone termed "a mutual cancellation—a matter-antimatter explosion, ending with a poof!"[13]

Not only did Firestone's "poof" trouble most nonfeminists and some second-wave liberal feminists, it also concerned some second-wave radical feminists, particularly those who wondered whether women would really gain true liberty by engaging in permissive sex, refusing to bear children, and becoming androgynous individuals. By the time the 1960s and 1970s had given way to the 1980s and the 1990s, these second-wave radical feminists—sometimes called "radical cultural feminists"[14] or "essentialists"[15]—began to caution that sex, usually understood as heterosexual sex, is more dangerous than pleasurable for most women. . . . Second-wave radical cultural feminists insisted that, as it has been experienced so far, heterosexuality is men's sexuality. . . . Freed from feeding men's sexual appetites, said radical cultural feminists, women would be able at last to nurture each other's sexual needs, embracing each other in joyous, gynocentric holds.

In addition to stressing the dangers of heterosexual relations and the pleasures of lesbian relations, second-wave radical cultural feminists emphasized that artificial reproduction would more likely disempower than empower women. . . . Unless women realize this, said second-wave radical cultural feminists, women might unwittingly forsake the ultimate source of their real power—namely, the ability to bring new life into the world through their bodies.[16]

Finally, second-wave radical cultural feminists rejected the idea of androgyny as a desirable goal for feminists, replacing pleas for it with proposals to affirm women's essential "femaleness."[17] Far from believing the liberated woman must exhibit both masculine and feminine traits and behaviors, second-wave radical cultural feminists expressed the view that it is better to be female/feminine than it is to be male/masculine. Women should not try to be like men, they said. On the contrary, they should try to be more like women, emphasizing the values and virtues culturally associated with women including "interdependence, community, connection, sharing, emotion, body, trust, absence of hierarchy, nature, immanence, process, joy, peace and life" and de-emphasizing the values and virtues culturally associated with men including "independence, autonomy, intellect, will, wariness, hierarchy, domination, culture, transcendence, product, ascetism, war and death."[18]

In proposing that women should try to be more like women, second-wave radical cultural feminists aimed to establish that all women are oppressed by men simply because they are women who think and act like females.[19] When some women protested that they did not experience themselves as being oppressed by men, and when other women insisted that they were anything but dependent, emotional, and overly compliant persons, second-wave radical cultural feminists accused these women either of "false consciousness."[20] or "male identification." . . .[21]

Not surprisingly, women accused of false consciousness and/or male identification did not welcome such harsh criticism from their supposed "sisters." They claimed that the radical-cultural-feminist construct, Woman, did not represent all women, but only a certain kind of woman—namely, Woman in the image and likeness of the women (radical cultural feminists) who had created her. U.S. women, they claimed, were not about to trade in Patriarchy for Matriarchy, nor were they about to deny their many differences in pursuit of a sameness they did not feel.

THE THIRD WAVE OF U.S. FEMINISM

The construct Woman proved to be the creation that signaled the end of second-wave feminism, for it mandated ways of doing, thinking, and being that an increasing number of American women were not ready, willing, or able to embrace. This led to the birth of a new form of feminism alert to women's differences, including ones of race, class, and national origin. This form of feminism, referred to as third-wave feminism, is a form of feminism that is still in the process of developing. Third-wave feminists want to understand the relationship between gender oppression and other kinds of human oppression, and they are willing to admit the ways in which they have sometimes oppressed others. In other words, they are self-critical feminists who aim to combine the best of second-wave liberal feminism and radical feminism with the best of black feminism, women-of-color feminism, working-class feminism, prosex feminism, and so on. . . . Third-wave difference feminists, sometimes referred to as postmodern feminists,[22] are not to be confused with second-wave radical cultural feminists. Whereas second-wave radical cultural feminists spoke of women's differences from men as women's departure from the culturally imposed norm Man, third-wave postmodern difference feminists spoke of women's difference "not as difference from a pre-given norm but as pure difference, difference itself, differences with no identity." . . .[23] In other words, as Teresa de Lauretis comments, whereas second-wave radical cultural feminists conceived women's "Nature" as some sort of biological or ontological given, third-wave postmodern difference feminists . . . maintained [that] we have no access to Woman as she is in Herself, but only to the enormous variety of women as they appear to us, to each other, and to themselves. Yet despite women's differences, in the same way we can recognize a triangle when we see one—be it scalene, isosceles, or equilateral—we can recognize a woman when we see one.

Choosing to resolve the perennial problem of the One and Many in feminist thought with an emphasis on women's differences, however, third-wave postmodern difference feminists lost their grip on women's sameness. Wondering what, if anything beyond two 'X' chromosomes women shared, some third-wave postmodern difference feminists worried, that in their stress on women's differences, they had lost feminism's rationale for collective political action on behalf of women's common interests. In an attempt to remedy this growing problem in feminist thought, de Lauretis suggested that when a woman (or man) becomes a feminist, she (or he) deliberately assumes a position or perspective[24] termed "gender" from which first "to interpret or (re)construct values and meanings"[25] and then to forge alliances aimed at increasing all women's freedom and well-being. . . .

Admitting that gender is not the only position or perspective from which feminists should coalesce for political action, de Lauretis nonetheless pressed Christine de Stephano's view that, in their desire to assume other positions or perspectives such as these of race and class, feminists might "lose" women.[26] According to de Stephano, even if gender is not the only perspective or position that matters in feminism, it remains basic to feminism, a difference that makes a difference. We must, said de Stephano, "repeatedly return . . . to the [figure of the shrinking woman] . . . because to ignore her altogether is to risk forgetting and thereby losing what is left of her."[27]

De Stephano's insistence that feminists require the position or perspective of gender is affirmed by third-wave multicultural and global feminists. Like third-wave postmodern difference feminists, third-wave multicultural and global feminists reject the second-wave radical-cultural feminist emphasis on women's *sameness*. . . .

In an attempt to clarify how assertions of "sameness" can serve to oppress people, multicultural and global feminist Elizabeth Spelman . . . urges feminists not to make the mistake made by historian Kenneth Stampp when he asserted "that innately Negroes are, after all, only white men with black skins, nothing more, nothing else."[28] Challenging white and "First-World" feminists in particular to ponder Stampp's words, Spelman asks why Stampp chose to describe *Negroes* as white men with black skins instead of choosing to describe *Caucasians* as black men with white skins. Could it be, probes Spelman, that Stampp was unconsciously committed to the view that "white" is the way all people really want to be? Moreover, could it also be that, like Stampp, white and First-World feminists unreflectively view "white" and "First World" as the preferred mode for all women's existence? . . .

No wonder, concludes Spelman, that so many women of color and Third-World women rejected second-wave feminist thought; it was too "white" and "First World" for them. A truly inclusive feminist theory cannot claim [that] all women are just like me, any more than it can claim that I am just like all other women; nor can it operate on the assumption that those who are different from me want to become like me, particularly if I do not want to become like them, but to remain myself. . . .

Although most third-wave multicultural and global feminists continue to doubt that "sisterhood" is a state of being all women can or should achieve, an increasing number of them are nonetheless optimistic that women who come from different "worlds" can come first to understand each other and then to work together on behalf of each other's specific interests. Among these more optimistic third-wave multicultural and global feminists is Spelman. She suggests that minimally, a way to get to know women different from one's self is to "read books, take classes, open your eyes and ears or whatever instrument of awareness you might be blessed with, go to conferences planned and produced by the people about whom you wish to learn and manage not to be intrusive."[29] A better but also more demanding way to get to know such women, adds Spelman, is to imagine their lives and to be tolerant of their differences from one's self no matter how threatening they might seem. Finally, concludes Spelman, the best and most demanding way to get to know such women is not simply to imagine their lives and to tolerate them but to perceive and welcome them. . . .

Stressing just how difficult it is for women from different worlds to perceive and welcome each other, third-wave multicultural and global feminists such as bell hooks caution white women and First-World women not to be disappointed if they are unable to achieve personal friendships with women of color and Third-World women. The kind of "friendship" or "sisterhood" third-wave multicultural and global feminists should seek is first and foremost political—not personal. There is, insists hooks, a major difference between "bourgeois-women's liberation,"[30] sisterhood, and third-wave multicultural and global feminist sisterhood. The former focuses on women supporting each other, where support serves "as a prop or a foundation for a weak structure,"[31] and where women, emphasizing their "shared victimization," give each other "unqualified approval."[32] The latter rejects this sentimentalized support system and offers in its stead a type of sisterhood that begins with women honestly acknowledging each other's differences, and ends with women using these very same differences to "accelerate their positive advance"[33] toward the goals they share in common. . . .

Using their differences as a source of the feminist strength, hooks affirms that third-wave multicultural and global feminists like Alison Jaggar advise contemporary U.S. feminists to "cross borders."[34] As they move toward the new millennium, Jaggar and other feminists with her perspective increasingly offer a *both/and* approach to resolving the tension between unity and diversity in feminist thought. As they see it, women from all over the world need to realize that despite all their differences, they also have some samenesses, and that they can become political allies even when they can't become personal friends. . . .

But First-World women who are sincere about eliminating all forms of human oppression, beginning with gender oppression, will need to do more than talk about the need to help Third-World women achieve all that is *rightfully* theirs as women. First-World women must, as Vandana Shiva and Maria Mies have suggested, be prepared to give up some of their luxuries so that Third-World women can attain most of their necessities. . . .[35]

That Mies and Shiva should call First-World women to task is not surprising, for, as they see it, what creates the greatest divide between people is some people having too much and other people having too little. In their estimation, one wrong way to resolve this undesirable state of affairs is for the "have nots" to wage war against the "haves." Little will be achieved by such violence except counterproductively reversing the membership of the "have" and "have not" classes.

Another wrong way to overcome the have/have not divide is for the haves to try to help the have nots join the class of haves. As Mies and Shiva see it, this strategy is destined for failure since there is no way that everyone can have everything in equal measure. . . .

A third way to overcome the gap between the haves and the have nots is, then, for First-World people to honestly confront the fact that their luxurious lifestyle is partially subsidized by a host of Third-World people who lead a Spartan lifestyle. Mies, Shiva, and other multicultural and global feminists urge privileged feminists, most of whom live in the First World, but some of whom live in the Third World, to voluntarily give up at least some of their excesses so that the basic needs of under-privileged women can be met. For example, says Mies, the wages of Third-World, women in the garment industry will be raised significantly only when First-World women are willing to pay more for imported garments.[36] The closets of many First-World women are bulging not only with clothes imported from the Third World but also with the "skeletons" of many Third-World women, most of whom have bare cup-boards as well as bare closets. This type of scenario suggests that a person ought not call herself or himself a feminist—someone committed to eliminating all forms of op-pression, particularly those forms that harm women—until he or she is willing to stop participating either explicitly or implicitly in oppressive systems, structures, and practices. Third-wave feminism is a most demanding form of feminism.

CONCLUSION

The message of third-wave U.S. feminism resonates in many ways with the messages of both first-wave and second-wave U.S. feminism. Nevertheless, when we compare such third-wave feminist documents as the 1995 Beijing Declaration with such second-wave feminist documents as NOW's 1967 Bill of Rights for Women and such first-wave feminist documents as the 1848 Declaration of Sentiments, we cannot fail to notice just how much feminism has changed since the late nineteenth century. The Declaration of Sentiments was, as its title implies, the expression of women's *feelings* of frustration, of their desire to break out in some measure from the narrow confines of the private realm into the broader purview of the public realm. It was written as a series of accusations against "He," the first and foremost accusation being that "he has never permitted her to achieve her inalienable right to the elective franchise."[37]

The central complaint of the Declaration is that Man has deprived Woman not only of her political and legal rights but also of her dignity. Indeed, the authors of the Declaration specifically bemoaned the fact that "He has endeavored, in every way that he could, to destroy her confidence in her own powers, to lessen her self-respect, and to make her willing to lead a dependent and abject life."[38] Of interest is the fact that the Declaration's authors viewed the Church as well as the State as play-ing a large role in subordinating Woman to Man, and they saw Academia as the quickest route to women's liberation. Also of interest is the fact that although the De-claration's authors faulted the so-called sexual double standard, they faulted it not because it restricted women's sexuality but because it failed to restrict men's sexu-ality. No plea was made to increase women's reproductive freedom, and it was simply assumed that the care of children was both woman's duty and first love. Pre-dictably, for the times, no mention was made of women's racial, class, or religious dif-ferences, as if all women were white, married or related to well-to-do men, and Christian.

The dominant messages of the Declaration of Sentiments were: (1) that men and women are created equal; (2) that it is the role of Government to help women as well as men secure their inalienable rights as human beings; and (3) that it is the responsibility of an oppressed group—in this case women—to refuse allegiance to any Government which denies them what it grants to the non-oppressed group—in this case men.

Over a century after the Declaration was proclaimed, NOW passed its 1967 Bill of Rights. Although women's suffrage was well established in law and practice by then, women continued to have far less [sic] opportunities than men to pursue their interests in the so-called public world. Unlike the authors of the Declaration of Sentiments, the authors of NOW's Bill of Rights identified women's childbearing ability and child-rearing role as the primary cause of women's inability to compete equally with men in the political forum, the academic arena, and the marketplace. Thus, NOW's authors pressed for more permissive contraception and abortion legislation, publicly subsidized child-care facilities, and maternity leave policies.

Expanding the limits of the Declaration even more, NOW's Bill of Rights mentioned race in its demand that "equal employment opportunity be guaranteed to all women, as well as men, by insisting that the EEOC enforces the prohibitions against racial discrimination."[39] And it made mention of class in its demand that "poor women be given the right" to secure job training, housing, and family allowances on equal terms with men, but without prejudice to a parent's right to remain at home to care for his or her children.[40] Like the authors of the Declaration of Sentiments, the authors of NOW's Bill of Rights stressed that women had a right "to be educated to their full potential equally with men,"[41] but unlike the Declaration of Sentiments' authors, the Bill of Rights' authors ignored topics such as morals, religion, and women's self-images. The dominant messages of NOW's Bill of Rights were: (1) that legislation can prevent the subordination of U.S. women to U.S. men; and (2) that what U.S. women want, more than anything, is equal opportunity to compete against men in the so-called public world.

Clearly, NOW's 1967 Bill of Rights forwarded a second-wave liberal feminist agenda focused on educational, economic, and political gender disparities. Thus, second-wave radical feminists were correct to challenge its authors for failing to highlight the ways in which women's sexual roles as well as women's reproductive roles contribute to the subordination of women to men. With reference to the issue of violence against women in pornography, prostitution, sexual harassment, rape, and domestic battery as well as the issue of women's sexual preference (heterosexual or lesbian), NOW's authors were silent. Like some of their first-wave predecessors, these second-wave feminists chose to downplay such issues on the grounds that they would unnecessarily alienate many men and non-feminist women.

NOW's aim was, it seemed, to produce a Bill of Rights that most mainstream Americans could accept. Therefore, only the most public of problems, such as education and employment, were addressed; more personal or private issues were avoided in this attempt to make the Bill of Rights acceptable to the mainstream. As a result, this Bill of Rights and second-wave liberal feminists managed to make few substantial changes in women's personal and private roles. They won for women the right to work a double day, to be the Superwoman who works as hard as a man during the day in the business world, and then works just as hard at night in her home cooking, cleaning, and caring for her loved ones.

In contrast to both the 1848 Declaration of Sentiments and the 1967 Bill of Rights, the 1995 Beijing Declaration was written with the realization that women are not the same, but very different from each other.[42] The authors of the Beijing Declaration admitted that women's overall estate was far better in the year 2000 than it had been in the year 1900, but that progress had been uneven. Mention was made of *men's* roles as well as women's roles in ending all forms of oppression, particularly gender oppression. Women's rights were repeatedly mentioned, but they were spoken of as women's *"human rights."*[43]

Moreover, reminiscent of the 1848 Declaration of Sentiments, mention was made of "the right to freedom of thought, conscience, religion and belief, thus contributing to the moral, ethical, spiritual and intellectual needs of women and men."[44] Unlike the authors of NOW's Bill of Rights, the authors of the Beijing Declaration used language that goes beyond "equal rights opportunities,"[45] and focuses on the implementation and realization of the goals set forth in the document. Although the Beijing Declaration's authors made it clear that women's political and personal freedom depends on women's economic well-being, they also made it clear that a free woman is a woman who is in charge of her procreative freedom and who does not live in fear of what pain men can inflict on her body and suffering on her spirit.

Clearly, the Beijing Declaration is sensitive to issues of race, class, national origin, and religion. Its message is not an individualistic assertion of rights, but a collective expression of people's basic needs. Its theme concerns women from all over the world working with each other and men to achieve equality in opportunity and access. This goal is akin to what Mies, Shiva, and other third-wave or global and multicultural feminists have termed a "subsistence life-style,"[46] the only lifestyle these feminists believe is compatible with gender equity. This kind of lifestyle demands much from First-World and Third-World people, but particularly from First-World people. It requires that everyone take as many of the following steps as possible.

1. People should produce only enough to satisfy fundamental human needs, resisting the urge to produce "an ever-growing mountain of commodities and money (wages or profit)"[47] in a futile attempt to still people's endless and insatiable wants.
2. People should use only as much of nature as they need to, treating it as a reality with "her own subjectivity;"[48] and people should use each other not to make money but to create communities capable of meeting people's fundamental needs, especially their need for intimacy.
3. People should replace representative democracy with participatory democracy so that each man and woman has the opportunity to express his or her concerns to everyone else.
4. People should develop "multidimensional or synergic"[49] problem-solving approaches, since the problems of contemporary society are interrelated.
5. People should combine contemporary science, technologies, and knowledge with ancient wisdom, traditions, and even magic.
6. People should break down the boundaries between work and play, the sciences and the arts, spirit and matter.
7. People should view water, air, earth, and all natural resources as community goods rather than as private possessions.

8. Men as well as women should adopt the socialist-transformative ecofeminist view, the subsistence perspective. . . .

9. Men as well as women should cultivate traditional feminine virtues (caring, compassion, nurturance) and engage in subsistence productions, for "only a society based on a subsistence perspective can afford to live in peace with nature, and uphold peace between nations, generations and men and women. . . ."[50]

10. Most importantly, people should realize that in order for each person to have enough, no person can "have it all. . . ."

The kind of third-wave feminist projected by the authors of the Beijing Declaration is very different from the kind of "feminist" that Naomi Wolf, Katie Roiphe, Camille Paglia, and René Denfield celebrate in their writings.[51] Terming themselves "power" as opposed to "victim" feminists,[52] these so-called postfeminists tend to focus on the sexual arena as the locus of women's empowerment. They want women to "have it all." For example, Wolf announces in her book that she wants "to be a serious thinker and not hide the fact that I have breasts; I want female sexuality to accompany, rather than undermine, female political power."[53]

Repeatedly, each of these postfeminists stresses that, at least in the United States, women are free to seize the day (carpe diem), to be whoever they want to be, and do whatever they want to do. Their only "enemy" is themselves. Forgetting that so much of the "power" they feel has to do with their advantaged socioeconomic position, these postfeminist celebrations of women's power are realized in selfishness, as portrayed by television characters such as Ally McBeal. . . .

Contemporary, third-wave, new-millennium feminism is difficult to describe succinctly and accurately. In fact, feminism has always been difficult to analyze. Even in 1913, a woman wrote: "I myself have never been able to find out precisely what feminism is. . . . I only know that people call me a feminist whenever I express sentiments that differentiate me from a doormat, or a prostitute."[54] The reason why it is not yet time to bid adieu to feminism is precisely the fact that so many pseudo-feminists like Ally McBeal have emerged on the scene. Admittedly, part of eliminating gender oppression is breaking into the "boy's club," as well as being as sexual as one desires, but this is only part of it. The other part is asking one's self some troubling questions about women who struggle to support their families on paltry wages, about shy girls who get pawed by predatory men, and about wondering how one's high salary and liberated sexuality might be contributing to the pain and suffering these women experience. Feminism is about justice, but it is also about caring—caring enough to make some sacrifices in one's own life so that women across the United States and around the globe, particularly women who may not be of one's own race or class, may experience more of life's opportunities.

Notes

1. Mary Wollstonecraft, *A Vindication of the Rights of Woman*, ed. Carol H. Poston (New York: W. W. Norton, 1975), 34.

2. Wollstonecraft, 61.

3. Sarah M. Grimké, *Letters on the Equality of the Sexes and the Conditions of Woman* (Boston: Isaac Knapp, 1838, reprinted by Source Book Press, New York, 1970), 9–10; 51; 85–86.

4. Judith Hole and Ellen Levine, *Rebirth of Feminism* (New York: Quadrangle Books, 1971), 434.

5. Hole and Levine, 434.

6. Caroline Bird, *Born Female* (New York: David McKay Company, 1968), 1.

7. Hole and Levine, 90.

8. Betty Friedan, "NOW—How It Began," *Women Speaking* (April 1967), 4.

9. "Declaration of Sentiments," *Self* (July 1998): 106–7.

10. "NOW (National Organization for Women) Bill of Rights" (Adopted at NOW's first national conference, Washington, D.C., 1967), in *Sisterhood is Powerful;* ed. Robin Morgan (New York: Random House, 1970), 513–14.

11. See Rosemarie Putnam Tong, *Feminist Thought: A More Comprehensive Introduction,* 2nd ed. (Boulder, CO: Westview Press, 1998), 47–48, for [the] distinction between radical-libertarian and radical-cultural feminists.

12. Shulamith Firestone, *The Dialectic of Sex* (New York: Bantam Books, 1970), 198.

13. Firestone, 190.

14. Tong, *Feminist Thought,* 47.

15. Linda Alcoff, "Cultural Feminism versus Poststructuralism: The Identity Crisis in Feminist Theory," *Signs: Journal of Women in Culture and Society* 13, no. 3 (1988): 488.

16. Adrienne Rich, *Of Women Born* (New York: W. W. Norton, 1976); Sara Ruddick. "Maternal Thinking," in *Mothering: Essays in Feminist Theory,* ed. Joyce Trebilcot (Totowa, N.J.: Rowman and Allanheld, 1984).

17. Alice Echols, "The New Feminism of Yin and Yang," in *Powers of Desire: The Politics of Sexuality,* ed. Ann Snitow, Christine Stansell, and Sharon Thompson (New York: Monthly Review Press, 1983), 445.

18. Alison M. Jaggar, "Feminist Ethics," in *Encyclopedia of Ethics,* eds. Lawrence Becker and Charlotte Becker (New York: Garland, 1992), 364.

19. Judith Grant, *Fundamental Feminism: Contesting the Care Concepts of Feminist Theory* (New York: Routledge, 1993), 25–26.

20. Grant, 31–33.

21. Grant, 32–33.

22. Tong, *Feminist Thought,* 6–7; 278.

23. Elizabeth Grosz, "Sexual Difference and the Problem of Essentialism," in *The Essential Difference,* eds. Naomi Schor and Elizabeth Weed (Bloomington, IN: Indiana University Press, 1994), 91.

24. Linda Alcoff, "Cultural Feminism versus Post-Structuralism: The Identity Crisis in Feminist Theory," *Signs: A Journal of Women in Culture and Society* 13, no. 3 (1988): 434–35.

25. Teresa de Lauretis, "The Essence of the Triangle or, Taking Risks of Essentialism Seriously," in *The Essential Difference,* ed. Schor and Weed (Bloomington: Indiana University Press, 1994), 10.

26. Christine de Stephano, "Dilemmas of Difference," in *Feminism/Postmodernism,* ed. Linda J. Nicholson (New York: Routledge, 1990), 75.

27. De Stephano, 63.

28. Elizabeth V. Spelman, *Inessential Woman: Problems of Exclusion in Feminist Thought* (Boston: Beacon Press, 1988), 12.

29. Spelman, 178.

30. bell hooks, *Feminist Theory: From Margin to Center* (Boston: South End Press, 1984), 404.
31. hooks, 404.
32. hooks, 404.
33. hooks, 404.
34. Alison Jaggar, "Globalizing Feminist Ethics," *Hypatia* 13, no. 2 (Spring 1998): 27.
35. Maria Mies, "The Myths of Catching-Up Development," in *Ecofeminism,* ed. Maria Mies and Vandana Shiva (London: Zed, 1993), 60.
36. Mies, "The Myths of Catching-Up Development," 67.
37. "Declaration of Sentiments," 107.
38. "Declaration of Sentiments," 107.
39. "NOW Bill of Rights," in *Sisterhood is Powerful,* ed. Robin Morgan, 513–14.
40. *Sisterhood is Powerful,* 513–14.
41. *Sisterhood is Powerful,* 513–14.
42. "The Beijing Declaration," in *Women in the Third World: An Encyclopedia of Contemporary Issues,* ed. Nelly P. Stromquist (New York: Garland, 1998), 673–75.
43. "The Beijing Declaration," 673.
44. "The Beijing Declaration," 673.
45. "The Beijing Declaration," 673.
46. Tong, *Feminist Thought,* 271.
47. Maria Mies, "The Need for a New Vision: The Subsistence Perspective," in *Ecofeminism,* ed. Maria Mies and Vandana Shiva (London: Zed, 1993), 319.
48. Mies, "The Need for a New Vision," 319.
49. Mies, "The Need for a New Vision," 320.
50. Mies, "The Need for a New Vision," 322.
51. Naomi Wolf, *Fire With Fire: The New Female Power and How It Will Change the Twenty-First Century* (New York: Random House, 1993); Katie Roiphe, *The Morning After: Sex, Fear, and Feminism on Campus* (New York: Little, Brown, 1993); Camille Paglia, *Sex, Art, and American Culture: Essays* (New York: Random House, 1992); René Denfield, *The New Victorians: A Young Woman's Challenges to the Old Feminist Order* (New York: Warner Books, 1995).
52. Leslie Heywood and Jennifer Drake, "Introduction," in *Third-Wave Agenda: Being Feminist, Doing Feminism,* ed. Leslie Heywood and Jennifer Drake (Minneapolis: University of Minnesota Press, 1997), 3.
53. Wolf, *Fire With Fire,* 185.
54. Nancy Gibbs, "The War Against Feminism," *Time* (March 9, 1992): 51.

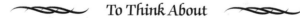

To Think About

1. Comment on the following statements:

    a. "Love is an institution where power expressions are found."   ***Kate Millet***

    b. "Men place women on pedestals because women bug them at eye level."
    Margaret Mead

    c. "Marriage means rape and life-long slavery."   ***Unknown***

    d. "In our society, men are unsexed by failure, women by success."
    Margaret Mead

e. "A woman can be seen as 'enslaved' because she persists in looking for her identity as a man." **Unknown**

2. On the thematic imperative: "Moral questing in a world without gods and miracles. Fatherless and motherless, we seek to discover our true brothers and sisters and lovers and siblings where goodness is possible." **Ann Rice**

3. "Sex is performed with strangers, romance is captured in brief affairs, friendship is assigned to friends. In this formula, one notices, the only stable element is friendship." **John White**

4. "With the collapse of other social values (those of religion, patriotism, the family and so on), sex has been forced to take up the slack, to become our sole mode of transcendence and our only touchstone of authenticity. . . . In our present isolation we have few ways besides sex to feel connected with one another; in the future there might be surer modes for achieving a sense of community." **John White**

5. "Our seemingly infinite longing for connection and intimacy with others coalesces uneasily with our seemingly infinite terror that others will subjugate and destroy our individuality and uniqueness. The passions are centered around the duality of our undeniable need for others and our felt danger at their approach." **Unknown**

6. "At the heart of liberty is the right to define one's own concept of existence, of meaning, of the universe, and of the mystery of human life." **David Souter**

7. "Men see objects, women see the relationship between objects. Whether the objects need each other, love each other, match each other, it is an extra dimension of feeling we men are without, and one that makes war abhorrent to all real women, and absurd." **John Fowles**

8. "What is the meaning in the profound love and joy we experience?" **Unknown**

9. "Any law that uplifts human personality is just. Any law that degrades human personality is unjust." **Martin Luther King, Jr.**

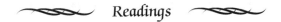

Readings

Jaggar, Alison M., and Iris M. Young, eds. *A Companion to Feminist Philosophy.* Malden, MA: Blackwell, 2000.

Meyers, Diana Tietjens, ed. *Feminist Social Thought: A Reader.* New York: Routledge, 1997.

Sterba, James P., ed. *Social and Political Philosophy: Contemporary Perspectives.* London: Routledge, 2001.

Tong, Rosemarie, and Nancy Tuana, eds. *Feminism and Philosophy: Essential Readings in Theory, Reinterpretation, and Application.* Boulder, CO: Westview Press, 1995.

48
Monarchy Is Best

Thomas Hobbes (1588–1679), *English political philosopher, is the author of* Leviathan *(1651) and a number of other treatises on human nature and society.*

There are many types of political and economic systems among the nations of the world. The economic systems range from almost complete free enterprise to total state control; the political systems range from democracy to strong central governments such as monarchies and dictatorships. These economic and political systems are seen in almost every possible combination. In this section we examine four forms of government: monarchy, communism, and two theories of democracy. Communism and democracy show strong links with economic theory, but all four positions have a basis in a general theory of human nature and society. Communism nearly always combines a state economic system with a dictatorship. Democracy most often is a combination of political democracy and capitalism, although it is also often combined with a modified government-controlled economy such as in the European socialist countries.

Thomas Hobbes, born, as he writes, "with the sound of cannon in my ear," is one of the greatest modern exponents of a theory identifying power and justice, arguing that it is not by nature, but by contract, that human beings enter into political association. Metaphysically a materialist and morally a relativist, Hobbes also based his political philosophy on his deep reading of history and the turmoil of seventeenth-century English political life. Humankind is fundamentally in a state of war or mutual conflict, and can preserve itself only by surrendering its natural rights and liberty to the authority of an absolute sovereign. The sovereign, in return for obedience, agrees to protect the lives of its subjects against domestic and foreign foes. So long as the sovereign preserves its power, its authority cannot be rescinded.

From Thomas Hobbes, *Leviathan,* Parts I and II, ed. Herbert W. Schneider, © 1958. Reprinted by permission of Prentice Hall, Inc., Upper Saddle River, NJ.

461

Sovereign power can rest in the hands of one person (monarchy), several (aristocracy), or all (democracy), but Hobbes has a clear preference for the efficiency of monarchical rule.

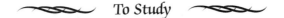 To Study

1. What does Hobbes mean by *power*? How important is it in human life?
2. What does Hobbes mean by *war*? What is the condition of humankind when war is present?
3. What is the state of nature according to Hobbes? Is there any law or morality in the state of nature?
4. What is the commonwealth? How does it secure peace for political subjects?
5. What three forms of commonwealth does Hobbes recognize? Why is monarchy superior to the others?

The POWER of a man, to take it universally, is his present means to obtain some future apparent good, and is either *original* or *instrumental*.

Natural power is the eminence of the faculties of body or mind, as extraordinary strength, form, prudence, arts, eloquence, liberality, nobility. *Instrumental* are those powers which, acquired by these or by fortune, are means and instruments to acquire more, as riches, reputation, friends, and the secret working of God, which men call good luck. For the nature of power is in this point like to fame, increasing as it proceeds; or like the motion of heavy bodies, which, the further they go, make still the more haste.

The greatest of human powers is that which is compounded of the powers of most men united by consent in one person, natural or civil, that has the use of all their powers depending on his will, such as is the power of a commonwealth; or depending on the wills of each particular, such as is the power of a faction or of divers factions leagued. Therefore to have servants is power; to have friends is power: for they are strengths united.

Also riches joined with liberality is power, because it procures friends and servants; without liberality, not so, because in this case they defend not, but expose men to envy, as a prey.

Reputation of power is power, because it draws with it the adherence of those that need protection.

So is reputation of love of a man's country, called popularity, for the same reason.

Also, what quality soever makes a man beloved or feared of many, or the reputation of such quality, is power, because it is a means to have the assistance and service of many.

Good success is power, because it makes reputation of wisdom or good fortune, which makes men either fear him or rely on him.

Affability of men already in power is increase of power, because it gains love.

Reputation of prudence in the conduct of peace or war is power, because to prudent men we commit the government of ourselves more willingly than to others.

Nobility is power, not in all places, but only in those commonwealths where it has privileges, for in such privileges consists their power.

Eloquence is power, because it is seeming prudence.

Form is power, because, being a promise of good, it recommends men to the favor of women and strangers.

The sciences are small power, because not eminent and therefore not acknowledged in any man; nor are at all but in a few, and in them but of a few things. For science is of that nature as none can understand it to be but such as in a good measure have attained it.

Arts of public use—as fortification, making of engines, and other instruments of war—because they confer to defense and victory, are power, and though the true mother of them be science—namely, the mathematics—yet, because they are brought into the light by the hand of the artificer, they be esteemed—the midwife passing with the vulgar for the mother—as his issue. . . .

So that, in the first place, I put for a general inclination of all mankind a perpetual and restless desire of power after power that ceases only in death. And the cause of this is not always that a man hopes for a more intensive delight than he has already attained to, or that he cannot be content with a moderate power, but because he cannot assure the power and means to live well which he has present without the acquisition of more. And from hence it is that kings, whose power is greatest, turn their endeavors to the assuring it at home by laws or abroad by wars; and when that is done, there succeeds a new desire—in some, of fame from new conquest; in others, of ease and sensual pleasure; in others, of admiration or being flattered for excellence in some art or other ability of the mind. . . .

Nature has made men so equal in the faculties of the body and mind as that, though there be found one man sometimes manifestly stronger in body or of quicker mind than another, yet, when all is reckoned together, the difference between man and man is not so considerable as that one man can thereupon claim to himself any benefit to which another may not pretend as well as he. For as to the strength of body, the weakest has strength enough to kill the strongest, either by secret machination or by confederacy with others that are in the same danger with himself.

And as to the faculties of the mind, setting aside the arts grounded upon words, and especially that skill of proceeding upon general and infallible rules called science—which very few have and but in few things, as being not a native faculty born with us, nor attained, as prudence, while we look after somewhat else—I find yet a greater equality among men than that of strength. For prudence is but experience, which equal time equally bestows on all men in those things they equally apply themselves unto. That which may perhaps make such equality incredible is but a vain conceit of one's own wisdom, which almost all men think they have in a greater degree than the vulgar—that is, than all men but themselves and a few others whom, by fame or for concurring with themselves, they approve. For such is the nature of men that howsoever they may acknowledge many others to be more witty or more eloquent or more learned, yet they will hardly believe there be many so wise as themselves; for they see their own wit at hand and other men's at a distance. But this proves rather that men are in that point equal than unequal. For there is not ordinarily a greater sign of the equal distribution of anything than that every man is contented with his share.

From this equality of ability arises equality of hope in the attaining of our ends. And therefore if any two men desire the same thing, which nevertheless they cannot both enjoy, they become enemies; and in the way to their end, which is principally their own conservation, and sometimes their delectation only, endeavor to destroy or subdue one another. And from hence it comes to pass that where an invader has no more to fear than another man's single power, if one plant, sow, build, or possess a convenient seat, others may probably be expected to come prepared with forces united to dispossess and deprive him, not only of the fruit of his labor, but also of his life or liberty. And the invader again is in the like danger of another.

And from this diffidence of one another there is no way for any man to secure himself so reasonable as anticipation—that is, by force or wiles to master the persons of all men he can, so long till he see no other power great enough to endanger him; and this is no more than his own conservation requires, and is generally allowed. Also, because there be some that take pleasure in contemplating their own power in the acts of conquest, which they pursue farther than their security requires, if others that otherwise would be glad to be at ease within modest bounds should not by invasion increase their power, they would not be able, long time, by standing only on their defense, to subsist. And by consequence, such augmentation of dominion over men being necessary to a man's conservation, it ought to be allowed him.

Again, men have no pleasure, but on the contrary a great deal of grief, in keeping company where there is no power able to overawe them all. For every man looks that his companion should value him at the same rate he sets upon himself; and upon all signs of contempt or undervaluing naturally endeavors, as far as he dares (which among them that have no common power to keep them in quiet is far enough to make them destroy each other), to extort a greater value from his contemners by damage and from others by the example.

So that in the nature of man we find three principal causes of quarrel: first, competition; secondly, diffidence; thirdly, glory.

The first makes men invade for gain, the second for safety, and the third for reputation. The first use violence to make themselves masters of other men's persons, wives, children, and cattle; the second, to defend them; the third, for trifles, as a word, a smile, a different opinion, and any other sign of undervalue, either direct in their persons or by reflection in their kindred, their friends, their nation, their profession, or their name.

Hereby it is manifest that, during the time men live without a common power to keep them all in awe, they are in that condition which is called war, and such a war as is of every man against every man. For WAR consists not in battle only, or the act of fighting, but in a tract of time wherein the will to contend by battle is sufficiently known; and therefore the notion of *time* is to be considered in the nature of war as it is in the nature of weather. For as the nature of foul weather lies not in a shower or two of rain but in an inclination thereto of many days together, so the nature of war consists not in actual fighting but in the known disposition thereto during all the time there is no assurance to the contrary. All other time is PEACE.

Whatsoever, therefore, is consequent to a time of war where every man is enemy to every man, the same is consequent to the time wherein men live without other security than what their own strength and their own invention shall furnish them withal. In such condition there is no place for industry, because the fruit thereof is uncertain: and consequently no culture of the earth; no navigation nor use of the commodities that may be imported by sea; no commodious building; no instruments of moving and removing such things as require much force; no knowledge of the face of the earth; no account of time; no arts; no letters; no society; and, which is worst of all, continual fear and danger of violent death; and the life of man solitary, poor, nasty, brutish, and short.

It may seem strange to some man that has not well weighed these things that nature should thus dissociate and render men apt to invade and destroy one another; and he may therefore, not trusting to this inference made from the passions, desire perhaps to have the same confirmed by experience. Let him therefore consider with himself—when taking a journey he arms himself and seeks to go well accompanied, when going to sleep he locks his doors, when even in his house he locks his chests, and this when he knows there be laws and public officers, armed, to revenge all injuries shall be done him—what opinion he has of his fellow subjects when he rides armed, of his fellow citizens when he locks his doors, and of his children and servants when he locks his chests. Does he not there as much accuse mankind by his actions as I do by my words? But neither of us accuse man's nature in it. The desires and other passions of man are in themselves no sin. No more are the actions that proceed from those passions till they know a law that forbids them, which, till laws be made, they cannot know, nor can any law be made till they have agreed upon the person that shall make it.

It may peradventure be thought there was never such a time nor condition of war as this, and I believe it was never generally so over all the world; but there are many places where they live so now. For the savage people in many places of America, except the government of small families, the concord whereof depends on natural lust, have no government at all and live at this day in that brutish manner as I said before. Howsoever, it may be perceived what manner of life there would be where there were no common power to fear by the manner of life which men that have formerly lived under a peaceful government use to degenerate into in a civil war.

But though there had never been any time wherein particular men were in a condition of war one against another, yet in all times kings and persons of sovereign authority, because of their independency, are in continual jealousies and in the state and posture of gladiators, having their weapons pointing and their eyes fixed on one another—that is, their forts, garrisons, and guns upon the frontiers of their kingdoms, and continual spies upon their neighbors—which is a posture of war. But because they uphold thereby the industry of their subjects, there does not follow from it that misery which accompanies the liberty of particular men.

To this war of every man against every man, this also is consequent: that nothing can be unjust. The notions of right and wrong, justice and injustice, have there no place. Where there is no common power, there is no law; where no law, no injustice. Force and fraud are in war the two cardinal virtues. Justice and injustice are none of the faculties neither of the body nor mind. If they were, they might be in a man that were alone in the world, as well as his senses and passions. They are qualities that relate to men in society, not in solitude. It is consequent also to the same condition that there be no propriety, no dominion, no *mine* and *thine* distinct; but only that to be every man's that he can get, and for so long as he can keep it. And thus much for the ill condition which man by mere nature is actually placed in, though with a possibility to come out of it consisting partly in the passions, partly in his reason.

The passions that incline men to peace are fear of death, desire of such things as are necessary to commodious living, and a hope by their industry to obtain them. And reason suggests convenient articles of peace, upon which men may be drawn to agreement. These articles are they which otherwise are called the Laws of Nature. . . .

The final cause, end, or design of men, who naturally love liberty and dominion over others, in the introduction of that restraint upon themselves in which we see them live in commonwealths is the foresight of their own preservation, and of a more contented life thereby—that is to say, of getting themselves out from that miserable condition of war which is necessarily consequent, as has been shown, . . . to the natural passions of men when there is no visible power to keep them in awe and tie them by fear of punishment to the performance of their covenants. . . .

The only way to erect such a common power as may be able to defend them from the invasion of foreigners and the injuries of one another, and thereby to secure them in such sort as that by their own industry and by the fruits of the earth they may nourish themselves and live contentedly, is to confer all their power and strength upon one man, or upon one assembly of men that may reduce all their wills, by plurality of voices, unto one will; which is as much as to say, to appoint one man or assembly of men to bear their person, and everyone to own and acknowledge himself to be author of whatsoever he that so bears their person shall act or cause to be acted in those things which concern the common peace and safety, and therein to submit their wills every one to his will, and their judgments to his judgment. This is more than consent or concord; it is a real unity of them all in one and the same person, made by covenant of every man with every man, in such manner as if every man should say to every man, *I authorize and give up my right of governing myself to this man, or to this assembly of men, on this condition, that you give up your right to him and authorize all his actions in like manner.* This done, the multitude so united in one person is called a COMMONWEALTH, in Latin CIVITAS. This is the generation of the great LEVIATHAN (or rather, to speak more reverently, of that *mortal god*) to which we owe, under the *immortal God,* our peace and defense. For by this authority, given him by every particular man in the commonwealth, he has the use of so much power and strength conferred on him that, by terror thereof, he is enabled to form the wills of them all to peace at home and mutual aid against their enemies abroad. And in him consists the essence of the commonwealth, which, to define it, is *one person, of whose acts a great multitude, by mutual covenants one with another, have made themselves every one the author, to the end he may use the strength and means of them all as he shall think expedient for their peace and common defense.* And he that carries this person is called SOVEREIGN and said to have *sovereign power;* and everyone besides, his SUBJECT. . . .

The difference of commonwealths consists in the difference of the sovereign, or the person representative of all and every one of the multitude. And because the sovereignty is either in one man or in an assembly of more than one, and into that assembly either every man has right to enter, or not every one but certain men distinguished from the rest, it is manifest there can be but three kinds of commonwealth. For the representative must needs be one man or more, and if more then it is the assembly of all or but of a part. When the representative is one man, then is the commonwealth a MONARCHY; when an assembly of all that will come together, then it is DEMOCRACY or popular commonwealth; when an assembly of a part only, then it is called an ARISTOCRACY. Other kind of commonwealth there can be none, for either one or more or all must have the sovereign power, which I have shown to be indivisible, entire.

There be other names of government in the histories and books of policy, as *tyranny* and *oligarchy;* but they are not the names of other forms of government, but of the same forms misliked. For they that are discontented under *monarchy* call it *tyranny,* and they that are displeased with *aristocracy* call it *oligarchy;* so also, they which find themselves grieved under a *democracy* call it *anarchy,* which signifies want of government, and yet I think no man believes that want of government is any new kind of government; nor by the same reason ought they to believe that the government is of one kind when they like it and another when they mislike it or are oppressed by the governors. . . .

The difference between these three kinds of commonwealth consists not in the difference of power but in the difference of convenience or aptitude to produce the peace and security of the people, for which end they were instituted. And to compare monarchy with the other two, we may observe, first, that whosoever bears the person of the people, or is one of that assembly that bears it, bears also his own natural person. And though he be careful in his politic person to procure the common interest, yet he is more or no less careful to procure the private good of himself, his family, kindred, and friends; and for the most part, if the public interest chance to cross the private, he prefers the private; for the passions of men are commonly more potent than their reason. From whence it follows that where the public and private interest are most closely united, there is the public most advanced. Now in monarchy the private interest is the same with the public. The riches, power, and honor of a monarch arise only from the riches, strength, and reputation of his subjects. For no king can be rich nor glorious nor secure whose subjects are either poor or contemptible or too weak through want or dissension to maintain a war against their enemies; whereas in a democracy or aristocracy, the public prosperity confers not so much to the private fortune of one that is corrupt or ambitious as does many times a perfidious advice, a treacherous action, or a civil war.

To Think About

1.   "Power tends to corrupt, and absolute power corrupts absolutely." ***Lord Acton***
2.   "Power gradually extirpates from the mind every human and gentle virtue. Pity, benevolence, friendship, are things almost unknown in high stations."

Edmund Burke

3. "Life is a search after power."   ***Ralph Waldo Emerson***

4. "Power corrupts the few, while weakness corrupts the many."   ***Eric Hoffer***

5. "Democracies are usually the best calculated to direct the end of law; aristocracies to invent the means by which that end shall be obtained; and monarchies to carry those means into execution."   ***Sir William Blackstone***

6. "If government is in the hands of a few they will tyrannize the many; if in the hands of the many, they will tyrannize the few. It ought to be in the hands of both, and they should be separated. . . . If separated, they will need a mutual check. This check is a monarch."   ***Alexander Hamilton***

7. "As virtue is necessary in a republic, and in a monarchy honor, so fear is necessary in a despotism."   ***Montesquieu***

<hr>

~~~ Readings ~~~

OAKESHOTT, MICHAEL. *Hobbes on Civil Association.* Berkeley: University of California Press, 1975.

SORELL, TOM, ed. *The Cambridge Companion to Hobbes.* Cambridge: Cambridge University Press, 1996.

STRAUSS, LEO. *The Political Philosophy of Hobbes.* Chicago: University of Chicago Press, 1984 (1952).

TUCK, RICHARD. *Hobbes.* Oxford: Oxford University Press, 1989.

49
Democracy Is Best

John Locke (1632–1704), English philosopher, wrote two major works regarded as classics, An Essay Concerning Human Understanding *(1690), which was discussed in Reading 27, and* Two Treatises of Government *(1689).*

John Locke, England's greatest political philosopher after Hobbes, differs sharply with Hobbes's pessimistic estimate of human nature and government while maintaining with him that political association arises out of human choice and contract. Human beings, while born in perfect liberty and equality, are prompted by reason and nature to cooperate and organize into political bodies. Having a natural right to life and property, they invest the sovereign with the authority to protect them against those who choose to live outside the law of nature but maintain the right to depose the sovereign if they think fit. Political power can be embodied in any number of persons, as Hobbes too had thought, but Locke argues that democracy best suits his theory of human nature. Locke's liberalism and republicanism deeply influenced the colonists of North America and served to justify their rebellion against the English king. Many of Locke's positions, and much of his language, find themselves in the American Declaration of Independence.

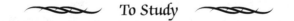 To Study

1. What does Locke mean by the *state of nature?* How does it differ from the state of war?
2. Is civil society "natural" for Locke? If not, how does it differ from the state of nature?
3. What is Locke's opinion on the nature of absolute monarchy?
4. What role does the majority play in Locke's conception of civil government?

From John Locke, *Second of Two Treatises of Government,* 1690, chapters 2, 3, 7, 8, 9, 10.

5. What does Locke mean by *property?* What is government's role in protecting it?

6. What forms of government does Locke recognize? Does he express preference for any one of them?

To understand political power aright, and derive it from its original, we must consider what estate all men are naturally in, and that is, a state of perfect freedom to order their actions, and dispose of their possessions and persons as they think fit, within the bounds of the law of Nature, without asking leave or depending upon the will of any other man.

A state also of equality, wherein all the power and jurisdiction is reciprocal, no one having more than another, there being nothing more evident than that creatures of the same species and rank, promiscuously born to all the same advantages of Nature, and the use of the same faculties, should also be equal one amongst another, without subordination or subjection, unless the lord and master of them all should, by any manifest declaration of his will, set one above another, and confer on him, by an evident and clear appointment, an undoubted right to dominion and sovereignty. . . .

But though this be a state of liberty, yet it is not a state of licence; though man in that state have an uncontrollable liberty to dispose of his person or possessions, yet he has not liberty to destroy himself, or so much as any creature in his possession, but where some nobler use than its bare preservation calls for it. The state of Nature has a law of Nature to govern it, which obliges every one, and reason, which is that law, teaches all mankind who will but consult it, that being all equal and independent, no one ought to harm another in his life, health, liberty or possessions. . . . Every one as he is bound to preserve himself, and not to quit his station wilfully, so by the like reason, when his own preservation comes not in competition, ought he as much as he can to preserve the rest of mankind, and not unless it be to do justice on an offender, take away or impair the life, or what tends to the preservation of the life, the liberty, health, limb, or goods of another. . . .

The state of war is a state of enmity and destruction; and therefore declaring by word or action, not a passionate and hasty, but sedate, settled design upon another man's life puts him in a state of war with him against whom he has declared such an intention, and so has exposed his life to the other's power to be taken away by him, or any one that joins with him in his defence, and espouses his quarrel; it being reasonable and just I should have a right to destroy that which threatens me with destruction; for by the fundamental law of Nature, man being to be preserved as much as possible, when all cannot be preserved, the safety of the innocent is to be preferred, and one may destroy a man who makes war upon him, or has discovered an enmity to his being, for the same reason that he may kill a wolf or a lion, because they are not under the ties of the common law of reason, have no other rule but that of force and violence, and so may be treated as a beast of prey, those dangerous and noxious creatures that will be sure to destroy him whenever he falls into their power.

And here we have the plain difference between the state of Nature and the state of war, which however some men have confounded, are as far distant as a state of peace, goodwill, mutual assistance, and preservation; and a state of enmity, malice, violence and mutual destruction are one from another. . . .

God, having made man such a creature that, in His own judgment, it was not good for him to be alone, put him under strong obligations of necessity, convenience, and inclination, to drive him into society, as well as fitted him with understanding and language to continue and enjoy it. The first society was between man and wife, which gave beginning to that between parents and children, to which, in time, that between master and servant came to be added. And though all these might, and commonly did, meet together, and make up but one family, wherein the master or mistress of it had some sort of rule proper to a family, each of these, or all together, came short of "political society," as we shall see if we consider the different ends, ties, and bounds of each of these. . . .

Man being born, as has been proved, with a title to perfect freedom and an uncontrolled enjoyment of all the rights and privileges of the law of Nature, equally with any other man, or number of men in the world, hath by nature a power not only to preserve his property—that is, his life, liberty, and estate, against the injuries and attempts of other men, but to judge of and punish the breaches of that law in others, as he is persuaded the offence deserves, even with death itself, in crimes where the heinousness of the fact, in his opinion, requires it. But because no political society can be, nor subsist, without having in itself the power to preserve the property, and in order thereunto punish the offences of all those of that society, there, and there only, is political society where every one of the members hath quitted this natural power, resigned it up into the hands of the community in all cases that exclude him not from appealing for protection to the law established by it. And thus all private judgment of every particular member being excluded, the community comes to be umpire, and by understanding indifferent rules and men authorised by the community for their execution, decides all the differences that may happen between any members of that society concerning any matter of right, and punishes those offences which any member hath committed against the society with such penalties as the law has established; whereby it is easy to discern who are, and are not, in political society together. Those who are united into one body, and have a common established law and judicature to appeal to, with authority to decide controversies between them and punish offenders, are in civil society one with another; but those who have no such common appeal, I mean on earth, are still in the state of Nature, each being where there is no other, judge for himself and executioner; which is, as I have before showed it, the perfect state of Nature.

And thus the commonwealth comes by a power to set down what punishment shall belong to the several transgressions they think worthy of it, committed amongst the members of that society (which is the power of making laws), as well as it has the power to punish any injury done unto any of its members by any one that is not of it (which is the power of war and peace); and all this for the preservation of the property of all the members of that society, as far as is possible. But though every man entered into society has quitted his power to punish offences against the law of Nature in prosecution of his own private judgment, yet with the judgment of offences which he has given up to the legislative, in all cases where he can appeal to the magistrate, he has given up a right to the commonwealth to employ his force for the execution of the judgments of the commonwealth whenever he shall be called to it, which, indeed, are his own judgments, they being made by himself or his representative. And herein we have the original of the legislative and executive power of civil society, which is to judge by standing laws how far offences are to be punished when committed within the commonwealth; and also by occasional judgments founded on the present circumstances of the fact, how far injuries from without are to be vindicated, and in both these to employ all the force of all the members when there shall be need.

Wherever, therefore, any number of men so unite into one society as to quit every one his executive power of the law of Nature, and to resign it to the public, there and there only is a political or civil society. And this is done wherever any number of men, in the state of Nature, enter into society to make one people one body politic under one supreme government: or else when any one joins himself to, and incorporates with any government already made. For hereby he authorises the society, or which is all one, the legislative thereof, to make laws for him as the public good of the society shall require, to the execution whereof his own assistance (as to his own decrees) is due. And this puts men out of a state of Nature into that of a commonwealth, by setting up a judge on earth with authority to determine all the controversies and redress the injuries that may happen to any member of the commonwealth, which judge is the legislative or magistrates appointed by it. And wherever there are any number of men, however associated, that have no such decisive power to appeal to, there they are still in the state of Nature.

And hence it is evident that absolute monarchy, which by some men is counted for the only government in the world, is indeed inconsistent with civil society, and so can be no form of civil government at all. For the end of civil society being to avoid and remedy those inconveniencies of the state of Nature which necessarily follow from every man's being judge in his own case, by setting up a known authority to which every one of that society may appeal upon any injury received, or controversy that may arise, and which every one of the society ought to obey. Wherever any persons are who have not such an authority to appeal to, and decide any difference between them there, those persons are still in the state of Nature. And so is every absolute prince in respect of those who are under his dominion. . . .

Men being, as has been said, by nature all free, equal, and independent, no one can be put out of this estate and subjected to the political power of another without his own consent, which is done by agreeing with other men, to join and unite into a community for their comfortable, safe, and peaceable living, one amongst another, in a secure enjoyment of their properties, and a greater security against any that are not of it. This any number of men may do, because it injures not the freedom of the rest; they are left, as they were, in the liberty of the state of Nature. When any number of men have so consented to make one community or government, they are thereby presently incorporated, and make one body politic, wherein the majority have a right to act and conclude the rest.

For, when any number of men have, by the consent of every individual, made a community, they have thereby made that community one body, with a power to act as one body, which is only by the will and determination of the majority. For that which acts any community, being only the consent of the individuals of it, and it being one body, must move one way, it is necessary the body should move that way whither the greater force carries it, which is the consent of the majority, or else it is impossible it should act or continue one body, one community, which the consent of every individual that united into it agreed that it should; and so every one is bound by that consent to be concluded by the majority. And therefore we see that in assemblies empowered to act by positive laws where no number is set by that positive law which empowers them, the act of the majority passes for the act of the whole, and of course determines as having, by the law of Nature and reason, the power of the whole.

And thus every man, by consenting with others to make one body politic under one government, puts himself under an obligation to every one of that society to submit to the determination of the majority, and to be concluded by it; or else this original compact, whereby he with others incorporates into one society, would signify nothing, and be no compact if he be left free and under no other ties than he was in before in the state of Nature. For what appearance would there be of any compact? What new engagement if he were no farther tied by any decrees of the society than he himself thought fit and did actually consent to? This would be still as great a liberty as he himself had before his compact, or any one else in the state of Nature, who may submit himself and consent to any acts of it if he thinks fit.

For if the consent of the majority shall not in reason be received as the act of the whole, and conclude every individual, nothing but the consent of every individual can make anything to be the act of the whole, which, considering the infirmities of health and avocations of business, which in a number though much less than that of a commonwealth, will necessarily keep many away from the public assembly; and the variety of opinions and contrariety of interests which unavoidably happen in all collections of men, it is next impossible ever to be had. And, therefore, if coming into society be upon such terms, it will be only like Cato's coming into the theatre, *tantum ut exiret.*[1] Such a constitution as this would make the mighty leviathan of a shorter duration than the feeblest creatures, and not let it outlast the day it was born in, which cannot be supposed till we can think that rational creatures should desire and constitute societies only to be dissolved. For where the majority cannot conclude the rest, there they cannot act as one body, and consequently will be immediately dissolved again.

Whosoever, therefore, out of a state of Nature unite into a community, must be understood to give up all the power necessary to the ends for which they unite into society to the majority of the community, unless they expressly agreed in any number greater than the majority. And this is done by barely agreeing to unite into one political society, which is all the compact that is, or needs be, between the individuals that enter into or make up a commonwealth. And thus, that which begins and actually constitutes any political society is nothing but the consent of any number of freemen capable of majority, to unite and incorporate into such a society. And this is that, and that only, which did or could give beginning to any lawful government in the world. . . .

If man in the state of Nature be so free as has been said, if he be absolute lord of his own person and possessions, equal to the greatest and subject to nobody, why

---

[1] So that he might just leave it. [ED.]

will he part with his freedom, this empire, and subject himself to the dominion and control of any other power? To which it is obvious to answer, that though in the state of Nature he hath such a right, yet the enjoyment of it is very uncertain and constantly exposed to the invasion of others; for all being kings as much as he, every man his equal, and the greater part no strict observers of equity and justice, the enjoyment of the property he has in this state is very unsafe, very insecure. This makes him willing to quit this condition which, however free, is full of fears and continual dangers; and it is not without reason that he seeks out and is willing to join in society with others who are already united, or have a mind to unite for the mutual preservation of their lives, liberties and estates, which I call by the general name—property.

The great and chief end, therefore, of men uniting into commonwealths, and putting themselves under government, is the preservation of their property; to which in the state of Nature there are many things wanting.

Firstly, there wants an established, settled, known law, received and allowed by common consent to be the standard of right and wrong, and the common measure to decide all controversies between them. For though the law of Nature be plain and intelligible to all rational creatures, yet men, being biased by their interest, as well as ignorant for want of study of it, are not apt to allow of it as a law binding to them in the application of it to their particular cases.

Secondly, in the state of Nature there wants a known and indifferent judge, with authority to determine all differences according to the established law. For every one in that state being both judge and executioner of the law of Nature, men being partial to themselves, passion and revenge is very apt to carry them too far, and with too much heat in their own cases, as well as negligence and unconcernedness, make them too remiss in other men's.

Thirdly, in the state of Nature there often wants power to back and support the sentence when right, and to give it due execution. They who by any injustice offended will seldom fail where they are able by force to make good their injustice. Such resistance many times makes the punishment dangerous, and frequently destructive to those who attempt it.

Thus mankind, notwithstanding all the privileges of the state of Nature, being but in an ill condition while they remain in it are quickly driven into society. Hence it comes to pass, that we seldom find any number of men live any time together in this state. The inconveniencies that they are therein exposed to by the irregular and uncertain exercise of the power every man has of punishing the transgressions of others, make them take sanctuary under the established laws of government, and therein seek the preservation of their property. It is this makes them so willingly give up every one his single power of punishing to be exercised by such alone as shall be appointed to it amongst them, and by such rules as the community, or those authorised by them to that purpose, shall agree on. And in this we have the original right and rise of both the legislative and executive power as well as of the governments and societies themselves. . . .

The majority having, as has been showed, upon men's first uniting into society, the whole power of the community naturally in them, may employ all that power in making laws for the community from time to time, and executing those laws by officers of their own appointing, and then the form of the government is a perfect democracy; or else may put the power of making laws into the hands of a few select men, and their heirs or successors, and then it is an oligarchy; or else into the hands of one man, and then it is a monarchy; if to him and his heirs, it is a hereditary monarchy; if to him only for life, but upon his death the power only of nominating a successor, to return to them, an elective monarchy. And so accordingly of these make compounded and mixed forms of government, as they think good. And if the legislative power be at first given by the majority to one or more persons only for their lives, or any limited time, and then the supreme power to revert to them again, when it is so reverted the community may dispose of it again anew into what hands they please, and so constitute a new form of government; for the form of government depending upon the placing the supreme power, which is the legislative, it being impossible to conceive that an inferior power should prescribe to a superior, or any but the supreme make laws, according as the power of making laws is placed, such is the form of the commonwealth.

To Think About

1. "The goal of democracy is freedom; of oligarchy, wealth; of aristocracy, the maintenance of education and national institutions; of tyranny, the protection of the tyrant."
   Aristotle

2. "The power of perpetuating our property in our families is one of the most valuable circumstances belonging to it, and that which tends the most to the perpetuation of society itself."
   Edmund Burke

3. In 1787 **Thomas Jefferson** said, "God forbid, we should ever be twenty years without such a rebellion." Elsewhere he elaborated: "What country can preserve its liberties, if its rulers are not warned from time to time, that this people preserve the spirit of resistance? Let them take arms. . . . The tree of liberty, must be refreshed from time to time, with the blood of patriots and tyrants."

4. "The true patriot is one who gives his highest loyalty not to his country as it is but to his own best conceptions of what it can and ought to be."
   Albert Camus

Readings

ASHCRAFT, RICHARD, ed. *John Locke: Critical Assessments.* London and New York: Routledge, 1991.

CHAPPELL, V. C., ed. *John Locke: Political Philosophy.* New York: Garland, 1992.

GOUGH, J. W. *John Locke's Political Philosophy: Eight Studies.* 2nd ed. Oxford: Clarendon Press, 1973.

LAMPRECHT, STERLING. *The Moral and Political Philosophy of John Locke.* New York: Russell & Russell, 1972.

50
Communism and
Nonalienated Labor Is Best

Karl Marx (1818–83) was born in Germany and lived in London after 1850. He wrote his Ph.D. thesis (1842) on Greek atomistic philosophy. Marx was the editor of Rheinische Zeitung *(1842), which was suppressed in 1843. He joined* **Friedrich Engels** *in Paris to develop the theory of socialism. He criticized Proudhon (1847) and founded the First International Workingmen's Association (1864). He is the author of* Communist Manifesto *(1847),* Das Kapital *(1867),* Civil War in France *(1871), and* Critique of Political Economy *(1859).*

Communism

As we have seen, there are many types of political and economic systems, ranging from almost complete free enterprise to almost total state economic control and from democracy to dictatorship. Among the best known of the many combinations of these systems are communism, which nearly always combines a state economic system with a dictatorship; fascism, which is a modified capitalism with a dictatorship; and democracy, which most often is a combination of political democracy with capitalism, although it is also often combined with a modified government-controlled economy such as in the European socialist countries.

The program of communism was set forth in 1848 by Marx in the famous *Communist Manifesto,* in which he applies his principles of materialism and dialectical method to the problems of society. It contains a general theory of history, an analysis of the ills of European society, a program of revolutionary action, and, finally, a plea for the union of the laboring classes.

From Karl Marx and Friedrich Engels, *Manifesto of the Communist Party,* trans. Samuel Moore, 1888, from the original German text of 1848, ed. Friedrich Engels (Moscow: Progress Publishers). Footnotes have been omitted.

To Study

1. Into what groups does Marx divide the history of man?
2. Into what groups does he divide present society? How are these groups defined?
3. What characteristics and social actions does Marx attribute to the bourgeoisie?
4. What economic acts does Marx attribute to the bourgeoisie? How does the bourgeoisie overcome its economic crises?
5. Who created the proletariat? How is it defined?
6. What happens to the middle class?
7. Why is the bourgeoisie unfit to rule?
8. What "measures" will the proletariat use to wrestle capital from the bourgeoisie, and so on? How many of these measures are incorporated in American life? Which would you like to see realized? Which removed?

A spectre is haunting Europe—the spectre of Communism. All the Powers of old Europe have entered into a holy alliance to exorcise this spectre: Pope and Czar, Metternich and Guizot, French Radicals and German police spies.

Where is the party in opposition that has not been decried as Communistic by its opponents in power? Where the Opposition that has not hurled back the branding reproach of Communism, against the more advanced opposition parties, as well as against its reactionary adversaries?

Two things result from this fact.

I. Communism is already acknowledged by all European Powers to be itself a Power.

II. It is high time that Communists should openly, in the face of the whole world, publish their views, their aims, their tendencies, and meet this nursery tale of the Spectre of Communism with a Manifesto of the party itself.

To this end, Communists of various nationalities have assembled in London, and sketched the following Manifesto, to be published in the English, French, German, Italian, Flemish and Danish languages.

I. BOURGEOIS AND PROLETARIANS

The history of all hitherto existing society is the history of class struggles.

Freeman and slave, patrician and plebeian, lord and serf, guildmaster and journeyman, in a word, oppressor and oppressed, stood in constant opposition to one another, carried on an uninterrupted, now hidden, now open fight, a fight that each time ended, either in a revolutionary re-constitution of society at large, or in the common ruin of the contending classes.

In the earlier epochs of history, we find almost everywhere a complicated arrangement of society into various orders, a manifold gradation of social rank. In ancient Rome we have patricians, knights, plebeians, slaves; in the Middle Ages, feudal lords, vassals, guild-masters, journeymen, apprentices, serfs; in almost all of these classes, again, subordinate gradations.

The modern bourgeois society that has sprouted from the ruins of feudal society has not done away with class antagonisms. It has but established new classes, new conditions of oppression, new forms of struggle in place of the old ones.

Our epoch, the epoch of the bourgeoisie, possesses, however, this distinctive feature: it has simplified the class antagonisms. Society as a whole is more and more splitting up into two great hostile camps, into two great classes directly facing each other: Bourgeoisie and Proletariat.

From the serfs of the Middle Ages sprang the chartered burghers of the earliest towns. From the burgesses the first elements of the bourgeoisie were developed.

The discovery of America, the rounding of the Cape, opened up fresh ground for the rising bourgeoisie. The East-Indian and Chinese markets, the colonisation of America, trade with the colonies, the increase in the means of exchange and in commodities generally, gave to commerce, to navigation, to industry, an impulse never before known, and thereby, to the revolutionary element in the tottering feudal society, a rapid development.

The feudal system of industry, under which industrial production was monopolised by closed guilds, now no longer sufficed for the growing wants of the new markets. The manufacturing system took its place. The guild-masters were pushed on one side by the manufacturing middle class; division of labour between the different corporate guilds vanished in the face of division of labour in each single workshop.

Meantime the markets kept ever growing, the demand ever rising. Even manufacture no longer sufficed. Thereupon, steam and machinery revolutionised industrial production. The place of manufacture was taken by the giant, Modern Industry, the place of the industrial middle class, by industrial millionaires, the leaders of whole industrial armies, the modern bourgeois.

Modern industry has established the world market, for which the discovery of America paved the way. This market has given an immense development to commerce, to navigation, to communication by land. This development has, in its turn, reacted on the extension of industry; and in proportion as industry, commerce, navigation, railways extended, in the same proportion the bourgeoisie developed, increased its capital, and pushed into the background every class handed down from the Middle Ages.

We see, therefore, how the modern bourgeoisie is itself the product of a long course of development, of a series of revolutions in the modes of production and of exchange. . . .

The bourgeoisie, wherever it has got the upper hand, has put an end to all feudal, patriarchal, idyllic relations. It has pitilessly torn asunder the motley feudal ties that bound man to his "natural superiors," and has left remaining no other nexus between man and man than naked self-interest, than callous "cash payment." It has drowned the most heavenly ecstasies of religious fervour, of chivalrous enthusiasm, of philistine sentimentalism, in the icy water of egotistical calculation. It has resolved personal worth into exchange value, and in place of the numberless indefeasible chartered freedoms, has set up that single, unconscionable freedom—Free Trade. In one word, for exploitation, veiled by religious and political illusions, it has substituted naked, shameless, direct, brutal exploitation.

The bourgeoisie has stripped of its halo every occupation hitherto honoured and looked up to with reverent awe. It has converted the physician, the lawyer, the priest, the poet, the man of science, into its paid wage-labourers.

The bourgeoisie has torn away from the family its sentimental zeal and has reduced the family relation to a mere money relation.

The bourgeoisie has disclosed how it came to pass that the brutal display of vigor in the Middle Ages, which Reactionists so much admire, found its fitting complement in the most slothful indolence. It has been the first to show what man's activity can bring about. It has accomplished wonders far surpassing Egyptian pyramids, Roman aqueducts, and Gothic cathedrals; it has conducted expeditions that put in the shade all former Exoduses of nations and crusades.

The bourgeoisie cannot exist without constantly revolutionising the instruments of production, and thereby the relations of production, and with them the whole relations of society. Conservation of the old modes of production in unaltered form, was, on the contrary, the first condition of existence for all earlier industrial classes. Constant revolutionising of production, uninterrupted disturbance of all social conditions, everlasting uncertainty and agitation distinguished the bourgeois epoch from all earlier ones. All fixed, fast-frozen relations, with their train of ancient and venerable prejudices and opinions are swept away, all new-formed ones become antiquated before they can ossify. All that is solid melts into air, all that is holy is profaned, and man is at last compelled to face with sober senses, his real conditions of life, and his relations with his kind.

The need of a constantly expanding market for its products chases the bourgeoisie over the whole surface of the globe. It must nestle everywhere, settle everywhere, establish connexions everywhere.

The bourgeoisie has through its exploitation of the world market given a cosmopolitan character to production and consumption in every country. To the great chagrin of Reactionists, it has drawn from under the feet of industry the national ground on which it stood. All old-established national industries have been destroyed or are daily being destroyed. They are dislodged by new industries, whose introduction becomes a life and death question for all civilized nations, by industries that no longer work up indigenous raw material, but raw material drawn from the remotest zones; industries whose products are consumed, not only at home, but in every quarter of the globe. In place of the old wants, satisfied by the productions of the country, we find new wants, requiring for their satisfaction the products of distant lands and climes. In place of the old local and national seclusion and self-sufficiency, we have intercourse in every direction, universal interdependence of nations. And as in material, so also in intellectual production. The intellectual creations of individual nations become common property. National one-sidedness and narrow-mindedness become more and more impossible, and from the numerous national and local literatures, there arises a world literature.

The bourgeoisie, by the rapid improvement of all instruments of production, by the immensely facilitated means of communication, draws all, even the most barbarian, nations into civilisation. The cheap prices of its commodities are the heavy artillery with which it batters down all Chinese walls, with which it forces the barbarians' intensely obstinate hatred of foreigners to capitulate. It compels all nations, on pain of extinction, to adopt the bourgeois mode of production; it compels them to introduce what it calls civilisation into their midst, *i.e.,* to become bourgeois themselves. In one word, it creates a world after its own image.

The bourgeoisie has subjected the country to the rule of the towns. It has created enormous cities, has greatly increased the urban population as compared with the rural, and has thus rescued a considerable part of the population from the idiocy of rural life. Just as it has made the country dependent on the towns, so it has made barbarian and semi-barbarian countries dependent on the civilised ones, nations of peasants on nations of bourgeois, the East on the West.

The bourgeoisie keeps more and more doing away with the scattered state of the population, of the means of production, and of property. It has agglomerated population, centralised means of production, and has concentrated property in a few hands. The necessary consequence of this was political centralisation. Independent, or but loosely connected, provinces with separate interests, laws, governments and systems of taxation, became lumped together into one nation, with one government, one code of laws, one national class-interest, one frontier and one customs-tariff.

The bourgeoisie, during its rule of scarce one hundred years, has created more massive and more colossal productive forces than have all preceding generations together. Subjection of Nature's forces to man, machinery, application of chemistry to industry and agriculture, steam-navigation, railways, electric telegraphs, clearing of whole continents for cultivation, canalisation of rivers, whole populations conjured out of the ground—what earlier century had even a presentiment that such productive forces slumbered in the lap of social labour?

We see then: the means of production and of exchange, on whose foundation the bourgeoisie built itself up, were generated in feudal society. At a certain stage in the development of these means of production and of exchange, the conditions under which feudal society produced and exchanged, the feudal organisation of agriculture and manufacturing industry, in one word, the feudal relations of property became no longer compatible with the already developed productive forces; they became so many fetters. They had to be burst asunder; they were burst asunder.

Into their place stepped free competition, accompanied by a social and political constitution adapted to it, and by the economical and political sway of the bourgeois class.

A similar movement is going on before our own eyes. Modern bourgeois society with its relations of production, of exchange and of property, a society that has conjured up such gigantic means of production and of exchange, is like the sorcerer, who is no longer able to control the powers of the nether world whom he has called up by his spells. For many a decade past the history of industry and commerce is but the history of the revolt of modern productive forces against modern conditions of production, against the property relations that are the conditions for the existence of the bourgeoisie and of its rule. It is enough to mention the commercial crises that by their periodical return put on its trial, each time more threateningly, the existence of the entire bourgeois society. In these crises a great part not only of the existing products, but also of the previously created productive forces, are periodically destroyed. In these crises there breaks out an epidemic that, in all earlier epochs, would have seemed an absurdity—the epidemic of overproduction. Society suddenly finds itself put back into a state of momentary barbarism; it appears as if a famine, a universal war of devastation had cut off the supply of every means of subsistence; industry and commerce seem to be destroyed; and why? Because there is too much civilisation, too much means of subsistence, too much industry, too much commerce. The productive forces at the disposal of society no longer tend to further the development of the conditions of bourgeois property; on the contrary, they have become too powerful for these conditions, by which they are fettered, and so soon as they overcome these fetters, they bring disorder into the whole of bourgeois society, endanger the existence of bourgeois property. The conditions of bourgeois society are too narrow to compromise the wealth created by them. And how does the bourgeoisie get over these crises? On the one hand by enforced destruction of a mass of productive forces; on the other, by the conquest of new markets, and by the more thorough exploitation of the old ones. That is to say, by paving the way for more extensive and more destructive crises, and by diminishing the means whereby crises are prevented.

The weapons with which the bourgeoisie felled feudalism to the ground are now turned against the bourgeoisie itself.

But not only has the bourgeoisie forged the weapons that bring death to itself; it has also called into existence the men who are to wield those weapons—the modern working class—the proletarians.

In proportion as the bourgeoisie, *i.e.,* capital, is developed, in the same proportion is the proletariat, the modern working class, developed—a class of labourers, who live only so long as they find work, and who find work only so long as their labour increases capital. These labourers, who must sell themselves piecemeal, are a commodity, like every other article of commerce, and are consequently exposed to all the vicissitudes of competition, to all the fluctuations of the market.

Owing to the extensive use of machinery and to division of labour, the work of the proletarians has lost all individual character, and, consequently, all charm for the workman. He becomes an appendage of the machine, and it is only the most simple, most monotonous, and most easily acquired knack, that is required of him. Hence, the cost of production of a workman is restricted, almost entirely, to the means of subsistence that he requires for his maintenance, and for the propagation of his race. But the price of a commodity, and therefore also of labour, is equal to its cost of production. In proportion, therefore, as the repulsiveness of the work increases, the wage decreases. Nay more, in proportion as the use of machinery and division of labour increases, in the same proportion the burden of toil also increases, whether by prolongation of the working hours, by increase of the work exacted in a given time or by increased speed of the machinery, etc.

Modern industry has converted the little workshop of the patriarchal master into the great factory of the industrial capitalist. Masses of labourers, crowded into the factory, are organised like soldiers. As privates of the industrial army they are placed under the command of a perfect hierarchy of officers and sergeants. Not only are they slaves of the bourgeois class, and of the bourgeois State; they are daily and hourly enslaved by the machine, by the overlooker, and, above all, by the individual bourgeois manufacturer himself. The more openly this despotism proclaims gain to be its end and aim, the more petty, the more hateful and more embittering it is.

The less the skill and exertion of strength implied in manual labor, in other words, the more modern industry becomes developed, the more is the labour of men superseded by that of women. Differences of age and sex have no longer any distinctive social validity for the working class. All are instruments of labour, more or less expensive to use, according to their age and sex.

No sooner is the exploitation of the labourer by the manufacturer, so far, at an end, that he receives his wages in cash, than he is set upon by the other portions of the bourgeoisie, the landlord, the storekeeper, the pawnbroker, etc.

The lower strata of the middle class—the small tradespeople, shopkeepers, and retired tradesmen generally, the handicraftsmen and peasants—all these sink gradually into the proletariat, partly because their diminutive capital does not suffice for the scale on which Modern Industry is carried on, and is swamped in the competition with the large capitalists, partly because their specialised skill is rendered worthless by new methods of production. Thus the proletariat is recruited from all classes of the population.

The proletariat goes through various stages of development. With its birth begins its struggle with the bourgeoisie. At first the contest is carried on by individual labourers, then by the workpeople of a factory, then by the operatives of one trade, in one locality, against the individual bourgeois who directly exploits them. They direct their attacks not against the bourgeois conditions of production, but against the instruments of production themselves; they destroy imported wares that compete with their labour, they smash to pieces machinery, they set factories ablaze, they seek to restore by force the vanished status of the workman of the Middle Ages.

At this stage the labourers still form an incoherent mass scattered over the whole country, and broken up by their mutual competition. If anywhere they unite to form more compact bodies, this is not yet the consequence of their own active union, but of the union of the bourgeoisie, which class, in order to attain its own political ends, is compelled to set the whole proletariat in motion, and is moreover yet, for a time, able to do so. At this stage, therefore, the proletarians do not fight their enemies, but the enemies of their enemies, the remnants of absolute monarchy, the landowners, the non-industrial bourgeois, the petty bourgeoisie. Thus the whole historical movement is concentrated in the hands of the bourgeoisie; every victory so obtained is a victory for the bourgeoisie.

But with the development of industry the proletariat not only increases in number; it becomes concentrated in greater masses, its strength grows, and it feels that strength more. The various interests and conditions of life within the ranks of the proletariat are more and more equalised, in proportion as machinery obliterates all distinctions of labour, and nearly everywhere reduces wages to the same low level. The growing competition among the bourgeois, and the resulting commercial crises, make the wages of the workers ever more fluctuating. The unceasing improvement of machinery, ever more rapidly developing, makes their livelihood more and more precarious; the collisions between individual workmen and individual bourgeois take more and more the character of collisions between two classes. Thereupon the workers begin to form combinations (Trades' Unions) against the bourgeois; they club together in order to keep up the rate of wages; they found permanent associations in order to make provision beforehand for these occasional revolts. Here and there the contest breaks out into riots.

Now and then the workers are victorious, but only for a time. The real fruit of their battles lies, not in the immediate result, but in the everexpanding union of the workers. This union is helped on by the improved means of communication that are created by modern industry and that place the workers of different localities in contact with one another. It was just this contact that was needed to centralise the numerous local struggles, all of the same character, into one national struggle between classes. But every class struggle is a political struggle. And that union, to attain which the burghers of the Middle Ages, with their miserable highways, required centuries, the modern proletarians, thanks to railroads, achieve in a few years.

This organisation of the proletarians into a class, and consequently into a political party, is continually being upset again by the competition between the workers themselves. But it ever rises up again, stronger, firmer, mightier. It compels legislative recognition of particular interests of the workers, by taking advantage of the divisions among the bourgeoisie itself. Thus the ten-hours' bill in England was carried.

Altogether, collisions between the classes of the old society further, in many ways, the course of development of the proletariat. The bourgeoisie finds itself involved in a constant battle. At first with the aristocracy; later on, with those portions of the bourgeoisie itself, whose interests have become antagonistic to the progress of industry; at all times, with the bourgeoisie of foreign countries. In all these battles it sees itself compelled to appeal to the proletariat, to ask for its help, and thus, to drag it into the political arena. The bourgeoisie itself, therefore, supplies the proletariat with its own elements of political and general education, in other words, it furnishes the proletariat with weapons for fighting the bourgeoisie.

Further, as we have already seen, entire sections of the ruling classes are, by the advance of industry, precipitated into the proletariat, or are at least threatened in their conditions of existence. These also supply the proletariat with fresh elements of enlightenment and progress.

Finally, in times when the class struggle nears the decisive hour, the process of dissolution going on within the ruling class, in fact within the whole range of old society, assumes such a violent, glaring character, that a small section of the ruling class cuts itself adrift, and joins the revolutionary class, the class that holds the future in its hands. Just as, therefore, at an earlier period, a section of the nobility went over to the bourgeoisie, so now a portion of the bourgeoisie goes over to the proletariat, and in particular, a portion of the bourgeois ideologists, who have raised themselves to the level of comprehending theoretically the historical movement as a whole.

Of all the classes that stand face to face with the bourgeoisie today, the proletariat alone is a really revolutionary class. The other classes decay and finally disappear in the face of modern industry; the proletariat is its special and essential product.

The lower middle class, the small manufacturer, the shopkeeper, the artisan, the peasant, all these fight against the bourgeoisie, to save from extinction their existence as fractions of the middle class. They are therefore not revolutionary, but conservative. Nay more, they are reactionary, for they try to roll back the wheel of history. If by chance they are revolutionary, they are so only in view of their impending transfer into the proletariat, they thus defend not their present, but their future interests, they desert their own standpoint to place themselves at that of the proletariat.

The "dangerous class," the social scum, that passively rotting mass thrown off by the lowest layers of old society, may, here and there, be swept into the movement by a proletarian revolution; its conditions of life, however, prepare it far more for the part of a bribed tool of reactionary intrigue.

In the conditions of the proletariat, those of old society at large are already virtually swamped. The proletarian is without property; his relation to his wife and children has no longer anything in common with the bourgeois family relations; modern industrial labour, modern subjection to capital, the same in England as in France, in America as in Germany, has stripped him of every trace of national character. Law, morality, religion, are to him so many bourgeois prejudices, behind which lurk in ambush just as many bourgeois interests.

All the preceding classes that got the upper hand, sought to fortify their already acquired status by subjecting society at large to their conditions of appropriation. The proletarians cannot become masters of the productive forces of society, except by abolishing their own previous mode of appropriation, and thereby also every other previous mode of appropriation. They have nothing of their own to secure and to fortify; their mission is to destroy all previous securities for, and insurances of, individual property.

All previous historical movements were movements of minorities, or in the interests of minorities. The proletarian movement is the self-conscious, independent movement of the immense majority, in the interest of the immense majority. The proletariat, the lowest stratum of our present society, cannot stir, cannot raise itself up, without the whole superincumbent strata of official society being sprung into the air.

Though not in substance, yet in form, the struggle of the proletariat with the bourgeoisie is at first a national struggle. The proletariat of each country must, of course, first of all settle matters with its own bourgeoisie.

In depicting the most general phases of the development of the proletariat, we traced the more or less veiled civil war, raging within existing society, up to the point where that war breaks out into open revolution, and where the violent overthrow of the bourgeoisie lays the foundation for the sway of the proletariat.

Hitherto, every form of society has been based, as we have already seen, on the antagonism of oppressing and oppressed classes. But in order to oppress a class, certain conditions must be assured to it under which it can, at least, continue its slavish existence. The serf, in the period of serfdom, raised himself to membership in the commune, just as the petty bourgeois, under the yoke of feudal absolutism, managed to develop into a bourgeois. The modern labourer, on the contrary, instead of rising with the progress of industry, sinks deeper and deeper below the conditions of existence of his own class. He becomes a pauper, and pauperism develops more rapidly than population and wealth. And here it becomes evident, that the bourgeoisie is unfit any longer to be the ruling class in society, and to impose its conditions of existence upon society as an over-riding law. It is unfit to rule because it is incompetent to assure an existence to its slave within his slavery, because it cannot help letting him sink into such a state, that it has to feed him, instead of being fed by him. Society can no longer live under this bourgeoisie, in other words, its existence is no longer compatible with society.

The essential condition for the existence, and for the sway of the bourgeois class, is the formation and augmentation of capital; the condition for capital is wage labour. Wage labour rests exclusively on competition between the labourers. The advance of industry, whose involuntary promoter is the bourgeoisie, replaces the isolation of the labourers, due to competition, by their revolutionary combination, due to association. The development of Modern Industry, therefore, cuts from under its feet the very foundation on which the bourgeoisie produces and appropriates products. What the bourgeoisie, therefore, produces, above all, is its own gravediggers. Its fall and the victory of the proletariat are equally inevitable.

Alienated Labor

Marx is usually thought of as the father of the ideology of communism, but in his early years he wrote some very important writings on alienation, especially alienation related to work. This problem, alienation, is one of the most serious problems of modern society. Marx contended that his work significantly defines a person and, further, the alienation of man from the products of his work alienates him from his essence. This especially occurs in the capitalist societies.

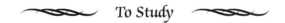

To Study

1. Explain: Labor creates the worker as a commodity.
2. What does *the alienation of the worker in his product* mean?
3. What does labor produce for the rich? For the poor?
4. What constitutes the alienation of labor?
5. Explain: Only in the final stage of the development of private property is its secret revealed.

We have now to grasp the real connection between this whole system of alienation—private property, acquisitiveness, the separation of labour, capital and land, exchange and competition, value and the devaluation of man, monopoly and competition—and the system of *money*.

From *Karl Marx: Early Writings*. T. B. Bottomore, trans. and ed. (New York: McGraw-Hill, 1964). Reprinted by permission of the publisher.

Let us not begin our explanation, as does the economist, from a legendary primordial condition. Such a primordial condition does not explain anything; it merely removes the question into a grey and nebulous distance. . . .

We shall begin from a *contemporary* economic fact. The worker becomes poorer the more wealth he produces and the more his production increases in power and extent. The worker becomes an ever cheaper commodity the more goods he creates. The *devaluation* of the human world increases in direct relation with the *increase in value* of the world of things. Labour does not only create goods; it also produces itself and the worker as a *commodity,* and indeed in the same proportion as it produces goods.

This fact simply implies that the object produced by labour, its product, now stands opposed to it as an *alien being,* as a *power independent* of the producer. The product of labour is labour which has been embodied in an object and turned into a physical thing; this product is an *objectification* of labour. The performance of work is at the same time its objectification. The performance of work appears in the sphere of political economy as a *vitiation* of the worker, objectification as a *loss* and as *servitude to the object,* and appropriation as *alienation.*

So much does the performance of work appear as vitiation that the worker is vitiated to the point of starvation. So much does objectification appear as loss of the object that the worker is deprived of the most essential things not only of life but also of work. Labour itself becomes an object which he can acquire only by the greatest effort and with unpredictable interruptions. So much does the appropriation of the object appear as alienation that the more objects the worker produces the fewer he can possess and the more he falls under the domination of his product, of capital.

All these consequences follow from the fact that the worker is related to the *product of his labour* as to an *alien* object. For it is clear on this presupposition that the more the worker expends himself in work the more powerful becomes the world of objects which he creates in face of himself, the poorer he becomes in his inner life, and the less he belongs to himself. It is just the same as in religion. The more of himself man attributes to God the less he has left in himself. The worker puts his life into the object, and his life then belongs no longer to himself but to the object. The greater his activity, therefore, the less he possesses. What is embodied in the product of his labour is no longer his own. The greater this product is, therefore, the more he is diminished. The *alienation* of the worker in his product means not only that his labour becomes an object, assumes an *external* existence, but that it exists independently, *outside himself,* and alien to him, and that it stands opposed to him as an autonomous power. The life which he has given to the object sets itself against him as an alien and hostile force.

Let us now examine more closely the phenomenon of *objectification;* the worker's production and the *alienation* and *loss* of the object it produces, which is involved in it. The worker can create nothing without *nature,* without the *sensuous external world.* The latter is the material in which his labour is realized in which it is active, out of which and through which it produces things.

But just as nature affords the *means of existence* of labour, in the sense that labour cannot *live* without objects upon which it can be exercised, so also it provides the *means of existence* in a narrower sense; namely the means of physical existence for the *worker* himself. Thus, the more the worker *appropriates* the external world of sensuous nature by his labour the more he deprives himself of *means of existence,* in two respects: first, that the sensuous external world becomes progressively less an object belonging to his labour or a means of existence of his labour, and secondly, that it becomes progressively less a means of existence in the direct sense, a means for the physical subsistence of the worker.

In both respects, therefore, the worker becomes a slave of the object; first, in that he receives an *object of work,* that is, receives *work,* and secondly, in that he receives *means of subsistence.* Thus, the object enables him to exist, first as a *worker* and secondly, as a *physical subject.* The culmination of this enslavement is that he can only maintain himself as a *physical subject* so far as he is a *worker,* and that it is only as a *physical subject* that he is a worker.

(The alienation of the worker in his object is expressed as follows in the laws of political economy: the more the worker produces the less he has to consume; the more value he creates the more worthless he becomes; the more refined his product the more crude and misshapen the worker; the more civilized the product the more barbarous the worker; the more powerful the work the more feeble the worker; the more the work manifests intelligence the more the worker declines in intelligence and becomes a slave of nature.)

Political economy conceals the alienation in the nature of labour in so far as it does not examine the direct relationship between the worker (work) and production. Labour certainly produces marvels for the rich but it produces privation for the worker. It produces palaces, but hovels for the worker. It produces beauty, but deformity for the worker. It replaces labour by machinery, but it casts some of the workers back into a barbarous kind of work and turns the others into machines. It produces intelligence, but also stupidity and cretinism for the workers. . . .

So far we have considered the alienation of the worker only from one aspect; namely, *his relationship with the products of his labour.* However, alienation appears not merely in the result but also in the *process* of *production,* within *productive activity* itself. How could the worker stand in an alien relationship to the product of his activity if he did not alienate himself in the act of production itself? The product is indeed only the *résumé* of activity, of production. Consequently, if the product of labour is alienation, production itself must be active alienation—the alienation of activity and the activity of alienation. The alienation of the object of labour merely summarizes the alienation in the work activity itself.

What constitutes the alienation of labour? First, that the work is *external* to the worker, that it is not part of his nature; and that, consequently, he does not fulfil himself in his work but denies himself, has a feeling of misery rather than well-being, does not develop freely his mental and physical energies but is physically exhausted and mentally debased. The worker, therefore, feels himself at home only during his leisure time, whereas at work he feels homeless. His work is not voluntary but imposed, *forced labour.* It is not the satisfaction of a need, but only a *means* for satisfying other needs. Its alien character is clearly shown by the fact that as soon as there is no physical or other compulsion it is avoided like the plague. External labour, labour in which man alienates himself, is a labour of self-sacrifice, of mortification. Finally, the external character of work for the worker is shown by the fact that it is not his own work but work for someone else, that in work he does not belong to himself but to another person. . . .

We began with an economic fact, the alienation of the worker and his production. We have expressed this fact in conceptual terms as *alienated labour,* and in analyzing the concept we have merely analyzed an economic fact.

Let us now examine further how this concept of alienated labour must press and reveal itself in reality. If the product of labour is alien to me and confronts me as an alien power, to whom does it belong? If my own activity does not belong to me but is an alien, forced activity, to whom does it belong? To a being *other* than myself. And who is this being? . . .

The *alien* being to whom labour and the product of labour belong, to whose service labour is devoted, and to whose enjoyment the product of labour goes, can only be *man* himself. If the product of labour does not belong to the worker, but confronts him as an alien power, this can only be because it belongs to *a man other than the worker.* If his activity is a torment to him it must be a source of *enjoyment* and pleasure to another. . . .

Thus, through alienated labour the worker creates the relation of another man; who does not work and is outside the work process, to this labour. The relation of the worker to work also produces the relation of the capitalist (or whatever one likes to call the lord of labour) to work. *Private property* is, therefore, the product, the necessary result, of *alienated labour,* of the external relation of the worker to nature and to himself.

Private property is thus derived from the analysis of the concept of *alienated labour,* that is, alienated man, alienated labour, alienated life, and estranged man.

We have, of course derived the concept of *alienated labour (alienated life)* from political economy, from an analysis of the *movement of private property.* But the analysis of this concept shows that although private property appears to be the basis and cause of alienated labour, it is rather a consequence of the latter, just as the gods are *fundamentally* not the cause but the product of confusions of human reason. At a later stage, however, there is a reciprocal influence.

Only in the final stage of the development of private property is its secret revealed, namely, that it is on one hand the *product* of alienated labour, and on the other hand the *means* by which labour is alienated, *the realization of this alienation.* . . .

Conclusion from Marx's Communist Manifesto

The Communists are distinguished from the other working-class parties by this only: 1. In the national struggles of the proletarians of the different countries, they point out and bring to the front the common interests of the entire proletariat, independently of all nationality. 2. In the various stages of development which the struggle of the working class against the bourgeoisie has to pass through, they always and everywhere represent the interests of the movement as a whole.

The Communists, therefore, are on the one hand, practically, the most advanced and resolute section of the working-class parties of every country, that section which pushes forward all others; on the other hand, theoretically, they have over the great mass of the proletariat the advantage of clearly understanding the line of march, the conditions, and the ultimate general results of the proletarian government.

The immediate aim of the Communists is the same as that of all the other proletarian parties: formation of the proletariat into a class, overthrow of the bourgeois supremacy, conquest of political power by the proletariat. . . .

The proletariat will use its political supremacy to wrest, by degrees, all capital from the bourgeoisie, to centralise all instruments of production in the hands of the State, *i.e.,* of the proletariat organised as the ruling class; and to increase the total of productive forces as rapidly as possible.

Of course, in the beginning, this cannot be effected except by means of despotic inroads on the rights of property, and on the conditions of bourgeois production; by means of measures, therefore, which appear economically insufficient and untenable, but which, in the course of the movement, outstrip themselves, necessitate further inroads upon the old social order, and are unavoidable as a means of entirely revolutionising the mode of production.

These measures will of course be different in different countries.

Nevertheless in the most advanced countries, the following will be pretty generally applicable.

1. Abolition of property in land and application of all rents of land to public purposes.
2. A heavy progressive or graduated income tax.
3. Abolition of all right of inheritance.
4. Confiscation of the property of all emigrants and rebels.
5. Centralisation of credit in the hands of the State, by means of a national bank with State capital and an exclusive monopoly.
6. Centralisation of the means of communication and transport in the hands of the State.
7. Extension of factories and instruments of production owned by the State; the bringing into cultivation of waste-lands, and the improvement of the soil generally in accordance with a common plan.
8. Equal liability of all to labour. Establishment of industrial armies, especially for agriculture.
9. Combination of agriculture with manufacturing industries; gradual abolition of the distinction between town and country, by a more equable distribution of the population over the country.
10. Free education for all children in public schools. Abolition of children's factory labour in its present form. Combination of education with industrial production, &c., &c.

When, in the course of development, class distinctions have disappeared, and all production has been concentrated in the hands of a vast association of the whole nation, the public power will lose its political character. Political power, properly so called, is merely the organised power of one class for oppressing another. If the proletariat during its contest with the bourgeoisie is compelled, by the force of circumstances, to organise itself as a class, if, by means of a revolution, it makes itself the ruling class, and, as such, sweeps away by force the old conditions of production, then it will, along with these conditions, have swept away the conditions for the existence of class antagonisms and of classes generally, and will thereby have abolished its own supremacy as a class.

In place of the old bourgeois society, with its classes and class antagonisms, we shall have an association, in which the free development of each is the condition for the free development of all. . . .

The Communists disdain to conceal their views and aims. They openly declare that their ends can be attained only by the forcible overthrow of all existing social conditions. Let the ruling classes tremble at a Communistic revolution. The proletarians have nothing to lose but their chains. They have a world to win.

WORKING MEN OF ALL COUNTRIES, UNITE!

<div align="center">~~~~ To Think About ~~~~</div>

1. "Heretofore philosophers have only *interpreted* the world differently: the point is, however, to *change* it."   ***Karl Marx***

2. "The goal of Marxism was that of the spiritual emancipation of man, of his liberation from the chains of economic determination, of restituting him in his human wholeness, of enabling him to find unity and harmony with his fellow man and with nature. Marx's philosophy was, in secular, nontheistic language, a new and radical step forward in the tradition of prophetic Messianism; it was aimed at the full realization of individualism, the very aim which has guided Western thinking from the Renaissance and the Reformation far into the nineteenth century."   ***A. K. Bierman***

3. "The dammed-up instinctual forces in civilized man are immensely destructive and far more dangerous than the instincts of the primitive, who in a modest degree is constantly living out his negative instincts. Consequently no war of the historical past can rival in grandiose horror the wars of civilized nations."   ***C. G. Jung***

4. "It is only from the selfishness and confined generosity of men, along with the scanty provision nature has made for his wants, that justice derives its origin."   ***David Hume***

5. "Religion is the sigh of the oppressed creature, the heart of a heartless world, just as it is the spirit of spiritless conditions. It is the *opium* of the people."   ***Karl Marx***

6. "To abolish religion as the *illusory* happiness of the people is to demand *their* real happiness."   ***Karl Marx***

7.   "The concepts of productive power and economic structure (unlike those of consciousness and culture) do not serve only to express a vision. They also assert their candidacy as the leading concepts in a theory of history, a *theory* to the extent that history admits of theoretical treatment, which is neither entirely nor not at all."   ***Robert Cohen***

8.   "What is society, whatever its form may be? The product of men's reciprocal activities. Are men free to choose this or that form of society? Not at all. Presuppose a particular state of development of men's faculties, and you will have a corresponding form of commerce and consumption. Presuppose a certain stage of development or production, commerce and consumption, and you will have a corresponding form of social constitution, a corresponding organization of the family, estates or classes, in a word, a corresponding civil society. Presuppose such a civil society, and you will have a corresponding political state, which is nothing but the official expression of civil society."   ***Robert Cohen***

9.   "Today tolerance appears again as what it was in its origins, at the beginning of the modern period—a partisan goal, a subversive liberating notion and practice. Conversely, what is proclaimed and practised as tolerance today, is in many of its most effective manifestations serving the cause of oppression."
                                                                                    Herbert Marcuse

10. "Adherents of the two great contrasting systems cast the same reproaches at each other. The one party considers economic freedom as one of the fundamental rights of the individual, and believes that it is in fact the very condition upon which the material and the moral health of a society depends. Therefore, it denounces economic planning as a form of tyranny which must be fought against in the name of the sacred value of liberty. The other party asserts that the liberation of individuals can be guaranteed only by an economic structure devoid of the faults of individual profit-seeking."   ***Joseph Post***

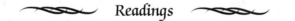

Readings

BERLIN, ISAIAH. *Karl Marx*. 4th ed. New York: Oxford University Press, 1996.

CARVER, TERRELL, ed. *The Cambridge Companion to Marx*. Cambridge: Cambridge University Press, 1991.

PLAMENATZ, JOHN. *Karl Marx's Philosophy of Man*. Oxford: Clarendon Press, 1975.

WOLFF, ROBERT PAUL. *Understanding Marx*. Princeton, NJ: Princeton University Press, 1984.

51

Democracy Can Have Serious Problems

Alexis de Tocqueville (1805–59) was a prominent French politician and writer born into an aristocratic family. In 1831 he visited the United States and traveled through-out the country, noting its institutional life and customs. The result of his work was Democracy in America, *recognized as perhaps the most penetrating analysis of American culture and society written in the nineteenth century. Holding a firm belief that democracy would ultimately triumph over prevalent European forms of aristo-cratic and monarchical government, Tocqueville nevertheless thought that much in American democratic life and action was unpromising, especially the kind of tyranny frequently imposed by the power of majority opinion.*

Tocqueville, like John Stuart Mill, fears the tyranny of the majority in a democracy. He argues that the majority, which is favorable to the legal despotism of the legisla-ture, is likewise favorable to the arbitrary authority of the magistrate. Thus he main-tains that the majority in the United States is invested with the right of making and of executing the laws far beyond the power of the kings of Europe. In this article he fails to mention the Bill of Rights as a restriction upon the majority, but as we know, even the First Amendment gets modified.

~~~~ To Study ~~~~

1. Why, according to Tocqueville, is any form of unlimited power bad and dan-gerous?
2. How might the three branches of American government be constituted so as to avoid tyranny?

Reprinted from *Democracy in America*, Part One, Chapter XV, translated by Henry Reeve (London: Saunders and Otley, 1835).

3. How, in the United States, does majority rule favor despotism and arbitrary power?

4. How is the power of public opinion in America greater than the power even of monarchies?

5. Why does Tocqueville claim that there is so little independence of mind and freedom of discussion in America?

6. What differences in types and instruments of oppression exist between monarchy and democracy?

7. Why is the moral character of citizens threatened in democracies?

8. Why in America is there an ever-present threat of anarchy?

I AM OF OPINION THAT SOME ONE SOCIAL POWER MUST ALWAYS BE made to predominate over the others; but I think that liberty is endangered when this power is checked by no obstacles which may retard its course, and force it to moderate its own vehemence.

Unlimited power is in itself a bad and dangerous thing; human beings are not competent to exercise it with discretion, and God alone can be omnipotent, because his wisdom and his justice are always equal to his power. But no power upon earth is so worthy of honour for itself, or of reverential obedience to the rights which it represents, that I would consent to admit its uncontrolled and all-predominant authority. When I see that the right and the means of absolute command are conferred on a people or upon a king, upon an aristocracy or a democracy, a monarchy or a republic, I recognize the germ of tyranny, and I journey onward to a land of more hopeful institutions.

In my opinion the main evil of the present democratic institutions of the United States does not arise, as is often asserted in Europe; from their weakness, but from their overpowering strength; and I am not so much alarmed at the excessive liberty which reigns in that country as at the very inadequate securities which exist against tyranny.

When an individual or a party is wronged in the United States, to whom can he apply for redress? If to public opinion, public opinion constitutes the majority; if to the legislature, it represents the majority, and implicitly obeys its injunctions; if to the executive power, it is appointed by the majority, and remains a passive tool in its hands; the public troops consist of the majority under arms; the jury is the majority invested with the right of hearing judicial cases; and in certain States even the judges are elected by the majority. However iniquitous or absurd the evil of which you complain may be, you must submit to it as well as you can.

If, on the other hand, a legislative power could be so constituted as to represent the majority without necessarily being the slave of its passions; an executive, so as to retain a certain degree of uncontrolled authority; and a judiciary, so as to remain independent of the two other powers; a government would be formed which would still be democratic without incurring any risk of tyrannical abuse.

I do not say that tyrannical abuses frequently occur in America at the present day, but I maintain that no sure barrier is established against them, and that the causes which mitigate the government are to be found in the circumstances and the manners of the country more than in its laws.

A distinction must be drawn between tyranny and arbitrary power. Tyranny may be exercised by means of the law, and in that case it is not arbitrary; arbitrary power may be exercised for the good of the community at large, in which case it is not tyrannical. Tyranny usually employs arbitrary means, but, if necessary, it can rule without them.

In the United States the unbounded power of the majority, which is favourable to the legal despotism of the legislature, is likewise favourable to the arbitrary authority of the magistrate. The majority has an entire control over the law when it is made and when it is executed; and as it possesses an equal authority over those who are in power and the community at large, it considers public officers as its passive agents, and readily confides the task of serving its designs to their vigilance. The details of their office and the privileges which they are to enjoy are rarely defined beforehand; but the majority treats them as a master does his servants when they are always at work in his sight, and he has the power of directing or reprimanding them at every instant.

In general the American functionaries are far more independent than the French civil officers within the sphere which is prescribed to them. Sometimes, even, they are allowed by the popular authority to exceed those bounds; and as they are protected by the opinion, and backed by the co-operation, of the majority, they venture upon such manifestations of their power as astonish a European. By this means habits are formed in the heart of a free country which may some day prove fatal to its liberties.

It is in the examination of the display of public opinion in the United States that we clearly perceive how far the power of the majority surpasses all the powers with which we are acquainted in Europe. Intellectual principles exercise an influence which is so invisible, and often so inappreciable, that they baffle the toils of oppression. At the present time the most absolute monarchs in Europe are unable to prevent certain notions, which are opposed to their authority, from circulating in secret throughout their dominions, and even in their courts. Such is not the case in America; as long as the majority is still undecided, discussion is carried on; but as soon as its decision is irrevocably pronounced, a submissive silence is observed, and the friends, as well as the opponents, of the measure unite in assenting to its propriety. The reason of this is perfectly clear: no monarch is so absolute as to combine all the powers of society in his own hands, and to conquer all opposition with the energy of a majority which is invested with the right of making and of executing the laws.

The authority of a king is purely physical, and it controls the actions of the subject without subduing his private will; but the majority possesses a power which is physical and moral at the same time; it acts upon the will as well as upon the actions of men, and it represses not only all contest, but all controversy.

I know no country in which there is so little true independence of mind and freedom of discussion as in America. In any constitutional state in Europe every sort of religious and political theory may be advocated and propagated abroad; for there is no country in Europe so subdued by any single authority as not to contain citizens who are ready to protect the man who raises his voice in the cause of truth from the consequences of his hardihood. If he is unfortunate enough to live under an absolute government, the people is upon his side; if he inhabits a free country, he may find a shelter behind the authority of the throne, if he require one. The aristocratic part of society supports him in some countries, and the democracy in others. But in a nation where democratic institutions exist, organized like those of the United States, there is but one sole authority, one single element of strength and of success, with nothing beyond it.

In America, the majority raises very formidable barriers to the liberty of opinion: within these barriers an author may write whatever he pleases, but he will repent it if he ever step beyond them. Not that he is exposed to the terrors of an *auto-da-fé,* but he is tormented by the slights and persecutions of daily obloquy. His political career is closed for ever, since he has offended the only authority which is able to promote his success. Every sort of compensation, even that of celebrity, is refused to him. Before he published his opinions he imagined that he held them in common with many others; but no sooner has he declared them openly than he is loudly censured by his overbearing opponents, while those who think like him, without having the courage to speak, abandon him in silence. He yields at length, oppressed by the daily efforts he has been making, and he subsides into silence, as if he was tormented by remorse for having spoken the truth.

Fetters and headsmen were the coarse instruments which tyranny formerly employed; but the civilization of our age has refined the arts of despotism, which seemed, however, to have been sufficiently perfected before. The excesses of monarchical power had devised a variety of physical means of oppression: the democratic republics of the present day have rendered it as entirely an affair of the mind as that will which it is intended to coerce. Under the absolute sway of an individual despot the body was attacked in order to subdue the soul, and the soul escaped the blows which were directed against it and rose superior to the attempt; but such is not the course adopted by tyranny in democratic republics; there the body is left free, and the soul is enslaved. The sovereign can no longer say, "You shall think as I do on pain of death"; but he says: "You are free to think differently from me, and to retain your life, your property, and all that you possess; but if such be your determination, you are henceforth an alien among your people. You may retain your civil rights, but they will be useless to you, for you will never be chosen by your fellow citizens if you solicit their suffrages, and they will affect to scorn you if you solicit their esteem. You will remain among men, but you will be deprived of the rights of mankind. Your fellow-creatures will shun you like an impure being, and those who are most persuaded of your innocence will abandon you too, lest they should be shunned in their turn. Go in peace! I have given you your life, but it is an existence incomparably worse than death."

Monarchical institutions have thrown an odium upon despotism; let us beware lest democratic republics should restore oppression, and should render it less odious and less degrading in the eyes of the many, by making it still more onerous to the few. . . .

The tendencies to which I have just alluded are as yet very slightly perceptible in political society, but they already begin to exercise an unfavourable influence upon the national character of the Americans. I am inclined to attribute the singular paucity of distinguished political characters to the ever-increasing activity of the despotism of the majority in the United States. When the American Revolution broke out they arose in great numbers, for public opinion then served, not to tyrannize over, but to direct the exertions of individuals. Those celebrated men took a full part in the general agitation of mind common at that period, and they attained a high degree of personal fame, which was reflected back upon the nation, but which was by no means borrowed from it. . . .

In free countries, where every one is more or less called upon to give his opinion in the affairs of state; in democratic republics, where public life is incessantly commingled with domestic affairs, where the sovereign authority is accessible on every side, and where its attention can almost always be attracted by vociferation, more persons are to be met with who speculate upon its foibles and live at the cost of its passions than in absolute monarchies. Not because men are naturally worse in these States than elsewhere; but the temptation is stronger, and of easier access at the same time. The result is a far more extensive debasement of the characters of citizens.

Democratic republics extend the practice of currying favour with the many, and they introduce it into a greater number of classes at once; this is one of the most serious reproaches that can be addressed to them. In democratic States organized on the principles of the American republics, this is more especially the case, where the authority of the majority is so absolute and so irresistible that a man must give up his rights as a citizen, and almost abjure his quality as a human being, if he intends to stray from the track which it lays down.

In that immense crowd which throngs the avenues to power in the United States I found very few men who displayed any of that manly candour and that masculine independence of opinion which frequently distinguished the Americans in former times, and which constitutes the leading feature in distinguished characters, wheresoever they may be found. It seems, at first sight, as if all the minds of the Americans were formed upon one model, so accurately do they correspond in their manner of judging. A stranger does, indeed, sometimes meet with Americans who dissent from these rigorous formularies; with men who deplore the defects of the laws, the mutability and the ignorance of democracy; who even go so far as to observe the evil tendencies which impair the national character, and to point out such remedies as it might be possible to apply; but no one is there to hear these things besides yourself, and you, to whom these secret reflections are confided, are a stranger and a bird of passage. They are very ready to communicate truths which are useless to you, but they continue to hold a different language in public. . . .

Despotism debases the oppressed much more than the oppressor: in absolute monarchies the king has often great virtues, but the courtiers are invariably servile. It is true that the American courtiers do not say 'Sire,' or 'Your Majesty'—a distinction without a difference. They are for ever talking of the natural intelligence of the populace they serve; they do not debate the question as to which of the virtues of their master is pre-eminently worthy of admiration, for they assure him that he possesses all the virtues under heaven without having acquired them, or without caring to acquire them; they do not give him their daughters and their wives to be raised at his pleasure to the rank of his concubines, but, by sacrificing their opinions, they prostitute themselves. Moralists and philosophers in America are not obliged to conceal their opinions under the veil of allegory; but, before they venture upon a harsh truth, they say: 'We are aware that the people which we are addressing is too superior to all the weaknesses of human nature to lose the command of its temper for an instant; and we should not hold this language if we were not speaking to men whom their virtues and their intelligence render more worthy of freedom than all the rest of the world.' It would have been impossible for the sycophants of Louis XIV to flatter more dexterously. For my part, I am persuaded that in all governments, whatever their nature may be, servility will cower to force, and adulation will cling to power. The only means of preventing men from degrading themselves is to invest no one with that unlimited authority which is the surest method of debasing them.

Governments usually fall a sacrifice to impotence or to tyranny. In the former case their power escapes from them; it is wrested from their grasp in the latter. Many observers, who have witnessed the anarchy of democratic States, have imagined that the government of those States was naturally weak and impotent. The truth is, that when once hostilities are begun between parties, the government loses its control over society. But I do not think that a democratic power is naturally without force or without resources: say, rather, that it is almost always by the abuse of its force and the misemployment of its resources that a democratic government fails. Anarchy is almost always produced by its tyranny or its mistakes, but not by its want of strength.

It is important not to confound stability with force, or the greatness of a thing with its duration. In democratic republics, the power which directs society is not stable; for it often changes hands and assumes a new direction. But whichever way it turns, its force is almost irresistible. The governments of the American republics appear to me to be as much centralized as those of the absolute monarchies of Europe, and more energetic than they are. I do not, therefore, imagine that they will perish from weakness.

If ever the free institutions of America are destroyed, that event may be attributed to the unlimited authority of the majority, which may at some future time urge the minorities to desperation, and oblige them to have recourse to physical force. Anarchy will then be the result, but it will have been brought about by despotism. . . .

To Think About

1. "Strong is never strong enough to be always the strongest, unless he transforms strength into right, and obedience into duty."   ***Jean-Jacques Rousseau***

2. "We were seeing the desperate attempt of a handful of pathetically unequipped children to create a community in a social vacuum. Once we had seen these children, we could no longer overlook the vacuum, no longer pretend that the society's atomization could be reversed. This was not a traditional generational rebellion. At some point between 1945 and 1967 we had somehow neglected to tell these children the rules of the game we happened to be playing. Maybe we had stopped believing in the rules ourselves, maybe we were having a

failure of nerve about the game. Maybe there were just too few people around to do the telling. These were children who grew up cut loose from the web of cousins and great-aunts and family doctors and lifelong neighbors who had traditionally suggested and enforced the society's values. They are children who have moved around a lot, *San Jose, Chula Vista, here.* They are less in rebellion against the society than ignorant of it, able only to feed back certain of its most publicized self-doubts, *Vietnam, Saran-Wrap, diet pills, the Bomb."*

                                                                    Joan Didion

3. "The passion for freedom of the mind is strong and everlasting which is fortunate, because so is the passion to squelch it."   ***A. M. Rosenthal***

4. "That one human being will desire to render the person and property of another subservient to his pleasures, notwithstanding the pain or loss of pleasure which it may occasion to that individual, is the foundation of government."

                                                                    James Mill

5. Distinguish between right, left, and center in social and political philosophy, and indicate where you stand and why. List specific groups in society that you think can reasonably be placed under each of these headings.

6. Indicate why you agree or disagree with the following statement by ***Samuel Eliot Morison*** in *Freedom in Contemporary Society:*

    > In my opinion, the growth of democracy in the United States has not contributed to the growth of political freedom. And the reasons, I think, are clear: (1) Political education has never caught up with political power. (2) The religious sanction to government has, declined, with commensurate loss of public virtue; character and intelligence are losing the race to greed and selfishness. It is only by comparison with totalitarian governments, where the religious sanction is wholly wanting, and where free rein is given to cruelty and other abominable traits of human nature, that we are reconciled to the milder ills and supportable disadvantages of democracy. (1956, p. 29)

7. "Adherents of the two great contrasting systems cast the same reproaches at each other. The one party considers economic freedom as one of the fundamental rights of the individual, and believes that it is in fact the very condition upon which the material and the moral health of a society depends. Therefore, it denounces economic planning as a form of tyranny which must be fought against in the name of the sacred value of liberty. The other party asserts that the liberation of individuals can be guaranteed only by an economic structure devoid of the faults of individual profit-seeking. . . ."   ***Joseph Post***

8. "An appeal to principles is the condition of any considerable reconstruction of society, because social institutions are the visible expression of the scale of moral values which rules the minds of individuals, and it is impossible to alter institutions without altering that valuation."   ***R. H. Tawney***

9. "It is not the business of government to make men virtuous or religious, or to preserve the fool from the consequences of his own folly. Governments should be repressive no further than is necessary to secure liberty by protecting the

equal rights of each from aggression on the part of others. . . . Out of the principle that it is the proper end and purpose of government to secure the natural rights and equal liberty of the individual, grows the principle that it is the business of government to do for the mass of individuals those things which cannot be done, or cannot be so well done, by individual action."   ***Henry George***

10. "There is, of course, a sphere within which the individual may assert the supremacy of his own will and rightfully dispute the authority of any human government—especially of any free government existing under a written constitution, to interfere with the exercise of that will."   ***Louis Brandeis***

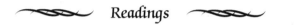

Readings

RAWLS, JOHN. *Political Liberalism.* New York: Columbia University Press, 1993.

WEST, CORNEL. *Democracy Matters: Winning the War against Imperialism.* New York: Penguin, 2004.

WOLIN, SHELDON S. *Tocqueville Between Two Worlds: The Making of a Political and Theoretical Life.* Princeton, NJ: Princeton University Press, 2001.

ZUNZ, OLIVER, AND ALAN S. KAHAN, eds. *The Tocqueville Reader: A Life in Letters and Politics.* Oxford: Blackwell, 2002.

52

Utopias Lead to Violence

Karl Popper (1902–94) was born in Vienna. He received a Ph.D. from the University of Vienna in 1928. In 1937 he emigrated to New Zealand, where he taught until 1945. He then moved to England and remained there until 1960 as a professor of philoso-phy at the London School of Economics. He was knighted by Queen Elizabeth II in 1964. Popper's major contributions to philosophy lie in the fields of scientific method and political theory. He called his position critical rationalism *and insisted that sci-ence progressed not inductively but by a method of* falsifiability, *whereby scientific theory was not so much confirmed as refuted by contrary evidence. In political the-ory he maintained a liberal democratic position, holding that both left-wing dogmas such as Marxism and right-wing dogmas such as fascism fail because of their non-scientific belief in historical inevitability. Popper's major writings include* The Open Society and Its Enemies *(1946),* The Logic of Scientific Discovery *(1959),* The Poverty of Historicism *(1961), and* Conjectures and Refutations *(1963), from which the fol-lowing reading is taken.*

The horrific events of September 11, 2001, have suggested to philosophers a new and compelling need to come to terms with the concept of terrorism and arguments ad-duced for and against its justification. But the conceptual problems involved are daunting. A recent estimate holds that there are at least one hundred definitions of ter-rorism in the current literature. Moreover, the experience of September 11 was un-precedented in our history. Never has the United States had to endure the kind of attack mounted by the terrorists, and opinions on dealing with future such threats vary widely. One undeniable feature of terrorism is the use of violence to pursue its aims. In the following essay, the distinguished philosopher of science Karl Popper exam-ines violence, in this case during a period more than half a century ago, the violence of the Second World War. He argues that it is a necessary component of idealistic utopian views of political association. Perhaps in our own time religious idealists,

Ch. 18 from *Conjectures and Refutations* by Karl Popper, first published 1963 by Routledge & Kegan Paul, London, reproduced by permission of the estate of Sir Karl Popper.

such as some Middle Eastern extremists, and democratic idealists, like some Western political leaders, hold similar utopian visions, that somehow the world will achieve a new period of glory if their own particular worldviews become realized. If Popper is right, violence must accompany their strategy. Utopian political schemes are perversely attached to an extreme rationalism. A critique of rationalism will entail a critique of utopianism and, finally, of the violent means needed by all utopian dogmatists to accomplish their aims.

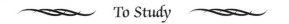 **To Study**

1. What does Popper mean by calling himself a *rationalist*?
2. What role does "intellectual humility" play in Popper's attitude of "reasonableness"?
3. What are some of the impediments to promoting Popper's form of rationalism?
4. How does Popper define *Utopianism*? How is it a form of rationalism?
5. How is Utopianism self-defeating? How does it tend to produce violence?
6. Popper distinguishes Utopianism from other forms of political reform and idealism. What characterizes acceptable reform in his opinion?
7. What attitude towards history does Popper have that convinces him of the false rationalism of Utopian schemes?
8. Popper argues that the problem of true and false rationalism is part of a larger problem. What is it? How does his version of rationalism help solve this larger problem?

THERE ARE many people who hate violence and are convinced that it is one of their foremost and at the same time one of their most hopeful tasks to work for its reduction and, if possible, for its elimination from human life. I am among these hopeful enemies of violence. I not only hate violence, but I firmly believe that the fight against it is not at all hopeless. I realize that the task is difficult. I realize that, only too often in the course of history, it has happened that what appeared at first to be a great success in the fight against violence was followed by defeat. I do not overlook the fact that the new age of violence which was opened by the two World wars is by no means at an end. Nazism and Fascism are thoroughly beaten, but I must admit that their defeat does not mean that barbarism and brutality have been defeated. On the contrary, it is no use closing our eyes to the fact that these hateful ideas achieved something like victory in defeat. I have to admit that Hitler succeeded in degrading the moral standards of our Western world, and that in the world of today there is more violence and brutal force than would have been tolerated even in the decade after the first World war. And we must face the possibility that our civilization may ultimately be destroyed by those

An address delivered to the Institute des Arts in Brussels in June 1947; first published in The Hibbert Journal, 46, *1948.*

new weapons which Hitlerism wished upon us, perhaps even within the first decade[1] after the second World war; for no doubt the spirit of Hitlerism won its greatest victory over us when, after its defeat, we used the weapons which the threat of Nazism had induced us to develop. But in spite of all this I am today no less hopeful than I have ever been that violence can be defeated. It is our only hope; and long stretches in the history of Western as well as of Eastern civilizations prove that it need not be a vain hope—that violence *can* be reduced, and brought under the control of reason.

This is perhaps why I, like many others, believe in reason; why I call myself a rationalist. I am a rationalist because I see in the attitude of reasonableness the only alternative to violence.

When two men disagree, they do so either because their opinions differ, or because their interests differ, or both. There are many kinds of disagreement in social life which must be decided one way or another. The question may be one which must be settled, because failure to settle it may create new difficulties whose cumulative effects may cause an intolerable strain, such as a state of continual and intense preparation for deciding the issue. (An armaments race is an example.) To reach a decision may be a necessity.

How can a decision be reached? There are, in the main, only two possible ways: argument (including arguments submitted to arbitration, for example to some international court of justice) and violence. Or, if it is interests that clash, the two alternatives are a reasonable compromise or an attempt to destroy the opposing interest.

A rationalist, as I use the word, is a man who attempts to reach decisions by argument and perhaps, in certain cases, by compromise, rather than by violence. He is a man who would rather be unsuccessful in convincing another man by argument than successful in crushing him by force, by intimidation and threats, or even by persuasive propaganda.

We shall understand better what I mean by reasonableness if we consider the difference between trying to convince a man by argument and trying to persuade him by propaganda.

The difference does not lie so much in the use of argument. Propaganda often uses argument too. Nor does the difference lie in our conviction that our arguments are conclusive, and must be admitted to be conclusive by any reasonable man. It lies rather in an attitude of give and take, in a readiness not only to convince the other man but also possibly to be convinced by him. What I call the attitude of reasonableness may be characterized by a remark like this: 'I think I am right, but I may be wrong and you may be right, and in any case let us discuss it, for in this way we are likely to get nearer to a true understanding than if we each merely insist that we are right.'

It will be realized that what I call the attitude of reasonableness or the rationalistic attitude presupposes a certain amount of intellectual humility. Perhaps only those can take it up who are aware that they are sometimes wrong, and who do not habitually forget their mistakes. It is born of the realization that we are not omniscient, and that we owe most of our knowledge to others. It is an attitude which tries as far as possible to transfer to the field of opinions in general the two rules of every legal proceeding: first, that one should always hear both sides, and secondly, that one does not make a good judge if one is a party to the case.

---

[1] This was written in 1947. Today I should alter this passage merely by replacing 'first' by 'second'.

I believe that we can avoid violence only in so far as we practise this attitude of reasonableness when dealing with one another in social life; and that any other attitude is likely to produce violence—even a one-sided attempt to deal with others by gentle persuasion, and to convince them by argument and example of those insights we are proud of possessing, and of whose truth we are absolutely certain. We all remember how many religious wars were fought for a religion of love and gentleness; how many bodies were burned alive with the genuinely kind intention of saving souls from the eternal fire of hell. Only if we give up our authoritarian attitude in the realm of opinion, only if we establish the attitude of give and take, of readiness to learn from other people, can we hope to control acts of violence inspired by piety and duty.

There are many difficulties impeding the rapid spread of reasonableness. One of the main difficulties is that it always takes two to make a discussion reasonable. Each of the parties must be ready to learn from the other. You cannot have a rational discussion with a man who prefers shooting you to being convinced by you. In other words, there are limits to the attitude of reasonableness. It is the same with tolerance. You must not, without qualification, accept the principle of tolerating all those who are intolerant; if you do, you will destroy not only yourself, but also the attitude of tolerance. (All this is indicated in the remark I made before—that reasonableness must be an attitude of *give and take.*)

An important consequence of all this is that we must not allow the distinction between attack and defence to become blurred. We must insist upon this distinction, and support and develop social institutions (national as well as international) whose function it is to discriminate between aggression and resistance to aggression.

I think I have said enough to make clear what I intend to convey by calling myself a rationalist. My rationalism is not dogmatic. I fully admit that I cannot rationally prove it. I frankly confess that I choose rationalism because I hate violence, and I do not deceive myself into believing that this hatred has any rational grounds. Or to put it another way, my rationalism is not self-contained, but rests on an irrational faith in the attitude of reasonableness. I do not see that we can go beyond this. One could say, perhaps, that my irrational faith in equal and reciprocal rights to convince others and be convinced by them is a faith in human reason; or simply, that I believe in man.

If I say that I believe in man, I mean in man as he is; and I should never dream of saying that he is wholly rational. I do not think that a question such as whether man is more rational than emotional or *vice versa* should be asked: there are no ways of assessing or comparing such things. I admit that I feel inclined to protest against certain exaggerations (arising largely from a vulgarization of psycho-analysis) of the irrationality of man and of human society. But I am aware not only of the power of emotions in human life, but also of their value. I should never demand that the attainment of an attitude of reasonableness should become the one dominant aim of our lives. All I wish to assert is that this attitude can become one that is never wholly absent—not even in relationships which are dominated by great passions, such as love.[2]

---

[2] The existentialist Jaspers writes 'This is why love is cruel, ruthless; and why it is believed in, by the genuine lover, only if it is so'. This attitude, to my mind, reveals weakness rather than the strength it wishes to show; it is not so much plain barbarism as an hysterical attempt to play the barbarian. (*Cf.* my *Open Society,* 4th edn., vol. II, p. 317.)

My fundamental attitude towards the problem of reason and violence will by now be understood; and I hope I share it with some of my readers and with many other people everywhere. It is on this basis that I now propose to discuss the problem of Utopianism.

I think we can describe Utopianism as a result of a form of rationalism, and I shall try to show that this is a form of rationalism very different from the form in which I and many others believe. So I shall try to show that there exist at least two forms of rationalism, one of which I believe is right and the other wrong; and that the wrong kind of rationalism is the one which leads to Utopianism.

As far as I can see, Utopianism is the result of a way of reasoning which is accepted by many who would be astonished to hear that this apparently quite inescapable and self-evident way of reasoning leads to Utopian results. This specious reasoning can perhaps be presented in the following manner.

An action, it may be argued, is rational if it makes the best use of the available means in order to achieve a certain end. The end, admittedly, may be incapable of being determined rationally. However this may be, we can judge an action rationally, and describe it as rational or adequate, only relative to some given end. Only if we have an end in mind, and only relative to such an end, can we say that we are acting rationally.

Now let us apply this argument to politics. All politics consists of actions; and these actions will be rational only if they pursue some end. The end of a man's political actions may be the increase of his own power or wealth. Or it may perhaps be the improvement of the laws of the state, a change in the structure of the state.

In the latter case political action will be rational only if we first determine the final ends of the political changes which we intend to bring about. It will be rational only relative to certain ideas of what a state ought to be like. Thus it appears that as a preliminary to any rational political action we must first attempt to become as clear as possible about our ultimate political ends; for example the kind of state which we should consider the best; and only afterwards can we begin to determine the means which may best help us to realize this state, or to move slowly towards it, taking it as the aim of a historical process which we may to some extent influence and steer towards the goal selected.

Now it is precisely this view which I call Utopianism. Any rational and non-selfish political action, on this view, must be preceded by a determination of our ultimate ends, not merely of intermediate or partial aims which are only steps towards our ultimate end, and which therefore should be considered as means rather than as ends; therefore rational political action must be based upon a more or less clear and detailed description or blueprint of our ideal state, and also upon a plan or blueprint of the historical path that leads towards this goal.

I consider what I call Utopianism an attractive and, indeed, an all too attractive theory; for I also consider it dangerous and pernicious. It is, I believe, self-defeating, and it leads to violence.

That it is self-defeating is connected with the fact that it is impossible to determine ends scientifically. There is no scientific way of choosing between two ends. Some people, for example, love and venerate violence. For them a life without violence would be shallow and trivial. Many others, of whom I am one, hate violence.

This is a quarrel about ends. It cannot be decided by science. This does not mean that the attempt to argue against violence is necessarily a waste of time. It only means that you may not be able to argue with the admirer of violence. He has a way of answering an argument with a bullet if he is not kept under control by the threat of counterviolence. If he is willing to listen to your arguments without shooting you, then he is at least infected by rationalism, and you may, perhaps, win him over. This is why arguing is no waste of time—as long as people listen to you. But you cannot, by means of argument, make people listen to argument; you cannot, by means of argument, convert those who suspect all argument, and who prefer violent decisions to rational decisions. You cannot prove to them that they are wrong. And this is only a particular case, which can be generalized. No decision about aims can be established by *purely* rational or scientific means. Nevertheless argument may prove extremely helpful in reaching a decision about aims.

Applying all this to the problem of Utopianism, we must first be quite clear that the problem of constructing a Utopian blueprint cannot possibly be solved by science alone. Its aims, at least, must be given before the social scientist can begin to sketch his blueprint. We find the same situation in the natural sciences. No amount of physics will tell a scientist that it is the right thing for him to construct a plough, or an aeroplane, or an atomic bomb. Ends must be adopted by him, or given to him; and what he does *qua* scientist is only to construct means by which these ends can be realized.

In emphasizing the difficulty of deciding, by way of rational argument, between different Utopian ideals, I do not wish to create the impression that there is a realm—such as the realm of ends—which goes altogether beyond the power of rational criticism (even though I certainly wish to say that the realm of ends goes largely beyond the power of *scientific* argument). For I myself try to argue about this realm; and by pointing out the difficulty of deciding between competing Utopian blueprints, I try to argue rationally against choosing ideal ends of this kind. Similarly, my attempt to point out that this difficulty is likely to produce violence is meant as a rational argument, although it will appeal only to those who hate violence.

That the Utopian method, which chooses an ideal state of society as the aim which all our political actions should serve, is likely to produce violence can be shown thus. Since we cannot determine the ultimate ends of political actions scientifically, or by purely rational methods, differences of opinion concerning what the ideal state should be like cannot always be smoothed out by the method of argument. They will at least partly have the character of religious differences. And there can be no tolerance between these different Utopian religions. Utopian aims are designed to serve as a basis for rational political action and discussion, and such action appears to be possible only if the aim is definitely decided upon. Thus the Utopianist must win over, or else crush, his Utopianist competitors who do not share his own Utopian aims and who do not profess his own Utopianist religion.

But he has to do more. He has to be very thorough in eliminating and stamping out all heretical competing views. For the way to the Utopian goal is long. Thus the rationality of his political action demands constancy of aim for a long time ahead; and this can only be achieved if he not merely crushes competing Utopian religions, but as far as possible stamps out all memory of them.

The use of violent methods for the suppression of competing aims becomes even more urgent if we consider that the period of Utopian construction is liable to be one of social change. In such a time ideas are liable to change also. Thus what may have appeared to many as desirable at the time when the Utopian blueprint was decided upon may appear less desirable at a later date. If this is so, the whole approach is in danger of breaking down. For if we change our ultimate political aims while attempting to move towards them we may soon discover that we are moving in circles. The whole method of first establishing an ultimate political aim and then preparing to move towards it must be futile if the aim may be changed during the process of its realization. It may easily turn out that the steps so far taken lead in fact away from the new aim. And if we then change direction in accordance with our new aim we expose ourselves to the same risk. In spite of all the sacrifices which we may have made in order to make sure that we are acting rationally, we may get exactly nowhere—although not exactly to that 'nowhere' which is meant by the word 'Utopia'.

Again, the only way to avoid such changes of our aims seems to be to use violence, which includes propaganda, the suppression of criticism, and the annihilation of all opposition. With it goes the affirmation of the wisdom and foresight of the Utopian planners, of the Utopian engineers who design and execute the Utopian blueprint. The Utopian engineers must in this way become omniscient as well as omnipotent. They become gods. Thou shalt have no other Gods before them.

Utopian rationalism is a self-defeating rationalism. However benevolent its ends, it does not bring happiness, but only the familiar misery of being condemned to live under a tyrannical government.

It is important to understand this criticism fully. I do not criticize political ideals as such, nor do I assert that a political ideal can never be realized. This would not be a valid criticism. Many ideals have been realized which were once dogmatically declared to be unrealizable, for example, the establishment of workable and untyrannical institutions for securing civil peace, that is, for the suppression of crime within the state. Again, I see no reason why an international judicature and an international police force should be less successful in suppressing international crime, that is, national aggression and the ill-treatment of minorities or perhaps majorities. I do not object to the attempt to realize such ideals.

Wherein, then, lies the difference between those benevolent Utopian plans to which I object because they lead to violence, and those other important and far-reaching political reforms which I am inclined to recommend?

If I were to give a simple formula or recipe for distinguishing between what I consider to be admissible plans for social reform and inadmissible Utopian blueprints, I might say:

Work for the elimination of concrete evils rather than for the realization of abstract goods. Do not aim at establishing happiness by political means. Rather aim at the elimination of concrete miseries. Or, in more practical terms: fight for the elimination of poverty by direct means—for example, by making sure that everybody has a minimum income. Or fight against epidemics and disease by erecting hospitals and schools of medicine. Fight illiteracy as you fight criminality. But do all this by direct means. Choose what you consider the most urgent evil of the society in which you live, and try patiently to convince people that we can get rid of it.

But do not try to realize these aims indirectly by designing and working for a distant ideal of a society which is wholly good. However deeply you may feel indebted to its inspiring vision, do not think that you are obliged to work for its realization, or that it is your mission to open the eyes of others to its beauty. Do not allow your dreams of a beautiful world to lure you away from the claims of men who suffer here and now. Our fellow men have a claim to our help; no generation must be sacrificed for the sake of future generations, for the sake of an ideal of happiness that may never be realized. In brief, it is my thesis that human misery is the most urgent problem of a rational public policy and that happiness is not such a problem. The attainment of happiness should be left to our private endeavours.

It is a fact, and not a very strange fact, that it is not so very difficult to reach agreement by discussion on what are the most intolerable evils of our society, and on what are the most urgent social reforms. Such an agreement can be reached much more easily than an agreement concerning some ideal form of social life. For the evils are with us here and now. They can be experienced, and are being experienced every day, by many people who have been and are being made miserable by poverty, unemployment, national oppression, war and disease. Those of us who do not suffer from these miseries meet every day others who can describe them to us. This is what makes the evils concrete. This is why we can get somewhere in arguing about them; why we can profit here from the attitude of reasonableness. We can learn by listening to concrete claims, by patiently trying to assess them as impartially as we can, and by considering ways of meeting them without creating worse evils.

With ideal goods it is different. These we know only from our dreams and from the dreams of our poets and prophets. They cannot be discussed, only proclaimed from the housetops. They do not call for the rational attitude of the impartial judge, but for the emotional attitude of the impassioned preacher.

The Utopianist attitude, therefore, is opposed to the attitude of reasonableness. Utopianism, even though it may often appear in a rationalist disguise, cannot be more than a pseudo-rationalism.

What, then, is wrong with the apparently rational argument which I outlined when presenting the Utopianist case? I believe that it is quite true that we can judge the rationality of an action only in relation to some aims or ends. But this does not necessarily mean that the rationality of a political action can be judged only in relation to an *historical* end. And it surely does not mean that we must consider every social or political situation merely from the point of view of some preconceived historical ideal, from the point of view of an alleged ultimate aim of the development of history. On the contrary, if among our aims and ends there is anything conceived in terms of human happiness and misery, then we are bound to judge our actions in terms not only of possible contributions to the happiness of man in a distant future, but also of their more immediate effects. We must not argue that a certain social situation is a mere means to an end on the grounds that it is merely a transient historical situation. For all situations are transient. Similarly we must not argue that the misery of one generation may be considered as a mere means to the end of securing the lasting happiness of some later generation or generations; and this argument is improved neither by a high degree of promised happiness nor by a large number of generations profiting by it. All generations are transient. All have an equal right to be considered, but our immediate duties are undoubtedly to the present generation and to the next. Besides, we should never attempt to balance anybody's misery against somebody else's happiness.

With this the apparently rational arguments of Utopianism dissolve into nothing. The fascination which the future exerts upon the Utopianist has nothing to do with rational foresight. Considered in this light the violence which Utopianism breeds looks very much like the running amok of an evolutionist metaphysics, of an hysterical philosophy of history, eager to sacrifice the present for the splendours of the future, and unaware that its principle would lead to sacrificing each particular future period for one which comes after it; and likewise unaware of the trivial truth that the ultimate future of man—whatever fate may have in store for him—can be nothing more splendid than his ultimate extinction.

The appeal of Utopianism arises from the failure to realize that we cannot make heaven on earth. What I believe we can do instead is to make life a little less terrible and a little less unjust in each generation. A good deal can be achieved in this way. Much has been achieved in the last hundred years. More could be achieved by our own generation. There are many pressing problems which we might solve, at least partially, such as helping the weak and the sick, and those who suffer under oppression and injustice; stamping out unemployment; equalizing opportunities; and preventing international crime, such as blackmail and war instigated by men like gods, by omnipotent and omniscient leaders. All this, we might achieve if only we could give up dreaming about distant ideals and fighting over our Utopian blueprints for a new world and a new man. Those of us who believe in man as he is, and who have therefore not given up the hope of defeating violence and unreason, must demand instead that every man should be given the right to arrange his life himself so far as this is compatible with the equal rights of others.

We can see here that the problem of the true and the false rationalisms is part of a larger problem. Ultimately it is the problem of a sane attitude towards our own existence and its limitations—that very problem of which so much is made now by those who call themselves 'Existentialists', the expounders of a new theology without God. There is, I believe, a neurotic and even an hysterical element in this exaggerated emphasis upon the fundamental loneliness of man in a godless world, and upon the resulting tension between the self and the world. I have little doubt that this hysteria is closely akin to Utopian romanticism, and also to the ethic of hero-worship, to an ethic that can comprehend life only in terms of 'dominate or prostrate yourself'. And I do not doubt that this hysteria is the secret of its strong appeal. That our problem is part of a larger one can be seen from the fact that we can find a clear parallel to the split between true and false rationalism even in a sphere apparently so far removed from rationalism as that of religion. Christian thinkers have interpreted the relationship between man and God in at least two very different ways. The sane one may be expressed by: 'Never forget that men are not Gods; but remember that there is a divine spark in them.' The other exaggerates the tension between man and God, and the baseness of man as well as the heights to which men may aspire. It introduces the ethic of 'dominate or prostrate yourself' into the relationship of man and God. Whether there are always either conscious or unconscious dreams of godlikeness and of omnipotence at the roots of this attitude, I do not know. But I think it is hard to deny that the emphasis on this tension can arise only from an unbalanced attitude towards the problem of power.

This unbalanced (and immature) attitude is obsessed with the problem of power, not only over other men, but also over our natural environment—over the world as a whole. What I might call, by analogy, the 'false religion', is obsessed not only by God's power over men but also by His power to create a world; similarly, false rationalism is fascinated by the idea of creating huge machines and Utopian social worlds. Bacon's 'knowledge is power' and Plato's 'rule of the wise' are different expressions of this attitude which, at bottom, is one of claiming power on the basis of one's superior intellectual gifts. The true rationalist, by contrast, will always know how little he knows, and he will be aware of the simple fact that whatever critical faculty or reason he may possess he owes to intellectual intercourse with others. He will be inclined, therefore, to consider men as fundamentally equal, and human reason as a bond which unites them. Reason for him is the precise opposite of an instrument of power and violence: he sees it as a means whereby these may be tamed.

To Think About

1. "Power and violence are opposites; where the one rules absolutely, the other is absent. Violence appears where power is in jeopardy, but left to its own course it ends in power's disappearance. This implies that it is not correct to think of the opposite of violence as nonviolence; to speak of nonviolent power is actually redundant. Violence can destroy power; it is utterly incapable of creating it."

   Hannah Arendt

2. "Power grows out of the barrel of a gun."   ***Mao Tse-tung***

3. "Examine the lives of the best and most fruitful men and people, and ask yourselves whether a tree, if it is to grow proudly into the sky, can do without bad weather and storms: whether unkindness and opposition from without, whether some sort of hatred, envy, obstinacy, mistrust, severity, greed, and violence do not belong to the favoring circumstances without which a great increase even in virtue is hardly possible."   ***Friedrich Nietzsche***

4. "After ages during which the earth produced harmless trilobites and butterflies, evolution progressed to the point at which it has generated Neros, Genghis Khans, and Hitlers. This, however, I believe is a passing nightmare; in time the earth will become once again incapable of supporting life, and peace will return."   ***Bertrand Russell***

5. "I would have supported the [French, ED.] Revolution if it had not begun with crimes. I will never regard murder as an object of admiration and a way to

achieve freedom. There is nothing more servile, despicable, cowardly and narrow-minded than a terrorist."   ***François René de Cheateaubriand***

6. "The story of the human race is war. Except for brief and precarious interludes there has never been peace in the world; and long before history began murderous strife was universal and unending."   ***Winston Churchill***

7. "Neither nature nor history can tell us what we ought to do. Facts, whether those of nature or those of history, cannot make the decision for us, they cannot determine the ends we are going to choose. It is we who introduce purpose and meaning into nature and into history. Men are not equal; but we can decide to fight for equal rights. Human institutions such as the state are not rational, but we can decide to fight to make them more rational."   ***Karl Popper***

8. "What causes the greatest crimes in history? The greatest bloodshed? The most murders? I would say two things: sincere love and a sincere devotion to liberty . . . If you kill out of love or for a perfect utopia, you never stop killing because human nature is always imperfect."   ***Peter Viereck***

Readings

ARENDT, HANNAH. *On Violence.* New York: Harcourt, Brace & World, 1970.

BAUDRILLARD, JEAN. *The Spirit of Terrorism and Other Essays.* New York: Verso, 2003.

HONDERICH, TED. *After the Terror.* Edinburgh: Edinburgh University Press, 2002.

NOTTURNO, MARK AMADEUS. *Science and the Open Society: The Future of Karl Popper's Philosophy.* New York: Central European University Press, 2000.

SCHILPP, PAUL ARTHUR, ed. *The Philosophy of Karl Popper.* La Salle, IL: Open Court, 1974.

53

Are Most Abortions Moral?

Jane English (1947–78) *taught at the University of North Carolina. She published several well-received articles and edited both* Sex Equality *(1977) and* Feminism and Philosophy *(1977).*

The final decades of the twentieth century saw a strong debate over the right to abortion, which was set off when the U.S. Supreme Court declared some abortions legal on the basis of the right to privacy. Those in favor of the right to abortion, the so-called pro-choice individuals, argue their position on two grounds: first, that a woman has a right to choose matters concerning her body and, second, that the fetus is not a person. In opposition the antiabortionists, the so-called pro-lifers, argue that the fetus is a person from conception.

The majority in *Roe* v. *Wade* (1973) argued that there is a constitutional right of privacy that protects the freedom to decide whether or not to have children. Thus a person has the freedom to terminate a pregnancy, although the Court recognized the state's interest in certain aspects of the practical exercise of that freedom—to protect a woman's health in the second trimester and to protect the life of a viable fetus in the third trimester. The underlying principle is nevertheless clear: the constitutional right of privacy allows every woman to make the choice for herself without government interference.

In the 1992 decision *Planned Parenthood* v. *Casey, Roe* was reaffirmed with some limitations regarding counseling, waiting period, and juvenile decision making. The majority held that there must be stability in the law and that there is a basic concept of liberty that embodies the right to privacy. The minority held that because the

Reprinted from the *Canadian Journal of Philosophy,* vol. 5, no. 2 (October 1975) by permission of the University of Calgary Press and the Jane English Memorial Trust Fund, University of North Carolina, Chapel Hill, NC.

right of privacy is not in the Constitution there is no such right, including that of abortion. They also held that the fetus is a potential human and therefore has a right to life.

Jane English's essay contends that conservatives who argue that abortion is wrong because it represents the murder of a human life that began at conception cannot justify their position, as there are some justifiable killings. On the other hand, liberals are wrong when they argue that because the fetus does not become a person until birth, abortion is never wrong. A woman cannot do whatever she wishes with her body during pregnancy. Animals are not persons, and yet to torture them is wrong. One great problem is that it is difficult to provide a satisfactory concept of a *person*. Nonetheless, that a fetus is a person does not mean that killing it is necessarily wrong, but if a fetus is not a person, abortion is not always morally permissible because in the last month a fetus closely resembles a person, and innocent persons should not be killed.

To Study

1. State the two most popular positions on abortion.
2. What are the five features Warren lists as criteria for personhood?
3. Are there any circumstances in which it is acceptable to kill an innocent person?
4. State some different historical views as to when a person comes into existence.
5. What premise does Judith Thomson say is needed in the conservative argument?
6. What reasons does English give to support her view that abortion is almost always justified?

The abortion debate rages on. Yet the two most popular positions seem to be clearly mistaken. Conservatives maintain that a human life begins at conception and that therefore abortion must be wrong because it is murder. But not all killings of humans are murders. Most notably, self defense may justify even the killing of an innocent person.

Liberals, on the other hand, are just as mistaken in their argument that since a fetus does not become a person until birth, a woman may do whatever she pleases in and to her own body. First, you cannot do as you please with your own body if it affects other people adversely.[1] Second, if a fetus is not a person, that does not imply that you can do to it anything you wish. Animals, for example, are not persons, yet to kill or torture them for no reason at all is wrong.

At the center of the storm has been the issue of just when it is between ovulation and adulthood that a person appears on the scene. Conservatives draw the line at conception, liberals at birth. In this paper I first examine our concept of a person and conclude that no single criterion can capture the concept of a person and no sharp line can be drawn. Next I argue that if a fetus is a person, abortion is still justifiable in

---

[1] We also have paternalistic laws which keep us from harming our own bodies even when no one else is affected. Ironically, anti-abortion laws were originally designed to protect pregnant women from a dangerous but tempting procedure.

many cases: and if a fetus is not a person, killing it is still wrong in many cases. To a large extent, these two solutions are in agreement. I conclude that our concept of a person cannot and need not bear the weight that the abortion controversy has thrust upon it.

I

The several factions in the abortion argument have drawn battle lines around various proposed criteria for determining what is and what is not a person. For example, Mary Anne Warren[2] lists five features (capacities for reasoning, self-awareness, complex communication, etc.) as her criteria for personhood and argues for the permissibility of abortion because a fetus falls outside this concept. Baruch Brody[3] uses brain waves. Michael Tooley[4] picks having-a-concept-of-self as his criterion and concludes that infanticide and abortion are justifiable, while the killing of adult animals is not. On the other side, Paul Ramsey[5] claims a certain gene structure is the defining characteristic. John Noonan[6] prefers conceived-of-humans and presents counterexamples to various other candidate criteria. For instance, he argues against viability as the criterion because the newborn and infirm would then be non-persons, since they cannot live without the aid of others. He rejects any criterion that calls upon the sorts of sentiments a being can evoke in adults on the grounds that this would allow us to exclude other races as non-persons if we could just view them sufficiently unsentimentally.

These approaches are typical: foes of abortion propose sufficient conditions for personhood which fetuses satisfy, while friends of abortion counter with necessary conditions for personhood which fetuses lack. But these both presuppose that the concept of a person can be captured in a strait jacket of necessary and/or sufficient conditions.[7] Rather, "person" is a cluster of features, of which rationality, having a self concept and being conceived of humans are only part.

What is typical of persons? Within our concept of a person we include, first, certain biological factors: descended from humans, having a certain genetic makeup, having a head, hands, arms, eyes, capable of locomotion, breathing, eating, sleeping. There are psychological factors: sentience, perception, having a concept of self and of one's own interests and desires, the ability to use tools, the ability to use language or symbol systems, the ability to joke, to be angry, to doubt. There are rationality factors: the ability to reason and draw conclusions, the ability to generalize and to learn

[2] Mary Anne Warren, "On the Moral and Legal Status of Abortion," *Monist* 57 (1973).

[3] Baruch Brody, "Fetal Humanity and the Theory of Essentialism," in Robert Baker and Frederick Elliston (eds.), *Philosophy and Sex* (Buffalo, N.Y., 1975).

[4] Michael Tooley, "Abortion and Infanticide," *Philosophy and the Public Affairs* 2 (1971).

[5] Paul Ramsey, "The Morality of Abortion," in James Rachels, ed., *Moral Problems* (New York, 1971).

[6] John Noonan, "Abortion and the Catholic Church: A Summary History," *Natural Law Forum* 12 (1967), pp. 125–31.

[7] Wittgenstein has argued against the possibility of so capturing the concept of a game. *Philosophical Investigations* (New York, 1958), §66–71.

from past experience, the ability to sacrifice present interests for greater gains in the future. There are social factors: the ability to work in groups and respond to peer pressures, the ability to recognize and consider as valuable the interests of others, seeing oneself as one among "other minds," the ability to sympathize, encourage, love, the ability to evoke from others the responses of sympathy, encouragement, love, the ability to work with others for mutual advantage. Then there are legal factors: being subject to the law and protected by it, having the ability to sue and enter contracts, being counted in the census, having a name and citizenship, the ability to own property, inherit, and so forth.

Now the point is not that this list is incomplete, or that you can find counter-instances to each of its points. People typically exhibit rationality, for instance, but someone who was irrational would not thereby fail to qualify as a person. On the other hand, something could exhibit the majority of these features and still fail to be a person, as an advanced robot might. There is no single core of necessary and sufficient features which we can draw upon with the assurance that they constitute what really makes a person; there are only features that are more or less typical.

This is not to say that no necessary or sufficient conditions can be given. Being alive is a necessary condition for being a person, and being a U.S. Senator is sufficient. But rather than falling inside a sufficient condition or outside a necessary one, a fetus lies in the penumbra region where our concept of a person is not so simple. For this reason I think a conclusive answer to the question whether a fetus is a person is unattainable.

Here we might note a family of simple fallacies that proceed by stating a necessary condition for personhood and showing that a fetus has that characteristic. This is a form of the fallacy of affirming the consequent. For example, some have mistakenly reasoned from the premise that a fetus is human (after all, it is a human fetus rather than, to say, a canine fetus), to the conclusion that it is *a* human. Adding an equivocation on "being," we get the fallacious argument that since a fetus is something both living and human, it is a human being.

Nonetheless, it does seem clear that a fetus has very few of the above family of characteristics, whereas a newborn baby exhibits a much larger proportion of them—and a two-year-old has even more. Note that one traditional anti-abortion argument has centered on pointing out the many ways in which a fetus resembles a baby. They emphasize its development ("It already has ten fingers . . . ") without mentioning its dissimilarities to adults (it still has gills and a tail). They also try to evoke the sort of sympathy on our part that we only feel toward other persons ("Never to laugh . . . or feel the sunshine?"). This all seems to be a relevant way to argue, since its purpose is to persuade us that a fetus satisfies so many of the important features on the list that it ought to be treated as a person. Also note that a fetus near the time of birth satisfies many more of these factors than a fetus in the early months of development. This could provide reason for making distinctions among the different stages of pregnancy, as the U.S. Supreme Court has done.[8]

---

[8] Not because the fetus is partly a person and so has some of the rights of persons, but rather because of the rights of person-like non-persons. This I discuss in part III, p. 146.

Historically, the time at which a person has been said to come into existence has varied widely. Muslims date personhood from fourteen days after conception. Some medievals followed Aristotle in placing ensoulment at forty days after conception for a male fetus and eighty days for a female fetus.[9] In European common law since the Seventeenth Century, abortion was considered the killing of a person only after quickening, the time when a pregnant woman first feels the fetus move on its own. Nor is the variety of opinions surprising. Biologically, a human being develops gradually. We shouldn't expect there to be any specific time or sharp dividing point when a person appears on the scene.

For these reasons I believe our concept of a person is not sharp or decisive enough to bear the weight of a solution to the abortion controversy. To use it to solve that problem is to clarify *obscurum per obscurius.*

II

Next let us consider what follows if a fetus is a person after all. Judith Jarvis Thomson's landmark article, "A Defense of Abortion,"[10] correctly points out that some additional argumentation is needed at this point in the conservative argument to bridge the gap between the premise that a fetus is an innocent person and the conclusion that killing it is always wrong. To arrive at this conclusion, we would need the additional premise that killing an innocent person is always wrong. But killing an innocent person is sometimes permissible, most notably in self defense. Some examples may help draw out our intuitions or ordinary judgments about self defense.

Suppose a mad scientist, for instance, hypnotized innocent people to jump out of the bushes and attack innocent passers-by with knives. If you are so attacked, we agree you have a right to kill the attacker in self defense, if killing him is the only way to protect your life or to save yourself from serious injury. It does not seem to matter here that the attacker is not malicious but himself an innocent pawn, for your killing of him is not done in a spirit of retribution but only in self defense.

How severe an injury may you inflict in self defense? In part this depends upon the severity of the injury to be avoided: you may not shoot someone merely to avoid having your clothes torn. This might lead one to the mistaken conclusion that the defense may only equal the threatened injury in severity; that to avoid death you may kill, but to avoid a black eye you may only inflict a black eye or the equivalent. Rather, our laws and customs seem to say that you may create an injury somewhat, but not enormously, greater than the injury to be avoided. To fend off an attack whose outcome would be as serious as rape, a severe beating or the loss of a finger, you may shoot; to avoid having your clothes torn, you may blacken an eye.

Aside from this, the injury you may inflict should only be the minimum necessary to deter or incapacitate the attacker. Even if you know he intends to kill you, you

---

[9] Aristotle himself was concerned, however, with the different question of when the soul takes form. For historical data, see Jimmye Kimmey, "How the Abortion Laws Happened," *Ms.* 1 (April, 1973), pp. 48ff, and John Noonan, *loc. cit.*

[10] J. J. Thomson, "A Defense of Abortion," *Philosophy and Public Affairs* 1 (1971).

are not justified in shooting him if you could equally well save yourself by the simple expedient of running away. Self defense is for the purpose of avoiding harms rather than equalizing harms.

Some cases of pregnancy present a parallel situation. Though the fetus is itself innocent, it may pose a threat to the pregnant woman's well-being, life prospects or health, mental or physical. If the pregnancy presents a slight threat to her interests, it seems self defense cannot justify abortion. But if the threat is on a par with a serious beating or the loss of a finger, she may kill the fetus that poses such a threat, even if it is an innocent person. If a lesser harm to the fetus could have the same defensive effect, killing it would not be justified. It is unfortunate that the only way to free the woman from the pregnancy entails the death of the fetus (except in very late stages of pregnancy). Thus a self defense model supports Thomson's point that the woman has a right only to be freed from the fetus, not a right to demand its death.[11]

The self defense model is most helpful when we take the pregnant woman's point of view. In the pre-Thomson literature, abortion is often framed as a question for a third party: do you, a doctor, have a right to choose between the life of the woman and that of the fetus? Some have claimed that if you were a passer-by who witnessed a struggle between the innocent hypnotized attacker and his equally innocent victim, you would have no reason to kill either in defense of the other. They have concluded that the self defense model implies that a woman may attempt to abort herself, but that a doctor should not assist her. I think the position of the third party is somewhat more complex. We do feel some inclination to intervene on behalf of the victim rather than the attacker, other things equal. But if both parties are innocent, other factors come into consideration. You would rush to the aid of your husband whether he was attacker or attackee. If a hypnotized famous violinist were attacking a skid row bum, we would try to save the individual who is of more value to society. These considerations would tend to support abortion in some cases.

But suppose you are a frail senior citizen who wishes to avoid being knifed by one of these innocent hypnotics, so you have hired a bodyguard to accompany you. If you are attacked, it is clear we believe that the bodyguard, acting as your agent, has a right to kill the attacker to save you from a serious beating. Your rights of self defense are transferred to your agent. I suggest that we should similarly view the doctor as the pregnant woman's agent in carrying out a defense she is physically incapable of accomplishing herself.

Thanks to modern technology, the cases are rare in which a pregnancy poses as clear a threat to a woman's bodily health as an attacker brandishing a switchblade. How does self defense fare when more subtle, complex and long-range harms are involved?

To consider a somewhat fanciful example, suppose you are a highly trained surgeon when you are kidnapped by the hypnotic attacker. He says he does not intend to harm you but to take you back to the mad scientist who, it turns out, plans to hypnotize you to have a permanent mental block against all your knowledge of medicine. This would automatically destroy your career which would in turn have a serious adverse impact on your family, your personal relationships and your happiness. It seems

---

[11] *Ibid.*

to me that if the only way you can avoid this outcome is to shoot the innocent attacker, you are justified in so doing. You are defending yourself from a drastic injury to your life prospects. I think it is no exaggeration to claim that unwanted pregnancies (most obviously among teenagers) often have such adverse life-long consequences as the surgeon's loss of livelihood.

Several parallels arise between various views on abortion and the self defense model. Let's suppose further that these hypnotized attackers only operate at night, so that it is well known that they can be avoided completely by the considerable inconvenience of never leaving your house after dark. One view is that since you could stay home at night, therefore if you got out and are selected by one of these hypnotized people, you have no right to defend yourself. This parallels the view that abstinence is the only acceptable way to avoid pregnancy. Others might hold that you ought to take along some defense such as Mace which will deter the hypnotized person without killing him, but that if this defense fails, you are obliged to submit to the resulting injury, no matter how severe it is. This parallels the view that contraception is all right but abortion is always wrong, even in cases of contraceptive failure.

A third view is that you may kill the hypnotized person only if he will actually kill you, but not if he will only injure you. This is like the position that abortion is permissible only if it is required to save a woman's life. Finally we have the view that it is all right to kill the attacker, even if only to avoid a very slight inconvenience to yourself and even if you knowingly walked down the very street where all these incidents have been taking place without taking along any Mace or protective escort. If we assume that a fetus is a person, this is the analogue of the view that abortion is always justifiable, "on demand."

The self defense model allows us to see an important difference that exists between abortion and infanticide, even if a fetus is a person from conception. Many have argued that the only way to justify abortion without justifying infanticide would be to find some characteristic of personhood that is acquired at birth. Michael Tooley, for one, claims infanticide is justifiable because the really significant characteristics of a person are acquired some time after birth. But all such approaches look to characteristics of the developing human and ignore the relation between the fetus and the woman. What if, after birth, the presence of an infant or the need to support it posed a grave threat to the woman's sanity or life prospects? She could escape this threat by the simple expedient of running away. So a solution that does not entail the death of the infant is available. Before birth, such solutions are not available because of the biological dependence of the fetus on the woman. Birth is the crucial point not because of any characteristics the fetus gains, but because after birth the woman can defend herself by a means less drastic than killing the infant. Hence self defense can be used to justify abortion without necessarily thereby justifying infanticide.

III

On the other hand, supposing a fetus is not after all a person, would abortion always be morally permissible? Some opponents of abortion seem worried that if a fetus is not a full-fledged person, then we are justified in treating it in any way at all.

However, this does not follow. Non-persons do get some consideration in our moral code, though of course they do not have the same rights as persons have (and in general they do not have moral responsibilities), and though their interests may be overridden by the interests of persons. Still, we cannot just treat them in any way at all.

Treatment of animals is a case in point. It is wrong to torture dogs for fun or to kill wild birds for no reason at all. It is wrong Period, even though dogs and birds do not have the same rights persons do. However, few people think it is wrong to use dogs as experimental animals, causing them considerable suffering in some cases, providing that the resulting research will probably bring discoveries of great benefit to people. And most of us think it all right to kill birds for food or to protect our crops. People's rights are different from the consideration we give to animals, then, for it is wrong to experiment on people, even if others might later benefit a great deal as a result of their suffering. You might volunteer to be a subject, but this would be supererogatory; you certainly have a right to refuse to be a medical guinea pig.

But how do we decide what you may or may not do to non-persons? This is a difficult problem, one for which I believe no adequate account exists. You do not want to say, for instance, that torturing dogs is all right whenever the sum of its effects on people is good—when it doesn't warp the sensibilities of the torturer so much that he mistreats people. If that were the case, it would be all right to torture dogs if you did it in private, or if the torturer lived on a desert island or died soon afterward, so that his actions had no effect on people. This is an inadequate account, because whatever moral consideration animals get, it has to be indefeasible, too. It will have to be a general proscription of certain actions, not merely a weighing of the impact on people on a case-by-case basis.

Rather, we need to distinguish two levels on which consequences of actions can be taken into account in moral reasoning. The traditional objections to Utilitarianism focus on the fact that it operates solely on the first level, taking all the consequences into account in particular cases only. Thus Utilitarianism is open to "desert island" and "lifeboat" counterexamples because these cases are rigged to make the consequences of actions severely limited.

Rawls' theory could be described as a teleological sort of theory, but with teleology operating on a higher level.[12] In choosing the principles to regulate society from the original position, his hypothetical choosers make their decision on the basis of the total consequences of various systems. Furthermore, they are constrained to choose a general set of rules which people can readily learn and apply. An ethical theory must operate by generating a set of sympathies and attitudes toward others which reinforces the functioning of that set of moral principles. Our prohibition against killing people operates by means of certain moral sentiments including sympathy, compassion and guilt. But if these attitudes are to form a coherent set, they carry us further: we tend to perform supererogatory actions, and we tend to feel similar compassion toward personlike nonpersons.

It is crucial that psychological facts play a role here. Our psychological constitution makes it the case that for our ethical theory to work, it must prohibit certain treatment of non-persons which are significantly person-like. If our moral rules allowed

---

[12] John Rawls, *A Theory of Justice* (Cambridge, Mass., 1971), §3–4.

people to treat some person-like non-persons in ways we do not want people to be treated, this would undermine the system of sympathies and attitudes that makes the ethical system work. For this reason, we would choose in the original position to make a mistreatment of some sorts of animals wrong in general (not just wrong in the cases with public impact), even though animals are not themselves parties in the original position. Thus it makes sense that it is those animals whose appearance and behavior are most like those people that get the most consideration in our moral scheme.

It is because of "coherence of attitudes," I think, that the similarity of a fetus to a baby is very significant. A fetus one week before birth is so much like a newborn baby in our psychological space that we cannot allow any cavalier treatment of the former while expecting full sympathy and nurturative support for the latter. Thus, I think that anti-abortion forces are indeed giving their strongest arguments when they point to the similarities between a fetus and a baby, and when they try to evoke our emotional attachment to and sympathy for the fetus. An early horror story from New York about nurses who were expected to alternate between caring for six-week premature infants and disposing of viable 24-week aborted fetuses is just that—a horror story. These beings are so much alike that no one can be asked to draw a distinction and treat them so very differently.

Remember, however, that in the early weeks after conception, a fetus is very much unlike a person. It is hard to develop these feelings for a set of genes which doesn't yet have a head, hands, beating heart, response to touch or the ability to move by itself. Thus it seems to me that the alleged "slippery slope" between conception and birth is not so very slippery. In the early stages of pregnancy, abortion can hardly be compared to murder for psychological reasons, but in the latest stages it is psychologically akin to murder.

Another source of similarity is the bodily continuity between fetus and adult. Bodies play a surprisingly central role in our attitudes toward persons. One has only to think of the philosophical literature on how far physical identity suffices for personal identity or Wittgenstein's remark that the best picture of the human soul is the human body. Even after death, when all agree the body is no longer a person, we still observe elaborate customs of respect for the human body; like people who torture dogs, necrophiliacs are not to be trusted with people.[13] So it is appropriate that we show respect to a fetus as the body continuous with the body of a person. This is a degree of resemblance to persons that animals cannot rival.

Michael Tooley also utilized a parallel with animals. He claims that it is always permissible to drown newborn kittens and draws conclusions about infanticide.[14] But it is only permissible to drown kittens when their survival would cause some hardship. Perhaps it would be a burden to feed and house six more cats or to find other homes for them. The alternative of letting them starve produces even more suffering than the drowning. Since the kittens get their rights second-hand, so to speak, *via* the need for coherence in our attitudes, their interests are often overridden by the interests of

---

[13] On the other hand, if they can be trusted with people, then our moral customs are mistaken. It all depends on the facts of psychology.

[14] *Op. cit.,* pp. 40, 60–61.

full-fledged persons. But if their survival would be no inconvenience to people at all, then it is wrong to drown them, *contra* Tooley.

Tooley's conclusions about abortion are wrong for the same reason. Even if a fetus is not a person, abortion is not always permissible, because of the resemblance of a fetus to a person. I agree with Thomson that it would be wrong for a woman who is seven months pregnant to have an abortion just to avoid having to postpone a trip to Europe. In the early months of pregnancy when the fetus hardly resembles a baby at all, then, abortion is permissible whenever it is in the interests of the pregnant woman and her family. The reasons would only need to outweigh the pain and inconvenience of the abortion itself. In the middle months, when the fetus comes to resemble a person, abortion would be justifiable only when the continuation of the pregnancy or the birth of the child would cause harms—physical, psychological, economic or social—to the woman. In the late months of pregnancy, even on our current assumption that a fetus is not a person, abortion seems to be wrong except to save a woman from significant injury or death.

The Supreme Court has recognized similar gradations in the alleged slippery slope stretching between conception and birth. To this point, the present paper has been a discussion of the moral status of abortion only, not its legal status. In view of the great physical, financial and sometimes psychological costs of abortion, perhaps the legal arrangement most compatible with the proposed moral solution would be the absence of restrictions, that is, so-called abortion "on demand."

So I conclude, first, that application of our concept of a person will not suffice to settle the abortion issue. After all, the biological development of a human being is gradual. Second, whether a fetus is a person or not, abortion is justifiable early in pregnancy to avoid modest harms and seldom justifiable late in pregnancy except to avoid significant injury or death.[15]

~~~~~~ To Think About ~~~~~~

1. In Brazil 40,000 women die each year because of botched abortions.

2. "Liberal abortion rules allow men to escape paternity consequences."
   Unknown Feminist

3. "U.S. women have three times as many abortions per group as does England, Sweden, or [the] Netherlands."   ***Guttmacher Institute***

4. "To regulate abortion at all is to treat men and women unequally."
   Unknown Feminist

5. "[We are not free, as slaves weren't] when some men decide that others are not fit to live . . . and abandoned in abortion."   ***Ronald Reagan***

6. Forty-two percent of pregnant women have an abortion in the United States. The average Russian woman has seven abortions during her life.

---

[15] I am deeply indebted to Larry Crocker and Arthur Kuflik for their constructive comments.

7.   "A state might properly fear the impact of widespread abortion on its citizens' instinctive respect for human life . . . which is a value for the maintenance of a just and decent civil society."   ***Ronald Dworkin***

8.   Chenyang Li's argument:

　　1.   An acorn is not an oak tree.

　　2.   There is no clear cut-off point between an acorn and an oak tree.
　　So it is false that there is one between conception and a baby.

9.   "There is no mention of privacy in our Bill of Rights but our decisions have recognized it as one of the fundamental values those amendments were designed to protect."   ***Justice William O. Douglas***

10.   The *potentiality principle* states that if there are properties possessed by *normal* adult human beings that endow any organism possessing them with a *serious* right to life, then at least one of those properties is such that any organism potentially possessing it has a serious right to life, simply by virtue of that potentiality.

11.   What are the rights of the fetus if any? At what stage do they begin?

12.   "Wrongfully prolonged life can be as tragic an error as wrongfully terminated life. In life's unhappier end games, there can be no 'safe side' to err on."   ***Joel Feinberg***

13.   "A newly fertilized ovum, a newly implanted clump of cells, is no more a person than an acorn is an oak tree. . . . Opponents of abortion commonly spend most of their time establishing that the fetus is a person, and hardly any time explaining the step from there to the impermissibility of abortion."   ***Judith Jarvis Thomson***

14.   Does life begin at conception or at implantation?

15.   "If one believes that the destruction of an embryo to isolate these (stem) cells is the moral equivalent of homicide, then why do we distinguish between private and public sponsorship of these activities (as the research will continue someplace)?"   ***H. T. Shapiro***

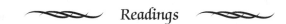 Readings

Feinberg, J., ed. *The Problem of Abortion.* Belmont, CA: Wadsworth, 1984.

Frey, R. G., and Christopher Heath Wellman. *A Companion to Applied Ethics.* Malden, MA: Blackwell, 2003.

Jung, Patricia Beattie, and Thomas A. Shannon, eds. *Abortion and Catholicism: The American Debate.* New York: Crossroad, 1988.

Marquis, Don. "An Argument That Abortion Is Wrong." In *Ethics in Practice: An Anthology*, ed. Hugh LaFollette, pp. 83–93. Oxford: Blackwell, 2002.

Pope John Paul II. *The Gospel of Life.* New York: Random House, 1995.

Thomson, J. "A Defense of Abortion." *Philosophy and Public Affairs* 1:1 (Fall 1971): 47–66.

54

Should Pornography
Be Censored?

David Ward (1949–) is a professor of philosophy at Widener University and has pub-lished in the area of political, legal, and social philosophy.

Recently we have observed the spectacle of government censorship of such well-known books as *Ulysses, Catcher in the Rye,* and *Slaughterhouse Five.* Many critics find such censorship so offensive that they believe the only just alternative is to elim-inate all laws against books and movies on sex. They argue that censorship is a viola-tion of the First Amendment and contend that adults should be allowed to make their own decisions as to what they read and see. After all, who can define the *obscene?*

In contrast, thoughtful arguments have also been made in favor of censoring pornographic materials. Supporters of this view believe that no society can be indif-ferent to the ways its citizens entertain themselves. They note that bearbaiting and cockfighting were outlawed, in part, because it was believed that these activities de-based and brutalized those who watched. Proponents of censorship argue that pornography debases sex; it insults a vital human relationship and thus harms those who view or read it. They believe that, if good books can *improve* people, then we must also believe that pornographic books can *harm* people. Further, they think that there may be a link between pornography and sexual crimes.

After consideration of such arguments, the U.S. Supreme Court established guidelines to determine if a work is obscene. Two cases are particularly important. In *Roth* (1957) the court ruled that a work should be censored if (1) its dominant theme shows a prurient interest in sex, (2) it is patently offensive to the average per-son, or (3) it is utterly without redeeming social value. Because of the difficulty of defining "the average person" and because all works have some social value (even if only to instruct us about sexual behavior), this legislation resulted in few

From David Ward, presentation to the North American Society for Social Philosophy, 1992. Reprinted by permission of the author.

convictions on obscenity charges. However, in a later case, *Miller* (1973), the courts ruled that "community standards" should determine whether a work is obscene. According to these guidelines a work is obscene if (1) "the average person, applying contemporary community standards," would find that the work, taken as a whole, appeals to prurient interests; (2) the work depicts or describes, in a patently offensive way, sexual conduct specifically defined by the applicable state law (i.e., describes ultimate sexual acts, masturbation, or excretory functions, or lewdly shows the genitals); (3) the work, taken as a whole, lacks serious literary, artistic, political, or scientific value.

David Ward argues that although some of the objections by women to pornography are valid, their objections often are censorious as well as demeaning of other groups such as blacks, Jews, homosexuals, and so on.

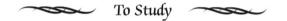 **To Study**

1. State Longino's definition of pornography.
2. According to Longino, how does pornography harm women?
3. With which of Longino's views does Ward agree?
4. What about gay men and pornography?
5. Discuss the problems of proving that pornography "causes" harm.
6. What is the possible cost of regulation of expression?
7. Which other groups are targets of harmful, degrading depictions in the culture?
8. What other institutions possibly degrade women besides pornography?
9. Discuss deontological objections to Longino's version of the principle of harm.

Some recent feminist writings have suggested that certain pornography is morally objectionable in ways that justify prohibiting its production, distribution and possession. While largely endorsing the feminist analysis of pornography accompanying these claims, I will argue that censorship of pornography that makes no use of children, mental incompetents, or nonconsenting adults is unjustified.

Quite a number of feminist writers have discussed this issue. Helen E. Longino gives a precise articulation of the pro-censorship position, and I will reply primarily on her work as representative of the censorship arguments I wish to oppose.

Longino's position can be summarized as follows:

1. Pornography can be defined, in the words of the Commission on Obscenity and Pornography, as ". . . explicit representations of sexual behavior which have as a distinguishing characteristic the degrading and demeaning portrayal of the role and status of the human female . . . as a mere sexual object to be exploited and manipulated sexually."[1]

---

[1] Helen E. Longino, "Pornography, Oppression and Freedom: a Closer Look," in Laura Lederer, ed., *Take Back the Night: Women in Pornography* (New York: William Morrow, 1980).

Longino makes clear that this definition should be taken to apply to material "... which represents or describes sexual behavior that is degrading or abusive to one or more of the participants *in such a way as to endorse the degradation.*"[2] Further characterizing pornography she adds, "Behavior that is degrading or abusive includes physical harm or abuse, and physical or psychological coercion. In addition, behavior which ignores or devalues the real interests, desires, and experiences of one or more participants in any way is degrading. Finally, that a person has chosen or consented to be harmed, abused, or subjected to coercion does not alter the degrading character of such behavior."[3]

2. Pornography is immoral because it is harmful to women. Pornography is harmful first because it lies. Longino says, "Pornography lies when it says that our sexual life is or ought to be subordinate to the service of men, that our pleasure consists in pleasing men and not ourselves, and that we are depraved, that we are fit subjects for rape, bondage, torture, and murder."[4] Pornography is thus immoral and harmful because it is libelous and defamatory.

Pornography also harms women because it supports the sexist objectification of women by men. It contributes to false, negative, and harmful images of women in the minds of men. Women's attitudes as well are warped by pornography, according to Longino. She says, "Women, too, are crippled by internalizing as self-images those that are presented to us by pornographers. Isolated from one another and with no source of support for an alternative view of female sexuality, we may not always find the strength to resist a message that dominates the common cultural media."[5] Most importantly, Longino believes, pornography is immoral and harmful because there is a "connection" between the consumption of pornography and the commission of other acts of sexual violence against women. She says, "Contrary to the findings of the Commission on Obscenity and Pornography, a growing body of research is documenting (1) a correlation between exposure to representations of violence and the committing of violent acts generally, and (2) a correlation between exposure to pornographic materials and the committing of sexually abusive or violent acts against women. While more study is needed to establish precisely what the causal relations are, clearly so-called hard-core pornography is not innocent."[6] Because pornography supports and reinforces the oppression and exploitation of women in these ways, Longino claims it is imperative that society not tolerate its production and distribution.

Before turning to the issue of censorship directly, let me first indicate the broad area of agreement I share with Longino concerning the nature of pornography and the undesirable effects of certain pornography on society in general. She is certainly correct in claiming that the feature which distinguishes pornographic (and immoral)

---

[2] *Ibid.,* p. 276.
[3] *Ibid.,* p. 277.
[4] *Ibid.,* p. 278.
[5] *Ibid.,* p. 279.
[6] *Ibid.,* p. 279.

depictions or descriptions of sexual behavior is the element of degradation. Erotica *per se* need carry no implication of degradation or of the endorsement of degradation. It is the addition of the element of degradation which both distinguishes pornography from the wider class of erotica and which makes pornography problematic.

The degradation is often explicit, involving portrayals of persons (men or women) in coercive and/or violent situations, portrayals in which the sexual subjugation and humiliation of one or more of the participants is central to the ideas communicated. Other (degrading) depictions are less explicit and grotesque, but undeniably degrading as well. Depictions of sexual behavior in which the pleasure or goals of some participants are treated as less worthy or important than those of others, or portrayals in which some participants are used, even consensually, as *mere* objects in the service of another's pleasure, are insidiously degrading and demeaning. They are degrading of human sexuality because they deny or undervalue the personhood of the persons portrayed.

Longino emphasizes how such portrayals degrade women, but it is important to note that they also degrade men. When men are portrayed as brutishly unconcerned with the pleasure, interests, or personhood of their sexual partners, *their* nature is degraded as well as that of their female partners. The image of men that much pornography puts forth is of people whose primary way of relating sexually involves brutal dominance, and concern with only the genitalia of their partners. This portrait of male sexuality ignores or denies entirely the capacity of men for tenderness and genuine, equal valuing of the personhood of their sexual partners. Women are degraded in pornography by being presented as fit objects for subjugation, rape, and abuse. Men are degraded by being pictured as brutes driven by desires to humiliate, subjugate, rape, and abuse women.

There are additional reasons to insist that the characterization of pornography be widened to include not just the degradation of women but of persons generally. Longino's characterization logically excludes the possibility of male homosexual pornography. If all the participants depicted are male, and a necessary condition for a portrayal's being pornographic is that it contain elements degrading to women, then no depiction which focuses exclusively on male homosexual conduct could count as pornographic. But many of the acts depicted which would clearly count as degrading if done to women (and therefore as pornographic) are also often included in male homosexual erotica. Depictions of coercive sexual violence, images of brutal subjugation, and the use of sexual partners as mere objects for the satisfaction of another are, unfortunately, at least as common in male homosexual erotica as in heterosexual pornography. Given that the degradation to which Longino correctly objects infects some homosexual erotica, as well as heterosexual depictions, it makes no sense to logically exclude all male homosexual erotica from being pornographic. Finally, though this is a relatively minor point, there is a sub-genre of heterosexual pornography in which the usual power relationships are reversed, and men are depicted as fit objects for humiliation, abuse, and violent subjugation by women.

One might still hold that pornography degrades only women by arguing that the power relationships that hold in society at large are so male-dominated that the treatment of men in these depictions as mere objects doesn't act to reinforce entrenched harmful attitudes and practices. In other words, depictions of men being treated in ways that would clearly count as degrading if done to women might not count as degrading because they would fail to have the same undesirable effects. This line of reasoning would be similar to that which holds that only whites can be racists, because blacks and members of other oppressed ethnic or racial minorities lack the power to act upon sentiments of racial hostility, while those in power, (i.e., whites) can and sometimes do act effectively to promote racist ideas.

But this reply would clearly not apply to male homosexual erotica, given that gay men clearly constitute an oppressed class of persons, persons whose sexuality has been pictured in a distorted way in the culture at large (as has female sexuality by the pornography to which Longino objects). Gay men as a class suffer disadvantages similar to those suffered by women as a class, in the case disadvantages related to the distorted stereotypical presentation of their sexuality.

Secondly, the reply speaks only to the purported effects of degrading depictions, and not to the issue of whether a depiction is intrinsically demeaning. One can grant that in general degrading depictions of women are more harmful to women (and to society in general) than those of men are to men (and to society in general) and still hold that pornography degrades men as well as women.

Let us turn to the issue of the harmful effects of pornography. The strongest claim made about the effects of pornography is that exposure to it *causes* violent or otherwise immoral behavior towards women. The issue of causality in human behavior is a vexed one in general, so we shouldn't be surprised if philosophical difficulties centering on free will and personal autonomy bedevil us in our specific consideration of pornography. There are layers of problems here. First, as Longino notes, the social science evidence concerning the putative negative effects of exposure to pornography is mixed. Further, most if not all of these studies deal with changes in *expressed attitudes* following exposure to pornography, and not with changes in *behavior.* The inference, on the basis of mixed and often contradictory results from social science concerning attitudinal changes after exposure to pornography, to the conclusion that pornography alters *behavior* is thus highly speculative even if we accept the philosophical presuppositions about the causal nature of human behavior underlying much social science research.

The most difficult issues in assessing the claim that exposure to violence, or pornography causes substantive behavioral changes are precisely the vexed questions: (1) Whether human behavior is to be explained exclusively or even primarily causally; and (2) What is the nature of causal connection *per se?* It is certainly not my intention to develop full answers to these questions here. But it is worth pointing out that the claim that human behavior is to be explained causally is, to say the least, philosophically tendentious. The conception of causality used in the kinds of social science research to which Longino refers amounts to nothing more than a formally specifiable relationship between independent and dependent variables in an experimental design. In such a design, if changes in the independent variable correspond with changes in the dependent variable, the relationship is said to be causal, *provided that there are no hidden or intervening variables affecting our results: that is, provided that all behaviorally relevant variables have been controlled for.* The manipulation of the independent variable is said to *produce* changes in the dependent variable. But the provision that all behaviorally relevant variables are controlled for merely refers us back to what I have already characterized as the philosophically tendentious assumption that what is behaviorally relevant, i.e., that what explains human behavior, is exclusively causal in the straightforward way in which chemical or physical changes are causal. This conception of causality in human action, from behaviorist psychology, makes no room for the possibility that autonomous judgment provided by consciousness intervenes crucially between the stimulus experience and changes in the independent variable. The simple causal model ignores the mediation of sensory stimulation by consciousness and rational judgment. If, as I would argue, judgment does intervene crucially between sensory input and resultant behavior in the sorts of cases under consideration, then the provision that all relevant intervening variables have been controlled for is necessarily unfulfilled. That is to say that no study of the sort to which Longino refers could possibly demonstrate a causal relationship between exposure to pornography and either attitudinal or behavioral change.

One important implication of this is that we are in some relevant sense *responsible* for our responses to exposure to such things as pornography, both in our attitudes and our behavior. If we pursue seriously the claim that exposure to pornography literally *causes* negative attitudinal or behavioral changes, we are dangerously close to absolving those with sexist attitudes and those who engage in sexual violence from responsibility for their actions. One is not usually held responsible for behavior one was caused to perform. If one is caused to perform some act, then one had no choice, no option other than to perform that act. Causes compel their effects. If we say that pornography *causes* sexist attitudes or behavior, how are we to answer the criminal who blames his attitudes or behavior on his prior exposure to pornography? Clearly people are responsible for any sexist attitudes they hold, and for their behavior. Longino's (appropriate) moral condemnation of sexism and sexual violence presumes moral responsibility, and moral responsibility is inconsistent with causality (at least with the notion of causality underlying the social science research she relies upon).

There is a second point to this metaphysical digression: regulation of expression has serious costs (a point I will take up later). Because of these costs, censorship shouldn't be undertaken lightly. We ought at least to have clear evidence of the means by which the speech or expression to be censored has the negative effects claimed for it. If we conceive of the negative influence of pornography in causal terms, this suggests remedies such as censorship. If a causal agent produces some undesirable effect, the most obvious solution is to eliminate that offending causal agent. If on the other hand, we conceive of the influence of pornography in terms of the persuasive power of speech, remedies other than censorship, such as counter-persuasion, suggest themselves. The burden of evidence lies heavily with those who support regulation of expression, and in the case at hand, the evidence of causal connection is simply too thin, speculative, and philosophically tendentious to support the prohibition of pornographic expression on causal grounds alone.

All this being said, it is crucial to acknowledge that in some philosophically less controversial sense, pornography as characterized by Longino is seriously harmful. But it is harmful in a more diffuse and indirect (but perhaps more insidious way) than Longino's language suggests. Like other kinds of speech and expression, pornography can persuade and influence. Even though the empirical evidence of harm is mixed at best, and even though metaphysical issues prevent us in any case from establishing a strictly causal relationship between exposure to pornography and behavior, it seems undeniable that the kinds of portrayals she discusses encourage, support, and disseminate degrading and demeaning attitudes towards women, and towards humans and human sexuality generally. This in itself is harmful and immoral, and therefore undesirable.

Further, many of the attitudes and ideas communicated by pornography coincide with sexist ideas in the general culture. Thus, the negative effects of pornography could be expected to be especially harmful because pornography acts to reinforce already embedded harmful ideas and attitudes.

Though our analyses differ slightly, Longino and I agree that (1) The distinguishing feature of pornography is its sexually degrading nature; and [that] (2) . . . pornography thus characterized is immoral and seriously harmful. What I sharply disagree with Longino about is the appropriate response to this harm. Longino's position involves appeal to one version of the principle of harm: that actions which harm innocent others are immoral *and therefore* may (or ought) to be forbidden. But the principle of harm is false. It does not follow from the fact that a particular action is harmful to innocents that it may be justifiably forbidden. There are two primary objections to this principle. On consequentialist grounds, one might hold that a harmful action ought to be forbidden only if the prohibition of that act causes less harm than permitting it. On deontological grounds, one might hold that persons are entitled to perform certain harmful actions in virtue of rights they possess, quite independently of the harmful nature of the consequences.

On both sorts of grounds, Longino's argument for censorship of pornography fails. Let us consider the consequentialist argument against censorship first. Censorship of any sort carries with it the following risks and costs: 1) Regulation of speech tends to have a "chilling effect" on expression, especially if the boundaries of forbidden expression are vaguely drawn. This problem is particularly salient in this case, given the obvious difficulty in explicitly or operationally defining the key terms in Longino's (and my) characterization of pornography. What exactly would be forbidden if we prohibited "degrading," "demeaning" depictions of women (or of human sexuality in general)? How could we hope to legislatively operationalize a prohibition against depictions of sexual subjugation? A key element of Longino's characterization is that pornography endorses the degradation depicted. How would such a determination be made in practice? Certainly there would be clear-cut cases, cases that would count as degrading if anything were to count as degrading, and cases in which the endorsement of the degradation could be uncontroversially read off the face of the depiction. But this characterization is so vague that the "gray area" between material patently degrading and that which is clearly not degrading is unworkably wide. It is a commonplace of jurisprudence that citizens have a right to know clearly what the law forbids. Under Longino's characterization we would have an unacceptably wide area of sincere and rationally defensible disagreement as to both the degrading character of portrayals and the point of view of those portrayals. (This objection has formed the basis of the judicial overthrow of local laws which proscribe the kinds of depictions to which Longino objects.) Longino's (correct) characterization fails radically to provide the precision needed for legislation, and I see no way in which her characterization could be modified to make it operationally acceptable without altering it essentially.

2) There is always a danger that once the principle of censorship is applied in one area that it will more easily be applied to another, and perhaps less desirable area of expression. This again applies with particular force in Longino's case. Why is it that she has singled out for protection a single class of persons (women) from a single sort of degrading depiction (sexual degradation)? Members of many groups are the targets of harmful degrading depictions in the culture at large: blacks, Jews, homosexuals, and so on. If women as a class are entitled to protection from these depictions by censorship, on what grounds could we allow speech degrading to other groups? To single out women as needing special protection from this sort of degrading material risks being patronizing to women by suggesting that women are weaker or more susceptible to damage than are members of other historically oppressed groups who have been subject to degrading depiction. Longino herself seems guilty of patronization when she claims that women are "crippled by internalizing as self-images those that are presented to us by pornographers. . . ."

And if the ground on which pornography is to be forbidden is not its sexual nature (and Longino carefully and correctly distinguishes her position from those who object to pornography on puritanical or prudish grounds, or on grounds that it offends modesty), what reasons would justify restricting only *sexually* degrading material? Wouldn't any degrading depiction of women be morally objectionable, and thus justifiably banned? Longino emphasizes that the degrading portrayals found in pornography are only one example of the demeaning view of women presented in the common cultural media, and that pornography derives much of its harmful influence precisely because it acts to reinforce attitudes already present in the wider culture.

Using Longino's application of the principle of harm, it would follow that degrading depictions which caused the most harm would be those most justifiably prohibited. But it is reasonable to suppose that the damage done by pornography is actually less than by the more subtle and insidious degradations found in mainstream culture. First, those from the mainstream culture are more widely disseminated. Second, pornography carries a degree of social stigma, and an element of shamefulness and sleaziness. Thus, consumers or casual observers could be expected to be less affected by pornography than by the less blatant sexist portrayals more clearly endorsed by the wider culture. At the least, we have no evidence that pornographic portrayals are more harmful than nonpornographic but degrading depictions. And we have no evidence that degrading depictions of women are more harmful to women (or society in general) than degrading depictions of oppressed minorities defined by race, ethnicity, religion, or sexual orientation are to members of those groups.

If, in the name of consistent application of the principle of harm, we contemplate forbidding a wider class of speech than the sexual degradation of women, a class that would include all harmfully degrading depictions of women, and all harmfully degrading depictions of other disadvantaged or oppressed groups (or of humans generally), we seriously risk suppressing the vigorous exchange of ideas that freedom of expression is intended to insure. There are, for example, doctrines from various religions, including fundamentalist Christianity and varieties of Islam which explicitly endorse the subordination and subjugation of women, and others which demean homosexuals by characterizing their sexual behavior as wicked. These religious doctrines are false, I would assert, but nonetheless within the realm of appropriately protected speech. The harm that would be done by such large-scale and vaguely defined rules of censorship would outweigh even the serious harm attributable to pornography or other degrading material.

There are deontological objections to Longino's version of the principle of harm as well. Deontological rights theories assert that persons are entitled to the exercise of a range of liberties not because each such exercise has desirable social consequences, but rather because rights embody and acknowledge the dignity of treatment due autonomous rational agents.

Longino's arguments are strictly consequentialist. She makes no attempt to answer rights-based deontological objections to censorship. And she provides no argument for the priority of consequentialist ethical theory over deontological views.

There are feminist writers who argue for the censorship of pornography on deontological as well as consequentialist grounds. They argue that degrading pornographic depictions violate the rights of women. But on what basis other than the consequentialist arguments already considered could one make this claim? One would need to argue that as a matter of *right,* and not just as a matter of moral or social desirability, women as a group ought not be degraded by the speech of others.

I know of no way to justify the claim that women or members of other groups have a *right* not to be degraded in speech. I grant that if a successful argument for censorship of pornography or other degrading material were to be made it would be on deontological grounds. In the absence of such an argument, however, the case for censorship of pornography fails.

It is essential to note that though the argument for censorship fails, it does not follow that nothing should or can be done about the negative influence of pornography or other degrading material. Longino and other feminist writers are undoubtedly correct in the claim that degrading depictions, especially those of historically oppressed groups, exert potent harmful influences. Issues of the regulation of expression are important precisely because of the immense power of speech.

Though speech does not *cause* attitudes or behavior, it persuades and influences, sometimes in seriously harmful ways. What can legitimately be done to counteract the harmful influence of pornography? As is often said, the cure for bad speech is good speech. Those of us who are aware of the insidious influence of pornography can speak against it, and point out the harm wrought by degrading portrayals of women and members of other groups. We can educate others about the more insidious effects of non-pornographic but equally sexist depictions of women, as Longino and others have done. And we can exert our economic influence, and encourage others to do the same, on those who purvey degrading material. We can expect success in this just insofar as people are responsive to reason, just insofar as autonomous rational judgment intervenes and mediates between sensory input and resultant behavior.

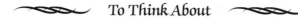

To Think About

1. "Only when obscene language is used to harass can it properly be made criminal."   ***Joel Feinberg***

2. "The invention of pornography came about in the early decades of the nineteenth century because of created 'secret museums' for objects 'pornographic,' and writings about prostitutes."   ***Walter Kendrick***

3. "Only since *Playboy* in 1953 has pornography been available to the middle classes and below."   ***James Gould***

4. "Pornography is not only words because it is reality; pornography should be banned because it silences women by making it more difficult to speak."
                                                                 C. MacKinnon

5. "Most pornography makes no contribution at all to political debate."
                                                              Ronald Dworkin

6. Andrea Dworkin claims that "women do not consume pornography," and yet a *Redbook* magazine (1987) survey revealed that 50 percent regularly watch it.

7. "TV talk shows are the new pornography."   ***James Gould***

8. "Whatever has social value isn't pornographic."   **Roth v. U.S.,** *1957*

9. Denmark has a low rate of coercive sex in spite of its liberal attitude toward pornography.

10. "Men often say that one cannot legislate morality. I say that we legislate hardly anything else."   ***Carl Rostow***

11. "Pornography degrades the relation between the sexes."   ***James Gould***

12. "Married couples need external sexual stimuli."   ***James Gould***

13. "Porn helps define what sex is." "It makes sex sexy."   ***James Gould***

55

Is Homosexuality Unnatural or Immoral?

James A. Gould (1922–) *is a professor of philosophy at the University of South Florida. He has published numerous texts and articles in the areas of logic and social philosophy. Professor Gould has lectured at Harvard, Stanford, Buffalo, Hawaii, Tokyo, Kent, and many other universities.*

A high percentage of Americans think that homosexuality is immoral and that it should be illegal. In *Bowers* v. *Hardwick* (1986) the Supreme Court declared in its majority decision that the right to engage in homosexual acts is not supported by the U.S. Constitution. Two basic arguments were given. Justice Burger held that such acts were illegal because they are unnatural, but he did not define *unnatural*. Determining the unnatural cannot be "based upon the operations of the physical world" because animals are a part of the physical world, and several of them perform homosexual acts. Nor can one call such acts immoral because they are abnormal. Most married people seldom make love for more than fifteen minutes, but to do so would not be considered immoral. On the other hand, if the natural means "present or existing from birth," then it can well be true of homosexuality, as has been held by the American Psychiatric Association, and hence nonblamable.

Justice White argued that homosexuality is not a right of privacy analogous to the right of marriage, contraception, procreation, and so on, and it is not a right long recognized in the history of this nation. For these reasons he held it not to be a constitutional right. In his dissent Justice Blackmun claimed that it is a right of privacy, and that homosexuality represents a freedom. A person achieves an identity in part through his or her sexual expression, and a person is freer through having a proper identity.

Reprinted by permission of the publishers from *International Journal of Applied Philosophy* (Fall 1988): 51–54.

In *Romer* v. *Evans* (1996) it was declared that the state of Colorado "shall not create regulations . . . whereby homosexual . . . orientation, conduct, practices or relationships will be illegal." This further enhanced the rights of the gay world.

Among the many critics of homosexuality are Paul Cameron and Lord Patrick Devlin. The former argues that there is a tilt toward homosexuality in our society for many reasons: the homosociality of children, the fact that males are more interested in sex than females, the fact that homosexual sex is more satisfying than heterosexual sex, and the egocentricity of the young. Nonetheless he is a strong critic: homosexuality produces a self-centered orientation, irresponsibility, and a tendency toward suicide and homicide. Devlin's position is discussed at length in the following essay.

> *It is argued by a recent head of the British judicial system, Lord Devlin, that a shared morality is what holds a society together and hence the enforcement of this shared morality is necessary to prevent society from collapsing or at least weakening. Consider some examples. During the time of the Vietnam War, American society was significantly split. Morality was not shared. Some were strongly for the war, and some violently against it. It was necessary for the war to end for society to feel united again. We can see other examples in the situations in Northern Ireland and in South Africa. The same situation has also existed in the United States regarding blacks. Devlin believes it is also true of homosexuality.*
>
> *Devlin holds two theories: (1) The disintegration thesis maintains that a society is held together by its shared morality, and hence the enforcement of this morality is necessary to prevent society from collapsing, or at least weakening. (2) On the other hand, his conservative thesis maintains that "the majority have a right to follow their moral convictions, viz., that their moral environment is a thing of value to be defended from change."*

In the following essay, several definitions of *unnatural* are examined, and none of them implies the unnaturalness of homosexuality. We now know, for example, that the male and female of certain species of pygmy apes engage in homosexual behavior. Can apes do the "unnatural"?

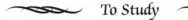 **To Study**

1. Explain the difference between the two meanings of *natural*.
2. Why don't these definitions show that homosexuality is unnatural?
    a. Based upon the operations of the physical world
    b. Possessing a normal connection with someone
    c. Present or existing from birth
    d. That which works
    e. Is in conformity with the laws of nature
    f. Artificial
    g. Used contrary to its principal function
3. What about evidence that homosexuality is a danger to the social fabric?
4. Sum up Lord Devlin's theories about homosexuality. What are the alleged dangers of Devlin's theories?

There are two traditional meanings of "the natural." The first is "the totality of existence." This includes everything we experience—people, tables, chairs and everything else in nature, even ourselves. Concurrent with this meaning of the natural is the concept of the unnatural as things imagined to exist, such as ghosts, utopias, etc. The mind in fact is natural, but the mind has objects beyond nature. The mind is then free to examine both nature and the unnatural. To love or hate is natural, and in general to be free to pursue what one wishes is natural. To know universals is not unnatural, but whether they exist naturally is a subject of debate. Nature itself may be a collective name for atomic existences, or it may be an organic structure. It could be either.

The second and more common meaning is that all of the natural is the "natural" world, excluding man and his works. According to this view, man grows up in nature and he never gets out of nature, but he is separate from it. Nature is external to man and his values, and is distinguished from culture, art, and history. Man, nonetheless, is not unnatural. The unnatural is what is external to the normal structure or occurrence of a thing. This second meaning of "the natural" is what the ordinary person considers correct.

Given that, in this view, man is separate from nature, are any of his acts unnatural? In 1986 the United States Supreme Court declared in its majority decision that the right to engage in homosexual acts is not supported by the U.S. Constitution.[1] This represents the only current written Supreme Court ruling on homosexuality. The Chief Justice, Warren Burger, wrote in this decision that such acts are illegal because they are "unnatural," and hence punishable. He provided no reasons whatsoever for holding them to be unnatural. Although Burger did not characterize "the natural" or the unnatural, others have tried to do so. Let us study the dictionary meanings. What can be said from them about the characteristics of this concept of "the natural"? Can any of the concurrent meanings of "the unnatural" be applied to homosexuality?

How has the concept been used in ordinary language? Dictionaries cite various uses. The first listed is: "based upon the operations of the physical world." If this is the case, then homosexuality is not unnatural, for animals are part of the physical world, and such mammals as mountain goats are well known for their homosexual behavior, as are other creatures. Homosexual activities occur among nature's animals. Freud is said to have believed that man is innately bisexual. Likewise, Wardell Pomeroy, Kinsey's successor to the Institute for The Advanced Study of Human Sexuality, contends that if cultural constraints did not play a role in the spectrum of sexual behavior in the United States, half of the male population would continue to be exclusively heterosexual and four percent would be exclusively homosexual. The rest would be bisexual to varying degrees.

A second definition of "the natural" found in dictionaries is "possessing a normal connection with someone." But what is "normal" is all too often simply a value

---

[1] *Bowers* v. *Hardwick,* 83–140, June 1986, Burger dissent. The only other significant Federal case wasn't adjudicated by the Supreme Court: *Doe* v. *City of Richmond,* 403 Fed. Supp. 1199. E.Q.Va. (1975). The other Supreme Court judges rejected homosexuality, in part basing their decision on the contention that homosexuality doesn't involve love as does a marriage.

judgment. Some so-called "crimes against nature," for example, are practiced by well over half the adult population. Hence, in a significant sense these acts are normal and are not in this sense unnatural. A third usage listed in dictionaries is "present or existing from birth." The American Psychiatric Association[2] recently declared that homosexuality often exists from birth and hence would in this sense be natural. So this third definition would not hold homosexuality to be unnatural.

A fourth definition is "that which works," a pragmatic doctrine suggested in an article by Herbert Schneider.[3] He offers this definition while at the same time noting its simplicity. It really is not *per se* helpful, but what is interesting is Schneider's further statement that "even the unnatural act may be a value an individual chooses," and perhaps be, in his mind, best for him. Hence, homosexuality may be deemed by an individual or by others as the best way of life for him. In a fifth definition, Professor Finnis[4] states that the natural "is that toward which one is naturally inclined." He maintains that although one is naturally inclined toward health, security, etc., one is not naturally inclined towards homosexuality. The American Psychiatric Association, however, has taken the position that homosexuality is not an illness, and hence can be a natural inclination. Thus under Finnis' definition homosexuality should not be held to be unnatural.

Another definition of the natural is that which "is in conformity with the laws of nature." But it has already been established that the homosexuality of a person can readily be held to be in accordance with the laws of nature, viz., the laws of observed human behavior. Furthermore, this definition is, of course, circular.

The unnatural has also been defined as the "artificial." Our lives are full of the artificial—clothes, instruments, plastics, etc. No one, however, considers that homosexual acts are artificial, even if such acts involve the use of artificial objects. So the artificial has no negating application to homosexuality as being unnatural.

It has been alleged that the unnatural occurs when a human organ is used for purposes contrary to its principle function. Such an argument involves the contention that sexual organs are principally used or are to be used for reproduction. The descriptive aspect of this contention (that human sexual organs *are* principally used for reproduction) is obviously false, as both the male and female sex organs are only occasionally used with conceptive intent. The prescriptive aspect raises the question of whether our organs should have only one particular act? Who is to say so? No one doubts that our eyes have the functions of observing and flirting, in addition to others. Our arms and legs also have several functions, and our sex organs as well have several functions. They both bring pleasure as well as seek successful reproduction.

In sum: Seven definitions of what is natural have been examined. None of them offer support that homosexuality is unnatural, and hence (as some argue) undesirable

---

[2] See *New York Times,* December 23, 1973, p. E5. It is not considered a "psychiatric disorder," but a "sexual deviation," viz., not normal.

[3] Schneider, Herbert, "The Unnatural," *Naturalism and the Human Spirit* (New York: Columbia University Press), 1944, pp. 121–32.

[4] Finnis, J., "Natural Law and Unnatural Acts," *Heythrop Journal,* vol. 11, no. 4, October 1970, 365–87.

in society. If that is the case, are there any reasons why a society should consider homosexuality among consenting adults undesirable and even illegal?

Are there any empirical data which indicate that homosexuals are a danger to society or to themselves? Before AIDS became a frightening phenomenon there was such evidence. One study of San Francisco at that time claimed that two-thirds of the gays living there had venereal disease at one time, and that the chances of getting such when visiting a bathhouse were one in three.[5] In addition, this study stated that the average homosexual had had five hundred lovers, while 28% of them had had one thousand. In those days such men were an obvious danger to themselves as well as to society.

Since that time, several studies have shown that gays have effected a marked decline in the number of sexual partners. In New York, the decline was 78%.[6] Sexual episodes involving an exchange of bodily fluids declined by 70%, and condom use during anal intercourse increased from 1.5 to 20%. Not only did 80% not use condoms, but abstinence from gay sex did not change over a period of one year. The number of sexual encounters remained the same as before. Given the fact of these incredibly numerous involvements, do these men have any time to give to supporting the needed volunteer groups which help make a society function? Society cannot adequately function without a significant number of its citizens playing volunteer roles, but if one's mental and physical activities are continuously concerned with sex, then the needed social roles are less likely to be filled. Is homosexuality thus to be morally undesirable on utilitarian grounds? Gays have a right to express their sexuality and experience the pleasure resulting there from; yet, the above-mentioned cases give some cause for homosexuals to use strong caution.

Prudentially given the present laws and public opinion in many states, one could argue that homosexual behavior is not wise. Not all people, however, choose freely to become homosexuals, and hence it is not fair to deny such people sexual expression.

What about harm to the young? Do homosexuals seduce and harm adolescents more than heterosexuals? There is no evidence to substantiate whether or not this is true, so no such charge should be made until definite evidence exists.

It is argued by a recent head of the British judicial system, Lord Devlin,[7] that a shared morality is what holds a society together and hence the enforcement of this shared morality is necessary to prevent society from collapsing or at least weakening. Consider some examples. During the time of the Viet Nam War, American society was significantly split. Morality was not shared. Some were strongly for the war, and some violently against it. It was necessary for the war to end for society to feel itself as one again. We can see other examples in the situations in Northern Ireland and in South Africa. The same situation has also existed here in the United States regarding the blacks. Devlin believes this is also true of homosexuality.

Devlin holds two theories. (1) The disintegration thesis maintains that a society is held together by its shared morality, and hence the enforcement of this morality is

---

[5] See *Newsweek,* September 29, 1980. Books.

[6] Martin, John L., "The Impact of AIDS on Gay Male Sexual Behavior Patterns in New York City," *American Journal of Public Health,* May 1987, vol. 77, no. 5, pp. 578–81.

[7] Devlin, Patrick. *The Enforcement of Morals* (Oxford: Oxford University Press), 1965.

necessary to prevent society from collapsing, or at least weakening. (2) On the other hand, his conservative thesis maintains that "the majority have a right to follow their moral convictions, *viz.,* that their moral environment is a thing of value to be defended from change." Consequently, Devlin sees two types of harm resulting from violations of the shared morality—tangible and intangible. First, the "tangible harm" seems to consist in a diminution of the physical strength of society. There are activities which are quite harmless to society when only a few of its members indulge in them, but which become harmful when the number of participants grows large. Devlin cites drunkenness as an example. He also argues that "unrestricted indulgence in vice" will weaken an individual to the extent that he ceases to be a useful member of society, and society will itself be weakened if it has a sufficient number of such weak members. Second, most men, he claims, take their morality as a whole, and immoral activity, by weakening belief in one part of society's shared morality, will probably result in the undermining of the whole morality. When there ceases to be common belief in the value of the moral code, society is threatened with disintegration.

Devlin's theory is interesting, but it has dangers. He says, for example, that if it is generally believed that deviations from the shared sexual morality will bring about the collapse of society, then this is sufficient to justify the suppression of the deviant conduct. But no one, even Devlin, with even a minimal respect for individual freedom, can possibly accept this. Religious intolerance, racial persecution, and the suppression of the fundamental liberties of minorities, can all be justified on this basis. By Devlin's dictum the first, fourth, sixth and fourteenth amendments could be rejected. None of us would want that to happen.

In sum: any criticism of homosexuality must be balanced with the obvious need of any human to have his or her sexual needs met. Homosexuality cannot be rejected by any definition of the unnatural. Hence, homosexuality should not be outlawed; rather, as it becomes more accepted by the general society these comments should be reflected upon by the gay community.

To Think About

1. "The Weinberg and Williams study of male homosexuals reports that just under fifty percent of the American population still finds homosexuality very obscene and vulgar, a marked difference from the readings of 5.4% for the Netherlands and 11.8% for Denmark."   ***Lee Rice***

2. "I feel that the right-wing doesn't really care about gays. They simply want to scare up voters to support their candidates."   ***Edmund White***

3. "Take that hard-ridden analogy between blacks and gays. Much of the ongoing debate over gay rights has fixated, and foundered, on the vexed distinction between 'status' and 'behavior.' The paradox here can be formulated as follows: Most people think of racial identity as a matter of (racial) status, but they respond to it as behavior. Most people think of sexual identity as a matter of (sexual) behavior, but they respond to it as status. Accordingly, people who fear and

dislike blacks are typically preoccupied with the threat that they think blacks' aggressive behavior poses to them. Hence they're inclined to make exceptions for the kindly, 'civilized' blacks: that's why 'The Cosby Show' could be so popular among white South Africans. By contrast, the repugnance that many people feel toward gays concerns, in the first instance, the status ascribed to them. Disapproval of a sexual practice is transmuted into the demonization of a sexual species."   ***Edmund White***

4. "In other cultures, love exists, but is given particular forms. Ancient Egyptian love poetry has no interest in the emotions of shame, guilt, or ambivalence. The Greeks thought nothing of homosexuality. Christianity proscribed the body and eroticized the soul."   ***Unknown***

5. Jesus doesn't attack homosexuality.

6. Therapy sessions reveal that gay bashers readily admit they fear that they themselves are at least latent homosexuals.

7. Although homosexuality is common among animals, it is rare for them to form serious lifelong relationships.

8. The average gay man dies at 47 in the United States (1995).

9. "The paradox is that if we don't name our difference in explicitly sexual terms, we remain invisible as lesbians—but if we do name it we're typecast as little more than sexual beings, and the vast complexity of our lives disappears."   ***Arlene Stein***

10. "It is possible, but not likely and not suggested by anything currently known, that a bisexual gene has achieved stable existence in the human gene pool. It is also quite unlikely, on equivalent analytical grounds and the virtual nonexistence of polymorphous animal sexuality in the wild, that males are primed only for an undifferentiated enjoyment of sex that is shaped by culture into heterosexuality."   ***Michael Levin***

11. "In masturbating, as in being masturbated or sodomized, one's body is treated as instrumental for the securing of the experiential satisfaction of the conscious self. Thus one disintegrates oneself in two ways, (1) by treating one's body as a mere instrument of the consciously operating self, and (2) by making one's choosing self the quasi-slave of the experiencing self which is demanding gratification."   ***John Finnis***

The Animal Rights Issue

56
Do Animals Have Rights?

Peter Singer (1946–) was born in Melbourne, Australia, and educated at the Universities of Melbourne and Oxford. In 1977 he was appointed to a chair of philosophy at Monash University in Melbourne and subsequently was the founding director of that university's Centre for Human Bioethics. In 1999 he became the Ira W. DeCamp Professor of Bioethics at Princeton University's Center for Human Values. He was the founding president of the International Association of Bioethics and, with Helga Kuhse, founding coeditor of the journal Bioethics. *Among his many publications are* Animal Liberation *(2nd ed., 1990),* Practical Ethics *(2nd ed., 1993),* The Expanding Circle *(1983),* How Are We to Live? *(1985),* Rethinking Life and Death *(1995),* A Darwinian Left *(1999),* Writings on an Ethical Life *(2000),* One World: The Ethics of Globalization *(2002), and* Pushing Time Away: My Grandfather and the Tragedy of Jewish Vienna *(2003). He is the author of the major article on ethics in the current edition of the* Encyclopedia Britannica.

"Man is a rational animal." So goes an ancient definition of humankind, perhaps first formulated by Aristotle. Much is made of the distinctiveness of human beings in the animal kingdom. But some philosophers think that similarities are more important, and that a number of human traits are in fact shared by many other animals. Animals feel, they have interests, they exhibit emotional lives, and many clearly have rudimentary intellectual lives. As such, some recent moralists maintain that animals have rights like human beings. Perhaps they do not have all of them, but certainly they have some basic ones, such as the right to be free from suffering and exploitation. The kind of respect we owe to each other, the argument goes, is owed just as much to other animals. In the following reading the history of animal liberation is described, along with arguments in its defense. Singer emphasizes the interests animals have rather than their rights. Relating his account to issues such as human nature, the value of personal liberty, and ethical ideals such as happiness and duty can enrich our understanding of such issues and perhaps show their application to other members of the animal kingdom.

From Peter Singer, "Animal Liberation at 30," *New York Review of Books,* May 30, 2003. Reprinted by permission of the author.

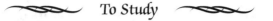

To Study

1. Define *speciesism*. How does it resemble forms of discrimination like racism or sexism?
2. How does Singer criticize arguments for speciesism drawn from the analogy between the family and the species?
3. What is meant by "the argument from marginal cases"? How does Singer respond to it?
4. Singer argues that "similar interests" rather than "rights" justify moral treatment of animals. Explain his position.
5. What effects have philosophical arguments had upon industrial and agricultural treatment of animals? Why is this situation worse in the United States than in Europe?
6. Why does animal liberation demand greater human altruism than other liberation movements?
7. What obstacles remain to the greater popular agreement with Singer's "basic idea" that shared interests of living things should be considered, regardless of species?

AMONG THE BOOKS MENTIONED IN THIS ARTICLE

Animal Rights and Wrongs
by Roger Scruton.
London: Metro, 2000.

The Animal Question:
Why Non-human Animals
Deserve Human Rights
by Paola Cavalieri,
translated from the Italian
by Catherine Woollard.
Oxford University Press, 2001.

Taking Animals Seriously:
Mental Life and Moral Status
by David DeGrazia.
Cambridge University Press, 1996.

Dominion:
The Power of Man,
the Suffering of Animals,
and the Call to Mercy
by Matthew Scully,
St. Martin's, 2002.

1.

The phrase "Animal Liberation" appeared in the press for the first time on the April 5, 1973, cover of *The New York Review of Books.* Under that heading, I discussed *Animals, Men and Morals,* a collection of essays on our treatment of animals, which was edited by Stanley and Roslind Godlovitch and John Harris.[1] The article began with these words:

> *We are familiar with Black Liberation, Gay Liberation, and a variety of other movements. With Women's Liberation some thought we had come to the end of the road.*

Discrimination on the basis of sex, it has been said, is the last form of discrimination that is universally accepted and practiced without pretense, even in those liberal circles which have long prided themselves on their freedom from racial discrimination. But one should always be wary of talking of "the last remaining form of discrimination."

In the text that followed, I urged that despite obvious differences between humans and nonhuman animals, we share with them a capacity to suffer, and this means that they, like us, have interests. If we ignore or discount their interests, simply on the grounds that they are not members of our species, the logic of our position is similar to that of the most blatant racists or sexists who think that those who belong to their race or sex have superior moral status, simply in virtue of their race or sex, and irrespective of other characteristics or qualities. Although most humans may be superior in reasoning or in other intellectual capacities to nonhuman animals, that is not enough to justify the line we draw between humans and animals. Some humans—infants and those with severe intellectual disabilities—have intellectual capacities inferior to some animals, but we would, rightly, be shocked by anyone who proposed that we inflict slow, painful deaths on these intellectually inferior humans in order to test the safety of household products. Nor, of course, would we tolerate confining them in small cages and then slaughtering them in order to eat them. The fact that we are prepared to do these things to nonhuman animals is therefore a sign of "speciesism"—a prejudice that survives because it is convenient for the dominant group—in this case not whites or males, but all humans.

That essay and the book that grew out of it, also published by *The New York Review*,[2] are often credited with starting off what has become known as the "animal rights movement"—although the ethical position on which the movement rests needs no reference to rights. Hence the essay's thirtieth anniversary provides a convenient opportunity to take stock both of the current state of the debate over the moral status of animals and of how effective the movement has been in bringing about the practical changes it seeks in the way we treat animals.

2.

The most obvious difference between the current debate over the moral status of animals and that of thirty years ago is that in the early 1970s, to an extent barely credible today, scarcely anyone thought that the treatment of individual animals raised an ethical issue worth taking seriously. There were no animal rights or animal liberation organizations. Animal welfare was an issue for cat and dog lovers, best ignored by people with more important things to write about. (That's why I wrote to the editors of *The New York Review* with the suggestion that they might review *Animals, Men and Morals,* whose publication the British press had greeted a year earlier with total silence.)

Today the situation is very different. Issues about our treatment of animals are often in the news. Animal rights organizations are active in all the industrialized nations. The U.S. animal rights group called People for the Ethical Treatment of Animals has 750,000 members and supporters. A lively intellectual debate has sprung up. (The most comprehensive bibliography of writings on the moral status of animals lists only ninety-four works in the first 1970 years of the Christian era, and 240 works between 1970 and 1988, when the bibliography was completed.[3] The tally now would probably be in the thousands.) Nor is this debate simply a Western phenomenon—leading works on animals and ethics have been translated into most of the world's major languages, including Japanese, Chinese, and Korean.

To assess the debate, it helps to distinguish two questions: First, can speciesism itself—the idea that it is justifiable to give preference to beings simply on the grounds that they are members of the species *Homo sapiens*—be defended? And secondly, if speciesism cannot be defended, are there other characteristics about human beings that justify them in placing far greater moral significance on what happens to them than on what happens to nonhuman animals?

The view that species is in itself a reason for treating some beings as morally more significant than others is often assumed but rarely defended. Some who write as if they are defending speciesism are in fact defending an affirmative answer to the second question, arguing that there are morally relevant differences between human beings and other animals that entitle us to give more weight to the interests of humans.[4] The only argument I've come across that looks like a defense of speciesism itself is the claim that just as parents have a special obligation to care for their own children in preference to the children of strangers, so we have a special obligation to other members of our species in preference to members of other species.[5]

Advocates of this position usually pass in silence over the obvious case that lies between the family and the species. Lewis Petrinovich, professor emeritus at the University of California, Riverside, and an authority on ornithology and evolution, says that our biology turns certain boundaries into moral imperatives—and then lists "children, kin, neighbors, and species."[6] If the argument works for both the narrower circle of family and friends and the wider sphere of the species, it should also work for the middle case: race. But an argument that supported our preferring the interests of members of our own race over those of members of other races would be less persuasive than one that allowed priority only for kin, neighbors, and members of our species. Conversely, if the argument doesn't show race to be a morally relevant boundary, how can it show that species is?

The late Harvard philosopher Robert Nozick argued that we can't infer much from the fact that we do not yet have a theory of the moral importance of species membership. "No one," he wrote, "has spent much time trying to formulate" such a theory, "because the issue hasn't seemed pressing."[7] But now that nearly twenty years have passed since Nozick wrote those words, and many people have, during those years, spent quite a lot of time trying to defend the importance of species membership, Nozick's comment takes on a different weight. The continuing failure of philosophers to produce a plausible theory of the moral importance of species membership indicates, with increasing probability, that there can be no such thing.

That takes us to the second question. If species is not morally important in itself, is there something else that happens to coincide with the human species, on the basis of which we can justify the inferior consideration we give to nonhuman animals?

Peter Carruthers argues that it is the lack of a capacity to reciprocate. Ethics, he says, arises out of an agreement that if I do not harm you, you will not harm me.

Since animals cannot take part in this social contract we have no direct duties to them.[8] The difficulty with this approach to ethics is that it also means we have no direct duties to small children, or to future generations yet unborn. If we produce radioactive waste that will be deadly for thousands of years, is it unethical to put it into a container that will last 150 years and drop it into a convenient lake? If it is, ethics cannot be based on reciprocity.

Many other ways of marking the special moral significance of human beings have been suggested: the ability to reason, self-awareness, possession of a sense of justice, language, autonomy, and so on. But the problem with all of these allegedly distinguishing marks is, as noted above, that some humans are entirely lacking in these characteristics and few want to consign them to the same moral category as nonhuman animals.

This argument has become known by the tactless label of "the argument from marginal cases," and has spawned an extensive literature of its own.[9] The attempt by the English philosopher and conservative columnist Roger Scruton to respond to it in *Animal Rights and Wrongs* illustrates both the strengths and weaknesses of the argument. Scruton is aware that if we accept the prevailing moral rhetoric that asserts that all human beings have the same set of basic rights, irrespective of their intellectual level, the fact that some nonhuman animals are at least as rational, self-aware, and autonomous as some human beings looks like a firm basis for asserting that all animals have these basic rights. He points out, however, that this prevailing moral rhetoric is not in accord with our real attitudes, because we often regard "the killing of a human vegetable" as excusable. If human beings with profound intellectual disabilities do not have the same right to life as normal human beings, then there is no inconsistency in denying that right to nonhuman animals as well.

In referring to a "human vegetable," however, Scruton makes things too easy for himself, for that expression suggests a being that is not even conscious, and thus has no interests at all that need to be protected. He might be less comfortable making his point with respect to a human being who has as much awareness and ability to learn as the foxes he wants to continue being permitted to hunt. In any case, the argument from marginal cases is not limited to the question of what beings we can justifiably kill. In addition to killing animals, we inflict suffering on them, in a wide variety of ways. So the defenders of common practices involving animals owe us an explanation for their willingness to make animals suffer when they would not be willing to do the same to humans with similar intellectual capacities. (Scruton, to his credit, is opposed to the close confinement of modern animal raising, saying that "a true morality of animal welfare ought to begin from the premise that this way of treating animals is wrong.")

Scruton is in fact only half-willing to acknowledge that a "human vegetable" may be treated differently from other human beings. He muddies the waters by claiming that it is "part of human virtue to acknowledge human life as sacrosanct." In addition, he argues that because in normal conditions human beings are members of a moral community protected by rights, even deeply serious abnormality does not cancel membership of this community. Thus even though humans with profound intellectual disability do not really have the same claims on us as normal humans, we would do well, Scruton says, to treat them as if they did. But is this defensible? Certainly if any sentient being, human or nonhuman, can feel pain or distress, or conversely can enjoy life, we ought to give the interests of that being the same consideration as we give to the similar interests of normal human beings with unimpaired capacities. To say, however, that species alone is both necessary and sufficient for being a member of our moral community, and for having the basic rights granted to all members of that community, requires further justification. We return to the core question: Should all and only human beings be protected by rights, when some nonhuman animals are superior in their intellectual capacities, and have richer emotional lives, than some human beings?

One well-known argument for an affirmative answer to this question asserts that unless we can draw a clear boundary around the moral community, we will find ourselves on a slippery slope.[10] We may start by denying rights to Scruton's "human vegetable," that is, to those who can be shown to be irreversibly unconscious, but then we may gradually extend the category of those without rights to others, perhaps to the intellectually disabled, or to the demented, or just to those whose care is a burden on their family and the community, until in the end we have reached a situation that none of us would have accepted if we had known we were heading there when we denied the irreversibly unconscious a right to life. This is one of several arguments critically examined by the Italian animal activist Paola Cavalieri in *The Animal Question: Why Nonhuman Animals Deserve Human Rights,* a rare contribution to the English-language debate by a writer from continental Europe. Cavalieri points to the ease with which slave-owning societies were able to draw lines between humans with rights and humans without rights.

That slaves were human beings was acknowledged both in ancient Greece and in the slaveholding states of the U.S.—Aristotle explicitly says that barbarians are human beings who exist to serve the good of the more rational Greeks,[11] and Southern whites sought to save the souls of the Africans they enslaved by making them Christians. Yet the line between slaves and free people did not slip significantly, even when some barbarians and some Africans became free, or when slaves produced children of mixed race. So, Cavalieri suggests, there is no reason to doubt our ability to deny that some humans have rights, while keeping the rights of other humans as secure as ever. But she is certainly not advocating that we do this. Her concern is rather to undermine the argument for drawing the boundaries of the sphere of rights so as to include all and only humans.

Cavalieri also responds to the argument that all humans, including the irreversibly unconscious, are to be elevated above other animals because of the characteristics they "normally" possess, rather than those they actually have. This argument seems to appeal to a kind of unfairness in excluding those who "fortuitously" fail to have the required characteristics. Cavalieri replies that if the "fortuitousness" is merely statistical, it carries no moral relevance, and if it is intended to suggest that the lack of the required characteristics is not the fault of those with profound intellectual disability, then that is not a basis for separating such humans from nonhuman animals.

Cavalieri states her own position in terms of rights, and in particular the basic rights that constitute what, following Ronald Dworkin, she calls the "egalitarian plateau." We want, Cavalieri insists, to secure a basic form of equality for all human beings, including the "non-paradigmatic" ones (her term for "marginal cases.") If the egalitarian plateau is to have a defensible nonarbitrary boundary that safeguards all humans from being pushed off the edge, we must select as a criterion for that boundary a standard that allows a large number of nonhuman animals inside the boundary as well. Hence we must allow onto the egalitarian plateau beings whose intellect and emotions are at a level that is shared by, at least, all birds and mammals.

Cavalieri does not argue that the rights of birds and mammals can be derived from self-evidently true moral premises. Her starting point, rather, is our prevailing belief in human rights. She seeks to show that all who accept this belief must also accept that similar rights apply to other animals. Following Dworkin, she sees human rights as part of the basic political framework of a decent society. They set limits to what the state may justifiably do to others. In particular, institutions like slavery or other invidious forms of racial discrimination that are based on violating the human rights of some of those over whom the state rules are, for that reason alone, illegitimate. Our acceptance of the idea of human rights therefore requires the abolition of all practices that routinely overlook the basic interests of rights-holders. Hence, if Cavalieri's argument is sound, our belief in rights commits us to an extension of rights beyond humans, and that in turn requires us to abolish all practices, like factory farming and the use of animals as subjects of painful and lethal research, that routinely overlook the basic interests of nonhuman rights-holders.

On the other hand, the rights for which Cavalieri argues are not supposed to resolve every situation in which there is a conflict of interests or of rights. Her notion of rights as part of the basic political framework of a decent society is compatible with specific restrictions of rights, as occurred for example when "Typhoid Mary" was compulsorily quarantined because she carried a lethal disease. A government may be entitled to restrict the movements of humans or animals who are a danger to the public, but it must still show them the concern and respect due to them as possessors of basic rights.[12]

My own opposition to speciesism is based, as I have already mentioned, not on rights, but on the thought that a difference of species is not an ethically defensible ground for giving less consideration to the interests of a sentient being than we give to similar interests of a member of our own species. David DeGrazia skillfully defends equal consideration for all sentient beings in *Taking Animals Seriously*. Such a position need not rely on prior acceptance of our current view of human rights—a view that, though widespread, can be rejected, especially once its implications in regard to animals are drawn out as Cavalieri draws them out. While the principle of equal consideration of interests is therefore more solidly based than Cavalieri's argument, however, it must face the difficulties that follow from the fact that interests, not rights, are now the focus of attention. That requires us to estimate what the interests are in an endless variety of different circumstances.

To take one case of particular ethical significance: the interest a being has in continued life—and hence, on the interests view, the wrongness of taking that being's life—will depend in part on whether the being is aware of itself as existing over time, and is capable of forming future-directed desires that give it a particular kind of interest in continuing to live. To that extent Roger Scruton is right about our attitudes to the deaths of members of our own species who lack these characteristics. We see it as less of a tragedy than the death of a being who is future-oriented, and whose desires to do things in the medium- and long-term future will therefore be thwarted if he or she dies.[13] But this is not a defense of speciesism, for it implies that killing a self-aware being like a chimpanzee causes a greater loss to the being killed than does killing a human being with an intellectual disability so severe as to preclude the capacity to form desires for the future.

We then need to ask what other beings may have this kind of interest in living into the future. DeGrazia combines philosophical insights and scientific research to help us answer such questions about specific species of animals, but there is often room for doubt, and the calculations required for applying the principle of equal consideration of interests can only be rough approximations, if they can be done at all. Perhaps, though, that is just the nature of our ethical situation, and rights-based views avoid such calculations at the cost of leaving out something relevant to what we ought to do.

The most recent addition to the literature of the animal movement has come from a surprising quarter, one deeply hostile to any discussion of the possibility of justifying the killing of human beings, no matter how severely disabled they may be. In *Dominion: The Power of Man, the Suffering of Animals, and the Call to Mercy* Matthew Scully, a conservative Christian, past literary editor of *National Review* and now speechwriter to President George W. Bush, has written an eloquent polemic against human abuse of animals, culminating with a devastating description of factory farming.

Since the animal movement has, for the past thirty years, generally been associated with the left, it is curious now to see Scully make a case for many of the same goals within the perspective of the Christian right, replete with references to God, interpretation of the scripture, and attacks on "moral relativism, self-centered materialism, license passing itself off as freedom, and the culture of death"[14]—but this time aimed at condemning not victimless crimes like homosexuality or physician-assisted suicide, but the needless suffering inflicted by factory farming and the modern slaughterhouse. Scully calls on all of us to show mercy toward animals and abandon ways of treating them that fail to respect their nature as animals. The result is a work that, although not philosophically rigorous, has had a remarkable amount of sympathetic publicity in the conservative press, which usually sneers at animal advocates.

3.

The history of the modern animal movement makes a nice counterexample to skepticism about the impact of moral argument on real life.[15] As James Jasper and Dorothy Nelkin observed in *The Animal Rights Crusade: The Growth of a Moral Protest,* "Philosophers served as midwives of the animal rights movement in the late 1970s."[16] The first successful protest against animal experiments in the United States was the 1976–1977 campaign against experiments conducted at the American Museum of Natural History on the sexual behavior of mutilated cats. Henry Spira, who conceived and ran the campaign, had a background of working in the union and civil rights movements, and had not considered, until he read the 1973 *New York Review* article, that animals are also worth the attention of those concerned about the exploitation of the weak. Spira went on to take on larger targets, such as the testing of cosmetics on animals. His technique was to target a prominent corporation that used animals—in the cosmetics campaign, he started with Revlon—and ask them to take reasonable steps to find alternatives to the use of animals. Always willing to engage in dialogue, and never one to paint the abusers of animals as evil sadists, he was remarkably successful in stimulating interest in developing ways of testing products without using animals, or with using fewer animals in less painful ways.[17]

Partly as a result of his work, there has also been a sizable drop in the number of animals used in research. In Britain official statistics show that roughly half as many animals are now experimented upon as were used in 1970. Estimates for the United States—where no official statistics are kept—suggest a similar story. From the standpoint of a nonspeciesist ethic there is still a long way to go for animals used in research, but the changes the animal movement has brought about mean that every year millions fewer animals are forced to undergo painful procedures and slow deaths.

The animal movement has had other successes too. Despite "fur is back" claims by the industry, fur sales have still not recovered to their level in the 1980s, when the animal movement began to target it. Since 1973, while the number of dogs and cats owned has nearly doubled, the number of stray and unwanted animals killed in pounds and shelters has been cut by more than half.[18]

These modest gains are dwarfed, however, by the huge increase in animals kept confined, some so tightly that they are unable to stretch their limbs or walk even a step or two, on America's factory farms. This is by far the greatest source of human-inflicted suffering on animals, simply because the numbers are so great. Animals used in experiments are numbered in the tens of millions annually, but last year ten *billion* birds and mammals were raised and killed for food in the United States alone. The increase over the previous year is, at around 400 million animals, more than the total number of animals killed in the U.S. by pounds and shelters, for research, and for fur combined. The overwhelming majority of these factory-reared animals now live their lives entirely indoors, never knowing fresh air, sunshine, or grass until they are trucked away to be slaughtered.

Against the confinement and slaughter of farm animals in America, the animal movement has, until quite recently, been impotent. Gail Eisnitz's 1997 book *Slaughterhouse* contains shocking, well-authenticated accounts of animals in major American slaughterhouses being skinned and dismembered while still conscious.[19] If such incidents had been documented in Britain they would have led to major news stories and the national government would have been forced to do something about it. Here the book passed virtually unnoticed outside the animal movement.

The situation is very different in Europe. Americans have often looked down on some European nations, especially the Mediterranean countries, for tolerating cruelty to animals. Now the accusing glance goes in the opposite direction. Even in Spain, with its culture of bull-fighting, most animals are better cared for than in America. By 2012, European egg producers will be required to give their hens access to a perch and a nesting box to lay their eggs in, and to allow at least 750 square centimeters, or

120 square inches per bird—dramatic changes that will transform the living conditions of more than two hundred million hens. United States egg producers haven't even started thinking about perches or nesting boxes, and typically give their fully grown hens just forty-eight square inches, or about half the area of a sheet of 8½-x-11-inch letter paper per bird.[20]

In the U.S. veal calves are deliberately kept anemic, deprived of straw for bedding, and confined in individual crates so narrow that they cannot even turn around. That system of keeping calves has been illegal in Britain for many years, and will become illegal throughout the European Union by 2007. Keeping pregnant sows in individual crates for their entire pregnancy, also the standard American practice, was banned in Britain in 1998, and is being phased out in Europe. These changes have wide support throughout the European Union, and the backing of leading European experts on the welfare of farm animals. They are a vindication of much that animal advocates have been saying for the past thirty years.

Are Americans simply less concerned with animal suffering than their European counterparts? Perhaps, but in *Political Animals: Animal Protection Policies in Britain and the United States,* Robert Garner explores several other possible explanations for the widening gap in animal welfare standards between the two nations.[21] By comparison with Britain, the US political process is more corrupt. Elections are many times more costly—the entire 2001 British general election cost less than John Corzine spent to win a single Senate seat in 2000. With money playing a greater role, American candidates are more beholden to their donors. Moreover, fund raising in Europe is largely done by the political parties, not by individual candidates, which makes it more open to public scrutiny and more likely to produce an electoral backlash for the entire party if it is seen to be in the pocket of a particular industry. These differences allow the agribusiness industry far greater control over Congress than it can hope to have over the political processes in Europe.

Consistent with that explanation, the most successful American campaigns— like Spira's campaign against the use of animals to test cosmetics—have concentrated on corporations rather than on the legislature or the government. Recently a ray of hope has come from an unlikely vehicle for change. After protracted discussions with animal advocates, started by Henry Spira before his death and then taken up by People for the Ethical Treatment of Animals, McDonald's agreed to set and enforce higher standards for the slaughterhouses that supply it with meat, and then announced that it would require its egg suppliers to provide each hen with a minimum of seventy-two square inches of living space—a 50 percent improvement for most American hens, but still only enough to bring these producers up to a level that is already on its way out in Europe. Burger King and Wendy's followed suit. These steps were the first hopeful signs for American farm animals since the modern animal movement began.

An even greater triumph was achieved last November by using another route around the legislative roadblock: the citizen-initiated referendum. With support from a number of national animal organizations, a group of animal activists in Florida succeeded in gathering 690,000 signatures to put on the ballot a proposal to change the constitution of Florida so as to ban the keeping of pregnant sows in crates so narrow that they cannot even turn around. Changing the constitution is the only way citizens can get a direct vote on a measure in Florida. Opponents of the measure, obviously unwilling to argue that pigs don't need to be able to turn around or walk, instead tried to persuade Florida voters that the confinement of pigs was not an appropriate subject for the state constitution. But by a margin of 55 to 45 percent, voters said no to sow crates, thus making Florida the first jurisdiction in the United States to ban a major form of farm-animal confinement. Though Florida has only a small number of intensive piggeries, the vote supports the idea that it is not hard hearts or lack of sympathy for animals but a failure of democracy that causes America to lag so far behind Europe in abolishing the worst features of factory farming.

4.

My original article in *The New York Review* ended with a paragraph that saw the challenge of the animal movement as a test of human nature:

> *Can a purely moral demand of this kind succeed? The odds are certainly against it. The book* [Animals, Men and Morals] *holds out no inducements. It does not tell us that we will become healthier, or enjoy life more, if we cease exploiting animals. Animal Liberation will require greater altruism on the part of mankind than any other liberation movement, since animals are incapable of demanding it for themselves, or of protesting against their exploitation by votes, demonstrations, or bombs. Is man capable of such genuine altruism? Who knows? If this book does have a significant effect, however, it will be a vindication of all those who have believed that man has within himself the potential for more than cruelty and selfishness.*

So how have we done? Both the optimists and the cynics about human nature could see the results as confirming their views. Significant changes have occurred, in animal testing and other forms of animal abuse. In Europe, entire industries are being transformed because of the concern of the public for the welfare of farm animals. Perhaps most encouraging for the optimists is the fact that millions of activists have freely given up their time and money to support the animal movement, many of them changing their diet and lifestyle to avoid supporting the abuse of animals. Vegetarianism and even veganism (avoiding all animal products) are far more widespread in North America and Europe than they were thirty years ago, and although it is difficult to know how much of this relates to concern for animals, undoubtedly some of it does.

On the other hand, despite the generally favorable course of the philosophical debate about the moral status of animals, popular views on that topic are still very far from adopting the basic idea that the interests of all beings should be given equal consideration irrespective of their species. Most people still eat meat, and buy what is cheapest, oblivious to the suffering of the animal from which the meat comes. The number of animals being consumed is much greater today than it was thirty years ago, and increasing prosperity in East Asia is creating a demand for meat that threatens to boost that number far higher still. Meanwhile the rules of the World Trade Organization threaten advances in animal welfare by making it doubtful that Europe will be able to keep out imports from countries with lower standards. In short, the outcome so far indicates that as a species we are capable of altruistic concern for other beings; but imperfect information, powerful interests, and a desire not to know disturbing facts have limited the gains made by the animal movement.

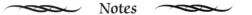 Notes

1. Taplinger, 1972.
2. Peter Singer, *Animal Liberation* (New York Review/Random House, 1975; revised edition, New York Review/Random House, 1990; reissued with a new preface, Ecco, 2001).
3. Charles Magel, *Keyguide to Information Sources in Animal Rights* (McFarland, 1989).
4. See, for example, Carl Cohen, "The Case for the Use of Animals in Biomedical Research," *New England Journal of Medicine,* Vol. 315 (1986), pp. 865–870; and Michael Leahy, *Against Liberation: Putting Animals in Perspective* (London: Routledge, 1991).
5. See Mary Midgley, *Animals and Why They Matter* (University of Georgia Press, 1984); Jeffrey Gray, "On the Morality of Speciesism," *Psychologist,* Vol. 4, No. 5 (May 1991), pp. 196–198, and "On Speciesism and Racism: Reply to Singer and Ryder," *Psychologist,* Vol. 4, No. 5 (May 1991), pp. 202–203; and Lewis Petrinovich, *Darwinian Dominion: Animal Welfare and Human Interests* (MIT Press, 1999).
6. Petrinovich, *Darwinian Dominion,* p. 29.
7. Robert Nozick, "About Mammals and People," *The New York Times Book Review,* November 27, 1983, p. 11; I draw here on Richard I. Arneson, "What, If Anything, Renders All Humans Morally Equal?" in *Singer and His Critics,* edited by Dale Jamieson (Blackwell, 1999), p. 123.
8. Peter Carruthers, *The Animals Issue: Moral Theory in Practice* (Cambridge University Press, 1992).
9. Daniel Dombrowski, *Babies and Beasts: The Argument from Marginal Cases* (University of Illinois Press, 1997).
10. See, for example, Carruthers, *The Animals Issue.*
11. Aristotle, *Politics* (London: J.M. Dent and Sons, 1916), p. 16.
12. As Dworkin himself argued in regard to the detention of suspected terrorists; see "The Threat to Patriotism," *The New York Review,* February 28, 2002.
13. See my *Practical Ethics* (Cambridge University Press, 1993), especially Chapter 4.
14. Quoted from Kathryn Jean Lopez, "Exploring 'Dominion': Matthew Scully on Animals," *National Review Online,* December 3, 2002.
15. See, for example, Richard A. Posner, *The Problematics of Moral and Legal Theory* (Belnap Press/Harvard University Press, 1999).
16. Free Press, 1992, p. 90.
17. See Peter Singer, *Ethics into Action: Henry Spira and the Animal Rights Movement* (Rowman and Littlefield, 1998).
18. *The State of the Animals 2001,* edited by Deborah Salem and Andrew Rowan (Humane Society Press, 2001).
19. Prometheus, 1997.
20. See Karen Davis, *Prisoned Chickens, Poisoned Eggs: An Inside Look at the Modern Poultry Industry* (Book Publishing Company, 1996).
21. St. Martin's, 1998.

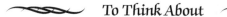

To Think About

1. "To undertake to lay down universally valid distinctions of value between different kinds of life will end in judging them by the greater or lesser distance at which they seem to stand from us human beings—as we ourselves judge. But that is a purely subjective criterion. Who amongst us knows what significance any other kind of life has in itself and as part of the universe?"

    Albert Schweitzer

2. "Animal liberationists do not separate out the human animal. . . . When it comes to having a central nervous system, and the ability to feel pain, hunger, and thirst, a rat is a pig is a dog is a boy. They're all mammals."   ***Ingrid Newkirk***

3. "'He was faced with a very difficult choice.' That is something you never would say of an animal. Neither would you say that the animal showed weakness or strength in making a choice.

    "Perhaps the chief reason why you cannot talk about the course of an animal's life, is that you cannot speak of progress or decline.

    "Neither can you say that the animal kept always to the same line, or that he was constantly jumping about from one thing to another. Since there are no occupations in an animal's life."   ***Rush Rhees***

4. "Animals do not have rights. This is not to say that we may do whatever we please to animals or that everything commonly done by humans to animals is justifiable. Not at all. It is morally right to use animals in medical research, but from this it does not follow that *any* use of them is right. Of course not. We humans have a universal obligation to act *humanely,* and this means that we must refrain from treating animals in ways that cause them unnecessary distress. Animals, to repeat what was said at the outset, are not lumps of clay, and they ought not to be dealt with as though they feel no pain."   ***Carl Cohen***

5. "I know that animals do many things better than we do, but this does not surprise me. It can even be used to prove they act naturally and mechanically, like a clock which tells the time better than our judgment does. . . . [I]f they thought as we do, they would have an immortal soul like us. This is unlikely, because there is no reason to believe it of some animals without believing it of all, and many of them such as oysters and sponges are too imperfect for this to be credible. . . . Please note that I am speaking of thought, and not of life or sensation. I do not deny life to animals, since I regard it as consisting simply in the heat of the heart; and I do not deny sensation in so far as it depends on a bodily organ. Thus my opinion is not so much cruel to animals as indulgent to men . . . since it absolves them from the suspicion of crime when they eat or kill animals."   ***René Descartes***

6. "What a pitiful thing, what poor stuff it is to say that animals are machines deprived of knowledge and feeling. . . . Barbarians seize this dog who so prodigiously surpasses man in friendship. They nail him to a table and dissect him alive to show you the mesenteric veins. You discover in him all the same organs

gans of feeling that you possess. Answer me, mechanist, has nature arranged all the springs of feeling in this animal in order that he should not feel? Does he have nerves to be impassive? Do not assume that nature presents this impertinent contradiction."   ***Voltaire***

7. "But so far as animals are concerned we have no direct duties. Animals are not self-conscious and are there merely as a means to an end. That end is man. We can ask, 'Why do animals exist?' But to ask, 'Why does man exist?' is a meaningless question. Our duties toward animals are merely indirect duties towards humanity. Thus, if a dog has served his master long and faithfully, his service, on the analogy of human service, deserves reward and when the dog has grown too old to serve, his master ought to keep him until he dies. Such action helps to support us in our duties towards human beings, where they are bounden duties. If then any acts of animals are analogous to human acts and spring from the same principles, we have duties toward the animals because thus we cultivate the corresponding duties toward human beings. If a man shoots his dog because the animal is no longer capable of service, he does not fail in his duty to the dog, for the dog cannot judge, but his act is inhuman and damages in himself that humanity which it is his duty to show towards mankind. If he is not to stifle his human feelings, he must practice kindness towards animals, for he who is cruel to animals becomes hard also in his dealings with men."   ***Immanuel Kant***

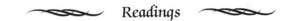

Readings

COETZEE, J. M. *The Lives of Animals.* Princeton, NJ: Princeton University Press, 1999.

FRANKLIN, JULIAN H. *Animal Rights and Moral Philosophy.* New York: Columbia University Press, 2005.

GAITA, RAYMOND. *The Philosopher's Dog: Friendships with Animals.* New York: Random House, 2002.

REGAN, TOM. *Defending Animal Rights.* Urbana: University of Illinois Press, 2001.

RHEES, RUSH. *Moral Questions.* New York: St. Martin's Press, 1999.

PART 9

AESTHETICS

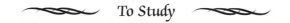

Are Artistic Judgments Subjective?

57
Tastes Cannot Be Disputed

Curt John Ducasse *(1881–1969) was president of the American Philosophical Association in 1936. His works include* Nature, Mind, and Death *(1951) and* Truth, Knowledge, and Causation *(1968).*

Is it fair to say that the person who enjoys Beethoven's music has better taste than someone who prefers punk rock? Can artistic judgments such as these ever be disputed? This question is constantly debated by both common people and philosophers. Ducasse maintains that the basic function of art is to express emotions rather than create beauty, but at the same time he holds that beauty is a legitimate standard in the criticism of works of art. He says that the choice of a standard is ultimately an expression of personal preference, and that taste is subjective and relative. There is, he concludes, no disputing among tastes for either the naive or the sophisticated.

To Study

1. What is Ducasse's definition of *beauty?* Why does he believe there is no such thing as authoritative opinion concerning beauty?
2. Why can't beauty be proved by an appeal to a consensus, the test of time, or the type of person who experiences it?
3. Why can't beauty be proved by appeal to technical principles? Discuss this question in terms of our personal reasons for disliking something, established canons of beauty, and the validity of professional opinion.
4. Can one criticize art objects in ethical terms?

From Curt J. Ducasse, *The Philosophy of Art,* Revised and Enlarged (New York: Dover, 1966), chap. 15. Reprinted by permission of the publisher.

5.   Regarding beauty, to what does ultimate analysis unavoidably lead?

6.   Can taste be refined? What does Ducasse conclude?

BEAUTY IS RELATIVE TO THE INDIVIDUAL OBSERVER

Beauty [is] defined as the capacity of an object aesthetically contemplated to yield feelings that are pleasant. This definition cannot be characterized simply either as objective, or as subjective. According to it, "beautiful" is an adjective properly predicable only of objects, by what that adjective does predicate of an object is that the feelings of which it constitutes the aesthetic symbol for a contemplating observer, are pleasurable. Beauty being in this definite sense dependent upon the constitution of the individual observer, it will be as variable as that constitution. That is to say, an object which one person properly calls beautiful will, with equal propriety be not so judged by another, or indeed by the same person at a different time.

There is, *then, no such* thing *as authoritative opinion concerning the beauty of a given object.* There is only the opinion of this person or that; or the opinion of persons of some specified sort. When one has stated the opinion and mentioned the person or class of persons who hold it, one has gone as far as it is possible to go in the direction of a scientifically objective statement relating to the beauty of the object. When some matter (as that of beauty) is not of the sort which "is so," or "not so," in an *absolute* sense, the nearest approach that one can make to the wished-for absoluteness lies in furnishing, as fully as possible, the data to which the matter in question is *relative;* and this is what one does in the case of beauty when one indicates just who it happens to be that judges the given object beautiful or the reverse.

All that was said . . . concerning aesthetic connoisseurship, i.e., concerning superior capacity for experiencing difference in aesthetic feeling in the presence of slight differences in the aesthetic object, applies equally here, where differences in the pleasantness of the feelings are particularly in question. There are connoisseurs of beauty, or, more often, of particular sorts of beauty; but their judgments of beauty are "binding" on no one. Indeed it is hard to see what could possibly be meant by "binding" in such a connection, unless it were an obligation on others to lie or dissemble concerning the aesthetic feelings which in fact they have or do not have on a given occasion. There is, of course, such a thing as good taste, and bad taste. But good taste, I submit, means either my taste, or the taste of people who are to my taste, or the taste of people to whose taste I want to be. There is no objective test of the goodness or badness of taste, in the sense in which there is an objective test of the goodness or badness of a person's judgment concerning, let us say, the fitness of a given tool to a given task.

BEAUTY CANNOT BE PROVED BY APPEAL TO CONSENSUS, OR TO THE "TEST OF TIME," OR TO THE TYPE OF PERSON WHO EXPERIENCES IT IN A GIVEN CASE

In the light of what precedes, it is obvious that the familiar attempts to prove the beauty of certain works of art by appeal to the consensus of opinion, or to the test of continued approval through long periods of time in the life either of society or of the individual, are, like the appeal to the connoisseur's verdict, entirely futile. Such tests cannot possibly prove the object's beauty to those who do not perceive any in it; and to those who do, they are needless. They prove nothing whatever, except that beauty is found in the object . . . by such as do find it there.

We might attempt to rank beauties on the basis of the particular aspect of human nature, or type of human being, that experiences aesthetic pleasure in given cases. This would lead to a classifying of beauties as, for instance, sentimental, intellectual, sexual, spiritual, utilitarian, sensuous, social, etc. We might well believe in some certain order of worth or dignity in the human faculties respectively concerned, but this would not lead to any aesthetically objective ranking of beauties. To suggest it would be as ludicrous as a proposal to rank the worth of various religions according to the average cost of the vestments of their priests. For a ranking of beauties, there are available only such principles as the relative intensity of the pleasure felt, its relative duration, relative volume, and relative freedom from admixture of pain. These principles, however, do not in the least release us from the need of relying upon the individual's judgment; on the contrary their application rests wholly upon it.

BEAUTY CANNOT BE PROVED BY APPEAL TO TECHNICAL PRINCIPLES OR CANONS

It may yet be thought, however, that there are certain narrower and more technical requirements in the various fields of art, without the fulfilling of which no work can be beautiful. Among such alleged canons of beauty may be mentioned the rules of so-called "harmony" in music; various precepts concerning literary composition; unity; truth to nature; such requirements as consistency, relevance, and unambiguity; and so on. There are indeed "rules" or "principles" of that sort, some of which are, I will freely declare, valid for me; so that when I find myself confronted by flagrant violations of them, I am apt to feel rather strongly, and to be impatient or sarcastic about "that sort of stuff." And indeed, on occasions when I have found myself inadvertently guilty of having drawn some line or written some sentence in violation of my own aesthetic canons, I have at times felt as ashamed of the line or the sentence as I should of having picked somebody's pocket. I admit having pronounced opinions about the beauty or ugliness of various things, and what is more, in many cases I am able to *give reasons* for my opinions.

But of what nature are those reasons? They are, ultimately, of the same nature as would be that offered by a man arguing that my pen had to fall when I let go of it a moment ago, *because of gravitation.* Gravitation is but the name we give to the general fact that unsupported objects *do* fall, and at a certain rate; but it is not a reason, or cause, or proof of that fact. To say that something always happens, is not to give any reason why it ever does. Therefore when I say that a certain design is ugly because it is against the "law of symmetry," I am not giving a reason why it *had* to give me aesthetic displeasure, but only mentioning the fact that it resembles in a stated respect certain others which as a bare matter of fact also do displease me. This character which displeases me and many persons, may, however, please others. And, what is more directly to the point, it not only may but it does,—jazzy or uncouth though I may call the taste of such persons. But what most obstinately drives me to the acquisition of a certain, at least abstract, sense of humor concerning the ravening intolerance and would-be authoritativeness of my own pet canons of beauty, is the fact that they have changed in the past, and that I see no reason why they should not change again in the future. For all I can see to prevent it, I may well to-morrow, next year, or in some future incarnation, burn what I aesthetically adore today, and adore what I now would burn. If this happens, I have no doubt at all that I shall then smugly label the change a progress and a development of my taste; whereas to-day I should no less smugly describe the possibility of a change of that sort in me, as a possibility that my taste may go to the devil. And, let it be noted, the sole foundation upon which either of the two descriptions would rest, would be the fact that the describer *actually* possesses at the time the sort of taste which he does. Tastes can be neither proved nor refuted, but only "called names," i.e., praised or reviled.

Certain limited and empirical generalizations have been found possible concerning factors upon which the aesthetic pleasure of most people, or of some kinds of people, appears to depend. Precarious generalizations of this sort may be found for instance in manuals of design and of pictorial composition, where they are often dignified by the name of "principles." People familiar with them may then be heard to say that a given picture, perhaps, is well composed and why; or that the tones, the masses, or the values are, as the case may be, well or ill balanced, and so on. Other statements that we may hear and which also imply "principles," would be that the color is clean, or else muddy; that the drawing is, perhaps, distorted; that the surfaces are well modelled; that the lines are rhythmical; that the color combinations are impossible; that the masses lack volume or solidity, etc. The words beauty and ugliness may not occur once, but it is nevertheless obvious that all such statements are not merely descriptive, but *critical*. They are not direct assertions of aesthetic value or disvalue, viz., of beauty or ugliness, but, taking it as an obvious fact, they attempt to trace it to certain definite sorts of features in the work. The more intelligent and better informed kind of art-criticism is of this analytical and diagnostic sort, and there is nothing beyond this that the art-critic could do.

All such comments, worded in the technical jargon of the particular craft, have the imposing sound of expert judgments based upon authoritative principles, and are likely to make the lay consumer of art feel very small and uninitiated. Therefore it cannot be too much emphasized here that a given picture is not ugly because the composition of it, or the color combinations in it, are against the rules; but that the rule against a given type of composition or of color combinations is authoritative only because, or if, or for whom, or when, compositions or combinations of that type are "*actually*" found displeasing. All rules and canons and theories concerning what a painting or other work of art should or should not be, derive such authority as they have over you or me or anyone else, solely from the capacity of such canons *to predict to us* that we shall feel aesthetic pleasure here, and aesthetic pain there. If a given rule predicts this accurately for a given person, that person's *actual* feeling of aesthetic pleasure or displeasure then, proves that this rule *was* a valid one so far as *he* is concerned. That is, the feeling judges the rule, not the rule the feeling. The rule may not be valid for someone else, and it may at any time cease to be valid for the given person, since few things are so variable as pleasure. The *actual* experience of beauty or ugliness by somebody is the final test of the validity of all rules and theories of painting, music, etc., and that test absolutely determines how far, and when, and for whom any given rule or theory holds or does not hold.

The difference between the criticisms of the professionals, and those of the people who, having humbly premised that they "know nothing about art," find little more to say than that a given work is in their judgment beautiful, or as the case may be, ugly or indifferent;—the difference, I say, between the criticisms of professionals and of laymen is essentially that the former are able to trace the aesthetic pleasure or displeasure which they feel to certain features of the object, while the latter are not able to do it. From this, however, it does not in the least follow that the evaluations of the professionals ultimately rest on any basis less subjective and less a matter of individual taste than do those of the layman. Indeed, so far as the nonprofessionals really judge at all, i.e., do not merely echo an opinion which they have somehow been bluffed into accepting as authoritative, their judgment is based on the fact that they actually feel something. The artists and professional critics, on the other hand, are exposed to a danger which does not threaten people who know nothing of the factors on which aesthetic pleasure or displeasure has in the past been found to depend for most people, or for some particular class of people,—the danger, namely, of erecting such empirical findings into fixed and rigid rules, and of judging the work of art no longer by the aesthetic pleasure it actually gives them, but by that which they think it "ought" to give them according to such rules. This danger is really very great, especially for the artist, who, in the nature of the case, is constantly forced to give attention to the technical means by which the objective expression of his feeling is alone to be achieved. Having thus all the time to solve technical problems, it is fatally easy for him to become interested in them for their own sake, and, without knowing it, to be henceforth no longer an artist expressing what he feels, but a restless virtuoso searching for new stunts to perform. This may be the reason why so many of the pictures displayed in our exhibits, although well-enough painted, make one feel as though one were receiving a special-delivery, registered, extra-postage letter, . . . just to say, perhaps, that after Thursday comes Friday.

Listening to the comments of artists and of some critics on a picture will quickly convince one that, strange as it sounds, they are as often as not almost incapable of seeing the picture about which they speak. What they see instead is brush work, values, edges, dark against light, colored shadows, etc. They are thus often not more but less capable than the untrained public of giving the picture *aesthetic* attention, and of getting from it genuinely aesthetic enjoyment. The theory that *aesthetic* appreciation of the products of a given art is increased by cultivating an amateur's measure of proficiency in that art, is therefore true only so far as such cultivation results in more intimate and thoroughgoing *aesthetic* acquaintance with the products of that art. This is likely to be the case in an interpretative art like music (not music-composing). But in an art which, like painting, is not so largely interpretative, and is at the same time dependent on rather elaborate technical processes, the amateur practitioner's attention is from the very first emphatically directed to these processes; and when it is directed to extant works of art it is directed to them as examples of a technique to be studied, not as aesthetic objects to be contemplated. The danger is then that such technical matters will come to monopolize his attention habitually, and that even in the face of nature he will forget to look at her, wondering instead whether the water or the sky be the brighter, or what color would have to be used to reproduce the appearance of a given shadow. Attention to technique is of course indispensable to the acquisition of it; and mastery of technique is in turn necessary to the production of art on any but the most humble scale. The risk is that the outcome of technical training will be not mastery of technique, but slavery to it. This risk disappears only when the technical apparatus has become as intimately a part of the artist as the hand is of the body for ordinary purposes, and is used without requiring attention. The attention can then turn from the means to the ends of art, viz., to the objective expression of feeling. But the stage at which technique has so become second-nature as to be forgotten, is not often fully reached. With most artists, what we may call their technical *savoir-faire* creaks more or less, as does the social *savoir-faire* of people who have become emilyposted but lately. Like the nouveaux gentlemen, such artists are too conscious of their technical manners, and forget what they are for.

CRITICISM OF AESTHETIC OBJECTS IN ETHICAL TERMS

Instead of asking whether a work of art or other aesthetic object is beautiful or ugly, i.e., whether the feeling obtained in aesthetic contemplation of it is pleasant or unpleasant, we may on the contrary disregard this and ask whether the feeling so obtained by a person is or may become connected with the rest of his life, and in what manner it may affect it for good or ill. The ethical or the religious worth of the feelings obtained in aesthetic contemplation of works of art, it will be recalled, would have been made by Plato and by Tolstoi the ruling standard in terms of which to judge art as good or bad. It is worth noting, however, that standards of evaluation cannot themselves be evaluated, except in terms of a standard not itself in any way vindicated but only dogmatically laid down. And any standard evaluated in this manner may itself equally well be laid down in turn as absolute, and be used to evaluate the standard which before was evaluating it. Arguments about the relative worth of various standards of worth are therefore wholly futile, inasmuch as, in the very nature of the logical situation, every such argument must to begin with beg as its premise the point essentially at issue. Ultimately, then, a given standard can only be sympathized with and adopted, or the reverse; and logic can come in only *after* this has occurred. Plato's and Tolstoi's choice of the ethical or religious nature of the aesthetic feelings imparted, as ruling standard for the evaluation of art, is legitimate, but it constitutes only a manifestation of their own ruling interest, and a different choice of ruling standard is equally legitimate by anyone else whose ruling interest happens to be different. With these remarks concerning the permissibility, but the arbitrariness, of describing any one standard of worth as "supreme" or "ruling," we may leave the matter, and now simply consider the question raised, namely, whether the feelings obtained in aesthetic contemplation may affect the rest of one's life, and how.

The value other than aesthetic that aesthetic feelings may have depends upon the fact that if, when a feeling has been obtained though aesthetic contemplation, the aesthetic attitude is then given up and replaced by the practical, that which had up to that moment the status of aesthetic feeling now assumes that of impulse.

So long as our state is properly describable as aesthetic feeling, its value is immediate and intrinsic, and consists in the pleasantness or unpleasantness of the state. But when our state comes to be properly describable as impulse, then its value is as usual to be measured in terms of the eventual significance of the impulse. An impulse is a seed of conduct, and an aesthetic feeling is at least a potential seed of impulse; the terms in which we commonly appraise conduct are therefore potentially applicable to it.

The impulse or embryonic conduct resulting from the transmutation of an aesthetic feeling through a shift to the practical attitude may be either a novel impulse in the life of the individual or not. If it is an impulse of a sort already experienced and more or less established with characteristic modes of manifestation in the life of the person concerned, then the reexperiencing of it as aftermath of aesthetic contemplation will not affect the individual's life qualitatively, but only quantitatively. It will be simply fuel to an engine already existing and functioning; it will add to the intensity of some aspect of life but will not alter it in kind, except perhaps indirectly if the changes of intensity involved are such as to upset an equilibrium previously existing, and thus force the recasting of life in a different qualitative pattern.

If however the impulse is a novel one in the life of the individual, then it constitutes directly the seed of a change in the kind of life that has been his. The evolution (whether towards good or evil) of the will-aspect of man's nature does not take place merely through increases in his knowledge of the facts and relations that constitute the field of action of his will, but also through the advent in him of qualitatively novel impulses. Indeed, it might well be argued that mere increase in the quantity as distinguished from the nature of one's knowledge and experience, only furnishes one with new means for the service of old ends, or makes one better aware of the ends to which one's hitherto blind impulses tended; but that, however such increase of knowledge may transform the manifestations of existing longings or impulses, it does not of itself alter their intrinsic nature. Transformation in the nature of the impulses themselves (apart from maturation) seems traceable to experiences of two sorts. One of them is awareness by the individual of the presence of a practically real situation novel in kind in his life. This may call forth in him an impulse hitherto foreign to him. The other is what we might call the surreptitious implantation of the impulse itself in him, through the transmutation which we are now considering of an aesthetic feeling into an impulse, by a shift to the practical attitude.

The aesthetic contemplation of nature and of various aspects of life is, through such a shift of attitude, a source of germs of new impulses and of food for old ones. Some persons are known to the writer, in whom the contemplation for the first time of the ocean, or of great mountains, seems to have produced feelings comparable in point of novelty and depth to those reported by the mystics, and the aftermath of impulse due to which gave to life a different pattern, somewhat as does a religious conversion. But art is capable of being as much more effective in the sowing of such seeds of novel impulse, as, for instance, the study of existing records is more effective than personal investigation in acquiring a knowledge of geography. For one thing, art is usually easier than nature to contemplate, being, we might almost say, made for that. Again, when nature was its model, art may be described as at least a drastic editing of nature, supplying what she forgot, omitting what was irrelevant, accenting her here or there into unambiguity. The work of art, being created specifically to give objective expression to a given feeling, is likely to have a pointedness of feeling-import which nature matches only by accident. The work of art, moreover, can be contemplated at length and returned to again and again, whereas natural facts and the aspects they show us are mostly beyond our control. They come and go heedless of the conditions which alone would make it possible for us to contemplate them adequately. But lastly, art, although in some ways it falls short of nature, has in another way a range of resources far greater than nature's, for it has at its command the boundless resources of the imagination. What it cannot present it often can represent, and thus set up before our attention objects of contemplation never to be found in nature. It can lead us into new worlds, in the contemplation of which our feeling-selves spontaneously burgeon and bloom in all sorts of new ways. Some poems, some music, some statues and pictures, have had in an extraordinary degree this power to bring to birth in people qualities of feeling that had remained latent in them. One such work of art is Leonardo's *Mona Lisa*. Art theorists whose fundamental dogma is that the end of painting is the representation of plastic form, and who find that picture but indifferently successful in this respect, cannot understand why the theft of it a few years ago should have been deemed a world-calamity. Their only explanation is the aesthetic ineptitude of mankind at large. They cannot see that design and the representation of plastic form is not the whole of the art of painting, but is rather a means which may be used to the ends of art, *when it is important to those ends.* Not the aesthetic ineptitude of mankind, therefore, but the sophomoric character of the measuring-rod by which such theorists would judge Leonardo's picture, is the lesson of the effect produced by that famous theft. There are doubtless people who, in a similar way, would insist on characterizing Socrates essentially as a Greek who was not a "good provider."

LIBERALISM IN AESTHETICS

The principal standards in terms of which works of art and aesthetic objects may be criticized have been considered above, and the general nature of the conclusions reached concerning the significance and validity of such criticisms may now be summarily characterized.

Judgments of mediate or instrumental value are capable of being proved or disproved. Their truth or falsity is objective, in the sense that it is not conferred upon them by the individual's taste, but is a matter of connections in nature independent of the critic's taste. But the *relevance* or importance, if not the truth, of any judgment of mediate value, is a matter of the individual critic's taste or constitution, since for any such critic that relevance depends on a judgment of immediate value by him.

As regards to judgments of immediate value, and in particular of beauty and ugliness, it seems to me that here as in other fields, ultimate analysis leads unavoidably to *the particular constitution of the individual critic* (no matter how he may have come by it); as the necessary and sufficient ground for all such judgments. The constitutions of numbers of individual critics may, of course, happen to be alike in some respects; or they can be made more or less alike by subjecting them to the sort of psychological pressure appropriate to the causation of such a result. If a number of critics are constituted alike in some respects, then any one of them will be able to formulate value judgments with which will agree as many of the other critics as are constituted like him in the respects needed for such agreement! I cannot see that "objective validity" in the case of a judgment of immediate value, means anything whatever but this; namely, several people judge alike because they are constituted alike. But whether a given taste be possessed by one person only, or by a thousand alike, the maxim that [there is no disputing about tastes] holds with regard to it.

Is there then no such thing as the refining and educating of taste? Certainly there is,—and there is also such a thing as perversion and deprivation of taste. But the question in any given case is, which is which? No one so far as I know has yet pointed out any way of answering this question otherwise than arbitrarily and dogmatically, i.e., otherwise than in terms of the taste actually possessed by some person or other, usually oneself, *arbitrarily* taken as standard. That question, indeed, is hardly ever frankly faced. Those who have approached it at all seem always to have labored under the strange delusion that if only they succeeded in showing that the tastes of a large number or a majority of people were alike, the question was answered; whereas the truth is on the contrary, as just pointed out, that mere numbers have no bearing whatever on the question. Taking a vote is only a device for ascertaining in advance what would be the outcome of a fight between two groups of people, if every person were as strong as every other and strength alone counted. "Proof" by appeal to a vote is obviously but a civilized form of . . . [arguing with the use of force].

It may be asked, however, whether in the absence of any standard of immediate value objectively valid in any sense other than that described above, it is not possible at least to point to some respects in which the (immediate) value judgments of all people whatever, would agree. Nobody whatever, it may be urged, likes great hunger or thirst or cold, or cuts or burns, etc. Now it may be granted that certainly not many do, but after all there are masochists and ascetics and martyrs. It may be true because tautologous that nobody likes pain; but we must keep in mind that pain and pleasure are the predicates, not the subjects, of immediate-value-judgments. Their subjects are things, situations, experiences. The question is thus not whether painfulness is ever pleasurable, but whether there are any *situations* or *experiences* which everybody without exception finds, for instance, painful. And this is very doubtful. We can probably say only that with regard to some situations or experiences, the dissentients are very few. And as we have just seen, numbers mean nothing at all in such a matter.

This brings us to what may be called a dogmatico-liberalistic position. Neither I nor anyone can refute anyone else's judgments of immediate value,—here, of beauty and ugliness; nor can anyone refute mine. This is the liberalistic aspect of the situation. The fullest insight into it, however, constitutes no reason whatever why any one should hold to his own immediate valuations any the less strongly. That our own opinion must in the nature of such matters be dogmatic is no reason why it should not be honest, vigorous, and unashamed.

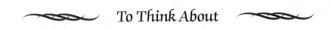

To Think About

1. "The thesis I wish to present here is that culture is not neutral politically, and that it is as impossible for it to be so as it is impossible for any other product of human labour to be detached from its conditions of production and reception. All culture serves someone's interest. Cultural products which present foreign wars as the heroic effort of a master race to ennoble mankind are, to the degree that they are successful as art, objectively in the interests of imperialists, who are people who make foreign wars against other races for profit. Cultural products that present people who have no money or power as innately stupid or depraved, and thus unworthy of money or power, are in the interests of the ruling class and the power structure as it stands. . . . In our times, to refrain from mentioning genocide, racism, cultural schizophrenia, sexual exploitation, and the systematic starvation of entire populations is itself a political act. For no one in our time can be awake enough to write and have avoided noticing these phenomena—though he may not recognize them for what they are. As our bankrupt civilization draws to its close, and as the violence of the powerful against the weak, of the rich against the poor, of the few against the many, becomes more and more apparent, until it becomes impossible to watch a news broadcast and remain unaware of it for a second—as this situation becomes exacerbated, to refrain from mentioning it becomes more and more clearly a political act, an act of censorship or cowardice."   **Meredith Tax**

2. "I'll give you a very simple answer. I'm not entertained by entertainment."
                                                                Cynthia Ozick

3. "Beauty in things exists in the mind which contemplates them." **David Hume**

4. "The stage began to be instructive.

   "Oil, inflation, war, social struggles, the family, religion, wheat, the meat market, all became subjects for theatrical representation. Choruses enlightened the spectator about facts unknown to him. Films showed a montage of events from all over the world. Projections added statistical material. And as the 'background' came to the front of the stage so people's activity was subjected to criticism. Right and wrong courses of action were shown. People were shown who knew what they were doing, and others who did not. The theatre became an affair for philosophers, but only for such philosophers as wished not just to explain the world but also to change it. So we had philosophy and we had instruction. And where was the amusement in all that?"   **Bertolt Brecht**

5. When asked, "What is art?" **Picasso** replied, "What isn't art?"

~~~~ Readings ~~~~

DANTO, ARTHUR. *The Abuse of Beauty: Aesthetics and the Concept of Art.* Chicago: Open Court, 2003.

DUCASSE, CURT. *Art, the Critics, and You.* New York: Bobbs-Merrill, 1944.

ISEMINGER, GARY. *The Aesthetic Function of Art.* Ithaca, NY: Cornell University Press, 2004

KIVY, PETER, ed. *The Blackwell Guide to Aesthetics.* Malden, MA: Blackwell, 2004.

Are Artistic Judgments Subjective?

58
Tastes Can Be Disputed

Monroe Beardsley (1915–81) was elected president of the American Society for Aesthetics in 1956. His works include Practical Logic *(1950),* Aesthetics *(1958), and* Aesthetics: A Short History *(1966).*

Beardsley disagrees with Ducasse about the subjectivity of beauty and maintains that one can and does dispute tastes. He says that when people critically comment on a work of art, they give reasons for saying that the work is good or bad. He discusses those features of art that prove its ability or inability to provide the audience with a deep aesthetic experience.

 To Study

1. What is the chief use of the maxim "There is no disputing about taste"? To what areas is the maxim most significantly applied?
2. Why do we believe there is no disputing about art, but there can be about political matters?
3. What is the theory of the aesthetic skeptic? How does Beardsley criticize this? Cite his reasons.
4. What is the value of works of art? Explain fully.

We are assured by an old and often-quoted maxim, whose authority is not diminished by its being cast in Latin, that there can be no disputing about tastes. The chief use of this maxim is in putting an end to disputes that last a long time and don't appear to be getting anywhere. And for this purpose it is very efficacious, for it has an air of

From Monroe Beardsley, "Tastes Can Be Disputed," *Swarthmore College Alumni Bulletin* 56 (October 1958): 1–5. Reprinted with permission of the publisher and the author.

profound finality, and it also seems to provide a democratic compromise of a dead-locked issue. If you can't convince someone that he is wrong, or bring yourself to admit that he is right, you can always say that neither of you is more wrong than the other, because nobody can be right.

Remarks that serve to close some people's debates, however, are quite often just the remarks to start a new one among philosophers. And this maxim is no exception. It has been given a great deal of thought, some of it very illuminating; yet there is still something to be learned from further reflection upon it. Nor is it of small importance to know, if we can, whether the maxim is true or false, for if it is true we won't waste time in futile discussion, and if it is false we won't waste opportunities for fruitful discussion.

The question whether tastes are disputable is one to be approached with wariness. The first thing is to be clear about what it really means. There are two key words in it that we should pay particular attention to.

The first is the word "taste." The maxim is perhaps most readily and least doubtfully applied to taste in its primary sensory meaning: some people like ripe olives, some green; some people like turnips, others cannot abide them; some people will go long distances for pizza pies, others can hardly choke them down. And there are no disputes about olives: we don't find two schools of thought, the Ripe Olive School and the Green Olive School, publishing quarterly journals or demanding equal time on television—probably because there simply isn't much you can say about the relative merits of these comestibles.

But we apply the word "taste," of course, more broadly. We speak of a person's taste in hats and neckties; we speak of his taste in poetry and painting and music. And it is here that the *non disputandum* maxim is most significantly applied. Some people like Auden and others Swinburne, some enjoy the paintings of Jackson Pollock and others avoid them when they can, some people are panting to hear Shostakovitch's latest symphony and others find no music since Haydn really satisfying. In these cases, unlike the olive case, people are generally not at a loss for words: there is plenty you can say about Shostakovitch, pro or con. They talk, all right; they may praise, deplore, threaten, cajole, wheedle, and scream—but, according to the maxim, they do not really dispute.

This brings us, then, to the second key word. What does it mean to say that we cannot *dispute* about tastes in literature, fine arts, and music, even though we can clearly make known our tastes? It certainly doesn't mean that we cannot disagree, or differ in taste: for obviously we do, and not only we but also the acknowledged or supposed experts in these fields. Consider James Gould Cozzens' novel, *By Love Possessed,* which appeared in August, 1957; consult the critics and reviewers to discover whether it is a good novel. Being a serious and ambitious work by a writer of standing, and also a best seller, it provoked unusually forthright judgments from a number of reviewers and critics—as may be seen in the accompanying quotations. "Masterpiece . . . brilliant . . . distinguished . . . high order . . . mediocre . . . bad"; that just about covers the spectrum of evaluation.

The International Council of the Museum of Modern Art recently took a large collection of American abstract expressionist paintings on tour in Europe. Its reception was reported in *Time.* In Spain some said, "If this is art, what was it that Goya painted?" and others cheered its "furious vitality" and "renovating spirit." In Italy one newspaper remarked, "It is not painting," but "droppings of paint, sprayings, burstings, lumps, squirts, whirls, rubs and marks, erasures, scrawls, doodles and kaleidoscope backgrounds." In Switzerland it was an "artistic event" that spoke for the genius of American art. And of course all these judgments could be found in this country too.

Not a dispute? Well, what is a dispute? Let us take first the plainest case of a disagreement (no matter what it is about): two people who say, "'Tis so!" and "'Tain't so!" Let them repeat these words as often as they like, and shout them from the housetops; they still haven't got a dispute going, but merely a contradiction, or perhaps an altercation. But let one person say, "'Tis so!" and give a *reason* why 'tis so—let him say, "Jones is the best candidate for Senator because he is tactful, honest, and has had much experience in government." And let the other person say, "'Tain't so!" and give a reason why 'tain't so—"Jones is not the best candidate, because he is too subservient to certain interests, indecisive and wishy-washy in his own views, and has no conception of the United States' international responsibilities." *Then* we have a dispute—that is, a disagreement in which the parties give reasons for their contentions. Of course this is not all there is to it; the dispute has just begun. But we see how it might continue, each side giving further reasons for its own view, and questioning whether the reasons given by the other are true, relevant, and compelling.

It is this kind of thing that counts as a dispute about the possibility of getting to the moon, about American intervention in the Middle East, about a Supreme Court decision, or anything else. And if we can dispute about these things, why not about art?

But here is where the *non disputandum* maxim would draw the line. We do not speak (or not without irony) about people's tastes in Senatorial candidates or missile policies (if the President replied to critics by saying, "Well, your taste is for speeding up the missile program and spending money, but that's not to my taste," we would feel he ought to back up his opinion more than that). Nor do we speak of tastes in international affairs, or laws, or constitutions. And that seems to be because we believe that judgments on these matters can be, and ought to be, based on good reasons—not that they always are, of course. To prefer a democratic to a totalitarian form of government is *not* just a matter of taste, though to like green olives better than ripe olives is a matter of taste, and we don't require the green olive man to rise and give his reasons, or even to *have* reasons. What kind of reasons could he have? "Green olives are better because they are green" would not look like much of a reason to the ripe olive devotee.

The question, then, is whether a preference for Picasso or Monteverdi is more like a preference for green olives or like a preference for a Senatorial candidate: is it *arguable?* can it be *reasoned?*

When we read what critics and reviewers have to say about the things they talk about, we cannot doubt that they do not merely praise or blame, but defend their judgments by giving reasons, or what they claim to be reasons. The judgments of *By Love Possessed,* here quoted out of context, are supplied with arguments, some of them with long arguments dealing in detail with the plot, style, characterization, structure, underlying philosophy, attitudes towards Catholics, Jews, and Negroes, and other aspects of the novel. Collect a number of these reviews together and it certainly *reads* like a dispute. Or here is one person who says, "Mozart's Quintet in E Flat Major for Piano and Winds (K. 452) is a greater piece of music than Beethoven's Quintet in E Flat Major for Piano and Winds (Op. 16) because it has greater melodic invention, subtlety of texture, a more characteristic scoring for the wind instruments, and a more expressive slow movement." And here is his friend, who replies, "The Beethoven quintet is greater because it has richer sonority, greater vigor and vitality, and a more powerful dynamic spirit." There's a dispute, or something that looks very much like one.

But according to the Aesthetic Skeptic—if I may choose this convenient name for the upholder of the "no disputing" doctrine—this is an illusion. The apparent reasons are not genuine reasons, or cannot be compelling reasons, like the ones we find in other fields. For in the last analysis they rest upon sheer liking or disliking, which is not susceptible of rational discussion. The defender of the Mozart Quintet, for example, seems to be trying to prove his point, but what he is actually doing (says the Skeptic) is better put this way: "*If* you like subtle texture and expressiveness in slow movements, *then* you (like me) will prefer the Mozart quintet." But what if his friend cares more for vigor and vitality? Then the so-called "argument" is bound to leave him cold. He can only reply, "*If* you like vigor and vitality, as I do, *then* you would prefer the Beethoven quintet." But this is no longer a dispute; they are talking completely at cross purposes, not even contradicting each other.

The Aesthetic Skeptic would analyze all apparent disputes among critics in these terms: the critic can point out features of the novel, the abstract expressionist painting, the quintet for winds, but when he does this he is taking for granted, what may not be true, that you happen to like these features. You can't, says the Skeptic, argue anybody into liking something he doesn't like, and that's why there's no disputing about tastes; all disputes are in the end useless.

Now this view, which I have here stated in a fairly rough way, can be worked out into a sophisticated and impressive position, and if it is mistaken, as I believe it is, its mistakes are not childish or simple-minded. Consequently, I cannot pretend to give here an adequate treatment of it. But I should like to consider briefly some of the difficulties in Aesthetic Skepticism, as I see it, and point out the possibility of an alternative theory.

The Skeptical theory takes people's likes and dislikes as ultimate and unappealable facts about them; when two people finally get down to saying "I like X" and "I don't like X" (be it the flavor of turnip or subtlety of texture in music), there the discussion has to end, there the dispute vanishes. But though it is true that you can't change a disliking into a liking by arguments, that doesn't imply that you can't change it at all, or that we cannot argue whether or not it *ought* to be changed. . . . But the fact remains that one person can give reasons to another why he would be better off if he *could* enjoy music or painting that he now abhors, and sometimes the other person can set about indirectly, by study and enlarged experience, to change his own tastes, or, as we say, to improve them. There is not just your taste and mine, but better and worse taste; and this doesn't mean just that I have a taste for my taste, but not yours—I might in fact have a distaste for the limitations of my own taste (though that is a queer way to put it). It is something like a person with deep-rooted prejudices, to which he has been conditioned from an early age; perhaps he cannot quite get rid of them, no matter how he tries, and yet he may acknowledge in them a weakness, a crippling feature of his personality, and he may resolve that he will help his children grow up free from them.

The Skeptic does not allow for the possibility that we might give reasons why a person would be better off if he liked or disliked *By Love Possessed* in the way, and to the degree, that it deserves to be liked or disliked. Sometimes, I think, he really holds that it would not be worth the trouble. After all, what does it matter whether people like green olives or ripe olives? We can obtain both in sufficient supply, and nothing much depends upon it as far as the fate of the world is concerned. That's another reason why we ordinarily don't speak of Senatorial candidates as a matter of taste—unless we want to be disparaging, as when people speak of the President's choice in Secretaries of State, to imply that he has no good reason for his choice. It does matter who is Senator, or Secretary of State—it matters a great deal. . . .

Now of course, if we are thinking of our two musical disputants about the relative merits of the two quintets, this is a dispute we may safely leave alone. Both quintets are of such a high order that it perhaps doesn't matter enormously which we decide to rank higher than the other, though there's no harm in trying to do this, if we wish. But the question about *By Love Possessed* is whether it is a "masterpiece" or "bad"; and the question about the paintings is whether they ought to be shown abroad at all. It may not matter so very much whether a person on the whole admires Mozart or Beethoven more, but what if he cannot make up his mind between Mozart and Strauss, or between Beethoven and Shostakovitch?

The fact is that the prevailing level of taste in the general public matters a great deal to me, for it has a great deal to do with determining what I shall have the chance to read, what movies will be filmed, shown, or censored, what music will be played most availably on the radio, what plays will be performed on television. And it has a great deal to do with what composers and painters and poets will do, or whether some of them will do anything at all. But more than that, even: if I am convinced that the kind of experiences that can only be obtained by access to the greatest works is an important ingredient of the richest and most fully developed human life, then do I not owe it to others to try to put that experience within their reach, or them within its reach? It might be as important to them as good housing, good medical and dental care, or good government.

But here is another point at which the Skeptic feels uneasy. Isn't it undemocratic to go around telling other people that they have crude tastes—wouldn't it be more in keeping with our laissez-faire spirit of tolerance, and less reminiscent of totalitarian absolutism and compulsion, to let others like and enjoy what they like and enjoy? Isn't this their natural right?

There are too many confusions in this point of view to clear them all up briefly. But some of them are worth sorting out. Of course it is a person's right to hear the music he enjoys, provided it doesn't bother other people too much. But it is no invasion of his right, if he is willing to consider the problem, to try to convince him that he should try to like other things that appear to deserve it. . . .

The distinction that many Skeptics find it hard to keep in mind is this: I may hold that there *is* a better and a worse in music and novels without at all claiming that *I know for certain* which are which. Those critics and reviewers who pronounced their judgments on *By Love Possessed* are not necessarily dogmatic because they deny that it's all a matter of taste (even though some of them were more positive than they had a right to be). They believe that some true and reasonable judgment of the novel is in principle possible, and that objective critics, given time and discussion, could in principle agree, or come close to agreeing, on it. But they do not have to claim infallibility—people can be mistaken about novels, as they can about anything else. Works of art are complicated. There need be nothing totalitarian about literary criticism, and there is nothing especially democratic in the view that nobody is wrong because there is no good or bad to be wrong about.

It would help us all, I think, to look at the problem of judging works of art in a more direct way. These judgments, as can easily be seen in any random collection of reviews, go off in so many directions that it sometimes seems that the reviewers are talking about different things. We must keep our eye on the object—the painting, the novel, the quintet. Because the composer's love affairs were in a sorry state at the time he was composing, people think that the value of the music must somehow be connected with this circumstance. Because the painter was regarding his model while he painted, people think that the value of the painting must depend on some relation to the way she really looked, or felt. Because the novelist is known to be an anarchist or a conservative, people think that the value of the novel must consist partly in its fidelity to these attitudes. Now, of course, when we approach a work of art, there are many kinds of interest that we can take in it, as well as in its creator. But when we are trying to judge it *as* a work of art, rather than as biography or social criticism or something else, there is a central interest that ought to be kept in view.

A work of art, whatever its species, is an object of some kind—something somebody made. And the question is whether it was worth making, what it is good for, what can be done with it. In this respect it is like a tool. Tools of course are production goods, instrumental to other instruments, whereas paintings and musical compositions and novels are consumption goods, directly instrumental to some sort of experience. And their own peculiar excellence consists, I believe, in their capacity to afford certain valuable kinds and degrees of aesthetic experience. Of course they do not yield this experience to those who cannot understand them, just as a tool is of no use to one who has not the skill to wield it. But we do not talk in the Skeptical way about tools: we do not say that the value of a hammer is all a matter of taste, some people having a taste for hammering nails, some not. No, the value resides in its capability to drive the nail, given a hand and arm with the right skill, and if the need should arise. And this value it would have, though unrealized, even if the skill were temporarily lost.

So with works of art, it seems to me. Their value is what they can do to and for us, if we are capable of having it done. And for those who do not, or not yet, have this capacity, it is not a simple fact that they do not, but a misfortune, and the only question is whether, or to what extent, it can be remedied. It is because this question sometimes has a hopeful answer that we dispute, and must dispute, about tastes. When the political disputant gives his reasons for supporting one Senatorial candidate over another, he cites facts about that candidate that he knows, from past experience, justify the hope of a good performance—the hope that the candidate, once elected, will do what a Senator is supposed to do, well. When the critic gives his reasons for saying that a work of art is good or bad, he is not, as the Skeptic claims, trying to guess whom it will please or displease; he is pointing out those features of the work—its qualities, structure, style, and so on—that are evidence of the work's ability or inability to provide qualified readers, listeners, or viewers, with a deep aesthetic experience.

To Think About

1. Plato, Tolstoy, and others have raised the question of the relation of art to morals. Is the production and enjoyment of art subject to the principles of ethics, or are art and morality two separate and autonomous fields? In your discussion, comment on the following: (a) "Art for art's sake"; (b) "Art, like other interests, can flourish only in a sound and whole society, and the law of soundness and wholeness in life is morality."   ***Ralph Barton Perry***

2. Should there be any censorship of art? Some groups vigorously oppose any type of censorship; others favor some censorship. Is censorship desirable? Give your reaction to the view that if censorship is ever tolerated, it should be limited to cases of obscenity not necessary to artistic effect and the depicting of crime and vice in such a way as to stimulate brutality.

3. ***Pablo Picasso,*** when asked to explain modern art, is said to have replied: "Do you require an explanation for the song of a bird?" Discuss this reply.

4. "This sense of art as process is crucial to the revitalization of it. As politics must teach people the ways and give them the means to take control over their own lives, art must teach people, in the most vivid and imaginative ways possible, how to take control over their own experience and observations, how to link these things with theory, and how to connect both with the experience of others."   ***Meredith Tax***

5. ". . . of rock stars becoming short-term divinities. A Boy George or Kiss or your Prince is celebrated, worshiped, listened to as if it were the ultimate creation of musical esthetics. Then all the sudden, they're gone. And all these kids with their Kiss masks, Prince posters and crap are left with the debris of a cult, and the music slips back to Sunday radio retrospectives.

    "That's not music, not art, and these poor youngsters have lost something they admired, possibly the only thing they cared about for a certain period of their life. And it gets replaced by something just as ephemeral and tawdry.

    "Instead of teaching them the beauty and wealth of nature and traditions, we watch them spend their youth and money and time on shallow little symbols of the marketplace. I grow so sad when I walk into a café or record store and see Prince or Boy George in duplicate, triplicate. They think that to be different they dress up *like* somebody else. Aping someone else is a badge of independence."   ***Unknown***

Readings

BEARDSLEY, MONROE. *Aesthetics: Problems in the Philosophy of Criticism.* New York: Harcourt Brace, 1958.

———. *Aesthetics, From Classical Greece to the Present.* New York: Macmillan, 1966.

HOFSTADTER, ALBERT. *Truth and Art.* New York: Columbia University Press, 1965. An evaluation of a number of recent philosophies of art.

JARRETT, JAMES L. *The Quest for Beauty.* Upper Saddle River, NJ: Prentice Hall, 1957. A general book dealing with aesthetics and art that brings in a considerable amount of illustrative material.

OSBORNE, HAROLD. *Aesthetics and Criticism.* London: Macmillan, 1956.

SIBLEY, FRANK. "Aesthetics and Nonaesthetics." *Philosophical Review* 74 (April 1965): 135–59.

STOLNITZ, JEROME. *Aesthetics.* Boston: Houghton Mifflin, 1958.

59

Art Purges the Emotions

Aristotle (384–322 B.C.), son of a physician, studied in Plato's Academy for twenty years before founding his own more empirical school, the Lyceum. He tutored Alexander the Great. He wrote on logic, ethics, aesthetics, metaphysics, biology, physics, psychology, and politics; further, he had an enormous influence on medieval Hebrew, Arabic, and Christian philosophers, especially on St. Thomas Aquinas and his later Scholastic followers.

The world's great tragedies, notably those of the Greeks, Sophocles and Euripides, and of Shakespeare, are considered by many people to be among the supreme works of art. *Oedipus Rex, Hamlet, Macbeth*—these creations are hardly surpassed by anything else in literature or indeed in any other work of art. The surprising fact is that we enjoy these tragedies, yet each is full of misery and suffering. This gives rise to the "paradox" of tragedy. Why is it that we enjoy these spectacles, which are so full of misery? Consider *Hamlet,* for example. In this play Ophelia dies, Polonius dies, and even Hamlet himself is killed, yet many people consider this to be the supreme work of art. In modern times, such a play as Miller's *Death of a Salesman* is considered to be among the greatest of twentieth-century works, and yet this too is filled with suffering. There have been many attempts to answer this paradox. One of the best-known answers has been given by Aristotle.

In Aristotle's *Poetics,* from which the following essay is taken, he analyzes the structure of tragedy, the nature of the tragic hero, and finally the paradox of tragedy itself. Aristotle explains the paradox with his doctrine of *catharsis,* which states that tragedy provokes emotions of pity and fear to the extent that they are purged from the individual, who takes pleasure in that purgation. His answer to the paradox of tragedy, then, is that there is a kind of pleasure that results from the purging of the emotions. Hence we enjoy these depictions of suffering.

From *The Poetics of Aristotle,* trans. by S.H. Butcher (London: Macmillan, 1895).

~~~~~~ To Study ~~~~~~

1. What is Aristotle's definition of *tragedy?* What are the six elements of tragedy?
    Which of them is most important?
2. What is the proper structure of the plot?
3. Why is poetry "a higher thing than history"? Give an example.
4. What are some elements of a perfect tragedy?
5. Discuss the role of pity and fear and their relation to pleasure in tragedies.

THE CATHARSIS THEORY

VI [Definition of tragedy. Six elements in tragedy. Plot, or the representation of the action, is of primary importance; character and thought come next in order.]

Tragedy, then, is an imitation of an action that is serious, complete, and of a certain magnitude; in language embellished with each kind of artistic ornament, the several kinds being found in separate parts of the play; in the form of action, not of narrative; through pity and fear effecting the proper purgation of these emotions. By "language embellished," I mean language into which rhythm, "harmony," and song enter. By "the several kinds in separate parts," I mean, that some parts are rendered through the medium of verse alone, others again with the aid of song.

Now as tragic imitation implies persons acting, it necessarily follows, in the first place, that Spectacular equipment will be a part of Tragedy. Next, Song and Diction, for these are the medium of imitation. By "Diction" I mean the mere metrical arrangement of the words: as for "Song," it is a term whose sense everyone understands.

Again, Tragedy is the imitation of an action; and an action implies personal agents, who necessarily possess certain distinctive qualities both of character and thought; for it is by these that we qualify actions themselves, and these—thought and character—are the two natural causes from which actions spring, and on actions again all success or failure depends. Hence, the Plot is the imitation of the action:—for by plot I here mean the arrangement of the incidents. By character I mean that in virtue of which we ascribe certain qualities to the agents. Thought is required wherever a statement is proved, or, it may be, a general truth enunciated. Every Tragedy, therefore, must have six parts, which parts determine its quality—namely, Plot, Character, Diction, Thought, Spectacle, Song. Two of the parts constitute the medium of imitation, one the manner, and three the objects of imitation, and these complete the list. These elements have been employed, we may say, by the poets to a man; in fact, every play contains Spectacular elements as well as Character, Plot, Diction, Song, and Thought.

But most important of all is the structure of the incidents. For Tragedy is an imitation, not of men, but of an action and of life, and life consists in action, and its end is a mode of action, not a quality. Now character determines men's qualities, but it is by their actions that they are happy or the reverse. Dramatic action, therefore, is not with a view to the representation of character: character comes in as subsidiary to the actions. Hence the incidents and the plot are the end of a tragedy; and the end is the chief thing of all. Again, without action there cannot be a tragedy; there may be without character. The tragedies of most of our modern poets fail in the rendering of character; and of poets in general this is often true. It is the same in painting; and here lies the difference between Zeuxis and Polygnotus. Polygnotus delineates character well: the style of Zeuxis is devoid of ethical quality. Again, if you string together a set of speeches expressive of character, and well finished in point of diction and thought, you will not produce the essential tragic effect nearly so well as with a play which, however deficient in these respects, yet has a plot and artistically constructed incidents. Besides which, the most powerful elements of emotional interest in Tragedy—Peripeteia or Reversal of the Situation, and Recognition scenes—are parts of the plot. A further proof is, that novices in the art attain to finish of diction and precision of portraiture before they can construct the plot. It is the same with almost all the early poets.

The Plot, then, is the first principle, and, as it were, the soul of a tragedy: Character holds the second place. A similar fact is seen in painting. The most beautiful colors, laid on confusedly, will not give as much pleasure as the chalk outline of a portrait. Thus Tragedy is the imitation of an action, and of the agents mainly with a view to the action.

Third in order is Thought,—that is, the faculty of saying what is possible and pertinent in given circumstances. In the case of oratory, this is the function of the political art and of the art of rhetoric: and so indeed the older poets make their characters speak the language of civic life; the poets of our time, the language of the rhetoricians. Character is that which reveals moral purpose, showing what kind of things a man chooses or avoids. Speeches, therefore, which do not make this manifest, or in which the speaker does not choose or avoid anything whatever, are not expressive of character. Thought, on the other hand, is found where something is proved to be or not to be, or a general maxim is enunciated.

Fourth among the elements enumerated comes Diction; by which I mean, as has been already said, the expression of the meaning in words; and its essence is the same both in verse and prose.

Of the remaining elements Song holds the chief place among the embellishments.

The Spectacle has, indeed, an emotional attraction of its own, but, of all the parts, it is the least artistic, and connected least with the art of poetry. For the power of Tragedy, we may be sure, is felt even apart from representation and actors. Besides, the production of spectacular effects depends more on the art of the stage machinist than on that of the poet.

VII [The plot must be a whole, complete in itself, and of adequate magnitude.]

These principles being established, let us now discuss the proper structure of the Plot, since this is the first and most important thing in Tragedy.

Now, according to our definition, Tragedy is an imitation of an action that is complete, and whole, and of a certain magnitude; for there may be a whole that is wanting in magnitude. A whole is that which has a beginning, a middle, and an end. A beginning is that which does not itself follow anything by causal necessity, but after which something naturally is or comes to be. An end, on the contrary, is that which itself naturally follows some other thing, either by necessity, or as a rule, but has nothing following it. A middle is that which follows something as some other thing follows it. A well-constructed plot, therefore, must neither begin nor end at haphazard, but conform to these principles.

Again, a beautiful object, whether it be a living organism or any whole composed of parts, must not only have an orderly arrangement of parts, but must also be of a certain magnitude; for beauty depends on magnitude and order. Hence a very small animal organism cannot be beautiful; for the view of it is confused, the object being seen in an almost imperceptible moment of time. Nor, again, can one of vast size be beautiful; for as the eye cannot take it all in at once, the unity and sense of the whole is lost for the spectator; as for instance if there were one a thousand miles long. As, therefore, in the case of animate bodies and organisms a certain magnitude is necessary, and a magnitude which may be easily embraced in one view; so in the plot, a certain length is necessary, and a length which can be easily embraced by the memory. The limit of length in relation to dramatic competition and sensuous presentment, is no part of artistic theory. For had it been the rule for a hundred tragedies to compete together, the performance would have been regulated by the water-clock,—as indeed we are told was formerly done. But the limit as fixed by the nature of the drama itself is this:—the greater the length, the more beautiful will the piece be by reason of its size, provided that the whole be perspicuous. And to define the matter roughly, we may say that the proper magnitude is comprised within such limits, that the sequence of events, according to the law of probability or necessity, will admit of a change from bad fortune to good, or from good fortune to bad.

VIII [The plot must be a unity. Unity of plot consists not in unity of hero, but in unity of action. The parts must be organically connected.]

Unity of plot does not, as some persons think, consist in the unity of the hero. For infinitely various are the incidents in one man's life which cannot be reduced to unity; and so, too, there are many actions of one man out of which we cannot make one action. Hence the error, as it appears, of all poets who have composed a Heracleid, a Theseid, or other poems of the kind. They imagine that as Heracles was one man, the story of Heracles must also be a unity. But Homer, as in all else he is of surpassing merit, here too—whether from art or natural genius—seems to have happily discerned the truth. In composing the Odyssey he did not include all the adventures of Odysseus—such as his wound on Parnassus, or his feigned madness at the mustering of the host—incidents between which there was no necessary or probable connection: but he made the Odyssey, and likewise the Iliad, to center round an action that in our sense of the word is one. As therefore, in the other imitative arts, the imitation is one when the object imitated is one, so the plot, being an imitation of an action, must imitate one action and that a whole, the structural union of the parts being such that, if any one of them is displaced or removed, the whole will be disjointed and disturbed. For a thing whose presence or absence makes no visible difference, is not an organic part of the whole.

IX [(Plot continued.) Dramatic unity can be attained only by the observance of poetic as distinct from historic truth: for poetry is an expression of the universal; history of the particular. The rule of probable or necessary sequence as applied to the incidents. The best tragic effect depends on the combination of the inevitable and the unexpected.]

It is, moreover, evident from what has been said, that it is not the function of the poet to relate what has happened, but what may happen—what is possible according to the law of probability or necessity. The poet and the historian differ not by writing in verse or in prose. The work of Herodotus might be put into verse, and it would still be a species of history, with meter no less than without it. The true difference is that one relates what has happened, the other what may happen. Poetry, therefore, is a more philosophical and a higher thing than history for poetry tends to express the universal, history the particular. By the universal I mean how a person of a certain type will on occasion speak or act, according to the law of probability or necessity; and it is this universality at which poetry aims in the names she attaches to the personages. The particular is—for example—what Alcibiades did or suffered. In Comedy this is already apparent: for here the poet first constructs the plot on the lines of probability, and then inserts characteristic names—unlike the lampooners who write about particular individuals. But tragedians still keep to real names, the reason being that what is possible is credible: what has not happened is manifestly possible: otherwise it would not have happened. Still there are even some tragedies in which there are only one or two well-known names, the rest being fictitious. In others, none are well known—as in Agathon's Antheus, where incidents and names alike are fictitious, and yet they give none the less pleasure. We must not, therefore, at all costs keep to the received legends, which are the usual subjects of Tragedy. Indeed, it would be absurd to attempt it; for even subjects that are known are known only to a few, and yet give pleasure to all. It clearly follows that the poet or "maker" should be the maker of plots rather than of verses; since he is a poet because he imitates, and what he imitates are actions. And even if he chances to take an historical subject, he is none the less a poet; for there is no reason why some events that have actually happened should not conform to the law of the probable and possible, and in virtue of that quality in them he is their poet or maker.

Of all plots and actions the episodic are the worst. I call a plot "episodic" in which the episodes or acts succeed one another without probable or necessary sequence. Bad poets compose such pieces by their own fault, good poets, to please the players; for, as they write show pieces for competition, they stretch the plot beyond its capacity, and are often forced to break the natural continuity.

But again, Tragedy is an imitation not only of a complete action, but of events inspiring fear or pity. Such an effect is best produced when the events come on us by surprise; and the effect is heightened when, at the same time, they follow as cause and effect. The tragic wonder will then be greater than if they happened of themselves or by accident; for even coincidences are most striking when they have an air of design. We may instance the statue of Mitys at Argos, which fell upon his murderer while he was a spectator at a festival, and killed him. Such events seem not to be due to mere chance. Plots, therefore, constructed on these principles are necessarily the best. . . .

XIII [(Plot continued.) What constitutes tragic action. The change of fortune and the character of the hero as requisite to an ideal tragedy. The unhappy ending more truly tragic than the "poetic justice" which is in favor with a popular audience, and belongs rather to comedy.]

A perfect tragedy should, as we have seen, be arranged not on the simple but on the complex plan. It should, moreover, imitate actions which excite pity and fear, this being the distinctive mark of tragic imitation. It follows plainly, in the first place, that the change of fortune presented must not be the spectacle of a virtuous man brought from prosperity to adversity: for this moves neither pity nor fear; it merely shocks us. Nor, again, that of a bad man passing from adversity to prosperity: for nothing can be more alien to the spirit of Tragedy; it possesses no single tragic quality; it neither satisfies the moral sense nor calls forth pity or fear. Nor, again, should the downfall of the utter villain be exhibited. A plot of this kind would, doubtless, satisfy the moral sense, but it would inspire neither pity nor fear; for pity is aroused by unmerited misfortune, fear by the misfortune of a man like ourselves. Such an event, therefore, will be neither pitiful nor terrible. There remains, then, the character between these two extremes—that of a man who is not eminently good and just, yet whose misfortune is brought about not by vice or depravity, but by some error or frailty. He must be one who is highly renowned and prosperous—a personage like Oedipus, Thyestes, or other illustrious men of such families.

A well-constructed plot should, therefore, be single in its issue, rather than double as some maintain. The change of fortune should be not from bad to good, but, reversely, from good to bad. It should come about as the result not of vice, but of some great error or frailty, in a character either such as we have described, or better rather than worse. . . .

In the second rank comes the kind of tragedy which some place first. Like the Odyssey, it has a double thread of plot, and also an opposite catastrophe for the good and for the bad. It is accounted the best because of the weakness of the spectators; for the poet is guided in what he writes by the wishes of his audience. The pleasure, however, thence derived is not the true tragic pleasure. It is proper rather to Comedy, where those who, in the piece, are the deadliest enemies—like Orestes and Aegisthus—quit the stage as friends at the close, and no one slays or is slain.

XIV [(Plot continued.) The tragic emotions of pity and fear should spring out of the plot itself. To produce them by scenery or spectacular effect is entirely against the spirit of tragedy.]

Fear and pity may be aroused by spectacular means; but they may also result from the inner structure of the piece, which is the better way, and indicates a superior poet. For the plot ought to be so constructed that, even without the aid of the eye, he who hears the tale told will thrill with horror and melt to pity at what takes place. This is the impression we should receive from hearing the story of the Oedipus. But to produce this effect by the mere spectacle is a less artistic method, and dependent on extraneous aids. Those who employ spectacular means to create a sense not of the terrible but only of the monstrous, are strangers to the purpose of Tragedy; for we must not demand of Tragedy any and every kind of pleasure, but only that which is proper to it. And since the pleasure which the poet should afford is that which comes from pity and fear through imitation, it is evident that this quality must be impressed upon the incidents. . . .

XV [The element of character in tragedy. The rule of necessity or probability applicable to character as to plot. The "deus ex machina." How character is idealized.]

In respect of Character there are four things to be aimed at. First, and most important, it must be good. Now any speech or action that manifests moral purpose of any kind will be expressive of character: the character will be good if the purpose is good. This rule is relative to each class. Even a woman may be good, and also a slave; though the woman may be said to be an inferior being, and the slave quite worthless. The second thing to aim at is propriety. There is a type of manly valor; but valor in a woman, or unscrupulous cleverness, is inappropriate. Thirdly, character must be true to life: for this is a distinct thing from goodness and propriety, as here described. The fourth point is consistency: for though the subject of the imitation, who suggested the type, be inconsistent, still he must be consistently inconsistent. As an example of motiveless degradation of character, we have Menelaus in the Orestes: of character indecorous and inappropriate, the lament of Odysseus in the Scylla, and the speech of Melanippe: of inconsistency, the Iphigenia at Aulis—for Iphigenia the suppliant in no way resembles her later self.

   As in the structure of the plot, so too in the portraiture of character, the poet should always aim either at the necessary or the probable. Thus a person of a given character should speak or act in a given way, by the rule either of necessity or of probability; just as this event should follow that by necessary or probable sequence. It is therefore evident that the unravelling of the plot, no less than the complication, must arise out of the plot itself, it must not be brought about by the *Deus ex Machina*—as in the Medea, or in the Return of the Greeks in the Iliad. The *Deus ex Machina* should be employed only for events external to the drama—for antecedent or subsequent events, which lie beyond the range of human knowledge, and which require to be reported or foretold; for to the gods we ascribe the power of seeing all things. Within the action there must be nothing irrational. If the irrational cannot be excluded, it should be outside the scope of the tragedy. Such is the irrational element in the Oedipus of Sophocles.

Again, since Tragedy is an imitation of persons who are above the common level, the example of good portrait-painters should be followed. They, while reproducing the distinctive form of the original, make a likeness which is true to life and yet more beautiful. So too the poet, in representing men who are irascible or indolent, or have other defects of character, should preserve the type and yet ennoble it. In this way Achilles is portrayed by Agathon and Homer.

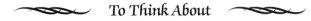

To Think About

1. "The tragic is an essential element of the universe itself."

2. Tragedy has always appeared at the mature period of a culture, not at its beginning.

3. "Tragedy must make life seem worth while."

4. "Miller's *Death of a Salesman* consists in the hero's glad acceptance of the conditions of life that will lead to his own annihilation."

5. "Americans have a kind of armor against tragic experience. It is due to our optimistic attitude and our lack of heroes."

6. "Everything in nature is lyrical in its ideal essence, comic in its existence and tragic in its fate."
   George Santayana

7. "Affirmation of life even in its strangest and sternest problems, the will to life rejoicing in its own inexhaustibility through the *sacrifice* of its highest types—*that* is what I called Dionysian, *that* is what I recognized as the bridge to the psychology of the *tragic* poet. *Not* so as to get rid of pity and terror, not so as to purify oneself of a dangerous emotion through its vehement discharge—it was thus Aristotle understood it—but, beyond pity and terror, to *realize in oneself* the eternal joy of becoming—that joy which also encompasses *joy in destruction*. . . . And with that I again return to the place from which I set out. *Birth of Tragedy* was my first revaluation of all values."
   Friedrich Nietzsche

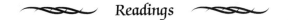

Readings

ELSE, GERALD F. *Aristotle's Poetics: The Argument.* Cambridge, MA: Harvard University Press, 1957.

HALLIWELL, STEPHEN. *The Aesthetics of Mimesis: Ancient Texts and Modern Problems.* Princeton, NJ: Princeton University Press, 2002.

HENN, T. R. *The Harvest of Tragedy.* 2nd ed. London: Methuen, 1966.

60
Magic or Amusement?

R. G. Collingwood (1889–1943), philosopher and historian, was Waynflete Professor of Metaphysical Philosophy, Oxford University. One of the most learned men of his generation, he had a remarkable breadth of interest and knowledge and originality of mind. He is the author of many notable books, including The Idea of History *(1946)*, An Autobiography *(1959)*, Essay on Metaphysics *(1940)*, Essay on Philosophical Method *(1933)*, The Idea of Nature *(1945)*, The New Leviathan *(1942)*, and, with J. N. L. Myres,* Roman Britain and the English Settlements *(1937).*

R. G. Collingwood contends that too much of what is claimed to be decent art is nothing but simple *amusement art:* such art has no value in itself, but is simply a way to discharge emotions. Some examples are pornography, detective stories, television, and football. In contrast, *art proper,* or what is called *magical art,* enlightens us about existence and makes us better civilized beings.

    Most so-called art is really amusement art. It performs the ideological function now that *panem et circenses* (bread and circuses) did in Roman times—it relieves our boredom. "The kinds of work on which the existence of a civilization like ours most obviously depends [are] an intolerable drudgery; . . . amusement art constitutes the feverish attempts to dispel this boredom by more amusement or by dangerous or criminal occupations." Amusement art is able to keep a civilization's discontent in thrall because it evokes emotion in its consumers and, by the device of make-believe, discharges those emotions within the content of the art itself. The emotions excited are not used to accomplish anything useful in society; they do not lead to action. Aestheticians ask us to distinguish between what is art proper and what is amusement art (not art proper) in order to help us escape the manipulation of amusement artists.

    From R. G. Collingwood, *The Principles of Art* (Oxford: Oxford University Press, 1938), 78–94. Reprinted by permission of Oxford University Press.

~~~~ To Study ~~~~

1. What is amusement as contrasted to practical life?
2. Distinguish between amusement art and art proper.
3. Discuss Collingwood's examples of amusement art. How can they be raised to the level of art proper?
4. Why is criticism impossible when art is identified with amusement?

---

1. Amusement Art

If an artifact is designed to stimulate a certain emotion, and if this emotion is intended not for discharge into the occupations of ordinary life, but for enjoyment as something of value in itself, the function of the artifact is to amuse or entertain. Magic is useful, in the sense that the emotions it excites have a practical function in the affairs of every day; amusement is not useful but only enjoyable, because there is a watertight bulkhead between its world and the world of common affairs. The emotions generated by amusement run their course within this watertight compartment.

Every emotion, dynamically considered, has two phases in its existence: charge or excitation, and discharge. The discharge of an emotion is some act done at the prompting of that emotion, by doing which we work the emotion off and relieve ourselves of the tension which, until thus discharged, it imposes upon us. The emotions generated by an amusement must be discharged, like any others; but they are discharged within the amusement itself. This is in fact the peculiarity of amusement. An amusement is a device for the discharge of emotions in such a way that they shall not interfere with the concerns of practical life. But since practical life is only definable as that part of life which is not amusement, this statement, if meant for a definition, would be circular. We must therefore say: to establish a distinction between amusement and practical life[1] is to divide experience into two parts, so related that the emotions generated in the one are not allowed to discharge themselves in the other. In the one, emotions are treated as ends in themselves; in the other, as forces whose operation achieves certain ends beyond them. The first part is now called amusement, the second part practical life.

In order that emotion may be discharged without affecting practical life, a make-believe situation must be created in which to discharge it. This situation will of course be one which "represents" . . . the real situation in which the emotion would discharge itself practically. The difference between the two, which has been indicated by calling them respectively real and make-believe, is simply this: the so-called make-believe situation is one in which it is understood that the emotion discharged shall be "earthed," that is, shall not involve the consequences which it would involve under the conditions of practical life. Thus, if one man expresses hatred for another by shaking his fist at him, threatening him, and so forth, he will ordinarily be regarded

---

[1] Aestheticians who discuss the relation between two mutually exclusive things called "Art" and "Life" are really discussing this distinction.

as a dangerous character, dangerous in particular to the man he has threatened, who will therefore take steps of one kind or another to protect himself: perhaps by appeasing the first, perhaps by attacking him and overpowering him, perhaps by obtaining police protection. If it is understood that nothing of this sort is to be done, that life is to go on exactly as if nothing had happened, then the situation in which the anger was expressed is called a make-believe situation.

Situations of this kind resemble those created by magic in being representative, that is, in evoking emotions like those evoked by the situations they are said to represent. They differ in being "unreal" or "make-believe"; that is, in that the emotions they evoke are intended to be earthed instead of overflowing into the situations represented. This element of make-believe is what is known as (theatrical) "illusion," an element peculiar to amusement art, and never found either in magic or in art proper. If in a magical ritual one says of a painting "this is a bison," or of a wax figure, "this is my enemy," there is no illusion. One knows perfectly well the difference between the two things. The make-believe of amusement art differs radically, again, from the so-called make-believe of childish games, which is not amusement but a very serious kind of work, which we call make-believe by way of assimilating it to something that occurs in our adult experience. Calling it by that misdescriptive name, we patronizingly license the child to go on with it; so that the child can work at the really urgent problems of its own life unhampered by the interference which would certainly be forthcoming if adults knew what it was doing.

Comparisons have often been made, sometimes amounting to identification, between art and play. They have never thrown much light on the nature of art, because those who have made them have not troubled to think what they meant by play. If playing means amusing oneself, as it often does, there is no important resemblance between play and art proper; and none between play and representative art in its magical form; but there is more than a mere resemblance between play and amusement art. The two things are the same. If playing means taking part in ritual games, art proper bears little resemblance to that, and amusement art even less; but such games, as we have already seen, not only resemble magic, they are magic. But there is another thing we call play: that mysterious activity which occupies the waking and working lives of children. It is not amusement, though we adults may amuse ourselves by imitating it, and even on privileged occasions taking part in it. It is not magic, though in some ways rather like it. Perhaps it is a good deal like art proper. Giambattista Vico, who knew a lot both about poetry and about children, said that children were "sublime poets," and he may have been right. But no one knows what children are doing when they play; it is far easier to find out what poets are doing when they write, difficult though that is; and even if art proper and children's play are the same thing, no light is thrown for most of us on art proper by saying so.[2]

---

[2] Dr. Margaret Lowenfeld (*Play in Childhood,* 1935) has devised a method for exploring the unknown world of children's play, and has made strange discoveries about the relation of this play to the child's health. My own interpretation of her discoveries may be expressed by saying that they suggest an identity between "play" in children and art proper.

There is a hedonistic theory of art: open, like all forms of hedonism, to the objection that even if the function of art is to give "delight" (as many good artists have said), still this delight is not pleasure in general but pleasure of a particular kind. When this objection has been met, the theory is a fair enough account of amusement art. The artist as purveyor of amusement makes it his business to please his audience by arousing certain emotions in them and providing them with a make-believe situation in which these emotions can be harmlessly discharged.

The experience of being amused is sought not for the sake of anything to which it stands as means, but for its own sake. Hence, while magic is utilitarian, amusement is not utilitarian but hedonistic. The work of art, so called, which provides the amusement, is, on the contrary, strictly utilitarian. Unlike a work of art proper, it has no value in itself; it is simply means to an end. It is as skillfully constructed as a work of engineering, as skillfully compounded as a bottle of medicine, to produce a determinate and preconceived effect, the evocation of a certain kind of emotion in a certain kind of audience; and to discharge this emotion within the limits of a make-believe situation. When the arts are described in terms implying that they are essentially forms of skill, the reference, as the terms are ordinarily used nowadays, is to this utilitarian character of amusement art. When the spectator's reception of them is described in psychological terms as a reaction to stimulus, the reference is the same. Theoretically, in both cases, the reference might be to the magical type of representation; but in the modern world that is generally ignored. For the student of modern aesthetic, it is a good rule, whenever he hears or reads statements about art which seem odd or perverse or untrue, to ask whether their oddity (or apparent oddity) may not be due to a confusion between art proper and amusement; a confusion either in the mind of their authors, or in his own.

2. PROFIT AND DELIGHT[3]

Magical function and amusement function in a work of art are of course mutually exclusive, so far as a given emotion in a given audience at a given moment is concerned. You cannot arouse in your audience a certain emotion (say, hatred of the Persians) and arrange at one and the same moment for its discharge in an amusement form, by raising a laugh at their expense, and in a practical form, by burning down their houses. But the emotion aroused by any given representation is never simple; it is always a more or less complicated stream or pattern of different emotions; and it is not necessary that all these should be provided with the same kind of discharge. In a general way, some are discharged practically, others earthed; the artist, if he knows his job, arranging which shall be discharged in this way, which in that. . . . "We do not write these novels merely to amuse," says Captain Marryat in *Midshipman Easy;* and goes on to boast that he has used his novels not unsuccessfully in the past to advocate reforms in naval administration. Mr. Bernard Shaw is another devout follower of Horace. There has

[3] The ends of all, who for the *Scene* does write; Are, or should be, to profit, and delight. (B. Jonson, *Epicaene, or The Silent Woman*)

never been any damned nonsense about art with him; he has careered through life most successfully as an entertainer, careful always to keep a few ball cartridges among his blank, and send his audience home indignant about the way people treat their wives, or something like that. But although he follows the same tradition as Marryat, it is doubtful whether he could claim an equal record of success as a pamphleteer. The difference is not so much between one writer and another as between one age and another. In the hundred years that have elapsed since *Midshipman Easy* was published, the ability of both artists and public to mix a dose of magic with their amusement has sensibly declined. Mr. Galsworthy began his career by putting so much *utile* and so little *dulce* into his stage-puddings that only very determined stomachs could digest them at all. So he gave up playing with magic, and specialized in entertaining a rather grim class of readers with the doings of the Forsyte family.

People who are not really competent in magic, as the fairytales wisely tell us, should be careful to leave it alone. One of the typical features of late nineteenth- and early twentieth-century literature is the way in which sound knockabout entertainers like Jerome K. Jerome or successful ginger-beer merchants like Mr. A. A. Milne suddenly come over all solemn, pull themselves together, and decide to become good influences in the lives of their audience. Nothing quite like it had ever happened before. It is a curious and unpleasant instance of the decline in taste which the nineteenth century brought in its train.

In general, the representational artist urgently needs to be a man of taste, in the sense that he must, on pain of professional disaster, know what emotions to excite. Unless he means to act as a magician, like Timotheus in Dryden's ode, and excite passions which those who feel them cannot discharge in anything short of practical acts, he must choose passions which, in the case of this particular audience, will submit to make-believe gratification. There is always a danger that, when once an emotion has been aroused, it may break down the watertight bulkhead and overflow into practical life; but it is the aim of both the amuser and the amused that this disaster shall not happen, and that by a loyal cooperation the bulkhead shall remain intact. The artist must steer a middle course. He must excite emotions which are closely enough connected with his audience's practical life for their excitation to cause lively pleasure; but not so closely connected that a breach of the bulkhead is a serious danger. Thus, a play in which a foreign nation is held up to ridicule will not amuse an audience in whom there is no sense of hostility towards that nation; but neither will it amuse one in whom this hostility has come near to boiling-point. A smoking-room story which amuses middle-aged clubmen would not amuse an old man who had outgrown sexual desire, nor a young man in whom it was agonizingly strong.

3. EXAMPLES OF AMUSEMENT ART

The emotions which admit of being thus played upon for purposes of amusement are infinitely various; we shall take a few examples only. Sexual desire is highly adaptable to these purposes; easily titillated, and easily put off with make-believe objects. Hence the kind of amusement art which at its crudest and most brutal is called pornography is very common and very popular. Not only the representation of nudity which reappeared in European painting and sculpture at the Renaissance, when art as magic was replaced by art as amusement, but the novel or story based on a sexual motive, which dates from the same period, is essentially an appeal to the sexual emotions of the audience, not in order to stimulate these emotions for actual commerce between the sexes, but in order to provide them with make-believe objects and thus divert them from their practical goal in the interests of amusement. The extent to which this make-believe sexuality has affected modern life can hardly be believed until the fact has been tested by appeal to the circulating libraries, with their flood of love-stories; the cinema, where it is said to be a principle accepted by almost every manager that no film can succeed without a love-interest; and above all the magazine and newspaper, where cover-designs, news-items, fiction, and advertisement are steeped in materials of the same kind: erotic stories, pictures of pretty girls variously dressed and undressed, or (for the female reader) of attractive young men: pornography homoeopathically administered in doses too small to shock the desire for respectability, but quite large enough to produce the intended effect. Small wonder that Monsieur Bergson has called ours an "aphrodisiac civilization." But the epithet is not quite just. It is not that we worship Aphrodite. If we did, we should fear these make-believe as a too probable cause of her wrath. An aphrodisiac is taken with a view to action: photographs of bathing girls are taken as a substitute for it. The truth may rather be that these things reveal a society in which sexual passion has so far decayed as to have become no longer a god, as for the Greeks, or a devil, as for the early Christians, but a toy: a society where the instinctive desire to propagate has been weakened by a sense that life, as we have made it, is not worth living, and where our deepest wish is to have no posterity.

The case of sexual fantasy is peculiar, because it seems in this way to have got out of hand, and thus to betray something amiss with our civilization as a whole. There are plenty of other cases where this complication is absent. For example, much pleasure may be derived from the emotion of fear; and today this is provided by a galaxy of talent devoted to writing stories of terrible adventure. The "thriller," to give the thing its current name, is not new. We find it on the Elizabethan stage, in the charnel-house sculpture of seventeenth-century tombs (the Last Judgements of medieval art were aimed not at making flesh creep but at reforming sinful lives), in the novels of Mrs. Radcliffe and "Monk" Lewis, in the engravings of Doré, and, raised to the level of art proper, in the first movement of Beethoven's Fifth Symphony and the Finale of Mozart's *Don Giovanni*. Among ourselves, the spread of literacy has begotten upon the old penny dreadful a monstrous progeny of hair-raising fiction concerned with arch-criminals, gunmen, and sinister foreigners. Why the ghost story, once so valuable for this purpose, has lost its efficacy, although heathenish rites, with much explicit bloodshed and even more hinted obscenity, are still in lively demand, is a curious problem for the historian of ideas.

The detective story, the most popular form of amusement offered by the profession of letters to the modern public, is based partly on appeal to the reader's fear, but partly on a rich medley of other emotions. In Poe the element of fear was exceedingly strong, and either because of his influence, or because of something ingrained in the civilization of the United States, the present-day American detective story shows a stronger inclination towards that type than those of any other nation. American corpses are the bloodiest and most horribly mangled; American police the most savage in their treatment of suspects.[4] Another emotion of great importance in such stories is the delight in power. In what may be called the Raffles period, this was gratified by inviting the reader to identify himself with a gallant and successful criminal; nowadays the identification is with the detective. A third is the intellectual excitement of solving a puzzle; a fourth, the desire for adventure, that is to say, the desire to take part in events as unlike as possible to the dreary business of actual everyday life. Members of the scholastic and clerical professions from time to time express a belief that young people who read these stories, and see films resembling them, are thereby incited to a career of crime. This is bad psychology. There is no evidence that stories of crime are the favourite reading of habitual criminals. In point of fact, those who constantly read them are on the whole thoroughly law-abiding folk; and this is only natural, for the constant earthing of certain emotions, by arousing and discharging them in make-believe situations, makes it less likely that they will discharge themselves in practical life.

No one has yet taken up the detective story and raised it to the level of genuine art. Miss Sayers, indeed, has given reasons why this cannot be done. Perhaps one reason is the mixture of motives which this *genre* has traditionally accepted as inevitable. A mixture of motives is, on the whole, favourable to good amusement, but it can never produce art proper.

Malice, the desire that others, especially those better than ourselves, should suffer, is a perpetual source of pleasure to man; but it takes different shapes. In Shakespeare and his contemporaries, bullying in its most violent form is so common that we can only suppose the average playgoer to have conceived it as the salt of life. There are extreme cases like *Titus Andronicus* and *The Duchess of Malfi*, where torture and insult form the chief subject-matter; cases like *Volpone* or *The Merchant of Venice*, where the same motive is veiled by a decent pretence that the suffering is deserved; and cases like *The Taming of the Shrew*, where it is rationalized as a necessary step to domestic happiness. The same motive crops out so repeatedly in passages like the baiting of Malvolio or the beating of Pistol, passages wholly unconnected with the plot of the play, so far as these plays have a plot, that it has obviously been dragged in to meet a constant popular demand. The theme is raised to the level of art proper here and there in Webster, in a few of Shakespeare's tragedies, and above all in Cervantes.

In a society which has lost the habit of overt bullying, the literature of violence is replaced by the literature of cattishness. Our own circulating libraries are full of what is grandiloquently called satire on the social life of our time; books whose popularity rests on the fact that they give the reader an excuse for ridiculing the folly of youth and the futility of age, despising the frivolity of the educated and the grossness of the uneducated, gloating over the unhappiness of an ill-assorted couple, or triumphing over the feebleness of a henpecked merchant prince. To the same class of

---

[4] Cf. Superintendent Kirk: ". . . I couldn't rightly call them a mellering influence to a man in my line. I read an American story once, and the way the police carried on—well . . . it didn't seem right to me." Dorothy L. Sayers, *Busman's Honeymoon*, p. 161.

pseudo-art (they are certainly not history) belong the biographies of cattishness, whose aim is to release the reader from the irksome reverence he has been brought up to feel for persons who were important in their day.

If the Elizabethan was by temperament a bully, the Victorian was by temperament a snob. Literature dealing with high life at once excites and in fancy gratifies the social ambition of readers who feel themselves excluded from it; and a great part of the Victorian novelist's work was devoted to making the middle classes feel as if they were sharing in the life of the upper. Nowadays, when "society" has lost its glamour, a similar place is taken by novels and films dealing with millionaires, criminals, film-stars, and other envied persons. There is even a literature catering for the snobbery of culture: books and films about Beethoven, Shelley, or, combining two forms of snobbery in one, a lady in high station who wins fame as a painter.

There are cases in which we find, not a mixture of amusement and magic, but a wavering between the two. A considerable literature exists devoted to sentimental topography: books about the charm of Sussex, the magic of Oxford, picturesque Tyrol, or the glamour of old Spain. Are these intended merely to recall the emotions of returned travellers and to make others feel as if they had travelled, or are they meant as an invocation—I had almost said, to call fools into a circle? Partly the one and partly the other; if the choice had been decisively made, literature of this kind would be better than it is. Similar cases are the sentimental literature of the sea, addressed to landsmen, and of the country, addressed to town-dwellers; folk-songs as sung not in pubs and cottages but in drawing-rooms; pictures of horses and dogs, deer and pheasants, hung in billiard-rooms partly as charms to excite the sportsman, partly as substitutes for sport. There is no reason why works of this kind should not be raised to the level of art, though cases in which that has happened are exceedingly rare. If it is to happen, there is one indispensable condition: the ambiguity of motive must first be cleared up.

4. REPRESENTATION AND THE CRITIC

The question may here be raised, how the practice of art-criticism is affected by identifying art with representation in either of its two forms. The critic's business, as we have already seen, is to establish a consistent usage of terms: to settle the nomenclature of the various things which come before him competing for a given name, saying, "this is art, that is not art," and, being an expert in this business, performing it with authority. A person qualified so to perform it is called a judge; and judgement means verdict, the authoritative announcement that, for example, a man is innocent or guilty. Now, the business of art-criticism has been going on ever since at least the seventeenth century; but it has always been beset with difficulties. The critic knows, and always has known, that in theory he is concerned with something objective. In principle, the question whether this piece of verse is a poem or a sham poem is a question of fact, on which every one who is properly qualified to judge ought to agree. But what he finds, and always has found, is that in the first place the critics as a rule do not agree; in the second place, their verdict is as a rule reversed by posterity; and in the third place it is hardly ever welcomed and accepted as useful either by the artists or by the general public.

When the disagreements of critics are closely studied, it becomes evident that there is much more behind them than mere human liability to form different opinions about the same thing. The verdict of a jury in court, as judges are never tired of telling them, is a matter of opinion; and hence they sometimes disagree. But if they disagreed in the kind of way in which art critics disagree, trial by jury would have been experimented with only once, if that, before being abolished for ever. The two kinds of disagreement differ in that the juror, if the case is being handled by a competent judge, has only one point at which he can go wrong. He has to give a verdict, and the judge tells him what the principles are upon which he must give it. The art critic also has to give a verdict; but there is no agreement between him and his colleagues as to the principles on which it must be given.

This divergence of principle is not due to unsolved philosophical problems. It does not arise from divergences between rival theories of art. It arises at a point in thought which is prior to the formation of any anesthetic theory whatever. The critic is working in a world where most people, when they speak of a good painting or a good piece of writing, mean simply that it pleases them, and pleases specifically in the way of amusement. The simpler and more vulgar make no bones about this; I don't know what's good, they say, but I know what I like. The more refined and artistic reject this idea with horror. It makes no difference whether you like it or not, they retort; the question is whether it is good. The protest is in principle perfectly right: but in practice it is humbug. It implies that whereas the so-called art of the vulgar is not art but only amusement, about which there is of course no objective goodness or badness but only the fact that a given thing amuses or does not amuse a given audience, the art of more refined persons is not amusement but art proper. This is simple snobbery. There is no difference in attitude between the people who go to see Gracie Fields and the people who go to see Ruth Draper except that, having been differently brought up, they are amused by different things. The cliques of artists and writers consist for the most part of a racket selling amusement to people who at all costs must be prevented from thinking themselves vulgar, and a conspiracy to call it not amusement but art.

The people who fancy themselves altogether above the vulgar level of amusement art, but are actually disporting themselves in that level and nowhere else, call their own amusements good art in so far as they find them amusing. The critic is therefore in a false position. He is committed, in so far as he himself belongs to these people and shares their shibboleths, to treating what is in fact a question of their likes and dislikes, their taste in amusements, as if it were that totally different thing, a question of merits and demerits in a given artist's work. And even that way of putting it makes his task seem easier than it really is. If these refined persons formed a perfectly compact psychological mob, what amused one would amuse all, as the same joke may please all members of a mess or a common-room. But in so far as their only bond is the negative one of refinement, which only means being unlike the people they regard as vulgar they cannot as a whole exhibit a compact mob-psychology, and different factions will be amused by different things. The critic's task is now hopeless, because the reasons why some people belonging to these circles call a book or a picture good will be the very same reasons why others, equally entitled to life, liberty, and the pursuit of amusement, will call it bad. And even if a certain kind of taste may for a time dominate the whole, or a large part of it, this is sure to be succeeded by another, from whose point of view the things that amused the earlier will be said to "date." . . .

The critic is generally despised, but he ought rather to be pitied. The villains of the piece are the self-styled artists. They have assured him that they are doing something which it will be worth his while to study, and have then done something else, on which no critic would waste an hour's thought. If the gigantic ramp by which the trade in genteel amusements passes itself off as art were once for all exposed, the critics could either come out frankly as the advertisement writers which many of them are, or stop bothering about sham art and concentrate, as some of them already do, on the real thing.

So long as art is identified with amusement, criticism is impossible; and the fact of its having been so long and so valiantly attempted is a remarkable proof of the tenacity with which the modern European consciousness sticks to its point that there is such a thing as art, and that some day we shall learn how to distinguish it from the amusement trade.[5] If art is identified with magic, the same conclusion follows; but this conclusion, in a society where magic is at all vigorous, may easily be masked by the substitution of a false objectivity for a true objectivity, an empirical generality for a strict universality. A matter of fact, as that this person did this act, or that this thing is a poem, is valid for everybody at every time and place. The "goodness" or "beauty" of a "work of art," if goodness or beauty means power of exciting certain emotions in the person using the word, has no such validity; it exists only in relation to the person in whom these emotions are aroused. It may happen that the same work will arouse the same emotions in others; but this will happen on a considerable scale only when the society in which it occurs thinks it necessary to its welfare.

That phrase is susceptible, we may note in passing, of two interpretations. (1) On a biological view of society, a society will consist of animals of a certain kind which through the action of such cases as heredity all possess a certain type of psychological organization. Owing to the uniformity of this organization, a stimulus of a specific kind will produce in all members of the society a specific type of emotion. The emotion will be necessary to the welfare of the society, because it is part and parcel of the psychological organization whose identity in all members of the society constitutes its principle of unity; and in so far as its members are conscious of this principle they will see that this emotional unanimity is necessary to their corporate existence, as a biological fact on which that existence depends. (2) On an historical view of society, a society will consist of persons who through communication by language have worked out a certain way of living together. So far as each one of them feels his own interests as bound up with those of the society, everything which forms

---

[5] It is hardly necessary to remark that the amusement racket has succeeded in corrupting quite a number of academic and other theoretical writers who base their aesthetic, or rather anti-aesthetic, on the identification of art with that which evokes a certain kind of emotion; with the consequence that "beauty" is "subjective," Man (and what a man!) is the measure of all things, and the critics, not (presumably) being Men but only heroes who have held a key-position of the civilized world for two centuries and a half against overwhelming odds, find that the pass has been sold behind their backs.

part of this common way of living will have to him an emotional value, the strength of this emotion being the force that binds the society together. In that case, anything intimately connected with their common way of living will arouse in all members of the society the same type of emotional response.

On either view, therefore, wherever there is a society of any kind, there will be certain established forms of corporate magic, whereby certain standard stimuli evoke certain standard emotional responses from all its members. If these stimuli are called "works of art," they are conceived as possessing a "goodness" or "beauty" which in fact is merely their power to evoke these responses. In so far as the society is really a society, the appropriate response is really evoked in all its members, and if they mis-use words in this way, they will all agree that the "work of art" is "good" or "beauti-ful." But this agreement is only an empirical generality, holding good within the society because the society just consists of those persons who share it. Enemies with-out, or even more foreigners, and traitors within, will just as necessarily disagree. So long as magic is taken for art, these agreements and disagreements will be taken for criticism; and in any given society it will be thought the mark of a good critic to in-sist that the common magic of the society is good art. . . .

To Think About

1. "Because art's role is now that of adapting the multitude to the dead mechani-cal existence of capitalist production, in which work sucks them of their vital energies without awakening their instincts, where leisure becomes a time to deaden the mind with the easy fantasy of films, simple wish-fulfilment writing, or music that is mere emotional massage—because of this the paid craft of writ-ing becomes as tedious and wearisome as that of machine-minder . . . (this art) is at once an expression of real misery and a protest against the real misery. This art, universal, constant, fabulous, full of the easy gratifications of instincts starved by modern capitalism, peopled by passionate lovers and heroic cow-boys and amazing detectives, is the religion of today, as characteristic an ex-pression of proletarian exploitation as Catholicism is of feudal exploitation. It is the opium of the people; it pictures an inverted world because the world of society *is* inverted."   ***Christopher Caudwell***

2. "Nobody seriously questions the principle that it is the function of mass culture to maintain public morale, and certainly nobody in the mass audience objects to having his morale maintained."   ***John Worsham***

3. "Poetry is a more philosophical and a more serious thing than history; for poetry is chiefly conversant about universal truth, history about particular." ***Aristotle***

4. "Once again I want to emphasize that literature does not present us with propo-sitions which are empirically verifiable like those of science and history; few if any statements in novels, that is, depicting the action or thought of a fictional character, can be verified in the way that informative propositions can. And yet they are true-*to*-human-nature as we know it. Thus in a way we *can* verify what

the artist has presented; we can verify his insights in our own further observations of people and actions." ***John Hospers***

5. "The artist picks out of reality something which we, owing to a certain hardening of our perceptions, have been unable to see ourselves." ***John Dewey***

6. "An artist is a disturber of the peace." ***James Baldwin***

7. "[C]apitalism and culture are almost doomed to lock horns. Capitalism requires a rational political order and a certain amount of discipline and restraint to plan for the future and ply its current wares. But a capitalist culture like the one that has developed in recent decades doesn't value the kind of patience and asceticism that sociologists like Max Weber associated with the origins of capitalism. Instead, capitalist culture values self-gratification and novelty. The result, Mr. Bell suggests, is a nihilistic culture commonly known as post-modern." ***E. Rothstein***

8. "I decline to accept the end of man. I believe that man will not only endure: He will prevail. He is immortal, not because he alone among creatures has an inexhaustible voice, but because he has a soul, a spirit capable of compassion and sacrifice and endurance. The poet's and writer's duty is to write about these things. It is his privilege to help man endure by lifting his heart, by reminding him of the courage and honor and hope and pride and compassion and pity and sacrifice which have been the glory of his past. The poet's voice need not merely be the record of man. It can be one of the props, the pillars to help him endure and prevail." ***William Faulkner***

PART 10

THE MEANING OF LIFE

What Gives Life Meaning?

61
Faith Provides Life's Meaning

Leo Tolstoy (1828–1910) was a Russian novelist and reformer. His great novels, including War and Peace *(1863–69) and* Anna Karenina *(1873–77), were written in the earlier period of his creative life. During the later period, he was principally concerned with religious, ethical, and aesthetic subjects.*

The question of the meaning and value of life has been debated by philosophers for centuries. Freud said that the moment a person questions the meaning of life, he or she is sick. In contrast, Karl Jaspers wrote that a person does not become really serious until he or she faces the question.

Perplexity about the meaning of life appears throughout the novels of Leo Tolstoy. He looks to science for answers to the meaning of suffering and death but finds no satisfactory solutions. He finds philosophy to be just as unsatisfactory in explaining the value of life. Unable to find answers through scientific and philosophical inquiry, Tolstoy turns to biblical Christianity. He thus accepts the Christian account of creation, purpose, and destiny of the world. Death is not a basis for despair or absurdity; it is the beginning of our best experience—communion with God. Christian doctrines give not only purpose and value to life, but also the promise of harmony of perspective for all existence.

To Study

1. Explain "an arrest of life." What happened to Tolstoy?
2. What is "the truth"?

From Leo Tolstoy, *My Confession,* trans. Leo Wiener (London: J. M. Dent & Sons, 1905).

3. What does Tolstoy say about art?
4. Does science give meaning to life? Do the working people? Rational people? Philosophers?
5. In what can one find the meaning of life?

Although I regarded authorship as a waste of time, I continued to write during those fifteen years. I had tasted of the seduction of authorship, of the seduction of enormous monetary remunerations and applauses for my insignificant labour, and so I submitted to it as being a means for improving my material condition and for stifling in my soul all questions about the meaning of my life and life in general.

In my writings I advocated, what to me was the only truth, that it was necessary to live in such a way as to derive the greatest comfort for oneself and one's family.

Thus I proceeded to live, but five years ago something very strange began to happen to me: I was overcome by minutes at first of perplexity and then of an arrest of life, as though I did not know how to live or what to do, and I lost myself and was dejected. But that passed and I continued to live as before. Then those minutes of perplexity were repeated oftener and oftener, and always in one and the same form. These arrests of life found their expression in ever the same questions: "Why? Well, and then?"

At first I thought that those were simply aimless, inappropriate questions. It seemed to me that that was all well known and that if I ever wanted to busy myself with their solution, it would not cost me much labour, that now I had no time to attend to them, but that if I wanted to I should find the proper answers. But the questions began to repeat themselves oftener and oftener, answers were demanded more and more persistently, and, like dots that fall on the same spot, these questions, without any answers, thickened into one black blotch.

There happened what happens with any person who falls ill with a mortal internal disease. At first there appear insignificant symptoms of indisposition, to which the patient pays no attention; then these symptoms are repeated more and more frequently and blend into one temporally indivisible suffering. The suffering keeps growing, and before the patient has had time to look around, he becomes conscious that what he took for an indisposition is the most significant thing in the world to him—his death.

The same happened with me. I understood that it was not a passing indisposition, but something very important, and that, if the questions were going to repeat themselves, it would be necessary to find an answer for them. And I tried to answer them. The questions seemed to be so foolish, simple, and childish. But the moment I touched them and tried to solve them, I became convinced, in the first place, that they were not childish and foolish, but very important and profound questions in life, and, in the second, that, no matter how much I might try, I should not be able to answer them. Before attending to my Samára estate, to my son's education, or to the writing of a book, I ought to know why I should do that. So long as I did not know why, I could not do anything. I could not live. Amidst my thoughts of farming, which interested me very much during that time, there would suddenly pass through my head a question like this: "All right, you are going to have six thousand desyatínas of land in the Government of Samára and three hundred horses—and then?" And I completely lost my senses and did not know what to think farther. Or, when I thought of the education of my children, I said to myself: "Why?" Or, reflecting on the manner in which the masses might obtain their welfare, I suddenly said to myself: "What is that to me?" Or, thinking of the fame which my works would get me, I said to myself: "All right, you will be more famous than Gógol, Púshkin, Shakespeare, Molière, and all the writers in the world—what of it?" And I was absolutely unable to make any reply. The questions were not waiting, and I had to answer them at once; if I did not answer them, I could not live.

I felt that what I was standing on had given way, that I had no foundation to stand on, that that which I lived by no longer existed, and that I had nothing to live by. . . .

All that happened to me when I was on every side surrounded by what is considered to be complete happiness. I had a good, loving, and beloved wife, good children, and a large estate, which grew and increased without any labour on my part. I was respected by my neighbours and friends, more than ever before, was praised by strangers, and, without any self-deception, could consider my name famous. With all that, I was not deranged or mentally unsound; on the contrary, I was in full command of my mental and physical powers, such as I had rarely met with in people of my age: physically I could work in a field, mowing, without falling behind a peasant; mentally I could work from eight to ten hours in succession, without experiencing any consequences from the strain. And while in such condition I arrived at the conclusion that I could not live, and, fearing death, I had to use cunning against myself, in order that I might not take my life.

This mental condition expressed itself to me in this form: my life is a stupid, mean trick played on me by somebody. Although I did not recognize that "somebody" as having created me, the form of the conception that some one had played a mean, stupid trick on me by bringing me into the world was the most natural one that presented itself to me.

Involuntarily I imagined that there, somewhere, there was somebody who was now having fun as he looked down upon me and saw me, who had lived for thirty or forty years, learning, developing, growing in body and mind, now that I had become strengthened in mind and had reached that summit of life from which it lay all before me, standing as a complete fool on that summit and seeing clearly that there was nothing in life and never would be: And that was fun to him—

But whether there was or was not that somebody who made fun of me did not make it easier for me. I could not ascribe any sensible meaning to a single act, or to my whole life. I was only surprised that I had not understood that from the start. All that had long ago been known to everybody. Sooner or later there would come diseases and death (they had come already) to my dear ones and to me, and there would be nothing left but stench and worms. All my affairs, no matter what they might be, would sooner or later be forgotten, and I myself should not exist. So why should I worry about all these things? How could a man fail to see that and live—that was surprising! A person could live only so long as he was drunk; but the moment he sobered up, he could not help seeing that all that was only a deception, and a stupid deception at that! Really, there was nothing funny and ingenious about it, but only something cruel and stupid.

Long ago has been told the Eastern story about the traveller who in the steppe is overtaken by an infuriated beast. Trying to save himself from the animal, the traveller jumps into a waterless well, but at its bottom he sees a dragon who opens his jaws in order to swallow him. And the unfortunate man does not dare climb out, lest he perish from the infuriated beast, and does not dare jump down to the bottom of the well, lest he be devoured by the dragon, and so clutches the twig of a wild bush growing in a cleft of the well and holds on to it. His hands grow weak and he feels that soon he shall have to surrender to the peril which awaits him at either side; but he still holds on and sees two mice, one white, the other black, in even measure making a circle around the main trunk of the bush to which he is clinging, and nibbling at it on all sides. Now, at any moment, the bush will break and tear off, and he will fall into the dragon's jaws. The traveller sees that and knows that he will inevitably perish; but while he is still clinging, he sees some drops of honey hanging on the leaves of the bush, and so reaches out for them with his tongue and licks the leaves. Just so I hold on to the branch of life, knowing that the dragon of death is waiting inevitably for me, ready to tear me to pieces, and I cannot understand why I have fallen on such suffering. And I try to lick that honey which used to give me pleasure; but now it no longer gives me joy, and the white and the black mouse day and night nibble at the branch to which I am holding on. I clearly see the dragon, and the honey is no longer sweet to me. I see only the inevitable dragon and the mice, and am unable to turn my glance away from them. That is not a fable, but a veritable, indisputable, comprehensible truth.

The former deception of the pleasures of life, which stifled the terror of the dragon, no longer deceive me. No matter how much one should say to me, "You cannot understand the meaning of life, do not think, live!" I am unable to do so, because I have been doing it too long before. Now I cannot help seeing day and night, which run and lead me up to death. I see that alone, because that alone is the truth. Everything else is a lie.

The two drops of honey that have longest turned my eyes away from the cruel truth, the love of family and of authorship, which I have called an art, are no longer sweet to me.

"My family—" I said to myself, "but my family, my wife and children, they are also human beings. They are in precisely the same condition that I am in; they must either live in the lie or see the terrible truth. Why should they live? Why should I love them, why guard, raise, and watch them? Is it for the same despair which is in me, or for dullness of perception? Since I love them, I cannot conceal the truth from them— every step in cognition leads them up to this truth. And the truth is death.

"Art, poetry?" For a long time, under the influence of the success of human praise, I tried to persuade myself that that was a thing which could be done, even though death should come and destroy everything, my deeds, as well as my memory of them; but soon I came to see that that, too, was a deception. It was clear to me that art was an adornment of life, a decoy of life. But life lost all its attractiveness for me. How, then, could I entrap others? So long as I did not live my own life, and a strange life bore me on its waves, so long as I believed that life had some sense, although I was not able to express it, the reflections of life in every description in poetry and in the arts afforded me pleasure, and I was delighted to look at life through this little mirror of art; but when I began to look for the meaning of life, when I experienced the necessity of living myself, that little mirror became either useless, superfluous, and ridiculous, or painful to me. I could no longer console myself with what I saw in the mirror, namely, that my situation was stupid and desperate. It was all right for me to rejoice so long as I believed in the depth of my soul that life had some sense. At that time the play of lights—of the comical, the tragical, the touching, the beautiful, the terrible in life—afforded me amusement. But when I knew that life was meaningless and terrible, the play in the little mirror could no longer amuse me. No sweetness of honey could be sweet to me when I saw the dragon and the mice that were nibbling down my support. . . .

In my search after the question of life I experienced the same feeling which a man who has lost his way in the forest may experience.

He comes to a clearing, climbs a tree, and clearly sees an unlimited space before him; at the same time he sees that there are no houses there, and that there can be none; he goes back to the forest, into the darkness, and he sees darkness, and again there are no houses.

Thus I blundered in this forest of human knowledge, between the clearings of the mathematical and experimental sciences, which disclosed to me clear horizons, but such in the direction of which there could be no house, and between the darkness of the speculative sciences, where I sunk into a deeper darkness, the farther I proceeded, and I convinced myself at last that there was no way out and could not be.

By abandoning myself to the bright side of knowledge I saw that I only turned my eyes away from the question. No matter how enticing and clear the horizons were that were disclosed to me, no matter how enticing it was to bury myself in the infinitude of this knowledge, I comprehended that these sciences were the more clear, the less I needed them, the less they answered my question.

"Well, I know," I said to myself, "all which science wants so persistently to know, but there is no answer to the question about the meaning of my life." But in the speculative sphere I saw that, in spite of the fact that the aim of the knowledge was directed straight to the answer of my question, or because of that fact, there could be no other answer than that I was giving to myself: "What is the meaning of my life?"—"None." Or, "What will come of my life?"—"Nothing." Or, "Why does everything which exists exist, and why do I exist?"—"Because it exists."

Putting the question to the one side of human knowledge, I received an endless quantity of exact answers about what I did not ask: about the chemical composition of the stars, about the movement of the sun toward the constellation of Hercules, about the origin of species and of man, about the forms of infinitely small, imponderable particles of ether; but the answer in this sphere of knowledge to my question what the meaning of my life was, was always: "You are what you call your life; you are a temporal, accidental conglomeration of particles. The interrelation, the change of these particles, produces in you that which you call life. This congeries will last for some time; then the interaction of these particles will cease, and that which you call life and all your questions will come to an end. You are an accidentally cohering globule of something. The globule is fermenting. This fermentation the globule calls its *life*. The globule falls to pieces, and all fermentation and all questions come to an end." Thus the clear side of knowledge answers, and it cannot say anything else, if only it strictly follows its principles.

With such an answer it appears that the answer is not a reply to the question. I want to know the meaning of my life, but the fact that it is a particle of the infinite not only gives it no meaning, but even destroys every possible meaning.

Those obscure transactions, which this side of the experimental, exact science has with speculation, when it says that the meaning of life consists in evolution and the cooperation with this evolution, because of their obscurity and inexactness cannot be regarded as answers.

The other side of knowledge, the speculative, so long as it sticks strictly to its fundamental principles in giving a direct answer to the question, everywhere and at all times has answered one and the same: "The world is something infinite and incomprehensible. Human life is an incomprehensible part of this incomprehensible *all*. . . . "

I lived for a long time in this madness, which, not in words, but in deeds, is particularly characteristic of us, the most liberal and learned of men. But, thanks either to my strange, physical love for the real working class, which made me understand it and see that it is not so stupid as we suppose, or to the sincerity of my conviction, which was that I could know nothing and that the best that I could do was to hang myself, I felt that if I wanted to live and understand the meaning of life, I ought naturally to look for it, not among those who had lost the meaning of life and wanted to kill themselves, but among those billions departed and living men who had been carrying their own lives and ours upon their shoulders. And I looked around at the enormous masses of deceased and living men—not learned and wealthy, but simple men—and I saw something quite different. I saw that all these billions of men that lived or had lived, all, with rare exceptions, did not fit into my subdivisions,[1] and that I could not recognize them as not understanding the question, because they themselves put it and answered it with surprising clearness. Nor could I recognize them as Epicureans, because their lives were composed rather of privations and suffering than of enjoyment. Still less could I recognize them as senselessly living out their meaningless lives, because every act of theirs and death itself was explained by them. They regarded it as the greatest evil to kill themselves. It appeared, then, that all humanity was in possession of a knowledge of the meaning of life, which I did not recognize and which I condemned. It turned out that rational knowledge did not give any meaning to life, excluded life, while the meaning which by billions of people, by all humanity, was ascribed to life was based on some despised, false knowledge.

The rational knowledge in the person of the learned and the wise denied the meaning of life, but the enormous masses of men, all humanity, recognized this meaning in

---

[1] Tolstoy previously observed that each of his peers assumed one of four attitudes toward life: They lived in ignorance of the problem of life's meaning; ignored the problem and pursued whatever pleasures possible; acknowledged the meaninglessness of life and committed suicide; or acknowledged the meaninglessness but lived on aimlessly, usually lacking the fortitude to take their own lives. See ch. 7 of *My Confession*. [ED.]

an irrational knowledge. This irrational knowledge was faith, the same that I could not help but reject. That was God as one and three, the creation in six days, devils and angels, and all that which I could not accept so long as I had not lost my senses.

My situation was a terrible one. I knew that I should not find anything on the path of rational knowledge but the negation of life, and there, in faith, nothing but the negation of reason, which was still more impossible than the negation of life. From the rational knowledge it followed that life was an evil and men knew it; it depended on men whether they should cease living, and yet they lived and continued to live, and I myself lived, though I had known long ago that life was meaningless and an evil. From faith it followed that, in order to understand life, I must renounce reason, for which alone a meaning was needed.

There resulted a contradiction, from which there were two ways out: either what I called rational was not so rational as I had thought; or that which to me appeared irrational was not so irrational as I had thought. And I began to verify the train of thoughts of my rational knowledge.

In verifying the train of thoughts of my rational knowledge, I found that it was quite correct. The deduction that life was nothing was inevitable; but I saw a mistake. The mistake was that I had not reasoned in conformity with the question put by me. The question was, "Why should I live?" that is, "What real, indestructible essence will come from my phantasmal, destructible life? What meaning has my finite existence in this infinite world?" And in order to answer this question, I studied life.

The solutions of all possible questions of life apparently could not satisfy me, because my question, no matter how simple it appeared in the beginning, included the necessity of explaining the finite through the infinite, and vice versa.

I asked, "What is the extra-temporal, extra-causal, extra-spatial meaning of life?" But I gave an answer to the question, "What is the temporal, causal, spatial meaning of my life?" The result was that after a long labour of mind I answered, "None."

In my reflections I constantly equated, nor could I do otherwise, the finite with finite, the infinite with the infinite, and so from that resulted precisely what had to result: force was force, matter was matter, will was will, infinity was infinity, nothing was nothing—and nothing else could come from it.

There happened something like what at times takes place in mathematics: you think you are solving an equation, when you have only an identity. The reasoning is correct, but you receive as a result the answer: $a = a$, or $x = x$, or $0 = 0$. The same happened with my reflection in respect to the question about the meaning of my life. The answers given by all science to that question are only identities.

Indeed, the strictly scientific knowledge, that knowledge which, as Descartes did, begins with a full doubt in everything, rejects all knowledge which has been taken on trust, and builds everything anew on the laws of reason and experience, cannot give any other answer to the question of life than what I received—an indefinite answer. It only seemed to me at first that science gave me a positive answer—Schopenhauer's answer: "Life has no meaning, it is an evil." But when I analyzed the matter, I saw that the answer was not a positive one, but that it was only my feeling which expressed it as such. The answer, strictly expressed, as it is expressed by the Brahmins, by Solomon, and by Schopenhauer, is only an indefinite answer, or an identity, $0 = 0$, life is nothing. Thus the philosophical knowledge does not negate anything, but only answers that the question cannot be solved by it, that for philosophy, the solution remains insoluble.

When I saw that, I understood that it was not right for me to look for an answer to my question in rational knowledge, and that the answer given by rational knowledge was only an indication that the answer might be got if the question were differently put, but only when into the discussion of the question should be introduced the question of the relation of the finite to the infinite. I also understood that, no matter how irrational and monstrous the answers might be that faith gave, they had this advantage that they introduced into each answer the relation of the finite to the infinite, without which there could be no answer.

No matter how I may put the question, "How must I live?" the answer is, "According to God's law." "What real result will there be from my life?"—"Eternal torment or eternal bliss." "What is the meaning which is not destroyed by death?"—"The union with infinite God, paradise."

Thus, outside the rational knowledge, which had to me appeared as the only one, I was inevitably led to recognize that all living humanity had a certain other irrational knowledge, faith, which made it possible to live.

All the irrationality of faith remained the same for me, but I could not help recognizing that it alone gave to humanity answers to the questions of life, and, in consequence of them, the possibility of living.

The rational knowledge brought me to the recognition that life was meaningless, my life stopped, and I wanted to destroy myself. When I looked around at people, at all humanity, I saw that people lived and asserted that they knew the meaning of life. I looked back at myself: I lived so long as I knew the meaning of life. As to other people, so even to me, did faith give the meaning of life and the possibility of living.

Looking again at the people of other countries, contemporaries of mine and those passed away, I saw again the same. Where life had been, there faith, ever since humanity, had existed, had given the possibility of living, and the chief features of faith were everywhere one and the same.

No matter what answers faith may give, its every answer gives to the finite existence of man the sense of the infinite—a sense which is not destroyed by suffering, privation, and death. Consequently in faith alone could we find the meaning and possibility of life. What, then, was faith? I understood that faith was not merely an evidence of things not seen, and so forth, not revelation (that is only the description of one of the symptoms of faith), not the relation of man to man (faith has to be defined, and then God, and not first God, and faith through him), not merely an agreement with what a man was told, as faith was generally understood—that faith was the knowledge of the meaning of human life, in consequence of which man did not destroy himself, but lived. Faith is the power of life. If a man lives he believes in something. If he did not believe that he ought to live for some purpose, he would not live. If he does not see and understand the phantasm of the finite, he believes in that finite; if he understands the phantasm of the finite, he must believe in the infinite. Without faith one cannot live. . . .

In order that all humanity may be able to live, in order that they may continue living, giving a meaning to life, they, those billions, must have another, a real knowledge of faith, for not the fact that I, with Solomon and Schopenhauer, did not kill myself convinced me of the existence of faith, but that these billions had lived and had borne us, me and Solomon, on the waves of life.

Then I began to cultivate the acquaintance of the believers from among the poor, the simple and unlettered folk, of pilgrims, monks, dissenters, peasants. The doctrine of these people from among the masses was also the Christian doctrine that the quasi-believers of our circle professed. With the Christian truths were also mixed in very many superstitions, but there was this difference: the superstitions of our circle were quite unnecessary to them, had no connections with their lives, were only a kind of an Epicurean amusement, while the superstitions of the believers from among the labouring classes were to such an extent blended with their life that it would have been impossible to imagine it without these superstitions—it was a necessary condition of that life. I began to examine closely the lives and beliefs of these people, and the more I examined them, the more did I become convinced that they had the real faith, that their faith was necessary for them, and that it alone gave them a meaning and possibility of life. In contradistinction to what I saw in our circle, where life without faith was possible, and where hardly one in a thousand professes to be a believer, among them was hardly one in a thousand who was not a believer. In contradistinction to what I saw in our circle, where all life passed in idleness, amusements, and tedium of life, I saw that the whole life of these people was passed in hard work, and that they were satisfied with life. In contradistinction to the people of our circle, who struggled and murmured against fate because of their privations and their suffering, these people accepted diseases and sorrows without any perplexity or opposition, but with the calm and firm conviction that it was all for good. In contradistinction to the fact that the more intelligent we are, the less do we understand the meaning of life and the more do we see a kind of a bad joke in our suffering and death, these people live, suffer, and approach death, and suffer in peace and more often in joy. In contradistinction to the fact that a calm death, a death without terror or despair, is the greatest exception in our circle, a restless, insubmissive, joyless death is one of the greatest exceptions among the masses. And of such people, who are deprived of everything which for Solomon and for me constitutes the only good of life, and who withal experience the greatest happiness, there is an enormous number. I cast a broader glance about me. I examined the life of past and present vast masses of men, and I saw people who in like manner had understood the meaning of life, who had known how to live and die, not two, not three, not ten, but hundreds, thousands, millions. All of them, infinitely diversified as to habits, intellect, culture, situation, all equally and quite contrary to my ignorance knew the meaning of life and of death, worked calmly, bore privations and suffering, lived and died, seeing in that not vanity, but good.

I began to love those people. The more I penetrated into their life, the life of the men now living, and the life of men departed, of whom I had read and heard, the more did I love them, and the easier it became for me to live. Thus I lived for about two years, and within me took place a transformation, which had long been working within me, and the germ of which had always been in me. What happened with me was that the life of our circle—of the rich and the learned—not only disgusted me, but even lost all its meaning. All our acts, reflections, sciences, arts,—all that appeared to me in a new light. I saw that all that was mere pampering of the appetites, and that no meaning could be found in it; but the life of all the working masses, of all humanity, which created life, presented itself to me in its real significance. I saw that that was life itself and that the meaning given to this life was truth, and I accepted it.

To Think About

1. "The idea of life as self-enclosed and purposeless is of course not simply a product of the despair of our own age. It is the natural product of the advance of science and has developed over a long period." ***Iris Murdoch***

2. "That human life has no external point or τέλος [purpose] is a view as difficult to argue as its opposite, and I shall simply assert it. I can see no evidence to suggest that human life is not something self-contained. There are properly many patterns and purposes within life, but there is no general and as it were externally guaranteed pattern or purpose of the kind for which philosophers and theologians used to search. We are what we seem to be, transient mortal creatures subject to necessity and chance. This is to say that there is, in my view, no God in the traditional sense of that term; and the traditional sense is perhaps the only sense. When Bonhoeffer says that God wants us to live as if there were no God I suspect he is misusing words. Equally the various metaphysical substitutes for God—Reason, Science, History—are false deities. Our destiny can be examined but it cannot be justified or totally explained. We are simply here. And if there is any kind of sense or unity in human life, and the dream of this does not cease to haunt us, it is of some other kind and must be sought within a human experience which has nothing outside it." ***Iris Murdoch***

3. "Every man, wherever he goes, is encompassed by a cloud of comforting convictions, which move with him like flies on a summer day." ***Bertrand Russell***

4. "If you look at a mythology of any tribe, you'll see that all mythologies give answers to certain primal and perennial human questions. Where did I come from, and where am I going? Who are my people, and what is my place? What is the meaning of suffering, what is the meaning of death, and what is sex about? How close should I be to people? For what am I guilty, and what should I avoid, what's taboo? In one sense, the modern myth was the myth that we didn't have myth because we had this scientific secular consciousness. I was raised in that, so were you. In seminary we talked about demythologizing, you know, we're going to get rid of all that primitive myth stuff.

   "Well, I began to examine my own experience at a very crucial and disturbed period in my life—when my own tenacious clinging to the Christian worldview and the Christian myth began to crumble, when I couldn't believe it anymore—and I had to ask myself the question, well, what do you believe? How do you find any rock upon which to put your feet? For a long time I was at a loss, and suddenly it occurred to me that instead of looking at the answers that myth gave, I could look at the questions. I began to interrogate my own life using those questions. Who are my heroes? Who are my villains? What is my source? Where did I come from? Who are my people? I discovered that I could find within my own autobiography, as it were, a complete but undeveloped mythology. And as I began to look at those stories and recover those stories for myself, I had a mythology that gave me a story by which I lived."

Sam Keen

5. "To the medieval Christian the meaning of human life was therefore perfectly clear. The stretch on earth is only a short interlude, a temporary incarceration of the soul in the prison of the body, a brief trial and test, fated to end in death, the release from pain and suffering. What really matters, is the life after the death of the body. One's existence acquires meaning not by gaining what this life can offer but by saving one's immortal soul from death and eternal torture, by gaining eternal life and everlasting bliss."   *Kurt Baier*

6. "However, let us be quite clear what is to be explained. There are two facts here, not one. The first is that the universe exists, which is undeniable. The second is that the universe must have originated out of nothing, and that is not undeniable. It is true that, *if it has originated at all,* then it must have originated out of nothing, or else it is not the universe that has originated. But need it have originated? Could it not have existed for ever?"   *Kurt Baier*

7. "What then, does all this amount to? Merely to the claim that scientific explanations are no worse than any other. All that has been shown is that all explanations suffer from the same defect: all involve a vicious infinite regress. In other words, no type of human explanation can help us to unravel the ultimate, unanswerable mystery. Christian ways of looking at things may not be able to render the world any more lucid than science can, but at least they do not pretend that there are no impenetrable mysteries. On the contrary, they point out untiringly that the claims of science to be able to elucidate everything are hollow. They remind us that science is not merely limited to the exploration of a tiny corner of the universe but that, however far our probing instruments may eventually reach, we can never even approach the answers to the last questions: 'Why is there a world at all rather than nothing?' and 'Why is the world such as it is and not different?' Here our finite human intellect bumps against its own boundary walls."   *Kurt Baier*

8. "Philosophers play a strange game. They know very well that one thing alone counts: Why are we born on this earth? And they also know that they will never be able to answer it. Nevertheless, they continue sedately to amuse themselves."   *Jacques Maritain*

9. "Death is the true inspiring genius, or the muse of philosophy. . . . Indeed, without death men could scarcely philosophize."   *Arthur Schopenhauer*

～～ Readings ～～

ALTHAUS, PAUL. "The Meaning and Purpose of History in the Christian View." *Universitas* 7 (1965): 197–204.

BENNETT. JAMES. "The Meaning of Life." *Canadian Journal of Philosophy* 14 (December 1984): 581–92.

BROWN, DELWIN. "God's Reality and Life's Meaning." *Encounter* 28 (Summer 1968): 252–62.

FACKENHEIM, EMIL. "Judaism and the Meaning of Life." *Commentary* 39 (1965): 45–55.

MAY, ROLLO. *Man's Search for Meaning.* New York: Norton, 1953.

SANDERS, E., ed. *The Meaning of Life.* Upper Saddle River, NJ: Prentice Hall, 1980.

62
Each Person Determines
His or Her Life's Meaning

Albert Camus (1913–60) was a French writer whose novels and plays are usually classified as "existentialist" literature. His writings, which earned him The Nobel Prize for literature in 1957, include The Stranger *(1942),* The Plague *(1947),* Man in Revolt *(1951), and* The Fall *(1957).*

"The Myth of Sisyphus" is a short essay in which Camus examines "the absurd hero," the person condemned to endless, meaningless toil. Camus paints a haunting picture, and it becomes even more so when we realize that Sisyphus is a symbol for all humankind: *all* human effort is equally devoid of meaning. Camus represents the agnostic existentialist position on the meaning of life. His agnosticism leads him to say, "I do not know a meaning that transcends life. I do not know that meaning and it is impossible for me to know it." That is why he calls the world absurd.* It is only in "this unintelligible and limited universe" that "man's fate assumes its meaning." Although this absurd world cannot guarantee a future, it *can* free the existential human being to become what he or she wishes. A person's life can have meaning even if the world does not. The meaning of life is cast in terms of two existentialist values: the revolt against conformity and the absurd, and the freedom felt through existentially free choices.

～ To Study ～

1. What is the only truly serious philosophical problem? Why is this so?
2. When does one choose death?
3. What is absurdity? When does the feeling of it arise?

*When Camus writes of "the absurd man," he refers to a person who is aware of and attempts to comprehend absurdity, and such an attempt he calls "absurd reasoning" or "absurd logic." [ED.]

From Albert Camus, *The Myth of Sisyphus and Other Essays,* trans. Justin O'Brien. Copyright © 1955 by Alfred A. Knopf, Inc. Reprinted by permission of the publisher.

4. Explain the statement "The revolt of the flesh is the absurd."
5. When does "man's fate assume its meaning"?
6. What is the connection between comparison and absurdity?
7. Explain the statement "Living is keeping the absurd alive."
8. What restores majesty to life?

ABSURDITY AND SUICIDE

There is but one truly serious philosophical problem, and that is suicide. Judging whether life is or is not worth living amounts to answering the fundamental question of philosophy. All the rest—whether or not the world has three dimensions, whether the mind has nine or twelve categories—comes afterwards. These are games; one must first answer. And if it is true, as Nietzsche claims, that a philosopher, to deserve our respect, must preach by example, you can appreciate the importance of that reply, for it will precede the definitive act. These are facts the heart can feel; yet they call for careful study before they become clear to the intellect.

If I ask myself how to judge that this question is more urgent than that, I reply that one judges by the actions it entails. I have never seen anyone die for the ontological argument. Galileo, who held a scientific truth of great importance, abjured it with the greatest ease as soon as it endangered his life. In a certain sense, he did right.[1] That truth was not worth the stake. Whether the earth or the sun revolves around the other is a matter of profound indifference. To tell the truth, it is a futile question. On the other hand, I see many people die because they judge that life is not worth living. I see others paradoxically getting killed for the ideas or illusions that give them a reason for living (what is called a reason for living is also an excellent reason for dying). I therefore conclude that the meaning of life is the most urgent of questions. . . .

Suicide has never been dealt with except as a social phenomenon. On the contrary, we are concerned here, at the outset, with the relationship between individual thought and suicide. An act like this is prepared within the silence of the heart, as is a great work of art. The man himself is ignorant of it. One evening he pulls the trigger or jumps. Of an apartment-building manager who had killed himself I was told that he had lost his daughter five years before, that he had changed greatly since, and that that experience had "undermined" him. A more exact word cannot be imagined. Beginning to think is beginning to be undermined. Society has but little connection with such beginnings. The worm is in man's heart. That is where it must be sought. One must follow and understand this fatal game that leads from lucidity in the face of existence to flight from light. . . .

But if it is hard to fix the precise instant, the subtle step when the mind opted for death, it is easier to deduce from the act itself the consequences it implies. In a sense, and as in melodrama, killing yourself amounts to confessing. It is confessing that life is too much for you or that you do not understand it. Let's not go too far in

---

[1] From the point of view of the relative value of truth. On the other hand, from the point of view of virile behavior, this scholar's fragility may well make us smile.

such analogies, however, but rather return to everyday words. It is merely confessing that life "is not worth the trouble." Living, naturally, is never easy. You continue making the gestures commanded by existence for many reasons, the first of which is habit. Dying voluntarily implies that you have recognized, even instinctively, the ridiculous character of that habit, the absence of any profound reason for living, the insane character of that daily agitation, and the uselessness of suffering.

What, then, is that incalculable feeling that deprives the mind of the sleep necessary to life? A world that can be explained even with bad reasons is a familiar world. But, on the other hand, in a universe suddenly divested of illusions and lights, man feels an alien, a stranger. His exile is without remedy since he is deprived of the memory of a lost home or the hope of a promised land. This divorce between man and his life, the actor and his setting, is properly the feeling of absurdity. All healthy men having thought of their own suicide, it can be seen, without further explanation, that there is a direct connection between this feeling and the longing for death.

The subject of this essay is precisely this relationship between the absurd and suicide, the exact degree to which suicide is a solution to the absurd. The principle can be established that for a man who does not cheat, what he believes to be true must determine his action. Belief in the absurdity of existence must then dictate his conduct. It is legitimate to wonder, clearly and without false pathos, whether a conclusion of this importance requires forsaking as rapidly as possible an incomprehensible condition. I am speaking, of course, of men inclined to be in harmony with themselves. . . .

In a man's attachment to life there is something stronger than all the ills in the world. The body's judgment is as good as the mind's, and the body shrinks from annihilation. We get into the habit of living before acquiring the habit of thinking. In that race which daily hastens us toward death, the body maintains its irreparable lead. In short, the essence of that contradiction lies in what I shall call the act of eluding because it is both less and more than diversion in the Pascalian sense.[2] Eluding is the invariable game. The typical act of eluding, the fatal evasion that constitutes the third theme of this essay, is hope. Hope of another life one must "deserve" or trickery of those who live not for life itself but for some great idea that will transcend it, refine it, give it a meaning, and betray it. . . .

All great deeds and all great thoughts have a ridiculous beginning. Great works are often born on a street-corner or in a restaurant's revolving door. So it is with absurdity. The absurd world more than others derives its nobility from the abject birth. In certain situations, replying "nothing" when asked what one is thinking about may be pretense in a man. Those who are loved are well aware of this. But if that reply is sincere, if it symbolizes that odd state of soul in which the void becomes eloquent, in which the chain of daily gestures is broken, in which the heart vainly seeks the link that will connect it again, then it is as it were the first sign of absurdity.

It happens that the stage sets collapse. Rising, streetcar, four hours in the office or the factory, meal, streetcar, four hours of work, meal, sleep, and Monday Tuesday

[2] Pascalian "diversion" is any undertaking, serious or trivial, that keeps one from thinking about oneself—of realizing "our feeble and moral condition, so miserable that nothing can comfort us when we think of it closely." See Pascal's *Pensées,* sections 139–43. [ED.]

Wednesday Thursday Friday and Saturday according to the same rhythm—this path is easily followed most of the time. But one day the "why" arises and everything begins in that weariness tinged with amazement. "Begins"—this is important. Weariness comes at the end of the acts of a mechanical life, but at the same time it inaugurates the impulse of consciousness. It awakens consciousness and provokes what follows. What follows is the gradual return into the chain or it is the definitive awakening. At the end of the awakening comes, in time, the consequence; suicide or recovery. In itself weariness has something sickening about it. Here, I must conclude that it is good. For everything begins with consciousness and nothing is worth anything except through it. There is nothing original about these remarks. But they are obvious; that is enough for a while, during a sketchy reconnaissance in the origins of the absurd. Mere "anxiety," as Heidegger says, is at the source of everything.

Likewise and during every day of an unillustrious life, time carries us. But a moment always comes when we have to carry it. We live on the future: "tomorrow," "later on," "when you have made your way," "you will understand when you are old enough." Such irrelevancies are wonderful, for, after all, it's a matter of dying. Yet a day comes when a man notices or says that he is thirty. Thus he asserts his youth. But simultaneously he situates himself in relation to time. He takes his place in it. He admits that he stands at a certain point on a curve that he acknowledges having to travel to its end. He belongs to time, and by the horror that seizes him, he recognizes his worst enemy. Tomorrow, he was longing for tomorrow, whereas everything in him ought to reject it. That revolt of the flesh is the absurd.[3]

A step lower and strangeness creeps in: perceiving that the world is "dense," sensing to what a degree a stone is foreign and irreducible to us, with what intensity nature or a landscape can negate us. At the heart of all beauty lies something inhuman, and these hills, the softness of the sky, the outline of these trees at this very minute lose the illusory meaning with which we had clothed them, henceforth more remote than a lost paradise. The primitive hostility of the world rises up to face us across millennia. For a second we cease to understand it because for centuries we have understood in it solely the images and designs that we had attributed to it beforehand, because henceforth we lack the power to make use of that artifice. The world evades us because it becomes itself again. That stage scenery masked by habit becomes again what it is. It withdraws at a distance from us. Just as there are days when under the familiar face of a woman, we see as a stranger her we had loved months or years ago, perhaps we shall come even to desire what suddenly leaves us so alone. But the time has not yet come. Just one thing: that denseness and that strangeness of the world is the absurd.

Men, too, secrete the inhuman. At certain moments of lucidity, the mechanical aspect of their gestures, their meaningless pantomime makes silly everything that surrounds them. A man is talking on the telephone behind a glass partition; you cannot hear him, but you see his incomprehensible dumb show: you wonder why he is alive. This discomfort in the face of man's own inhumanity, this incalculable tumble before the image of what we are, this "nausea," as a writer of today calls it, is also

---

[3] But not in the proper sense. This is not a definition, but rather an *enumeration* of the feelings that may admit of the absurd. Still, the enumeration finished, the absurd has nevertheless not been exhausted.

the absurd. Likewise the stranger who at certain seconds comes to meet us in a mirror, the familiar and yet alarming brother we encounter in our own photographs is also the absurd.

I come at last to death and to the attitude we have toward it. On this point everything has been said and it is only proper to avoid pathos. Yet one will never be sufficiently surprised that everyone lives as if no one "knew." This is because in reality there is no experience of death. Properly speaking, nothing has been experienced but what has been lived and made conscious. Here, it is barely possible to speak of the experience of others' deaths. It is a substitute, an illusion, and it never quite convinces us. That melancholy convention cannot be persuasive. The horror comes in reality from the mathematical aspect of the event. If time frightens us, this is because it works out the problem and the solution comes afterward. All the pretty speeches about the soul will have their contrary convincingly proved, at least for a time. From this inert body on which a slap makes no mark the soul has disappeared. This elementary and definitive aspect of the adventure constitutes the absurd feeling. Under the fatal lighting of that destiny, its uselessness becomes evident. No code of ethics and no effort are justifiable *a priori* in the face of the cruel mathematics that command our condition. . . .

Whatever may be the play on words and the acrobatics of logic, to understand is, above all, to unify. The mind's deepest desire, even in its most elaborate operations, parallels man's unconscious feeling in the face of his universe: it is an insistence upon familiarity, an appetite for clarity. Understanding the world for a man is reducing it to the human, stamping it with his seal. The cat's universe is not the universe of the anthill. The truism "All thought is anthropomorphic" has no other meaning. Likewise, the mind that aims to understand reality can consider itself satisfied only by reducing it to terms of thought. If man realized that the universe like him can love and suffer, he would be reconciled. If thought discovered in the shimmering mirrors of phenomena eternal relations capable of summing them up and summing themselves up in a single principle, then would be seen an intellectual joy of which the myth of the blessed would be but a ridiculous imitation. That nostalgia for unity, that appetite for the absolute illustrates the essential impulse of the human drama. But the fact of that nostalgia's existence does not imply that it is to be immediately satisfied. For if, bridging the gulf that separates desire from conquest, we assert with Parmenides the reality of the One (whatever it may be), we fall into the ridiculous contradiction of a mind that asserts total unity and proves by its very assertion its own difference and the diversity it claimed to resolve. This other vicious circle is enough to stifle our hopes. . . .

Hence the intelligence, too, tells me in its way that this world is absurd. Its contrary, blind reason, may well claim that all is clear; I was waiting for proof and longing for it to be right. But despite so many pretentious centuries and over the heads of so many eloquent and persuasive men, I know that is false. On this plane, at least, there is no happiness if I cannot know. That universal reason, practical or ethical, that determinism, those categories that explain everything are enough to make a decent man laugh. They have nothing to do with the mind. They negate its profound truth, which is to be enchained. In this unintelligible and limited universe, man's fate henceforth assumes its meaning. A horde of irrationals has sprung up and surrounds him until his ultimate end. In his recovered and now studied lucidity, the feeling of the absurd becomes clear and definite. I said that the world is absurd, that is all that can be said. But what is absurd is the confrontation of this irrational and the wild longing for clarity whose call echoes in the human heart. The absurd depends as much on man as on the world. For the moment it is all that links them together. It binds them one to the other as only hatred can weld two creatures together. This is all I can discern clearly in this measureless universe where my adventure takes place. Let us pause here. If I hold to be true that absurdity that determines my relationship with life, if I become thoroughly imbued with that sentiment that seizes me in face of the world's scenes, with that lucidity imposed on me by the pursuit of a science, I must sacrifice everything to these certainties and I must see them squarely to be able to maintain them. Above all, I must adapt my behavior to them and pursue them in all their consequences. I am speaking here of decency. But I want to know beforehand if thought can live in those deserts. . . .

All these experiences agree and confirm one another. The mind, when it reaches its limits, must make a judgment and choose its conclusions. This is where suicide and the reply stand. But I wish to reverse the order of the inquiry and start out from the intelligent adventure and come back to daily acts. The experiences called to mind here were born in the desert that we must not leave behind. At least it is essential to know how far they went. At this point of his effort man stands face to face with the irrational. He feels within him his longing for happiness and for reason. The absurd is born of this confrontation between the human need and the unreasonable silence of the world. This must not be forgotten. This must be clung to because the whole consequence of a life can depend on it. The irrational, the human nostalgia, and the absurd that is born of their encounter—these are the three characters in the drama that must necessarily end with all the logic of which an existence is capable. . . .

If I accuse an innocent man of a monstrous crime, if I tell a virtuous man that he has coveted his own sister, he will reply that this is absurd. His indignation has its comical aspect. But it also has its fundamental reason. The virtuous man illustrates by that reply the definitive antinomy existing between the deed I am attributing to him and his lifelong principles. "It's absurd" means "It's impossible" but also "It's contradictory." If I see a man armed only with a sword attack a group of machine guns, I shall consider his act to be absurd. But it is so solely by virtue of the disproportion between his intention and the reality he will encounter, of the contradiction I notice between his true strength and the aim he has in view. Likewise we shall deem a verdict absurd when we contrast it with the verdict the facts apparently dictated. And, similarly, a demonstration by the absurd is achieved by comparing the consequences of such a reasoning with the logical reality one wants to set up. In all these cases, from the simplest to the most complex, the magnitude of the absurdity will be in direct ratio to the distance between the two terms of my comparison. There are absurd marriages, challenges, rancors, silences, wars, and even peace treaties. For each of them the absurdity springs from a comparison. I am thus justified in saying that the feeling of absurdity does not spring from the mere scrutiny of a fact or an impression, but that it bursts from the comparison between a bare fact and a certain reality, between an action and the world that transcends it. The absurd is essentially a divorce. It lies in neither of the elements compared; it is born of their confrontation.

In this particular case and on the plane of intelligence, I can therefore say that the Absurd is not in man (if such a metaphor could have a meaning) nor in the world, but in their presence together. For the moment it is the only bond uniting them. If I wish to limit myself to facts, I know what man wants, I know what the world offers him, and now I can say that I also know what links them. I have no need to dig deeper. A single certainty is enough for the seeker. He simply has to derive all the consequences from it. . . .

And carrying this absurd logic to its conclusion, I must admit that that struggle implies a total absence of hope (which has nothing to do with despair), a continual rejection (which must not be confused with renunciation), and a conscious dissatisfaction (which must not be compared to immature unrest). Everything that destroys, conjures away, or exorcises these requirements (and, to begin with, consent which overthrows divorce) ruins the absurd and devaluates the attitude that may then be proposed. The absurd has meaning only in so far as it is not agreed to. . . .

There exists an obvious fact that seems utterly moral: namely, that a man is always a prey to his truths. Once he has admitted them, he cannot free himself from them. One has to pay something. A man who has become conscious of the absurd is forever bound to it. A man devoid of hope and conscious of being so has ceased to belong to the future. That is natural. But it is just as natural that he should strive to escape the universe of which he is the creator. All the foregoing has significance only on account of this paradox. . . .

It is a matter of living in that state of the absurd. I know on what it is founded, this mind and this world straining against each other without being able to embrace each other. I ask for the rule of life of that state, and what I am offered neglects its basis, negates one of the terms of the painful opposition, demands of me a resignation. I ask what is involved in the condition I recognize as mine; I know it implies obscurity and ignorance; and I am assured that this ignorance explains everything and that this darkness is my light. But there is no reply here to my intent, and this stirring lyricism cannot hide the paradox from me. One must therefore turn away. Kierkegaard may shout in warning: "If man had no eternal consciousness, if, at the bottom of everything, there were merely a wild, seething force producing everything, both large and trifling, in the storm of dark passions, if the bottomless void that nothing can fill underlay all things, what would life be but despair?" This cry is not likely to stop the absurd man. Seeking what is true is not seeking what is desirable. If in order to elude the anxious question: "What would life be?" one must, like the donkey, feed on the roses of illusion, then the absurd mind, rather than resigning itself to falsehood, prefers to adopt fearlessly Kierkegaard's reply: "despair." Everything considered, a determined soul will always manage. . . .

ABSURD FREEDOM

Now the main thing is done, I hold certain facts from which I cannot separate. What I know, what is certain, what I cannot deny, what I cannot reject—this is what counts. I can negate everything of that part of me that lives on vague nostalgias, except this desire for unity, this longing to solve, this need for clarity and cohesion. I can refute everything in this world surrounding me that offends or enraptures me, except this chaos, this sovereign chance and this divine equivalence which springs from anarchy: I don't know whether this world has a meaning that transcends it. But I know that I do not know that meaning and that it is impossible for me just now to know it. What can a meaning outside my condition mean to me? I can understand only in human terms. What I touch, what resists me—that is what I understand. And these two certainties—my appetite for the absolute and for unity and the impossibility of reducing this world to a rational and reasonable principle—I also know that I cannot reconcile them. What other truth can I admit without lying, without bringing in a hope I lack and which means nothing within the limits of my condition?

If I were a tree among trees, a cat among animals, this life would have a meaning, or rather this problem would not rise, for I should belong to this world. I should *be* this world to which I am now opposed by my whole consciousness and my whole insistence upon familiarity. This ridiculous reason is what sets me in opposition to all creation. I cannot cross it out with a stroke of the pen. What I believe to be true I must therefore preserve. What seems to me so obvious, even against me, I must support. And what constitutes the basis of that conflict, of that break between the world and my mind, but the awareness of it? If therefore I want to preserve it, I can through a constant awareness, ever revived, ever alert. This is what, for the moment, I must remember. At this moment the absurd, so obvious and yet so hard to win, returns to a man's life and finds its home there. At this moment, too, the mind can leave the arid, dried-up path of lucid effort. That path now emerges in daily life. It encounters the world of the anonymous impersonal pronoun "one," but henceforth man enters in with his revolt and his lucidity. He has forgotten how to hope. This hell of the present is his Kingdom at last. All problems recover their sharp edge. Abstract evidence retreats before the poetry of forms and colors. Spiritual conflicts become embodied and return to the abject and magnificent shelter of man's heart. None of them is settled. But all are transfigured. Is one going to die, escape by the leap, rebuild a mansion of ideas and forms to one's own scale? Is one, on the contrary, going to take up the heart-rending and marvelous wager of the absurd? Let's make a final effort in this regard and draw all our conclusions. The body, affection, creation, action, human nobility will then resume their places in this mad world. At last man will again find there the wine of the absurd and the bread of indifference on which he feeds his greatness.

Let us insist again on the method: it is a matter of persisting. At a certain point on his path the absurd man is tempted. History is not lacking in either religions or prophets, even without gods. He is asked to leap. All he can reply is that he doesn't fully understand, that it is not obvious. Indeed, he does not want to do anything but what he fully understands. He is assured that this is the sin of pride, but he does not understand the notion of sin; that perhaps hell is in store, but he has not enough imagination to visualize that strange future; that he is losing immortal life, but that seems to him an idle consideration. An attempt is made to get him to admit his guilt. He feels innocent. To tell the truth, that is all he feels—his irreparable innocence. This is what allows him everything. Hence, what he demands of himself is to live *solely* with what he knows, to accommodate himself to what is, and to bring in nothing that is not certain. He is told that nothing is. But this at least is a certainty. And it is with this that he is concerned: he wants to find out if it is possible to live *without appeal*. . . .

Now I can broach the notion of suicide. It has already been felt what solution might be given. At this point the problem is reversed. It was previously a question of finding out whether or not life had to have a meaning to be lived. It now becomes clear, on the contrary, that it will be lived all the better if it has no meaning. Living an experience, a particular fate, is accepting it fully. Now, no one will live this fate, knowing it to be absurd, unless he does everything to keep before him that absurd brought to light by consciousness. Negating one of the terms of the opposition on which he lives amounts to escaping it. To abolish conscious revolt is to elude the problem. The theme of permanent revolution is thus carried into individual experience. Living is keeping the absurd alive. Keeping it alive is, above all, contemplating it. Unlike Eurydice, the absurd dies only when we turn away from it. One of the only coherent philosophical positions is thus revolt. It is a constant confrontation between man and his own obscurity. It is an insistence upon an impossible transparency. It challenges the world anew every second. Just as danger provided man the unique opportunity of seizing awareness, so metaphysical revolt extends awareness to the whole of experience. It is that constant presence of man in his own eyes. It is not aspiration, for it is devoid of hope. That revolt is the certainty of a crushing fate, without the resignation that ought to accompany it.

This is where it is seen to what a degree absurd experience is remote from suicide. It may be thought that suicide follows revolt—but wrongly. For it does not represent the logical outcome of revolt. It is just the contrary by the consent it presupposes. Suicide, like the leap, is acceptance at its extreme. Everything is over and man returns to his essential history. His future, his unique and dreadful future—he sees and rushes toward it. In its way, suicide settles the absurd. It engulfs the absurd in the same death. But I know that in order to keep alive, the absurd cannot be settled. It escapes suicide to the extent that it is simultaneously awareness and rejection of death. It is, at the extreme limit of the condemned man's last thought, that shoelace that despite everything he sees a few yards away, on the very brink of his dizzying fall. The contrary of suicide, in fact, is the man condemned to death.

That revolt gives life its value. Spread out over the whole length of a life, it restores its majesty to that life. To a man devoid of blinders, there is no finer sight than that of the intelligence at grips with a reality that transcends it. The sight of human pride is unequaled. No disparagement is of any use. That discipline that the mind imposes on itself, that will be conjured up out of nothing, that face-to-face struggle have something exceptional about them. To impoverish that reality whose inhumanity constitutes man's majesty is tantamount to impoverishing him himself. I understand then why the doctrines that explain everything to me also debilitate me at the same time. They relieve me of the weight of my own life, and yet I must carry it alone. At this juncture, I cannot conceive that a skeptical metaphysics can be joined to an ethics of renunciation.

Consciousness and revolt, these rejections are the contrary of renunciation. Everything that is indomitable and passionate in a human heart quickens them, on the contrary, with its own life. It is essential to die unreconciled and not of one's own free will. Suicide is a repudiation. The absurd man can only drain everything to the bitter end, and deplete himself. The absurd is his extreme tension, which he maintains constantly by solitary effort, for he knows that in that consciousness and in that day-to-day revolt he gives proof of his only truth, which is defiance. This is a first consequence. . . .

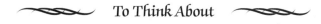

To Think About

1. "To lose one's life is a little thing and I shall have the courage to do so if it is necessary; but to see the meaning of this life dissipated, to see our reason for existing disappear, that is what is unbearable. One cannot live without meaning."
   Albert Camus

2. "The Symbolism of Christianity is wonderful beyond words, but when people try to make a philosophical system out of it, I find it disgusting."
   Ludwig Wittgenstein

3. "Could a man's life have or fail to have meaning, without his knowing?"
   Ronald Hepburn

4. "Let us note here too what is not Hamlet, what is not Don Quixote. That is to say, what is not the intellectual: the man of ordinary consciousness who lives by deliberately blurring the meaning of any act of his on the immediate horizon with its meaning on the ultimate horizon of his life. This, which the ordinary man does constantly, the intellectual must at all costs avoid ever doing."
   Lionel Abel

5. "Theism seeks to give meaning and purpose to human life in a morally objectionable way. Understanding one's life as given purpose by God involves a thoroughgoing self-abasement or self-annulment quite incompatible with the stance of a moral agent."
   Kurt Baier

6. "Does the life of a flower have meaning?"
   Ronald Hepburn

7. "To look for a purpose in Life outside Life itself amounts to killing Life. Reason is given by Life, not vice versa. Life is prior to meaning. Life does not die, sing the Vedas. Christ came so that we may have Life, say the Gospels. Ah, these terrific Westerners who anguish over questions other cultures ask with more detachment and serenity, who are believers to the marrow even in their desacralized existence! Human life is joyful interrogation. Any answer is blasphemy."
   Raimon Panikkar

8. "You were born without purpose, you live without meaning, living is its own meaning. When you die, you are extinguished. From being you will be transformed to non-being. A god does not necessarily dwell among our increasingly capricious atoms.

   "This insight has brought with it a certain security that has resolutely eliminated anguish and tumult, though on the other hand I have never denied my second (or first) life, that of the spirit."
   Ingmar Bergman

9. *"Life's but a walking shadow; a poor player,"*
    That struts and frets his hour upon the stage,
    And then is heard no more: it is a tale
    Told by an idiot, full of sound and fury,
    Signifying nothing."   **William Shakespeare,** from *Macbeth*

10. Joseph Campbell's life work was to seek out the themes common to all myths
    that reveal the human psyche's need for profound principles to live by.
    > Moyers: "You're talking about a search for the meaning of life?" I asked.
    > Campbell: "No, no, no," he said. "For the *experience* of being alive."
    > **Bill Moyers**

11. "How terrifying and glorious the role of man if, indeed, without guidance and with-
    out consolation he must create from his own vitals the meaning for his existence
    and write the rules whereby he lives."   **Thornton Wilder,** from *Julius Caesar*

12. "In broad terms, the destiny of man on earth has been made clear by evolu-
    tionary biology. It is to be the agent of the world process of evolution, the
    sole agent capable of leading it to new heights, and enabling it to realize new
    possibilities."   **Julian Huxley**

13. "Man can will nothing unless he has first understood that he must count on
    no one but himself; that he is alone, abandoned on earth in the midst of his
    infinite responsibilities; without help, with no other aim than the one he sets
    himself, with no other destiny than the one he forces for himself on this
    earth."   **Jean-Paul Sartre**

14. "Perhaps the most majestic feature of our whole existence is that while our in-
    telligences are powerful enough to penetrate deeply into the evolution of this
    quite incredible Universe, we still have not the smallest clue to our own fate."
    Fred Hoyle

15. "In a universe suddenly divested of illusions and lights, man feels an alien, a
    stranger. His exile is without remedy since he is deprived of the memory of a lost
    home or the hope of a promised land. This divorce between a man and his life, the
    actor and his setting, is properly the feeling of absurdity."   **Albert Camus**

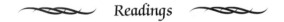 **Readings**

AYER, A. J. "The Claims of Philosophy." In *Philosophy of the Social Sciences,* ed. M.
    Natanson, pp. 468–86. New York: Random House, 1963.

BAIER, KURT. "Meaning and Morals." In *Moral Problems in Contemporary Society,* ed.
    Paul Kurtz, pp. 33–47. Upper Saddle River, NJ: Prentice Hall, 1969.

BREE, GERMAINE. *Camus.* New Brunswick, NJ: Rutgers University Press, 1959.

JOSKE, W. D. "The Meaning of Life." *Australasian Journal of Philosophy* 52 (1974): 93–104.

KLEMKE, E. D. *The Meaning of Life.* New York: Oxford University Press, 1981.

Glossary

Absolute   whatever is absolute would be underived, complete, perfect, unconditioned, and unchangeable in any way. An absolute moral principle is universally binding.

Aesthetics   the area of philosophy that studies beauty, especially in the arts.

Agnosticism   the view that God's existence can be neither proved nor disproved.

Analogy   when one reasons by analogy, one concludes that because two or more entities share one aspect, they share another as well.

Analytic   in epistemology, a particular kind of statement in which the predicate merely spells out what the subject implies, for example, "a bachelor is an unmarried man."

A posteriori   concerns knowledge gained through experience.

A priori   concerns knowledge that is gained prior to experience.

Atheism   denial of theism; it does not believe in a Supreme Being who created and cares for people, but it does not necessarily deny the existence of nontheistic gods.

Axiom   a proposition regarded as self-evident or true.

Bourgeoisie   those who own the means of production.

Categorical imperative   Immanuel Kant's ethical standard: so act as if the maxim by which you act were to become a universal law.

Catharsis   Aristotle's doctrine that states that tragedy provokes emotions of pity and fear to the extent that they are purged from the individual, who takes pleasure in that purgation.

Coherence theory   the view contending that truth is a property of a related group of consistent statements.

Communitarianism   a critique of classical social and political liberalism, stressing the central importance of the community group over the autonomous individual in the formulation of political and economic rights and obligations.

Compatibilism   another name for soft determinism.

Contingent   something that may be and also may not be.

Correspondence theory   the view contending that truth is an agreement between a proposition and a fact.

Cosmology   the study of the way by which the world unfolds and evolves.

Creationism   the theory that life originated through an act of the Creator; it strongly criticizes the theory of evolution.

Deduction   logical reasoning to necessary conclusions.

Deism   the view that God, having created the universe, remains apart from it and administers it through natural laws.

Denotation   defining a term by providing examples.

Deontology   in ethics, the theory that emphasizes obligations as primary.

Determinism   the view that everything that happens is caused.

Dialectical method   a method, used by Socrates, Hegel, and Marx, of asking questions and critically analyzing answers as a way to arrive at propositions that can be accepted as true.

Dualism   the view that reality is composed of two different substances, so that neither one can be related to the other, thus: spirit/matter, mind/body, good/evil.

Egoism   an ethical theory that contends that we act morally when we act for our own interests.

Emotivism   the metaethical position that ethical statements fundamentally express emotions.

Empiricism   the view that knowledge has its origins in and derives all of its content from experience.

Epistemology   the area of philosophy that investigates the nature, sources, limitations, and validity of knowledge.

Essence   the qualities without which any particular object/event would not exist or would be a distinctly different kind of object/event. The qualities necessary for anything to be what it is.

Ethical egoism   the belief that all people ought to seek their own interests.

Ethical relativism   the position that moral principles vary from individual to individual, from culture to culture; it denies the existence of universal, objective moral principles.

Ethics   the area of philosophy that analyzes the good and right thing to do.

Existentialism   the philosophy that argues that we create our own essence through free action.

Fascism   an organic view of the state in which the supreme value is placed on the state rather than on the individual.

Fatalism   the view that events are fixed, usually by a divine being.

Forms   a metaphysical term used by Plato to refer to nonmaterial, eternal, and changeless entities that constitute reality; examples of Plato's Forms are beauty, justice, man, and so on.

Free will   the view that human acts are not completely determined.

Hedonism   in ethics, the doctrine that pleasure is the ultimate goal of life that does and should determine our behavior.

Hedonistic calculus a series of calculations used to evaluate the particular ends, either pleasures or avoidance of pains, that humans seek.

Hypothetical imperative a command that is useful to attain some end.

Idealism in metaphysics, the position that reality is nonmaterial; in epistemology, the view that all we know are our ideas.

Indeterminism the view that some individual choices are not caused by earlier events.

Induction logical reasoning to probable conclusions.

Inference an argument using induction or deduction.

Innate ideas ideas that are inborn or naturally born.

Instinctive natural.

Instrumental value the worth that something has because of its use.

Intrinsic value the inherent worth that something has.

Intuition a source of knowledge that does not rely immediately on the senses or reason but on direct awareness.

Laissez-faire in economics, the act of government noninterference.

Law of contradiction a law of logic that states that a proposition and its negation cannot both be true at the same time.

Leap of faith an expression used by Kierkegaard to refer to the unquestioned acceptance of God.

Libertarianism the metaphysical view that humans have free will in spite of any past events; this is the theory of Sartre and Richard Taylor.

Logic the branch of philosophy that studies the methods and principles of correct reasoning.

Materialism the metaphysical view that holds that only physical entities are real or exist.

Metaethics the study of the meanings of ethical words and of the sentences in which they appear.

Monotheism the belief in a single God.

Morals a person's principles concerning what is right or wrong.

Naturalism the worldview that holds that there is but a single order of reality, that of matter-in-motion.

Nihilism the view that nothing has value.

Nominalism the position that only particular entities are real and that universals represent detectable likeness among particulars.

Normative ethics the area of ethics that makes judgments about obligation and value.

Omnipotent all-powerful.

Omnipresent being everywhere at once.

Omniscient all-knowing.

Pantheism the belief that everything is God.

Polytheism belief in many Gods.

Pragmatism   the philosophy that rejects all first principles and tests truth through workability.

Predestination   the view that every aspect of our lives has been divinely determined from the beginning of time.

Predeterminism   the belief that events (either some or all) throughout eternity have been foreordained by some supernatural power (usually God).

Predicate   that which is affirmed or denied of a subject or substance.

Proletariat   the worker or the members of the working class.

Proposition   a true or false statement.

Psychological egoism   the belief that individuals always seek their own interests.

Rational   based on or appealing to reason.

Rationalism   the theory of knowledge that holds that the ultimate source of knowledge is reason.

Realism   the view that to be real is to exist apart from perception.

Relativism   the view that one's moral views are conditioned by factors such as acculturation and personal bias.

Secondary qualities   according to Locke, qualities that we impose on an object: color, smell, texture, and so on.

Sense data   images or sense impressions.

Skepticism   the view that either doubts all assumptions until proved or claims that no knowledge is possible.

Social humanism   the political philosophy of John Dewey, which holds that every mature human being must be allowed to participate in the formation of the values that regulate the living of people together.

Social philosophy   the application of moral principles to the problems of freedom, equality, and justice.

Soft determinism   attempts to reconcile freedom and responsibility with determinism.

Solipsism   the doctrine that only "I" exists.

Soul   the immaterial entity that is identified with consciousness, mind, or personality.

Subjective   that which refers to the knower; that which exists in the consciousness but not apart from it.

Subjective idealism   the view that all we ever know are our own ideas.

Substance   in metaphysics, an entity that can have properties indicated of it but cannot itself be a predicate of any object.

Summum bonum   in ethics, the Ultimate Good of human existence, that is, the final good toward which all our endeavors should be directed.

Synthetic   a statement in which the subject term does not contain the predicate.

Tautology   a proposition that is true because of the meanings of its words.

Teleology   the theory that deliberate, purposive activity, rather than mere chance, is involved in some process.

Tenacity establishing one's beliefs through one's parents and/or one's environment.

Theology the study of God, including religious doctrines.

Totalitarianism the political view that the state is of paramount importance.

Truth the approximation of thought to reality.

Universal that which is predictive of many particular entities; thus, "human" is a universal, because it is predictive of individual humans.

Utilitarianism the view that each of us should seek the greatest good for the greatest number of people.

Validity refers to an argument whose conclusion follows by logical necessity.